Standing Tall

How a Man Can Protect His Family

Steve Farrar

MULTNOMAH BOOKS

STANDING TALL
© 1994 by Steve Farrar

Published by Multnomah Books
a part of the Questar Publishing Family

Edited by Larry R. Libby
Cover design by David Uttley

Printed in the United States of America.

International Standard Book Number: 0880-70-618-X

For information:
Questar Publishers, Inc.
Post Office Box 1720
Sisters, Oregon 97759

94 95 96 97 98 99 00 01 — 10 9 8 7 6 5 4 3 2 1

To Mary

For nearly twenty years we have ridden
the river of life together.
There have been times when we
lashed ourselves together
because the rapids and white water
were severe and rocky.
And then there were those
sections of water where
together we savored
the placid stillness
and gazed upon the dazzling beauty
that surrounded us.
We have navigated rough waters
and we have enjoyed calm waters
and there will be more of each ahead.
That's just the way the Lord
has designed His rivers.
Smooth and quiet one minute,
wild and treacherous the next.
But that's okay.
We're in this canoe together.
And never has a man enjoyed
the ride more than I.

CONTENTS

It has been said that if you see a turtle sitting on a fencepost, it's for sure he had some help getting up there. The same could be said for me. I had a tremendous amount of help getting here from some very gifted and dedicated compatriots.

• Larry Libby is an editor with a unique combination of abilities. Editorially speaking, Larry threw some key blocks for me when I was hemmed in. That's why Larry has my vote for All-Pro. I can't tell you how glad I am that we're playing on the same team.

• Don Jacobson, Dan Rich, Steve Cobb, Doug Gabbert, and Eric Weber are key players in the excellent publishing team known as Questar. Many thanks to them for their professionalism and their desire to speak truth. These are men who, when they make a promise, keep a promise. It's a genuine pleasure to be in the harness with them.

• Stu Weber, Gary Rosberg, Andy McQuitty, Jim Litchfield, Steve Lawson, and my wife, Mary, all took their valuable time to evaluate the manuscript and make insightful comments and suggestions. Their encouragement especially fueled this project when we were nearing the finish line.

• Bob and Judy Brown graciously allowed me to hide out in the canyon at a time when solitude was needed and necessary. A week without a ringing phone is worth at least a pound of gold. And so are good friends.

• David Uttley came up not only with the cover, but with the title of this book as well. Way to hum, David.

• John Bethany, Mike Miller, Deedee Smith, and Mike Wolverton are a staff sent from heaven. They covered a multitude of bases at the office when I was both preoccupied and occupied with this book. Thanks, guys, for a job well done.

9

I don't smoke cigarettes or rob banks. But I do write books. And believe me, *any* of those activities can kill you.

In the classic Hollywood western, *Butch Cassidy and the Sundance Kid*, the two wily outlaws find themselves hemmed in by an angry posse. Completely outflanked by rifle-toting deputies, they are backed up against the edge of a hundred-foot cliff. Looking over the precipice behind them, they see a raging, frothy river clawing its way through the canyon far below.

Butch suggests they jump.

Sundance refuses. Butch won't give up the idea and Sundance continues to resist. Finally, with the lawmen closing in for the kill, Butch asks in desperation why Sundance won't jump. Meekly, Sundance admits that he can't swim.

Butch laughs and then utters those immortal words: "You can't swim? Shoot, the *fall* will probably kill you anyway!"

With that, they both step off the cliff.

This book has just about done me in. I knew it might, back when I stepped off the cliff four months ago. Here's the problem: The stuff I am writing about is heavy stuff. Every man in America who loves his family should be aware of these issues, but...taking them on is no Sunday picnic. These are intense, gut-wrenching questions that can consume huge hunks of emotional energy.

As you read the pages that follow, you'll see just what I mean. Some of these issues will probably make you angry, frustrated, and intense. And frankly, they *need* to upset you. If you're not upset when you finish some of these chapters, then I haven't done a good job.

But the purpose of this book is not to kill you. The purpose of this book is to wise men up to some conditions that threaten not only our children, but our very existence as a nation.

Yes, there are some pretty heavy chapters. These are chapters that talk about the overwhelming need for male leadership in families across America. I'll be trying to divulge the strategies of the Enemy to utterly destroy the once-strong pillars of biblical morality on which this nation was founded.

But as I said, I'm not writing just to raise men's blood pressure. I don't want to send any guys packing from hyper-tension or coronary arrest. For that reason, there are other chapters that will remind us that God is in charge, that He is working His plan, and that He will take care of us as we seek to take care of our families.

In other words, these pages have some warning, some encouragement, and some hands-on help for standing tall in a culture that wants Christian men to check out of any significant involvement in the destiny of our nation.

I have carried the message of this book in my heart for over a year now. I am convinced it is a message the Enemy does not want you to hear. For if you hear the message, then you will be motivated to square your shoulders, step up to the line, and fight for your family as perhaps never before. And the *last* thing the Enemy wants is for God's men to be charged up and ready to take on the very gates of hell.

But that's exactly what we have to do, gentlemen.

Because the gates of hell have set up shop just outside our front doors. The gates of hell cast their shadows into our schools, the media, the movies, the TV sitcoms, and the morals of our nation.

Enough is enough. It's time to stand tall.

So if you're with me, let's take a flying leap over the edge.

It should be quite a ride.

CHAPTER ONE

Ridin' for the Brand

Unprincipled men and women,
disdainful of their moral heritage and skeptical of Truth itself,
are destroying our civilization by weakening
the very pillars upon which it rests.

CHARLES COLSON

The Brand.

Every man and boy in the Old West knew the importance of a brand. A brand was the mark that a rancher would burn on his stock.

But it was more than that. Much more.

When a man hooked up with a certain outfit, it was then said that he was "ridin' for the brand." Louis L'Amour, the great storyteller of the American West, etches out for us the significance of those four potent words:

The term "riding for the brand" was an expression of loyalty to a man's employer or the particular outfit he rode for. It was considered a compliment of the highest order in an almost feudal society. If a man did not like a ranch or the way they conducted their affairs he was free to quit, and many did, but if he stayed on he gave loyalty and expected it.

A man was rarely judged by his past, only by his actions. Many a man who came west left things behind him he would rather forget, so it was not the custom to ask questions. Much was forgiven if a

13

man had courage and integrity and if he did his job. If a man gave less than his best, somebody always had to take up the slack, and he was not admired.[1]

This is a book for men. Men who are ridin' for the brand. To be more specific, it's written to men who are not their own. The reason they are not their own is simple. They've been bought with a price.

Every man I know who is ridin' for the brand has things in his past he wishes he could go back and undo. But that really isn't necessary. Once you've been called to ride for the brand, your past is taken care of. Totally and completely. Because you've been bought with a price. And the blood that bought you covers it all. Your past, your present, and your future.

What is this brand? Let me suggest that it's the Two-One-Two brand. The Two-One-Two is very direct and to the point. It signifies two nails in His hands, one spear in His side, and two more nail scars in His feet. That's why we're not our own, and that's the price He paid. For you. For me. We're ridin' for the brand.

Ridin' for the brand is a high calling. No, that's not quite right. It is *the* highest calling. It's the brand that is above every other brand and every other name. For it signifies the name of the Lord Jesus Christ. When a man begins to understand the privilege and responsibility of owning this brand, he will give it nothing less than his best. A man who is ridin' for the brand is not judged by his past, but he is expected to have courage, integrity, and to do his job.

What is that job? What are the duties of a man who rides for the brand? That question deserves a definitive answer. And there's no better place to start than with some other guys, in another time, in another place. Why would we start with them? Simple. They were ridin' for the brand.

GUMLESS WARRIORS

When you buy a Bible, it usually doesn't come with a slab of bubble gum. The only thing I remember that comes with a slab of bubble gum is a pack of baseball cards. But that's exactly why every Bible should come with bubble gum. For every Bible contains 1 Chronicles 11 and 12. Those two chapters are a set of baseball cards. Well, not baseball cards. *Warrior* cards.

When I was a kid, I had hundreds of baseball and football cards. Back in the fifties, it was not unusual for me to invest my allowance in complete sets of the American and National Leagues in baseball, plus the NFL. Each of those cards had a picture of the player on the front. On the back, it had a brief biography, a few important stats, and one or two of the player's most outstanding achievements. I know a lot of guys who still collect baseball cards, football cards, basketball cards, and even *hockey* cards, for crying out loud.

But I don't know anyone with a set of warrior cards. That's why we need 1 Chronicles 11 and 12. These stirring Old Testament chapters are the equivalent of going down to the drugstore, laying down your money, and collecting a package of cards with a slab of bubble gum. This section in Chronicles doesn't come with pictures, but it does have brief biographies, a few stats, and some of the more outstanding achievements of a group of guys known across the territory as David's Mighty Men.

God's men have never been strangers to battle. In the days of King David, God's men were often fighting physical battles. That's part of riding for the brand. Today, in our culture, God's men are fighting spiritual battles. That's also riding for the brand. The stakes are high. For two very sacred and fundamental components of our lives are under attack from our culture.

What are these two sacred factors that we are sworn to defend?

It is our faith and it is our families.

That's why we are going to battle. In our culture, a man who is riding for the brand is going to have to stand tall against his enemies. And at some point, he's going to have to fight. There's no getting around it.

ONWARD CHRISTIAN SOLDIERS

David was a gifted man. He was a poet, a musician, and a king. But above everything else, David was a warrior. David was no stranger to war or bloodshed. That's why you should know David well. You may not be a poet, a musician, or a king, but if you are a Christian husband and father, you are a warrior.

You see, over time, a man who is riding for the brand will be called by different names. In one culture it's "warrior," in another it might be "cowboy," in another, "conquistador." But it's really the same thing. It's just another way of describing a man who is riding for the brand.

David was a commander and a leader. That kind of warrior always draws other men to his cause. David had some spectacular warriors in his army. They were so remarkable that Scripture reports not only their names, but their exploits.

You've probably never heard of these guys. But if you'd been around in David's day, you would have recognized them immediately. They were known men. Guys such as Ahiezer, the head of the tribe of Benjamin. Ahiezer's warriors were respected and feared throughout that chunk of the world. Men such as Joash, the two brothers Jeziel and Pelet, Beracah, Jehu the Anathothite, and Ishmaiah the Gibeonite.

Tough men. Dangerous men. Men who were absolutely fearless.

These were the men who came to David at Ziklag, while he was banished from the presence of Saul son of Kish (they were among the warriors who helped him in battle; they were armed with bows and were able to shoot arrows or to sling stones right-handed or left-handed)(1 Chronicles 12: 1-2, NIV).

Did you notice that these guys were switch hitters? That was very important for a warrior back then, for if you were wounded in your right arm, and you were a natural right hander, then you were probably dead meat. But these guys had thought of that possibility. I wonder how many hundreds, if not thousands, of hours they spent working with sling and swords with their natural hand and their unnatural hand. So if they were wounded in one shoulder, no problem. They'd just switch hands, suck it up, and keep fighting.

As good as these men were, David had others just as good. The same account in 1 Chronicles 12 also records the exploits of the Gadites (v. 8). The Gadites were a company of crack troops who just showed up one day at David's door. The son of Jesse looked outside one morning and—bang— there they were. That was the interesting thing about David's army. None of these men were drafted; they were all volunteers. They believed in David and they believed in his cause. They wanted to back David's star and ride in

David's posse. The young general from Judah must have been mighty glad to see them.

Scripture describes them this way:

They were brave warriors, ready for battle and able to handle the shield and spear. Their faces were the faces of lions, and they were as swift as gazelles in the mountains (1 Chronicles 12: 8, NIV).

These guys were not only tough, they were *fast*. Speed has always been important in warfare, and the men from Gad had it. They were fierce and they were quick. Their chief was Ezer, but also mentioned by name are Obadiah, the second in command, Eliab their third, Mishmannah the fourth, Jeremiah the first, Attai the sixth, Eliel the seventh, Johanan the eighth, Elzabad the ninth, Jeremiah the tenth, and Macbannai the eleventh. The reason they are referred to this way is that they were each commanders. Here are their stats: "These Gadites were army commanders; the least was a match for a hundred, and the greatest for a thousand" (1 Chronicles 12:14).

These guys could handle themselves. They were sort of David's Navy SEALS. Verse 9 records that they were the ones "who crossed the Jordan in the first month when it was overflowing their banks, and they put to flight everyone living in the valleys, to the east and to the west."

The first month was flood season, and when the Jordan flooded, it was serious stuff. You're talking about getting across a raging, fast moving, torrent of water a mile wide and 150 feet deep. That's no exaggeration. In other words, these guys weren't swimming laps at the "Y." These Gadites were the original Ironmen. A triathlon would have been a piece of cake to the boys from Gad.

Why were they willing to make such a dangerous crossing at such a treacherous time of year? They wanted to ride for the brand.

First Chronicles 12 goes on to list a number of other warriors who joined David when he was at a place called Hebron. All of these men were clear-eyed, battle-hardened soldiers. The best Israel had to offer. They were the top riders, the Special Forces, the Green Berets of the nation. They were David's Doomsday Defense. They are listed by tribe, and in some cases, by exploit, as the men of Zebulun, who are described as "experienced soldiers prepared for battle with every type of weapon" (v. 33, NIV).

In the midst of this all-star lineup of warriors in 1 Chronicles 12, is a reference to a group of men who were absolutely unique to any army that has ever been gathered. These men were not listed by their names. Only their tribe is mentioned. They are not described as warriors who could fight with either hand or swim across the Jordan at flood stage.

So who were they, and what could they do?

They were the "men of Issachar, *who understood the times and knew what Israel should do*" (v. 32).

Now don't get me wrong. The men of Issachar could fight or they wouldn't have been listed with the others. These guys could hold their own against anyone. But they had another dimension to them. And quite frankly it was a dimension the others apparently didn't have. But David desperately needed their contribution, and so did the entire nation. These men understood the times and as a result, they knew what Israel should do.

In other words, these men had two things that made them a cut above the rest:

• The men of Issachar had discernment.

• The men of Issachar had direction.

The men of Issachar saw what others didn't see. They looked behind the physical events and circumstances and realized there were spiritual forces influencing the conditions and situations of the nation from behind a parted curtain. That's why the men of Issachar were so valuable for warfare. They had discernment. They could stare a hole right through the obvious and see what wasn't obvious. Because of their discernment, they were then able to offer direction. Direction that was accurate and on target.

The men of Issachar were worth their weight in gold because they understood the times. Because they understood their culture and the forces at work behind the scenes, they knew what Israel should do.

As I read through 1 Chronicles 11 and 12, I was impressed by the thousands of men from each tribe who were listed in David's army. Thousands upon thousands. Yet when it came to the men of Issachar, it mentions only their two hundred chiefs. These men appear to be the cream of the crop.

There weren't twenty thousand of them, there were just two hundred. Yet their influence left its mark on all the rest.

They had discernment.

All of David's mighty men rode for the brand. But the men of Issachar saw what the other men didn't see, perceived what the other men didn't perceive.

As a result, they knew what needed to be done.

Gentlemen, we are living in a culture that is changing so fast it's hard to assimilate the changes. And the changes are not for the good. America is deteriorating morally and spiritually at an alarming rate. There are spiritual forces behind those changes. If you are going to function effectively as the spiritual leader of your home, you must be able to discern what is happening in this culture. You must do for your family what the men of Issachar did for Israel.

You must understand the times.

And if you understand the times, then you will know what your family should do.

This book is an attempt to help us understand our times. For—in the sovereignty of God—these are the very times when a lot of us happen to be raising our families. Our children are living in a culture that is light years different from the culture in which we were raised. You may be raising your family in the same town in which you grew up. Your kids might even go to the same schools you attended. You might drive the same streets on which you used to ride your bike as a kid. On the surface, it may look pretty much the same.

But that's an illusion.

The streets may be the same, the schools may be the same, the neighborhoods may be the same, but that town is a different town than it was thirty years ago because at least two things have changed.

• The thinking has changed.

• The values have changed.

Because the thinking has changed and the values have changed, our outlook for the future has changed.

Peggy Noonan writes a profoundly accurate picture of where many of us baby-boomers are:

I don't know many people aged 35 to 50 who don't have a sense that they were born into a healthier country, and that they have seen the culture deteriorate before their eyes....

You don't have to look far for the fraying of the social fabric. Crime, the schools, the courts. Watch Channel 35 in New York and see your culture. See men and women, homo- and hetero-, dressed in black leather, masturbating each other and simulating sadomasochistic ritual. Realize this is pumped into everyone's living room, including your own, where your 8-year-old is flipping channels. Then talk to a pollster. You too will declare you are pessimistic about your country's future; you too will say we are on the wrong track.[2]

The America we remember from our youth and the America in which we are raising our kids are so different it's almost as if they're two different countries. In a sense, they are different countries. Today's America is being ripped by forces our parents and grandparents would never have dreamed of. It is the clash of these forces that is becoming known in our day as "the Cultural War."

THE CULTURAL WAR

The Cultural War is a reality. But what is it? Tom Bethell has done as good a job as anyone in giving a summary of the Cultural War:

"The culture" really refers to a widely held set of beliefs about the purpose of life and the way in which society should be organized as a consequence. Those beliefs, in the U.S. as in the West generally, were for a long time broadly Judeo-Christian. Those who did not share these underlying religious beliefs were nonetheless for the most part willing to assent to them, and to accept the resulting framework of law and custom: abortion is wrong and should be illegal, homosexual behavior is shameful and should be frowned on, at best closeted; sexual intercourse should await matrimony and thereafter be confined to one's spouse.

All those beliefs have for a long time been under attack and have now been very widely discarded. Laws have been changed to reflect the new "reality." The results of abandoning the old culture are now apparent in the gay bathhouses and the AIDS wards, in the addiction treatment centers, in the crumbling inner cities, in the street gangs of the underclass, in the abortion clinics, in the high-school clinics that distribute condoms and Norplant, in the welfare offices, in the public housing projects, in the crime and illegitimacy rates, and most recently in the activities of the serial killer from Michigan, Jack Kevorkian.[3]

If any more evidence is really necessary to prove that America has changed, William Bennett can provide it. Bennett, the former Secretary of Education, has recently published his Index of Leading Cultural Indicators. The results are astonishing and demonstrate just how great the changes in this country have been since the early 1960s. I suggest that you read this next paragraph slowly and thoughtfully.

[During this] same 30 year period there has been a 560 percent increase in violent crime; more than a 400 percent increase in illegitimate births; a quadrupling in divorce rates; a tripling of the percentage of children living in single-parent homes; more than a 200 percent increase in the teenage suicide rate, and a drop of almost 80 points in the S.A.T. scores.[4]

Bennett has proven our suspicions. This country has changed. We are being defeated, not by some outside threat, but by our own choices. We are hemorrhaging internally, and if the bleeding isn't stopped, this nation will not survive.

Is there any doubt that America has changed? The statistics prove it, our eyes behold it, and sometimes, friends, our minds simply can't believe it. America has changed as a nation and we have changed from the inside.

I can remember as a kid when there was a great rush in this country to build bomb shelters. Everyone knew that the Soviet Union had the ability to rain missiles down just about anywhere in our country. Who would have believed back then that what would ultimately bring America down was not the Russians, but *ourselves*.

Paul Harvey illustrates the point by telling a rather gruesome story. It's a story about hunting. More precisely, it's a story that describes the process an Eskimo uses to hunt down a wolf.

First, the Eskimo coats his knife blade with animal blood and allows it to freeze. Then he adds another layer of blood, and another, until the blade is completely concealed by frozen blood.

Next, the hunter fixes his knife in the ground with the blade up. When a wolf follows his sensitive nose to the source of the scent and discovers the bait, he licks it, tasting the fresh frozen blood. He begins to lick faster, more and more vigorously, lapping the blade until the keen edge is bare. Feverishly now, harder and harder the wolf licks the blade in the Arctic night. So great becomes his cravings for blood that the wolf does not notice the razor-sharp sting of the naked blade on his own tongue, nor does he recognize the instant at which his insatiable thirst is being satisfied by his own warm blood. His carnivorous appetite just craves more—until the dawn finds him dead in the snow.[5]

A cagey wolf might have thought his greatest enemy was man. Not so. His greatest enemy was himself. The wolf was destroyed by internal lust. The real threat was not from the outside, it was from the inside. As it was with the wolf so it is with America. For there are forces at work within this country that are as insidious as any that can ever come from the outside. It is these forces that day by day are eroding the moral infrastructure of this great land.

I believe it was Pogo who said, "We have seen the enemy, and he is us."

THE LOWEST COMMON DENOMINATOR

When I read Bennett's report of the decline of the nation, I found it difficult to assimilate all of that information. Quite frankly, I was overwhelmed not only by the statistics, but the complexity and scope of our social and moral deterioration. It quickly became apparent that I was going to have to reduce all of those statistics down to their lowest common denominator.

You remember "the lowest common denominator," don't you? It's the single most important principle to successfully working fractions. It is also very effective in working *fractures*. Fractured children, fractured families, and fractured nations.

I believe that when you look at every major pressing social issue in this country, whether it's teenage pregnancy, child abuse, drive-by shootings, teenage suicide, or the divorce rate, and reduce each of those problems down to their lowest common denominator, you will find in each case the same root cause.

That cause is a lack of male leadership.

Somewhere and in some way, with every major social problem in America, a father has failed to give leadership to his family. That's the root cause of every pressing social issue in this country. The deterioration of our culture has accelerated dramatically because fathers who are willing to lead are in the minority. And that's the lowest common denominator. Daniel Patrick Moynihan observed this fact in 1965:

> From the wild Irish slums of the 19th century Eastern seaboard to the riot-torn suburbs of Los Angeles, there is one unmistakable lesson in American history: a community that allows a large number of young men (and women) to grow up in broken families, dominated by women, never acquiring any stable relationship to male authority, never acquiring any set of rational expectations about the future...that community asks for and gets chaos.[6]

Chaos.

That word accurately describes what is coming in our country because of the breakdown of male leadership. When authority breaks down, first in the home and then consequently, in the nation, chaos is the inevitable and frightening result.

We are closer to chaos than one might want to believe. When authority breaks down, and the consequences of breaking authority cease to exist, then you can be assured that we, as a nation, are well on our way to chaos. You've heard the phrase, "Crime doesn't pay." The truth of the matter is that in this culture of ours, those who abuse authority and despise authority are paid very well indeed.

Senator Phil Gramm recently wrote a piece for the *New York Times* where he cited a recent study from Texas A&M that calculated the amount of time that a person committing a crime in 1990—the last year for which we have complete statistics—could reasonably expect to spend in prison. The conclusions were shocking. On average,

- a person committing murder can expect to spend 1.8 years in prison;
- the expected punishment for rape is sixty days;
- robbery will bring an average prison time of twenty-three days;

• a person convicted of arson can expect 6.7 days;

• aggravated assault averages 6.4 days;

• a person stealing a car can reasonably expect to spend a day and a half in jail.[7]

With the breakdown of authority that began in our homes and spread to our schools and courts, it becomes clear that crime does pay. And it pays very well. America is quickly becoming a country that is sending a message to scores of young people and the message is this:

• authority is not important;

• you can willfully break authority (although we would prefer that you don't);

• if you choose to break authority and punishment cannot be avoided, we will make it as easy on you as we possibly can.

It has been a time-honored tradition in New York City for kids to try to open fire hydrants on hot summer days to cool off. The Fire Department would then come along and close the hydrants so that the water pressure could be kept up. Columnist John Leo reports that lately this "game" has been getting ugly.

Now, the kids open the hydrants and if they are pugnacious about it, the firefighters back down and the kids win. In certain areas, rocks and bottles are tossed whenever hydrant closers arrive. The standard practice of offering free spray caps hasn't worked. In one case, a hard spray was aimed at the cab of a fire truck, causing it to crash. It's not just about access to water during a heat wave. There's a sense that turf is somehow being invaded by the fire department and that the firefighters are authority figures worth rebelling against.

So the fire department issued a new directive. Now firefighters are under orders to back off from confrontations, though they are allowed to try closing the hydrants "at a later time." (Perhaps in the fall?)

In effect the city has "solved" its problem by turning control of the hydrants over to potential troublemakers. On the street, everyone now knows that firefighters will fade away even if growled at. A letter to the editor of New York's *Daily News* correctly called it a scary precedent that borders on anarchy. What's next, the letter writer asked, police avoiding gun-bearing thugs?

Policies such as these are as demoralizing as major crimes. Cities are haunted by the fear that no one is really in charge, that the nominal government can't or won't keep order, that it will cede any ground and collapse any standard to avoid trouble. Authorities keep backpedaling. Menaces aren't confronted. They are adjusted to and become part of the system.[8]

The lowest common denominator in this story about kids playing with fire hydrants is the absence of male leadership. Thirty years ago, if a kid was fooling around with a fire hydrant and then spoke disrespectfully to a fireman, his father would have taken down the strap and given him a few well placed licks on his rear end. Today, there is no father present in the home, and if he was there, and if he did take down his strap, some bureaucrats would have his rear end in jail for damaging the psyche of his son.

We need to get something straight. Ridin' for the brand means that a man leads his family. That's part of the high calling. It's such a necessary part that the Scriptures clearly teach that a man who doesn't lead his family and control his children is unfit for leadership in the church. Why would family leadership be a prerequisite for a man who is called to serve as leader in his church?

Ridin' for the brand means that you are a man who is salt and light. A society cannot survive without male leadership. For when male leadership ceases to be a reality in the home, we are only one generation away from anarchy in the streets. This is the direction that our nation is going. If we lose male leadership in Christian families, then this country is finished for sure.

Ridin' for the brand means that a man is not a follower. He stands tall. He is a leader. And that's the name of the game, gentlemen. It's leadership.

If you are a leader instead of a follower, or if up to now you have been a follower, but have a *desire* to be a leader of your family, then I think I can make you a promise. This book will make you a more effective husband and a more effective father, because this book will enable you to discern more accurately the forces that are actively at work in our nation to bring down everything that you value and love.

But if a man doesn't understand what the forces and issues are, then how can he give effective leadership to his family? How can he give direction to his children? How can he prepare them for what they are going to face if he doesn't know what they are going to face?

Our children are facing and will face moral challenges that were absolutely unthinkable when we were growing up. That's why we must familiarize ourselves with the forces that are at work to destroy the innocence of our children in this culture.

These forces are serious. Deadly serious.

That's why we have to be like the sons of Issachar.

The men of Issachar had vision, and we must have vision.

Soon after the completion of Disney World, someone said, "Isn't it a shame Walt Disney didn't live to see this?"

Mike Vance, creative director of Disney Studios, replied, "He *did* see it. That's why it's here."

This is a book for men. It's a book on how to lead your family in the midst of a culture hostile to Christian principles. It is designed to help you discern, and it is designed to help you give direction. Quite frankly, it's a follow up to *Point Man,* a book I wrote to men a few years ago on how to spiritually lead a family.

If you are a husband and father, then you are leading your family through the moral chaos of this culture. You are the point man. There is an enemy who is very real, and he has a plan to pick you off and neutralize you from leading your family. When you are the point man, to a great degree, the very survival of your family depends upon the caliber of your leadership.

The book that you hold in your hands is designed to familiarize you with the changing spiritual influences that we are fighting against. Battles change with time, and this battle is no different. We need to clearly see what we are up against.

There is nothing worse than a blind point man. Helen Keller was once asked if there was anything worse than being blind. "Yes, there is," she replied. "It is having sight but no vision."

Let me be honest with you. I am genuinely amazed at how many blind Christian men I run into. Now don't get me wrong. They have physical vision.

They might even be 20-20 when it comes to seeing stuff on the surface. What they are missing is *spiritual vision*. They don't have spiritual discernment. They don't understand the times, and most tragically, when it comes to spiritual matters, they don't have a clue as to what their families should do.

I see it in the choices they make. I see it in the lack of direction they give to their children. I see it when Christian fathers allow their children to attend certain movies. A man of discernment would never allow his children to attend that movie. A man without vision thinks to himself, "It's just a movie." A man of vision knows that it's more than a movie. It's a carefully crafted and marketed piece of propaganda promoting a value system contrary to everything right, just, godly, and good.

But the man without vision doesn't see that. So he hands his ten-year-old a ticket and throws him to a pack of morally-rabid, Hollywood-bred pit bulls.

That's like a guy leading a patrol through enemy-occupied territory noticing a trip wire partially exposed in the underbrush, just off the dimly marked path. If he thinks to himself, "It's just a wire," he will soon be headed home either in a helicopter or a body bag. A man giving leadership to a patrol or a family must have eyes to see and understand what isn't apparent on the surface.

A man with vision is a man of discernment.

And what is discernment?

Discernment is looking at the same thing as everyone else and seeing something very different. You see the unseen and the inevitable implications that will come from what seems to be just an isolated situation. A man who can't see with discernment is not an effective husband or father. He has to see the bigger picture. He has to have vision. He must be a man of action.

In Lewis Carrol's *Alice in Wonderland,* there is a particular dialogue between Alice and the Cheshire Cat. Alice inquires of the cat, "Would you tell me, please, which way I ought to go from here?"

"That depends a good deal on where you want to get to," the Cat replies.

"I don't much care where," says Alice.

"Then it doesn't matter," returns the Cat, "which way you go."

You wouldn't be reading this book if you didn't care where your family was going. You care, and you care deeply. That's precisely why you need vision to discern this culture in which you are raising your family. Men who ride for the brand are men of vision. They understand the times and they know what their families should do.

How much vision do we need?

Just enough to see the barbarians.

1. Read 1 Chronicles 11:15-19 and 12:16-18. Describe the character of the loyalty of these men to David and to the Lord. What can we as men learn from these displays of unflinching, unintimidated loyalty to their cause?

2. Review 1 Chronicles 12:32. In view of the conditions in America today, how can we be more like the sons of Issachar?

3. Look again at 1 Chronicles 12:33. What might the biblical writer have had in mind when he described the men of Zebulun as men of "undivided heart"? What kinds of influences in our contemporary culture might give Christian men a *divided* heart? What will it take for us to ride for the brand like those guys from Zebulun?

4. Note the last words in 1 Chronicles 12: "There was joy indeed in Israel." What do you see in the preceding verses of the chapter, particularly in verses 38 through 40, that might have brought such joy? What clues does the writer leave that might make us more joyful men today—even in a country where Christian values are being trashed?

5. Take a moment to look up Proverbs 29:18. If you have copies of the New International Version, the New American Standard Version, and the King James Version, check out the differences in wording. Solomon seems to be equating "vision," with prophetic vision or divine revelation. In other words, the Scriptures! What evidence in today's culture do you see of Solomon's warning about those who remove such "vision" from a nation or people?

CHAPTER TWO

The Whites of Their Eyes

At what point, then, is the approach of danger to be expected?
I answer, if it ever reaches us it must spring up amongst us;
it cannot come from abroad.

ABRAHAM LINCOLN

I live in Texas. There are still a lot of cowboys wherever you go in Texas. Whether it's San Antonio, El Paso, Tyler, or Dallas, you'll see cowboys everywhere. And the telltale sign of a genuine Texas cowboy is his Stetson hat.

All over Texas you'll run into men wearing their Stetsons. Texas is full of cowboys and cowboy hats. You will also see a lot of pickups. And that explains something that you might not know if you live outside Texas.

Do you know why cowboys always roll the brims of their Stetsons up on the sides? It's so three of them can fit in the cab of a pickup.

Attila the Hun didn't wear a Stetson and he didn't drive a pickup. But he was as wild as any cowboy who ever rode in Texas. Attila the Hun was a barbarian. The words "Hun" and "barbarian" go hand in hand. Wess Roberts describes the men who followed Attila's leadership:

Individually, the Huns were a spirited, perfidious [I don't know what perfidious means, but it sure sounds good] people without common purpose other than to establish their next campsite. Commodities for internal trade didn't exist, so they sought out villages to lay waste to in

31

order to obtain booty that would later be used as barter for food and other supplies necessary for their survival....

Clad in the skins and the furs of beasts, many of the Huns were characterized by somber, yellowish skin, long arms, large chests, and narrow, slanted eyes with a dull glitter of mingled cunning and cruelty. Their warriors had skulls deformed in childhood by a wooden apparatus held fast by leather tongs. The scant beards of the warriors were the result of their cheeks having been seared with hot irons in their youth to retard the growth of facial hair.

They ate raw meat toughened by having been carried in pouches between their thighs or between the flanks of their horses. A portion of their nutrition came from drinking mare's milk.

The weapons of the horde were considered unsophisticated and outlandish even in their own time. Their spirit as warriors was driven by a lust for rapid and sustained movement in pursuit of a paradise of glory filled with pillage and booty.

To the civilized world they were barbarians not far removed from wild animals in both appearance and lifestyle. The mere presence of the horde often instilled sufficient terror in the people of the region that they abandoned their villages without resistance or subsequent reprisal.[9]

CHOOSING SIDES

The Green Bay Packers were the team of sixties, the Pittsburgh Steelers the team of the seventies, and the San Francisco 49ers owned the eighties. Which team would you choose over the others? That's a tough call.

There are some who would pick Attila and the Huns as the greatest warriors in history. Others would take Alexander the Great and his crew. Personally, I'll stick with David and his Mighty Men. I'll stack them up against a bunch of wild-eyed barbarians anytime. For David's men had Someone on their side that no other nation in history can claim in the same way. His name is Yahweh, the Creator and Ruler of all things.

Why did God give David such a group of mighty warriors? David had his Mighty Men because Israel would need such men to protect them from the barbarian hordes that surrounded them on every side. David and all of Israel were encircled by barbarians.

By the way—so are we.

The only difference is that the barbarians in our culture don't *look like* barbarians. That's precisely why you need discernment. Without discernment, you won't be able to recognize the barbarians.

Charles Colson delivers this sobering diagnosis:

I believe that we do face a crisis in Western culture, and that it presents the greatest threat to civilization since the barbarians invaded Rome. I believe that today in the West, and particularly in America, the new barbarians are all around us. We have bred them in our families and trained them in our classrooms. They inhabit our legislatures, our courts, our film studios, and our churches. Most of them are attractive and pleasant; their ideas are persuasive and subtle. Yet these men and women threaten our most cherished institutions and our very character as a people.... Today's barbarians are ladies and gentlemen. Yet behind their pleasant, civilized veneer lurks an unpleasant intolerance that threatens the very processes of pluralism and freedom they claim to defend.[10]

I recently came across one of these new barbarians in one of my children's schools. I got so close that I could see the whites of his eyes. As a matter of fact, I had to go toe-to-toe with him in front of two hundred people.

The last thing he looked like was a barbarian. Truthfully, he was a well-dressed, very pleasant looking gentlemen in his early forties. He certainly did not look threatening. He looked like a nice, average American who would live across the street from you. He was married and had two children. He was a nice guy, with a nice job, with a nice family, from a nice neighborhood.

He was also a barbarian.

In our state, there have been several attempts in recent years by Planned Parenthood and their philosophical cohorts to mandate sex education courses in public schools, beginning with kindergarten. These people, along with Surgeon General Joycelyn Elders, believe that five-year-olds should be given information that will help them determine their "sexual orientation." That is nothing short of criminal.

Last year in Texas, a new bill was introduced that was very, very vague. It was vague by design. In their previous attempts to pass mandated sex education that would take the control out of the local school boards, the Planned Parenthood proposals were soundly defeated. So they decided to be delightfully non-specific. There were several meetings called by concerned parents in our community. One was called by a group of mothers who opposed the bill. I made sure that I attended that one. Another was called two weeks later by some people who were for the bill. I decided I had better show up at that one as well.

When I arrived for the meeting, things had already gotten underway. There were close to two hundred parents in the cafeteria. The sponsors made it very clear that the meeting was not sponsored by the school district. Rather, it was being called by a man in our community who was concerned that the previous meeting had been too conservative and one-sided. He had invited an official of Planned Parenthood to debate the issues with a lady who represented the other side.

Because I got to the meeting late, I was unaware of the arrangements. The lady "representing the conservative side" was so inarticulate and non-committal that I thought throughout the evening that she, too, was representing the side of Planned Parenthood.

It wasn't much of a debate.

Basically, the guy from Planned Parenthood spent two hours giving half truths, inaccurate statistics, and evasive responses to written questions. The man who had called the meeting announced that no questions would be taken from the floor. All question were to be written. The moderator read through the questions and submitted the ones he thought the guest should answer. That's called censorship.

After about forty-five minutes of hearing the moderator lob the Planned Parenthood representative nice, easy, and mostly irrelevant questions, a man to my left spoke from the floor. He was told that questions weren't being taken from the floor. He replied that *his* question was not being addressed and he went directly into his question. It was a very good question. He had obviously done his homework and the man from Planned Parenthood hemmed and hawed but could not give a definitive response. For the first time, someone had called his bluff. He wasn't looking very sharp as he took the first "unscreened" question from the floor.

That's when I decided to speak up.

The moderator reminded me that questions were not being taken from the floor. I replied that my question was germane to the discussion and was being ignored. So I went ahead and asked my question.

"Sir, two years ago a group known as APPAC (Adolescent Pregnancy and Parenthood Advisory Council) made some recommendations to the state legislature encouraging the passing of a mandatory sex education curriculum."

"Yes," replied the man. "I was a part of that committee."

"In your recommendations you advised the state to adopt a curriculum that included a 'Bill of Rights' for adolescents. I am quoting from the Bill of Rights that you encouraged the state to adopt."

I then read a section of the document that said that every adolescent has a "right" to "confidential reproductive health care services."

"Sir, as I understand this 'right' that you feel that young children should have, it means that my daughter could walk into one of your clinics at school, be given advice and encouragement that is contrary to the moral values that my wife and I have taught, and I would never know about it. She could also be given a birth control device without my knowledge. Why is it that you believe that your counselors have a moral viewpoint superior to ours—and why is it that your counselors should have access to my child in such a way that undercuts my parental authority?"

A murmur rippled through the audience.

The Planned Parenthood spokesman then began a lengthy and evasive response that appealed to some Supreme Court decision on the question of "privacy." As he continued his verbal gymnastics he made a reference that was very innocuous and harmless on the surface.

That's when I jumped in again.

"Sir, by that reference, aren't you referring to abortion?"

The room suddenly got very quiet because I had said the "A" word. His reply was nothing short of phenomenal.

"I was not referring to abortion. *Planned Parenthood has nothing to do with abortion.*"

I couldn't believe my ears. I looked around and saw a few others shaking their heads in disbelief. The tragedy was that a number of people in the room believed him. After all, he was such a nice guy with such a nice family.

"Sir," I said, "you are deliberately misstating the truth."

Immediately some people began to boo and hiss at me. Others started to applaud.

"I am not. Planned Parenthood has nothing to do with abortion. I'm the director and I ought to know."

"That is exactly right, sir. You should know and you *do* know, and I know. You are deliberately attempting to persuade this audience of something that is not true."

The booing got louder and the hisses became more pronounced. A woman turned around right in front of me and declared that she found my remarks offensive. I smiled at her and kept going.

The guest speaker was now backtracking by citing another Supreme Court decision. I responded by reminding him that the Supreme Court, in its Dred Scott decision, had ruled that black people were nothing but chattel. In other words, the Supreme Court could be very, very wrong.

It was getting late and the meeting was hastily brought to a conclusion. It was then that the man from Planned Parenthood walked up to me.

"So you think I lied to this audience tonight?"

"Sir," I replied, "I know that you did. And so do you."

He then proceeded to explain to me that "technically" they did not directly do abortions in their office. However, they did underwrite the budgets of twenty-something abortion clinics in several counties. He then detailed other activities they supported that directly encouraged and funded abortions.

"Sir, why didn't you say all of this up in front of the audience? You deliberately withheld this information—and you did it in order to leave an impression that was blatantly untrue."

"Well," he replied, "I must say that I am deeply disturbed by the hatred, fear tactics, and half-truths being spread by the other side!"

"So what you are doing bothers you, right?"

He looked at me completely confused. "Of course not! I was referring to the other side!"

"Oh," I responded. "After watching your performance this evening, I was sure that you were referring to yourself." I then smiled and said, "It's nothing personal." In my mind I thought, *It's just that you want my children. And that's not going to happen.*

I don't enjoy people booing and hissing at me. But do you know why I spoke up? I spoke up because I'm riding for the brand. To have *not* spoken up would have been nothing less than a betrayal of the Lord Jesus Christ. I guarantee that *He* would have spoken up because the lives of little children are at stake. In my opinion, that's something worth standing up for.

You see, gentlemen, because we are surrounded by these new barbarians, it means that Christian husbands and fathers are going to have to do three things. A man who is going to ride for the brand and fight the good fight must (along with his wife):

- discern his culture;

- defend his convictions;

- disciple his children.

That's it. That's the abbreviated job description of a point man in this culture. That's what it's going to take to battle the barbarians. That's what it's going to take to stand tall and defend your family.

I took the time to recount my experience to you because it demonstrates in microcosm the real issue going on in this country. What was it about this nicely dressed gentleman that was so barbaric? It was what he believed. You see, this man believes in something called *moral relativism*. I believe in *moral absolutes*. And so do you. I seriously doubt that you would be reading this if you didn't believe in moral absolutes. It used to be that the vast majority of Americans believed in moral absolutes, but that is no longer the case. As Pat Buchanan observed, "Americans of left and right no longer share the same religion, the same values, the same codes of morality; we only inhabit the same piece of land."

In case someone is still unclear as to what we mean when we refer to moral absolutes, allow me to offer the following examples:

• "I am the LORD your God, who brought you out of the land of Egypt, out of the house of slavery. You shall have no other gods before Me."

• "You shall not make for yourself an idol, or any likeness of what is in heaven above or on the earth beneath or in the water under the earth. You shall not worship them or serve them; for I, the LORD your God, am a jealous God, visiting the iniquity of the fathers on the children, on the third and fourth generations of those who hate Me, but showing lovingkindness to thousands, to those who love Me and keep my commandments."

• "You shall not take the name of the LORD your God in vain, for the LORD will not leave him unpunished who takes His name in vain."

• "Remember the Sabbath day to keep it holy."

• "Honor your father and mother, that your days may be prolonged in the land which the LORD your God gives you."

• "You shall not murder."

• "You shall not commit adultery."

• "You shall not steal."

• "You shall not bear false witness against your neighbor."

• "You shall not covet your neighbor's house; you shall not covet your neighbor's wife."

These examples of moral absolutes are brought to you through the courtesy of Moses and Western civilization as founded on the Word of God as recorded in Exodus 20:1-17. For hundreds and hundreds of years, anyone who did not believe these particular moral absolutes was considered to be, quite frankly, a barbarian.

THE BARBARIAN COAST

Why is moral relativism so barbaric? It is barbaric because of what it believes. Here's the bottom line. A person who believes in moral relativism basically believes in two things:

• There is no absolute truth, therefore;

• Everything is permitted.

Moral relativism took off in this country in the sixties. A case could be made that the first capital of moral relativism was the Haight-Ashbury district of San Francisco. San Francisco was once known as the Barbary Coast; what it gave birth to in the sixties was nothing less than the Barbarian Coast of free love, free speech, and moral relativism.

This was the thinking behind the cultural shift that took place in America right around 1968. It was taught in our universities and spread like wildfire through the collective consciousness of students all over America. But those students of the sixties are no longer students. They are professors, members of Congress, judges, school board members, and presidents of the United States. What they believe is that there is no absolute truth, therefore, everything is permitted.

In the sixties, it was called "doing your own thing." If you bought into moral relativism in the sixties, you could let your hair grow, sleep around, smoke dope, and basically do whatever you wanted. That's what it looked like on the surface. But underneath, it was even more terrifying. In Colson's words, moral relativism means that:

> In every decision a person stands alone. Because there are no moral absolutes, there are no value-associated reasons to make one decision over another. We may as readily choose to ignore a neighbor rather than help him, to cheat rather than be honest, to kill rather than let live...the outcome of our choices carries no moral weight.
>
> No longer are we guided by virtue or tradition. Selfish passions breed freely.... Gone are any notions of duty to our fellow man and to the Creator. As a result, there is no straight edge of truth by which to measure one's life. Truth is pliable and relative; it can take whatever shape we want.[11]

IN AGAINST THE NIGHT

Gentlemen, we are raising our kids in this sewer of moral relativism. If your kids buy into this philosophy, it will ruin their lives. Here's the deal, guys. Our kids won't know anything else unless they see it in our lives. Our kids won't know that there are moral absolutes unless they absolutely see those truths *lived out* in our lives.

In thirty years, moral relativism has swept through our culture with blinding speed and pervasiveness. It's everywhere. Our kids read it in the newspapers and magazines, watch it on TV, hear it on the talk shows, listen to it on CDs and cassettes, and are taught it in the majority of public schools.

You see, when I was a kid the Ten Commandments were posted in our classroom. As a result, every kid in my public school classroom knew that it was wrong to steal, wrong to cheat, wrong to murder, and wrong to lie. Why did we know that? Because Almighty God said so. It was God who had given that moral code to Moses on Sinai.

But today, our kids are growing up in a culture where someone will say, "Well, that may be wrong for *you*, but that doesn't mean it's wrong for *me*." That is moral relativism.

The point is this, gentlemen: We can't rely on the culture to back up what we are trying to teach to our children. That's the way it was in the fifties, when I was growing up. Generally speaking, the culture was going to back up the values that my parents were trying to teach me. That's why Ozzie didn't leave Harriette, David, and Ricky, and run off with some sweet young thing he met at the office. (Did Ozzie ever go into the office?) The culture and the media upheld and sustained the moral absolutes of the Ten Commandments, therefore it was unthinkable for Ozzie to commit adultery. But those days are gone.

We have now completely lost our moral compass in this country. In modern America, bad is good and good is bad. Listen to the network anchors, listen to the Donahues and Oprahs and Geraldos, listen to the godless messages of the TV sitcoms, listen to the messages written on the editorial pages of this nation's newspapers. They are all saying that on the moral compass south is north and north is south.

They are wrong.

Almighty God determined the magnetic fields that causes compasses to point north and He wrote the moral law that gives civilized people equilibrium and balance. And He has revoked neither the magnetic fields nor His moral law.

North is still north.

South is still south.

Homosexuality is still perversion.

Abortion is still the taking of innocent human life.

Yet the media is working in a concerted effort with the other elitists to give the impression that their distorted morality is the "consensus" of this country. They use the power of vicious sarcasm and slanted reporting to shout down anyone who would stand up to their twisted and convoluted morality. Their primary weapon is sheer intimidation. Saying that there is such a thing as absolute truth is the very thing that moral relativism detests and despises.

THE WAY WE WERE

Allan Bloom knew American culture. His book, *The Closing of the American Mind*, was viciously attacked by liberals when it was released. Bloom, who recently passed away, was a liberal Jewish scholar greatly respected in academic circles. At least he was until he wrote his critique of American higher education. Bloom describes what has happened to the average American family as a result of moral relativism:

> Parents do not have the legal or moral authority they had in the Old World. They lack self-confidence as educators of their children, generously believing that they will be better than their parents, not only in well-being, but in moral, bodily, and intellectual virtue. There is always a more or less open belief in progress, while the past appears poor and contemptible. The future, which is open-ended, cannot be prescribed to by parents, and it eclipses the past which they know to be inferior....

> Parents can no longer control the atmosphere of the home and have even lost the will to do so. With great subtlety and energy, television enters not only the room, but also the tastes of old and young alike, appealing to the immediately pleasant and subverting whatever does not conform to it. Nietzsche said that the newspaper had replaced prayer in the life of the modern bourgeois, meaning that the busy, the cheap, the ephemeral, had usurped all that remained of the eternal in his daily life. Now television has replaced the newspaper.[12]

But today, television is perhaps the primary spokesman for moral relativism. Approximately one hundred years prior to the 1950s, philosopher

Soren Kierkegaard wrote: "Suppose someone invented an instrument, a convenient little talking tube which, say, could be heard over the whole land.... I wonder if the police would not forbid it, fearing that the whole country would become mentally deranged if it were used."[13]

Kierkegaard feared that we might become mentally deranged. What has happened is that we *have* become morally deranged. I believe that, to a great degree, that derangement is the result of American families becoming morally crippled by an unstructured and malnourishing diet of cable and network television. At the bottom of it all is a blind point man who either doesn't know or doesn't care that his home is under attack.

What many men don't realize is that someone or something is leading your family. Now is it you or is it television? Is it you or the peers of your children? Make no mistake, *someone* is leading. Do you know who that someone or something is?

A family needs discernment and direction. Where are they going to find it? The ideal answer is that they get it from their fathers. Without your discernment and direction, my friend, the chances are extremely high in this culture that your children will become morally deranged.

Bloom made the statement that "parents can no longer control the atmosphere of the home and have even lost the will to do so." Generally speaking, I think Bloom is right. But he was off just a hair. His statement would be much more accurate if he had said, "*Fathers* no longer control the atmosphere of the home and have even lost the will to do so."

Not too long ago, my son called me from the home of a friend.

"Dad, can I watch MTV?" he asked.

"No," I replied. "Son, I really appreciate your calling and asking me. I wish I could let you watch it. But there is stuff on MTV that will hurt you. I'm not going to let them do that to you. Why don't you bring your friend down here to our house and you guys can watch one of your videos."

My son was just seven years old when he made that call. He was phoning from the home of a good family with a good dad and a good mom. I know where they worship and it's a fine, Bible teaching church where Jesus Christ is honored. But my question is, why is this guy allowing MTV to be pumped into his house to influence his three kids under the age of ten?

It may surprise you that my seven-year-old called to ask if he could watch 〉 Good
that program. The reason he did is because we've worked with all of our kids 〉 tending
on this issue. If they are at a friend's house, we have emphasized the impor- 〉 Thought
tance of calling us and checking if they can watch a particular video or program that we don't watch at home. The reason we have done this is that we
have discovered some very fine people dropping the ball when it comes to television. I used to assume that I could trust the discernment of other parents. I
don't make that assumption anymore. That's why I have asked my kids to call.

My son's friend has a dad who's a good guy—but doesn't control the
atmosphere of his own home. Would he ever allow some sexual deviate into
his home to have free reign in influencing his children? Of course not. It's
amazing to me how some guys will let someone into their home to influence
their kids through television who they would never allow in the front door.

Are you familiar with Butthead and Beavis? When I was kid, we'd come
home from school and watch a half-hour of Huckleberry Hound. Now it's
Butthead and Beavis on MTV. Bob DeMoss of Focus on the Family offers
the following description of this popular program:

> This daily half-hour "cartoon" combines ridiculous and vulgar
> "adventures" with clips of two idiots (after whom the show is
> named) sitting on the sofa babbling about music videos (mostly
> heavy metal) which play on the screen. Whether mocking the
> Challenger disaster or mooning "The Brady Bunch," these two
> delinquents take television to an all-time low.

> Beavis and Butthead's conversation resorts to scatological name-call-
> ing and comments about erections, urination, sadomasochism,
> mucous, flagellation, vomiting, and masturbation....

> The boys show disrespect for all authority. The exploits also include
> stealing and destroying property, verbally assaulting a schoolmate
> ("Do you got periods?") and voyeurism (leering at girls in music
> videos, peering into a van at a couple having sex, and so on)....

> In essence, this MTV feature presents two juvenile media junkies
> left to follow their own standards of morality and conduct—which,
> in some ways, probably mirror the values of the executives at MTV
> who program such twaddle.[14]

Allow me to make a suggestion. If MTV is being piped into your home through cable, I'd like to tactfully suggest that you get rid of it as soon as possible. If you were to find that your home's water supply was contaminated with E. coli bacteria or cancer-causing PCBs, then you would take immediate and drastic steps to protect your family from the water.

If your kids have access to MTV, then they are in as much spiritual danger from the moral raw sewage as they would be from any physical danger.

Get rid of it, my friend.

Your kids may scream, yell, cry, and say that everyone else watches it. The reason their friends watch it is that they have fathers who aren't leading the family. Your first step of leadership is to cut off that vile runoff from polluted minds.

Now you may be saying, "I don't let my kids watch MTV," or "we don't have MTV at our house." That's great to hear. But may I remind you that the major networks are doing all they can to follow MTV's lead? They're only a step or two behind, and gaining rapidly. Personally, I don't let my kids watch MTV or prime-time network TV for the same reason that I don't encourage them to drink water from the toilet. As I write these words, groups of well-dressed executives at ABC, CBS, NBC, and Fox are sitting around walnut conference tables thinking up new ways to swim in the sewage race with MTV.

Why I am going into all of this? It's easy to look at the nation as a whole and be concerned about the overwhelming social issues. But the question is this: What am I as a father doing to keep my kids from becoming a part of these negative social issues? The only way to cut down the numbers of kids involved in everything from teen-pregnancy to drive-by shootings is to get fathers involved in *leading* their homes.

Why in the world should you allow the Attilas who program the networks to come riding into your house and pick off your kids? Gentlemen, if we want to see the nation changed, then let's begin in our own living rooms.

Yes, you will probably be accused of being "strict." My kids think I'm strict. They think that because I am. When they tell me I'm strict I immediately agree with them. And then I tell them that in twenty years when they are the parents they will be stricter than I am.

This book is an attempt to help you discern the times so that you can be a better husband, a better father, and a more effective spiritual leader in your home. In an age where moral relativism, like a huge, national vacuum, has sucked away nearly every vestige of decency, truth, and goodness, it is not too late to establish those ideals in the life of your family. But it will take a godly, clear-eyed, modern-day son of Issachar riding out ahead of the family wagon.

A man who is sure and confident in the truth of the Scriptures.

A man who taps into the Spirit's willingness and ability to guide him through the moral storms that are seething just over the horizon.

America is headed for dark days, for America has crossed the line of no return. We have crossed that line morally and we have crossed it spiritually. To be quite honest, America is in deep yogurt, and there will likely be dark days ahead for those of us who hold to the moral absolutes of the Scriptures.

What your family needs in these troubled days is leadership. And it must come from you. For it is the observation of truth lived in your life that will make the difference in their lives.

But may I ask you a direct question? How about your family? How are they doing for leadership? Do they have a man at the helm who has a firm grip on the wheel? Or are things drifting?

Today is the day to stop the drift.

Today is the day to reassess your priorities.

Today is the day to begin making the Bible the center of your home instead of the television.

In other words, if you have lost control, *take* control.

Today is the day to start standing tall.

Read Proverbs 24 and discuss the following questions.

1. In verses 5 and 6, what elements do you see that could help Christian men fighting the cultural war in America? How can we avoid the shame and humiliation implied in verse 10?

2. What do verses 11 and 12 have to say to Christian men who shrug their shoulders or turn a blind eye to issues such as abortion and the savage war for the hearts and minds of America's children?

3. As we wage this battle with enemies of all that is right and good and decent in this country, what note of caution does Solomon add in verses 17 and 18? Bring these two verses into today's arena, and put them into your own words.

4. What encouragement can a present-day warrior engaged in America's cultural war gain from the "big picture perspective" presented in verses 24 and 25?

5. What does the little story in verses 30 through 34 have to say to Christian men about vigilance in view of what's happening in our country? What application could we make to the "garden" of our own spiritual lives and relationship with Jesus Christ?

CHAPTER THREE

Dads Who Draw the Line

The best time to tackle a minor problem is before he grows up.

RAY FREEDMAN

The teenage son picked up the phone on the first ring.

His dad whispered, "If it's the office, tell 'em I'm not here."

That evening when the family went out for dinner, the father looked over the check and noticed the waiter had undercharged him.

"If they're not smart enough to total up a check correctly, then it's *their* problem, not mine," said the dad.

All of this didn't escape the notice of the son, whom the father had grounded just the week before for cheating on a test at school. There was nothing wrong with that boy that a moral relative couldn't take care of.

The opening chapters of this book have traced the moral deterioration of our once great nation. But it must be pointed out that every nation is compromised of individual families. A nation is only as strong as its families. That's why every family needs a moral relative at the helm. Believe it or not, history teaches that the very survival of a nation can depend upon a child having a father who is a moral relative. A dad who is a moral relative knows how to draw the lines in the necessary places.

And he also knows when *not* to draw a line.

As I write these words, Halloween is just several days away. I was speaking last night to a group of men, and one of them asked me a very good question about Halloween. He mentioned that Halloween is a big problem in their family because of the origins of the holiday. In other words, because of the pagan beginnings of Halloween, he and his wife didn't let their kids observe it. He then asked me what we did with Halloween.

My reply was that Halloween did have pagan origins. But in our family, when we think of Halloween, we're not thinking of anything pagan. We're just thinking about how much candy we can accumulate in about two hours. We have the mentality of chipmunks gathering acorns before the winter. We want to get as many Hershey bars as we possibly can for the long, cold winter ahead. Our goal is to plunder the neighborhood the way the children of Israel plundered the Egyptians before they headed out for the Promised Land.

My kids have had Christian teachers who told them that Halloween was the Devil's day and that they should not trick or treat. I did not appreciate that comment. And I did not appreciate the legalism. If you read Romans 14, and Colossians 2:16-17, you will find that some issues are issues of conscience. Some Christians observe a particular day as the Sabbath, others consider every day alike. According to 1 Corinthians 8, some Christians eat meat offered to idols, others do not (that's not a big deal in our culture, but it certainly was in theirs). Some Christians get steamed over Halloween, others plunder the neighborhood in the name of Jesus.

The point of Romans 14 is that these are issues that Scripture doesn't specifically cover. So, Paul says let each man be fully convinced in his own mind. One believer will, one believer won't. Each man should have a personal conviction. But if your neighbor has a different conviction, then don't try to persuade him that yours is superior. And don't condemn him.

What I have said to my kids is that Halloween does have some pagan roots. But we're not pagans. We love Jesus. Halloween to your six-year-old probably doesn't mean satanic worship. It means candy. So every Halloween I take my kids out to get candy. That's what Halloween means at my house. In other words, guys, I'm going to have to draw *enough* lines where the

interesting observations about Halloween

scriptures *are* clear. If I don't have to draw a line, believe me, I'm not going to draw it. Especially when a Hershey bar is at stake.

My kids aren't Satan worshipers. But they do like Hershey bars. So we go out on Halloween and have a lot of fun getting candy, then we eat too much candy, and then we throw up later that night. We like to think of it as quality time.

PRIME TIME

Good dads have the biblical wisdom to know when to lighten up. They also know when to draw a line, and how to draw a line. That's why Hollywood mocks the God-ordained institution of fatherhood.

We live in a culture where the entertainment industry consistently criticizes and belittles fathers. Michael Medved offers a common sense analysis of Hollywood's view of the family:

> In addition to its relentless antimarriage messages that undermine the connection between husbands and wives, the popular culture also helps to poison relationships between parents and children. No notion has been more aggressively and ubiquitously promoted in films, popular music, and television than the idea that children know best—that parents are corrupt, hypocritical clowns who must learn decency and integrity from their enlightened offspring.[15]

As usual, the entertainment moguls have it dead wrong. But the Scriptures have it right. There is a script in the Old Testament that would make a blockbuster movie, but don't hold your breath for Hollywood to produce it, since Cecil B. De Mille is now deceased. Yet this is a script that every father in America should be aware of. It's the story of a man who was a moral relative. His name was Mordecai. His moral leadership in the life of his adopted little girl saved an entire nation. This is no phony "docu-drama" or made-for-TV movie. It really happened. And it could still happen today.

The book of Esther begins with a Persian king by the name of Ahasuerus. (Some versions refer to him as Xerxes. Both names are correct.) Ahasuerus gets upset with Vashti, the queen of his nation. He gets so upset that he decides to replace her the way Richard Nixon replaced Spiro Agnew with Gerald Ford. In other words, he launches a nationwide search for a new queen. You can read all of this for yourself in the opening chapters of Esther. We pick up the story in chapter 2, verse 5:

Now there was a Jew in Susa the capital whose name was Mordecai, the son of Jair, the son of Shimei, the son of Kish, a Benjamite, who had been taken into exile from Jerusalem with the captives who had been exiled with Jeconiah king of Judah, whom Nebuchadnezzar the king of Babylon had exiled. And he was bringing up Hadassah, that is Esther, his uncle's daughter, for she had neither father nor mother. Now the young lady was beautiful of form and face, and when her father and her mother died, Mordecai took her as his own daughter.

So it came about when the command and decree of the king were heard and many young ladies were gathered to Susa the capital into the custody of Hegai, that Esther was taken to the king's palace into the custody of Hegai, who was in charge of the women. Now the young lady pleased him and found favor with him. So he quickly provided her with cosmetics and food, gave her seven choice maids from the king's palace, and transferred her and her maids to the best place in the harem. Esther did not make known her people or her kindred, for Mordecai had instructed her that she should not make them known. And every day Mordecai walked back and forth in front of the court of the harem to learn how Esther was and how she fared...

So Esther was taken to King Ahasuerus to his royal palace in the tenth month which is the month Tebeth, in the seventh year of his reign. And the king loved Esther more than all the women, and she found favor and kindness with him more than all the virgins, so that he set the royal crown on her head and made her queen instead of Vashti. Then the king gave a great banquet, Esther's banquet, for all his princes and his servants; he also made a holiday for the provinces and gave gifts according to the king's bounty.

And when the virgins were gathered together the second time, then Mordecai was sitting at the king's gate. Esther had not yet made known her kindred or her people, even as Mordecai had commanded her, for Esther did what Mordecai told her as she had done when under his care (Esther 2: 5-11,16-20).

MORAL RELATIVISM OR MORAL RELATIVE?

Every child in America needs a moral relative. A strict moral relative. And that strict moral relative should be Dad. America desperately needs some strict fathers. There are hundreds of thousands of children walking around our schools, streets, and malls who desperately need someone in their lives who loves them enough to say "no."

The first two chapters of this book outlined a rough sketch of the moral deterioration taking place in this country. May I suggest to you that one of the root causes of our breakdown as a nation is a lack of men who love their families enough to be strict.

"Strict" is a very unpopular word today. Yet it is a very necessary word. We have lost fathers in this nation who know how to be strict—in the best sense of the term. We have fathers in this nation who are more interested in being popular with their kids than they are in being respected. And therein lies our problem.

Nearly forty years ago, in an effort to beat back a rising crime rate among juveniles, the Houston Police Department undertook a massive public relations campaign. Chuck Swindoll was a young man in Houston during this time, and recounts the effort in his first book, *You and Your Child*.[16] Billboards were placed all over the city with pertinent messages to parents about raising children. One of the most well received messages was a pamphlet entitled "Twelve Rules for Raising Delinquent Children."

1. Begin with infancy to give the child everything he wants. In this way he will grow up to believe the world owes him a living.

2. When he picks up bad words, laugh at him. This will make him think he's cute.

3. Never give him any spiritual training. Wait until he is twenty-one and then let "him decide for himself."

4. Avoid the use of "wrong." He may develop a guilt complex.

This will condition him to believe later, when he is arrested for stealing a car, that society is against him and he is being persecuted.

5. Pick up everything he leaves lying around. Do everything for him so that he will be experienced in throwing all responsibility on others.

6. Let him read any printed matter he can get his hands on. Be careful that the silverware and drinking glasses are sterilized, but let his mind feast on garbage.

7. Quarrel frequently in the presence of your children. In this way they won't be so shocked when the home is broken up later.

8. Give a child all the spending money he wants. Never let him earn his own.

9. Satisfy his every craving for food, drink, and comfort. See that his every sensual desire is gratified.

10. Take his part against neighbors, teachers, and policemen. They are all prejudiced against your child.

11. When he gets into real trouble, apologize for yourself by saying, "I could never do anything with him."

12. Prepare for a life of grief. You will be likely to have it.

Those twelve rules are just another way of saying to parents, whatever you do, don't be strict. Let me go on record as saying that strict can be very, very good. It isn't inherently bad, as many would lead us to believe in our day and age.

A family had taken shelter in the basement as a severe storm passed over their town. The radio warned that a tornado had been spotted. When the storm had passed by, the father opened the front door to look at the damage. A downed power line was whipping dangerously on the street in front of their house. Before the father realized what was happening, his five-year-old daughter ran right by him, headed for that sparkling wire in the street.

"Laurie, stop!" he yelled.

Laurie just kept going.

"Laurie, STOP!"

Laurie ran right for the enticing cable.

"STOP NOW, Laurie!"

Little Laurie reached down to pick up the wicked power line and was instantly killed.

What a heart-breaking tragedy. But the real tragedy is that it happened because a little girl had never been taught that when her father said "no," he really meant "no." It cost him the life of his daughter.

When Esther was still a little girl, she learned from Mordecai that "no" meant "no." He loved her enough to train her to obey, and that obedience not only saved her life, but the lives of all the Jews. "Esther did what Mordecai told her as she had done when under his care." Esther did not start obeying when she was twenty-one. It started much earlier than that. And it began with a man who loved her enough to be strict.

Allow me to clarify up front what I *don't* mean when I refer to a "strict father."

- Strict fathers aren't mean to their kids.
- Strict fathers aren't aloof from their kids.
- Strict fathers aren't distant from their kids.
- Strict fathers aren't harsh with their kids.
- Strict fathers aren't verbally abusive to their kids.

The kind of strict fathers that our nation needs are men who fit the following criteria:

- We need strict fathers who love their kids.
- We need strict fathers who are affectionate with their kids.
- We need strict fathers who verbally praise their kids.
- We need strict fathers who emotionally support their kids.

The strict fathers I'm referring to aren't out of balance. They are in balance. Their strictness is balanced by a host of positive qualities that gave their kids a context of unconditional love and acceptance.

As a matter of fact, we are going to have to redefine the normal definitions of the word "strict." Dictionaries define words in different ways with slightly different nuances. I marked several variations after a brief search. Strict is...

"marked by careful attention to relevant details;"

"incapable of changing or being changed;"

"extremely severe or stern;"

"given to or characterized by strict discipline or firm restraint;"

"conformable to a fact or a standard."

A LOOK AT A SUCCESSFUL, STRICT FATHER

Let's examine each of these definitions of "strict" one-by-one, for they each have something significant to offer. And let's examine them through the lens of Mordecai.

1. Strict fathers are marked by careful attention to relevant details.

A lot of us guys are not detail oriented. But when it comes to our kids, there are certain details we need to be aware of. If you read through the book of Esther (and I suggest that if you haven't done it recently, you quickly review the book), you will find that Mordecai was always hanging around the gate of the palace. Why would he do that? It's simple. Mordecai wanted to know what was going on in Esther's life. He wanted to know the details. Not because he was pushy, but because he knew she was in uncharted territory. So he made himself accessible.

Some of you guys have daughters that are beginning to date. This is when you need to be aware of some details. As an example, the first detail should be "*who* is she going out with?"

Fathers in America have been taken out of the dating process. It's time they got back in. *Fast.* A teenage daughter needs her father to be very much involved in this part of her life. Let me ask a question to you guys who have daughters who are dating: "Do you know the guy that your daughter is going out with?" And perhaps more importantly, "Does he know you?"

My daughter is beginning the dating process. That means I am beginning the dating process, too. The young men who take out our daughters need to understand that we, as fathers, are going to be involved in the details. But before we get to the details, they need to understand that it is a *privilege* to take out our daughters. Not a right, but a privilege. And privileges are earned.

Does this seem old-fashioned to you? That's exactly what it is. It may not be in fashion for a father to be involved in the dating life of his daughter, but may I submit that's exactly why we have such incredible problems in this society. Bill Bennett pointed out that since 1962, illegitimate births have gone up 400 percent. I can't help but think that if more fathers were involved in the details of their daughter's lives, that statistic would drop dramatically.

Fathers have not been involved. They have been relegated to the sidelines. But those days are over. I can't do a lot about society as a whole, but I can definitely go against the tide of male passivity that is ruining our families and make a difference in my own family. How do I do that? By exerting some loving, strict, family leadership.

My daughter is now fourteen, but when she's twenty-five and starts dating(!), I plan on figuring into the dating equation in a way that will honor her. I'm not talking about embarrassing our daughters, guys. I'm talking about protecting them. We obviously want to make our influence known in a way that doesn't give our daughters a reputation of having a "weird" father. And we can do that. We can get the message across without being weird or forcing the young man to sit through a cross-examination that will guarantee he will never come back.

What I am saying, gentlemen, is that your influence and presence must be realized and *felt.* There are appropriate ways to do that without putting a kid through the inquisition.

I want to meet a young man before he takes my daughter out. I want him to know that I'm interested in the details. I want to know where they are planning on going, of course, and make it clear what time I expect them to be back home. And I will remind him in an appropriate way that I am trusting him to honor the plan that has been set forth for the evening, and that if any pertinent changes come up, I expect them to check in with me.

If a young boy knows that a father is interested in the details, that will make a major difference in how he treats not only the events of the evening, but your daughter. Gentlemen, if you let him know by your actions that you consider her to be very valuable, then he will treat her accordingly. Especially if he knows that you are in the picture. The fear of a father is the beginning of wisdom. Especially when it comes to dating.

We should be just as involved in the details of our sons' dating lives. We should let them know that we expect them to be gentlemen at all times and to handle themselves according to a different standard than the one that many of their friends will follow.

Sons should be coached by fathers—and not just in Little League. If you will take time to give your son some "tips" on how a gentleman treats a lady, then he will be miles ahead of his peers.

2. Strict fathers are not incapable of changing or being changed.

The second definition of "strict" that I found was "incapable of changing or being changed." That's a somewhat skewed definition of "strict," in my book. Quite frankly, it needs to be changed. For the purposes of our discussion, let's alter this particular definition to "a father who is capable of changing when it is appropriate, but who has the guts to stick to his guns when he needs to." Now that definition probably wouldn't make it into Webster's, but I sort of like the way it flows. It has a nice ring to it.

Good fathers are capable of change. But strict fathers know there are times when the worst thing a father can do is alter the guidelines he has laid down. The effective, strict fathers that I know are entirely capable of change. But they know that changing the rules because a child pleads for you to do so is a very poor excuse for being an effective dad.

Mordecai was a man who taught little Esther to obey him and God. But you don't get the idea that Mordecai was overbearing. As I read this story I don't pick up any hostility between Mordecai and Esther. It seems to me that they had a very healthy relationship as adults—which tells me they had a healthy relationship as she was growing up. As the story develops, the wicked bureaucrat Haman plots to destroy the Jews. When Esther reveals the plot to Mordecai, she gives her foster-dad some specific directions. The Scripture says "So Mordecai went away and did just as Esther had commanded him" (Esther 4:17).

I get the strong sense that Mordecai was a guy who knew how to draw the line...but also had a teachable spirit. In other words, he knew when to submit. That's the mark of good leaders. They know how to submit to good counsel. I pick up the picture that Esther respected Mordecai because he was capable of change when it was appropriate.

When I was a sophomore in high school, we moved to a new town and a new high school. It was the typical scenario of being the new kid who didn't know anyone. One of the fastest ways to make friends in that situation is to go out for a sport. In about two days, you know more guys from playing ball than you could meet in three months.

Normally, I would have gone out for basketball. But I had done something very foolish. I had brought home a "D" on my last report card. The only reason I had gotten a "D" was that I had horsed around in the class and basically exhibited some very irresponsible behavior in turning in papers. My dad had a rule for the three boys in our family, and the rule was this: if any of us got anything lower than a "C" in a class, we couldn't play ball. He didn't demand that we get straight "A's" or make the honor roll. My dad knew that the only reason any of us would get a "D" was that we were fooling around instead of acting in a responsible way.

As a result, I didn't go out for basketball. Now my dad was all for me playing ball. He had been all-state in both basketball and football in high school, went to college on a basketball scholarship, and after World War II, was offered a contract to play football for the Pittsburgh Steelers. My dad was not against sports. He wanted me to play. But he was more interested in developing my character than he was in developing my jump shot. My dad had some long terms goals for me that were more important than basketball. He knew it would be very good for me to have to live with the consequence of sitting out a basketball season due to my lackadaisical behavior.

One day I was in my Physical Education class, and we were playing basketball. I didn't know it but the varsity coach was in the bleachers watching the pickup game. After we went into the locker room he came up to me and asked me who I was and why I wasn't out for varsity basketball. I told him that we had just recently moved into town and that I'd come out for basketball next year. He said that he wanted me to come out this year.

I told him that my dad had a rule about getting any grade lower than a "C."

The coach said, "But according to the school rules you're still eligible to play if you have just one 'D'."

"Yessir, I realize that," I replied. "But you have to understand that my dad has his own eligibility rules."

"What's your phone number?" the coach asked. "I'm going to call your dad."

I responded, "I'll be happy to give you the phone number, but it will be a waste of your time."

This coach was a big, aggressive guy. He was about 6'2 and 220 pounds which put him one inch shorter and twenty pounds lighter than my dad. Coach was used to getting his own way. But he hadn't met my dad. I knew before the coach ever called what my dad's answer would be.

Was my dad capable of change? Sure he was. Was he going to change because he got a call from the varsity coach? Of course not. A lot of dads would have been so flattered that they would have compromised on the consequences. But my dad wouldn't, because my dad was strict. And I thank God that he was.

That night after dinner Dad told me the coach had called. He told me he had told the coach no. He then reminded me of the importance of being responsible in class and that he really *wanted* me to play basketball. But the ball was in my court (no pun intended). If I wanted to play ball it was up to me. At that point, I was very motivated to work hard in class so that I could play basketball the next season.

The next morning the coach came up to me in the locker room.

"I talked to your dad yesterday afternoon and he wouldn't budge. I explained the school eligibility rules, but he wouldn't change his mind. I don't have very much respect for your father."

I couldn't believe my ears. *This coach didn't respect my father.* Even I had enough sense to know my dad was doing the right thing. Sure, I wanted to play ball but I knew my dad was a man of his word and he was right in not letting me play. I couldn't believe this coach would say such a thing.

"Coach," I said. "I can tell you that I highly respect my dad. And I also want you to know that I will *never* play basketball for you."

I never did. I got my grades up, but I never went out for varsity basketball. I refused to play for a man who didn't respect my dad for doing what was right. That was the end of my high school basketball career because that man coached basketball for my remaining years in high school.

Why wouldn't I play for him? Because he didn't respect my father. If he didn't have the sense to respect my dad then I sure as heck wasn't going to play for him. Come to think of it, the real reason I wouldn't join his team was that I didn't respect *him*. He was a compromiser and I suspected that he would do anything to win. My dad was a man of conviction and a man of character. And any coach who couldn't see that was not the kind of man I wanted to associate with.

My dad was strict and unwilling to change his conviction even though it hurt him for me not to play ball. My dad was capable of change, but he was unwilling to change because he had a long-term objective for my life that the coach didn't have.

The coach wanted to win games.

My dad wanted to build a son.

The issue was character.

My dad had it and he was trying to build it into me. As far as I was concerned, the coach didn't have it. I decided to stick with the strict guy. It was one of the better decisions I have ever made.

3. *Strict fathers should not be extremely severe or stern.*

One definition of strict is "extremely severe or stern." As my kids like to say, *"Not!"* Let's get one thing clear. Extremely severe or stern is not what makes for a good family. Extremely severe fathers ruin their children's lives. Ephesians 6:4 couldn't be any plainer: "Fathers, do not provoke your children to anger…" Colossians 3:21 says the same thing…with a different twist: "Fathers, do not exasperate your children, that they may not lose heart."

Fathers who practice the wrong kind of "strict" cause their children to lose heart. One wise scribe commented on Colossians 3:21 by saying "a child frequently irritated by over severity or injustice, to which, nevertheless, it must submit, acquires a spirit of sullen resignation, leading to despair."[17]

There is a time to be strict but there is also a time to lighten up and chill out. Good dads have happy homes with happy kids. Overbearing fathers tend to lose their kids as their kids get older. That's a tragedy. The relationship with a child should only get better as the child develops. But that won't happen if a father is severe or stern.

Mordecai and Esther were close. That should tell us that Mordecai was not some legalistic nut who set stringent and unnecessary rules in Esther's life. Good dads draw the lines where they have to be drawn, but leave plenty of room for fun and good times.

Homes are like restaurants in that every restaurant has a certain atmosphere. So do homes. Most guys that I know are only concerned about the quality of food when they consider a restaurant. But sometimes our wives like to go on special occasions to restaurants that have good food and good atmosphere. Some restaurants work very hard to develop "ambiance." Ambiance is a classy, upscale French word. I think it means expensive.

Have you noticed that the nicer the atmosphere in a restaurant the greater the check at the end of the meal? Atmosphere is expensive. By the way, do you know why there are no restaurants on the moon? There's no atmosphere.

Every home has an atmosphere. And generally speaking the atmosphere is one of two kinds. The atmosphere in your home is either *constructive* or it is *destructive*. In other words, in your home people are either built up or they are torn down. Construction or destruction. Building up or ripping down. Which one is behind your front door?

Gentlemen, we set the atmosphere. We determine whether the atmosphere is positive or negative. We can talk all day long about the deterioration of this nation, but what about your home? Are your kids falling apart under the constant stream of criticism that comes from your mouth? Are your kids having a tough time responding to you because you are one way at church and another way at home?

Let me put my cards on the table. Fathers who are overly strict are lousy fathers. Men who are rigid, authoritarian, suppressive, tyrannical, domineering, and legalistic are men who turn their kids away from Jesus Christ. Kids don't want to be around people like that. I sure don't want to be around people like that. Men who establish an atmosphere that is repressive, legalistic, and harsh are destroying their own children.

The story is told of the old Persian ruler who wanted to impress a visiting dignitary. He showed the official a glass cage and inside the cage a lion was resting comfortably next to a little lamb.

The guest couldn't believe his eyes. "How can a lion and lamb coexist?" he asked.

"I believe that it is possible for natural enemies to find peace," replied the ruler.

"But how can a lion and a lamb possibly get along in the same cage?" asked the guest.

"It's simple," said the ruler. "Every morning I put in a new lamb."

Children are not replaced on a regular basis. That's why they must be nurtured in an environment that is firm, yet appropriately flexible. It was Sam Goldwyn, the Hollywood mogul at MGM who said to his staff after six straight box office flops, "I want you to tell me exactly what's wrong with me and MGM. Even if it means losing your job."

That's not exactly the kind of atmosphere that builds healthy relationships within a company. And it doesn't seem to work well with kids, either. Kids need strict fathers who know how to lighten up and have a good time. They don't need dads who are wound so tightly that everyone is wondering when they are going to snap next. That doesn't make for a home of construction. In a nation that is falling apart, we need families that aren't.

4. *Strict fathers are characterized by discipline and firm restraint.*

I admit that I am reading between the lines when it comes to Mordecai and Esther. The Scripture doesn't give us a lot of details from the early years. But I am convinced the reason Esther obeyed Mordecai later in life was that she learned to obey him early in life.

The story is told of a judge in the wild West who had a strange custom. This judge had a practice of giving condemned criminals a choice between hanging and the "big, black door."

The time for execution would inevitably arrive, and the judge would go to the cell of the prisoner. "Well, what'll it be? The rope or the big, black door?"

Nearly everyone who was given that option wound up taking the rope.

A sheriff once asked the judge why the prisoners always chose hanging over the big, black door. The judge replied, "They always prefer the known to the unknown. People fear what they don't know. Yet, we gave them a choice."

"What lies beyond the big door?" asked the sheriff.

"Freedom," replied the judge. "But very few men are brave enough to choose the option of the unknown."[18]

A good father knows that discipline and firm restraint are the doors to lifelong freedom for his children. It is the father who chooses to not discipline who is condemning his children to a life of difficulty and hardship.

In the history of Israel, there is another account of a particular man who chose not to discipline his sons. His name was Eli and his is a tragic story. Eli was a priest, yet his sons were men whose hearts were far from the Lord. Eli was one of those guys who wasn't a strict father. And it just about did him in.

The story is outlined for us in 1 Samuel 2, beginning with verse 12: "Now the sons of Eli were worthless men; they did not know the LORD and the custom of the priests with the people."

The account goes on to explain that Eli's sons appropriated the people's animal sacrifices for their own meals. If anyone resisted them, they threatened them with force. Scripture describes their activity in this way: "Thus the sin of the young men was very great before the Lord, for the men despised the offering of the LORD" (1 Samuel 2:17).

The rebellion of Eli's sons became the talk of the town.

Now Eli was very old; and he heard all that his sons were doing to all Israel, and how they lay with the women who served at the doorway of the tent of meeting. And he said to them, "Why do you do such things, the evil things that I hear from all these people? No, my sons; for the report is not good which I hear the Lord's people circulating" (1 Samuel 2:22-24).

Eli presented his sons with a very profound question. He asked his sons why they were doing such evil things. That was a great question.

Unfortunately, Eli was a major part of the answer. Why were his sons doing such things? Listen to the words the Lord spoke to young Samuel in 1 Samuel 3:11-13:

> And the LORD said to Samuel, "Behold, I am about to do a thing in Israel at which both ears of everyone who hears it will tingle. In that day I will carry out against Eli that I have spoken concerning his house, from beginning to end. For I have told him that I am about to judge his house forever for the iniquity which he knew, because his sons brought a curse on themselves and he did not rebuke them."

Why were the sons of Eli involved in such wicked activity? Because they had a father who didn't rebuke them. Esther obeyed Mordecai later in life because she obeyed him earlier in life. Eli's sons didn't obey him because they apparently had never been rebuked by their father. He didn't rebuke them as men because he hadn't rebuked them as children. In other words, discipline and firm restraint were new concepts to them—especially when it came to their father. Boys who are not used to discipline and restraint grow up to be men who have severe problems. If you have any doubt about that, just ask a prison chaplain. Why is it that our prisons are bulging at the seams? A lack of strict fathers who don't love their sons enough to exercise discipline and firm restraint.

There is an old story that has made the rounds. Two fathers of teenagers were having a cup of coffee. "Do you strike your sons?" the one father asked. "Only in self-defense," came the response. There's another dad who didn't rebuke his sons early.

Skillful fathers are men who know that their children need discipline and firm restraint. Michael Green wrote:

> Loose wires give out no musical notes, but when their ends are fastened, the piano, the harp, or the violin is born. Free steam drives no machine, but harnessed and confined with piston and turbine it makes possible the great world of machinery. An unhampered river drives no dynamos, but dam it up and you can generate sufficient power to light a great city.[19]

Strings that are tightened, steam that is captured, rivers that are harnessed, and children that are disciplined can produce astonishing results.

Roy Lessin put it best: "Rules for children are like a pole that is placed alongside a tall plant growing in the garden. The pole is not there to stop the plant's development, but to help guide it into maturity and productivity."

Eli never put those poles in place, and it cost him the joy of watching his sons become mature and productive men in his old age. What a tragic waste of potential.

5. *Strict fathers conform to a fact or a standard.*

There is a better way of saying this one. Instead of saying that strict fathers conform to a fact or a standard, it's much better to say that every child needs a dad who is a moral relative. He models the standard by his life and his behavior. He isn't perfect, but he is consistent. A father who is a moral relative is raising his children in a culture which practices moral relativism. They must see the difference in his life. That's why consistency is so important.

Ken Canfield has done some great work with fathers. One of the principles Ken emphasizes is the area of consistency:

How does a man become a more consistent person and thus a more effective father? One way is for him to understand all the different ways in which his children need him to demonstrate consistency. The research shows that an effective father is consistent in his:

- mood swings;
- presence in the family;
- keeping of promises;
- morality and ethics;
- daily schedule;
- hobbies and schedules.[20]

I see symptoms of consistency throughout the life of Mordecai. He might have had a temper and he might have been impatient. I really don't know what his faults were. But I can tell you this. There was a little girl who saw enough *consistent* love in his life that she was willing to follow his counsel and put her life on the line.

Stuart Briscoe tells the following true story of leadership:

One of my young colleagues was officiating at the funeral of a war veteran. The dead man's military friends wished to have a part in the service at the funeral home, so they requested the pastor lead them down to the casket, stand with them for a solemn moment of remembrance, and then lead them out the side door. This he proceeded to do, but unfortunately the effect was somewhat marred when he picked the wrong door. The result was that they marched with military precision into a broom closet, in full view of the mourners, and had to beat a hasty retreat covered with confusion.

This true story illustrates a cardinal rule or two. First, if you're going to lead, make sure you know where you are going. Second, if you are going to follow, make sure that you are following someone who knows what he is doing![21]

Leaders not only need to know where they are going, they need to see the big picture. It is the father's job to see the larger picture that a child doesn't see.

I recently heard a story about Earl Weaver, the former manager of the Baltimore Orioles, and how he handled his star player, Reggie Jackson. Weaver had a rule that no one could steal a base unless given the steal sign. This upset Jackson because he felt *he* knew the pitchers and catchers well enough to judge who he could and could not steal off of.

So one game he decided to steal without a sign.

Jackson got a good jump off the pitcher and easily beat the throw to second. As he shook the dirt off is uniform, Jackson smiled with delight, feeling he had vindicated his judgment to his "strict" manager.

Later, Weaver took Jackson aside and explained why he hadn't given the steal sign. First, the batter was Lee May, his best power hitter other than Jackson. When Jackson stole second, first base was left open, so the other team walked May intentionally, taking the bat out of his hands.

Second, the following batter hadn't been strong against that pitcher, so Weaver felt he had to send up a pinch hitter to try to drive in the men on base. That left Weaver without bench strength later in the game when he needed it.

The problem was, Jackson saw only his relationship to the pitcher and catcher. Weaver was watching the whole game. A case could be made that Weaver was a "strict manager." Perhaps that's why he was such an effective manager. Weaver saw the big picture and so did Mordecai. Mordecai was a man who knew where he was going, and what he was doing.

A lovely lady named Esther learned this firsthand. In the face of incredible, overwhelming odds, one man squared his shoulders and stood tall. One little girl was fortunate enough to grow up in the security of his long shadow.

The bottom line is this. His leadership ultimately saved her life. But it not only saved her life, it saved *his* life. In fact, it saved a nation.

Every child needs a moral relative, a dad who can draw the line. And guess what, guys. We've been nominated.

Do you accept? Or do you decline? Grab a Hershey bar and think it over.

1. What can you discern about the "father-daughter" relationship between Mordecai and Esther from Esther 2:10-11,20, and 4:1-17? How had Mordecai's training of Esther prepared her for life circumstances that were perplexing, heart-breaking, and dangerous?

2. Review Ephesians 6:1-4, restating in your own words both sides of the parent-father "contract." What is the likely result of a dad who insists on verses 1 and 2, without providing the *context* of verse 4? What additional insight does Paul provide in Colossians 3:21?

3. Look again at 1 Samuel 2:12-17 and 3:10-14. Where does the Lord lay the blame for the evil that shadowed the sacred Tent of Meeting? What can we learn about the violence and corruption in our own culture from this account?

4. As you weigh the necessity of becoming a dad who "draws the line," carefully consider Paul's words in Ephesians 4:29-32. How do these biblical instructions modify your view of what a "strict father" looks like?

CHAPTER FOUR

When America Lynched Common Sense

The Christian world is in a deep sleep.
Nothing but a loud voice can waken them out of it.

GEORGE WHITEFIELD, 1739

They were called line riders.

In many ways, it was the loneliest job on a large ranch.

The designated cowboy would load up his bedroll, fill his saddlebags, and head out to the farthest boundaries of the spread. He would then make a long circuit around the far-flung borders of the ranch. Depending on the size of the boss's range, the job could take days—or weeks—in the saddle.

Along the way, the rider made certain that cattle with the ranch brand didn't stray too far from home range, and that stock from neighboring ranches didn't wander in to sample the grass. He checked the herd for sickness, noted the condition of watering holes, and kept his lariat handy in case he had to rope an adventurous cow out of a bog. Armed with a .45 pistol on his hip and a Winchester in the saddle boot, the lonely rider kept his eyes open for rustlers, cougars, or wolves who might prey on the stock—especially the young.

Even in the years before fences began criss-crossing the wide rangelands, there really wasn't much problem with boundaries. Everyone pretty much knew where they were. The landmarks were clear: a creek, a long ridge, a butte, a stand of timber, a well-rutted trail, a single, wind-twisted cottonwood. There were a thousand ways to recognize the borders of the home range.

In later years, of course, the line riders became fence riders, inspecting the fences and making repairs wherever there was a break. If cattle had drifted through a break, the cowboy would gather them, if possible, and drive them back toward home.

Everyone used to know the *moral* boundaries in America, too.

It was a community that would "ride the fences," keeping watch over the young and dispatching the wolves and rustlers who had somehow slipped on to the home range. In recent years, however, most of America's moral fences have been systematically removed.

There are even those who would deny they were ever there at all.

THE TRUE FOUNDATION

When John Hubbard, the former president of the University of Southern California, made a trip to the Middle East, he was astonished to meet so many graduates of USC halfway around the world from L.A. In the government alone he could count four cabinet ministers and fourteen deputy ministers as USC alumni, plus some of USC's most prosperous businessmen.

Dr. Hubbard was the guest of honor at a large banquet. Lamb and pilaf. He brought with him the filmed highlights of recent USC seasons. One was a USC-Notre Dame game, when USC trailed 24-6 at the half. The robed and bearded audience groaned. The USC Trojans came back with forty-nine points in the second half to win. The audience cheered, play by play, touchdown by touchdown. When the lights went on, the host of the alumni meeting, filled with the spirit of victory, made a pronouncement.

"Gentlemen," he said, "Allah is a Trojan."[22]

That was a pretty funny line. With a room full of USC alumni in Saudi Arabia, a person who didn't know the background of USC could have very easily gotten the impression that USC was a Moslem school. The fact is that USC was originally chartered as a *Methodist* university. But most people don't know that. Especially in the middle of an alumni meeting in the Middle East.

Just as there are graduates of USC who probably don't know the historical context of the founding of USC, so there are many people today who don't realize the historical context of the founding of the United States. Allah is not a Trojan and God is not an American. That does not mean, however, that the Word of God did not play a key role in the founding of our nation. The Bible did play a central role in the minds and hearts of the vast majority of our founding fathers.

Does that mean that America was a Christian nation? John Eldredge of Focus on the Family answers:

> If by the phrase "Christian nation" one means that every citizen of the United States at its founding was a disciple of Jesus, or required to be one, the answer is obviously "no." ...If by the phrase "Christian nation" one implies that somehow the United States exhibited all of the virtues of the Christian ethic in its laws and institutions, the answer is also "no." Slavery should remove any doubt that the new nation failed to fulfill Christ's vision for humanity.[23]

We must be very careful in saying that America was a Christian nation. That is not only a loaded statement but it is somewhat imprecise. Well, in one sense it is, and in one sense it isn't. Eldredge hits the nail on the head when he writes that "precision is absolutely essential when discussing the role of the Christian faith in America's founding and the First Amendment in particular."

However, there is absolutely no doubt that America's founders unashamedly were shaped in their thinking by the Bible. No, this was not a Christian nation in the sense that everyone had a personal relationship with Jesus Christ. On the other hand, there was no other teaching or people who played a more vital role in the development of this nation than those who recognized the God of Abraham, Isaac, and Jacob. Quite frankly, most Americans have no idea how central the Bible was to our founding fathers.

If you have any doubt about that, you probably haven't visited

Washington, D.C. Everywhere you look in Washington you see Scripture. In Congress, you will see massive paintings that portray the centrality of Scripture. You will see Pilgrims kneeling on the soil of their new country with the Bible opened before them. You will see Scripture chiseled in marble on building after building, monument after monument. And thank God it was chiseled! Because if it wasn't, it would have been removed long ago.

When we go back and read the statements of the founding fathers, it is clear that Scripture was central in their thinking as they constructed the framework of this nation. The central book in their minds was not the Koran, or the writings of Confucius or Buddha. It was the Bible. That is historical fact.

Let's ride on in and take a closer look.

A CLOSER LOOK

Just what exactly was the moral foundation of this country? As David Noebel has pointed out, "There can be no denying that the United States was originally founded on Christian principles and values."[24] In order to prove the validity of that statement, allow me to machine gun some historical quotes and information that you probably never heard in school.

John Adams, a member of the committee appointed to draft the Declaration and a former president of the United States, says, "Our Constitution was made only for a moral and religious people. It is wholly inadequate for the government of any other."[25]

It was James Madison who declared, "We have staked the whole future of American civilization not upon the power of government—far from it, but we have staked the future of all of our political institutions upon the capacity of mankind for self government, upon the capacity of each and all of us to govern ourselves, to control ourselves, to sustain ourselves according to the Ten Commandments of God."[26]

Madison was one of the chief architects of the Constitution, yet the Supreme Court of our day would not allow Madison to post the Ten Commandments in a public school. Even though the founding fathers had staked the entire American future upon them.

George Washington made it clear where he stood when he declared, "It is impossible to rightly govern without the Bible." The beliefs of Washington are clearly documented. Much of what our kids hear today in school about Washington is sheer myth. David Barton has written a booklet entitled, *The Bulletproof George Washington.* It tells a story that was widely published and printed in all textbooks—until 1934. Because of its strong allusions to Christianity, it has been eradicated from the texts in favor of the cherry tree story.

Barton's booklet is worth obtaining to read to your family. Briefly, he recounts a fierce battle that Washington, then a twenty-three-year-old colonel, took part in during the French and Indian War. This particular battle was so intense that his life literally hung in the balance for two hours. Washington's assignment was to communicate orders from the general to the other officers in the field. This necessitated Washington being on horseback during the entire battle. The Indian sharpshooters had been given specific directions to shoot the officers. As a result, sixty-three of the eighty-six officers were casualties.

After the battle, Washington wrote a letter to his brother, describing his acknowledgment of the hand of God that secured his safety:

By the all-powerful dispensations of Providence, I have been protected beyond all human probability or expectation; for I had four bullets through my coat, and two horses shot under me, yet [I] escaped unhurt, although death was leveling my companions on every side of me![27]

Fifteen years later, the Indian chief who was in charge during the battle, met Washington and related to him the following account:

I called to my young men and said, "Mark yon tall and daring warrior [Washington]? Himself alone is exposed. Quick, let your aim be certain, and he dies." Our rifles were leveled, rifles which, but for you, knew not how to miss—'twas all in vain, a power mightier far than we shielded you. Seeing you were under the special guardianship of the Great Spirit, we immediately ceased fire at you.... I come to pay homage to the man who is the particular favorite of Heaven, and who can never die in battle.[28]

God sovereignly kept His hand on the young man who was to become a key player in the formulation of a new nation—a nation that had a unique place in the plan of God. But whatever we do, let's not let our school children hear that story! It might cause them to think that there really is a God who oversees and controls the affairs of men.

Are you familiar with John Jay? No, he didn't play third base for the Reds in 1947. John Jay was the first Chief Justice of the Supreme Court. He was appointed Chief Justice of the first Supreme Court by George Washington. Jay had this to say about the Christian foundation of this new nation: "Providence has given to our people the choice of their rulers, and it is a duty as well as a privilege and interest of our Christian nation to select and prefer Christians to be their rulers."[29]

Note that the first Chief Justice of the United States had no problem back then with referring to America as a "Christian nation." The influence of Christianity and the Bible had permeated every strata of life in early America. Including politics.

James Wilson holds a unique place in American history, in that he was one of only six men to sign both the Declaration of Independence and the Constitution. Wilson, a highly respected judge who was also appointed by George Washington, was the second most frequent speaker at the Constitutional Convention. It was Judge Wilson who said, "Christianity is a part of the common law of America."[30]

On July 4, 1776, Benjamin Franklin, John Adams, and Thomas Jefferson were appointed as a committee to prepare a Seal of the United States of America. Some of the ideas they came up with show the centrality of the Bible in their thinking. Your kids, however, will never read this in their public school textbooks.

Various suggestions were offered for the design of the Seal. Franklin wanted a design featuring Moses. Moses! In the background, the troops of Pharaoh would be seen drowning in the Red Sea and the message would be: "Rebellion to tyrants is obedience to God." Can you believe that? The ACLU (if they had been around back then) would have filed a suit so fast that Ben wouldn't have believed it. Jefferson suggested that the Seal show that the children of Israel in the wilderness were "led by a cloud by day and pillar of fire by night."[31]

What kind of coffee were these guys drinking? What about the separation of church and state? These were gentlemen who didn't believe in the separation of *sense* and state.

Some would object to these references by saying that some of these men such as Franklin and Jefferson weren't Christians at all. They were deists, men who believed that "God created the world as a watchmaker makes a watch, and then wound it up and let it run. Since God was a perfect watchmaker, there was no need of his interfering with the world later."[32]

Francis Schaeffer, the late twentieth-century prophet, explains the meaning of the word, "Christian."

Not all the individual men who laid down the foundation for the United States Constitution were Christians; some, in fact, were deists. But we should realize that the word "Christian" can legitimately be used in two ways. The primary meaning is: an individual who has come to know God through the work of Christ. The second meaning must be kept distinct but also has validity. It is possible for an individual to live within the circle of that which a Christian consensus brings forth, even though he himself is not a Christian in the first sense.... Some of the men who laid the foundation of the United States Constitution were not Christians in the first sense, and yet they built upon the Reformation...to whatever degree a society allows the teaching of the Bible to bring forth its natural conclusions, it is able to have form and freedom in society and government.[33]

Most Americans are very familiar with Patrick Henry and his famous statement, "Give me liberty or give me death." But there is another comment from the lips of Patrick Henry that gives particular insight into his view of the founding of America:

It cannot be emphasized too strongly or too often that this great nation was founded, not by religionists, but by Christians; not on religions, but on the Gospel of Jesus Christ. For this very reason people have been afforded asylum, prosperity, and freedom to worship here.[34]

America was built on the foundations of biblical Christianity. Can you imagine the public outcry if Patrick Henry, John Adams, Benjamin

Franklin, and Thomas Jefferson were alive today and made some of those comments in public?

First of all, they would be barbecued in the media. They would be scolded for their lack of sensitivity and accused of being messengers of hate and prejudice, completely lacking in tolerance. Newspaper editorials would accuse them of being out of touch with multiculturalism and the mainstream of American thought.

I can imagine that the next step would be to appoint a special prosecutor to investigate, intimidate, and instigate possible criminal proceedings for their questionable roles in such procedures that blur the line that separates church and state.

It's amazing how much can change in two hundred years.

MORAL ABSOLUTES? ABSOLUTELY!

There is no question that the Bible was the foundational and pivotal book in this country for decade upon decade. Every home had a Bible. The Bible represented the value system of most Americans. Even if someone didn't have a personal relationship with Jesus Christ, they still had a Bible, and would try to live their lives according to the Ten Commandments. At work and in their personal relationships, they would practice the Golden Rule.

In other words, the vast majority of Americans were directly influenced by the Bible and took their moral code from it. The moral boundaries were clear and obvious. As a result, most Americans believed that certain things were right and that certain things were wrong. They believed in moral absolutes. They believed it was wrong to lie, to steal, to kill, and to commit adultery.

In other words, they had common sense.

Have your ever referred to a friend or neighbor and made the observation that they had a lot of "common sense." Sure you have. When we use the term "common sense," what we are saying is that the person has a kind of wisdom. Common sense is a synonym for wisdom. It's just another way of saying that the person uses wisdom in making their choices.

It used to be that most people in America had common sense. America was characterized by "common sense." You could find common sense in our schools, in our courts, and in our personal relationships. Why was that true?

Quite simply, America had common sense because we shared a common morality and a set of common values. Now the question is this: Where did that morality and where did those values come from?

The answer is the Bible.

The Scriptures permeated American culture. Do you see why there was such common sense in America? The Scriptures were central. But those days are over, gentlemen. It's a whole new ball game. And the rules have changed.

I recently came across a pithy little poem that summarizes the moral slide we have all witnessed. Arthur Guiterman penned these words:

> First dentistry was painless;
>> Then bicycles were chainless
>> And carriages were horseless
>> And many laws enforceless.
> Next, cookery was fireless,
>> Telegraphy was wireless,
>> Cigars were nicotineless
>> And coffee, caffeinless.
> Soon oranges were seedless,
>> The putting green was weedless,
>> The college boy hatless,
>> The proper diet, fatless.
> Now motor roads are dustless,
>> The latest steel is rustless,
>> Our tennis courts are sodless,
>> Our new religions, godless.

You might be interested to know that Guiterman wrote those words in 1936.

THE ASSASSINATION OF COMMON SENSE

For the last fifty years, and especially since the 1960s, moral relativism has been taught in our universities. That's why there are so many teachers, judges, congressmen, and white collar professionals who subscribe to it.

That's exactly why America has lost its common sense.

America has had its share of assassinations. But there is an assassination that takes place every day in this country that goes unreported in the media. It is the assassination of common sense. Nearly every time I pick up a newspaper, I read of a situation where common sense has been assassinated. In fact, I have a file that is tabbed "The Assassination of Common Sense." It is to my left as I write these words. The file is packed. Allow me to pull out just a few examples.

• What should be the penalty for carrying a gun into a high school? Most of us would agree that's a very serious offense. Back when I was in high school, if a kid were to bring a gun to school, he would have been expelled on the spot. Today, in New York City, if a student brings a gun to school, the student will be suspended and transferred to another school.[35] Now there's a real stroke of genius. Why wouldn't they expel a kid? Because it might violate his rights. Does anyone ever think of the rights of the other kids to go to school without fear of being shot? The answer is no. That would make too much sense. Let's transfer him to another school and let him shoot a kid from another part of town.

• A man in Massachusetts stole a car from a parking lot and then died in a traffic accident while making his getaway. His estate sued the parking lot for letting him steal the car.[36]

• A burglar was robbing a school. As he was traversing the roof in darkness, he fell through a skylight. His attorneys charged the school with negligence and won $260,000 in damages plus a $1,200 monthly payment to the burglar for his injuries.[37]

• In York, Pennsylvania, after ax murderer Karl Chambers had been found guilty of robbing, beating, and killing a seventy-year-old woman, his sentence was voided and a new hearing ordered because the District Attorney *quoted from the Bible.* To be more specific, in his closing remarks the District Attorney said, "The Bible says, 'The murderer shall be put to death.' " For that reason the judge ordered that the ax murderer be resentenced. I wonder how the seventy-year-old woman whom he murdered would have felt about that?[38]

• Recently in Dallas, a woman was throwing a paper route on a quiet, residential street early in the morning. She had a regular day job, but had taken on the paper route to help pay for some expenses that her elderly mother had incurred. A man, recently released from a mental hospital, stepped out of the darkness, walked up behind her and shot her dead in cold blood. Approximately one year later, as the judge released the man to freedom, he said, "Sir, I want you to do what is right. That means that you are to take your medication every day." With that, he set the man free. He walks the streets of Dallas today. Since my family lives in Dallas, I certainly hope that guy is taking his medication.

When I read of that judge's decision, I wanted the opportunity to say to him, "Judge, why don't *you* do what is right?" What he did was nonsensical. It was wildly unjust. What about the woman that was killed? What about her grieving husband and children? They never came into consideration. Why? Because we have numerous judges in this country who assassinate common sense every day.

Why did that judge let that man walk out of the courtroom? As I thought about it for awhile, I came up with an answer. That judge had no fear of the Lord.

The Scriptures are very clear: "The fear of the Lord is the beginning of wisdom" (Proverbs 9:10). Would it be incorrect to say that the fear of the Lord is the beginning of common sense? I don't think so. But as America has taught moral relativism in its educational institutions, we have developed a solid line of judicial and political leaders who have lost any touch with reality and common sense because they have no fear of God.

MEGADITTOES

This is getting pretty heavy so perhaps we ought to stop for a minute, go to the refrigerator, pull out a Snapple, and talk about Rush Limbaugh.

Rush Limbaugh.

The very name elicits one of two reactions. Generally speaking, if you like Rush, you probably believe in moral absolutes. If you don't like Rush, you probably believe in moral relativism.

As you probably know, Rush is host of the largest radio talk show in

America. Literally millions of people—twenty million as of this writing—tune into Rush's "Excellence in Broadcasting Network" at any given moment of the day. Five years ago, nobody outside of Sacramento knew who Rush was. But now they do.

I like Rush Limbaugh. I agree with him about 97 percent of the time. And so do a lot of other people who are tired of the twisted and biased coverage that comes from the majority of the media. Rush is right when he says, "I *am* equal time."

Recently, I was speaking at a Christian conference center and over dinner, the conversation turned to Rush Limbaugh. The guy next to me asked me what I thought about Rush.

"I think he's great," I replied.

The man was shocked. "He is such an egotist! How can you like someone who thinks he is so great?"

I explained to the man that Rush is not only a commentator, he is also an *entertainer*. That's part of Rush's shtick. He does all of that "half my brain tied behind my back" stuff with tongue in cheek. When Rush says he does it "with talent on loan from God," he's right.

As Rush explains it, this phrase is "often misunderstood by hypercritical and sensitive types to mean [I think] I am God. On the contrary, I believe that I am what I am because of the grace of God and that my time on earth, as is everyone's, is temporary. We are all on loan from God, you see."[39]

I'll be honest with you. I'm grateful for Rush Limbaugh. And so are many of you reading this book. First of all, if it hadn't been for Rush, you wouldn't have discovered Diet Snapple Peach Iced Tea. Second, if it wasn't for guys like Rush and Cal Thomas, there would be very little common sense at all in the media. My one concern for Rush is that sometimes he gets risqué and off color when he's horsing around. Rush really doesn't need to do that. He's too classy a guy for that.

Have you ever wondered how Rush came out of the blue to be so popular? Have you ever wondered why this guy's program is rewriting the broadcasting record books? My theory is that Rush Limbaugh represents the thinking of the average American thirty years ago. Rush represents what America used to be like before moral relativism took over the media and education. To put it another way, Rush has common sense.

Rush has common sense because he espouses a Christian worldview—the view of the average American just thirty years ago. What I mean by that is that Rush views the world from a biblical perspective. If you read his book, *The Way Things Ought to Be,* you will quickly see that his perspective is indeed Christian. For instance, Rush makes fun of the foolishness of "animal rights" because as he puts it:

> In my opinion, at the root of the assertion that animals have rights is the belief that animals and men are equal in creation, that man evolved from apes, and that creation is an allegorical myth contained in that wonderful piece of literature known as the Bible. There is no escaping the connection between humanism and animal rights activism.

> The Bible teaches that God created man in His own image and that He placed him on this earth in a position superior to all other creatures, and gave him dominion over animals and nature. God did not create other animals in His own image.[40]

Way to go, Rush. Teach that theology! Do you see what I mean? The reason he believes what he does about animal rights, abortion, homosexuality, femi-nazis, and other issues is that Rush views the world from the lens of the Christian perspective.

Wait a minute! Doesn't Rush say "damn" and "hell" from time to time? As a matter of fact he does. And because he does, it keeps the liberals from labeling him as a member of the Religious Right. I'm not condoning his language, I'm just saying that it baffles the media (as well as some Christians) to hear a guy taking the stands that Rush does who is not an apparent member of the Religious Right. Recently, Rush showed some cards in an interview with the *Wittenberg Door* that may be of interest to you.

Door: "Why are people so unhappy in this country? What does make a person happy? Where do we go to find what gives life meaning?"

Rush: "Jesus."

Door: "What?"

Rush: "Jesus. Jesus holds the answers to all of the everyday problems that you face. I am talking about an acceptance and belief in Jesus, heaven, and God. I guess you can deal with your problems on your own without those beliefs, but it's much, much tougher."[41]

Some people act like Rush is the messiah. He'd be the first to tell you he's not. He's just a guy who is speaking common sense. And now we know where it comes from.

THE SEPARATION OF SENSE AND STATE

Speaking of a lack of common sense, let's look at the Supreme Court. The other day I was discussing a particular moral issue with a very fine Christian man. He is active in his church, which is a Bible-believing fellowship. In our discussion, he made it clear that although he felt that we as Christians were to definitely base our personal choices on the Scriptures, we should not be involved in the political process because of the separation of church and state. Quite frankly, I was somewhat stunned by his statement. What he was saying was that, yes, we Christians do have our standards of morality, but we should not impose those on others, because of the separation of church and state.

This guy has been conned. Who conned him?

Unless I miss my guess, it was the public school system, the courts, and the media.

The problem with that view is two-fold. First of all, every law ever written has "imposed morality." There are laws all over America, mandating that it is legal to drive only twenty miles per hour in school zones. Why is that the case? Because it would be immoral to allow someone to drive fifty-five miles per hour in a school zone! The chances are great that numerous children would be struck by fast moving cars. Thus, in order to keep that from happening, morality has been imposed upon the populous. Every law legislates morality!

The question is this: whose morality is going to be the standard? For nearly two hundred years in this country, the Scriptures were the basis of law. It was the principles of the Bible that held this country together. As we have seen, the vast majority of people in this country believed in moral absolutes, because that was the value system of the Scriptures. In other words, certain things were right, and certain things were wrong.

But now we are fighting a battle with those who believe in moral relativism. They reject the moral absolutes of the Bible, and seek to impose their morality on the rest of us. And supposedly, we Christian men are supposed to stand around and let it happen because of "the separation of church and state."

The separation of church and state has become the most basic principle defining religious liberty in this country. More has been done to take away religious freedoms under the guise of the separation of church and state than any other principle. But do you realize that the term "separation of church and state" does not appear in the Constitution? It is not found in the Declaration of Independence, or in the Bill of Rights. As a matter of fact, it is not to be found in any legal document of this country. Read the entire Federalist Papers! It's not there. Not even once.

Then where in the world did it come from? It goes back to our friends on the Supreme Court. In 1947, a case called *Everson v. The Board of Education* came out before the Supreme Court. This was the first case the Court decided on the principle of the separation of church and state. So if that phrase or concept doesn't come from any of our founding documents, then where in the world did the Supreme Court come up with it?

In 1802, Thomas Jefferson wrote a letter to the Danbury, Connecticut, Baptist Association. There were rumors that the Congress was considering establishing a national church in the United States, just as the Anglican church was the Church of England. Thomas Jefferson used the phrase "separation of church and state" to actually acknowledge the concept that had been first used by Roger Williams, the Rhode Island Baptist. In other words, Jefferson was picking up on the term first used by Williams to denote that it would not be proper to establish a national church in America.

In *Everson v. The Board of Education*, the Court went to a private letter and used a term from this correspondence as their bulwark reasoning in limiting religious freedom. In doing so, they violated every historical and legal precedent. So the concept of separation of church and state does not even have its roots in the Constitution. The Supreme Court had to do some shameful gymnastics to twist the true intent of the founders of this country. The separation of the church and state is the result of the separation of sense from state.

Now the principle of the separation of church and state has become the bedrock legal principle in limiting religious freedom. Hitler was right: "If you tell any lie long enough, often enough, and loud enough, people will come to believe it."

THE SEMI-SUPREME COURT

Let me say a word about the Supreme Court.

They're not.

Do your kids say "not?" Mine do. "Not" is a pretty good word. Especially when it comes to the Supreme Court. As I understand it, they are the Supreme Court *of the United States of America.* They may be the highest court in this land, but there is another Court that is far superior. One day, every justice who has ever served on the Supreme Court of the United States of America will kneel before *The* Supreme Court and give an account to the real Chief Justice, the Lion of Judah, for every one of their opinions.

Some of them, no doubt, will say in their defense that they did not want to inflict their morality on anyone else. That's no defense at all. They were never asked to impose their morality. They were responsible to be true to the Constitution. And they all swore on His eternal Word that they would do it. Some justices have been true, and more recently, some justices haven't.

The Supreme Court, beginning in 1962, began to hand down decisions that were the first legal jackhammers to penetrate our nearly two hundred-year-old biblical foundation. Since 1962, the Supreme Court has declared the following:

• Prayer in public schools is unconstitutional.

• The posting of the Ten Commandments is prohibited in public schools.

• Prayers of any type at graduation ceremonies are not allowed.

• Abortion, without consent of parents or husbands (as the case may be), is a woman's right to privacy under the constitution.

I wonder what Benjamin Franklin and some of the other founding fathers would have thought if they could have looked ahead two hundred years to a Supreme Court that would emasculate this country by removing prayer from its classrooms.

What is the point of all of this? The point is this:

• America was founded on Scriptural principles.

• The vast majority of Americans believed in moral absolutes.

• There is now a new and powerful element that believes moral relativism.

• In this new culture of openness and tolerance there is room for any and every viewpoint except one—and it's ours.

Let me make a comment about the removal of prayer and Bible reading from the schools. The Supreme Court took prayer out of the schools, but they did not take it out of the home. The Supreme Court took prayer out of the classroom, but they didn't take it out of the family. At least, not yet.

Gentlemen, you may be for prayer in the schools, but the question is, do you have prayer in your home? You may be for Bible-reading in the schools, but my question is do *you* read the Bible in your home with your family? Those two exercises are not illegal. But to look at many Christian homes, you would get the impression that they are illegal.

Yes, the Supreme Court took prayer and Bible-reading out of the schools. But have you as a father taken prayer and the Bible out of your own home? Nothing would please the Enemy more than to get us all ticked off at the Supreme Court, forgetting in the process to exercise our religious freedom by praying and reading the Scriptures with our own families. My friend, if you have unwittingly taken prayer and Scripture out of your home, allow me to make a suggestion. Put it back in.

You may say "my son plays on two soccer teams and my daughter is in dance class three nights a week! We have no time to read the Bible every night." You don't have to read it every night. But you ought to consider doing it two or three nights a week. You may need to have your son play on only one soccer team, and your daughter may only be able to go to dance class two nights a week. I don't know how you will work out all the scheduling with your wife. *But sit down with her and work it out.* And by the way, if you do something like this, you will probably upset the coach and the dance teacher. But that's okay. There's only one Person you need to please, and that's the Lord Jesus.

You are the spiritual leader. Leaders lead. Your kids need the Word of God and they need prayer. If you don't do it now when you have the religious freedom, what makes you think you will do it if we lose that freedom?

A family that is in the Book and on their knees will be blessed by God. That same approach brought God's blessing to this nation. Maybe the nation has forgotten, but guys, we can't afford to forget. This is how you protect your family. So, let's turn off the TV, pass out the Bibles, and get our families on their knees. 'Nuff said.

THINKING THE UNTHINKABLE

I would like very much to put a positive spin on what I see going on around us. But it would be a wrong spin. I think that the imminent persecution of the church of Jesus Christ is blowing in faster than any of us can imagine. Gentlemen, the unthinkable is about to happen in the United States of America.

I read last week that Chuck Colson thinks we have five years to turn things around in this nation. I think he's right. He also said that he thought we were only five years away from blatant persecution of believers in this nation.

The storm clouds are rolling in.

When Christians are viewed as "threats," that ought to tell us something.

In a recent poll of leaders across America (business leaders, government leaders, academics, priests, and rabbis, for instance), evangelicals came out the highest as a perceived "threat to democracy." Can you believe that?

Thirty-four percent of academics rate evangelicals as a menace to democracy, compared with only fourteen percent who see any danger from racists, the Ku Klux Klan, and Nazis.[42] So when it comes to the menaces of society you have your Nazis, your skinheads, and the Ku Klux Klan, but leading the way are those dangerous Christians. That's why at the recent gay rights march in Washington, D.C., many of the marchers were shouting,

"Bring back the lions." They weren't referring to the Detroit Lions, they were referring to the lions in Rome who would maul and eat the Christians in the Coliseum.

There seems to be a move to give everyone the right to say anything they want—except Christians. You can count on it, folks. The Left has an agenda and they intend to do whatever they can do to silence the biblical voice which they find so irritating and upsetting. We are the target, for we are the Religious Right.

Who comprises the Religious Right? Chances are, since you're reading this book, you do. You are an official member of the Religious Right if you believe in the authority of the Bible, the Trinity, the deity of Jesus Christ, the virgin birth, the substitutionary atonement, and the resurrection of Christ; if you believe that abortion is murder, homosexuality is perversion, and sexual permissiveness is wrong; if you agree with the statement made by Patrick Henry, then you are the new enemy in this country. For it is those principles that characterize the Religious Right. In other words, if you believe the things that the vast majority of the Founding Fathers of this country believed, then you are the problem.

You may think that the unthinkable won't happen. Quite frankly, I hope with all my heart that you are right. But I say, *think again.* Who would have thought five years ago that the Soviet Union would fall apart at the seams? That was unthinkable, yet it is precisely what happened. Who would have ever imagined five years ago that the Berlin Wall would come down. Three years ago they were still shooting people who tried to get across that wall! Today, the wall is gone. The unthinkable happened. For the second time.

Just in the last three years, we have seen some of the most unthinkable things we could ever imagine come to pass. And I think that we are going to see one more. And it's one we don't want to think about.

It's the persecution of believers in the United States of America.

Two hundred years ago, most Americans did not speak of their "First Amendment rights." But they did often refer to the "rights of Englishmen." Two hundred years ago, Americans were proud to have the "rights of Englishmen," and it was unthinkable that those rights would ever be taken from them.

What were the rights of the Englishmen, and why are they remarkably relevant to us? The rights of Englishmen were drawn from the various documents that made up England's constitution. The Petition of Right (1628) spelled out in detail many of the rights of Englishmen upon which the colonists were relying. More were added by the "Bill of Rights" of 1689. Colonists everywhere were familiar with the writings of William Blackstone, the famous common-law expert whose commentaries on English law contained whole chapters about the rights of Englishmen.

From the time of Patrick Henry's famous House of Burgesses speech in 1765, through the spring of 1774, the claim to the "rights of Englishmen" led the day.

Then the unthinkable happened.

Certain powerful members of Parliament began insisting that the colonists were no longer Englishmen or citizens. Word came to the colonists that the majority party considered them to be outside the British constitution and that their charters were meaningless. Some British leaders were saying that the colonists no longer had any rights.

The colonists were stunned. It took them months to believe and sort through what had actually happened. They were finally convinced that their appeals were falling upon deaf ears when in August of 1775, the king refused to see Richard Penn and receive the "Olive Branch Petition" from the colonists. That same day, the king declared the colonies were in rebellion and must be crushed. So much for the rights of Englishmen.[43]

Literally overnight, the rights which the colonists thought to be inherently theirs, disappeared. The unthinkable took place.

It could happen again.

Allow me to take one of the above paragraphs and make a few alterations that demonstrate how quickly we could find ourselves in the state our forefathers found themselves over two hundred years ago:

Then the unthinkable happened.

Certain powerful members of Congress began insisting that the Religious Right were no longer Americans or citizens. Word came to the Christians that the majority party considered them to be outside the American constitution and that their interpretation of the First Amendment was meaningless. Some American leaders were saying that the Religious Right no longer had any rights.

A chilling thought? Yes. An unthinkable thought? No. Not with the way things are going in this country. Consider this extract from the 1959 edition of the World Book Encyclopedia. In the article on the United States Constitution, the paragraph that specifically deals with the First Amendment contains this editorial comment:

> None of the rights protected in Amendment I can be considered as absolute. For example, Congress cannot prohibit the free exercise of religion, but it could pass legislation against any sect which practiced customs contrary to morality.[44]

This has already happened in America. Two different cases were brought against Christian institutions and in each case the court ruled that the state's compelling interest in homosexual rights and racial equality overruled the First Amendment rights of the institutions. Those are two very chilling precedents. In other words, if the courts find a particular issue to their liking, they will not hesitate to use that issue to set aside the First Amendment. My friend, if you are counting on the First Amendment to guarantee your religious freedom you are on thin ice indeed.

Until now, it has been socially acceptable to be a Christian. I think the days are quickly coming when it will be socially unacceptable to be a follower of Christ.

The lines have been drawn and it's time to make a decision.

We either stand tall and follow Christ with all of our hearts or we don't.

It's that simple. Either get on the ark or get off.

The reason it's that simple is that up until recent times it has been convenient in this country to be a believer. But it is going to quickly become inconvenient.

We have never experienced anything like this in America before. This is a completely new chapter for us. But there are some remarkably similar parallels from history that can give us insight into what God may possibly do in our situation. More importantly, these parallels can give us a hope in the midst of a new and changing high pressure system.

Historically, whenever persecution has come to the people of God, two very positive changes have taken place:

• The church has been purified.

• The church has been empowered.

Judgment begins with the household of God. The church has been weakened by the virus of sexual immorality that has spread through its leadership. God is going to do what needs to be done to bring the church back to holiness. That's where persecution could come in. This won't be the first time that God's people have lived in hostile circumstances. But it's the first time that we have. And it's going to require a warrior mentality.

Walking Tall into Danger

Llamas are warriors, in their own way.

Llamas?

Several years ago, numerous sheep ranchers in a section of Montana were losing sheep at an alarming rate to marauding coyotes. The ranchers tried everything to protect their flocks. Electric fences, odor spray, and traps all failed. The coyotes kept coming. One lady lost fifty lambs—nearly one a week—to the relentless predators.

Nothing worked. Until she got the llama. Llamas are strange-looking animals that have a warrior mentality. Llamas don't appear to be afraid of *anything*. When they see something, they put their head up and walk straight toward it. The coyotes couldn't handle the courage of the llamas. So they finally left the sheep alone.

Gentlemen, we don't know what's coming. But may I suggest to you that when we see it, we lift our heads, level our gaze, and walk right toward it.

I am writing these words just several miles away from the nation's largest llama ranch. I saw quite a few of them this morning as I was driving to a men's breakfast. As I looked at those llamas, they had a certain aura about them that attracted me. I couldn't figure out what it was about them that made them so appealing.

But I just figured it out. The thing I like about llamas is that they are always standing tall. Literally. And because they are standing tall, they are willing to lift their heads and walk straight toward the unknown.

We of all men should be able to stand tall. And it's for one reason. We don't know the future, but we know Who holds the future. That's why we can lift our heads and walk right into it.

The Lord Jesus has us covered.

1. In what ways can alert Christian men be like the "line riders" of the Old West?

2. As you consider the message of this chapter, what new significance do you find in verses such as Proverbs 11:11 and 14:34? Looking back over our nation's history, in what ways has America been "exalted"? What now is our growing "disgrace"?

3. Carefully consider Proverbs 9:9-12. Take a moment to apply the truth of these words to our nation as whole.

4. As you soberly reflect on the probability of Christians facing persecution in our country, discover afresh Paul's description of the "last days" in 2 Timothy 3:1-5. In view of what all godly Christians must face in such a time (vv. 12-13), what is Paul's prescription for standing tall?

5. Take a moment to ponder the *ultimate* Supreme Court at the end of time, as described in Revelation 20:11-15. Then turn back to Philippians 2:9-12 to consider the ultimate Chief Justice. In what way is the concept of "moral absolutes" rooted in a Person? What then, does acceptance or rejection of that Person ultimately imply?

CHAPTER FIVE

Showdown in Samaria

It is bad to live under a prince who permits nothing,
but much worse to live under one who permits everything.

JOHN CALVIN

Since I'm a native Californian, I never expected to move to Little Rock, Arkansas. But that's what we did in 1986. And that's when I became familiar with...a certain couple.

I was somewhat familiar with them before we moved to Little Rock, but it was after we settled into life in Arkansas that I began to pay much more attention to who they were and what they stood for.

Both husband and wife were deeply involved in politics. In fact, their marriage seemed more of a political alliance than a relationship. The husband sought power and was extremely ambitious. The wife sought power and was extremely ambitious. Both were leaders and both were aggressive. He was a driven man and thought through his political moves very carefully. But if possible, she was even more driven and ambitious than her husband, and would seemingly do whatever was necessary to build her own power base.

This couple resided in a region where religion was popular. Part of the heritage. Part of the culture. So, good politicians that they were, they, too, were religious. They attended religious services consistently—and made sure everyone noticed.

As time went by, however, it became obvious to me that this couple's religious involvement was superficial. As I spent more and more time observing them, it became clear that their positions on moral and social issues were usually the *opposite* of biblical values. If this couple was "religious," then it was in name only. When it came to applying the truth of the Scriptures to their political decisions and choices, it was apparently the furthest thing from their mind.

The reason for this was that although they were religious, their moral and spiritual values did not come from the Scriptures. It became clear that they were primarily influenced by the value system of moral relativism that had so permeated their culture. The other thing that became plain was their deep resentment toward those who did hold to biblical morality. Not only did they loathe those who firmly held to biblical principles, but they worked politically to make sure those biblical values (upon which their country had been founded) were kept out of the law of the land.

Whether the issue was homosexuality, the killing of children, or any other major pressing social issue, this couple worked overtime to make sure that biblical teaching had no influence on the political process. They willfully and consistently opposed those who sought to bring Scriptural principles into the discussion.

As they gained more and more attention in a larger sphere, this couple made alliances with other influential groups who also stood against biblical values. It began to look as if there was no one to oppose them.

As a family, we were enjoying our time in Little Rock. But as I continued to watch this couple, I became increasingly aware of the fact that they viewed those who held biblical moral convictions as "troublesome." And it became clear to me that under the guise of "tolerance" was what can only be described as a deep-seated hatred for the truth of God. At a certain point I realized that this couple would have no trouble wielding their power to actively stand against those who held to biblical morality.

At seemingly every opportunity, they would do whatever they could to neutralize true and godly religion and those who practiced it. At the same time, they would elevate and lift those who practiced abhorrent lifestyles of perversion to positions of power and influence and attempt to make them look good and acceptable.

Make no mistake about it. This couple was powerful. Ambitious. Shrewd. And they had an agenda.

I think by now you may have an idea of who I am referring to. It's hard to believe that anyone could miss who this couple is—especially if you are familiar with the Scriptures. Their story is outlined for us in the pages of the Old Testament.

Their names were Ahab and Jezebel.

It was in 1986, after we had moved to Little Rock, that I began studying certain sections of the Old Testament in more detail than I had ever done before. In my studies I became increasingly aware of this couple who brought so much despair and hardship to their nation.

DON'T KNOW MUCH ABOUT HISTORY

There's an old song that says, "Don't know much about history, don't know much geography...." For most of us, when it comes to the Old Testament, that's true. We don't know much about the history of the Old Testament, and we don't know much about the geography of the Old Testament. But there is a particular clip of Israel's history that every man ridin' for the brand needs to know. And he needs to know it well.

America is in a moral and spiritual freefall. From a biblical perspective, we are unraveling at a breathtaking rate. Where we are as a country is not unlike where Israel was after the death of David. From then on, it was downhill. The glory of the former days were gone. Israel was no longer the country of prosperity and blessing that it was under David. The slide started when Solomon came to the throne. As Solomon began to deteriorate personally, the nation followed suit. Israel became like a gigantic runaway snowball, picking up speed and critical mass with each revolution. This is exactly where we are today.

Maybe when you hear the word "history" you immediately tune out. When you think of history, you think of those boring classes you had to sit through in high school. Making history out to be boring should be a felony! History is the most exciting thing in the world! There is so much to learn from it. So if you're one of those guys who goes into a "sleep" mode, when you hear "history," don't! This stuff is critical! As one great mind once put it,

"Those who refuse to learn from history are doomed to repeat it."

Let's start with something most of know a little about. How about the Civil War? Most of us could place the Civil War roughly around 1860. The Civil War was a time in our country when our nation divided. We actually became two countries.

Did you know that the same thing happened in Israel? Israel had three kings. The first was Saul, the second was David, and the third was Solomon. That's pretty basic stuff that many of us got in Sunday school. But it's after Solomon that things start getting murky. That's where we need to fill in some blanks.

Why in the world would you keep reading to fill in the blanks of Israel? Unless I miss my guess, you're a fairly busy person. You have a lot on your plate. I doubt if one of your pressing felt needs in life is to know more about the history of Israel in the Old Testament. But listen guys, there's a good reason to take a few minutes and check this out. If you are a husband and father, then you are leading your family in a culture that is about as screwed up morally and spiritually as it could possibly be. And right here in the era of the Old Testament kings, God has given a detailed road map that shows how to pick your way through the rubble of a collapsing society.

But there's good news here, too! Even in the midst of a fast-track national decline, there were still individuals and families who did not cave in.

Instead of falling apart, they held together.

Instead of letting their culture color them, they colored their culture.

That's why this period of history is so important! It lets us know that God always has His men. Even in a time of absolute spiritual and moral decadence like ours. So let's learn a little bit of history. I guarantee that it will make you a better leader of your family.

HIGHLIGHT CLIPS

I'm a 49ers fan. However I live in Dallas, Texas. There is a football team in Dallas known as the Cowboys. Most people in Dallas would rather watch the Cowboys than the San Francisco 49ers. So there are many Sunday afternoons when I'm stuck with the Cowboy game instead of the 'Niners. When this happens, I make sure that I tune into Sports Center on ESPN. That way, I can at least catch the highlights of my team. I know that I won't get the whole game, but at least I get a few of the high spots.

That's how we are going to do this little history lesson that will make you a better spiritual leader. We are going to hit the highlights. Or to put it more accurately, the lowlights. As you will see, it was a pretty dismal time in the life of Israel, God's covenant people.

We have Saul down, right? He was the first king. We have the second king down, too. David was a man after God's own heart. David had a son by the name of Solomon, and Solomon was appointed by God to be king number three. Now here's where it gets a little murky for most of us, so stay tuned to these ESPN highlights.

Solomon had a son by the name of Rehoboam (by the way, if your wife is pregnant and you are looking for a distinctive name, we are going to come across some real winners on this list of kings). Solomon had started his reign with a gift of wisdom. Unfortunately, his son Rehoboam had the gift of foolishness. Rehoboam immediately kicks off his administration by imposing severe taxation. (Why does that sound familiar?) Jeroboam, an officer in the army, says no way, and leads ten of the twelve tribes in revolt. Rehoboam was such a lousy leader that a large contingent of people turned to Jeroboam and decided that he ought to be king. Rehoboam was so hated by the people that ten of the twelve tribes of Israel backed Jeroboam. Suddenly they were a nation split in two.

The two tribes that stuck with Rehoboam were Benjamin and Judah. They were known as the southern kingdom, or "Judah." The other ten tribes formed a new nation called "Israel." For the next several hundred years, God's chosen people existed as two nations, with two different governments. Can you imagine the North and the South in the United States being divided for over two hundred years? Well that's what happened here. And believe me, Jeroboam and Rehoboam were the first in two lines of some of the sorriest leaders in history.

A CASE FOR TERM LIMITS

The eighth king to come along in the northern kingdom was Ahab. Ahab had to be one of the original inspirations for the concept of term limits. He was nothing less than a total catastrophe for Israel. We are introduced to him in 1 Kings 16:

> In the thirty eighth year of Asa king of Judah, Ahab son of Omri became king of Israel, and he reigned in Samaria over Israel twenty two years. Ahab son of Omri did more evil in the eyes of the Lord than any of those before him. He not only considered it trivial to commit the sins of Jeroboam son of Nebat, but he also married Jezebel daughter of Ethbaal king of the Sidonians, and began to serve Baal and worship him. He set up an altar for Baal in the temple of Baal that he built in Samaria. Ahab also made an Asherah pole and did more to provoke the Lord, the God of Israel, to anger than did all the kings of Israel before him (vv. 29-33, NIV).

In the history of Israel, Ahab is remembered for two things. First, he is remembered as the wickedest king in the history of the nation. Ahab was the guy who introduced Baal worship to Israel. As we shall soon see, it doesn't get any worse than Baal worship. Second, he topped that off by marrying a woman who was even more godless than he was.

By himself Ahab would have been a menace. Plainly an opportunist, he seems to have had few convictions or scruples. But he was not by himself. Jezebel was at his side, using her prestige and influence as insidiously and maliciously as possible. Like Solomon's foreign wives, she continued her pagan worship, maintaining it on a lavish scale. When the prophets of Yahweh opposed her heathen ways, she ruthlessly set out to destroy them.

Having bent every effort to suppress true prophetic activity, Jezebel imported to her court hundreds of false prophets dedicated to Baal. Such zeal in so strategic a position posed an incalculable threat to Israel's historic faith. The corruption of Canaanite religion had long been seeping in from the Israelites' Canaanites neighbors, but under Jezebel it was pumped from the palace with the pressure of a fire-hose.[45]

Ahab did not lead his family. Jezebel called the shots in their relationship. God has called men to lead their homes, and it follows logically that a couple who were so set against God as individuals would also show their perversity in their own marriage relationship. As in so many areas of their lives, they modeled the opposite of what God intended. It started in their own marriage. Ahab was the front man, but every one knew who was Number One. And it wasn't Ahab.

A LACK OF MALE LEADERSHIP IN ISRAEL

Ahab's first mistake was marrying a woman from a foreign land that he was clearly forbidden to marry. Once they were married, he allowed her to do whatever she wanted. It was Jezebel's agenda to bring Baal worship to Israel and to make it the religion of choice. It was Jezebel who imported 850 missionaries of Baal and Asherah (a closely related cult) and fed them at her own table (1 Kings 18:19). That's an entitlement if I ever saw one.

But Jezebel was just getting rolling.

As Ahab gave her more and more rope she eventually killed the true prophets of God (1 Kings 18:4). Do you see how out of control this woman was? She was the leader, not only of her home, but of the nation.

Ahab had basically given up. That's why after she had killed the prophets, she had no hesitancy to go after Elijah (1 Kings 19:1-2). This woman was on a rampage. And it all stemmed from a wimpy husband who refused to set the standards for his own home.

What is fascinating is that Ahab and Jezebel had at least three sons— and all three of them were named after Yahweh! His three boys were Jehoram ("Yahweh is high"), Ahaziah ("Yahweh has taken hold"), and Athaliah ("Yahweh is strong").[46] In those days, children were not named loosely. I would put money on the table that Ahab and Jezebel had it out every time they had to settle on a name. Jezebel's own father was named Ethbaal, which meant "with Baal." It had to tick her off when Ahab stuck with three names that were based on Yahweh. But apparently, those were about the last shreds of Ahab's waning influence. Ahab had the presence of mind in his early days at least to name his children after Yahweh instead of Baal. But as he gave in more and more to Jezebel, the influence of Yahweh on his home was lost to the influence of Jezebel.

Ahab was just one of many kings in the split nations of Israel and Judah who did not lead their families spiritually. Out of all the kings, and in total there were forty-two, only five lived complete lives without denying or rebelling against God. The five were David, Jehoshaphat, Jotham, Hezekiah, and Josiah. Yet even the best of the men were woeful failures when it came to the leadership of their own families.

> The sons of each of these good kings turned out to be disappointing failures, either divided or completely ungodly men. Thus the breakdown of godliness from father to son in even the best of Jewish homes led to increased idolatry and Baal worship in Israel.[47]

INHALING BAAL

Ahab ruled over Israel for twenty-two years. Twenty-two years under this guy! People thought it had been bad under his father, Omri. Omri ruled for twelve years, and I'm sure many folks thought it couldn't get any worse. They were wrong. Ahab came along and it got much worse. You've heard of sons trying to outdo their fathers? Ahab was one of those sons. Unfortunately, he was successful. That's why the Scripture clearly says that he did more evil than any of the kings who went before him (including his dad).

What is it after all these years that Ahab and Jezebel are remembered for? Ahab and Jezebel introduced Baal worship to Israel. That's their legacy. Baal worship was a very complex religion, but there were four distinguishing characteristics of Baal worship that have particular relevance to our culture.

You might be amazed at how current these four characteristics are to our own culture. Why do they sound like current events? Because America is bowing at the altar of Baal. Our new administration is leading us down the same path of spiritual and moral deterioration that brought down Israel three thousand years ago. We just haven't realized it.

Characteristic #1: *Baal worshipers were pro-choice.* We're familiar with pro-choice, right? These Baal worshipers were a little different. They were pro-choice *after* the child was born. They commonly killed newborn children in the worship of Baal.

Characteristic #2: *Baal worshipers held the environment in high esteem and considered Baal as the one who determined and controlled the environment.*

Characteristic #3: *Baal worship encouraged and promoted rampant sexual immorality, particularly homosexuality, as a normal and natural alternative lifestyle.*

Characteristic #4: *Baal worship sought to coexist as a legitimate religious viewpoint alongside Judaism.*

Let's take these one by one, for all can be found in the account that describes Israel under the leadership of Ahab and Jezebel. Let's go back to characteristic #1.

CHARACTERISTIC #1: BAAL WORSHIPERS WERE PRO-CHOICE

Immediately after introducing Ahab and Jezebel, the Scriptures then describe what seems to be a very weird situation that doesn't have much to do with Israel. But it is very significant.

> In Ahab's time, Hiel of Bethel rebuilt Jericho. He laid its foundations at the cost of his firstborn son Abiram, and he set up its gates at the cost of his youngest son Segub, in accordance with the word of the LORD spoken by Joshua the son of Nun (1 Kings 16:34, NIV).

This passage is a reference to the man who attempted to do what God said would never be done. He attempted to rebuild Jericho but was foiled, for God said Jericho would never be rebuilt. This attempt took place during the reign of Ahab. But what should be noted is the fact that Hiel possibly buried his sons in the foundations of Jericho. It appears to have been a practice of Baal worshipers, not only to kill their newborn children, but to bury them in the foundation of a house or wall. Archaeologists have found several remains of small children in the ancient ruins of homes and fortified walls.

Baal worshipers also were known for making their sons pass through the fire. This even became a practice in Israel after Ahab introduced Baal worship to the nation. The point is this: human life was cheap in Israel and Judah and it is cheap in America. Generally speaking, we don't practice the killing of infants (although some doctors have done it after a botched abortion), but we do sanction the killing of children in the womb.

As I write these words, there is a bill pending in Congress called the Freedom of Choice Act. This legislation would give a woman the right to abort her child anytime during the pregnancy. That means that if she were on the delivery table, and just fifteen minutes away from birth, she could legally decide to abort the child. What is the difference between killing a child fifteen minutes before birth or killing it fifteen minutes after birth? About thirty minutes. That's the only difference.

The following sketch shows the steps of the new D&X abortion procedure that will flourish if the Freedom of Choice Act is enacted. If it passes, Mr. Clinton has indicated that he supports this piece of legislation and will sign it into law. This picture shows the barbaric steps that are used to "abort" the fetus. That's not a fetus, guys, that's a *baby*. And remember, when the Freedom of Choice Act becomes law, it will be perfectly legal to take the life of a baby who is full-term. Two of our children were born premature, one six weeks early and the other five. When they came out of the womb, they were not fetal tissue. They were little, fully-developed human beings made in the image of God. And they could feel pain. Wouldn't *you* feel pain if some doctor thrust a pair of scissors into the back of *your* neck?

This D&X procedure has Baal written all over it. All that's missing are an altar and an idol. Recently in a meeting with Southern Baptist leaders, President Clinton indicated his personal opposition to abortion, but said he did not want to violate a woman's right to choose. To use the biblical term, that's "dung." It is also godless.

Life is cheap in America. Yet as a nation, we know in our hearts what we are doing. Those aren't fetuses, they are babies. In a revealing article in the *Dallas Morning News,* Janie Bush, director of the Choice Foundation made the following astonishing admission:

> We have learned a great deal from the movement that calls itself pro-life. We were hiding [from themselves and other women] some pieces of the truth about abortion that were threatening. It is a kind of killing, and most women seeking abortion understand that.

Ms. Bush's amazingly candid admission was not well received by other abortion advocates. Kate Michelman, president of the National Abortion Rights Actions League said, "I would never tell someone they are killing. It is a loaded term." So what would Ms. Michelman tell them? She would say "they are terminating a stage of fetal development and potential life."[48]

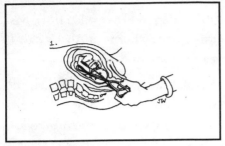

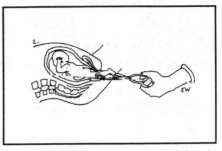

1. The abortionist grasps one of the baby's legs with forceps.

2. The leg is pulled into the birth canal.

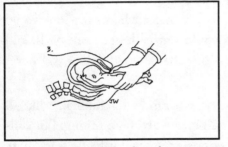

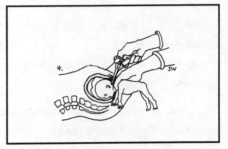

3. Using his hands the abortionist delivers the baby's body. The head remains inside.

4. The abortionist forces scissors into the base of the baby's skull. He then opens the scissors to enlarge the hole.

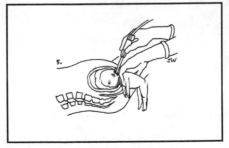

5. A suction catheter is inserted into the hole, and the baby's brains are sucked out. The child is then removed.

Ms. Bush was very honest in her comments. So honest that her peers could not handle it. They are experts in denial. I wonder how Ms. Michelman would have justified the sacrifice of newborns in Ahab's day. If we keep going the way we are, in a few years we will find out.

The point is simply this. In the spiritual deterioration of Israel, the killing of children was acceptable behavior. No wonder we witness the same spirit in our nation as we continue to watch our moral infrastructure erode.

Recently Vice President Al Gore, in his book, *Earth in the Balance,* registered his concern over the burning of the rain forests. Gore writes, "according to our guide, the biologist Tom Lovejoy, there are more different species of birds in each square mile of the Amazon than exist in all of North America—which means we are silencing thousands of songs we have never heard."[49] It is somewhat baffling that a family man such as Mr. Gore would be so concerned about the songs that would not be heard from birds, and apparently so unconcerned about the songs that aborted babies will never have the opportunity to sing.

Birds are important, but they can't hold a candle to children. I like to hear the songs of both, for both have been created by God to sing. But children are superior to birds and more important than birds. At least that's what Jesus taught: "Look at the birds of the air, that they do not sow, neither do they reap, nor gather into barns, and yet your heavenly Father feeds them. Are you not worth much more than they?" (Matthew 6:26).

Jesus made it very clear that human life is more important and more valuable than the life of a bird. Unfortunately, it doesn't seem to be as clear to some of our elected officials.

CHARACTERISTIC # 2: BAAL WORSHIPERS WERE OBSESSED WITH THE ENVIRONMENT

Baal worshipers held the environment in high esteem and considered Baal as the one who determined and controlled the environment. Elijah tackled that issue the very first time he went one-on-one with Ahab.

Now Elijah the Tishbite, from Tishbe in Gilead, said to Ahab, "As the Lord, the God of Israel, lives, whom I serve, there will be neither dew nor rain in the next few years except at my word" (1 Kings 17:1).

There is more here than meets the eye. Elijah is not just showing up to give Ahab the latest forecast from The Weather Channel. Elijah is laying down a challenge and stating a fact. Now this was the first public appearance of Elijah. Up until now, he was just some guy from Tishbe. But never again could he fade into the scenery. Elijah was a marked man because he had taken on Ahab. But more importantly, he had taken on Baal.

Why did Elijah talk to Ahab about the weather? He could have addressed a number of issues, but why the weather? The answer is this: Ahab and the other Baal worshipers thought that Baal was the one who controlled the weather. And they worshiped him as such. But they were wrong.

Baal was known by his many strengths, but primarily he was known as the storm god: "As the god of the storm, whose voice resounded through the heavens in the form of thunder."[50] Elijah was stealing Baal's thunder. "Baal was a god of many faces, being a god of rain, fertility, and the personification of the sun"[51] To be more precise, Elijah was challenging Baal's ability to make thunder, and then rain.

Oswald Sanders wrote:

The worship of Baal...one of the oldest superstitions in the world, was the worship of the sun, regarded as the king of heaven. The Baalim were the gods of the land, owning and controlling it, and the increase of the crops, fruit, and cattle was supposed to be under his control.[52]

We're talking the environment here, guys.

Baal worship was all wrapped up in depending upon Baal to take care of the environment. Baal worship was built around the environment. They worshiped the creation over the Creator. They put a high value on animal life and the ecosystem while discounting human life the way that Wal-Mart might discount a bag of Oreos.

This stuff has been around for a long time. We are not the first culture to have a vocal group that seeks to elevate the environment to a place of deity. The animal rights activists and ecology groups of our time are the modern day equivalent of Baal worshipers. They have a value system, just as the prophets of Baal had a value system, and they are working feverishly to get their curriculum and influence into our schools, our movies, and our kids' cartoons.

In other words, they want the minds of our children.

Let me give you one more illustration from Al Gore on the environment. In arguing for the preservation of the rain forest, Gore says,

> If we allow this destruction to take place, the world will lose the richest storehouse of genetic information on the planet, and along with it possible cures for many of the diseases that afflict us. Indeed, hundreds of possible medicines now common use are derived from plants and animals of the tropical forests. When President Reagan was struggling to survive his would-be assassin's bullet, one of the critical drugs used to stabilize was a blood pressure medication from an Amazon bush viper.[53]

So far, so good. That's a good reason not to have the wholesale destruction of the rain forest. I agree with his point. It makes sense to me that we were able to save Mr. Reagan's life because of the medicine that was derived from the bush viper. So, let's save the rain forest in order to get medicines from plants and animals to save human lives. Doesn't that seem to be his point here? Well, hold on for the very next paragraph.

> Most of the species unique to the rain forests are in imminent danger, partly because there is no one to speak up for them. [Farrar editorial comment: Once again Mr. Gore is very concerned about speaking up for something like a bird or a tree which can't speak. Why isn't this man consistent in giving the same concern to unborn children as he does to the yew tree?] In contrast, consider the recent controversy over the yew tree, a temperate forest species, one variety of which now grows only in the Pacific Northwest. The Pacific yew can be cut down and processed to produce a potent chemical, taxol, which offers some promise of curing certain forms of lung, breast, and ovarian cancer in patients who would otherwise die.

> It seems an easy choice—sacrifice the tree for a human life—until one learns that three trees must be destroyed for each patient treated, that only specimens more than one hundred years old contain the portent chemical in their bark, and that there are very few of these yews remaining on earth. Suddenly we must confront some tough questions. Are those of us alive today, entitled to cut down all of

these trees to extend the lives of a few of us, even if it means that this unique form of life will disappear forever, thus making it impossible to save human lives in the future?[54]

It is here that Mr. Gore reveals the true colors of his position. Mr. Gore speaks of the tough questions. Quite frankly, these questions are not tough at all. They are only tough if you buy into a philosophy that puts people and trees on the same playing field. Mr. Gore points out that it is an easy choice to sacrifice a tree for a human life—until one realizes several things:

• In actuality it takes three trees to save a life.

• The tree must be over one hundred years old.

• There are few yew trees left.

According to Gore, here's where it "gets tough." Allow me to offer some answers to Mr. Gore.

Question: Are those of us alive today entitled to cut down all of these trees to extend the lives of a few of us?

Answer: *Yes.* Mr. Gore speaks of the few whose lives would be extended. That's an interesting comment. The few of which he speaks are those who suffer from lung cancer, breast cancer, and ovarian cancer. For some reason, the number of people suffering from such diseases strike me as being more than a "few." My field is not medicine, but it would be my guess that thousands, if not hundreds of thousands, of people fall within the confines of those three types of cancer.

What if the yew tree was known to be a cure for AIDS? Would Mr. Gore have the same reservation about "sacrificing" the tree in that case? For some reason, I have my doubts. Or what if it were discovered that the yew tree was the only resource for a mysterious illness that was killing off thousands of dolphins? Would the vice president still be facing some tough questions? I think it's possible that Mr. Gore and his friends would be oiling their chain saws as quickly as possible in an attempt to save as many "Flippers" as they could. But humans suffering with cancer? Well, that's a tough one.

I can say this. If my wife, or one of my children, was suffering from one of those forms of cancer, and the cost was three trees, then that is a no brainer. Quite frankly, if it were three hundred trees—or a *forest*—I would not hesitate. It wouldn't be tough at all. I sincerely doubt that Mr. Gore would hesitate to bring down three hundred trees if it meant sustaining the life of one of his loved ones.

Question: Are we entitled to cut down all of the yew trees, even if it means that this "unique" form of life will disappear forever, thus making it impossible to save human lives in the future?

Answer: *Yes.* We are entitled because if you believe that the Scriptures are God's divine revelation, God makes it clear that He has given mankind dominion over the earth. Men and women, boys and girls, and unborn children are made in the image of God. Trees aren't.

The yew tree may be "unique" but it is not nearly "unique" as any person who walks this earth. And how do we know that if the yew trees are saved they would be sacrificed in the future to help meet the needs of people?

Excuse me for going into such detail, but gentlemen, we need to understand that these beliefs have very serious implications. The modern-day environmental movement is committed to cutting no trees down, regardless of who it might benefit. Therein lies the danger. They have elevated the earth to the same plane as people. That is wrong. It is simply another form of Baalism that is just as insidious and dangerous as their philosophical ancestors in Israel.

Why in the world are we talking about trees in a book that is aimed at men who want to spiritually lead their families? We are talking about it because our children are being bombarded every day with this extreme environmental garbage that is both inhuman and ungodly.

Now let me set the record straight. I'm all for trees and I'm all for the environment. I just spent $400 in an effort to save two pecan trees in my front yard. I like those trees. They are beautiful and majestic. But they are not as important as people. Should we destroy the earth and be irresponsible with our stewardship? Of course not. Adam was told to subdue the earth, not ruin it. But should we forget that people are made in the image of God while animals and trees are not? Of course not. Yet that's exactly what we're doing. And the fingerprints of Baal are all over that kind of thinking.

Gentlemen, we need to teach our kids the truth about the environment from the Scriptures. Take them back to Genesis and show them that God created the environment. Show them that God then created man and gave man authority over the creation. Show them that people are made in the image of God. In other words, guys, give your kids a biblical perspective so that they can fight off this dangerous and deceptive worship of the environment that destroys the lives of people. Teach them the Word of God and you will give them a foundation on which they can stand tall and fight off the false teachings about pro-choice and the environment that are a direct perversion of God's plan for the earth. Read through Francis Schaeffer's classic treatment of the environment, *Pollution and the Death of Man.* It will give you a balanced presentation that you can adapt as you talk to your kids about these issues.

We have only covered two of the four characteristics of Baal worship. We'll hit the last two in the next chapter. And believe me, it gets worse. Much worse. But I think you're probably starting to get a flavor for this insidious belief system that brought down Israel. Perhaps "flavor" is a poor choice of terms. I think Elijah might refer to it as a "stench."

It was Elijah whom God used to confront Ahab and Jezebel over the issue of their wicked leadership in Israel. We will devote an entire chapter to Elijah later in this book, but suffice it to say for now that Elijah could spot a Baalist at fifty miles. And he could smell one from a hundred.

What do you think the reaction of Elijah would be if he were to make an appearance in the United States of America in the 1990s? I think he would immediately pick up the stench that now permeates virtually every part of this nation. He could walk from sea to shining sea and see the spiritual devastation that accompanies the presence of Baal. Most Americans don't even know who Baal is, let alone what he stands for. But Elijah does. And I wouldn't be surprised if he were to make his way to the capital of this nation as he once made his way to the capital of Israel. And for some reason I have the sneaking suspicion that his message would be the same message of God's judgement.

And because Elijah was such a straight shooter, I think he would deliver his message to any and all of our leaders who have bowed to Baal. He would declare it to the Executive branch, the Legislative branch, and the Judicial branch. He would tell it straight to Democrats, Republicans, and

Independents alike. He would ignore such religious affiliations as Methodist, Baptist, Episcopalian, Roman Catholic, or any other denominational tag. You see, back when Elijah spoke for God, there were no denominations. You were either on the Lord's side or you weren't. You either submitted to the authority of God or you didn't. You either promoted the holiness of God or you mocked it.

That's why Elijah could spot a Baalist at fifty miles. The lines were clearly drawn. And I think Elijah would quickly and powerfully redraw those lines for our leaders who have erased them like a lead-off hitter who takes his foot and deliberately wipes away the chalk in a freshly marked batter's box.

I think Elijah would immediately pick up that the same forces that destroyed Israel are destroying us. And that's why he would stand tall, redraw the lines, and courageously remind our leaders of the Sovereign and Immutable God of Abraham, Isaac, and Jacob who is still calling the shots. He might even quote Psalm 2:10-12:

> Now therefore, O kings, show discernment;
> Take warning, O leaders of the earth.
> Worship the LORD with reverence,
> And rejoice with trembling.
> Do homage to the Son, lest he become angry,
> and you perish in the way,
> For His wrath may soon be kindled.

1. Briefly review the steep downhill slide on which Israel found itself because of its evil leadership. Check out 1 Kings 16:12-13,18-19,25-26,30-33. What kind of trend do you see here? In your view, is America at the beginning of such a trend...or are we already quite a ways "down the slide"? Explain your answer.

2. Elijah stood tall in the face of terrible evil and terrible danger (1 Kings 17:1-9). Why do you suppose God suddenly pulled him from the front line and gave him an extended time of "R&R"? As Christian men face the intensity of an emotionally-exhausting, sometimes-dangerous "culture warfare" in our country, how can we find a balance between fighting the good fight and simply enjoying life with our families?

3. Review the Creator's intentions for man and his "environment" in Genesis 1:26-29, and 2:15,19-20. How has today's environmental movement twisted God's mandate for the world? What can we as dads do to help our kids stand tall against the nonstop brainwashing on this issue that so saturates our culture?

4. Look back in this chapter at the first two characteristics of Baal worship. How long ago did these "warning signs" appear in our country in a major way? In what ways do you see them growing more and more prevalent as time goes by?

CHAPTER SIX

High Noon for a Nation
(Gay Wrongs, Part 1)

When principles that run against your deepest convictions
begin to win the day, then battle is your calling,
and peace has become sin; you must, at the price of dearest peace,
lay your convictions bare before friend and enemy,
with all the fire of your faith.

ABRAHAM KUYPER

In the classic 1952 western *High Noon,* Gary Cooper gives an Academy-Award winning performance as a U.S. marshal waiting the arrival of four vengeful gunmen bent on shooting him down.

Three of the killers clean their guns and bide their time at the station. The train bearing their leader is scheduled to roll into the placid little desert town at 12:00 P.M.

High noon.

Throughout the taut drama, director Fred Zinneman skillfully and repeatedly intersperses the action with two haunting images. The first image is that of empty train tracks stretching off into a heat-distorted horizon. Down those tracks, just out of sight, a relentless evil is bearing down on a peaceful town. The second image is that of ticking clocks. Lots of clocks. Wall clocks. Grandfather clocks. Desk clocks. Pocket watches. All of them ticking down the hours and minutes and seconds until the howling locomotive rolls into the station bearing bitterness and death for a good man who must stand alone against the evil, against the odds.

Throughout the movie, Cooper approaches citizen after citizen, appealing for deputies to stand beside him as the inevitable showdown draws nearer. No one is willing to risk his life. Not even the men he called "old friends." At the eleventh hour, Cooper interrupts the Sunday service of the town's church. These are good people, he reasons, people who ought to be willing to stand tall against the shadow creeping toward their town. The pastor, however, finds himself in a moral dilemma and can't recommend anything. The mayor rises to counsel prudence, and suggests that the marshal simply flee. The men in the church debate the issue, leaning first this way, then that way—paralyzed by timidity and indecision. In the end, Cooper walks out alone.

He loves life. He would love to leave on his honeymoon with his new wife (you would too if you'd just married Grace Kelley), but he knows in his heart he can't run. He has to take a stand, even though it will most likely mean his life.

One jaded old lawman, played by Lon Chaney, tells Cooper the bitter truth: "People don't care. They just don't care."

An interesting thing happened as Warner Brothers filmed the fateful approach of the noon train. They just about lost their cameraman.

He was lying on his stomach in the middle of the tracks focusing on the locomotive rushing in from the horizon. It was such a dramatic shot. The train rushed closer and closer, billowing white smoke. Then, as it drew nearer, it billowed black smoke. What a great effect! The cameraman was relishing every exciting frame. What he didn't understand was that the black smoke was meant to be a *distress signal.* The train had lost its brakes.

Looking through the lens, he watched the death train hurtle toward his camera. But wasn't the engineer overdoing it a little on the whistle? And why wasn't he hearing the squeal of brakes? And my goodness, the thing didn't seem to be slowing down! At the last possible second, the cameraman hurled his camera to one side and leaped off the tracks as the locomotive screamed right on through the station. The camera was destroyed by the impact, but the film cartridge remained intact. Fortunately, so did the cameraman.

Gentlemen, I don't mean to sound theatrical or melodramatic, but it is high noon for America. In fact, it may be closer to 12:30. An unbelievably destructive evil has rolled into our cities and towns and communities, bring-ing death, perversion, and the destruction of many cherished values and ideals. We'll talk about that evil in the next two chapters.

Yes, it may be too late to stop the train, but it's never too late for good men to make a determined stand in defense of their homes and families.

We need men who are willing to stand tall, and we need them now.

Why now?

In our last chapter we saw how our nation has fallen into the same kind of Baal worship that seduced and ultimately destroyed the northern king-dom of Israel. We zoomed in on the first two characteristics of Baal worship:

#1. Baal worshipers were pro-choice after the child was born.

#2. Baal worshipers held the environment in high esteem and consid-ered Baal as the one who determined and controlled the environment.

In this chapter, we will consider the last two traits of Baal worship:

#3. Baal worship encouraged and promoted rampant sexual immorality, particularly homosexuality, as a normal and natural alternative lifestyle.

#4. Baal worship sought to coexist as a legitimate religious viewpoint alongside Judaism.

TIME CHANGES ITS TUNE

I recently came across a somewhat inflammatory statement about homosexuality. Instead of letting you know who made the statement, allow me to quote it…and then let's talk about the source:

> Even in purely nonreligious terms, homosexuality represents a mis-use of the sexual faculty and, in the words of one…educator, of "human construction." It is a pathetic little second-rate substitute for reality, a pitiable flight from life. As such it deserves fairness, compassion, understanding, and, when possible, treatment. But it deserves no encouragement, no glamorization, no rationalization, no fake status as a minority martyrdom…

Now who made the statement? Let's make it multiple choice. Was it:

A. Pat Buchanan.

B. Jerry Falwell.

C. Rush Limbaugh.

D. An essay in *Time* magazine.

The answer is "D." It is a direct quote from an issue of *Time* that I recently came across. I couldn't believe my eyes. I did not expect that kind of thinking from *Time*. That's when I noticed the date of the issue.

January 21, 1966.

If an editor at *Time* were to make a statement like that today it would be the end of his journalistic career. He would be ostracized from the honorable practice of free expression forever. The reason he would be ostracized is that free expression in the American press is, generally speaking, a thing of the past. That statement would never appear in *Time* because it is not politically correct. The problem with the paragraph is that it does not speak of homosexuality in glowing terms. And that is a problem! According to the writer, "homosexuality is a pathetic little second-rate substitute for reality." That is not acceptable in *Time* or in any other self-respecting news magazine of the 1990s.

In America in the 1990s, homosexuality is not "second rate," it is first rate. And not only is it accepted, it is encouraged. And God help the writer at *Time* or any other newsmagazine who would dare to differ.

I recently spent some time on a Saturday at the library of a major university. I was sitting at a computer in the periodical library doing a literary search of articles written on homosexuality. I started in the 1950s and worked my way up to the 1990s. It was one fascinating ride through the annals of American thought. What I discovered was this. Up until 1968, the reporting in *Time* and other popular magazines concerning homosexuality reflected a value system that was based on moral absolutes. In other words, the writers at *Time* were working from a framework of Judeo-Christian moral absolutes that viewed homosexuality as wrong and abnormal.

That all changed with one article in 1968. In that one article, *Time* made an amazing leap to the viewpoint of moral relativism. With one stroke of the pen, *Time* was on a crusade to not only approve homosexuality, but to justify it.

This is a book to Christian men. And what Christian men need to understand is that *the greatest moral threat to your family in this country is militant homosexuality.*

We'll talk about that, but first allow me to make an important distinction. I have met some very fine people who have struggled with the issue of homosexuality in their lives. It is something they know is wrong and many of them have taken significant steps to bring this issue of their lives under the control of the Holy Spirit.

I know of others, who, after pursuing for a time the gay lifestyle, turned to Christ as a result of discovering they have AIDS. They regret their behavior in the past and have repented of it at the foot of the cross. They have met Jesus Christ as their Lord and Savior.

I had breakfast with a friend this morning. My friend's brother, who lives in another state, is dying of AIDS. But as my friend described it, his brother has received a transfusion of the blood of Christ, and he has received eternal life.

I know people who have deeply struggled with homosexual tendencies in their lives and continue to struggle. They have my most sincere concern and sympathy. As I have met with them in the confidentiality of a counseling session, I have assured them that I am on their team. Some of you reading this have struggled firsthand with homosexuality because of a missing emotional piece in your relationship with your father. The only response to a man who is working through this issue is biblical love and compassion.

But there is another group who demands their actions be accepted and approved. Any hesitancy to do either prompts them to cry "bigot" or "homophobe." These are the *militant* gays. We are talking about a very powerful and wealthy group of individuals who have a clear strategy and agenda. Try as they may to cloak that agenda in the media (since it isn't socially acceptable), their goals have been clearly spelled out in print by their own writers. In a nutshell, the militant homosexual community desires to bring about two radical changes to our society:

1. They want to remove the sodomy laws from the books.

2. They want to remove the age of consent laws from the books.

For all intents and purposes, they have effectively achieved their first goal. For even in states where sodomy laws are still in effect, they are conveniently ignored by the authorities.

What is frightening is their desire to remove the age of consent laws from our legal framework. Now, I want to be fair on this point. Not all homosexuals want to lower or remove the age of consent laws. However, after reading the literature of the gay rights movement, one can only conclude that for what appears to be a significant and vocal number, that indeed is their aim.

I find that many Christian men are ignorant of this side of the homosexual agenda. Quite frankly, the ramifications of such a change are so staggering and so wicked that they defy description. But make no mistake. This is the agenda. It's high noon, gentlemen, and this is no time to be naive.

I recently had a Christian father tell me that he was more concerned about someone speeding down his residential street than he was about the homosexual agenda. This man, though highly educated, is not thinking clearly. He has completely fallen for the homosexual propaganda that flows out of the media with the steady and unrelenting pressure of a firehose. Of course this father should be concerned about speeding cars in his neighborhood. That is an apparent threat to his children. But he should not be unaware of the hidden threat of the gay agenda.

If your reaction to what you are reading is "this is homophobic, reactionary, alarmist, or hateful," then you, my friend, have also been taken in. And you will live to see the day that you regret it.

Let us make no mistake about it. Gay rights is not about the normative rights that all citizens enjoy. Men and women who practice homosexuality have the same rights as those of us who don't practice homosexuality. Gay rights is about *special rights*. It is these special rights that will ultimately bring down judgment upon this nation.

Why am I writing about militant homosexuality in this book to men? I am writing about it because it an issue that you will soon have to face in your community. It's an issue that you can't escape. The train has already rolled into town. The destroyers are already in the streets.

I have met Chuck McIlhenny on several occasions. Chuck is a

level-headed man who loves his family and the church that he pastors in San Francisco. I like Chuck because he, too, rides for the brand. He is a man of courage who has stood tall for the truth against unbelievable opposition. His home and church have been firebombed, he has been sued on more than one occasion, and his children have been sexually threatened. Here's what Chuck says to those of us who don't live in San Francisco:

> Whether you want to or not, you will eventually have to deal with the gay rights movement. It may first appear as a "human rights ordinance" at your local city council; or it may turn up as a pro-homosexual teen counseling center at your local junior and senior high school, or perhaps as a safe-sex education program for your children, teaching them that homosexual sex and same-sex partnerships are just as "normal" as heterosexual marital relationships. ALL of these things are in effect in San Francisco at the present time. Regardless of how it comes to your community, you and your children will eventually be *forced* to submit to the homosexual agenda—or face legal sanctions.[55]

Chuck knows first-hand of what he speaks. I know of two other men who have also paid a tremendous price for taking a moral stand on the issue of homosexuality. Both men were in highly visible positions in two of America's largest cities. Although their competency and excellence in their respective positions were beyond reproach, they were both the objects of direct and concerted public campaigns to drive them from their positions. Both men were relieved of their duties because they dared to stand in opposition to the homosexual agenda.

Now what we should understand is that neither one of these men went out of their way to take on the homosexuals. They didn't picket anybody, they didn't lead a demonstration, and they didn't file a lawsuit. They were persecuted and eventually railroaded out of their positions because somewhere in the normal course of their life they stated in a way *unrelated* to their jobs that they opposed homosexuality on moral grounds.

How did homosexuals get so much power?

How did a sexual practice that even *Time* magazine considered to be less than normal fewer than three decades ago gain such prominence and clout?

Roger Magnuson speaks of "a great iron triangle of a special-interest group [the homosexual lobby], the media [filled with issues consultants], and compliant legislators who insure that programs are sensitive to homosexuals."[56]

Let me reiterate what I said previously. If you think that I am panicking, resorting to hyperbole, or overstating my concerns, then you are the very man who needs to read on. How did a group that was outside of the boundaries of morality just ten, fifteen, or twenty years ago, suddenly become mainstream? How is it that anyone who dares to speak in opposition is looked upon as prejudiced, hateful, and intolerant? If the homosexual movement has gained this much power in the last twenty years, how much more will they gain in the next twenty?

Chuck McIlhenny issues a warning:

The homosexual movement is coming after your right to free speech, to religious freedom, and, most importantly, after your public school children through homosexual recruitment programs disguised as "safe sex" and/or AIDS education classes, alternative lifestyle classes, or through counseling services for teens run exclusively by gays and lesbians. And, no, your private Christian school will not be spared if anti-discrimination/sexual orientation ordinances are passed in your community. There will be no exceptions allowed in their bid for political rule over community after community—and why should there be? These are two mutually-exclusive moralities; one based on the Word of God, and the other based on the arbitrary will of men.[57]

Once again, we are back to the clash between those who believe in moral absolutes and those who believe in moral relativism.

What will you do if your state passes a law that prohibits "discrimination" against homosexuals or any adulterer, and even includes a prohibition against speaking or writing anything critical of such immoral conduct? Will your church take a stand? Will your pastor take a stand? Will you support your pastor if he does take a stand, even though your reputation in the community may suffer? Or will you compromise and allow legislated immorality to take over your community in the name of freedom? Will you allow your children to be recruited by such ungodliness in your tax-funded public schools and organizations? Only you can answer these questions.[58]

GEORGIA ON MY MIND

Marietta, Georgia, is a peaceful, family-oriented suburb just north of Atlanta. A recent *USA Today* article describes what happened when two thousand gay activists swarmed the town square park to protest the passage of legislation in Cobb County declaring homosexuality "incompatible with community standards." The homosexuals took over the park, which is usually a haven for families, and held a "Queer Family Picnic."

We have friends who live in Marietta. We know several couples in Marietta who love Jesus Christ and are raising their families in homes where the Scriptures are central. But our friends are now having to defend the well-being of their children. The article goes on to say that similar battles are unfolding in Idaho, Maine, Oregon, Florida, Michigan, Missouri, and Washington. No one is immune from the gay agenda.

When the battle for gay rights comes to your community, gentlemen, I suggest that you be there. This is the only Christian thing for a man to do. This is a battle over the children, and I will speak to that in just a moment. The homosexual militants play hardball. They loudly condemn the "intolerance" and "hate tactics" of those who oppose them. Yet they are well-known for their own confrontational tactics of interrupting church services and threatening those who dare to stand publicly against them.

Gary Bauer, president of the Family Research Council, is one of the bravest men you'll ever meet. He continues to speak the truth on this issue even at great personal risk. Recently, Gary wrote an article in the *Washington Post* against the removal of the ban that keeps homosexuals from serving in the military. Gary's wife received a call that evening from a man who told her that if the family didn't leave Washington within one week, he would kill all of them. Gary and his family didn't flinch. They stayed at the post and kept being faithful. They didn't give in to intimidation.

Because of the tactics of the militant gays, I suggest this is an issue that requires male leadership. Contrary to popular opinion, real men—especially Christian men—don't send women into combat. When we are surrounded by militant homosexual barbarians who are bent on nothing less than the destruction of every moral load-bearing wall left in this country, then it is the *men* whom God calls to go to battle. That is our situation, gentlemen. I believe that God is looking for men who have such a deep love for Jesus Christ and for their families, that they will put themselves on the line. God's men don't put their wives or their kids on the front lines, they put themselves on the line. That's what it's going to take in this assault on morality and godliness.

That's why it's our responsibility, gentlemen, to defend our families from the homosexuals who desire to break down the laws that protect decency and innocence. Martin Luther spoke with a prophetic voice when he said:

If I profess with the loudest voice and clearest exposition every portion of the truth of God except precisely that little point which the world and the Devil are at that moment attacking, I am not confessing Christ, however boldly I may be professing Christ. Where the battle rages, there the loyalty of the soldier is proved, and to be steady on all the battlefield besides, is mere flight and disgrace if he flinches at that point.

Martin Luther rode for the brand. And he is calling us to do the same.

I don't know too many men who relish the idea of getting into a confrontation with a group that throws bricks through windows, leaves butchered animals on doorsteps, paints lewd slogans on the opposition's building, or calls in bomb threats to disrupt the normal activity of those who are willing to stand against them. Focus on the Family has experienced all of those things since they supported the passage of Amendment 2 in Colorado. Dr. James Dobson has been the subject of vicious rumors that have been pushed without confirmation or hesitation by most of the media.

Why is Jim Dobson and Focus on the Family under such attack for taking a moral stand? They are under attack because they had the courage to take a stand against a movement that would give homosexuals special rights that no legitimate minority or any other group in this country enjoys. That was the "hate crime" of Focus on the Family.

As for me and my house, we're standing with Focus. And we're standing with them for one reason. They're standing tall.

WHO ARE THEY AND WHAT DO THEY WANT?

Militant homosexuals like to paint themselves as a minority. That is by design. Marshall Kirk and Erastes Pill published an article in the homosexual magazine, *Guide,* in November 1987. The article, "The Overhauling of Straight America," outlines a strategy by which homosexuals can best implement their agenda. Here are the main points as outlined in the gay strategy:

1. *Desensitization.* "To desensitize the public is to help it view homosexuality with indifference instead of with keen emotion."

2. *Portray gays as victims, not as aggressive challengers.* "In any campaign to win over the public, gays must be cast as victims in need of protection so the straights will be inclined by reflex to assume the role of protector." In other words, make homosexuals a minority.

3. *Give the protectors a just cause.* "Our campaign should not demand direct support for homosexual practices, but instead make anti-discrimination as its theme."

4. *Make the victimizers look bad.* "To be blunt—they must be vilified.... The public should be shown images of ranting homophobes whose secondary traits disgust middle America. These images might include the Ku Klux Klan demanding that gays be burned alive or castrated."[59]

Marshall Kirk has one other bit of advice for those trying to elicit sympathy for the plight of the gay movement:

> In the early stages of the campaign, the public should not be shocked and repelled by premature exposure to homosexual behavior itself. Instead, the imagery of sex per se should be down-played, and the issue of gay rights reduced as far as possible, to an abstract social question."

A shrewd strategy? You'd better believe it.

A COUNTER-STRATEGY

Part of the problem with this whole issue is that very few people understand the activities of homosexuals. If they did they would get physically ill. Did you notice the suggestions made by the gay activists? In their own words they said that "the public should not be shocked and repelled by premature exposure to homosexual behavior itself." Now why do they stress such a strategy? They stress it because if the public knew what homosexuals did they would be precisely shocked and repelled! But that is part of the scam! In other words, if people don't know what homosexuals do, all the while being told that they are a minority, and that homosexuality is not a choice but genetic factor, then the homosexual strategists have won the hearts of a lot of people.

That's the strategy. And that's why I want to offer a counter-strategy.

This is a book to men. For that reason, I am going to give you some information that for obvious reasons should be marked "highly sensitive." Gentlemen, we have to understand that this movement is perverse. That's why I am going to give you some descriptions of homosexual behavior in the next few pages. For if more people knew the facts about homosexual behavior, the gay agenda would be stopped dead in its tracks. There would be no more talk about gay counselors in schools, or gays teaching sex education courses, or gay speakers being invited to schools to share the "gay alternative." Not a chance.

The following material is obscene and it is shocking.

If you would rather not be exposed to this information, then I suggest that you quit reading here and pick it up a little further down the road. I do want to encourage you to read this, however—especially if you are a father. For those of us with children cannot afford to be uninformed. The fact of the matter is that some of you men reading this have children who have already been exposed to this information. And it happened without your knowledge or consent.

Dr. Stanley Monteith reports the following information about homosexual behavior.[61]

• One hundred percent of homosexuals engage in fellatio, which is either insertive or receptive oral sex.

• Ninety-three percent engage in rectal sex, which is anal intercourse.

• Ninety-two percent are active in "rimming," which is licking with the tongue in and around the partner's anus, and inserting the tongue into the same. Dr. Monteith points out that with such behavior, the ingestion of some fecal matter is inevitable.

• Forty-seven percent of homosexuals practice "fisting." Fisting is where the hand and arm are inserted into another person's rectum. Recently a brochure was handed out to high school students in New York City. The brochure was graphically illustrated and informed the students "to use latex gloves when fisting. Don't insert the fist past the length of the glove."[62] Using a latex glove when fisting is obviously what some homosexuals consider to be "safe sex."

• Twenty-nine percent of homosexuals participate in "golden showers." This is where one man lies naked on the ground and is urinated upon by others.

• Seventeen percent of homosexuals are involved in "scatting." Scatting is either the eating of human feces or the smearing of human feces over one's body.

• Closely related is the practice of "mudrolling," which is rolling naked in human feces.

May I suggest to you that there is nothing normal, natural, or genetic about such behavior. I might add that we have not mentioned any details about sado-masochism, which according to Dr. Monteith's studies, show that 37 percent of homosexuals engage in sado-masochistic behavior. But we should point out that the average homosexual has twenty to 106 partners each year, and that 28 percent of homosexuals have committed sodomy with over one thousand men.

After reading this mind-boggling facts, is it any wonder that the average homosexual is:

• eight times more likely to contract hepatitis;

• fourteen times more likely to get syphilis;

• and five thousand times more likely to contract AIDS than a heterosexual man?

Now perhaps we understand why the gay agenda is to make sure that the public isn't shocked and repelled by premature exposure to homosexuality itself. If the facts were known, they would never get past the parking lot of a school. Up until twenty or so years ago when common sense about homosexuality was assassinated in this country, they were kept out of the schools.

But no longer.

Is it any wonder that recently San Francisco attorney Melvin Belli complained that eleven-year-old girls, nauseated by a classroom presentation of "gay sex" by activists, were not allowed to leave the room. Many of the girls have reported recurring nightmares. If the thought of little girls being forced to view such trash in a public school doesn't nauseate you, then perhaps this fact will. The city of San Francisco gives the gay activists $124,000 each year to go into the schools to "educate" the children.[63]

Whoever heard of education that makes little girls vomit? You'll find it alive and well in a city that has caved in to the homosexual agenda.

High noon in America has come and gone. If you've been a casual observer, laying on the tracks and watching the locomotive roll in from a safe distance, you'd better think about taking some action. Bob Dylan used to sing a song about a slow train comin'. This is no slow train, my friend. It's a bullet train.

And it's heading directly your way.

1. Read Paul's prophetic words in Romans 1:18-32. Describe the progression (regression?) that begins in verse 18 and ends in the depravity and perversion in verses 24 through 32. With Paul's warnings ringing in your ears, draw parallels with what you see in today's America.

2. In view of Romans 1:18-22,28-32, discuss this statement: A society that removes prayer, the Ten Commandments, and a belief in the Creator from its schools, can expect to reap a deadly harvest in the following generations.

3. Review Leviticus 18:22,24-30 and 20:13. Summarize God's view of homosexual relations, using some of the strong terms that He uses.

4. Take time to consider again Martin Luther's statement, relating it to the militant homosexual's battle for "rights" within your community:

> If I profess with the loudest voice and clearest exposition every portion of the truth of God except precisely that little point which the world and the Devil are at that moment attacking, I am not confessing Christ, however boldly I may be professing Christ. Where the battle rages, there the loyalty of the soldier is proved, and to be steady on all the battlefield besides, is mere flight and disgrace if he flinches at that point.

CHAPTER SEVEN

When the House Begins to Fall
(Gay Wrongs, Part 2)

To the pure, all things are pure,
but to those who are corrupted and
do not believe, nothing is pure.
In fact, both their minds and consciences
are corrupted

(TITUS 1:15, NIV).

When I finally got my luggage off the carousel, I walked out the glass doors and saw the hotel shuttle pull right up in front of me.

That's what you call timing.

The driver helped haul my stuff on board and we took off for the hotel.

"Ever been to Kansas City before?" he asked.

"No," I replied. "It's my first trip."

The driver then began to tell me a little bit about his town. He was in his fifties and had lived in Kansas City all his life. We continued to talk as the shuttle merged into the exit lane for downtown. That's when I asked a very simple question and got a very unexpected answer.

"How long have you worked at the hotel?"

"Since the first day that it opened in 1980. I've been here the whole time. I was even here the night of the accident."

"Accident? What accident?"

"I was here the night the balconies collapsed. It was the most horrible thing I've ever seen in my life. As long as I live, I'll never be able to get those screams out of my mind. There were people crushed under the weight of the falling balconies—pinned to the floor—but we couldn't get the balconies off of 'em."

And then the man choked up. In the rear view mirror, I could see his eyes welling up with tears. He wasn't able to say anything more for several minutes. Matthys Levy and Mario Salvadori are two structural engineers who describe what the driver of the hotel shuttle was not able to:

In July 1980 the plushest and most modern hotel in Kansas City, Missouri, the Hyatt Regency, was ready for occupancy after two years of design and two more years of construction....

The Hyatt Regency complex consists of three connected buildings: a slim reinforced concrete tower on the north end, housing the guests' bedrooms and suites; a 117-by-145-foot atrium with a steel and glass roof 50 feet above the floor; and at the south end a four-story rein-forced concrete "function," containing all the service areas—meeting rooms, dining rooms, kitchens, etc. The tower was connected to the function block by three pedestrian bridges, or walkways, hung from the steel trusses of the atrium roof: two, one above the other, at the second- and fourth-floor levels near the west side of the atrium and one at the third-floor level near the east side of the atrium. Restaurant service was available at a bar set under the two stacked walkways on the west side of the atrium. The main purpose of the walkways was to permit people to pass between the tower and function block without crossing the often crowded atrium.

At 7:05 P.M. on Friday, July 17, 1981, the atrium was filled with more than sixteen hundred people, most of them dancing to the music of a well-known band for a tea dance competition, when suddenly a frightening, sharp sound like a thunderbolt was heard, stopping the dancers in mid-step. Looking up toward the source of the sound, they saw two groups of people on the second—and fourth-floor walkways, observing the festivities and stomping in rhythm with the music. As the two walkways began to fall, the observers were seen holding on to the railings with terrified expressions on their faces. The fourth-floor walkway dropped from the hangers holding it to the roof structure, leaving the hangers dangling like impotent stalactites. Since the second-floor walkway hung from the fourth-floor walkway, the two began to fall together. There was a large roar as the concrete decks of the steel-framed walkways cracked and crashed down, in a billowing cloud of dust, on the crowd gathered around the bar below the second-floor walkway. People were screaming; the west glass wall adjacent to the walkways shattered, sending shards flying over 100 feet; pipes broken by the falling walkways sent jets of water spraying the atrium floor. It was a nightmare the survivors would never forget.... The final count reported 114 dead and over 200 injured, many maimed for life. It was indeed the worst *structural* failure ever to occur in the United States.[64]

It's a tragedy when two balconies holding hundreds of people fall down.

It's an even greater tragedy when a nation collapses.

For when a nation collapses, the lives of hundreds of thousands are crushed by tragedy. That's what happened to Israel. Israel collapsed under the weight of Baal worship just as those two balconies at the Hyatt collapsed under the weight of the crowd.

In both cases, the tragedy was the result of a serious, ultimately fatal structural defect.

FATAL FLAWS IN THE STRUCTURE

The acceptance and promulgation of homosexuality in a nation is the moral equivalent of a structural defect in a building or a bridge. At a certain point, the weight of the moral wickedness will cause the nation irreparable harm and the nation will collapse. Dr. Armand Nicholi, eminent psychiatrist and faculty member of the Harvard Medical School, describes the structural problem of a nation that embraces homosexuality:

No society past or present, has ever tolerated the institutionalization of homosexuality, for to do so would be to sow the seeds for its own extinction because homosexuality undermines the basic unit of society—the family—and of course precludes procreation, which means extinction of the race.

This is pure common sense. But in America, when the issue of homosexuality comes up, common sense is routinely assassinated.

Solomon had it right when he declared that there is nothing new under the sun. As we view the spiritual deterioration of our nation, we are reminded of the same deterioration that took place in Israel under Ahab and Jezebel. Homosexuality fits into that structural breakdown that was known back then as Baal worship.

Remember the third distinguishing characteristic of Baal worship? Baal worship encouraged and promoted rampant sexual immorality, particularly homosexuality, as a normal and natural alternative lifestyle.

The religion of Baal promoted homosexual activity as part of its worship. It was a religion orchestrated by Satan himself, so it stands to reason that it would violate the holiness and purity of Almighty God. There were three kinds of cultic prostitutes in Baalism: male prostitutes, female prostitutes, and sodomite prostitutes. In their public worship and festivals, they would recreate the sexual perversion that are a part of the Baal myths. These public displays were so vile that they cannot be put in print.

The actions of the male sodomite prostitutes of Baal were so filthy that the Hebrew metaphor chosen to describe them was "dog."[65] That's pretty strong language. It's another way of saying their behavior was worse than animals. Why worse? Because animals don't even do the things those guys did.

Now let's be very clear here. Scripture uses the term "dog" to describe the men who were engaged in these activities because what they were doing was an abomination to God. Ahab and Jezebel were not only protecting these prostitutes, but by their association and allegiance with them they were directly condoning and encouraging such a lifestyle.

The use of the word "abomination" is found 117 times in the Old Testament. The word, which literally means "a detestable thing," has a deep ethical meaning. It covers such things as witchcraft, sorcery, child sacrifices, and the worship of the sun, moon, and stars. In the Old Testament, the Law demanded death for those who practiced such things. Why? Because God knew that those were the kind of inherent structural defects that would bring down the nation.

A study of the word "abomination" makes it clear that there are some practices, specifically in the context of religion, which God abhors. *These are sins against the person of God Himself.* To understand the sense of the word "abomination," it is helpful to think of some synonyms. A thesaurus lists words such as "aversion," "hate," "hatred," "loathing," "repugnance," "horror," "repulsion," and "revulsion."

We are quickly getting to a point in America where even *speaking* against homosexuality is considered a "hate crime." There are some courts that would have to find God and the Bible guilty, because God says that homosexuality is an abomination.

Abominations are abominations because they are unnatural. They run directly counter to the way God created the world. We are His creation, and He is the ultimate judge of what is natural and what isn't. Our mighty Creator despises sexual perversion, and what it does to the souls and lives of those who practice it. To put it plainly, God is strict. He has drawn some very important moral lines. What else would you expect from a perfect heavenly Father?

Does that mean He won't forgive homosexuality? Of course not.

Or do you not know that the unrighteous shall not inherit the kingdom of God? Do not be deceived; neither fornicators, nor idolaters, nor adulters, nor effeminate, nor homosexuals, nor thieves, nor the covetous, nor drunkards, nor revilers, nor swindlers, shall inherit the kingdom of God. And such were some of you; but you were washed, but you were sanctified, but you were justified in the name of the Lord Jesus Christ, and in the Spirit of our God (1 Corinthians 6: 9-11).

The church is made up of forgiven people. There is no sin that God will not forgive, except the refusal to receive the sacrifice of His Son. But when a person refuses to admit that his behavior is wrong, he embarks on a downward spiral that takes him further and further from the forgiveness of God. That's certainly the message of Romans 1:18-32.

STEP ONE: SUPRESSION OF TRUTH

For the wrath of God is revealed from heaven against all ungodliness and unrighteousness of men, who suppress the truth in unrighteousness, because that which is known about God is evident within them; for God made it evident to them. For since the creation of the world His invisible attributes, His eternal power and divine nature, have been clearly seen, being understood through what has been made, so that they are without excuse.

STEP TWO: APATHY

For even though they knew God, they did not honor Him as God, or give thanks; but they became futile in their speculations, and their foolish heart was darkened. Professing to be wise, they became fools, and exchanged the glory of the incorruptible God for an image in the form of corruptible man and of birds and four-footed animals and crawling creatures.

STEP THREE: LUST

Therefore God gave them over in the lusts of their hearts to impurity, that their bodies might be dishonored among them. For they exchanged the truth of God for a lie, and worshiped and served the creature rather than the Creator, who is blessed forever. Amen.

STEP FOUR: PERVERSION

For this reason God gave them over to degrading passions; for their women exchanged the natural function for that which is unnatural, and in the same way also the men abandoned the natural function of the woman and burned in their desire toward one another, men with men committing indecent acts and receiving in their own persons the due penalty of their error.

STEP FIVE: DEPRAVED THINKING

And just as they did not see fit to acknowledge God any longer, God gave them over to a depraved mind, to do those things which are not proper, being filled with all unrighteousness, wickedness, greed, evil; full of envy, murder, strife, deceit, malice; they are gossips, slanderers, haters of God, insolent, arrogant, boastful, inventors of evil, disobedient to parents, without understanding, untrustworthy, unloving, unmerciful; and, although they know the ordinance of God, that those who practice such things are worthy of death, they not only do the same, but also give hearty approval to those who practice them.

By today's standards, Romans 1 is "intolerant." But that only demonstrates how far we have slid in twenty-five years.

Quite frankly, the homosexuals of this new Baal movement are gaining incredible acceptance in our society. And they have an agenda. If environmentalists want the minds of children, homosexuals want the *bodies* of children. We've already looked at what homosexuals do. Now let's look at who they are.

WHO THEY ARE

Are homosexuals in America, in fact, a legitimate minority group, disadvantaged and under-privileged? Hardly. As a demographic group:

• the average income for homosexuals is $59,000 per year versus an annual income of $32,000 for heterosexuals;

• 59.6 percent of homosexuals are college graduates, compared to 18 percent for the national average;

• 49 percent of gays hold professional/managerial positions, compared to 15.9 percent for the national average;

• 26.5 percent are frequent fliers, compared to 1.9 percent of the general population;

• the total homosexual market is estimated to be approximately $400 billion.[66]

This group that is seeking "minority" status is extremely well-heeled. They are smart, well-financed, and well-connected. And yes, they have an agenda. Homosexuals recruit. They have to recruit. They recruit children and adolescents because they cannot reproduce.

In Boston there is a gay newspaper by the name of the *Gay Community News.* The February 15, 1987, edition contained a lengthy statement by a radical homosexual named Michael Swift. Some have viewed this as the gay rights' Statement of Faith. I have selected the following excerpts:

We shall sodomize your sons, emblems of your feeble masculinity, of your shallow dreams and vulgar lies. We shall seduce them in your schools, in your dormitories, in your gymnasiums, in your locker rooms, in your sports arenas, in your seminaries, in your youth groups, in your movie theater bathrooms, in your army bunkhouses, in your truck stops, in your all-male clubs, in your houses of Congress, wherever men are with men together. Your sons shall become our minions and do our bidding. They will be recast in our image. They will come to crave us and adore us....

All laws banning homosexual activity will be revoked. Instead, legislation shall be passed which engenders love between men....

Homosexuals must stand together as brothers; we must be united artistically, philosophically, socially, politically, and financially. We will triumph only when we present a common face to the vicious heterosexual enemy....

If you dare to cry faggot, fairy, queer, at us, we will stab you in your cowardly hearts and defile your dead, puny bodies....

There will be no compromises. We are not middle-class weaklings. Highly intelligent, we're the natural aristocrats of the human race, and steely-minded aristocrats never settle for less. Those who oppose us will be exiled....

The family unit—spawning grounds of lies, betrayals, mediocrity, hypocrisy, and violence—will be abolished. The family unit, which only dampens imagination and curbs free will, must be eliminated. Perfect boys will be conceived and grown in a genetic laboratory. They will be bonded together in a communal setting, under the control and instruction of homosexual savants....

All churches who condemn us will be closed. Our holy gods are handsome young men....

Since we are alienated from middle class heterosexual conventions, we are free to live our lives according to the dictates of pure imagination. For us too much is not enough....[67]

When I read this for the first time, three thoughts came to my mind.

The first was "in your dreams." After I calmed down, the second was that I would like to sit down with the man who wrote this and find out about his relationship with his father. I can assure you that there is a major fissure in this man's life with his dad. The third thought was that this angry and bitter man desperately needs to know Jesus Christ.

Gentlemen, some things are worth fighting for. I had an evangelical pastor tell me last week that he didn't mind if his kids had *seven* homosexual teachers. How tolerant. And how naive. I got the strong sense that this man was not willing to take a stand. He reminded me of a certain Old Testament character named Lot. Lot, you'll remember, got so desensitized to immorality in Sodom that he never did take a stand. As a result, he lost his own family.

God help us if we don't draw the lines *now.* If we don't stand tall as men right now, then the same rights that are being given to homosexuals will soon be given to those who desire to legalize their incest, bestiality, and other unspeakable acts.

It was Blaise Pascal who once said that "those who indulge in perversion tell those who are living normal lives that it is they who are deviating from what is natural." That is the message of the homosexual movement. And it has the fingerprints of Baal all over it.

WHAT THEY WANT

We have just seen that homosexuals want access to our children. The question is, how will they obtain that access? The answer is, they must first acquire special rights which is also known as gay rights.

What is "gay rights"?

Put plainly, gay rights laws are meant to protect men and women who practice oral and anal copulation with members of the same sex. In about half the states, their behavior violates criminal laws.... [68]

The test, then, is one of behavior, not status. Homosexuals can be characterized by what they do (sodomy) and with whom they do it (their own sex). According to Magnuson, what gay rights laws ask for is a special privilege for homosexuals not generally available to other groups, such as those who commit incest, bestiality, pedophilia or, for that matter, any other criminal or antisocial behavior.

Robert Knight, the cultural director of the Family Research Council, describes the gay rights issue with keen insight:

> Contrary to their claims of "discrimination," there is no effort to deny homosexuals the same rights guaranteed to all Americans. The truth is that homosexuals have the same rights, with the restrictions, as everyone else. Homosexuals have the right to free speech, freedom of religion, due process under the law, the right to engage in commerce, to enter in contracts, own property, vote, along with a host of other rights. In fact, an ACLU handbook lists dozens of rights homosexuals already enjoy. In this country all citizens are guaranteed equal protection under the law. Homosexuals do not need equal protection.[69]

Despite the fact that homosexuals do not need special rights, since they enjoy the same rights as all Americans, they employ militant tactics to obtain their objectives and intimidate their opposition. Militancy is the logo of the gay rights movement. Their modus operandi is to intimidate rather than reason. Magnuson describes the logical consequences of such a militant strategy:

> The strategic vision of "total acceptance" articulated by (militant) homosexuals...means public legitimacy, credibility, and community endorsement: in short, making sexual deviance as acceptable as sexual normalcy.[70]

To accomplish that objective, homosexuals now fight tactical battles on three fronts:

1. Where homosexuality is prohibited by law, as in the case of laws prohibiting sodomy, homosexuals seek to repeal those laws or have them declared unconstitutional by the courts.

2. Where there are practices permitted by the law to heterosexuals but not to homosexuals (for example, marriage or adoption of children), homosexuals seek equal privileges for themselves.

3. Where the personal discretion or decision making of individuals impinges on homosexuals—a landlord's choice not to rent to practicing homosexuals, for example—homosexuals seek to pass laws that actually create special privileges for homosexual behavior ("gay rights laws") that are not available for people with more normal behavior.

THE REAL CONSEQUENCES OF GAY RIGHTS

If a gay rights bill or legislation comes to your town (and it inevitably will), then the granting of special rights to homosexuals would also *take* rights from other people in the community—people such as you, your family, and your church. Robin Knight outlines the actual consequences of such legislation:

• Parents would lose the right to protect their children from exposure to homosexuality.

• Private religious and civic groups would no longer be able to exclude homosexuals. The Boy Scouts of America are being sued in several states for refusing to admit homosexuals. These attacks on the Scouts convey the message that parents will no longer be free to ensure that organizations to whom they entrust their children will convey the parent's values.

• Landlords, even those in duplexes and family-centered complexes, could be forced to rent to open homosexuals.

• Good people of conscience would lose the right to disagree. For example, two Madison, Wisconsin, women were forced to pay fines, attend a political re-education class, write a letter of apology, and were informed that they were to be monitored by a public agency for two years because they declined to room with a lesbian.[71]

Nothing illustrates the twisted and depraved strategy of the gay rights movement more than their assault on the Boy Scouts. What parents in their right minds would want their son to have a homosexual scoutmaster? Yet, such companies as Levi Strauss actually pulled their funding of the Boy Scouts because of that organization's refusal to knuckle under to militant homosexual demands. Levi Strauss is one of a handful of companies that offer benefits to homosexuals and their "partners" as if they were married couples. Interestingly enough, they pulled their corporate donation to the Boy Scouts about the same time they offered benefits to homosexual couples. As George Grant points out, "Though company representatives insisted their decision was motivated solely by principle, the San Francisco-based company happily admits that 'three out of four gay men prefer Levi's jeans...over other brands.' "[72]

Could that juicy little fact have anything to do with the fact that Levi Strauss thinks that gays should qualify as scoutmasters for the Boy Scouts?

In 1988, an army NCO was a troop leader at Ft. Hood, Texas. He bound up the young boys and sodomized them with a nightstick while he videotaped their agonized screams.[73] I wonder what kind of jeans he prefers?

Fortunately, the Boy Scouts have not lost their common sense. They know that many homosexuals would like access to the boys, and some unfortunately, deceive their way into positions of trust. But at least the Scouts are attempting to keep the barbarians from storming the gates, with no thanks to Levi Strauss.

It is an established fact that homosexuality is tied with child molestation.

At least 30 percent of convicted male child molesters have committed homosexual acts and at least 91 percent of those who molested non-familial boys admitted to no sexual contact ever in their lives except with homosexuals.[74]

In France, 129 convicted gays said they had had contact with a total of 11,007 boys (an average of eighty-five per man).[75] Of four hundred consecutive Australian cases of molestation, 64 percent of those assaults were homosexual.[76]

Dr. Paul Cameron has written an excellent pamphlet on this subject. Cameron comments that:

Study after nationwide study has yielded estimates of male homosexuality that range between 1% and 3%. The proportion of lesbians in these studies is almost always lower, usually half that of gays. So, overall, perhaps 2% of adults regularly indulge in homosexuality. Yet, they account for between 20% to 40% of all molestations of children.

Child molestation is not to be taken lightly. Officials at a facility which serves about 1,500 runaway youngsters each year estimate that about half of the boys have been homosexually abused.... Investigation of those suffering chronic mental illness implicates child molestation as a primary cause.

If 2% of the population is responsible for 20% to 40% of something as socially and personally troubling as child molestation, something must be desperately wrong with that 2%. Not every homosexual is a child molester. But enough gays do molest children so that the risk of a homosexual molesting a child is 10 to 20 times greater than that of a heterosexual.[77]

George Grant reports that a recent poll was taken by the National Gay Task Force. The two major priorities of the homosexuals surveyed was the right for admitted homosexuals to be public school teachers and the right of homosexuals to adopt children.[78] They are well on their way to achieving both goals.

ACHIEVING THE UNTHINKABLE

This leads us to NAMBLA. That stands for the North American Man/Boy Love Association. This perverse group is taking the philosophy of the homosexual movement to its horrible, yet logical, conclusion. "If there is no such thing as perversion and if sex is good, the exercise of the merely physical appetite, then why should children be denied this good?"[79] Here are some statements from NAMBLA that will make you sick, but gentlemen, we'd better know what these people are up to! They want nothing less than unrestricted access to your children.

NAMBLA takes the view that sex is good, and that homosexuality is good not only for adults, but for young people as well. We support all consensual sexual relationships regardless of age. As long as the relationship is mutually pleasurable and no one's rights are violated, sex should be no one else's business....

Sexual liberation cannot be achieved without the liberation of children. This means many things. Children need to gain control over their lives, a control which they are denied on all sides. They need to break the yoke of 'protection' which alienates them from themselves, a 'protection' imposed upon them by adults—their family, the schools, the state, and prevailing sexual and social mores....

There is no age at which a person becomes capable of consenting to sex. The age of sexual consent is just one of many ways in which adults impose their system of control of children.[80]

Those statements are nothing less than demonic. Yet I believe that the pressure to endorse homosexuality is so strong in this country that *in the next ten years we will see states begin to either ignore or do away with the age-of-consent laws*. In other words, it's just a matter of time before NAMBLA will reach its stated goals.

The only barrier standing in their way is God's men.

May God grant us the courage and strength to stand tall.

BORN TO CHOOSE

A modern piece of propaganda is that homosexuals are born that way. And if they are, then their propensity for children should be excused. Or at least that's the reasoning behind NAMBLA. It seems that every month or so the media reports a study that shows that homosexuality is "genetic." Suffice it to say that you can't believe everything you read in the newspaper. Robert Knight adds a bit of common sense to the equation:

Flawed or misreported science can have enormous political ramifications, as shown by the willingness of the popular journals to tout studies that bolster gay activist' views while ignoring others that contradict them. The now-discredited Kinsey-based myth that 10 percent of the population is homosexual is a prime example. Although numerous studies from many nations indicate that the percentages are 2 percent or less, the 10 percent myth lives on.[81]

Knight cites the recent findings of Drs. William Byne and Bruce Parsons who examined past and current claims that homosexuality is genetic. They concluded that "there is no evidence at present to substantiate a biologic theory.... The appeal of current biologic explanations for sexual orientation may derive more from dissatisfaction with the present status of psycho social explanations than from a substantiating body of experimental data."[82] At last, a little bit of common sense from two doctors who are not intimidated by a very powerful group of homosexuals.

Gentlemen, this is a serious threat. Homosexuality has always been around, even when we were children. But the difference is that now homosexuals are attempting to legitimize their access to children through the courts. We cannot sit by and let this happen. For there is an agenda. And it is horrific.

CHURCHES EMBRACING BAAL

Affirmation, Glad, Honesty, Integrity, and Dignity sound like five points you might pick up from a motivational talk on positive thinking. But that's not what they are. These are the names of gay groups lobbying within denominations for acceptance, approval, and sanction. Affirmation is a Methodist group, Glad is with the Disciples of Christ, Honesty is trying to get in with the Southern Baptists, and Integrity is an Episcopalian group.

In addition to these, other gay organizations are American Baptists Concerned (someone needs to start a group called American Baptists Alarmed), the Brethren and Mennonite Council for Lesbian and Gay Concerns, the Presbyterians for Lesbian and Gay Concerns, the Seventh-Day Adventist group by the name of Kinship, and the United Church Coalition for Lesbian and Gay Concerns, which is tied up with the United Church of Christ. The Catholics have two groups bothering them, Dignity and the Catholic Coalition for Gay Civil Rights, while Axios is the gay group in the Greek Orthodox Church.

In addition to these, there are the independent groups working to get into non-denominational evangelical and charismatic churches. I refer to groups such as Evangelicals Concerned, Evangelicals Together, Lambda Christian Fellowship, and the National Gay Pentecostal Alliance. There is also the first gay denomination, the Metropolitan Community Church, which is seeking to join the World Council of Churches.[83]

I would like to offer a suggestion to all of these groups. My suggestion is that they all get together and rent a small banquet room in a hotel (they would only need a small room since all of these groups are very small in number). The purpose of the meeting would be to join together and streamline their efforts. I think they should join together and adopt a common name.

The name that I would like to suggest is "Apostasy."

I think that has a very nice ring to it. Plus, it fits. According to the Oxford English Dictionary, apostasy is "the abandonment or renunciation of one's religious faith or moral allegiance." As the shoe salesmen said to me recently, "If the shoe fits, wear it."

The fourth characteristic of Baal worship is that it attempted to come alongside of Judaism and be regarded as a legitimate part of the worship of Israel. At least that certainly appears to have been the agenda of Jezebel when she married Ahab. That same attempt is being made today in the church of Jesus Christ by homosexual activists.

Today's culture, obviously, doesn't like this kind of "intolerant" talk. But it's about time somebody stood up and told the truth about this stuff. The militant homosexual rights groups such as Act Up and Queer Nation, and homosexual churches such as the Metropolitan Community Churches and the so-called Cathedral of Hope in Dallas, are the modern-day equivalents of Baal worship. They are tied into the same thinking that brought Baal to Israel...and brought Israel to destruction.

Homosexuality is not a sickness or a disease. It is sinful behavior. Adultery is sinful, alcoholism is sinful, and overeating is sinful. Yet we tend to view all of those as sicknesses. They may be compulsive behaviors, but they are still sin. Each person is still responsible for the choices that he or she makes.

Jay Adams comments:

One is not a homosexual constitutionally any more than one is an adulterer constitutionally. Homosexuality is not considered to be a condition, but an act. It is viewed as a sinful practice which can become a way of life. The homosexual act, like the act of adultery, is the reason for calling one a homosexual. (Of course one may commit homosexual sins of the heart, just as one may commit adultery in his heart. He may lust after a man in his heart as another may lust after a woman).[84]

EVANGELICAL FUDGE

A recent article in *Christianity Today* was entitled "Homosexuality Debate Strains Campus Harmony: Homosexuals at Christian colleges press for acceptance." The lead paragraph of the story was revealing: "Christian college campuses across the country have become the setting for an intense struggle over homosexuality, involving free-speech rights, academic freedom, and theological beliefs."[85]

The article reported a debate that is taking place at Calvin College, Eastern College, and Gordon College concerning homosexuality. According to the article, "four students from Eastern attended the Gay March on Washington in April with a banner proclaiming 'Christian, Gay and Proud—Eastern College Gay and Lesbian Community.'"

The question is this: What is there to debate? The answer is if one takes a high view of Scripture there is *nothing* to debate.

Dr. Stanton Jones of Wheaton College is exactly right when he says that the "reason homosexuality is an important issue is that what the Bible treats as an isolated act to be condemned—people of the same gender having sex—our society treats as a fundamental element of personal identity."[86] Jones also is dead on target when he makes two other statements. The first is: "Every time homosexual practice is mentioned in the Scriptures, it is condemned."[87] The second is: "There are only two ways one can neutralize the biblical witness against homosexual behavior: by gross misinterpretation or by moving away from a high view of Scripture."[88]

This is the essence of these debates at "Christian" colleges. They are retreating from a high view of Scripture. Lewis Smedes, professor of theology at Fuller Theological Seminary has also retreated from the scriptural line. In 1976, Smedes wrote a book entitled, *Sex for Christians*. In referring to homosexuality, Smedes discusses a concept he calls "creative compassion" for the homosexual who suffers from constitutional homosexuality. This, according to Smedes, is the homosexual, who—although responsible for his choices and having gone through therapy—finds that he *cannot* change. The emphasis on "cannot" is pivotal.

As Smedes puts it in his book:

Within his [the homosexual who cannot change] sexual experience, he ought to develop permanent associations with another person, associations in which respect and regard for the other person dominates their sexual relationship.

To develop a morality for the homosexual life is not to accept homosexual practices as morally commendable. It is, however, to recognize that the optimum moral life within a deplorable situation is preferable to a life of sexual chaos.[89]

Teaching that homosexuals cannot change is not only unbiblical, it runs contrary to proven fact.

Dr. Reuben Rine, director of the New York Center for Psychoanalytic Training, has found that almost any program dedicated to helping homosexuals wishing to get out of the lifestyle to be successful. A large percentage have, indeed, given up homosexuality under all kinds of treatment programs. "The misinformation that homosexuality is untreatable by psychotherapy does incalculable harm to thousands of men and women."[90]

If psychotherapy can help change homosexuality, certainly the Word of God can, too.

To further drive home the point that homosexuals indeed can change, Dr. Joseph Nicolosi has written a book entitled *Repairative Therapy of Male Homosexuality*. It's the kind of book to keep on the bedstand for some light reading before you fall off to sleep (just kidding). Allow me to sum up Dr. Nicolosi's theory, for it is critical to this concession that so many Christians are making that homosexuals "cannot" change their behavior. Nicolosi's counseling technique is based on

a developmental view that the homosexual condition is the result of incomplete gender-identity development arising when there is conflict and subsequent distancing from the father. This defensive detachment is the psychological mechanism by which the pre-homosexual boy removes himself emotionally from the father (or father figure) and fails to establish a male identity. Many homosexuals are attracted to other men because they are striving to complete their own gender-identification.[91]

Nicolosi's basic thesis is that homosexuals have been emotionally cut off from proper identification and relationship with their fathers. That is a condition, that once understood, can be repaired through *rightly* relating emotionally to other men or father figures. Nicolosi has had unusual success with homosexual men who *have changed* their identity and behavior. The reason I am quoting these two psychologists is that there are psychologists who are saying that homosexuality is a behavior that *can* be changed, then it is a tragedy when those in the church say that it *cannot* be changed. The reason it is a tragedy is that the Scriptures clearly state that homosexuals can change (1 Corinthians 6:9-11).

Smedes is to be commended for his desire to express compassion to the person who is struggling with homosexuality. But the kind of compassion that anyone needs is not creative compassion but *biblical* compassion. In his attempt to extend compassion, what Smedes has done is to grant permission for someone to continue in a type of sexual conduct that the Bible expressly forbids. That, ultimately, is not compassion. Jesus made it clear to His disciples that if they were to be His disciples, then they were to abide in His word, and the truth would set them free (John 8:31-32).

Compassion without truth sets no one free. And advancing the myth that homosexuals cannot change simply gives permission to practice a behavior that the Scripture clearly condemns.

One of the leading spokesmen for the gay rights agenda is Dr. Mel White. White is a former professor at Fuller Theological Seminary. In fact, he taught there when Smedes released his book. White now calls himself a gay Christian and is the director of media for a large gay church in Dallas. According to the *Dallas Morning News*, Mel White came out of the closet in the early 1980s.[92] He divorced his wife of twenty-two years and left her and their two children for the homosexual life. Mel has been with his current partner for nine years. I recently saw Mel White on the Larry King Show. Time and time again, he alluded to his sexuality as something that one "cannot" change.

When I first read of Mel White's change several months ago, the first thought that came to my mind was Lewis Smedes's book. In his book, Smedes opened the door and Mel White walked through it. Smedes's "creative compassion" was wrong in 1976 and it's wrong today. But it is definitely gaining acceptance in evangelical churches where the lines are being moved to stay in step with a culture that is marching to the drumbeat of Baal.

Why have I written two chapters on this topic?

One reason. Our children are at risk.

Yes, homosexuality has always been around. But it has not always demanded authentication and acceptance from the rest of society as the movement is now doing. They are not content to just have their own neighborhoods and sections of a city. They want into the schools. They want to adopt kids. And they want special rights. For now, the churches and Christian schools will be exempted. For now. But we are kidding ourselves to think those exemptions will last.

Men, it's time to draw a line, and draw it right here.

When this issue comes up at a school board meeting, *be there.*

When a gay rights bill comes before your city council, *be there.*

Don't send your wife while you stay home to watch the ball game. You go to the meeting. Go prepared, and don't go alone. Take some guys with you and pray for one another during the meeting.

What else can you do to stand tall?

I'll make it easy.

Take the time to obtain a copy of the twenty-minute video, "The Gay Agenda." This has been shown to members of Congress and throughout the Pentagon. The gay community is well aware of the power of this video, because it presents the facts they don't want presented. You can obtain it from: "The Gay Agenda," The Report, 42640 North 10th Street, Lancaster, California 93534, (805) 940-4700. Show it to your school board members and show it to some of your city council members. Show it to the principal of your child's school. Show it to the pastor of your church, and then have him show it to the rest of the church board. Just by doing that, by touching decision makers with this common sense truth, you *will* make a difference. And hey, it's not tough. Anyone can shove a video cassette into a VCR.

I opened this discussion in the last chapter by referring to the shift that *Time* magazine made in its acceptance of homosexuality in 1968. Let me relate something that happened to me just yesterday. Before boarding a flight from Chicago to Portland, I picked up the latest *Time* at the newsstand. As I flipped through the issue I came across an article titled, "For the Love of Kids: What should be done with a teacher who belongs to a pedophile group but has a spotless record?"[93]

The article is about a New York City school teacher who is also a member of NAMBLA. I must tell you that this article will be as significant to the acceptance of pedophiles as the *Time* article of 1968 was to homosexuals. While the magazine does not condone his behavior, they do paint him as an innocent victim. This is the first "pedophile victim" story I've ever seen in a major news magazine. Mark my words, guys, it's just the first of many. The opening paragraphs of the article are classics:

> The principle behind a legal defense based on civil liberty is often illustrated by the famous lament of a Dachau prisoner: "They came first for the communists, and I didn't speak up because I wasn't a communist. Then they came next for the Jews, and I didn't speak up because I wasn't a Jew." And so on, through the trade unionists and the Catholics, until, "Then they came for me, and by that time no one was left to speak up."
>
> The question in the case of New York City teacher Peter Melzer is, Is it possible, in all sincerity, to begin that recitation, "They came for the pedophiles…?[94]

Gentlemen, this bullet train has just sped up. What should be done with a teacher who belongs to a pedophile group but has a spotless record? Most people will tell you what should be done—because they have still a line or two they're willing to stand behind. And one of those lines is sex with children. But that line is going to be challenged just as the homosexual line was challenged and erased twenty years ago.

Are you ready to draw the line? Are you willing to say, "It's here and no further"?

If godly men won't draw it, then who will?

The answer is *no one* will.

But you and I will show up at the school board meeting. We'll show up at the city council meeting. We'll square our shoulders, stand tall, and take the heat. And we will also fast and pray, because this battle is ultimately a spiritual one.

But one thing is for sure, we will *not* retreat.

We *will* protect our children.

And we will do it because we're ridin' for the brand.

1. Allow me to put a reverse spin on an old football cliché and say, *The best defense is a good offense.* As you consider the powerful, mysterious words of Paul in Ephesians 5:22-33, describe how biblically-obedient, Christ-centered marriages can turn back the creeping shadows of depravity and perversion in our country.

2. As you continue to reflect on the above passage, why does the Lord place so much importance on the "object lesson" of a loving husband and wife living together in sexual purity? Why does the perversion of that divinely ordained model cause the Lord so much grief and righteous anger?

3. It's very easy to read a chapter like this and become "worked up." That's not so bad. A lot of us need to be worked up over what's happening in our country. But as men who ride for the Lord Jesus, we need to display the kind of balance that He displayed when faced with a hostile, hateful world. Compare His reactions to the following situations:

Jesus in the temple (John 2:12-17).

Jesus at the feast (John 7: 30-38).

Jesus approaches Jerusalem (Luke 13:34-35; 19:41-44).

Jesus with the teachers and Pharisees (Matthew 23:13-36).

Jesus with the crowds (Matthew 9:36; 11:28-30).

How can we bring that kind of balance to our struggle with epidemic immorality and perversion in our country?

CHAPTER EIGHT

Elijah Stands Tall

Tolerance is the virtue of people who don't believe in anything.

G.K. CHESTERTON

Orestes Lorenzo Perez loved his country, but he couldn't stomach what was happening in it.

So in March of 1991, Lorenzo got into his MiG-23 fighter jet, flew it under U.S. radar, and safely landed in Key West, Florida. Upon defecting, he figured that Castro, embarrassed to have one of his top pilots defect, would immediately release Lorenzo's wife and his young sons to join him.

Lorenzo was wrong.

But Lorenzo wasn't through

For the next twenty-one months, Lorenzo worked every waking hour to get his family out. After months of frustration, Lorenzo decided on a plan that was crazy. He decided that his only chance was to fly back to Cuba and get his family. Only this time he didn't have a jet. He had a little thirty-one-year-old Cessna.

On December 19, 1992, at 5:05 P.M., Lorenzo took off from Florida for a little seaside village in Cuba. He had been able to smuggle a message to his wife to tell her of the plan. But his chances of getting through the net of radar and MiGs that surrounded Cuba were slim and none. If he was spotted, it would be over in an instant. So he flew in just as he had flown out, skimming scant inches over the waves.

At 5:43 P.M. his wife, Victoria, spotted the plane, as he was attempting to land on the busy highway just two blocks from the beach. She grabbed her boys and they started running.

Lorenzo brought the little Cessna down on the highway, narrowly missing a boulder in the middle of the road. Then he pulled to a stop just ten yards short of a head-on collision with a wide-eyed truck driver.

Lorenzo says that the hardest part (and the part that still pains him) was when Victoria and the boys jumped in—and he didn't even have time to hug or kiss them.

"Shut up and sit down!" he yelled. "I have to fly the plane!"

They hit American airspace twenty-one minutes later, and that's when the hugs and kisses started flowing.

The night before he took off, Lorenzo was praying in a small chapel. A woman came up to him and said, "Don't be afraid. Your trip will be a success." Lorenzo didn't know this woman and immediately wondered how she could know of his plans for the next day. He could only believe that God was speaking to him, assuring him that he would not be flying alone.[95]

There can be no doubt that Orestes Lorenzo Perez is a man of courage, conviction, and character. He's a man who stands tall.

You might say that he's flyin' for the brand.

ANOTHER TIME AND ANOTHER PLACE

Elijah loved his country, but he couldn't stomach what was happening in it.

So Elijah decided to take a little trip to Jerusalem to speak directly to King Ahab. We don't know how he got there and we don't know how he got past the guards to see the king. Elijah had a way of just showing up. And Ahab had to be as shocked to see Elijah as that truck driver was to see Lorenzo.

You see, God had had it with Ahab and Baal worship. It was killing the nation of Israel, God's chosen nation. Ahab was bringing down Israel like those balconies came down in Kansas City. So God looked for a man that he could trust to deliver a message to Ahab.

Now Elijah the Tishbite, from Tishbe in Gilead, said to Ahab, "As the Lord, the God of Israel, lives, whom I serve, there will be neither dew nor rain in the next few years except at my word" (1 Kings 17:1, NIV).

Elijah was pretty direct. With that brief announcement to Ahab, he had fired off a direct challenge to this false god, Baal, who was bringing down the entire nation.

Why was it a direct challenge to Baal? Because they all thought Baal controlled the rain. Oswald Sanders nails it down for us when he writes; "Baal was a god of many faces—being a god of rain, fertility, and the personification of the sun."[96] A common name for Baal was "The Rider of the Clouds." It was Baal who determined when the rain would fall and where the rain would fall.

Elijah looked around and saw that Israel was falling apart. He saw the immorality and apostasy. He saw Ahab and Jezebel and their troop of 850 prophets. And he saw that their belief system was destroying the moral and spiritual infrastructure of the nation. He also saw that they played hardball. They had killed the other prophets that had stood up to them. They had killed so many that Elijah legitimately thought he was the only one left. So what did Elijah do in the midst of those overwhelming odds?

Did he retreat?

No.

He stood tall and spoke the truth. No matter what the outcome, no matter what the cost, no matter what the odds against him, he took a stand. He was not going to let the moral erosion continue unchecked. Matthew Henry summarizes the situation:

Never was Israel so blessed with a good prophet as when it was so plagued with a bad king. Never was a king so bold to sin as Ahab, never was a prophet so bold to reprove and threaten as Elijah.... He only, of all the prophets, had the honor of Enoch, the first prophet, to be translated, that he should not see death, and the honor of Moses, the great prophet, to attend our Savior in his transfiguration. Other prophets prophesied and wrote, he prophesied and acted, but wrote nothing; but his actions cast more luster on his name than their writings did on theirs.[97]

Now remember, Ahab was the king of *Israel*. Israel wasn't just any nation, it was God's nation. These were God's people who had been called for a specific purpose. They were to be distinct and different because God has something very special for them to accomplish as a nation in His plan for the world.

The problem was Ahab and Jezebel. They thought Israel belonged to them. They were having a great time leading the nation down a path of godlessness, immorality, and wickedness. And they were getting away with it, or so it seemed, until Elijah showed up.

Who was Elijah? Quite simply, Elijah was a man who couldn't be bought. You've heard it said that every man has his price? Not Elijah. Elijah was sold out 100 percent to the God of Israel, Yahweh. Elijah was ridin' for the brand.

Elijah showed up and did something that was very, very foreign to Ahab and Jezebel.

He told the truth.

You see, Elijah had no interest in public opinion polls. The leather-clad prophet from the back-country of Gilead had no inclination to please special interest groups. Elijah was not one to make promises to any audience for any reason, just to secure their support. Elijah wasn't a politician. Elijah was a prophet. That simply means that he spoke the Word of God. Period.

It didn't matter what it was that God wanted him to say.

If it was politically incorrect, he said it.

If it was unpopular, he said it.

If it was offensive, he said it.

If people didn't understand, he said it.

If people were going to ridicule him and talk behind his back, he said it.

Elijah spoke the truth of God.

As suddenly as Elijah showed up, he then left. He was gone for three years. Elijah might have left, but his message didn't. Another drop of rain never dared to hit the ground after Elijah, the servant of God had spoken. This was all painfully clear to Ahab and Jezebel.

Gentlemen, what Elijah did took tremendous courage. Elijah faced Ahab by himself. A lesser man would have worried about the possibility of losing his life after speaking so directly to a king. But not Elijah. Elijah was a man of courage. He delivered the message and then:

> The word of the LORD came to him saying, "Go away from here and turn eastward, and hide yourself by the brook Cherith, which is east of the Jordan. And it shall be that you shall drink of the brook, and I have commanded the ravens to provide for you there." So he went and did according to the word of the LORD, for he went and lived by the brook Cherith, which is east of the Jordan. And the ravens brought him bread and meat in the morning and bread and meat in the evening, and he would drink from the brook (1 Kings 17:2-6).

There is a very simple reason God told Elijah to go to Cherith. It was for his protection. As the weeks and months went by, and no rain appeared, Ahab got hotter and hotter (no pun intended). The reality of Elijah's prophecy began to hit home. Baal or no Baal, it really wasn't going to rain until Elijah said so. If Ahab was angry, Jezebel must have been livid. For she was the one who had brought Baal with her when she married Ahab. And it was Jezebel who really ran the show. As several commentators have pointed out, she ruled Ahab, therefore she ruled the nation.

The name Jezebel means "unmarried" or "without cohabitation."[98] As one reads the pages of the Old Testament, it becomes quite clear that the marriage of Ahab and Jezebel was nothing more than a clever political alliance. When two people of such character deficit as Ahab and Jezebel get together in marriage, the focus isn't intimacy and romance, it's nothing less than naked ambition and raw power.

J. Vernon McGee described Jezebel as "a masculine woman with strong intellectual powers and a fierce passion for evil. She was strong-willed and possessed a dominant personality, but she had no moral sense. She was hardened into insensibility. She was unscrupulous and the most wicked person in history—bar none."[99] Those are pretty strong words. They also happen to be right on track. In Revelation 2:20, Jesus spoke to the church at Thyatira:

> I have this against you, that you tolerate the woman Jezebel, who calls herself a prophetess, and she teaches and leads My bond-servants astray, so that they commit acts of immorality and eat things sacrificed to idols.

Why would two people such as Ahab and Jezebel ever let Elijah out of the palace alive? I think that they must have been so surprised by his entrance and so stunned by his boldness that they didn't know what hit them. He delivered his message and then in the stunned silence following that prophetic concussion bomb, he was gone. You can put your money on the fact that a likeness of the prophet's mug soon graced every post office across Israel. As far as Ahab and Jezebel were concerned, he was "most wanted." The Scriptures indicate that there was not a nation or kingdom where Ahab hadn't looked for Elijah (1 Kings 18:10).

There is much speculation about the location of Cherith, but frankly, no one knows for sure where it was. More importantly, Ahab didn't know where it was. We don't know *where* it was, but we do know *what* it was: It was a place of protection where God took care of Elijah's needs.

Sometimes we are hesitant to speak out when we should. In our hearts, we know that we should, but we are reluctant because it might cost us something to do so. The story of Elijah reminds us that God is our protector. He has a way of looking out for those who are willing to stand tall and speak out for truth. God has ways of protecting us and our families that we would never dream of. One man experienced that protection in a most extraordinary way.

Elmer Bendiner flew numerous bombing runs over Germany in World War II. In his book, *The Fall of the Fortresses*, he recalls one bombing run that he will never forget.

> Our B-17 *[The Tondelayo]* was barraged by flak from Nazi antiaircraft guns. That was not unusual, but on this particular occasion our gas tanks were hit. Later, as I reflected on the miracle of a twenty-millimeter shell piercing the fuel tank without touching off an

explosion, our pilot, Bohn Fawkes, told me it was not quite that simple.

On the morning following the raid, Bohn had gone down to ask our crew chief for that shell as a souvenir of unbelievable luck. The crew chief told Bohn that not just one shell but eleven had been found in the gas tanks—eleven unexploded shells where only one was sufficient to blast us out of the sky. It was as if the sea had parted for us. Even after thirty-five years, so awesome an event leaves me shaken, especially after I heard the rest of the story from Bohn.

He was told that the shells had been sent to the armorers to be defused. The armorers told him that Intelligence had picked them up. They could not say why at the time, but Bohn eventually sought out the answer.

Apparently, when the armorers opened each of those shells, they found no explosive charge. They were clean as a whistle and just as harmless. Empty? Not all of them.

One contained a carefully rolled piece of paper. On it was a scrawl in Czech. The Intelligence people scoured our base for a man who could reach Czech. Eventually, they found one to decipher the note. It set us marveling. Translated, the note read: "This is all we can do for you now."[100]

Perhaps the idea of taking a stand on the issue of homosexuality is more than you can handle. Or it may be taking a stand at your office or your place of employment. We tend to worry about what might happen if we take a stand for the Lord. The Lord has promised to protect us just as He did Elijah. He knows how to get us to a brook where our needs will be met, and He knows how to keep our enemies from finding us.

A little lady by the name of Amy Carmichael spent her life for the gospel in India. She became aware of the horrible practice that was so common at the Hindu temples. Little girls as young as six and seven would be sold by their parents into lives of prostitution. Amy Carmichael could not bear the thought of such brutality to little girls. So she decided to do something about it.

Through miraculous means, the first little girl was brought to her in 1901. The little seven-year-old girl showed Amy her hands that had been branded with hot irons because she had tried to escape once before. By 1943, Amy was taking care of nearly eight hundred children, and she was a hated woman by a powerful system of prostitution that been in effect for nearly a thousand years. But God protected this woman who had the courage to stand for the Word of God. Gentlemen, if God could protect Amy Carmichael over all of those years, then we should ask God to give us just a tenth of her courage.

MAN OF CONVICTION, MAN OF COMPROMISE

We could spend an entire book on the life of Elijah. Since we can't do that, let's jump nearly three years ahead when Elijah shows himself again to Ahab.

Now it came after many days, that the word of the LORD came to Elijah in the third year, saying, "Go, show yourself to Ahab, and I will send rain on the face of the earth." So Elijah went to show himself to Ahab. Now the famine was severe in Samaria. And Ahab called Obadiah who was over the household. (Now Obadiah feared the LORD greatly; for it came about, when Jezebel destroyed the prophets of the LORD, that Obadiah took a hundred prophets and hid them by fifties in a cave, and provided them with bread and water.) Then Ahab said to Obadiah, "Go through the land to all the springs of water and to all the valleys; perhaps we will find grass and keep the horses and mules alive, and not have to kill some of the cattle." So they divided the land between them to survey it; Ahab went one way by himself and Obadiah went another way by himself.

Now as Obadiah was on the way, behold, Elijah met him, and he recognized him and fell on his face and said, "Is this you, Elijah my master?" And he said to him, "It is I. Go, say to your master, 'Behold, Elijah is here.' " And he said, "What sin have I committed, that you are giving your servant into the hand of Ahab, to put me to death? As the LORD your God lives, there is no nation or kingdom where my master has not sent to search for you; and when they said, 'He is not here,' he made the kingdom or nation swear that they could not find you. And now you are saying, 'Go, say to your master, "Behold, Elijah is here." ' And it will come about when I leave you that the Spirit of the LORD will carry you where I do not know; so when I come and tell Ahab and he cannot find you, he will kill me, although I your servant, have feared the LORD from my youth. Has it not been told to my master what I did when Jezebel killed the prophets of the LORD, that I hid a hundred prophets of the LORD by fifties in a cave, and provided them with bread and water? And now you are saying 'Go, say to your master, "Behold, Elijah is here" '; he will then kill me." And Elijah said, "As the LORD of hosts lives, before whom I stand, I will surely show myself to him today."

So Obadiah went to meet Ahab and told him; and Ahab went to meet Elijah (1 Kings 18: 1-16).

This dialogue between Elijah and Obadiah is critical. As we know, Elijah is a man of courage, conviction, and character. I want to suggest to you that Obadiah, although the text states very clearly that he is a believer, is a man in contrast to Elijah. Obadiah is a picture of a compromiser. Instead of courage, conviction, and character, he demonstrates cold feet, compromise, and convenience.

Elijah	*Obadiah*
courage	cold feet
conviction	compromise
character	convenience

Warren Wiersbe has noted some rather marked differences between Elijah and Obadiah:

Elijah was serving the Lord publicly and without fear; Obadiah was serving Ahab and trying to serve the Lord secretly. Elijah was "outside the camp" (Hebrews 13:13); Obadiah was inside the court. Elijah knew the will of God; Obadiah did not know what was going on. While Elijah was laboring to save the nation, Obadiah was out looking for grass to save the horse and mules. When Elijah confronted Obadiah, the frightened servant did not trust the prophet. And note that Obadiah had to "brag" about his secret service to impress Elijah with his devotion.[101]

THE QUESTION OF LEADERSHIP

There's an age-old question about leaders. Are they born or are they made? All leaders must be born...and from there they are constantly learning.

I believe that what is going to be required for this new era of American history are two things: courage and holiness. That's why some of you who are reading this are going through such difficult experiences in your personal lives right now. God is getting you ready for leadership. God is getting His men and women ready who will take a moral stand for Christ in a generation that is becoming increasingly hostile to the gospel.

"Wait a minute!" you may be saying. "I'm not a leader. And I'm not sure I have what it takes to be a leader in that kind of climate."

Sure you do. I recently came across what I consider to be a very insightful column on leadership. It was written to business entrepreneurs, but I think the parallels to our discussion will be quite clear. Wilson L. Harrell writes:

Psychologists claim that leadership asserts itself early in life. They're wrong. How many voted "most likely to succeed" at your school ever amounted to anything? Leadership is acquired—forged in the hell of combat. Being called upon to "face fire" transmutes ordinary men into leaders. It matters not whether the bullets are the lead kind or the more insidious projectiles of corporate battle.

A few years after every war, there is an explosion of entrepreneurship. Why? Because many of us discover courage we never knew we had. Courage is the kernel of leadership. In World War II, I was a combat fighter pilot flying a P38, giving "close support" to General Patton in his march through France. Our mission was to bomb and strafe enemy positions ahead of his troops. One day, my flight of four planes was ordered to take out a German airfield 100 miles behind their lines. We zoomed down, made our run, and survived the antiaircraft fire. As we pulled up, I saw in the distance what looked like a big flock of buzzards. Then I realized: "Those aren't buzzards. Those are airplanes...German airplanes!"

I got on the intercom and called in to my leader, Jerry Gardner. In a voice two octaves above high C, I yelled: "Jerry, there's a whole mess of bogeys at 10 o'clock low! Jerry looked up. After a moment of silence, he said calmly, "Let's go get 'em."

Off we went, four idiots chasing what turned out to be 67 enemy fighters—the dreaded Hermann Goering yellow-nose fighters. Toward the end of the war, America had destroyed most of the Luftwaffe, so General Goering brought together his best pilots into one invincible unit. They'd had a field day bombing our airfields and killing our troops. They'd never been challenged—until now.

As we got closer, we could see that they carried bombs and belly tanks. They were off bombing some unsuspecting airfield and not eager to play with four. Then they turned into us—67 of them head-on. Almost in range. My backside was chewing up the seat. Now, there is one sacred rule in the Air Force: Always keep formation. The only way to survive air-to-air combat is to stay together and protect each other. At that moment, Jerry got on the horn and uttered some immortal words:

"Every man for himself."

We zoomed right into the middle of their formation. I ended up on the tail of a German general leading the group with his three wingmen. Nobody behind me could shoot at me for fear of hitting the general—a no no for any German pilot who didn't want to face a firing squad. I shot down the three wingmen without even getting shot at.

Then the general and I had ourselves one hell of a dogfight. He probably flew into my fire, since from the beginning I was squeezing every trigger in the cockpit. He went down.

The next second, every #*&%#@ that wasn't shooting at Jerry and my other two buddies opened up on me. My plane and I caught fire.

I bailed out, pulled my rip cord, and looked up. My chute was on fire.... Luckily , I was so low that my chute swung only a couple of times before I hit the ground, badly burned, and was picked up by the French underground. Eleven days later, when I was near death, Patton sent in a squadron of tanks to get me out of there.

The day of our dogfight, 47 yellow-nose fighters were shot down.... All four of us survived and earned Presidential citations. But the real question is: Why? Why did three pilots willingly follow Jerry into what we knew was most certain death?

Jerry Gardner was a leader. Remembering his example, I became one.[102]

That's precisely why we are looking at the example of Elijah. That's why I would suggest that you take some time and read the entire Scriptural account of the life of Elijah. It really doesn't take that long to get through his biography. You start in 1 Kings 17 and read through 2 Kings 2:14. That's a total of about seven chapters. And in those seven chapters you'll see first-hand the example of Elijah's leadership.

Elijah wasn't perfect. There was a brief time after his mighty victory over the four hundred prophets of Baal that he lost perspective. That often happens after a great victory. It's after a great triumph that a man is most susceptible to depression. And that's what happened to Elijah. As James tells us, "Elijah was a man with a nature like ours" (James 5:17).

But the clear and steady evidence shows Elijah to be a man of courage, conviction, and character. Obadiah, on the other hand, was a man who tried to play both ends against the middle. And that is the road to ruin.

Quite frankly, Obadiah is a puzzle to me. He also puzzles Old Testament commentators. Obadiah is a mystery because he had behaviors that are contradictory. On one hand he appeared to be committed, but on the other...what was he doing *working for Ahab?* Someone recently reminded me that Daniel, too, worked in a high government position for pagan kings. So what was wrong with Obadiah being in that position?

Nothing was wrong with him having the position. What was wrong was that he *held on* to the position instead of standing up to Ahab.

It's apparent from Obadiah's conversation with Elijah that Obadiah was more concerned about saving his life than he was in speaking the truth. Daniel would never have done that. Daniel never compromised his faith, that's why he spent some time at the lion exhibit in the Babylon zoo. Think about Shadrach, Meshach, and Abed-nego. They were willing to walk into the fire rather than compromise their convictions. But Obadiah was trying to play both sides. And that was his problem. Obadiah was a believer and he had convictions. His problem was that he was way too willing to compromise those convictions in ways that Daniel, Shadrach, Meshach, and Abed-nego never would have.

Obadiah was a compromiser. Elijah told it straight and took the heat. Obadiah had a great job and career that was hard to give up. Elijah lived day to day in complete dependence on the Holy One of Israel. Obadiah was part of a group that promoted wickedness, killing, and immorality—although he himself found those things to be wrong.

The problem with Obadiah was that he was like a chameleon. A chameleon is a small lizard that can change colors to fit into its environment. The problem with that is simply that our colors should be clear.

I walked into my study this morning to find the following statement on my desk. My daughter had made some copies of this quote for her high school Bible study and had inadvertently left one on my desk. It makes the point about as clearly as it can be made. I would give the person who wrote it credit, but I don't know where it came from. However, it is worth repeating:

I am part of the Fellowship of the Unashamed. I have the Holy Spirit's power. The die has been cast. I have stepped over the line. The decision has been made. I am a disciple of Jesus Christ. I won't look up, let up, slow down, back away, or be still. My past is redeemed, my present makes sense, and my future is secure. I am finished and done with low living, sight walking, small planning, smooth knees, colorless dreams, tame visions, mundane talking, chintzy giving, and dwarfed goals.

I no longer need pre-eminence, prosperity, position, promotions, plaudits, or popularity. I don't have to be right, first, tops, recognized, praised, regarded, or rewarded. I now live by presence, lean by faith, love by patience, lift by prayer, and labor by power. My pace is set, my gait is fast, my goal is heaven, my road is narrow, my way is rough, my companions few, my guide reliable, my mission clear. I cannot be bought, compromised, deterred, lured away, turned back, diluted, or delayed. I will not flinch in the face of sacrifice, hesitate in the presence of adversity, negotiate at the table of the enemy, ponder at the pool of popularity, or meander in the maze of mediocrity. I won't give up, back up, let up, or shut up until I've preached up, prayed up, stored up, and stayed up the cause of Christ.

I am a disciple of Jesus Christ. I must go until Heaven returns, give until I drop, preach until all know, and work until He comes. And when He comes to get His own, He will have no problem recognizing me. My colors will be clear.

This author of this statement is ridin' for the brand. Elijah would have signed off on this, too, because he was also ridin' for the brand. But Obadiah, well, Obadiah was just ridin'. Sometimes he was riding for the brand and other times he was just riding. In other words, Obadiah's colors weren't always clear. But they needed to be. What a pity it is that I know some high school girls who are more willing than their fathers to let their colors be clear. What those girls need are dads who are willing to stand tall.

How about your colors? Are they clear or are they muddled? Are your colors clear in your career? Are they clear with your kids? Are they clear with the IRS? Are they clear when it comes to sexual purity? Are you ridin' for the brand, or are you just ridin'? Are you standing tall, or just standing around?

To put it in a nutshell, guys, I believe every Christian family needs a man of courage, character, and guts at the helm. A man willing to stand tall no matter what. That's the kind of leadership it's going to take to lead a family in a culture that is becoming more and more hostile every day to Christianity. These are times of great necessities and great pressure for God's people. That's why God is looking for his men to step up to the plate and be great leaders.

Great and extraordinary undertakings require character, conviction, and courage. Louis Adamic wrote: "There is a certain blend of courage, integrity, character, and principle which has no satisfactory dictionary name but has been called different things at different times in different countries." Our

American name for it is "guts." Elijah had guts. And so did Peter Cartwright.

Peter Cartwright was a circuit-ridin' Methodist preacher back in the nineteenth century. He stood tall, he shot straight, and he rode for the brand. On one occasion Cartwright was getting ready to preach to a very large congregation when he was told that President Andrew Jackson would be in the audience. His friends, who knew Mr. Cartwright well, asked him to make sure that his remarks were positive and unoffensive.

Peter Cartwright preached his sermon. Somewhere in that sermon he said, "I have been told that Andrew Jackson is in this congregation. And I have been asked to guard my remarks. What I must say is that *Andrew Jackson will go to hell* if he doesn't repent of his sin."

The congregation, of course, was aghast. Yet after the service, President Jackson made his way to Peter Cartwright and extended his hand.

"Sir," the president said, "if I had a regiment of men like you, I could whip the world."

Do you know what I think? I think God is looking for some Peter Cartwrights today. I think He's scanning the horizon for an Elijah or two. I think He is looking for some men who have a great love for Jesus Christ and a great love for their families and a great love for this nation. The light in America has grown dim, but the light is still on. I don't know of too many guys who climb into a Cessna in Havana and land on a road in Florida to rescue their families and then hightail it back to Cuba. America is not what it used to be morally or spiritually, but the light is still on and it still beats the alternative.

But if the light is going to *remain* on and if—in God's great grace—the light is going to get stronger, then you can count on the fact that God will work through His men to lead the charge.

Men who love Jesus Christ more than they love personal peace.

Men who love their families more than they love their comfort.

Men who love holiness more than they love popularity.

Men who love their country enough to get on their knees to ask God to bring a genuine revival to this nation.

Men who are willing to go to battle to protect their families and save their nation.

Are you willing to put yourself on the line? Are you willing to even put your job on the line? If you're not, then do yourself a favor and stop reading this book right now. But if you are willing to go to battle, if you are willing to stand up and speak the truth, if you are willing to be persecuted, if necessary, for righteousness' sake, then read on. You're ridin' for the brand.

The great comedian of old movies, W. C. Fields, once said, "A dead fish can float downstream, but it takes a live one to swim against the current." The easy thing is to float. But it's tough, especially in this culture, to swim against the current. But that's exactly what it's going to take.

We're raising our children under an administration that has more in common with the Baal-worshiping kings of the Old Testament than with our founding fathers. For the first time in our history, we are under leaders who are fundamentally opposed to the moral absolutes upon which this country was founded.

So what is our response to all of this? To be more specific, what is your response going to be?

One option is to do nothing. Just raise our hands in disgust and become reconciled to the fact that there is nothing we can do to stem the tide. But I don't think that's the correct response. Elijah certainly didn't do that. Elijah got involved. You might even say that he got involved politically, since he personally confronted the king.

If you are a Christian father and husband, then you are salt and you are light. And if salt and light doesn't start making an appearance all over this country, then we can go ahead and just hand over the key to our cities and towns to the new Baal worshipers.

Some will say that we shouldn't get involved in politics or in school boards. The liberals are definitely saying that, but unfortunately, there are some Christians saying the same thing. Christians shouldn't be involved in politics, because politics is "worldly."

I must heartily disagree. The fact of the matter is this: the political issues of our day, issues such as homosexual rights, abortion rights, sex education in the classroom, values clarification in the classroom, etc. *are at their core not political issues* but spiritual issues. I read somewhere that we are to be in the world but not of the world. Therefore we cannot retreat, because the future of our children and their children are on the line. That's why Orestes Lorenzo Perez was willing to put it all on the line.

Something interesting has been happening over the last year or two. During that time I've been praying that God would raise up one million men who would be willing to put it all on the line for the Lord. About six months ago, I was talking with Randy Phillips, the executive director of Promise Keepers. When I mentioned that I had been praying about God raising up a million men to spiritually lead their families, Randy said, "That's our vision as well. We're praying the same prayer."

I think that more people than we know are praying that prayer. At first, a million men seems like a lot. But when you realize that the population of this country is over 250 million, a million guys is not that many. But a million guys, who are committed to their Lord and committed to their families could shake things up a little bit across this nation. Can you imagine the impact that one million Elijahs could have in their communities? Imagine that!

One million guys who love their wives, one million guys who aren't going to flake out and pursue another woman, one million guys who won't be afraid to take a stand in their community on moral issues, one million guys who aren't taking public opinion polls to find our where they should stand, one million guys who will turn off the TV and read the Bible to their kids.

Gentlemen, God always has His Elijahs. God always has his men. Are you going to be an Elijah or an Obadiah?

The King of Kings awaits your answer.

1. Elijah wasn't afraid to take on the political powers-that-be in an Israel that had tossed aside its godly heritage. Read Matthew 3:7-10 and Mark 6:14-20 to see how the New Testament "Elijah," John the Baptist, took off on the same confrontational track. Compare the willingness of these two men to deliver a "politically incorrect" message in the presence of entrenched governmental evil. What principles can we learn from their example?

2. Compare what you've learned about Obadiah to the story of Nicodemus in John 3:1-12. What do these men have in common? What do they have in common with many Christian men in today's world?

3. Right in the middle of a fast-paced account of Elijah, Ahab, Jezebel, and Obadiah, the biblical writer tells a story about a widow and her son in a place called Zarephath (1 Kings 17:7-24). The placement of this story seems strange. Why do you think the Holy Spirit might have directed the writer to place this little "aside" right in the middle of the larger story? What lessons can we learn from this brief-but-amazing encounter?

4. Read again Warren Wiersbe's contrast of two godly but very different men:

> Elijah was serving the Lord publicly and without fear; Obadiah was serving Ahab and trying to serve the Lord secretly. Elijah was "outside the camp" (Hebrews 13:13); Obadiah was inside the court. Elijah knew the will of God; Obadiah did not know what was going on. While Elijah was laboring to save the nation, Obadiah was out looking for grass to save the horse and mules. When Elijah confronted Obadiah, the frightened servant did not trust the prophet. And note that Obadiah had to "brag" about his secret service to impress Elijah with his devotion.

As we view the emerging "culture war" exploding on all sides of us, what does an "Elijah" look like in today's America? What does an "Obadiah" look like?

5. Think out loud about the impact one million "Elijahs" could make on our country over the next few years.

CHAPTER NINE

Fighting the Good Fight

If the foundations are destroyed, what can the righteous do?
(PSALM 11:3).

I had a pretty good idea why they wanted to meet.

While speaking at a men's conference, I met a group of guys who were all in the same accountability group. They asked if we might be able to get together for a half hour or so. We decided to meet that night after the evening session.

I knew from our initial conversation that although these six guys were in a group that met every week, they were from two different churches. It was when they told me which two churches they were members of that I had a pretty strong clue as to what they wanted to discuss. It really didn't take a genius to figure it out.

What they had in common was this. Both groups of men had senior pastors who had been asked to step down because of moral failure in their personal lives. And it had devastated both churches.

These two churches were not small. As a result, the failure of both pastors sent Richter-scale shock waves up and down their part of the country.

Both of these pastors had very high profiles. Both were remarkably gifted as speakers. They could mesmerize people with their humor, their exposition, and their personalities. As a result, their churches were growing with unbelievable strides. Thousands of people were coming to hear each of these men.

That's why their fall was so cataclysmic. They effected thousands as they climbed the numerical ladder and they effected even more when they fell off.

What was interesting was that I met both of these men fifteen years ago. I spent some time with each of them. After spending the afternoon with the first pastor, I remember being somewhat stunned as I drove home. As Mary and I talked over dinner, I told her a little bit of our conversation. To tell you the truth, it was very eye opening to spend several hours with this guy. Although we had just met, a mutual friend was with us, with whom he felt very comfortable. As a result his guard was down. That's why at dinner that night I said something that really surprised my wife.

"Mary, I think that guy is headed for a major fall."

I'm no prophet. But something was obviously wrong in this man's life, and the unguarded signals were so clear that even I could see them.

He talked freely of his dreams, his aspirations, the books he was reading, and his latest successes. What was very clear was that there were a number of influences in his life, but the New Testament apparently wasn't one of them. He sounded like a guy looking to get to the top and get there in a hurry.

That's what he did. He got to the top in a hurry. He got there so fast that he fell off. It happened ten years after our meeting. After allegations of sexual involvement with a woman associate, he divorced his wife and left his children.

I met the other pastor about a year later, and we had the opportunity to spend an entire weekend together. What a great weekend that was. This guy had a love for Jesus Christ and a love for the Scriptures that was very apparent. He also seemed to have a great love for his wife. He talked about her throughout the weekend and how they were so very careful to protect their marriage and sustain it. This guy was solid. He was the exact opposite of the other pastor. I greatly benefited from our time together and wished that it could have continued. That's why I was absolutely shocked to hear that he had resigned from his church because of moral reasons. I was stunned, jarred, startled, and shaken. I was also in a state of disbelief. In fact, I didn't believe it until I talked with his associate, and the facts were confirmed.

FIGHTIN' FOR THE BRAND

The Christian life is a violent life. Does that surprise you? It shouldn't. The Christian life is a life of warfare, a life of high-stakes spiritual combat. The Bible clearly states that we are in a battle with the world, the flesh, and the Devil. That's precisely why Paul told Timothy to "fight the good fight."

Satan may be many things, but he is no fool. He is very strategic in his efforts. That's why he goes after those in leadership. If a highly visible spiritual leader can be brought down, then the fallout will be great. That's why we should be praying for our pastors and for other leaders who have been given a place of wide ministry.

It's also why we should be praying for ourselves.

You don't have to be well-known speaker to be the recipient of the Enemy's attack. He is more than happy to bring down a Sunday school teacher or any other person of influence in a local congregation. That's why we all have to stand tall and fight the good fight.

The question that these broken-hearted church leaders put before me that evening was this: "How is it that men who have had such influence in the body of Christ can suddenly fall into sexual immorality?"

The answer I offered was that it probably wasn't "sudden." It seemed sudden, but that's only because we couldn't see the private choices that these men had been making over the last several years. When sexual immorality hits in the life of a spiritual leader it is usually the accumulated, tragic result of a series of poor and very private choices.

That's what Paul was trying to get across to Timothy. Paul wanted Timothy to be successful. That's why Paul's words to this young pastor have such relevance to all of us who want to be people of character. In fact, it is impossible to climb the character ladder without applying these words to our lives. Every day.

This command I entrust to you, Timothy, my son, in accordance with the prophecies previously made concerning you, that by them you may fight the good fight (1 Timothy 1: 18).

The Mentoring Epistles

The New Testament letters of 1 and 2 Timothy, along with Titus, are frequently called the Pastoral Epistles. Timothy and Titus were young pastors, and Paul was writing to them to give some tangible principles that would enable them to be successful in their work. Today, we might say that Paul was mentoring these young men.

What is a mentor? John Gardner says that a mentor is an older person who actively helps young people along the road to leadership—as a friend, an advisor, a teacher, a coach, a listener, or a resource. Gardner writes that "mentoring may be as formal as a master-apprentice relationship or as informal as an older friend helping a younger one."[103]

If you ever benefited from the wisdom and counsel of an older person who took an interest in you, then you know first hand how meaningful a mentor can be to a younger person. And it's people who have personally profited from that kind of valued relationship who make excellent mentors themselves.

Paul and Timothy had a father-son relationship. They were exceptionally close and Paul had a vested interested in Timothy's well-being. Timothy was a young man in a difficult situation (it's funny how often that is the case!).

Timothy was not happy. He was in over his head at Ephesus. But Paul needed Timothy to do at least three things: appoint elders in the church, combat false doctrine and false teachers, and supervise the church as Paul's personal representative. That was a tall order for a young man like Timothy.

Timothy's main problem was that he wasn't Paul. He didn't have Paul's age or wisdom or in-your-face personality. Timothy was a non-confronter in a situation that cried out for confrontation.

No Place to Run

The real estate broker was driving slowly down a residential street looking for a new listing. As he came to the house, he noticed next door a little boy straining to reach the doorbell. The little boy was up as far as he could get on his tip-toes, but he still couldn't reach the doorbell.

The man smiled as he watched the scene, and then walked over to the door and rang the doorbell for the little fellow. The little boy looked up at the man and said, "Now *run!*"

Paul's young buddy Timothy wanted to run, too.

That's why earlier in the chapter, in verse 5, Paul had to urge him to "remain on at Ephesus." Timothy didn't want to stick around Ephesus. He wanted to find the back door, and slip through it as soon as possible. But Paul had other plans for him. Paul wanted him to "fight the good fight." In other words, it was time for Timothy to stand tall.

Mentors know when their protégés need some encouragement. That's why Paul reminded Timothy of the prophecies that were made concerning him. We are not privy to the content of these prophecies, but apparently someone, speaking by the Spirit, predicted the kind of ministry Timothy would have. These prophecies were a source of encouragement to the young pastor. That's why Paul brought them up.

Paul was Timothy's coach. It's almost as though Paul, although writing from a distance, was trying to psych Timothy up for the game, not unlike a coach in a locker room. Paul wanted Timothy to get in there and fight!

But Timothy hated fighting. It just wasn't his personality.

I remember very well the first root canal I ever had. I was twelve years old and my tooth started to abscess one night as we were eating dinner. My mom called the dentist and he said to bring me right in. As I was stepping into the room for my root canal, Cassius Clay was stepping into the ring to meet Sonny Liston. It was 8:45 P.M., Tuesday evening, February 25, 1964, in Miami for the boxing match, and 5:45 P.M. in San Francisco for the root canal. My dentist had the fight going full blast on the radio as he was working on me.

This was the first big fight of Cassius Clay's career. We now know Cassius Clay as Mohammed Ali, one of the greatest fighters of all time. But on that night, he was just a young, loud-mouthed kid, up against the man known as the "The Bear." I can remember the week before the fight seeing a full-page picture of Sonny Liston and thinking to myself, *That guy is the meanest and toughest guy I've ever seen. Cassius Clay is going to get killed.*

That was pretty much the consensus before the fight. Hardly anyone gave Clay a chance. I didn't think I'd survive the root canal or that Clay would survive Liston. But I was wrong on both counts. My dentist knocked out the knotty nerve and Clay knocked out the menacing bear.

Timothy was no Cassius Clay. It wasn't his personality. Yet he was called to "fight the good fight." And so are we. We are called to fight it every day. But here's the question—and it is an extremely important question.

How do I fight the good fight?

The reason that question is so critical is that so many in the body of Christ are not fighting the good fight. They have been disqualified, and they have not gone the distance.

I want to fight the good fight. Timothy wanted to fight the good fight. The question is *how.* How do I do it?

Paul gives the answer in the next verse. "Keeping faith and a good conscience, which some have rejected and suffered shipwreck in regard to their faith" (1 Timothy 1: 19).

KEEPING FAITH AND A GOOD CONSCIENCE

Yogi Berra once said, "If you come to a fork in the road, take it." Now, that doesn't make much sense. Usually a fork means you have to go left or go right. How does one fight the good fight? By doing two things: keeping faith and a good conscience. You have to do both. If you just keep faith, then you won't fight the good fight. If you just keep a good conscience, without keeping faith, you won't fight the good fight. You have to do both. Let's take them in order.

"Keeping faith."

What in the world does that mean? Well, let's think it through. Where does faith come from? Ephesians 2:8 is very clear that faith is a gift of God. But how does God distribute this faith? Through what means does faith come into our lives? According to Romans 10:17, "faith comes from hearing, and hearing by the word of Christ."

It is impossible to separate faith from the Word of God. And what is the Word of God? According to Hebrews 4:12, the "word of God is living and active and sharper than any two-edged sword, and piercing as far as the division of soul and spirit, of both joints and marrow, and able to judge the thoughts and intentions of the heart."

When Paul instructs Timothy to fight the good fight by "keeping faith," Paul is referring to the doctrinal purity that comes only from the Word of God. He is reminding Timothy that he must stay in the Word of God if his faith is going to remain clear, clean, and pure.

The Enemy loves to downplay the importance of the Bible in our lives. That's why he works so hard to keep us from interacting with Scripture! Mark this: If I'm not in the Word, it is *impossible* for me to fight the good fight. Moses certainly didn't downplay Scripture. Note his words in Deuteronomy 32:46-47: "Take to your heart all the words which I am warning you today, which you shall command your sons to observe carefully, even all the words of this law. For it is not an idle word for you; indeed *it is your life.*"

That's a pretty strong statement. But it fits perfectly with what Jesus said about the character of Scripture. When Jesus was being tempted by Satan in the wilderness, He responded to the first temptation with the words, "It is written, Man shall not live by bread alone, but on every word that proceeds out of the mouth of God." We live off of the Scripture. It is our life. The word of God contains the spiritual vitamins and minerals that we need to "fight the good fight." Without the nutrition of the Scripture, it is impossible to fight well. Without the Scripture there is no vitality, no energy, no health. No wonder Oswald Chambers said,

> The mere reading of the Word of God has power to communicate the life of God to us mentally, morally, and spiritually. God makes the words of the Bible a sacrament, i.e., the means whereby we partake of His life, it is one of His secret doors for the communication of His life to us.[104]

No wonder the Enemy wants to keep me away from my Bible!

"A good conscience."

But there's a second aspect to fighting the good faith. Paul emphasized to Timothy that he must keep a *"good conscience."* That's the tough part about fighting the good fight. This war is fought on two fronts. We find ourselves fighting on both fronts simultaneously. If you put all of your effort into keeping faith, you will be leaving your flank wide open. Or if you are completely focused on keeping a good conscience, you are just as vulnerable. In order to fight the good fight, we have to do both. We have to be keeping faith *and* a good conscience. At the same time.

The priority of a good conscience is a theme Paul rides hard all the way through this letter to Timothy. That makes complete sense, since 1 Timothy is really a handbook on spiritual leadership. It's impossible to be an effective spiritual leader without paying attention to the condition of one's conscience.

A couple of years ago I was invited to speak to a chapel service for the Cincinnati Bengals. I had my two boys with me and we had a great time meeting many of the players at chapel and then watching the Bengals play the Steelers on a crisp December afternoon with a fifteen-degree temperature. We went through a lot of hot chocolate that afternoon! We had some free time after the chapel service and before the kickoff, so I was reading the Sunday sports page.

That's when my eye caught the NFL injury list for that weekend's games around the league. The injury list contains the name of each injured player and the particular injury they are experiencing (knee, Achilles tendon, wrist, etc.). Each player is then listed as out, probable, or doubtful.

On that particular list were the names of around fifty players. These men had an incredible list of injuries: broken arms, broken legs, broken jaws, pulled hamstrings, turf toes, and hyper-extended elbows. But what was fascinating to me was that none of those players was on the injury list for leprosy. That's right. Leprosy.

Most of us in this country don't think about leprosy. We may think of the possibilities of having a heart attack, or some type of cancer, but unless I miss my guess the idea that you might get leprosy has never crossed your mind. Generally speaking, leprosy is not an American disease, although there is a leprosarium still functioning in Louisiana. But leprosy is associated more with Third World countries than with the United States. Consequently, most of us have very little understanding of what leprosy really is.

I remember as a young boy, watching a movie that a missionary from India was showing to our church. It was my first visual exposure to leprosy. I'll never forget seeing those black and white images of people who had lost their toes, feet, fingers, and hands. I thought for some reason leprosy was a disease of the skin. Years later I found out leprosy is not a skin disease, it's a *nerve* disease.

A person with leprosy has lost the ability to feel. In a Third World country, a leprous man can be walking down a street barefoot, step on a piece of glass, and keep right on walking. He doesn't even realize there's an injury, because there is no pain. No feeling. Nothing. It's not until he looks down and sees the blood that he realizes something is wrong. By that time, the hunk of glass may have worked its way further up into his foot. A normal person would feel all of these things, but the person with leprosy is unable to feel the throbbing sensations.

A woman with leprosy could pick up a cast iron skillet and not even realize the skillet was horribly hot, even as it seared the skin right off of her hand. That's the problem with leprosy. Lepers have lost the ability to feel because their nerves are dead. That's how they wind up losing toes, feet, fingers, and hands.

There is a spiritual nerve located down deep in every one of us. It is the nerve of conscience. You have heard it said, "Let conscience be your guide." That's not quite right. The guide to right and wrong is the Scripture. The Bible is the basis of our moral value system. Conscience is a nerve that begins to pulsate when we depart from what we know to be right. As we begin to move from right toward wrong, the nerve of conscience begins to send messages to us. It is letting us know something is wrong. It warns us that we are moving into dangerous territory.

There is a tragic explanation in 1 Timothy of something that is going to happen in the last days. In 1 Timothy 4:1, Paul tells Timothy:

The Spirit explicitly says that in later times some will fall away from the faith, paying attention to deceitful spirits and doctrines of demons.

What is interesting here is the reason some will fall away. They have not kept faith! Instead of listening to the doctrinal purity of the Word of God they have paid attention to deceitful spirits and doctrines of demons! But Paul continues in the next verse to explain how they paid attention to such wrong doctrine. They listened to false teachers. Note Paul's explanation of *why* certain men will be false teachers: "By means of the hypocrisy of liars *seared in their own conscience* as with a branding iron" (1 Timothy 4:2).

Did you catch the significance of what Paul said? The reason these men can teach such doctrinal deceit which they *know* to be wrong is because they are men without conscience. It's almost as though they took a white-hot poker and thrust it down deep into the depths of their souls. These men have cauterized their own consciences and they don't feel anything anymore. They are spiritual lepers.

How does one become a spiritual leper? Believe me, there are many of them walking around. One becomes a spiritual leper by consistently *not* keeping a good conscience. A spiritual leper is someone who consistently chooses not to listen to his conscience when his conscience indicates that he is deviating from what he knows to be true. It's not that these folks don't know what is right. The issue is, they refuse to *do* what is right.

Every time the Spirit of God impresses our conscience and we fail to respond to His prompting, we are coating our sensitive nerve with another layer of resistance, and we are taking a step toward leprosy. Over a long period of time, our consciences become hard and callused.

That is a very dangerous state for any nerve. Especially the nerve of conscious. It is possible for that nerve to become so callused that when the Holy Spirit touches, it feels absolutely nothing. Not even one impulse.

That my friend, is a graphic description of a spiritual leper. And they are everywhere.

The key to keeping a good conscience is not so much in the big choices, but the little ones. It's those seemingly small and tiny choices of the inner man that no one else ever sees. That's why we are so shocked when we hear of the immorality of a very public preacher. Perhaps we have benefited greatly from the person's teachings over the radio or through cassette tapes. The problem is this: You can't look into someone's conscience over the radio. You can't look into a conscience at all. But that's where the real fight takes place. Only the Holy Spirit, the Enemy, and ourselves, are able to see into that very private arena.

Standing tall in private is just as important as standing tall in public. Maybe more so.

Have you noticed that wherever there is sexual immorality, there is also deceit? Deceit and sexual immorality always go hand in hand. Because when something is wrong in our lives—such as sexual immorality—we will go to great lengths in order to deceive others about the reality of the situation. But before we deceive others, we first deceive ourselves. Before we lie to others, we first lie to ourselves. And that's where heeding the first impulses of the Holy Spirit on our nerves of conscience can save us from choices that will cause our lives to completely unravel. Lying must be nipped in the bud. It is lying out of control that leads to deceit of ourselves, our spouses, our children, and our friends.

Let me give you a personal example.

THE PRICE OF A CLEAN CONSCIENCE

A number of years ago, when Mary and I were pulling out of our tough chapter, we were really counting our pennies. We were even counting our half pennies. In order to make our budget shrivel even more, we decided that I would take my lunch to the office rather than buy lunch. I committed to do that every day. No problem.

But one particular morning was extremely hectic. The alarm didn't go off, and everyone was late. As I hustled to get out the door, I forgot my lunch. But I didn't realize it until later. I was studying that morning for my sermon on Sunday. As lunch time approached, I went to get my lunch and then realized I had left it at home. I decided just to keep studying through my normal lunch time because I really could use the extra time.

By about 2:30, however, I started to get a headache, and I usually don't get headaches. I then realized I hadn't eaten since about 7:00 that morning.

I made a quick run over to McDonald's and ordered a Quarter Pounder with cheese and a medium Diet Coke. (I'm sort of a health nut.) By the time I actually ate it was 3:00 in the afternoon. I went back to the office, did some more studying, and left for home a little earlier than usual. We were going to some event that evening as a family, and it required about a hour's drive in rush-hour traffic. We were having an early dinner so we could get a head start on traffic and hopefully arrive at our destination on time.

As I walked in the door, the kids were already at the table. "Your timing is perfect," Mary said. "We're ready to eat!"

As I sat down, she added, "You forgot your lunch today. What did you do for lunch?"

I replied, "I didn't eat lunch."

That's what is known as a lie.

Mary said, "You must really be hungry if you didn't eat lunch."

"I sure am!"

I wasn't. I had just eaten about an hour and half before at McDonald's. I sat down and ate enough to make it look like I was indeed hungry when in actuality I wasn't hungry at all.

Several days later I was in my office, going over my sermon notes for Sunday. I was done with my preparation and was going over my outline and praying that God would be pleased to use me that coming Sunday. I was asking Him to use me in a powerful way to communicate the message of His Word. It was a time of quiet meditation. No one else was in the room. Just me, my Bible, and my notes.

And the Holy Spirit.

As I was praying, I suddenly felt something. What I felt was one of my nerves. To be more specific, it was the nerve of conscience. Something was flicking the nerve of my conscience. I knew who was doing it and I knew what it was about. It was the Holy Spirit. He was impressing my conscience that I had deviated from what I knew to be right and true. I had lied to my wife. That's when the rationalizations started.

It was only $2.89. What's $2.89? It's no big deal.

Another flick.

So I didn't tell her the truth. I just won't do it again.

Another flick. A little stronger this time.

If I tell her that I lied to her, she's going to think I'm a real jerk. My credibility isn't worth destroying over $2.89.

It was right there that I was on dangerous territory. My credibility was already gone. Mary just didn't know about it. Finally, I did what I really wanted to avoid. I picked up the phone and dialed. Mary answered.

"Mary? How's it going?"

"Fine, sweetheart. What's up?"

"Mary, umm, do you remember the other day when I forgot my lunch and when I got home you asked me what I did for lunch and I said that I didn't eat lunch?"

"Sure I do."

"Well, I ate lunch. I went to MacDonald's and spent $2.89 for a Quarter Pounder with cheese and a medium Diet Coke."

"Steve," she said with amusement, "why didn't you just tell me?"

"I honestly don't know," I replied. "Maybe I was embarrassed that I broke my promise about eating lunch out. But whatever the reason, I'm calling to tell you that I lied to you. Mary, would you forgive me for lying to you?"

"Of course I forgive you. Thanks for calling and telling me the truth."

I'll be honest with you. I really didn't want to make that call. After all, it was only $2.89. But in reality, a lot more was at stake than $2.89.

What was at stake was the trust in my marriage.

What was at stake was letting a small crack run unchecked in the sanctity of our home.

What was at stake was whether or not I was going to fight the good fight or just pretend to fight sin in my own life.

So I made the call. Too much was on the line to let it pass.

How does a man in spiritual leadership who has had such an impact in your life suddenly fall into sexual immorality? Well, it starts with something around $2.89. Something small. Something insignificant. Instead of obeying the nudge of the Holy Spirit, he lets it pass. Then when the next small thing happens, well, he lets that one go, too. And over a period of weeks and months, a series of seemingly small and insignificant choices are being made that no one else sees. The Spirit of God is trying to get the man's attention, but he is now walking around with a nerve that has become more callused. And the more callused the nerve, the easier it is to ignore the Spirit of God.

Then one day, "she" walks into his life. He will soon be in a situation that would have absolutely been unthinkable just a year or two ago. But now it's not only possible, it's probable. Why? Because that nerve of conscience which helps us fight the good fight has been severely damaged by neglect. Long before a spiritual leader ever climbs into the bed of immorality, God has been trying to get his attention.

But there is nerve damage. Severe nerve damage.

At that first "private" meeting, just to have lunch or to meet to talk about some church activity, you can be sure the Spirit of God twinged that minister's conscience, and at that moment he knew the meeting was inappropriate. But instead of heeding the impulse of the Spirit on his nerve of conscience, they decided to meet again. Once again, the Holy Spirit hit the nerve. But he didn't respond. On and on it goes. That is the pattern that leads to sexual immorality in the life of anyone. And believe it or not, it can start with something as small as $2.89.

What's the $2.89 in your life? Have you dealt with it? Or are you still rationalizing and coddling it?

That's why it is so important to heed the Spirit's prompting early. If we hesitate, if we rationalize, if we try to bypass the twinging nerve of conscience, we are only going to find ourselves in an increasingly tangled web of emotions that get more and more difficult to break away from.

How do we avoid becoming trapped in Satan's deceptive web? It's simple. We determine to acknowledge the Holy Spirit every time He touches our inner nerve of conscience. That's how He gets our attention. What happens if we don't quickly acknowledge the Spirit's promptings? Then we are on our way to shipwreck. At least that's the metaphor Paul uses to describe it.

THREE SHIPS THAT NEVER SAILED HOME

What do the *Titanic,* the *Hymenaeus,* and the *Alexander* have in common? All three experienced horrible shipwrecks.

But only the *Titanic* was a ship. Hymenaeus and Alexander were men.

The *Titanic* has been found at the bottom of the Atlantic. Hymenaeus and Alexander can be found on the pages of the New Testament.

Specifically in 1 Timothy:

> Keeping faith and a good conscience, which some have rejected and suffered shipwreck in regard to their faith. Among these are Hymenaeus and Alexander, whom I have delivered over to Satan, so that they may be taught not to blaspheme (1:19-20).

Shipwrecked lives, shipwrecked dreams, shipwrecked families, and shipwrecked churches. Shipwrecks are always great tragedies. But to shipwreck spiritually is the greatest tragedy of all. That's what happened to Hymenaeus and Alexander. And it's happening with increasing frequency in the church today.

We are missing a great deal of the puzzle of circumstances that fit around the story of Hymenaeus and Alexander. But Paul knew the missing pieces and so did Timothy. That's why he mentioned them to Timothy. What we do know is that they shipwrecked. And they shipwrecked for one of two reasons:

- They didn't keep sound doctrine.
- They didn't keep a good conscience.

The *Exxon Valdez* shipwrecked and coated the Alaska coastline with oil. As I write these words, the 89,700 ton tanker *Braer* has run aground in the Shetland Islands of Scotland. It is carrying twice the amount of oil that was on the *Exxon Valdez* and therefore has the potential to be an even greater disaster.

There is more than one way to be shipwrecked. But in the body of Christ, the amount of shipwrecks that are attributed to sexual immorality are growing every day. Paul wanted Timothy to fight the good fight. That's why he put such an emphasis on keeping faith and a good conscience. Both must be well in hand if our credibility is to be restored. Our walk must back up our talk.

The same question burned in the minds of the six men I met with at the men's conference: "How in the world did our pastor get involved in immorality?" I asked them if they were in the morning session and they nodded that they were. In that session I taught the concepts and the passage that is in this chapter. As we thought through the circumstances of each pastor, the answer started to emerge.

The first pastor shipwrecked because he had not kept faith. He became enamored with pop psychology. His love for the Scripture gradually gave way to the desire to speak "relevant" messages in the pulpit. He gradually lost his ability to see how "relevant" the Scriptures really are. Truth is always relevant. He shipwrecked because he lost his love for the purity of the Word, and as he lost his commitment to the Scripture, his conscience started to give way as well.

The second pastor was on the other end of the spectrum. He loved the Scriptures and was powerful in the Scriptures. But he allowed himself to get into some compromising situations. When a close friend approached him about it, he explained the situation away as harmless. I'm sure that Another approached him as well over the years—the Holy Spirit. But he didn't respond to those impulses on the nerve of his conscience, and that's how he shipwrecked. He was doctrinally pure, but he still shipwrecked.

Both of these men were gifted. That's why some are attempting to get them back into "ministry," even when there has been repentance that is shallow at best. "But they are so gifted!" comes the reply. There can be no denying their giftedness. But the issue is not giftedness, it is character.

John Luther states the matter brilliantly.

Good character is more to be praised than outstanding talent. Most talents are, to some extent, a gift. Good character, by contrast, is not given to us. We have to build it piece by piece, thought by thought, choice by choice, which requires great courage and determination.[105]

It's easy to point at spiritual leaders and see their weaknesses. But the question that I pose to you is the one that I frequently pose to myself. Are you fighting the good fight? Are you standing tall in private, when no one sees? Are you keeping faith and a good conscience? Those are questions that only you can answer.

There is an old poem that sums up Paul's instruction to young Timothy:

When wealth is lost, nothing is lost;

When health is lost, something is lost;

When character is lost, everything is lost.

Let me be very direct. If you are involved in some type of sexual sin, please don't take a stand against homosexuality in your community. Please don't attend a school board meeting and voice your conviction against a sex education curriculum. And please...don't join a church board or teach a Sunday school class. Why? Because you can be sure your sin will find you out. When it does, the moral stands that you took will be discredited.

And so will the name of Jesus Christ.

If there is any kind of sin in your life that you have not confessed, then it is impossible for you to fight the good fight. You may fight, but it won't be the good fight.

And that's no fight at all.

1. I have stated that the Christian life is a violent life. In what way is this more—or less—apparent in our day than it was in our fathers' and grandfathers' generations? Review Peter's strong counsel to men in 1 Peter 5:1-11. What are three or four key principles the apostle offers for fighting the good—and sometimes violent—fight?

2. Young Timothy was incredibly blessed to have a loyal, battle-scarred veteran in his corner. When Paul commanded Timothy to "fight the good fight," Timothy knew he had a lot more than his friend's verbal backing. He had Paul's example, Paul's abiding interest and concern, and Paul's constant prayers behind him. Discuss the role of "mentors" among Christian men in the church. When have you benefited most from a concerned, older man willing to stay in your corner? When have you longed for such an individual, but never found one? How can guys today who want to fight the good fight find a mentor...or become one?

3. What are some of the ways we men can encourage each other to "keep faith" by staying in the Word?

4. Reflect on a time when you attempted to "stuff" the voice of your conscience in an area of your life. Were you "successful" in your attempts? What happened as a result? How can we restore the nerve of conscience after it has been deadened by repeated disobedience? How can we help each other as men to restore and maintain a good conscience?

5. Review Proverbs 20:30; 27:5-6; 28:23; and Psalm 141:4-5. What would you do if you suspected that one of your close Christian friends was headed toward moral shipwreck? What would the risks be of damaging your relationship—or getting punched in the mouth? What would the risks be of remaining quiet and turning a blind eye?

CHAPTER TEN

Seven Ways to Help Your Kids Stand Tall

Without God, we cannot.
Without us, God will not.

AUGUSTINE

The prayer of a righteous man
is powerful and effective.

JAMES

Eli Whitney is famous for inventing the cotton gin. But Whitney didn't get his money from the cotton gin. Whitney became a wealthy man by inventing and manufacturing firearms. One of the men he teamed up with was Sam Colt.

Colt was a marketing genius who knew how to use advertising to spread the fame of the Colt revolvers. But Whitney was the actual hands-on genius. It was the collective efforts of Sam Colt and Eli Whitney that formulated one of the most popular weapons in the old West that eventually brought law and order to a rapidly changing society.

Another powerful weapon in the old West was the printing press. But it was bigger than just the old West. The printing press changed the whole world. And it was Johannes Gutenberg, a man who lived back in the 1400s, who came up with it. How in the world did Gutenberg come up with an invention that changed the world? He did it by connecting two things that were previously unconnected.

Gutenberg took the wine press and the coin punch and came up with the printing press. The function of the wine press was to apply a force over a large area in order to squeeze juice out of grapes. The purpose of the coin punch was to leave an image on a small area such as a gold coin.[106] Johannes took two very good concepts and turned them into something revolutionary.

When you look at your kids, what do you see? Do you see them as they are now…or do you see them as what they will become? I think a lot of guys look at their four-year-olds and just see four-year-olds. And we need to value them and appreciate them as four-year-olds. But on the other hand, we also need to clearly see that these four-year-olds won't always be four. In ten years, they'll be fourteen, chompin' at the bit to get their driver's licenses in a couple of years.

He will also be under tremendous peer pressure.

In just ten years, your four-year-old will be making some of the most critical choices of his entire life. The decision he will make every day is whether he will be a leader or a follower.

I'm convinced we need to "Gutenberg" our kids. Just as Johannes took a press and a punch and turned them into a printing press, so we dads need to take our kids and shape their character so we turn them into leaders. Now obviously some kids are natural leaders. They'll grab the initiative and make things happen. But what I'm talking about is turning your kids into *moral and spiritual* leaders. I'm talking about turning your kids into men and women of character who can make the kind of tough character choices that few leaders in our contemporary world seem able to make.

The time to begin doing that is now.

Something happens when a kid hits adolescence. When kids are small, they tend to think their dad hung the moon. When kids hit adolescence sometimes they begin to think their dad should go to the moon. To take it a step further, when a boy or girl hits adolescence, one of two things is going to happen. An adolescent will either go to his peers and critique his parents, or go to his parents and critique his peers. Obviously, we want our kids to come to us.

To put it another way, a child is going to be either a leader or a follower. Teenagers are having to decide this every day of their lives. There is pressure to do drugs, have sex, and do whatever it is that everyone else is doing. So how do we combat that? We combat it by Gutenberging our kids into leaders. And we get after it right away.

Roger von Oech tells the story of a terrible plague that swept through Lithuania. No one could quite figure it out.

What was curious about this disease was its grip on its victim; as soon as the person contracted it, he would go into a very deep almost deathlike coma. Most individuals would die within twenty four hours, but occasionally a hardy soul would make it back to the full bloom of health. The problem was that since early eighteenth-century medical technology wasn't very advanced, the unafflicted had quite a difficult time telling whether a victim was dead or alive. This didn't matter too much, though, because most of the people were, in fact, dead.

Then one day it was discovered that someone had been buried alive. This alarmed the townspeople, so they called a town meeting to decide what should be done to prevent such a situation from happening again. After much discussion, most people agreed on the following solution. They decided to put food and water in every casket next to the body. They would even put an air hole up from the casket to the earth's surface. These procedures would be expensive, but they would be more than worthwhile if they would save some people's lives.

Another group came up with a second, less expensive right answer. They proposed implanting a twelve inch long stake in every coffin lid directly over where the victim's heart would be. Then whatever doubts there were about whether the person was dead or alive would be eliminated as soon as the coffin lid was closed. [107]

Thousands of adolescents are buried alive by peer pressure each year. Not only are they buried alive, but in each coffin there's a twelve inch stake that goes right into their hearts. A number of twelve-, thirteen-, and fourteen-year-old kids (not to mention fifteen-, sixteen-, and seventeen-) are emotionally killed because they haven't been *trained* to withstand the pressure from their peers. Good dads make sure their kids have airholes and plenty of emotional food and water. They also plan way in advance to keep the coffin of a sick and godless culture from slamming shut on their adolescent.

In our MTV culture, the majority of teenagers are swimming with the current (and so are their parents). I want my kids to swim upstream. I don't want my kids to be swept along in the current of peer pressure. I want them to be secure enough in who they are and what they believe that they will be confident to swim *against* the current. Followers go with the current. Leaders go against it.

LEADERSHIP: WHAT IS IT?

What is leadership? That's a question that has received a lot of attention. A friend of mine wrote his doctoral dissertation on leadership and found 165 published definitions. Some of those definitions are pretty complex and dazzling. Dr. Howard Hendricks, distinguished professor at Dallas Theological Seminary, has come up with the best definition of a leader I've ever heard. According to Dr. Hendricks, "a leader is someone who leads." Don't let the simplicity of that definition fool you. It is pregnant with meaning.

Recently a man handed me his business card. It was impressive. Nicely designed. Gold-embossed logo. It listed his position as chief executive officer and president. I later found out this man is a poor excuse for a leader. Yet his card is impressive. This man has positional leadership, but an illustrious business card or title doesn't make someone a leader. As John Gardner puts it:

> We must not confuse leadership with status. Even in large corporations and government agencies, the top-ranking person may simply be bureaucrat number 1. We have all occasionally encountered the top persons who couldn't lead a squad of seven-year-olds to the ice cream counter.[108]

In other words, you are only a leader if you lead.

Leaders come in many forms, with many styles and diverse qualities. There are quiet leaders and leaders one can hear in the next county. Some find their strength in eloquence, some in judgment, some in courage…

The fact that there are many kinds of leaders has implications for leadership education. Most of those seeking to develop young potential leaders have in mind one ideal model that is inevitably constricting. We should give young people a sense of the many kinds of leaders and styles of leadership, and encourage them to move toward those models that are right for them."[109]

It's important we distinguish between leading and "managing." Managing is usually tied in with some type of organizational structure. The true leader may have no organizational structure at all. He simply leads.

In 1947, a professor at the University of Chicago, Dr. Chandrasekhar, was scheduled to teach a class in advanced astrophysics. The professor was living in Wisconsin where he was doing some research for an upcoming conference. His plan was to commute to Chicago twice a week, even though the class was held during the winter quarter, and he would encounter the very worst weather the Midwest could throw at him.

The professor had second thoughts about teaching the class when he heard that only two students had signed up for his course. He thought of the distance, he thought of the time away from his family, and he thought of the snow and ice. But then he thought of the two students. He decided to follow through on his commitment to teach. He had obviously hoped for more than two students, yet perhaps those two students would be worth the time investment.

Ten years later, Dr. Chandrasekhar was very pleased to hear that the two young men who made up his class were progressing along quite nicely. Chen Ning Yang and Tsung-Dao Lee both were awarded the Nobel prize in physics in 1957. In 1983, Dr. Chandrasekhar was awarded the same honor. You might say the class was worth the effort. The professor who demonstrated his leadership in being willing to teach just two, young, motivated students obviously passed along some values and character as well as a syllabus.

Gentlemen, your kids are your students. You're teaching the class on leadership every day. And whether you realize it or not, they are watching your example like hawks. You may only have one or two. But a man with vision knows that the opportunity to shape the lives of his children with godly character is simply too good to pass up. It's worth whatever sacrifice is necessary.

I've been thinking about this process of turning kids into leaders for quite some time. Not only have I been thinking about it, I have been *working* on it. I have some good friends who are in the same process. From time to time we will compare notes for the simple reason that none of us really have our act together. So we check in with one another as much as possible and talk shop about raising our kids to be leaders.

I have come up with seven principles which could help your kids stand tall. Interestingly enough, I see all seven in the leadership style of our old friend, Mordecai. Mordecai did a pretty fair job of raising Esther to be a leader. His leadership of Esther gave her what it took to be a leader when her life was literally on the line.

1. BE A LEADER YOURSELF.

Dave Johnson is a friend of mine in San Jose who rides for the brand. For years Dave rode for the brand on a Harley. But now he rides in a patrol car. Dave is a police officer in San Jose who wrote a fascinating book about his experiences as a street cop. Dave has plenty of stories that are hilarious, but here's one that could make you weep:

Frank and I had just finished a call, and climbed into our police cars.... As I started my car, I heard the police radio call out Frank's unit number. The dispatcher reported a young boy missing from his residence. I heard the address and the description: two years old, wearing tennis shoes, coveralls, and a light blue T-shirt. The dispatcher said the mother had lain down on the couch and fallen asleep, and discovered the boy missing when she awoke fifteen minutes later.

Frank acknowledged the call, and began driving to the address. I picked up my radio and told the dispatcher I would respond to the area to help in the search.

I was driving directly behind Frank's car. Our sergeant, Dennis Busch, had also heard the call and, because he was nearby, radioed back that he would also respond.

Suddenly the dispatcher alerted Frank, Dennis, and myself: "The lost boy has been located—in the next-door neighbor's swimming pool."

Adrenaline shot through my veins as I reached for the control switch to activate my red lights. I saw Frank's lights jump on at the same time. We both accelerated. I began praying that the people who found the boy knew CPR—cardio-pulmonary resuscitation— and were attempting to revive him.

As Frank and I rounded the corner near the address, we saw several men standing on the sidewalk in front of a house. Dennis was just getting out of his police car and talking with the group of people. As I began getting out of my car, I suddenly saw Dennis bolt toward a gate at the side of the house. As Frank and I got closer, one of the men pointed and told us what he must have told Dennis: "The boy's in the pool in that backyard." I could hardly believe what I'd heard.

Frank and I both ran through a narrow side yard that led to the swimming pool. As we rounded the corner of the house we could see Dennis pulling the boy's limp body out of the pool, lifting him by the back of shirt.

Dennis laid the boy on the cold cement at the pool's edge and began administering CPR, and Frank knelt down to help.

With Frank and Dennis hovering over the motionless body, attempting to breathe life back into the child, I was left with nothing to do except watch—which is hard for most police officers to do in a life-and-death situation. Unable to help, I searched the boy's face, looking for any sign of life that might flicker there. If only *I could do something....*

Dennis continued to breathe for the boy, while Frank kept com pressing his small chest, trying to get his heart going again.

My eyes fell to the coveralls that hung wet on his little body. I thought how much they looked like the ones my girls wore when they were that age. I saw the small tennis shoes on his limp feet, and noticed that one was untied. I wondered if he would ever have someone tie his shoes again.

I desperately tried to choke back the lump tightening in my throat, and could feel tears coming down my cheeks.

I turned, walked a few steps, and took out my handkerchief to wipe my eyes. As I put it back in my pocket, I saw four men standing and watching Dennis and Frank work. I recognized them as part of the group standing out front when we arrived.

I felt anger welling up inside me. "Who found the boy in the pool?" I asked.

They looked at me, but none of them said a word.

I repeated the question, surprised at how loud my voice came out. Then I continued, "Why did you just leave him in the pool? Why didn't you at least pull him out?"

They only hung their heads, and stared at the ground.

Just then the fire department arrived. Soon an oxygen mask was secured around the small face that hadn't changed expression. The firefighters took over the CPR. Dennis was still kneeling, softly stroking the boy's small, closed hand, and staring into his lifeless face...

I looked up again at the four men still standing in their group. Suddenly, as if directed by some unseen instructor, they all turned and walked out of the yard, none of them saying a word.[110]

I don't know anything else about those four men. I don't know where they worked, I don't know their ages, I don't know if they were married, and I don't know if they were Democrats or Republicans. But there's something that I do know. None of those four men were leaders. Every one of them were followers.

Allow me to surmise something else about each of these four men. If any of them had children, my guess is that you would find them doing the same things that their fathers were doing.

Standing around.

Generally speaking, men who are followers produce children who are followers. And followers are very good at just standing around in a crisis.

That little two-year-old boy lost his life because four men were followers. It's my conviction that children all over America are dying emotionally, spiritually, and morally because the men in their lives are just standing around. That's absolutely the worst thing that any man with children could ever do. Passivity is death! Whatever you do, don't stand around!

What should you do?

Sit down and write out a plan.

Set some goals for your family.

Take a successful dad out for breakfast and tap into his methods.

Get with a small group of guys and encourage and sharpen each other.

Come to one of our Point Man Conferences.

You'll join thousands of other men who have walked out of that conference with a plan on how to lead your family! But whatever you do, don't stand around!

I don't remember who said it, but they were right on target: "There is as much risk in doing nothing as in doing something." And doing nothing with kids in regard to leadership is simply asking for tragedy in the teenage years. Horace Bushnell once said, "Somewhere under the stars God has a job for you to do and no one else can do it." That job, my friend, is to lead them by your example.

So what's it going to be, Dad? Are you standing tall...or just standing around?

Edmund Burke was right on the money: "Example is the school of mankind and they will learn at no other."

2. BE A SPIRITUAL SUBMARINE UNDER THE SURFACE OF YOUR CHILDREN'S LIVES.

Tom Clancy knows submarines. That why he writes the following words with such certainty:

Submarine. The very word implies stealth and deadliness. Of all the conventional weapons used by world's armed forces these days, none is more effective or dangerous that the nuclear attack submarine (SSN). Since its creation in the United States some forty years ago, the SSN has become the most feared weapon in the oceans of the world. The modern SSN is a stealth platform with 70 percent of the world's surface under which to hide, its endurance determined not by fuel but by the amount of food that may be crammed into the hull, and its operational limitations determined more by the skill of the commander and crew than by external factors....

Visually, a submarine is the least impressive of physical artifacts. Its hull does not bristle with weapons and sensors as do surface warships, and for one to see its imposing bulk, it must be in dry-dock. On those rare moments when a submarine is visible, this most lethal of ships appears no more threatening than a huge sea turtle. Yet despite that, the true capabilities of the modern SSN are most easily understood in terms of myth or the modern equivalent, a science fiction movie.

Here is a creature that, like Ridley Scott's *Alien,* appears when it wishes, destroys what it wishes, and disappears immediately to strike again when *it* wishes.[111]

May I submit to you, gentlemen, that God has called you to be a SSN for your children. When it comes to spiritual battle, you should understand that you have been given awesomely powerful weapons.

In my estimation, Ephesians 6 is telling us that godly men who are leading their families have the potential to be nothing less than the stealth warships of spiritual warfare who lurk just beneath the surface of their children's activities and affairs:

Put on the full armor of God, that you may be able to stand firm against the schemes of the devil. For our struggle is not against flesh and blood, but against rulers, against the powers, against the world forces of this darkness, against the spiritual forces of wickedness in the heavenly places. Therefore, take up the full armor of God , that you may be able to resist in the evil day, and having done everything, stand firm. Stand firm therefore, having girded your loins with truth, and having put on the breastplate of righteousness, and having shod your feet with the preparation of the gospel of peace; in addition to all, taking up the shield of faith with which you will be able to extinguish all the flaming missiles of the evil one. And take the helmet of salvation, and sword of the Spirit, which is the word of God. With all prayer and petition pray at all time in the Spirit, and with this in view, be on the alert with all perseverance and petition for all the saints (Ephesians 6: 11-18).

A godly father is the unseen spiritual submarine who lurks below the surface of every activity of his child's life. A man who has put on the full armor of God and with that armor, goes to warfare on his knees for his children, is a force to be reckoned with. The prayers of a man who has put on the full armor of God are lethal. Effective. Protective. God responds to the prayers of such a man who is alert to pray with perseverance for his children.

We understand, gentlemen, that we cannot be with our children twenty-four hours a day. We cannot be with them every time they encounter peer pressure. You may be out of sight, but like a submarine, that does not mean you are without influence. We are in spiritual warfare. A man in the full armor of God is nothing less a force than a SSN. Through your prayers you have the ability to affect situations where you are not physically present. You may be undetected but that does not mean that you are ineffective.

The next five points will not take as much explanation. They're simple and direct. But don't let that fool you. They're also *strategic*.

3. EXPECT YOUR CHILDREN TO BE LEADERS.

"I don't know what to do," a man said to his therapist. "My wife thinks she's a piano."

"Well, then, bring her in for an appointment."

"Are you crazy? exclaimed the husband. "Do you have any idea what it costs to move a piano?"

The moral of the story? If you *think* your kids are leaders and expect them to be leaders, then your kids will begin to see themselves as leaders.

What are your expectations? Do you expect your kids to go along with the crowd? Then they most likely will. Do you expect them to fight their way up upstream when everyone else is floating with the downstream current? Then they probably will. Expect your children to be leaders. If it's important to you it will be important to them.

4. ENCOURAGE YOUR CHILDREN TO BE LEADERS.

Every leader gets discouraged. That's why they need encouragement. "Encouragement" is a great word. It means "to put courage in." That's the job of a dad. It's tough being a teenager who goes against conventional wisdom; sometimes kids can become weary in well doing. That's especially when you must put courage in.

Two psychiatrists were at a convention. "What was your most difficult case?" one asked the other.

"Once I had a patient who lived in a pure fantasy world," replied his colleague. "He believed that a wildly rich uncle in South America was going to leave him a fortune. All day long he waited for a make-believe letter to arrive from a fictitious attorney. He never went out or did anything. He just sat around and waited."

"What was the result."

"It was an eight-year struggle, but I finally cured him. And then that stupid letter arrived..."

The last thing we want to do is to discourage our children in any way. We don't want to discourage their dreams, their hopes, their aspirations, or their moral courage. We want to help them become optimistic about what God has in store for them to be and to do.

Thomas Fuller once said that a young trooper should have an old horse. Guess what my friend, you are the horse. And your name isn't Trigger, Champion, or Silver. Your name had better be Encouragement.

5. REMIND YOUR CHILDREN THAT THEY ARE LEADERS.

"Dad," a polar bear cub asked his father, "am I 100 percent polar bear?"

"Of course you are," answered the father bear. "My parents are 100 percent polar bear, which makes me 100 percent polar bear. Your mother's parents are 100 percent polar bear, so she's 100 percent polar bear. Yep, that makes you 100 percent polar bear. Why do you ask?"

"I'm *freezing* out here, Dad."

Kids need to be frequently reminded who they are. When I drop my kids off at school, I often say to them as they get out of the car, "Be a leader today." Why do I do that? Because they need to be reminded.

Recently I was talking to one of my boys about a particular behavior. I reminded him that our family didn't do such things. I said to him, "Papa Jim doesn't do that. Uncle Mike doesn't do that. Uncle Jeff doesn't do that. And I don't do that. Farrars don't do that, and you are a Farrar."

Young polar bears may need to be reminded who they are when they feel the cold. Our kids need to be reminded when they start following the crowd that leaders don't do that. They are *leaders*, not followers. It's your job to remind them when they begin to doubt. It was Leo Tolstoy who commented, "We lost, because we told ourselves we lost." Remind your kids that they are leaders. Frequently.

6. SUPPORT THEM IN THEIR LEADERSHIP.

Professional golfers play every tournament round with a caddie. The caddie is more than an extra shoulder to hoist a bag of clubs. A caddie is there for support. A good caddie can be a tremendous support in the heat of competition.

Tommy Bolt was one of the greatest golfers of all time. But he had a legendary temper that almost outshone his reputation as a golfer. Tommy was playing in a tournament in southern California one year, and he was still ticked off from his score from the day before. He told his caddie not to say a word to him.

Tommy hit his first tee shot and it came to rest behind a tree. He asked his caddie what he thought about a 5-iron. The caddie didn't reply. Tommy hit the 5-iron and made an unbelievable shot that landed on the green.

Tommy turned to his caddie and proudly said, "Well, what do you think about that?"

"It wasn't your ball, Tommy," said the caddie as he picked up the bag and headed toward the green.

One of the greatest ways you can support your kids is to listen to them. When they need to talk, then you listen. When there's something eating 'em up, you find out what's going on inside their hearts. It will not be easy for your kids to be leaders when most of their friends are moral followers. And there will be times when they just need to talk. So *be there*, my friend. Be there with very large ears and a very large heart. If you do that, they will know that they are supported. Because you cared enough to listen.

This is what Ross Campbell calls "Focused Attention." Ross is a physician who has written an excellent book I have been recommending for years: *How to Really Love Your Child.*

Ross puts it this way:

What is focused attention? Focused attention is giving a child our full, undivided attention in such a way that he feels without doubt that he is completely loved. That he is valuable enough in his own right to warrant parents' undistracted watchfulness, appreciation, and uncompromising regard.[112]

Believe me, gentlemen. The child who gets focused attention will feel your complete support.

7. REWARD THEM FOR DEMONSTRATING LEADERSHIP.

When a child leads he should be rewarded. When your child eats lunch at school with a kid who the other kids make fun of, then he should be rewarded. When your teenager stands tall in the howling winds of peer pressure and does what is right, then he should be rewarded. But how do you reward him?

When I say reward, I don't mean money and I don't mean giving a gift. Now there is certainly a time and place for that. But there are other ways of giving a child a reward.

One of the better ways to reward your sons and daughters is with your words. Acknowledge their achievement or accomplishment verbally. There is a reason why I think this is important. When your kid does the right thing you can count on the fact that he will be criticized. Criticism always follows leaders. Men and women and boys and girls who stand tall always make the easiest targets.

A young boy had practiced for years to become a great pianist. Finally the night of his debut concert arrived. The auditorium was jammed. The teenage boy played his heart out for the audience. Yet when the newspapers came out, the critics ripped apart his performance. A wise old musician put his arm around the boy and said, " Remember, young man, there is no city in the world where they have erected a statue to a critic."

Your child will have plenty of critics. Just make sure that you are not one of them. Words are very important. We all remember the childhood rhyme, "Stick and stones may hurt my bones, but words will never hurt me." Nothing could be further from the truth. Many of us have broken bones and have recovered very nicely in a month or so. But is it not true that we can still remember the critical words that were hurled at us on a playground twenty, thirty, forty, even fifty years later? Words can hurt like nothing else.

Gentlemen, let's reward with our words. Samuel Goldwyn, who was the Yogi Berra of the film industry, once said of a director, "We are overpaying him, but he's worth it." When your kids demonstrate leadership, overpay them with your words.

You and I both know they're worth it.

BUT THERE ARE NO GUARANTEES

Ken Canfield makes a great point when he compares fathering to farming. There are no guarantees in either profession. A farmer can do all the right things and still lose a crop. So can a father. The farmer can till the ground at the right time, put in the right seed, and irrigate and fertilize according to the textbook. But that does not guarantee a crop.

A dad can implement all of the seven principles we've enumerated and still lose the crop. And there is nothing more heartbreaking. I'm aware of a man who in the estimation of many godly people had done an excellent job of cultivating his children. But recently one of his teenager daughters became pregnant.

Gentlemen, it could happen to any of us. All we can do is the best we can do. Perhaps you have a hard time understanding how a man could be such an outstanding leader and have one of his kids fail morally. The answer to that is that our kids are still kids. Because of circumstances, peer pressure, and lack of experience, they will make some choices at times that will not be the choices we had hoped for. Just like we did when we were their age.

My point in writing this chapter is not to say that we can be such great fathers as to guarantee that our kids will exhibit spiritual leadership in every situation they face in life. They won't, because they are human. But I am writing to say that the farmer who tills the soil, plants good seed, and irrigates his crop has a much better hope for a good crop than the man who doesn't plant any seed to begin with.

But there are no guarantees. I have the ability to make choices and so do my kids. And if God has blessed your life with kids that have—up to now—made the right choices, then be careful. Be grateful but also be careful.

In September of 1985 a party was held at one of the largest city pools in New Orleans. The reason for the festive occasion? The summer of 1985 was the first summer in years that a drowning did not occur at a New Orleans city pool. The summer was now officially over and two hundred guests were at the celebration, including over one hundred certified lifeguards.

It was a great party! All were thrilled at the accomplishment of the summer. It wasn't until the party was over that they noticed the fully-clothed man at the bottom of the pool near the drain. They attempted to revive him, but it was too late. The man had drowned, surrounded by life guards who were celebrating their success.

God has been good to many of us with our kids. But before we get carried away celebrating our successes, let's not forget to stay on our knees.

Let me also say a word to those of you who may have had a tough time with this chapter. You have a child who is not responding to the principles you have carefully instilled into his or her life. Perhaps your teenager has recently made a choice that has apparently torpedoed much of what you had hoped and dreamed for that young life. Don't lose heart my friend. You may be thinking that the crop you had worked and hoped for in the life of your son or daughter may never come in.

That's how the father of the prodigal son must have felt for quite awhile. There had to be nights when he felt that the crop he had hoped to reap in the life of his son was lost forever.

But it ain't over until it's over.

Prodigals have a way of coming home. That's why you might want to keep a fatted calf ready. Or at least a few extra steaks in the freezer. You never know when that crop might come pulling into the driveway.

1. Do you find yourself moved or convicted by Officer Dave Johnson's story of the four men who "just stood around," instead of pulling the little boy out of the pool? When it comes to being a spiritual leader in your home, do you ever feel as though you're doing a lot of standing around? How has this book helped or encouraged you to break that pattern?

2. Take a moment to review the following scriptures: Ephesians 6:18, Philippians 4:6-7, Colossians 4:2,12-13, and James 5:16. As you consider the implications of fighting spiritual battles in your child's life, look again at Colossians 4:12-13. Describe the kind of prayer ministry a guy named Epaphras was having in the lives of the Colossian believers. What do you think it means to "labor earnestly" (NASB) or "wrestle" (NIV) for someone in prayer? What kind of impact could that kind of prayer—coming from you, their dad—have in the lives of your kids down through the years? Is it a ministry you've seriously considered before now? How can we as men encourage one another in this crucial area of helping our kids stand tall?

3. Consider again Dr. Ross Campbell's explanation of supporting your child through focused attention:

> Focused attention is giving a child our full, undivided attention in such a way that he feels without doubt that he is completely loved. That he is valuable enough in his own right to warrant his parents' undistracted watchfulness, appreciation, and uncompromising regard.

As you look back over the last couple of weeks, have you been giving each of your kids the benefit of such attention? What are some ways a man might remind himself to carve out some focused time for each child during the course of a week?

4. Take a 3x5 card and write out the seven steps I've outlined in this chapter. If you're serious about this business of helping your sons and daughters stand tall, stick the card someplace where your eyes will fall on it every day. Tape it to the bathroom mirror where you shave, or tape it to the dashboard of your car. It could provide some stimulating conversation in the old car pool!

CHAPTER ELEVEN

Womenfolk

I don't mind living in a man's world
as long as I can be a woman in it.

SUSAN BARKELY

I have never been tortured.

But last week I had an impacted wisdom tooth removed. In my mind, there seems to be a direct correlation between the two experiences. They put me out to remove the tooth, so I really don't know how they got it out. But the way my jaw feels, I suspect they blasted it out.

That's why I was up last night at 2:30 A.M. And that's why I was watching an old episode of *Rawhide*. Rawhide was one of the great TV westerns. Even with my pain, it brought back good memories to watch Gil Favor, Rowdy Yates, and Wishbone.

Last night, Gil and Rowdy had to ride into town to find some of the boys who got drunk at the saloon. As I watched them walk through town, I began to notice something about the way they interacted with people. Every time they would pass by a woman, they would tip their hats. When they addressed a woman, they called her "Ma'am." These two rough and tumble trail drivers were very careful with their manners when it came to "womenfolk."

What struck me about these cowboys was that they were *respectful* of women. That's the way real men would relate to "womenfolk" in the Old West. And real men do the same thing today.

One of the tell-tale signs of our rapid national erosion is the way women are treated in our land. To put it on the table, we are developing into a nation where women are not respected. And the flaw has been in the moral fabric for quite awhile.

I'll never forget the first time an abused woman walked into my office. I hadn't been pastoring long and I wasn't happy with the way she had been treated. Her eye was bruised and her lip was split and broken. After I talked with her and got her some medical attention, I drove down to her husband's place of employment.

This guy sold new cars. As I walked into the showroom I could tell he was a little surprised to see me.

I walked up to him and said, "I'd like to make a deal with you."

So we went into one of those little white offices and sat down, just like we were going to negotiate on a car. But I wasn't there to talk about a car.

"Let me offer you a deal," I told him. "The next time you decide you want to hit somebody, I want you to call me up. I'll come over to your house and you can hit me and I won't hit you back. That's the deal. But if you ever strike your wife again, our elder board will press charges against you faster than you can believe."

This guy was pretty tough with a woman. That's why he wasn't a real man. Real men don't strike women. But unless I miss my guess, the reason this guy hit women was because he was raised in a home where women were struck. In other words, he didn't know how to respect a woman because his father never *taught* him to respect women.

Gentlemen, if you would like to make a difference in this nation, let me suggest to you that you teach your sons to respect women. Our country is crying out for men who know how to treat women in a biblical and gracious manner.

A recent commentary from Chuck Colson underscores the need for such behavior from young men in a culture that has lost its moral mind.

According to Colson, there is a new fad going on in public swimming pools in New York City. It's called "whirlpooling." Colson writes:

> Twenty to thirty boys link arms in a circle and surround a solitary girl. The boys close in on her, dunk her head under water, and frequently tear off her bathing suit and grab at her.
>
> The problem has grown so severe that in New York City several teenage boys have actually been arrested. Some girls say they're afraid to go to the pool alone…
>
> The underlying philosophy that spawns this ugliness was uncovered in an informal survey by the *New York Times*. Reporters asked several teens how they accounted for the boys' predatory behavior in the swimming pools.
>
> "It's nature," one boy replied. "Look at a female dog and a male dog. It's the same thing: you see 20 male dogs on a female dog. It's the male nature, in a way."
>
> How utterly repugnant. But how utterly consistent with what these kids are being taught in public schools. The great prophet of sex education was Alfred Kinsey, who built his theory of sexuality squarely on the foundation of scientific naturalism. Humans are part of nature, Kinsey taught—nothing more…
>
> The Bible does not teach that we are mere dogs in heat. It teaches that we are bearers of the image of God.[113]

I don't know anymore details about "whirlpooling" than what Colson reported. But there are two things that come to mind. I would have liked to have seen Gil Favor and Rowdy Yates show up at that swimming pool. And secondly, none of those boys who were in involved in such a sick activity were taught by their fathers to respect women.

Women are not being respected in our culture. It's just another sign of the moral and spiritual sickness that plagues our nation. Women are hit, raped, abused, grabbed, and harassed. Is there anything we can do about this problem that plagues us? Yes, there is. We can teach our sons *early* to respect women.

Just think about the problem and its root causes. They all go back to the home.

• Men who strike women were not taught to respect women.

• Men who rape women were not taught to respect women.

• Men who divorce their wives for younger women were not taught to respect women.

• Men who sexually harass women with crass innuendoes were not taught to respect women.

• Men who don't live with their wives in an understanding way were not taught to respect women.

• Men who don't grant their wives honor as a fellow-heir of the grace of life were not taught to respect women.

Now the key question is this: When is it in his life that a man learns to respect women? The answer is that a man should learn to respect a woman when he is a boy. *And he should learn it from his father.*

My wife told me of a recent situation that she witnessed between a ten-year-old boy and his mother. It should also be pointed out that the boy's father had just left his mother for another woman. It was a public setting and the woman asked the boy to get his things so that they could get into the car and go pick up his younger brother.

"I'll go when I'm ready," said the boy.

"We have to go now," said the mother.

"Shut up," retorted the boy.

"Don't talk to me that way!"

"I'll talk to you any way I want to," said the boy as he stalked off.

The mother, who had just been through the humiliation of having her husband leave her for a younger woman, was now publicly embarrassed by a ten-year-old who was completely out of control. She stood in a group of watching adults, deeply humiliated by a boy who was emulating the example of his dad. Like father, like son.

Last summer, my wife and I were invited to speak at the Christian Business Men's Committee national convention in Orlando. The hotel was right next door to Disney World and we had a great time with our family that week. Our sessions were in the morning, so we were free in the afternoons and evenings to go to Disney World.

I was committed for an evening meeting on Tuesday, so I left Mary and the kids at Epcot and went back to the conference. Mary recounted an interesting experience she had when they returned to the hotel. As they came into the lobby at about 10:00 P.M., Mary asked one of our boys, to go to the coffee shop with the rest of the group, while Mary dropped some packages in the hotel room.

"Mom, can I go find Dad?" he asked.

"No, I want everyone to stay together. You stay with the kids and go to the coffee shop. I'll be right there and Dad is planning on meeting us there."

"Yes, ma'am," he said.

As Mary got into the elevator a lady got in with her.

"I want you to know that I was very impressed with your son back there," she said.

"Oh, really?" replied Mary.

"We have been at Disney World all week and it seems that all I have seen this week are children who don't know how to obey their parents. All week long I have had my fill of spoiled kids arguing with their parents in the most abusive terms when they didn't get their way. It was absolutely refreshing to see a boy who knew how to obey his mother."

Now that is quite a social commentary. Please don't get the idea that things always work that way at our house. I could enumerate a number of stories where the outcome of the discussion wasn't resolved as it was that evening. But the point here is that a watching stranger found my son's simple obedience to his mother so *unusual* that she felt compelled to comment on it. That is a very sad commentary.

One of the key times in the life of boys and girls is adolescence. This is often the time when the parameters are tested. And this is often the time when a wrong pattern of acting disrespectfully takes root. As a boy grows in physical stature, it becomes quite tempting to try his wings with his new found size and physical strength. This is precisely where the respect for a mother will be tested. The reason I know this is that I remember being thirteen years old. In twelve months' time, I grew from 5'7" and 130 pounds to 6'3" and 190 pounds. Believe me, I was feeling my oats.

I can remember a talk I had with my dad like it was yesterday afternoon. The topic of our conversation was my tone of voice and the content of my speech to my mother. I may have been impressed with my new found size but my dad wasn't impressed in the least. He wouldn't have been impressed if I had been 7'3". You see, I was impressed with physical size. My dad was impressed with the size of character and attitude. And the purpose of our discussion was to cut me down to size.

What size did my dad whittle me down to? He brought me down to the reality that no matter how tall I was, or how much I weighed, or how old I was, I was *under* the authority of my mother. He reminded me that this wasn't between me and my mother. It was between me and him.

I recently came across a "Calvin and Hobbes" cartoon that captures the idea. Calvin says to Hobbes, "I feel bad that I called Susie names and hurt her feelings. I'm sorry I did it."

"Maybe you should apologize to her," Hobbes suggests.

Calvin thinks about this momentarily and then retorts, "I keep hoping there's a less obvious solution."

I had to laugh recently when a friend of mine had a similar encounter with his soon-to-be-thirteen-year-old boy. The boy was starting to display some very disrespectful behavior to his mother. My friend made it clear to him that this was not going to continue. The boy would do well for awhile…and then he would get upset and start running off his mouth to his mother.

The father was getting ready to go on a business trip for a couple of days. He sat down and talked with his son and reminded him that he fully expected him to speak respectfully to his mother while he was away. If he did not, there would be certain severe consequences upon his return. The first night away, the dad called the son, and in the course of their conversation, he reminded him about his expectation of his behavior.

The next night that dad got in from the airport at about 10:30 P.M. As he walked in the door, he wife looked very discouraged. She then proceeded to tell him about the latest bout of disrespect. The dad listened, took his suitcase upstairs, and went into his son's bedroom. He got the boy out of bed, and they went into the family room to talk. He went back over his instructions. The boy agreed that he understood the instructions.

The father then commenced to apply knowledge to the seat of understanding. But he was not through. He was just beginning. He then told his son that he was at a crossroads. A very important crossroads. He explained to the son that it was his desire for his son to enjoy life. But it was the boy's decision whether or not that would happen.

The father was very direct in explaining to his son that another verbal barrage on his mother would mean that his choice had been made. One more bout of disrespect would mean that the boy was done with football and done with all social activities at school. This father wasn't kidding around. A man who respects his wife protects his wife.

Fortunately, this dad had a large amount of credibility capital with his son. The boy knew his dad meant every word. He knew that his father would pull him off the football team without even thinking twice. His father reminded him that football and social activities were privileges that were earned. They were not rights. The father then reminded the son that this was not an issue between the boy and the mother, but between him and his boy. He also let the boy know that it was the boy who would make the choice of living a miserable existence. If there was one more episode, football was over in mid-September.

Over the next few weeks there was an amazing transformation of character. The boy suddenly became very careful of his speech. He seemed to work overtime to be kind and loving to his mother. Why was the boy suddenly motivated to bring about such a change in character?

I believe the term is known as "fear."

And just as the fear of the heavenly Father is the beginning of wisdom, so the fear of an earthly father is also the beginning of wisdom.

One thing needs to be pointed out. This father deeply loves his son. He loves his son more than words could ever express. He is deeply committed to his son living a full, productive, and meaningful life. This father wants his son to have a good marriage and great relationships with his children. Those are the motives behind the father's remarks.

One more thing. It was all the father could do to keep from laughing when he was talking with his son. Because he kept remembering a similar talk that his father had with him when he was approximately the same age. When he heard himself using some of the exact words and phrases that his father had used with him over thirty years prior, it was all he could do to keep a straight face. And in thirty or so years in the future, his son will also have to work very hard to keep a straight face when he repeats those same phrases to his boy.

There's yet another interesting twist to this story. Weeks later, this man was talking to his wife about the remarkable character transformation in the life of their son. Now the boy hadn't become perfect, but when he started to slip into disrespect he would catch himself and quickly shift attitudinal gears.

That's when the wife said, "In all of our years of marriage you have done some wonderful things for me. You have given me wonderful gifts and we have taken some very special trips. But nothing you have ever done for me has meant more to me than the way that you demanded that our son respect me. You will never know how much that let me know how much you love me and value me."

Whoa! This guy was completely blown away. He couldn't believe the impact that his actions with his son had had on his wife (not to mention his son).

Gentlemen, this is what you call male leadership. This is the solution to the sexual harassment problem, the rape problem, the physical abuse problem, and a few other problems that we probably haven't even thought about. Let me put it another way. Boys who love and respect their mothers don't abuse women and they don't rape women. But you take away the respect from an adolescent boy and you are asking for trouble that will affect all of society.

In George Bernard Shaw's *Pygmalion,* Eliza Doolittle married Freddy Eynsford-Hill because she knew that she would always be a cockney flower girl to Professor Henry Higgins. She knew that he could never accept the change in her, but would always see her as she used to be. As she told Freddy, "The difference between a lady and a flower girl is not how she behaves but how she's treated. I shall always be a flower girl to Professor Higgins because he always treats me as a flower girl and always will; but I know I can be a lady to you because you always treat me like a lady and always will."[114]

I realize that there are cases when an innocent man is accused of sexual impropriety and there is nothing to the allegations. But I am not speaking of such cases. My comments are directed to the situations where women are taken advantage of by men. The time to cure an increasing problem with irresponsible men who don't know how to treat a woman respectfully is not at age thirty or forty or fifty. It is at twelve or thirteen. Quite frankly, gentlemen, anything past that is too late.

The mighty Niagara river plummets some 180 feet at the American and Horseshoe Falls. Before the falls, there are violent, turbulent rapids. Farther upstream, however, where the river's current flows more gently, boats are able to navigate. Just before the Welland River empties into the Niagara, a pedestrian walkway spans the river. Posted on this bridge's pylons is a warning sign for all boaters: DO YOU HAVE AN ANCHOR? DO YOU KNOW HOW TO USE IT?[115]

There is a point on the Niagara River that is the point of no return. There is a point in the lives of our children where they, too, will be caught up in an irresistible current. That current is a combination of adolescent experimentation and cultural attitudes to God-ordained authority that—if unchallenged—will sweep our children over the falls to a life of relational chaos. They will *drown* in those wrong attitudes. Not only will they drown, but they will take others with them.

Do you want to do something to stop the moral deterioration of our nation? Then anchor your son.

A father is the anchor that God has placed in the life of a child. It is the father's role and responsibility to dig deeply into the solid rock of Christ in order to tether a young boy headed in the wrong direction. Every boy needs the bone-jarring yank that occurs when the anchor takes hold.

That yank of a loving father has kept many a boy from going over the falls. And the astonishing thing about that fact is this: that yank on the life of your boy just won't save him alone. An anchor that holds that deeply into the bedrock of Christ will save not only your boy, but *his* boy, and *his* boy. Real men yank on the chain of the generations and demand respect for women.

And here's the deal on this chain. It's real long and it's real strong. It goes way back, further than you may have imagined. For on the other end of the anchor is the One who in His last moments on the cross thought not of himself, but of a woman, and entrusted her care into the hands of a trusted friend. He not only died for His mother, but He respected His mother. And we can do no less than to uphold His example of ideal masculinity for our families.

The term "womenfolk" may be outdated, but the term "respect" is not. For godly men it is still very much in vogue.

Drop the anchor, my friend, and pull hard on the chain. And you will save your family from sure disaster.

1. What does it mean to treat a woman in a "biblical" way? Take a few minutes to consider the following scriptures: John 19:25-27; 1 Timothy 5:1-2; 1 Peter 3:7; Ephesians 5:25-30,33; Colossians 3:19. Looking through a wide-angle lens, what are some of the main attitudes and actions conveyed by these biblical writers?

2. Now, looking through a zoom lens, focus in on 1 Peter 3:7, and then verses 8 and 9 following. Summarize Peter's thoughts in your own words. Talk about the impact on your sons and daughters as they see you living with your wife in the way Peter describes.

3. To what degree have you seen your attitude toward your wife reflected in your son or daughter's attitude toward their mother? In what way would you like to see that reflection improve or change?

CHAPTER TWELVE

Outposts of Civilization

*We act as though it were our mission
to bring about the triumph of truth,
but our mission is only to fight for it.*

BLAISE PASCAL

A TV news camera crew was on assignment in southern Florida film-
ing the widespread destruction of Hurricane Andrew. In one scene,
amid the devastation and debris stood one house on its foundation. The owner was cleaning up the yard when a reporter
approached him.

"Sir, why is your house the only one in the entire neighborhood that is standing?" asked the reporter. "How did you manage to escape
the severe damage of the hurricane?"

"I built this house myself," the man replied. "I also built it according to
the Florida state building code. When the code called for 2x6 roof trusses, I
used 2x6 roof trusses. I was told that a house built according to code could
withstand a hurricane. I did and it did. I suppose no one else around here
followed the code."[116]

A house built to the moral code of Scripture can also withstand a *moral*
hurricane. And that's what we are in, gentlemen. A hurricane. But we

should remember that as bad as hurricanes can be, some houses remain standing. But the house must be built according to code.

Most men don't take the time or effort to build according to code. They would rather take the shortcuts. But your shortcuts will find you out! Just ask the people who lost their homes in Hurricane Andrew. In that entire neighborhood, only one house remained standing. And it was the house of a man who built it himself according to the predetermined standards of the code. He didn't do what everyone else did. In fact, he did what everyone else *didn't* do. When all else fails, read the directions. Oh, yeah, there's one more thing. Don't just don't read the directions. *Follow* the directions.

Just because we are in the hurricane doesn't mean that we have to be pessimistic. Some people are negative all the time. One guy described his outlook on life with this statement, "I was going to read a book on positive thinking. But then I thought, *what good will do that do?*" That's certainly not the Christian perspective.

I like the perspective characterized by a good ol' boy from the backwoods by the name of Jeb. Wolves were picking off the livestock of ranchers at an alarming rate, so the state offered a bounty of $5,000 for every wolf killed. Jeb and his friend, Ernie, decided to go into the wolf hunting business. They had been out huntin' wolves all day and into the night, and made camp way up in the mountains near a beautiful little stream. About four o' clock in the morning, Jeb woke up to see their camp surrounded by thirty or forty wolves. In the light of the dying campfire, he could see the blood-lust in their eyes, and the white of their exposed, razor-sharp teeth. He could also see that they were about ready to spring.

"Hey, Ernie," he whispered. "Wake up! *We're rich!*"

Now that's a man with a positive attitude.

Guys, as we look at what's happening around us, we should understand that we are rich. Rich with opportunity, that is. The early days of America were no piece of cake. Building a new nation with new opportunity meant plenty of risk. It meant putting yourself on the line. Men died for the freedoms we enjoy today, just as they have done at various times in our two hundred-year history. It was in those early days of great risk and uncertainty that Abigail Adams wrote a letter to Thomas Jefferson. In that letter, dated

1790, Mrs. Adams had a bit of wisdom for the ages.

She wrote: *"These are the hard times in which a genius would wish to live. Great necessities call forth great leaders."*

Abigail Adams took a long look at the world around her and saw it brimming with threats and difficulties. And she realized she was rich. That woman was a leader.

Gentlemen, we are living in days of great necessities. That's why you're rich. For you have an opportunity to offer great leadership to your family. Who is the man who is the great leader? It is the man who builds his family according to code.

There was another time in history where there were great necessities. After the fall of the Roman Empire, things were so bad historians have called that period "The Dark Ages." In the midst of the ravaging, marauding bands from the east, the great Roman Empire gradually fell to the invaders over a period of approximately fifty years. Society as it had been known broke down.

But here and there were pockets of civility in the midst of barbarism.

Why was there civility? Because some folks were building according to code.

There was a group of men who stood against the culture and infiltrated the culture, and eventually they changed the culture. Even though things were dark, they believed in the Light of the gospel. It not only made a difference in their lives, but in the lives of all whom they touched.

In the fifth century, it appeared that Western Europe was headed for nothing less than total barbarism. As Charles Colson so brilliantly described in his book, *Against the Night,* only one force prevented barbarism from taking Europe. And that force was the church. Allow me to quote from Colson, and then draw a parallel to where we are today in America.

> Instead of conforming to the barbarian culture of the Dark Ages, the medieval church modeled a counterculture to a world engulfed by destruction and confusion. Thousands of monastic orders spread across Europe, characterized by discipline, creativity, and a coherence and moral order lacking in the world around them. Monks

preserved not only the Scriptures but classical literature as well; they were busy not only at their prayers but in clearing land, building towns, and harvesting crops. When little else shone forth, these religious provided attractive models of communities of caring and character, and in the process they preserved both faith and civilization itself...by holding on to such vestiges of civilization—faith, learning, and civility—these monks and nuns held back the night, and eventually the West emerged from the Dark Ages into a renewed period of cultural creativity, education, and art. The barbarians could not withstand this stubborn preservation of culture.[117]

The monks preserved Christian civilization in a dark age by building little outposts of civilization across Europe. And when they built their outposts, they built them according to the code.

As we have seen, we live in a culture that contains powerful groups hellbent on removing every vestige of the Bible from our society. You recall that earlier, we cited an incredible event where common sense was assassinated. A convicted murderer's sentence to life in prison was revoked because one of the attorneys quoted a phrase from the Bible in his closing argument. He didn't even quote a verse, just a phrase, and the sentence of the murderer was revoked. I think that most of us by now would agree that our civilization is serious lacking in one attribute and that attribute is *civilization*.

Now my question is this. We are living in an age growing darker by the day. Who is going to preserve the message of the Scriptures as the monks did in their little groups during the first Dark Ages?

The answer to that is Christian men are going to do it.

Christian men are going to emphasize the Scriptures in the enclaves of their own homes even as the culture attempts to eradicate the Bible from the life of our nation. For that is how civilization is kept within civilization. Our job is the same as the monks. We are to build outposts of civilization. And we are to build them according to code.

Those little monastic orders were the instruments God used to preserve His truth. He wants to do the same thing in this culture with your family and my family, for the family is the church in miniature.

In those little outposts:

- God's Word was read and obeyed.

- Prayer was a source of focus and encouragement.

- Women were respected.

- Leaders were developed.

- Morality was practiced.

- Discipline was expected.

- Accountability was the order of the day.

Gentlemen, those same factors must characterize our families. May I suggest to you that this is how a man disciples his children? He raises them in a family that is an outpost of civilization. And the father makes sure that the outpost is built according to code.

Where is the code found? It is found in various parts of the Scriptures, but you can get right to the essence of it in Deuteronomy 6. Note how Moses addresses the men of Israel:

> Now this is the commandment, the statutes and the judgments which the LORD your God has commanded me to teach you, that you might do them in the land where you are going over to possess it, so that you and your son and your grandson might fear the LORD your God, to keep all His statutes and His commandments, which I command you, all the days of your life, and that your days may be prolonged. O Israel, you should listen and be careful to do it, that it may be well with you and that you may multiply greatly, just as the LORD, the God of your fathers, has promised you, in a land flowing with milk and honey.

> Hear, O Israel! The LORD is our God, the LORD is one! And you shall love the LORD your God with all your heart and with all your soul and with all your might. And these words, which I am commanding you today, shall be on your heart; and you shall teach them diligently to your sons and shall talk of them when you sit in your house and when you walk by the way and when you lie down and when you rise up (Deuteronomy 6:1-7).

Out of Moses' instruction to the men of Israel, I see that the code pre-scribes two iron-clad essentials for discipling your children.

• A man is to be with his children.

• A man is to teach his children.

When you stop and think about it, this is precisely how Jesus discipled the twelve. He was with them and He taught them.

We're all fighting a battle for enough family time. Everyone is busy and it seems that we are going in three directions at once. So the first question is this: How are you doing in the "with" category? For you see, if you are going to build according to code, there has to be time just to be "with."

A number of years ago, Dr. Robert Schuller was on a whirlwind book promotion tour, visiting eight cities in four days. It was an exhausting sched-ule in addition to the normal duties that Dr. Schuller had on his shoulders as pastor of a large church. As he was going over his schedule with his secre-tary for his return home, she reminded him that he was scheduled to have lunch with the winner of a charity raffle. Tickets had been raffled for a lunch with Dr. Schuller. Schuller was suddenly sobered when he found out the winner of the raffle, for he happened to know that the $500 the person bid to have lunch with him represented that person's entire life savings.

How did he know that?

The person who was willing to spend $500 to have lunch with Dr. Schuller was his own teenage daughter.

Dr. Schuller obviously loves his family as much as any of us do. He gra-ciously allowed Paul Harvey to tell this story in his column. It simply reminds us fathers that we can be so busy doing what is good, that we forget what is of real importance. So many of the things we believe are "caught" by our kids when they are "with" us. That's the value of time.

According to the code, the second task is to *teach*. Guys, let me shoot absolutely straight with you. This is so basic and fundamental that the ten-dency—the very strong tendency—would be to put this book down.

But I have a question for you: Whose job is it to teach your kids the Scriptures? The Sunday school teacher, the youth pastor, the pastor?

According to Deuteronomy 6, it's *your* job. And no one has been a bigger failure at this than me.

For years, we never had a consistent family devotional time during the week. From time to time I'd take a stab at it—only to watch my kids' eyes glaze over and roll back in their heads. But about a year ago I woke up and realized what was going on. My kids are being raised in Baal-like culture. If I don't give them the Word of God then no one will give them the Word of God. Sure, they'll get it at Sunday school, but guys, forty-five minutes in Sunday school is not going to counterbalance a Baal-possessed culture that they function in the other six-and-a-half days.

Let me tell you what I stumbled across. It's a plan that's so simple it's absolutely profound. About a year and a half ago, Mary suggested to me that as a family, we read the Bible together.

That's it?

That's it.

What we do is we make sure the homework is done and the TV is off. Any dad in the world can lead his family spiritually by turning off the TV and getting everyone together in the family room. Everyone opens their Bible and we start reading. What we do is read right through a book. We've read through Esther, Ruth, 1 Kings, and a bunch of other books. What I do is look at the chapter and see how many verses there are. Then I divide the chapter by three (because I have three kids) and let them each take their turn reading.

If your kids are small and can't read, then you should get them *The Beginner's Bible.*[118] Kids absolutely go crazy over *The Beginner's Bible*. It's at their level of understanding so that when Dad reads to them they won't fall asleep. It's also a great first Bible for a child just learning to read.

Our kids are older, so we vary from a regular Bible translation to *The Wonder Bible.*[119] *The Wonder Bible* is a great tool for kids between eight and twelve. It summarizes everything in the Scriptures without compromising the essence, and makes for a much easier read for kids. Each of the kids has a *Wonder Bible*. It's a great tool. Of course, as your kids are older, they can begin reading directly from the Scriptures.

We don't do this every night, because life is nuts! But we shoot for two to three nights a week. We read the Word and then sometimes we have great discussions and other nights we don't. That will take care of itself.

Any guy in the world can do this. If your kids ask you a question that you don't know, then *tell* them you don't know. That's no disgrace! But make sure you follow up and get back to them. If you get stuck, give your pastor a call. He'll be more than happy to help a man who is leading his family in the study of God's Word.

Guys, let me tell you why this is so important. I'm dead serious, this is real life stuff. Note what Moses said to the men of Israel about their job of building their outpost of civilization according to code: "So the LORD commanded us to observe all these statutes, to fear the LORD our God for our good always *and for our survival,* as it is today (Deuteronomy 6:24)."

Did you catch that?

It for our SURVIVAL.

Moses knew that Israel was going into Canaan. But guess who was waiting in Canaan? Baal was in Canaan, waiting to swallow the families of Israel that didn't have a man at the helm who was smart enough to build his outpost according to code.

Hey, guys, Baal worship is everywhere in this country. How in the world are your kids ever going to learn to filter the demonic teaching and thinking that barrages them twenty-four hours a day? Their only hope for survival is that you give them the Word of God. With the Word of God they will be able to filter out the lies of the culture. And as they watch you love your Lord, love your wife, and take a stand for truth in this culture, believe me, they are going to put the pieces together.

Baal has invaded our land as he once invaded Israel. Alasdair MacIntyre has pondered our secular situation and reached this conclusion:

If my account of our moral condition is correct, we ought to conclude that for some time now we too have reached the turning point. What matters at this stage is the construction of local forms of community with which civility and the intellectual and moral life can be sustained through the new dark ages which are already upon us. And if the tradition of the virtues was able to survive the horrors of the last dark ages, we are not entirely without grounds for hope.

He's talking about building an outpost of civilization. But guys, it will only stand if it's built to the standards of the code. The only way to do that is to put the Bible back in the central place of your home. You must read the Scriptures personally and then read them to your children. For without the Scriptures, our culture has no hope and your children have no hope. If your children are not equipped in the Scriptures, then how will they maintain the truth to pass on to their children?

Generations of the past knew this. Allan Bloom describes the way it used to be:

It was the home (and the houses of worship related to it) where religion lived. The holy days and the common language and set of references that permeated most households constituted a large part of the family bond and gave it a substantial content. Moses and the Table of the Law, Jesus and his preaching of brotherly love, had an imaginative existence. Passages from the Psalms and the Gospels echoed in children's heads. Attending church or synagogue, praying at the table, were a way of life, inseparable from the moral education that supposed to be the family's special responsibility in this democracy. Actually, the moral teaching was the religious teaching. There was no abstract doctrine. The things one was supposed to do, the sense that the world supported them and punished disobedience, were all incarnated in the Biblical stories. The loss of the gripping inner life vouchsafed those who were nurtured by the Bible must be primarily attributed not to our schools or political life, but to the family, which, with all its rights to privacy, has proved unable to maintain any content of its own. *The dreariness of the family's spiritual landscape passes belief.* It is as monochrome and unrelated to those who pass through it as are the barren steppes frequented by nomads who take their mere substance and move on. The delicate fabric of the civilization into which the successive generations are woven has unraveled, and children are raised, not educated.

I am speaking here not of the unhappy, broken homes that are such a prominent part of American life, but the relatively happy ones, where husband and wife like each other and care about their children, very often unselfishly devoting the best parts of their lives to them. But they have nothing to give their children in the way of a vision of the world, of high models of action or profound sense of connection with others. The family requires the most delicate mixture of nature and convention, of human and divine, to subsist and perform its function. Its base is merely bodily reproduction, but its purpose is the formation of civilized human beings. In teaching a language and providing names for all things, it transmits an interpretation of the order of the whole of things. It feeds on books, in which the little polity—the family—believes, which tell about right and wrong, good and bad, and explain why they are so. The family requires a certain authority and wisdom about the ways of the heavens and of men. The parents must have knowledge of what has happened in the past, and prescriptions for what ought to be, in order to resist the philistinism or the wickedness of the present.... The family, however, has to be a sacred unity believing in the permanence of what it teaches, if its ritual and ceremony are to express and transmit the wonders of the moral law, which it alone is capable of transmitting and which makes it special in a world devoted to the humanly, all too humanly, useful. When that belief disappears, as it has, the family has, at best, a transitory togetherness. People sup together, travel together, but they do not think together. Hardly any homes have any intellectual life whatsoever, let alone one that informs the vital interests of life. Educational TV marks the high tide for family intellectual life.[120]

I was driving home last night and a song came on the radio that I had never heard before. It was so profound, that I tracked down the lyrics this afternoon.

> Grandpa, tell me 'bout the good old days,
> Sometimes it feels like this world's gone crazy.
> Grandpa, take me back to yesterday.
> When the line between right and wrong didn't seem so hazy.
> Did lovers really fall in love to stay,
> Stand beside each other come what may?

A promise really something people kept,
Not just something they would say,
And then forget?
Did families really bow their heads to pray?
Daddies really never go away?
Grandpa, tell me 'bout the good old days.[121]

Gentlemen, our kids don't need to be told about the good old days. They need to be *shown* the good old days. And the one to show them is you. In your home.

There are no shortcuts to building your outpost of civilization. But quite frankly, it really isn't that difficult. If you will take the time to turn off your in-house direct link to the nightly network feed of Baal thinking, God will make a difference in your family. In turn your family will be able to make a difference in some other family who's following Baal—even though they don't know who he is.

Just as the monks brought light and hope and civility to their troubled and dark times, may I suggest today that God desires to use Christian churches and families in the same way? As we stand tall and lead and love our families in the midst of a culture growing weaker by the day, may history one day look upon us and perhaps describe us in the following manner:

Instead of conforming to the barbarian culture of moral relativism, the Christian church and family in the 1990s modeled a counter-culture to a world engulfed by moral destruction and confusion. Thousands of Christian families were found across America, and they were characterized by discipline, creativity, and a coherence and moral order lacking in the culture around them. Christian fathers preserved the Scriptures by reading the Word of God to their families and introducing them to the collective wisdom of its pages. Christian families were busy, but not too busy to meet most evenings for the reading of Scripture and prayer. But they also worked hard in their appointed tasks and contributed to society by doing so. When little else shone forth, these Christian families, led by Christian fathers and husbands, provided attractive models of communities of caring and character. In the process, they preserved both faith and civilization itself. By holding on to such vestiges of civilization—faith, learning, and civility—these Christian husbands and wives and single parents, held back the night. Eventually, America emerged from the Dark Ages of moral relativism as revival swept the land. This launched the nation into a renewed period of cultural creativity, education, and art that reflected their trust and confidence in a holy and sovereign God.

If you will build according to the code, your house will be standing when the others are in shambles. And they will notice, and they will ask you what you did. And you can show them the code and introduce them to the One who wrote the code.

LORD OF LORDS

In the New Testament, Baal is known as Beelzebul, which literally means "Lord of the House." In Matthew 12:24-27, Jesus clearly identifies Beelzebul (Baal) as Satan.

Gentlemen, every house has a "lord." That's why Joshua was so emphatic to state "That as for me and my house, we shall serve the LORD" (Joshua 24:15).

There are many homes in this nation that have become outposts of Baal. He has deceived them and he ultimately is directing them. These homes of Baal desperately need to see the truth of the Lord of Lords. Satan (Baal) is the great deceiver. Do you remember that one of the names of Baal was "Rider of the Clouds"? That term came from an ancient poem about Baal that hit the chart in Elijah's day. The poem literally reads:

Seven years shall Baal,
Eight the Rider of the Clouds,
No Dew, No Rain,
No welling up of the deep,
No sweetness of Baal's voice."[122]

Baal, you'll remember, was widely thought to control the weather and the rainfall. This poem, which was known in the households of Baal, taught that Baal controlled the rain and even the dew!

But Elijah knew this was a fraud. When Elijah showed up for the first time before Ahab, he specifically said, "As the LORD, the God of Israel lives, before whom I stand, surely there shall be *neither dew nor rain* these years, except by my word (1 Kings 17:1)."

Elijah walked right into a household of Baal and spoke the real truth. Baal doesn't control the dew and rain. The God of Israel controls the dew and the rain. Satan has always been a deceiver and a deceiver of households and families. No wonder he had the gall to refer to Baal as the "The Rider of the Clouds."

Baal is not the rider of the clouds. The Lord Jesus Christ is the Rider of the Clouds:

> And I saw heaven opened; and behold, a white horse, and He who sat upon it is called Faithful and True; and in righteousness He judges and wages war. And His eyes are a flame of fire, and upon His Head are many diadems; and He has a name written upon Him which no one knows except Himself. And He is clothed with a robe dipped in blood; and His name is called The Word of God. And the armies which are in heaven, clothed in fine linen, white and clean, were following Him on white horses. And from His mouth comes a sharp sword, so that with it He may smite the nations; and he will rule them with a rod of iron; and He treads the wine press of the fierce wrath of God, the Almighty. And on His robe and on His thigh He has a name written, KING OF KINGS, AND LORD OF LORDS (Revelation 19:11-16).

Jesus Christ is Lord of all who desire to make their homes an outpost of civilization. One day the Lord Jesus is going to come back to this earth. He's coming to settle up. The Lord Jesus Christ not only rides for the brand, He is the brand. His name is above every name and His brand is above every brand. To those of us who have been chosen to ride for the brand, and stand for the brand, and fight for the brand, it should be said that of all men, we are most privileged. For it is our honor and our duty to occupy until He comes.

Until then, men, stand tall.

1. Review Moses' solemn charge in Deuteronomy 6:1-7. Note especially the instructions in verse 7. In Moses' day, families *walked* together to get places. It made for an ideal teaching time as dads could talk about the Lord, the Scriptures, and important issues as they were "on the way." Today's world is more hectic and fast-paced, but the need to "teach your children" is more important than ever. What are some practical ways dads can get alongside their sons and daughters in the course of a normal week? What role could outdoor activities play in this critical responsibility?

2. Moses speaks of teaching our children when we "lie down" and "rise up." How could this work in a typical American household? What are the most likely things that could get in the way of such teaching times? Why is such teaching becoming more and more crucial?

3. How long has it been since you've invited another Christian single, couple, or family into your home to share a meal, tap into a Bible study, or to watch you burn some hamburgers on the grill? Have you ever had a visiting missionary over for an evening of mutual encouragement? Have you considered hosting a neighborhood evangelistic Bible study in your home? In other words, are your kids getting the idea that your home is an *outpost* for the love and light of Jesus in a world growing darker by the day? What are some other ways you could help your family catch that vision?

1. Louis L'Amour, *Riding for the Brand* (New York: Bantam, 1986), 1.

2. Peggy Noonan, "You'd cry too if it happened to you," *Forbes*, 14 September 1992, 58.

3. Tom Bethell, "Culture War II," *The American Spectator*, July 1993, 16.

4. William J. Bennett, *The Index of Leading Cultural Indicators*, March 1993, Vol. I (Washington, D.C.: The Heritage Foundation).

5. Paul Harvey as quoted in *Leadership*, Winter 1987, Vol. VIII, No. I, 41.

6. Daniel Patrick Moynihan, cited by James Dale Davidson and Lord William Rees-Moog, *The Great Reckoning* (New York: Simon and Schuster, 1993), 291.

7. Phil Gramm, "Don't let judges set crooks free," *New York Times*, 8 July 1993, A13.

8. John Leo, "When cities give up their streets," *U.S. News and World Report*, 26 July 1993, 20.

9. Wess Roberts, *Leadership Secrets of Attila the Hun* (New York: Warner Books, 1985), iv, 2.

10. Charles W. Colson, *Against the Night* (Ann Arbor, Mich.: Servant Books, 1989), 23, 46.

11. Ibid., 39.

12. Allan Bloom, *The Closing of the American Mind* (New York: Simon and Schuster, 1987).

13. Colson, *Against the Night*, 41.

14. Bob DeMoss, "The Wise Watch What They Watch," Parental Guidance, *Focus on the Family*, August 1993, Vol. 4, No. 2.

15. Michael Medved, *Hollywood vs. America* (New York: Harper Collins, 1992), 147.

16. Charles R. Swindoll, *You and Your Child* (Nashville: Thomas Nelson Publishers, 1977), 64.

17. T. K. Abbott, cited by Fritz Rienecker, *A Linguistic Key to the Greek New Testament* (Grand Rapids, Mich.: Regency Reference, 1976), 582.

18. *Leadership*, Vol. XIV, No. 4, Fall 1993, 56. I have taken the liberty of changing some of the details of this story to fit the narrative.

19. Michael Green, source unknown.

20. Ken R. Canfield, *The 7 Secrets of Effective Fathers* (Grand Rapids, Mich.: Zondervan, 1992), 79.

21. Stuart Briscoe, source unknown.

22. Adam Smith, *Paper Money* (New York: Summit Books, 1981), 230.

23. John Eldredge and Greg Jesson, *Community Impact Curriculum*, Focus on the Family, Colorado Springs, 20.

24. David A. Noebel, *Understanding the Times* (Manitou Springs, Colo.: Summit Press, 1989), 622.

25. Cited by David A. Noebel, Richard John Neuhaus, *The Naked Public Square* (Grand Rapids, Mich.: Eerdmans, 1984), 95.

26. Cited by D. James Kennedy, "The Separation of Church and State," *American Family Association Journal*, January 1993, Vol. 17, No. 1, 18.

27. David Barton, *The Bulletproof George Washington* (Aledo, Texas: Wallbuilders Press, 1990).

28. Ibid., back cover.

29. Kennedy, "The Separation," 18.

30. Ibid.

31. Bruce L. Shelley, *Church History in Plain Language* (Waco, Tex.: Word, 1982), 361.

32. Ibid., 334.

33. Francis A. Schaeffer, *The Complete Works of Francis A. Schaeffer: A Christian Worldview, Volume Five, A Christian View of the West* (Westchester, Ill.: Crossway Books, 1982), 139.

34. Eldredge and Jesson, *Community Impact Curriculum*, 21.

35. Edward L. Lederman, "When Students Take Guns into School," *Human Events*, 9 May 1992.

36. Charles Colson, "Clogged Courts Drain the Nation," *Jubilee*, April 1992, 7.

37. Ibid., 7.

38. Eldredge and Jesson, *Community Impact Curriculum*, 7. Also *National & International Religion Report*, 18 November 1991, Vol. 5, No. 24, 7.

39. Rush Limbaugh, *The Way Things Ought to Be* (New York: Pocket Books, 1992), 299.

40. Ibid., 104.

41. *The Wittenberg Door*, Interview with Rush Limbaugh, November 1993.

42. Os Guiness, *The American Hour* (New York: The Free Press, 1993), 180.

43. Gary T. Amos, *Defending the Declaration* (Brentwood, Tenn.: Wolgemuth & Hyatt, 1989), 39.

44. "United States Constitution," *World Book Encyclopedia*, Vol. 17 (Chicago: Field Enterprises, 1959), 8370.

45. William Sanford Lasor, David Allan Hubbard, and Frederic William Bush, *Old Testament Survey* (Grand Rapids, Mich.: Eerdmans Publishing, 1982), 266.

46. Leon Wood, *A Survey of Israel's History*, 310.

47. James Edward Anderson, "The Idolatrous Worship of Baal by Israel," unpublished doctoral dissertation, Dallas Theological Seminary, 1975, 396.

48. Gayle Reaves, "Abortion Rights Backers, Foes Re-examining Tactics," *Dallas Morning News*, 28 June 1993, 1A.

49. Albert Gore, *Earth in the Balance* (New York: The Penguin Group, 1993), 23.

50. John Aaron Flack, "The Influence of Canaanite Civilization on the Children of Israel," unpublished master's thesis, Dallas Theological Seminary, 1958, 11.

51. Charles Swindoll, *The Life and Times of Elijah* (Anaheim, Calif.: Insight for Living, 1992), 4.

52. J. Oswald Sanders, *Robust in Faith* (Chicago: Moody Press, 1965), 125.

53. Gore, *Earth in the Balance*, 119.

54. Ibid.

55. Chuck and Donna McIlhenny, *When the Wicked Seize a City* (Lafayette, La: Huntington House, 1993), 40.

56. Roger J. Magnuson, *Are Gay Rights Right?* (Portland, Ore.: Multnomah Press, 1990), 15.

57. McIlhenny, "When the wicked seize a city," 126.

58. Ibid., 127.

59. Ibid., 18.

60. Cited by George Grant and Mark A. Horne, *Legislating Immorality* (Chicago: Moody, 1993), 33.

61. Dr. Stanley Monteith, cited by "The Gay Agenda" video tape, "The Report" (Lancaster, Calif.).

62. Robert H. Knight, "The Homosexual Agenda in Schools," *Family Research Council Insight*, 11 June 1993, 2.

63. Family Research Report, July-August 1992, 1. (Address: P.O. Box 2091, Washington, D.C., 20013.)

64. Matthys Levy and Mario Salvadori, *Why Buildings Fall Down* (New York: W. W. Norton & Company, 1992), 221.

65. James Edward Anderson, *The Idolatrous Worship of Baal*, unpublished doctoral dissertation, Dallas Theological Seminary, May 1975, 159.

66. McIlhenny, "When the wicked seize a city," 78.

67. Ibid., 212.

68. Magnuson, *Are Gay Rights Right?*, 31.

69. Robert H. Knight, "Homosexuality Is Not a Civil Right" (Washington: Family Research Council In Focus).

70. Magnuson, *Are Gay Rights Right?*.

71. Knight, "Homosexuality Is Not a Civil Right," 4.

72. Grant, *Legislating Immorality*, 67.

73. Robert H. Knight, Key finding of an analysis of one hundred punitive separations for homosexual conduct from the U. S. Army, 1989-1992, Family Research Council In Focus, 700 Thirteenth St. NW, Suite 500, Washington, D.C. 20005.

74. Grant, *Legislating Immorality*, 43.

75. Dr. Paul Cameron, "Child Molestation and Homosexuality," Family Research Institute, 3.

76. Ibid., 4.

77. Ibid., 5-6.

78. Grant, *Legislating Immorality*, 42.

79. Magnuson, *Are Gay Rights Right?*, 13.

80. Ibid., 14.

81. Robert H. Knight, "Flawed Science Nurtures Genetic Origin for Homosexuality," Family Research Council In Focus.

82. Ibid., 1.

83. Grant, *Legislating Immorality*, 170. (Author's note: I am indebted to George Grant for supplying this information on homosexual groups.)

84. Ibid., 197.

85. *Christianity Today*, "Homosexual Debate Strains Campus Harmony," 22 November 1993, 38.

86. Stanton L. Jones, "The Loving Opposition, Speaking the truth in a climate of hate," *Christianity Today*, 19 July 1993, 24.

87. Ibid., 20

88. Ibid.

89. Lewis Smedes, *Sex for Christians* (Grand Rapids, Mich.: William B. Eerdmans, 1976), 72.

90. Cited by Trudy Hutchens, "Homosexuality: Born or Bred?" Family Voice Magazine, Concerned Women of America, June 1993.

91. Joseph Nicolosi, Ph.D., *Repairative Therapy of Male Homosexuality* (Northvale, N.J.: Jason Aronson, 1991), inside cover flap.

92. *Dallas Morning News*, 27 June 1993, 1A.

93. "For the Love of Kids: What should be done with a teacher who belongs to a pedophile group but has a spotless record?" *Time*, 1 November 1993, 51.

94. Ibid.

95. "100 Minutes to Freedom," *People Weekly Magazine*, 11 January 1993, 52.

96. J. Oswald Sanders, *Robust in Faith* (Chicago, Ill.: Moody Press, 1965), 126.

97. Matthew Henry, *Commentary on the Whole Bible* (Grand Rapids, Mich.: Zondervan Publishing House, Regency Reference Library, 1961), 385.

98. J. Vernon McGee, *Through the Bible*, Vol. II (Nashville, Tenn.: Thomas Nelson Publishers, 1982), 282.

99. Ibid.

100. Cited in *Leadership*, Spring 1983, Vol. IV, No. 2, 93.

101. Warren W. Wiersbe, *Wiersbe's Expository Outlines on the Old Testament* (Wheaton, Ill.: Victor Books, 1993), 318.

102. Wilson L. Harrell, "Facing Fire: Combat Creates Entrepreneurial Leaders," *Success Magazine*, February 1993, Vol. 40, No. 1, 9.

103. John Gardner, *On Leadership* (New York: The Free Press, 1990), 169.

104. Oswald Chambers, source unknown.

105. John Luther, source unknown.

106. Roger von Oech, *A Whack on the Side of the Head* (New York: Warner Books, 1983), 6.

107. Ibid., 25.

108. Gardner, *On Leadership* , 2.

109. Ibid., 4.

110. David R. Johnson, *The Light Behind the Star* (Sisters, Ore.: Questar Publishers, 1989), 93-96.

111. Tom Clancy, *Submarine: A Guided Tour Inside a Nuclear Warship* (New York: Berkley Books, 1993), xix.

112. Ross Campbell, *How to Really Love Your Child* (Wheaton, Ill.: Victor Books, 1984).

113. Chuck Colson, "The Human Animal," *Breakpoint*, 10 August 1993, No. 30810.

114. Cited by Warren Bennis, *On Becoming a Leader* (New York: Addison Wesley Publishing, 1989), 197.

115. *Leadership*, To Illustrate, Summer 1992, Vol. XIII, No. 3, 47.

116. *Leadership*, To Illustrate, Winter 1993, Vol. XIV, No. 1, 49.

117. Colson, *Against the Night*.

118. Karyn Henley, *The Beginner's Bible* (Sisters, Ore.: Questar Publishers, 1989).

119. Mack Thomas, *The Wonder Bible* (Sisters, Ore.: Questar Publishers, 1993).

120. Allan Bloom, *The Closing of the American Mind* (New York: Simon and Schuster, 1987).

121. "Grandpa (Tell Me 'Bout the Good Old Days)," The Judds, ©1986, RCA.

122. Cited by Anderson, *The Idolatrous Worship*, 355.

10-23

W9-ANV-165

Early Dutch
Painting

Albert Châtelet

Early Dutch Painting

Painting in the northern Netherlands in the fifteenth century

Translated by Christopher Brown and Anthony Turner

The Fondation Education et Recherche, the Ministère des Universités, and the Université des Sciences humaines in Strasbourg have provided grants for the publication of this book.

Published by
WELLFLEET PRESS
110 Enterprise Avenue
Secaucus, New Jersey 07094

World English language rights reserved by
William S. Konecky Associates, Inc.
New York, N.Y. 10011

ISBN: 1-55521-255-7

Printed and bound in Italy.

Contents

This book is dedicated to my father,
Albert Châtelet (1884–1960),
on the twentieth anniversary
of his death.

Acknowledgment

The study presented in this book is the result of thirty years of research, which explains the amount of help, support and understanding from family, friends, colleagues and acquaintances that it required. Therefore, to all those I cannot mention by name, I want to proffer my heartfelt thanks.

My first grateful thoughts are also for those art historians who are no longer with us and who so generously received and counselled me: Max J. Friedländer, Friedrich Winkler, Erwin Panofsky, Ludwig Baldass, Frits Lugt, Hoogewerff, Byvanck, Horst Gerson, S. J. Gudlaugsson, Frithjof van Thienen, Jacques Lavalleye, Paul Coremans, Bob Delaissé, Albert Philippot; and those who guided my studies: Michel Florisoone, Edouard Michel, Elie Lambert, Georges Gaillard, as well as those who helped them along: Professors Vittorio Viale and Luigi Malle.

Several institutions provided support at decisive points: the French Ministry of Foreign Affairs, the National Centre for Scientific Research (CNRS), the government of the Netherlands, the Rijksbureau voor Kunsthistorische Documentatie, the Institut royal du Patrimoine artistique, the Brussel's Art Seminar, the Fondation Custodia, the department of paintings at the Louvre, Paris, and that museum's curator-in-chief, Germain Bazin, as well as all his assistants during the 1950's, university libraries such as the Jacques Doucet in Paris and the ones in Lille and Strasbourg, and the conservation library of the Louvre, the library of the Lille museum and the Strasbourg museum and the Université des sciences humaines in Strasbourg.

Many people in Holland helped me in numerous ways: Professors van Regteren Altena, van Gelder, Josua Bruyn, K. G. Boon, the foremost expert on the period under study here, whom I never consulted in vain, although our methods and opinions are at variance, Professor Jongkees, the archivists Misses Prinsen and Kurtz, Messieurs Ooosterbann and Temminck, the scholar Michel Thierry de Bie Doleman and Dr. Bouvy.

Specialists from other countries also gave of their time; in Belgium: Hermann Liebaers, Roger Sneyers, Roger d'Hulst, Suzanne Sulzberger, Nicole Veronee-Verhaegen, Antoine de Schryver, Jacqueline Folie, Micheline Comblen-Sonkes; in Germany: Paul Pieper: in Italy: Michelangelo Muraro, Anna Serena Fava, Dr. Molfese and his aunts; in Austria: Professor G. Heinz and Dr. Knab; in the United States: Robert Calckins, Creighton Gilbert, Haverkamp Begemann and James Marrow.

In France, Charles Sterling, to whom I owe so much, deserves particular tribute, as do all those who, with him, provided the university backing and sanction for this project: André Chastel, Louis Grodecki and Pierre Chaunu. Nor could I forget Countess de Charnacé, daughter of Count Durrieu, nor especially Mrs Gruner Schlumberger, who spontaneously and very generously gave the support of her foundation so that this book could be published.

I also want to thank my original publishers, Office du Livre, and their director, Jean Hirschen, as well as all the people there who undertook to produce this beautiful art book. To my translators too, Christopher Brown and Anthony Turner, I owe a debt of gratitude for their fine English translation.

And finally, I can never forget all the precious aid provided by my family: my father and mother, my wife, Liliane Châtelet-Lange, who with great patience translated this book into German, and my sisters Suzanne and Yvonne Châtelet, as well as my aunt, Maria Châtelet.

My thoughts gratefully dwell on all of these people, here or in the hereafter, as we go to print on this book, which owes so much to them, and in this small way I would like to associate their names to the completion of this study.

Mundolsheim, July 1980

Introduction

The murder of John the Fearless on the bridge at Montereau in 1419 had consequences which were not merely political. It precipitated a significant change in the world of art which had been in the making for some years and was to culminate in the collapse of the position of Paris as the artistic centre of northern Europe. John's successor as Duke of Burgundy, Philip the Good, abandoned the King of France's party and retired to his territories in the north, where he set out to create a court glittering enough to attract artists who in the past would have sought their fortunes at the royal court or in the service of French dukes.

These events encouraged the emergence of a new style of painting which had its beginnings in the studios of Robert Campin (the Master of Flémalle) at Tournai, of Jan van Eyck, first at The Hague and later at Lille and Bruges, and, lastly, of Rogier van der Weyden at Tournai and then at Brussels. Without disappearing completely, the Gothic elegance of the Parisian court of the fourteenth century came largely to be superseded by a scrupulous realism, alive to the appearances of the everyday world. The completion in 1432 of the polyptych 'The Mystic Lamb' (in the Church of St. Bavo at Ghent) was a supremely important landmark in this style of art, which was to continue to flourish until the beginning of the sixteenth century. Three generations of artists worked in this realistic manner: after that of its founders came the generation of Dieric Bouts and Petrus Christus, followed by that of Hans Memling, Hugo van der Goes and Gerard David.

These 'early Dutch painters' came to dominate northern European painting: both French and German art were to be profoundly influenced by them. Since the beginning of the present century a number of important exhibitions, above all the Bruges Exhibition of 1902 and those held in Paris in 1935 and 1947, have made us familiar with their works. Eminent art historians, among them Max J. Friedländer, Charles de Tolnay and Erwin Panofsky,[1] have studied and analysed their style.

However, the precise geographical area of their activity remains vague. Certainly, no scholar would think of confining it to the county of Flanders. Tournai, where Robert Campin (the Master of Flémalle) worked, was a free city, directly linked to the French crown, while surrounded by the lands of the county of Hainault. Consequently, there is a great temptation to equate the limits of the Flemish Primitives' activity with the physical boundaries of the territories which Philip the Good and Charles the Bold united under their control: Flanders, Artois, Hainault and Brabant, as well as the county of Holland and Zeeland and even Luxembourg and Guelders, including such enclaves as Tournai. In effect, this is to confine the activity of these painters within the areas which, together with the ecclesiastical principalities of Liège and Utrecht, were to form the three modern states of Belgium, the Netherlands and Luxembourg.

Nevertheless, as early as 1894, A. Pit tried to establish that the area which forms the modern Netherlands had possessed a distinct and independent artistic tradition since the fourteenth century. It was the same idea which, more or less explicitly, was to inspire two important exhibitions, one held in 1935 at the Boymans Museum in Rotterdam (*Jeroen Bosch—Noord-Nederlandsche Primitieven*) and the other in 1958 at the Rijksmuseum in Amsterdam (*Middeleuwse Kunst der Noorderlijke Nederlanden*). In 1936 and 1937 Hoogewerff was likewise to attempt, not without an element of chauvinism, to present a synthesis of this pictorial art in the first two volumes of his study *De Nord-nederlandsche Schilderkunst.*[2]

At about the same time, A. Byvanck, while engaged in cataloguing illuminated manuscripts made in the northern Netherlands, discovered that he was dealing with a style of art which had little in common with the Flemish miniature.[3] In contrast with the refined and cultivated world of the latter, these were unsophisticated works, humbler in appearance. In a brilliant essay, Delaissé set himself to define the style of the men who created them, whom he saw as deeply influenced by the new piety (the 'Devotio Moderna') which had its birth in the circle of Geert Groote at the end of the fourteenth century.[4]

It was here that art historians found common ground with the historians, who had long before shown that, even after its annexation by Philip the Good, the county of Holland and Zeeland had retained more contact with the ecclesiastical principality, i.e. Utrecht, and with Guelders than with Flanders or even with Hainault, although like them it had long been under the domination of the House of Bavaria.[5] Of course, one could not go so far as to talk of a Dutch 'nation': as Huizinga rightly insisted,[6] such a concept did not exist at the time. However, there were enough common interests to give substance to the notion of a certain unity of the northern Netherlands.

The question, therefore, could and should be raised of the existence of such a unity of the north Netherlands in terms of painting.[7] Here the answer was more difficult to establish: the existing paintings are few, many having been destroyed during the iconoclasm of the sixteenth century, and the written evidence is sparse. Already, in 1604, the painter Karel van Mander (the so-called Vasari of the North) was experiencing difficulty in gleaning information about fifteenth-century artists, although he did succeed in establishing their existence and their importance. And so it became a matter of undertaking a thorough archaeological analysis of the surviving works, of relating them to the few accessible documents, of placing them in a chronological development, of attempting an examination of the methods of their creation from the few remaining examples, of defining, in fact, the originality of this art. Such a study is undertaken here. And more than one reader, faced with the artistic personalities as presented, will doubtless experience reactions similar to those of Karel van Mander, who wrote in 1604 on the subject of Albert van Ouwater: 'I came to realise, somewhat to my surprise, that he revealed himself at a very early stage as an oil painter of great distinction and... that he was a contemporary of Jan van Eyck'.[8] Nowadays, Geertgen tot Sint Jans, for example, is not unknown, but there was a time when he was regarded—rather too hastily, it would seem—as a second-rate follower of Hugo van der Goes. As for the Master of the *Virgo inter Virgines*, he deserves to be ranked almost with Bosch.

Examination of the surviving evidence has also served to underline the importance of the stay of Jan van Eyck in The Hague from 1422 to 1424. The presence of a painter from the southern Netherlands must have made a decisive contribution to the formation of a new and original art. He was certainly to play an integral part in the history of those painters whom we propose to label 'early Dutch painters'.

Publisher's Note: The numbers in italics in parentheses refer to the catalogue numbers. The numbers in the margins refer to the caption numbers in both text and the catalogue.

I. The beginnings
The age of the counts of Holland and the House of Bavaria-Straubing

The historical setting

Although the Hundred Years War left its mark on the powers of western Europe during the second half of the fourteenth century, the Netherlands remained untouched. The ties of kinship which at one time united the Bavarian ruling family with the French crown[1] did not draw those rulers and their domains into the conflict.[2]

At that moment, the towns of the north were at the height of their prosperity. The cities of the Rhine, from Guelders to Dordrecht, grew rich on the flourishing river traffic. Dordrecht alone, clinging too firmly to its almost unenforceable right to exact a shipping toll, began slowly to decline. The towns of the county of Holland were expanding their industrial activities, which depended on the agriculture of the countryside.

Altogether, this would have seemed a favourable state of affairs were it not for the worsening political situation affecting Holland and Guelders, though not, at that time, the ecclesiastical principality. The two counties were torn periodically by clashes between opposing factions. In Holland the struggle, ostensibly over the succession, was between the *Kabeljauwen* ('codfish') and the *Hoeksen* ('fish-hooks'). When William IV[3] died childless in 1345, the *Hoeksen* pressed the claims of his sister, wife of the Emperor Louis of Bavaria, while the *Kabeljauwen* took up the cause of the son of the Emperor William. The background to this feud was, of course, fraught with deeper and more complex issues.

Fired originally by rivalry between opposing groups of nobles, the conflict can ultimately be seen as a local manifestation of a more general state of affairs: the revolt, throughout Europe, of the prosperous urban bourgeoisie against the privileged lives of the aristocracy.[4] The *Hoeksen* represented the interests of the old nobility. They were led by the Brederode in association with the traditional rulers of the counties, the Wassenaar, Montfoort and Duvenwoorde families. Although able, from time to time, to win the loyalty of a town from their rivals—in the case of Delft, for instance—or occasionally to call upon the support of artisans by opposing the patrician bourgeoisie, they were essentially attached to the privileges of a society in the process of disintegration.

Their rivals, the *Kabeljauwen*, were led by the noble Arkel, Egmont and Borselen families. The strength of this group, however, lay in the support of commercial towns, chiefly Dordrecht, still at that time the richest and most thriving, but also Rotterdam, Schiedam, Delft (at least in the beginning), Haarlem and Amsterdam. In these towns it was the bourgeoisie who held the real power, and their prosperity derived from the thriving agriculture of the countryside, their expanding commercial activities and their ports, which were among the busiest in northern Europe. The very name of this faction—whether chosen by its members or a gibe in which they gloried—bears witness, if this were needed, to the important part played by the bourgeoisie of the ports. Even their hat, the sign to which they rallied, was unmistakably bourgeois.

The conflict within Guelders followed a similar pattern: disputes over the right to succession after the death of Reynald II, which provoked discord between his two sons Reynald III and Edward, and later their half-sisters Matilda and Maria. Here again, behind the opposing factions lay class rivalry. It was above all the Rhenish towns of Nijmegen and Arnhem which were trying to escape as far as possible from the counts' control.

Only the ecclesiastical principality was relatively free of troubles. After a certain amount of conflict preceding the nomination as bishop of Jan van Arkel (1342–64) there followed a succession of strong prelates who imposed their authority on the entire principality: Jan van Virneburg (1364–71), formerly bishop of Münster: Arnoul van Hoorn (1371–8), a canon from Cologne who came to Utrecht from the Avignon curia; Floris van Wevelinchoven (1379–98), who also came from the episcopal seat of Münster; and finally the former bishop of Strasbourg, Fredrik van Blankenheim (1393–1423). All of them placed temporal matters before spiritual duties and crushed any attempt at uprising or claim to independence. This situation greatly favoured the interests of the episcopal town of Utrecht, which profited so much from this administration that its artisans, painters and sculptors, as well as other professions, all flourished.

If the bishops were first and foremost temporal rulers, they were nevertheless concerned with the religious life of their

1 *Epitaph of Canon Hendrik van Rijn*, c.1363, Antwerp,
Musée des Beaux-Arts (*1*)

subjects. They held regular diocesan synods, and it was in this atmosphere, inspired by the charismatic personality of Geert Groote, that the 'Devotio Moderna' first took hold. The bishops made no opposition to the movement and in fact even encouraged the establishment, in their own lands and elsewhere, of the Brethren of the Common Life and the Congregation of Windesheim.[5]

Works of the fourteenth century

Before 1400, panel painting was virtually unknown in the north Netherlands and in most of northern Europe. There are only two works, or 'epitaphs', which testify to its existence, the epitaph of Hendrik van Rijn (in the Musée Royal des Beaux-Arts at Antwerp) and that of the Lords of Montfoort (in the Rijksmuseum in Amsterdam). The fact that these are rare and isolated examples might discourage us from studying them in any depth: nevertheless, it is worth looking at them fairly closely, for the first, at least, has some surprising qualities.

Both paintings came originally from the bishopric of Utrecht. The older can be dated around 1363, the year in which Hendrik van Rijn died, according to an inscription on the painting itself (*1*). Its technique is close to that of Master Theodoric, who was working at Karlstein at about the same time.[6] The panel has a gold background on which there is a pattern stamped in relief—here made up of squares each containing an encircled lion—which means that the painted areas lie in a slight depression. Two characteristics meet and yet are also opposed in the painting of the figures. The stereotyped linearity of the folds of the robes of the Virgin and St. John and the shape of their silhouettes derive from the Gothic tradition, which had become hackneyed through over-use. The large part played by these two figures in the impression of the whole might detract from the panel's interest; however, the painting of the body of Christ and the face of the kneeling donor is surprisingly vigorous. A fairly heavy application of paint gives them volume, as do the dull colour tones, which now appear even darker because of the dirt which has lodged in the depressions of the surface. On one side there is an emaciated body, its flesh withered and limp, blue in

death and stained with blood; on the other a simple face, not
beautiful but very striking. The style of this figure has often been
compared with that of the contemporary portrait of *John the Good*
(in the Louvre in Paris).[7] The incisiveness and sense of plasticity
of the latter are invariably so highly praised that the Utrecht
epitaph appears weak in contrast. We should not, however, lose
sight of the considerable difference in scale between the two
works, as well as their different functions: while one is a portrait
in the true sense of the term, the other is merely a face inserted
into a religious scene. Bearing these differences in mind, the two
works appear to have rather more in common. The clear line of
John the Good's profile is achieved through the use of a plain
gold background, while the insertion of a small face amidst the
decorative stamping of the Utrecht epitaph makes such precise
definition impossible. On the other hand, the actual modelling
of the features is almost identical in the two panels. The quality
of the Utrecht painting is revealed more clearly if it is compared
with the works of Master Theodoric at Karlstein. The two
artists worked in an identical technique, yet in one case the
Gothic tradition is still dominant whereas, in the other, all linear
grace has been cast aside in favour of a greater expressiveness.

Whatever critical reservations may have been expressed
about the *Epitaph of Hendrik van Rijn,* it must be placed among
the rare examples of a great tradition during the second half of
the fourteenth century. It may be less advanced in style than the
works of Theodoric or even, in certain respects, of the *John the
Good,* but it still belongs to that tradition.

The second painting might, on the other hand, tend to detract
from the importance of the episcopal workshops—in the first

analysis, at least. It is more trite in style and its execution is
rather poor. On their epitaph (*2*), the Lords of Montfoort are
lined up in a rather simple, uninteresting manner. There is no
attempt at modelling, the workmanship is poor, the firmly
drawn outlines follow late Gothic models. Just as the *Calvary of
the Tanners* is a poor example of the tradition of painting in
Bruges, so the Rijksmuseum picture appears surprisingly weak
when compared with the more distinguished quality of the
epitaph in the museum at Antwerp.

However, we should not remain content with a first
impression. Although the composition and placing of the
figures are undeniably weak, the general arrangement of the
picture and certain of its details reveal a link with a more
sophisticated centre of painting. The Virgin's throne, architec-
turally conceived, is of the type so brilliantly developed by
André Beauneveu in the Duke of Berry's Psalter. It is also to be
found in manuscript illuminations of the Master of the
Parement de Narbonne and the artists who followed him in the
Très Belles Heures de Notre Dame. It is in this group that we find
similarities to the Virgin and Child of the Amsterdam panel and
its probable source, the *Coronation of the Virgin* on folio 100 verso
of the volume known as the *Turin-Milan Hours.*[8] The establishment of this connection would suggest a date for the Amsterdam picture as late as around 1375–80.

At that date, the painting would still bear witness to a contact
with a more cultivated *milieu.* Whether this was Paris, where the
Master of the Parement de Narbonne worked, or Liège, is of

2

little importance[9]: in either case, the Amsterdam painting can only appear as a rather inept derivation of a work in a more sophisticated style. It does, however, confirm that the episcopal workshops were open to outside influences, and, despite its poor quality, testifies quite as much as the *Epitaph of Hendrik van Rijn* to the existence of an important artistic tradition during the second half of the fourteenth century.

The beginning of the fifteenth century in the ecclesiastical principality and in Guelders

The first decades of the fifteenth century left behind them little evidence of artistic activity in the ecclesiastical principality. There is however one notable exception: a fresco worth consideration here by virtue of the quality of its execution, and its reasonably satisfactory state of preservation (*3*). This is a *Crucifixion* in an arch of the second chapel in the south aisle of Utrecht Cathedral, dedicated to Guy d'Avesnes, bishop from 1301 to 1317. When its coating of dirt was removed, it became clear that the fresco dated from a later period than the chapel itself. The figures, the costumes, and the composition as a whole, still belong to the tradition of the fourteenth century and so it is unlikely to have been painted later than the early years of the fifteenth century.

The fresco's originality is not to be found, however, in its composition, which is still close to that of the *Epitaph of Hendrick van Rijn,* but in its technique. The expressions of the figures are rendered in fine brush-strokes which accentuate the features and refine their forms. The face of St. John, raised towards heaven, is marked by bitter grief. That of the agonised Christ, surrounded by a web of matted hair, is already emaciated and relaxed in the serenity of death. In the context of the Gothic style which still pervades the whole, such sensitive treatment is remarkable. We can find similarities in contemporary miniatures. The most beautiful example is the frontispiece to the *Bressanone Missal* made for Bishop Zweder van Culemborgh in about 1425.[10] This last composition reflects a search for volume, a desire for a simplification of line which would seem to point to a more advanced tradition.

This fresco therefore assumes a particular importance in that it bears striking witness to the existence of a tradition of painting in Utrecht in the early decades of the fifteenth century. The works executed in Guelders on the other hand—or more precisely those of whose production in Guelders we can be certain—are rare and of no great importance. The most remarkable is the large altarpiece of the Church of Saint Walburga at Zutphen (*4*). In the centre are the Virgin and St. John the Evangelist, one on either side of the Cross. The Cross is now empty but must once have supported the figure of Christ, probably sculpted in wood. On the wings are Mary Magdalene and Mary Cleophas. The four figures stand out

against a dark-blue sky scattered with golden stars. They are stiff, a little dry, probably fairly late provincial imitations of the International Gothic style. It is very difficult to give a precise date to works of this type: this kind of slightly mechanical interpretation of models which were perhaps well-known could only have developed at a relatively late date, about 1425–30.

With so few examples to judge from, any attempt to establish the existence of an artistic tradition in Guelders might seem vain. Recently there have been animated discussions about the origin of certain manuscript illuminations which some writers believe were made in Guelders and others in the diocese of Utrecht.[11] Archival evidence suggests that the problem is really a false one, as it is known that some artists worked in both places. Jan van Merlo, who acquired citizenship of Utrecht in 1398, appears to have come originally from Guelders. In 1415, at the time of the banishment of the Lochorst faction, he was among the exiles and probably followed the dean of the Cathedral chapter into Guelders. William de Engelsman did not become a citizen of Utrecht until 1415, but in that year he also was exiled and is mentioned as the 'servant of the dean' of the cathedral, whom he doubtless followed into Guelders.[12] As far as the manuscripts themselves are concerned, we can establish certain close similarities. Even if we agree with G. I. Lieftinck[13] that the Master of Otto of Moerdrecht is not an individual so much as a style, we find this style in a manuscript made in Arnhem such as the *Breviary of Mary of Guelders*[14] and in another made in Utrecht such as the *Treatise of Nicholas of Lyra* written for the Carthusian of Utrecht, Otto of Moerdrecht.[15] It would certainly appear that there were frequent contacts and exchanges between the two neighbouring regions.

The style of the manuscript illuminations leads us to similar conclusions, for it is virtually impossible to distinguish between a Guelders and a Utrecht 'manner'. There is no marked difference of style between the illustrations of the *Treatise of Dirc van Delft,* probably written near Utrecht at the Charterhouse of Nieuwlicht[16] in about 1404, and the *Breviary of Mary of Guelders,* written at the convent of Marienborn near Arnhem in about 1415.[17] In both works the main artist is less concerned with the minute description of detail but has some happy inventions in his evocation of the different scenes and attitudes of the figures. The principal artist of the *Breviary* is probably more familiar with the products of the great Parisian workshops and there is a certain grace about the rhythm of his compositions. But the sense of expression and the remarkably naturalistic treatment of religious scenes are common to both works.[18]

And so it would seem, as far as manuscript illumination is concerned, that the regions of Guelders and Utrecht formed a single artistic *milieu.* This idea is implicit in recent writings, but no author has stated it openly. K.G. Boon proposes the hypothesis of a movement of artists from the court of Guelders to Utrecht on the death of Duke Reynald IV in 1423.[19] Hoogewerff, who wants to isolate a Guelders tradition, does not

3 *Christ on the Cross, c.*1410, Utrecht, cathedral (*3*) ▷

even admit the participation of Utrecht artists in the illustration of the *Bible of Lochorst,* thought to have been written during the exile in Arnhem of the dean of the Cathedral. V. Finke takes the opposite view, defending the pre-eminence of the episcopal city and underlining the importance of the artists' travels.[20]

This situation, which as far as manuscripts are concerned seems quite clearcut, may well also apply to painting. The rarity of extant works does not allow us to form conclusions. Nevertheless it would be misleading to state categorically that pictures which seem to reflect the art of Guelders could not have been painted in Utrecht. However, there were painters from Guelders who found fame through their work in noble courts elsewhere. We must therefore look at their art in an attempt to establish the extent to which they retained something of the style of their native country.

The *émigrés* from Guelders: Jean Malouel

The work of Friedrich Gorissen has established that four famous artists came originally from Nijmegen: Jean Malouel and his nephews, the Limbourg Brothers.[21] Jean, the son of Willem Malouel, worked in 1396 for Queen Isabella of Bavaria and then went into the service of Philip the Bold, Duke of Burgundy. He may have returned to his native town in 1405; he was certainly there in 1413. He preserved links with his native country, if only because of the interests he retained there. The same is true of his nephews, Paul, Herman and Johan, sons of his sister and the sculptor Arndt. Herman and Paul are mentioned for the first time in 1399; they entered the service of the Duke of Burgundy in 1402 and then that of John of Berry in 1411. But we also find mention of them from time to time in their native town: Herman and Johan in June 1410, Jean on 5 December 1413, Paul and Jean on 6 and 15 March 1415.

This clearly poses the problem of their collaboration. In the case of the Limbourgs, the question is answered almost as soon as it is posed. A document of 1400 tells us that Jean Malouel sent for his nephews 'Herman and Jacquemin in order that they should learn the goldsmith's craft from Alebret de Bolure, goldsmith living in Paris.' Only in the case of Paul is the situation more complicated since there is no mention of him before 1402, in Dijon. It seems probable, however, that he like his brothers had previously gone abroad to learn his trade. It remains open to question whether this training took place only in France, at the royal and ducal courts, or in Italy as the recurrence of certain reminiscences of Italian works of art in the *œuvre* of the three brothers suggests.[22]

The case of Malouel is far less easy to resolve. Although we can follow his move from the service of the Queen of France to that of the Duke of Burgundy, we have no precise knowledge of his career before his arrival at the Parisian court. However, both his father Willem and his uncle Hermann are mentioned as

painters working in Nijmegen[23] and therefore it seems likely that he was trained locally.

The only way to test this hypothesis is to examine the works or rather the one certain work by Jean Malouel which has survived, *The Christ on the Cross with the Martyrdom of St. Denis* (Paris, Louvre 6). His authorship of even this painting has been doubted;[24] and indeed the question of its attribution is complex. It was part of the Bartholomey collection in Dijon, which was sold in 1843. It was then thought to have come from the Charterhouse of Champmol. It is known that in 1398 five altarpieces were ordered from Malouel and in 1416 Henri Bellechose, his successor as *valet de chambre* to the Duke of Burgundy, received ground pigments in order to 'parfaire' (literally perfect) a painting depicting the life of St. Denis. The Louvre painting was therefore attributed to him and considered to be a work left unfinished by Malouel at his death and completed by Bellechose. The identification was reinforced by the fact that the document of 1398 gave the measurements of '5 tables de bois pour autel' (five panels of wood for altarpieces) ordered from the carpenter Daniel Hobel[25] and one of these would seem to correspond more or less with the measurements of the painting in the Louvre. Nicole Reynaud, however, discovering that these measurements had been read incorrectly, considered that this identification should be questioned.

In the months following the purchase of the wood, Malouel also acquired some knives 'pour racler plusieurs tables et tableaux que ledit peintre fait pour les autels de l'église des Chartreux'[26] (in order to scrape several panels which the said painter is making for the altars of the church of the Carthusians). The artist therefore himself prepared the wood, which had been delivered to him untreated. The possibility cannot be excluded that he even recut the panels which had been delivered to him already assembled but not cut to size. However, even if the five panels delivered to him were of the same length, they were of differing widths. It is hard to reconcile this with the usual practice in the case of panels prepared for painting, which dictated that the ratio between length and breadth accord with a more elaborate system of measurement. This is clear if we think in terms of unprepared panels made up of planks of wood which may have come from one or more trees, and which would be of the same length but of differing widths according to the way in which they had been cut. Moreover in 1401 Malouel was paid for 'l'entaillure de un grant pannone' (the shaping of a large panel).[27] This was in fact a painting which he had to adapt for a new location, but it confirms that the artist was able to carry out such routine preparatory work.

There is more to add. It is known, in fact, that six altars were consecrated in the Charterhouse in March 1389, those of St. Peter, St. Agnes, the Chapter itself, St. Denis, the Sacristy and Our Lady.[28] The most important, that of Our Lady, was to have been surmounted by an altarpiece by Jacques de Baerze and Melchior Broederlam. The paintings ordered from Malouel must therefore have been destined for the other five altars, and indeed there was among them an altar dedicated to St. Denis. In 1791 the original picture was no longer in the Charterhouse.

There were, however, in the inventory of that year two canvases by Carle van Loo which were pendants on the altars of the brothers' choir, one of which was dedicated to St. George and the other to St. Denis.[29] There is in the Louvre an altarpiece of the same size as that of the *Martyrdom of St. Denis,* which retains essentially the same composition but is dedicated to St. George and includes a Carthusian donor. Its style, however, would seem to place it 30 or 40 years later. It also comes from the Bartholomey collection and is also said to have come from the Charterhouse.[30] The situation is therefore clear. In the course of the fifteenth century a second altarpiece dedicated to St. George was commissioned by a monk in imitation of the first dedicated

4 MALOUEL. *Christ on the Cross and Martyrdom of St. Denis,* Paris, Louvre (6)

to St. Denis. In the eighteenth century these paintings were replaced by those of van Loo and then they passed at an unknown date into a private collection or alternatively were acquired directly from the Charterhouse by Bartholomey.

These facts make it apparent that the Louvre painting was indeed one of those ordered from Malouel in 1398. Therefore the term 'parfaire' (perfect) in the document of 1416 should be accepted in its true sense of completion. The relative participation of the two painters remains to be determined. A panel such as this, painted with a gold background, required, before the

17

5 MALOUEL. *Christ on the Cross and Martyrdom of St. Denis*, detail, Paris, Louvre (*6*)

application of the gold leaf, a drawn outline of the composition. Bellechose received pigments but no gold in 1416. The painting must therefore have already been at a fairly advanced stage when he began work on it; he would not have been able to make significant changes, tied as he was to the basic composition defined by the areas of gold and by the design sketched out on the prepared surface of the panel. Moreover, painters followed a prescribed routine in which they invariably proceeded from the top to the bottom of the panel. It is therefore in the upper part of the painting that we are likely to find Malouel's original work.[31]

Placed in this context, the analysis of the *Martyrdom of St. Denis* would appear more straightforward and perhaps becomes clearer if we compare it with two other works which also probably come from the Charterhouse of Champmol and are

now in the Louvre: the Large[32] and Small tondos depicting the Pietà. There is a close relationship between the Small tondo and the upper part of the *Martyrdom* and particularly with the figure of God the Father and his halo of angels. In both cases the faces are graceless but very expressive. A technique which is at the same time precise and painterly is employed in the depiction of the flesh and the hair. The latter is rendered in characteristically fine, wavy brushstrokes. The composition of the Small tondo has the abrupt, jerky appearance, which is so striking a feature of the *Martyrdom of St. Denis*. In both works, the masses are disposed on the principle of axial symmetry but in a very summary fashion and the forms are rather stiffly related to one another.

In contrast, the large tondo is painted in a softer flowing style. The forms are more elegant and naturally fit within the circular

7

5

7

4

154

154

6 MALOUEL. *Virgin and Child with butterflies*, Berlin, Staatliche Museen (*8*) ▷

18

shape which they seem to emphasise. The treatment is very much smoother; it does not accentuate the details of the faces and softens the modelling, which is barely suggested. Compare the crude faces of the angels of the halo of God the Father in the *Martyrdom* with the almost gracious little figures in the Large tondo, whose forms fail to achieve a convincingly sorrowful expression. These angels are close relations of those which we find in the lower part of the large Louvre painting, behind Christ and next to St. Denis. The hair seems to be treated in the same way, but here it is more precisely drawn with each strand clearly delineated. It is tempting to see the hand of Bellechose here. There remains however one last problem: the Large tondo carries on the reverse the arms of Burgundy in the form adopted by Philip the Bold. This would suggest that the painting was executed prior to 1404, at which date we know nothing of Bellechose. It is not impossible, however, that he was then already in the workshop of Malouel and that they worked together. The official painter of the Duke would have had too many commissions to carry out without assistance, and it would seem logical that he would be succeeded by his principal collaborator.

If we accept these arguments, the interpretation of the astonishing *Virgin and Child with Butterflies*, recently discovered in Berlin (*8*), is very much easier. While it is difficult to place the work between the large tondo and the *Martyrdom of St. Denis* in the *œuvre* of the same artist, as do Millard Meiss and Colin Eisler, the same obstacles do not exist if we attribute it to Malouel. The three angels in the left foreground in the Berlin painting are close to those of the large tondo and the lower part of the *Martyrdom*. Here, however, they possess that vigour of expression and slight trace of vulgarity which characterises the angels of God the Father's halo in the Louvre painting. The composition itself has a clumsy grace. The hand of the Virgin, instead of following a gentle curve, falls as if broken. The drapery falls in confused folds on the right, and the massed heads of the angels are irregularly grouped on either side of the principal figure. It seems more convincing to explain this vigorous treatment as characteristic of a particular artist rather than to explain the stylistic evolution from the large tondo to the Berlin painting in terms of the influence of Sluter's naturalism. Such an argument would necessitate having to justify a return to an earlier manner in the *Martyrdom of St. Denis*.

11 MALOUEL (?). *Crucifixion* (inner panel of a quadriptych), Baltimore, Walters Art Gallery (5)

The problem had now been opened up, and it was boldly discussed by Nicole Reynaud in her review of the Hamburg exhibition.[42] For her, the 'religious expressionism' of the master is analogous with that of the Book of Hours in the Library at Liège which was made in Guelders. This similarity, however, is merely the result of an apparently undeniable closeness of spirit and not of common sources. It is clear that the violence of the gestures, the harshness of the faces and the cramped composition of the Master of Hamburg are closer to the illuminations of Guelders than to the work of Conrad of Soest, for example. Is that enough to establish a common source? Perhaps not.

In fact the precise links of the artist with Guelders are difficult to define. The recurrence of an iconographic formula like that of the *Adoration of the Magi* in the version taken to be Eyckian and 166

12 MALOUEL (?). *Resurrection* (inner panel of a quadriptych), Antwerp, Mayer van den Bergh Museum (5)

remains to be proved that the latter was so called because he came from Zutphen. Such a description may already have possessed a patronymic connotation and have attested simply to his father's place of origin, or even that of a more distant ancestor.[41] Although we know that there was a Dominican monastery at Zutphen, no trace of the painter-monk has ever been discovered.

Any discussion must therefore be based on the works alone. Up until fairly recently, no scholar had seen traces of the art of Guelders in the work of the Master of Hamburg. For Bella Martens, the painter was influenced only by developments in Paris. The studies published on the occasion of the exhibition in 1969 made it clear that this thesis was too rigid in its conclusions. The exhibition itself, based on the work of Bella Martens, also revealed the tenuousness of certain of the stylistic links which were presented as crucial.

often followed in the northern Netherlands hardly provides proof, since that formula was widely imitated. The most significant comparisons which can be made only concern works by emigrants from Guelders, the Limbourgs (as Nicole Reynaud suggests) and also Malouel. The Hamburg *Man of Sorrows*[43] presents a clear similarity with *The Virgin and Child with Butterflies* (8) by the painter of John the Fearless: the treatment of the hands in particular has a similar decorative aspect in the two works that have the same sense of contained violence.

In the present state of our knowledge of Master Francke himself, as of the art of Guelders, it seems impossible to come to a firm conclusion about his origins. It is possible but by no means certain that he was trained in Guelders. Such a training would account for his artistic approach, but his sources remain mysterious. We might therefore ask whether the painter, from a family in Guelders, was not simply drawn towards artists from the same region during his travels in France. In other words, his style may have been formed by contact with other *émigrés* from Guelders. This is only a working hypothesis, but one which makes it clear that the art of Master Francke should not be considered part of the art of Guelders.

Therefore it is only through a study of the paintings produced in emigration that we can try to gauge what was produced in Guelders and the ecclesiastical principality in these early times. That a tradition had been established there seems likely, judging by the artistic achievements of the emigrants. A little later the citizens of Bruges had to fight against the importation of illuminated manuscripts from Utrecht.[44] One can understand therefore that the best painters, lacking a sufficient market for their work, turned towards the rich courts. Malouel's is the only case in which we have positive proof. But perhaps one day it will be established that the Master of the Rohan Hours shared this background. The expressive power of his art is matched, though less strikingly, by other illuminators. One cannot help being struck by the marked similarity between the representation of the creation of the soul in the book now in the Walters Art Gallery (W. 171 f25) and the scene of the dead man before his judge in the Rohan Hours.[45] This remains pure hypothesis, but nevertheless it underlines the rich artistic possibilities of the Guelders-Utrecht *milieu*, capable of providing other regions with artists of the first rank.

◁ 13 MALOUEL (?). *Baptism of Christ* (outer panel of a quadriptych), Baltimore, Walters Art Gallery (5)

II. Jan van Eyck in Holland

The evidence for artistic activity in the county of Holland is more recent than that recorded for the ecclesiastical principality of Utrecht and Guelders. Nevertheless, the existence of an active court at The Hague and the commercial activity of the harbour towns could have led to the creation of numerous works of art, despite the disturbed climate of the county. The absence of any known example at the present time should therefore not be taken as conclusive.[1]

The court of The Hague

It is with the last two counts of the house of Bavaria-Straubing, William VI and John of Bavaria, that we find evidence of princely commissions. This is not surprising: both princes were intimates of the Parisian court of Charles VI. Queen Isabella was their first cousin. William VI intervened in French affairs on several occasions and his presence in Paris is often mentioned. He married his daughter Jacqueline to the Dauphin, John of Touraine. As for John, we know that he surrounded himself with a splendid retinue[2] and that he, too, frequented the court of his cousin Isabella and her husband Charles VI. Such princes were naturally anxious to surround themselves with works of art.

The accounts of Duke William VI mention several commissions given to an artist who remains mysterious, but who doubtless belonged to that generation of late-fourteenth-century painters of whom as yet we know little. His name was Dirck de Maelre, and he is mentioned for the first time in 1398–9 for the painting of coats of arms and for the last time in 1434 in the accounts of the Oude Kerk at Delft. He was probably a native of that great commercial centre and must have lived there. In 1410–11 he provided a crucifix for the court chapel and in 1414 paintings and images for the 'chapel next to the towers'. The only work about which we have more information is the one he painted in 1428 for the Nieuwe Kerk at Delft. This was a large picture of St. Christopher and was placed in the choir near the tabernacle.[3] One wishes that this painting by a 'good artist', *een guet constenair*, had survived the Wars of Religion to give us an idea of his art.

We do not know much more about the first artist mentioned in the service of John of Bavaria. According to Pinchart, who does not name his sources, a *Heynrich Melre* illuminated a book decorated with gold letters for Elizabeth of Luxembourg in 1421.[4] Could this Henry be identical with Henric Mande, the Windesheim priest who, according to his biographer, worked during his early years on the copying and illuminating of manuscripts at the court of William of Bavaria? It is an attractive hypothesis, and such an identification would shed new light on the relationship between the world of Netherlandish art and the 'Devotio Moderna.'

In addition, we cannot forget that William VI was in Hainault and that he could have called upon the services of artists from that province. What of one Ghiskin Zalme, mentioned in the Hainault accounts as court painter to John of Touraine, Jacqueline of Bavaria's husband?[5] Was he from Hainault or Holland? It is difficult to be sure, for we find an artist of the same name, Michiel Zalme, mentioned at The Hague between 1455 and 1458,[6] at a period when the links between Hainault and Holland no longer seem to have been so close. The nature of the artistic relationship between the two counties in the early fifteenth century is unclear. It could explain the knowledge of certain works by the Master of Flémalle in the northern Netherlands, which will be pointed out later on. But maybe one day we shall have to emphasize the influences which flowed in the opposite direction, using them to throw light on the common inspiration of the expressive power of the Master of Flémalle and the similar feeling in the productions of the northern manuscript illuminators.[7]

The reputation of John of Bavaria as a patron rests, however, on surer foundations than his possible employment of Henric Mande. In 1422 he was able to secure the services of a painter whose choice bears witness to his taste, since it was none other than Jan van Eyck. This appointment, however, was perhaps the result of non-artistic causes. We know that the artist was probably a native of the ecclesiastical principality of Liège, which the prince had abandoned several years earlier to launch himself on the conquest of his brother's inheritance. We also know that several people named 'Eyck' are mentioned in the prince-bishop's entourage.[8] The artist may, therefore, have been recommended to him by family connections or more simply by fellow-countrymen. However, it is unlikely that Jan van Eyck was a mere novice in 1422. He probably already had a notable career behind him, even if no evidence of it has come down to us.[9] The prince's choice must have been determined not only by personal acquaintance, but also by an established artistic reputation.

The accounts of The Hague show payments to the painter from 1422 to the end of 1424.[10] Unfortunately, they only mention the money paid and do not specify the kind of work demanded of him. In the very first entry, however, mention is made of an assistant and the following entry mentions two. This is worthy of note, for it is quite rare to find artists accompanied by collaborators or assistants. The second entry even specifies the role of these, or of one of them at least, by saying that 'he works with him'. He was therefore an apprentice or a journeyman, and his presence indicates the amount of work undertaken as well as the fame of Jan van Eyck. It is probably on the strength of this one reference that various authors have asserted that Jan van Eyck painted frescoes in the count's residence at The Hague: the idea is certainly plausible, but there are no grounds for considering it an established fact.[11]

A remarkable ensemble, which can be ascribed very precisely to this period, has survived. An analysis of it is necessary here: the presence of an artist of Jan van Eyck's stature in Holland cannot have passed unnoticed, and may have influenced local artists. The work in question consists of illuminations for a book of hours which had belonged to Duke John of Berry and which in an incomplete form came into the possession of John of Bavaria. This work is commonly known as the *Turin* or *Milan-Turin Book of Hours,* according to whether one is referring to the part formerly at Turin and now destroyed, or the part which belonged to the Counts Trivulzio at Milan and which has been given to the city of Turin, or even as the *Turin-Milan Book of Hours* when one is referring to the original ensemble.

The nobleman who commissioned these illuminations was at first believed to be William VI, and the best pages were seen as collaborations between the two van Eyck brothers, Hubert and Jan. It now seems certain that the book was commissioned by John of Bavaria, and must therefore be dated after 1417, in other words after the death of William VI.

The Sovereign's Prayer (14)

The history of the manuscript and the theories to which it has given rise are particularly complex and cannot be discussed here.[12] It is nevertheless worth pausing for a moment over the illumination which has most often been at the heart of the debate, as its interpretation is particularly significant. The illustration of this leaf, which is now lost, showed a prince on horseback followed by a troop of horsemen; with his hands clasped together, he seems to be addressing a prayer to God the Father who appears in the sky. The scene is set on the seashore and a princess, accompanied by female attendants, advances on

foot and bows before the troop which is making towards her. In the midst of the escort a mounted soldier carries a banner with the arms of Bavaria, which are clearly recognisable even though their elements have been reversed.

An initial reading is required. This picture illustrates the text which is written on the same leaf, a prayer for the use of a sovereign prince imploring the protection of God for himself and for his people, *ac cunctum populum mihi commissum.* In the illumination the prince is the only person praying, and his people are represented not only by the troop accompanying him but also by a peasant in the foreground who kneels while baring his head. The text of the same prayer appears in several books of hours belonging to the Duke of Berry, a prince of the royal blood who had legitimate aspirations to the throne. It is strange that a prince of the house of Bavaria should have kept it in a volume for his own use and even more so that he should have had it illustrated with such a large miniature. In the *Petites Heures* of the Duke of Berry, the same text has as its only illustration the Duke kneeling at his prie-dieu before a vision of the Lord.[13] The power of the dukes of Bavaria is doubtless justified by the illumination in the lower margin: in a vast plain with rich pastures the only figures are three women and two horsemen with drawn swords which they hold up in front of them. This last detail is significant: it is, according to medieval tradition, a sign of power.[14] It alludes to the power which John of Bavaria considered himself to have acquired in Holland by grant of the Emperor.

To restrict oneself to this would, however, be facile. Such a wealth of details in the illumination suggests some allusion to contemporary events. From the moment this famous page was discovered, this was exactly the interpretation placed on it by all the historians who sought to unravel its mystery by direct examination. Some years ago, Frédéric Lyna believed he could demonstrate that the illumination was a reversed reproduction of an earlier work. Whether one retains this hypothesis or rejects it, following Charles Sterling,[15] is ultimately of little consequence. The extraordinary pictorial quality of the page, still easily discernible in surviving photographs and especially their enlargements, suffices to show that, if it was a copy, it was a copy from the hand of an exceptional master who re-adapted an earlier work of his own to a new purpose. He would therefore have had to adapt to the illustration of a sovereign prince's prayer a scene which originally had a completely different meaning. But if we concede that the work was not a copy, the complexity of the scene so far exceeds that of a pictorial commentary on a sovereign's prayer, unusual as that was, that we must suppose it to have had a wider implication.

The crux of the explanation must lie in the strange relationship between the prince's troop and the greeting of the young princess surrounded by her ladies-in-waiting. This young lady, linked in this way to the house of Bavaria, can only be the famous Jacqueline, whose life was romantic in the extreme. If

14 JAN VAN EYCK. *Sovereign's Prayer* (destroyed illumination from the *Turin Hours*), enlarged approx. 2 × (14) ▷

28

the prince depicted were her father William VI, she should appear even younger—she was only sixteen years old at the time of his death. Moreover, in an illumination which symbolises the power of a great lord, she would have been shown as the natural heiress of that power, a position in which William VI had striven to have her recognised.

Whether the princess is making a gesture of greeting or is about to curtsey in homage, she is clearly in a position inferior to the prince on horseback. And that accords well with the aims of her uncle John of Bavaria who, from 1417 onwards, was trying to seize her inheritance. It is even possible that the scene represents a specific episode in the struggle between uncle and niece, so closely do the details appear to match the accounts of one such episode, the Peace of Woodrichem. In 1419, after the siege of Dordrecht, whose outcome was settled by a decisive victory for John of Bavaria, John the Fearless, Duke of Burgundy, disturbed by the developments of this conflict, had despatched a mediator to the belligerents in the person of his son the Count of Charolais, the future Philip the Good. Under his auspices, a delegation from Duke John of Bavaria negotiated with Jacqueline and her second husband, John of Brabant, at Woodrichem. When the agreement was concluded, Duke John arrived on the scene himself, by boat from Dordrecht, with a magnificent entourage. He was greeted by his nephews, John of Brabant and Philip, Count of Charolais, who then accompanied him to Woodrichem where Jacqueline awaited him.[16] There are certainly two princes riding behind the sovereign and they are clearly distinguished from the armed retinue by their costumes. One of them wears a breastplate and a hood; this must be the future Duke of Burgundy, Philip the Good. Near him a richly-dressed young man executes a caracole on the fringe of the procession. His thin, sickly face, despite its tiny dimensions, bears a striking resemblance to the portrait of John of Brabant as it appears in the *Recueil Succa*.[17]

On a first analysis there is only one serious objection to the identification: the landscape. The admirable background represents, without a shadow of doubt, a beach. Even the width of the Waal near Woodrichem cannot give this impression of the open sea. Should this be considered an obstacle? Probably not, for the representation of a seashore, with a large number of ships in the distance, could assume a symbolic significance here. At Woodrichem, the possession of southern Holland with its many notable ports including Dordrecht was officially accorded to John of Bavaria. The homage of the peasant who kneels on the ground before the prince could well symbolise the recognition of his sovereignty over that rich territory.

It is no doubt the same meaning which is conveyed by the illumination in the lower margin, which is, as has been mentioned, one of Holland's first realistic landscapes. The riders bear witness, in the name of the Emperor, to the power of the duke over this land—and in particular that of Duke John, since they are wearing curious straw hats, unusual for armed horsemen, which doubtless correspond to the 'townsmen's grey caps' that the *Kabeljauwen*, Duke John's partisans, had adopted for mutual recognition.[18]

The probability of this interpretation is strengthened by the existence of a second example, though of very inferior artistic quality. This is a drawing from the Louvre, recently published but incorrectly interpreted (*21*). It is a reversed copy of a composition whose original was probably once included in the Imperial collections in Vienna. The leaf brings together two compositions which must originally have been pendants as two separate 'tableaux', rounded at the top. On either side of a river two groups face one another, one consisting of men, the other of women. Among the men, three wear the chain of the Order of St. Anthony, which brings us back once more to the counts of Hainault, and so to the dukes of Bavaria-Straubing.

Two figures dominate the male group. One, sumptuously dressed, wears not only the Order of St. Anthony but also a jewelled collar and a pendant on his cap. The other, standing slightly apart, seems more quietly dressed, but his separateness gives him a sort of pre-eminence which is confirmed by the curious staff which he holds in his right hand. The first can scarcely be other than one of the two last dukes, William VI or John of Bavaria. As for the second, although his appearance and bearing are unfamiliar in the guise of a young man, he is rather reminiscent of Philip the Good, who liked to carry a staff.

It is a third character, the young man standing back behind the Bavarian duke, that gives us the clue to the meaning of this unusual scene. His sickly mien and hollow cheeks are the very features of John of Brabant in the portrait handed down to us by Succa. In the drawing at the Louvre the identification is much more obvious than in the Turin manuscript. The male protagonists are therefore identical in the two scenes. It is hard to believe that this peaceful hunting scene could be another illustration of the meeting at Woodrichem. In fact, the same personages had already met two years earlier, but this time at Biervliet. Philip, Count of Charolais, was already acting as a mediator, but on this occasion to facilitate the arrangement of the marriage between John of Brabant and Jacqueline of Bavaria. On the female side the principal actors were the Duchess Margaret of Bavaria and, of course, her daughter Jacqueline; these could be the two women who clearly take precedence in the left-hand group. This would explain the pronounced symmetry of the male and female groups, as well as the symbolism of the hunting and fishing which occur frequently in the late Middle Ages in scenes of similar subjects.[19] The drawing in the Louvre seems to be a fairly free interpretation of the original. If the figures seem to have been copied with an obvious regard for exactness, this is not so with the setting. The landscape has been transposed more freely and is strongly redolent of the sixteenth century in its treatment. For this reason it is difficult to be assertive in suggesting the name of the artist of the original. Otto Kurz thought of Jan van Eyck; one is tempted to follow him, looking at the full but supple lines of these figures and the characterisation (but not caricature) of

15 JAN VAN EYCK. *Nativity of St. John the Baptist* (illumination from the *Milan-Turin Hours*). Turin, Museo Civico, enlarged approx. 2× (*18*) ▷

e uentie matis mee uocauit me dns
nomine meo. et posuit os meū siait
gladium acutum sub tegumento
manus sue protexit me posuit me

17 JAN VAN EYCK. *Baptism of Christ* (illumination from the *Milan-Turin Hours*), Turin, Museo Civico, enlarged approx. 2 × (*18*)

dimensional diagrams he has substituted an illusion. The scene is set out before us as if behind an open window, and in order to stress this, Jan van Eyck actually shows us, in the *Requiem Mass* (*19*), an unfinished church, whose rising walls frame an opening though which we view the scene. This is one of van Eyck's most novel and far-reaching advances, but one which his successors were far from adopting without reservations. However, beyond these limits, there is yet another new element in these two leaves, one which bears less on the idea of illusion and which constitutes one of the most delightfully poetic aspects of van Eyck's art. It is the pre-eminence and splendour of light. For light features not only as the source of chiaroscuro, but also has its scope extended in both scenes with unusual breadth and imagination. In the *Nativity of St. John the Baptist* (*18*), it seems omnipresent, playing on the smallest reflective surfaces—

window-panes, pewter and copper; its beams pierce the gloom of a corridor and add new depth to the room. In the church of the *Requiem Mass* (*19*), candle-flames dance and stained glass sparkles. Need one recall here that this vision of glistening, glowing light contributed to van Eyck's mature art and to indications of his more than purely painterly interest in light, as revealed by the analyses of Charles de Tolnay?[21]

It is these two contributions, the illusion of reality and the poetry of light, which make the landscapes of this manuscript what they are. Only one has survived, that of the illumination at the bottom of the *Nativity of St. John the Baptist* leaf, depicting the Baptism of Christ. The light plays on the water, brushes against the foliage of the trees, illuminates the far distance and models the little clouds scattered across the sky. The view is essentially realistic in that it depicts a well-characterised and credible landscape reminiscent of places along the Meuse. But the specific description is transcended by the effect of the light which creates an atmosphere, constructs real space rather than lines of perspective, and, above all, renders brightness in its

19 JAN VAN EYCK. Detail from the *Baptism of Christ* (ill. 17), Turin, Museo Civico, enlarged approx. 1.5 ×

◁ 18 JAN VAN EYCK. Detail from the *Virgin with Chancellor Rolin*, Paris, Louvre, enlarged approx. 1.5 ×

rarest form, gilding shapes and clothing them in a precious substance.

Any remaining doubt as to whether these illuminations are the work of Jan van Eyck will easily be dispelled by this scene beneath the *Nativity of St. John the Baptist*. When a detail of the landscape is compared with the corresponding detail from the *Virgin and Child with Chancellor Rolin*—in two photographs enlarged by the same factor—the identity of the technique becomes startlingly apparent. The waves in the *Baptism of Christ* recur in the Louvre panel—not only are they drawn in an identical way, but the execution, too, is similar: a dark, discontinuous round brushstroke is joined to a light brushstroke which doubles it in places and conveys the play of the light. Other analogies can be found between the reflections of the buildings in the water, the rendering of windows by means of small dark irregular rectangles, and the human figures suggested by what may best be called 'macchiette' sparkling with light blobs. Comparisons between the *Burial* below the *Requiem Mass* (*19*) and the *St. Barbara* in Antwerp are also significant: in both works we find the same rendering of gestures and poses, the same slightly stooping postures, thick-set silhouettes, curved legs, and detailed drawing of the feet, whether clothed in peasants' or noblemen's hose. Here we clearly have the personal

18, 19

24, 25

20 JAN VAN EYCK. Illumination from the foot of the page of the *Sovereign's Prayer* (destroyed illumination from the *Turin Hours*), enlarged approx. 2 × (*14*)

touch of one painter, the graphic notations which are typical of his handling and testify to his originality.

We should, however, be restricting the extent of van Eyck's advances in the realm of landscape if we were to analyse them solely on the basis of this surviving illumination. This piece of evidence has a further merit; it gives us a better understanding of the photographs of the pages burnt in 1904, particularly those of the *Sovereign's Prayer* (*14*) and the *Voyage of SS. Julian and Martha* (*17*). The realism of the conception is accompanied here, perhaps more obviously than in the *Baptism of Christ,* by a sensitivity close to that of the greatest modern artists. The background of the *Sovereign's Prayer* (*14*) is a remarkable depiction of the Dutch coast after a shower of rain, when the returning sun puts a sparkle on the sea-foam, gilds the sand and imparts an especially dazzling whiteness to the dappled clouds. Though one may think here of the great seventeenth-century Dutch landscapists, Jan van Eyck's art differs from theirs not

14, 22

14

21 JAN VAN EYCK. *Requiem Mass* (illumination from the *Milan-Turin Hours*), Turin, Museo Civico, enlarged approx. 2 × (*19*) ▷

34

least in its microcosmic vision, suggesting the richness of the world by the precise representation of its tiniest details.

The three large scenes containing landscapes are composed on the same principle. The lower half is enlivened by figures, the upper half contains the landscape and sky. The horizon is set three quarters of the way up the picture. This approach, completely different from that required for illuminations in lower margins, whose oblong shape imposes its own rhythm, was dictated by a desire to cover or rather make use of the entire area of a vertical picture. The scale of the figures is also much smaller than was then customary in such manuscripts: comparison between the van Eyck leaves and earlier or even contemporary illustrations brings this out clearly. Such an approach was dictated by a concern for unity and coherence. The painter sets his figures in the very heart of his landscapes and links them to their setting. *The Voyage of SS. Julian and Martha* (*17*) provides the best example of this. The boat is not only visible on the great river, but also absorbed into the countryside as a whole, as if the painter had wanted to emphasise its fragility amidst the raging waters. If one recalls the depiction of Mary Magdalene's voyage on one of the panels of the *Tiefenbronn Altarpiece* by Lucas Moser, the originality of van Eyck's conception will be even more apparent. The German painter's choice of a formula which gave greatest prominence to the saints was dictated by the need to obtain a monumental effect in an altarpiece. This observation leads, by contrast, to the conclusion that a book of hours, because of its particular purpose, permitted the use of conventions that were hardly acceptable in painting. Placed on a prie-dieu to encourage prayer and meditation, such a volume could open a window for a single person; it could aim at the greatest realism and intimacy since it was, in principle, intended to be seen by only one pair of eyes, at very close range.

The real extent of the last innovation in the known pages is more difficult to assess today. This is the nocturne effect aimed at in the *Kiss of Judas* scene (*15*). The printed reproductions of the surviving photographs are unsharp. Count Durrieu described the original as worn. Perhaps it was partly unfinished. However, a good quality enlargement taken from the surviving negative gives the impression of a remarkable effort to convey the glare of torches in the night. Light glints on all the helmets and picks out the faces of the two protagonists, with their heads close together. Most remarkable of all is the depiction of the city by moonlight, with its white, almost ghostly roofs. A comparison between this page and the 'Boutsian' panel in Munich (*55A*), which is obviously inspired by it, is to the disadvantage of the latter which contents itself with an approximation. All the same, it is not surprising that a painter who uses light to build up his view of the world should take pleasure in depicting the glint of moonbeams and torches in the night.

◁ 22   JAN VAN EYCK. *Voyage of St. Julian and St. Martha* (destroyed illumination from the *Turin Hours*), enlarged approx. 2 × (*17*)

23   JAN VAN EYCK. *Crucifixion*, New York, Metropolitan Museum (*20*)   ▷

24 JAN VAN EYCK. *St. Barbara*, detail. Antwerp, Musée des Beaux-Arts, enlarged approx. 1.5 ×

25 JAN VAN EYCK. *Burial*, illumination from the foot of the page from the *Milan-Turin Hours*, detail, Turin, Museo Civico, enlarged approx. 1.5 × (*19*)

As well as the *Turin-Milan Hours*, one other work bears witness to Jan van Eyck's activity in Holland, but it is known only through copies. This is a *Carrying of the Cross* of which the painted replica in the Budapest Museum was compared to the art of van Eyck by Winkler as early as 1916 (*22*). What is most remarkable in the Budapest painting, and links it with the illuminations, is the relationship between the landscape and the figures. As in Turin, the actors stand out because of their position rather than their size. Round about them the landscape unfolds coherently and without any clear-cut break in continuity. The relation of the different planes and their articulation are even emphasised with a certain pedantry by two parallel paths, one going up to Golgotha, the other cutting across an undulating meadow on the right.

Here Jan van Eyck displays a fondness for anecdote which allows picturesque touches to proliferate around the main group: richly-dressed peasants, peasant women going to market, Jews mocking the condemned man, people running to follow the group. This is realism with an eye for the contemporary world, but also for the everyday world. Anecdote merges easily into satire, very noticeably in the variety of poses which are all observed with remarkable exactness, even if they seem somewhat stiffened in the literalness of the copy. This outlook is at one with that which placed everyday secondary characters in

front of the *Nativity of St. John the Baptist* (*18*). Yet the painting reveals the same interest now directed towards the world of peasants, with a vividness which strikingly foreshadows the art of Bruegel.

The *Carrying of the Cross* may seem at first sight to belong to the tradition, so strong in manuscript illumination, of multiple scenes in an artificially divided landscape. Its originality lies, however, in its insistence on a unity of place by the linking of the various planes, as well as on a unity of time. Here the secondary scenes are simultaneous with the main one. In the left background we see the preparations for the crucifixion, a scene which could well have been enacted during the actual ascent to Calvary depicted in the lower section. We have, superimposed on a medieval form, a realistic and almost rationalist outlook which in the early fifteenth century was the mark of a singularly independent spirit. This fact is worth noting, for the lesson seems to have been grasped in the northern Netherlands.

To gain a better idea of the lost original we must compare the photograph of it with the *Crucifixion* (*20*) from the New York diptych. For here is a painting in which we can recognise the hand of Jan van Eyck and which could well have been executed during his two years in Holland. But why only the *Crucifixion*, in an ensemble which, in its present state, consists of two panels? Because the *Last Judgement*, interesting though it is, is less novel in conception and less brilliant in execution, suggesting the collaboration of some assistant.

The *Crucifixion* is as surprising in its understanding of space as the *Carrying of the Cross* (*22*). In developing the theme, Jan van

26 JAN VAN EYCK. *Crucifixion*, New York, Metropolitan Museum, detail (*20*)

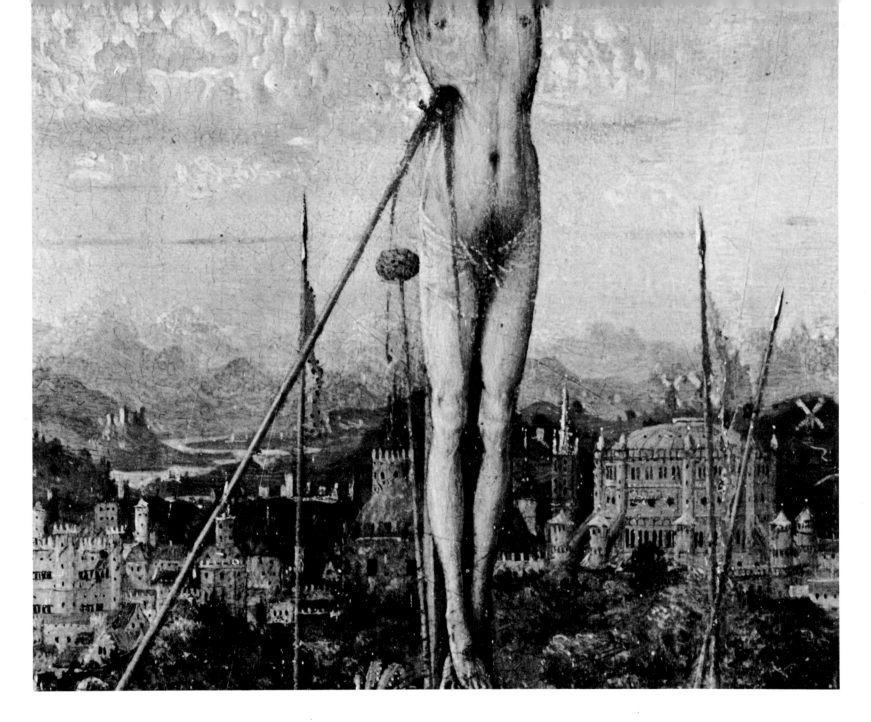

27 JAN VAN EYCK. *Crucifixion*, New York, Metropolitan Museum, detail of landscape, enlarged approx. 2 × (20)

Eyck perhaps drew inspiration from Italian examples. He has distributed the scene between two principal foci of interest: the crucified men, surrounded by the crowd of gawpers and unbelievers, who abuse and mock Christ, and the grief-stricken believers, who surround the fainting Virgin. Between these two groups, some soldiers, seen from behind and carefully situated, lead the eye from one to the other and establish a spatial link.

Behind the crosses, and reduced to some very sketchy indications, is a whole marvellous landscape enclosed by a mountain range. We even find the windmills of the Budapest painting again, but this time depicted on their exact scale and suggested as silhouettes rather than rendered in detail: it was a landscape of this kind, conveyed by suggestions which create a deep, airy space, that the copyist of the *Carrying of the Cross* must have clumsily misrepresented in his desire to make it exact and unnecessarily detailed.

Master H

The originality of Jan van Eyck's output in Holland is even more noticeable when his works are compared with those of a painter then working alongside him, 'Master H'. The latter derives his designation from the letter of the alphabet assigned to his share in the illumination of the *Turin-Milan Hours* in 1911 by Hulin de Loo. Though it no longer seems possible to follow Hulin de Loo in identifying this artist as Jan van Eyck himself, it is no easier to accept Friedländer's theory, taken up by Panofsky, which dates his share in the illustration of the book between 1435 and 1440: the objection lies in the presence, in a manuscript from the hand of this master, of a praying nobleman who can only be John of Bavaria as he is seen in the *Sovereign's Prayer* (14).[22]

14

27

162

This artist is both very close to and very different from Jan van Eyck. The impression of fullness given at first glimpse by such compositions as the *Jesus in the Garden of Gethsemane* (*27*) or the *Pietà* (*26*) inevitably recalls the monumentality of the outer panels of the *Mystic Lamb*, for example. The composition of the illuminator's 'tableaux' is imbued with an unusual concern for clarity which also brings out the family resemblance of the two approaches.

And yet their outlooks are very far apart. What is most striking initially is that Master H puts his main accent on the figures. It is the dramatis personae who occupy most of the area of the *Jesus in the Garden of Gethsemane* (*27*), of the *Pietà* (*26*) and even of the *Crucifixion* (*28*). The oddest case is that of the *Finding of the Cross* (*29*), often attributed indeed to Master G, i.e. Jan van Eyck. The scene is set in a landscape, but this plays little part in the organisation of the picture. It constitutes a background on the right of the composition. The very soil on which the characters move is only suggested in an almost abstract manner, in a rather stereotyped green hue. One only needs to compare such a depiction with that of the *Sovereign's Prayer* (*14*) to understand what separates the two artists. In the latter the figures are integrated into the landscape and not presented against a backdrop. This result is also obtained by the scrupulous

28 MASTER H. *St. Thomas in his cell* (destroyed illumination from the *Turin Hours*) (*24*)

40

enumeration of precise, realistic details, like the depiction of a meadow strewn with daisies instead of the commonplace soil of Master H. While Jan van Eyck creates depth and atmosphere by delicate shading, by his interlocking of planes so as to avoid any abrupt transitions, H methodically divides up the page with a succession of rounded hills whose tops stand out clearly, almost starkly. This technique appears not only in the *Finding of the Cross* (*29*), but in all the pages by this painter which feature outdoor settings.

These two techniques are very much in the tradition of manuscript illumination. This is why, when one leafs through the Turin volume, one does not immediately notice the pages illustrated by Master H: they do not stand out from the others by their conception, whereas with Jan van Eyck's the eye is riveted by the depiction of another world. Besides, it is quite probable that Master H was trained as a manuscript illuminator. Apart from these fundamental characteristics, we can also distinguish in his work a style and some techniques which were prevalent among early fifteenth-century illuminators. Firstly, there is the habit of colouring surfaces with tints laid on flat and then adjusting them with stippling. To add shadows or simply to modulate the tints, one tone is set off against another by a simple gradation. This technique also occurs in the work of the Limbourgs, in the *Heures d'Ailly* for example, and in that of the Boucicaut Master. The insistence on having the ground at an angle to the plane of the page is also an illuminator's technique rather than a painter's.

Nevertheless, Master H was profoundly influenced by Jan van Eyck. But this influence only bore on secondary aspects of his outlook, without transforming its fundamental characteristics. Compared with Jan van Eyck, Master H is a poor landscapist; yet in contrast to his contemporaries and successors, he seems to sense the qualities of light or of a sky. The clouds in the *Finding of the Cross* (*29*) are clumsy in comparison with those of the *Sovereign's Prayer* (*14*) or of the *Voyage of SS. Julian and Martha* (*17*); but not until Marmion will we find others as successful in Flemish illumination. The atmosphere is conveyed without great subtlety; and yet there are felicities like the picking out of a town by a ray of light while the surrounding hills are less brightly lit. This technique was soon to become common in north Netherlandish manuscript illumination.

Master H's importance lies in the fact that his art was closer to tradition and that he was content to innovate in secondary aspects only. Whereas van Eyck's inventiveness was to have no heirs, whether in illumination or in panel painting, the art of this master, albeit secondary, was to be frequently imitated in many respects. His approach to the subjects is also more popular. With him, anecdote is given free rein and overshadows the main theme. A cat and a dog in the foreground of the *Nativity of St. John the Baptist* (*18*) are only noticed at a second glance, as the distribution of colour first draws the eye towards the new-born baby. But in the *Finding of the Cross* (*29*), the eye lingers on the peasants busy with their spades around the crosses and needs to explore the rest of the composition to discover, amidst a close-packed retinue, a queen who must be St. Helena. Likewise,

29 MASTER H. *The Virgin amongst the virgins* (destroyed illumination from the *Turin Hours*) (*23*)

30 MASTER H. *God the Father enthroned* (destroyed illumination from the *Turin Hours*) (*25*)

31 MASTER H. *Pietà* (destroyed illumination from the *Turin Hours*) (*26*)

the sleeping apostles, so convincingly realistic in their poses that one can almost hear old St. Peter snoring, are given as much prominence in the scene of *Jesus in the Garden of Gethsemane* (*27*) as Christ at prayer.

However, when the accent is laid more on the central theme, as in the *Pietà* (*26*), concentration on drama and pathos makes itself felt. Grief is manifested on each face, trembling hands are clasped together. The expressions of the Virgin and St. John the Evangelist at the foot of the Cross, despite their solemn, simple poses—which may well suggest a drawing by Jan van Eyck, worked up and finished by Master H—are contorted in a way which conveys rather crudely the violence of their grief. Jan van Eyck's humanity, his humour, his emotion, all take on a more familiar and accessible form in Master H's work.

Several paintings may be the work of this illuminator. They must be later and would not normally concern us here. But they are remarkable for remaining true to the style of the miniaturist and to the themes of Jan van Eyck's early work. The Ca' d'Oro Museum possesses a *Crucifixion* (*32*) which almost exactly follows the illumination in the *Milan Hours,* itself very probably inspired by a lost original by Jan van Eyck. There are strong indications that this work could actually have been painted in Italy during the 1440s. Master H thus deliberately adopted an

archaising style, perhaps exploiting the celebrity of the name and formulae of the man whose collaborator he had been. In the same period, he produced a *St. Jerome* (*33*) bearing the date 1442, which takes up the motifs of the *Turin Hours* illumination (*24*) representing St. Thomas. In it, the artist's hesitancy reveals itself: he has mastered neither perspective nor pictorial effects, although he strives to emulate the charm of the Eyckian microcosm of the *Nativity of St. John the Baptist*.

When he displays more independence with regard to Eyckian models, Master H still remains very faithful to their spirit. It is to him that we owe *St. Francis receiving the stigmata* (*30*) (Philadelphia), handled with all the minuteness of an illumination. The landscape seems very close to its models in the sensitivity of its

32 MASTER H. *Jesus in the Garden of Gethsemane* (illumination from the *Milan-Turin* ▷ *Hours*), Turin, Museo Civico (*27*)

33 MASTER H. *Invention of the Cross* (illumination from the *Milan-Turin Hours*), Turin, Museo Civico (*29*)

and he practised the craft himself, which would account for the importance of this technique in the artist's training. Nevertheless, the hypothesis remains unsubstantiated and one would need other evidence to propose it with confidence.

In this way, *pace* Dvořák and his followers, all the illuminations from the hands of Hulin de Loo's G and H can be seen to add up to no more than a temporary artistic immigration into the northern Netherlands, brought about by princely patronage. An analysis of it has however been necessary in the context of this study, principally because it has been forcefully interpreted as exemplifying the art of this region and has been linked with the enigma of Albert van Ouwater. But if such conclusions have seemed possible, it is only because these two artistic careers seem to have had such a strong influence on the future development of northern art. Knowledge of this corpus of work is convincingly attested by frequent reworkings of the most popular compositions, such as the *Finding of the Cross* or the   33
Carrying of the Cross, in various manuscripts of undeniably   162
northern origin.[23]

A direct, immediate influence of the presence in Holland of Jan van Eyck and his collaborators is not strikingly noticeable. No doubt the destruction of many works of art, especially during the Reformation, has helped to obscure these influences. But at least two works bear witness to them. The first is often attributed to Hubert or Jan van Eyck: this is a drawing in the

34 MASTER H. *St. Francis receiving the stigmata*, Philadelphia, Museum of Art (*30*)

lighting, especially in the background to which the lighting gives depth. It differs from them in having a much less skilful structure, which contrasts the planes abruptly, and in its resemblance to a stage set rather than to natural scenery, setting it back from the figures instead of enveloping them. Similarly, this artist's third known treatment of the *Crucifixion* (*31*) (Berlin) abruptly juxtaposes the plane containing the cross with that of the distant landscape instead of observing the principle of transition introduced by the work of Jan van Eyck, copied in the *Milan Hours.*

Master H's considerable part in the illumination of the *Turin-Milan Hours* lends plausibility to the notion of his having been one of the two servants who worked with Jan van Eyck. However, the archives of The Hague have not preserved their names and shed virtually no further light on the mystery of Master H's identity. It is only an assortment of cross-references that leads us to set the artist's later activity in Bruges. And among the masters whose activity is known to us, it is Jan Coene whose description answers best to that of our mystery man. His name is that of a family of illuminators (one of them has been tentatively identified with the Master of the Boucicaut Hours),

III. The northern Netherlands from Philip the Good to Philip the Handsome (1428–1505)

Philip the Good and Charles the Bold

Placed under the provisional authority of Philip the Good from 1428 onwards, the county of Holland and Zeeland was permanently incorporated into his territories in 1433. Did the region thus lose its identity and become merged into the Burgundian dominions? It seems not.[1]

The dukes displayed little personal affection for the county. Their presence was rare. Philip the Good honoured Holland with just one great celebration, the ninth chapter of the Order of the Golden Fleece, an occasion for the sumptuous festivities which took place at The Hague in 1456, in the great hall of the old county palace.[2] Charles the Bold was even less attached to the region when he became count. Perhaps he had unpleasant memories of his quarrel with his father between 1462 and 1464, when he had taken refuge in the Dutch lands assigned to him in 1459, Gorkum and the lordships of Putten and Strijden.

The county was governed in the name of the dukes by stadhouders: Hugues de Lannoy (1433–40), Guillaume de Lalaing (1440–5) Jean de Lannoy (1448–63) and Louis de Gruuthuse (1463–77) succeeded one another in this capacity. None of them seems to have played the part of a 'viceroy', substituting for the sovereign in his pomp, among other things. One can discern no interest on their part in Netherlandish artists. They behaved more like absentee overlords milking a lucrative post.

Until the death of Charles the Bold, disturbances were rare. The rival factions of *Hoeksen* and *Kabeljauwen* were not much in evidence. They sprang to life again for a moment in 1445 with a rising of the Kabeljauwen at Amsterdam and Haarlem, which necessitated the presence first of the Duchess of Burgundy, then of the Duke himself, in order to restore calm. A similar revolt, of short duration, at Rotterdam in 1452 was the only other event of this kind.

The two reigns were marked most of all by a remarkable economic expansion. All things considered, the conflict between the Dutch towns and the Hansa was of little importance and scarcely interfered with the former's development. In any case, hostilities were brief: they lasted from 1438 to 1440 and were then interrupted by a ten-year truce, before the struggle was renewed in 1451 and turned rapidly in favour of the Dutch. Finally, at the Peace of Utrecht between England and the Hansa in 1474, the towns obtained further advantages.

The towns of Holland, the most urbanised of the Burgundian territories, then enjoyed a period of prosperity. Amsterdam laid the foundations of its future power. While the southern Netherlands did not escape the depression in the reign of Charles the Bold, Holland continued its expansion. In 1473, the county contributed as much as Flanders itself to the *aide* of 500,000 crowns levied by Charles the Bold on his dominions—another sign of undeniable prosperity.

When one looks at the duchy of Guelders and the ecclesiastical principality, one cannot fail to be struck by the contrast between their condition and that of the county. Struggles over ducal power consumed the entire reign of Arnold van Egmond (1423–73), who successively had to deal with his rivals, then with his own relatives, his wife and his son, and also with the impatience of the towns, anxious to free themselves as much as possible from his grip. At his death in 1473 the inheritance fell to Charles the Bold, but the latter was obliged to mount a full-dress campaign, with a siege of Nijmegen, to give some substance to his power.

The situation was scarcely better in the principality. The death of Fredrik van Blankenheim in 1423 was the signal for a contest between a candidate supported by Guelders and one put forward by the cathedral chapter. The latter's death in 1433 did not, however, leave the coast clear for the former, Rudolph van Diepholt, despite the confirmation of his nomination by Pope Eugenius IV in the previous year: the chapter put up another competitor. And even when an agreement had been reached with some difficulty, the bishop was still not left in peace. His involvement in the Rhineland struggles soon earned him the enmity of the towns and above all of Utrecht.

In 1456, Philip the Good managed to set his illegitimate son, David of Burgundy, formerly bishop of Thérouanne, on the episcopal throne. This success, achieved by a combination of diplomacy and force, was precarious: it took many years of strife and guile before the new prelate finally succeeded, in 1470, in imposing himself as the true temporal prince and spiritual head.

Such a state of affairs was evidently not very favourable to the economy and social life of the two provinces, whose development lagged behind that of the Dutch towns.

From Mary of Burgundy to Philip the Handsome

The death of Charles the Bold at Nancy in 1477 precipitated a period of disturbance and crisis for the whole of the Netherlands. The towns asserted themselves once more and took advantage of the brief reign of Mary of Burgundy (1477–82), then of the regency of Maximilian in the name of his son Philip the Handsome, to try to recover some of the power that the dukes of Burgundy had progressively taken from them. This time, Holland and Zeeland did not hold themselves aloof and the uprisings spread to the ecclesiastical principality and to Guelders. The factions sprang to life again. The *Hoeksen*, under Jan van Montfoort, led the revolt in all the northern provinces, causing uprisings in Haarlem, The Hague, Hoorn and above all Leiden; but they also seized power in Utrecht, of which they were masters from 1481 to 1483.

It required a full-scale military campaign by the 'mambour' Maximilian, with German troops led for a time by Albert of Saxony, gradually to restore peace. In 1491–2 new rebellions affected Alkmaar, Haarlem and Kennemerland: the cause this time was economic distress resulting from the devastation of the countryside by the soldiery. It was not until 1494, when

37 *Hours of Catherine of Cleves*. Adoration of God the Father by saintly knights and monks. The first saintly knight may have the features of Duke Arnold of Guelders (*37-P 66*)

Maximilian gave up the regency, that some semblance of calm returned. But it was at this moment that trouble broke out again in Guelders: Charles of Egmond, Duke Adolf's son, tried to recover the inheritance of which he had been dispossessed. France and the Empire interfered surreptitiously in the quarrel, which thus became European and was only ended by the pretender's death in 1538.

The new sovereign, Philip the Handsome, was no more interested than his predecessors in his northern territories. He honoured them with a single visit, of around 40 days, in 1497; his accession to the throne of Castile, in 1504, seems to have inspired reciprocal indifference on the part of his subjects in Holland and Guelders.

The political and economic condition of the Netherlandish provinces did not encourage artistic development. No doubt one ought to stress the extent to which the county of Holland and Zeeland constituted a relative oasis of tranquillity and wealth between 1428 and 1477, by comparison with the ecclesiastical principality and the duchy of Guelders, which were the victims of constant disturbance. Certainly, one may also note that the death of Charles the Bold formed an important turning-point and ushered in a period of uncertainty which lasted till the end of century. Once again Holland emerged earlier from its difficulties and seems to have suffered less economically, largely because of the expansion of Amsterdam.

However, these are only very vague indications. We must add the disappearance of the princely courts, for during this whole period only one survived—the modest one of Duke Arnold of Guelders, a constant prey to financial hardship. It was none the less for this court that one of the major works of the time was produced, the *Book of Hours of Catherine of Cleves*.

The orientation of the three provinces remained quite different. On the one hand, Holland and Zeeland, under Burgundian control, were theoretically linked to the southern provinces of Flanders, Brabant and Hainault. Nevertheless, they pursued an independent policy, developing their economy at the expense of the southern commercial centres. The political ties seem to have been loosened after 1477 and were only strengthened in the very last years of the fifteenth century. On the other hand, the ecclesiastical principality, through the personality of its bishops and of some of its priests, and through its dependence on the archbishopric of Cologne, maintained fairly extensive relations with both north Germany and the Rhine valley. The situation of Guelders was fairly similar but for different reasons. Because of the Rhenish trade it was orientated towards Germany; the quarrels in which it was involved brought it into confrontation with the neighbouring German states, Cleves and the archbishopric of Cologne.

Religious life

When Cardinal Nicholas of Cues was appointed legate by Pope Nicholas V in 1451, his mission led him first of all to the

38 PIETER GERRITSZ (?), *St. Bavo's, Haarlem*, 1518 (?), Haarlem, St. Bavo's

northern Netherlands. He was obliged to devote much of his time to resolving temporal problems, especially conflicts of jurisdiction with civil courts and the struggle which still raged between Bishop Rudolph van Diepholt and his rival Walraven van Meurs, elected by the chapter. However, he was no less preoccupied by spiritual affairs. And one cannot fail to be impressed by the attention he gave to the establishments of the Windesheim congregation. If one adds to this the fact that he had asked Dionysius the Carthusian to accompany him, one can easily gauge the importance he attached to the spiritual life of the north.

The movement of the Devotio Moderna, issued from the teachings of Geert Groote, was then at its peak.[3] The most original of the creations arising from it was that of the 'Brethren and Sisters of the Common Life'. This took on substance with the foundation in 1391 of the 'house of Florent' at Deventer which was soon followed by others. In the northern Netherlands alone there appeared, one after the other, the houses of Delft (1403), Hoorn (which was short-lived), Albergen (1406, transformed in 1447 into a Windesheim monastery), Hulsbergen (1407), 's Hertogenbosch (1424), Groningen (between 1426 and 1432), Hardewijk (1441), Gouda (1445), Utrecht (1474), Nijmegen (1469 or 1470) and Berliksum. They were not very numerous, but in them the founder's ideas were followed with great fervour. They did not claim to be monastic establishments, but rather to be communities—in our modern sense—of priests, scholars and laymen living in the world. Their life was expected to be one of example and practice. They were to serve an evangelical function, but also, for those hesitant at the prospect of a monastery, as a prelude to and trial of a regular life.

The brethren's vocation was modified by a broad extension of the teaching activity that Groote himself had practised. In this sphere, however, their work was not as decisive as has often been alleged. The brethren co-operated in the running of existing schools more often than they started their own, and even then they did not hesitate to call on the services of masters who did not belong to their community. Mainly, they set up lodging-houses for the pupils of the schools and thus only exerted their influence on education indirectly.[4]

The brethren also had an important rôle as copyists, inspired from the very beginning by Geert Groote himself. Behind this certainly lay the desire to generate an income for the houses from the volumes produced. The work was also seen as an exercise in spiritual reflection. The brethren were exhorted to meditate on the texts they were copying and to compile collections of quotations or 'rapiaria'.

The form of communal life most often adopted by Groote's disciples was that of the convents of the Windesheim congregation. Founded in 1386–7, the latter expanded rapidly, and initially in the northern Netherlands. In 1424, at the death of Prior Jan Vos van Heusden, it numbered 24 monasteries and

49

39 *Portrait of Thomas à Kempis*, Zwolle, Historical Museum

expansion. In primarily advocating the development of the inner life at the expense of the liturgy, the Devotio Moderna had a universal appeal and may be seen not as a path reserved for monks and priests, but as a doctrine of life which brought devotion into the everyday world. It advocated 'exercises' that were within the capacity of everyone, meditation before an image or preferably after the reading of a text, and reflection on prayer which must not be a mere litany, but a starting-point from which God might be reached by meditation. It was certainly associated with moral strictness. Continuous reflection on Christ's sacrifice heightened the awareness of sin. This spirituality was based on an emotionalism accessible to all, which sometimes acquired a mystical impetus.

Groote himself left few writings and his influence, though crucial and profound, depended less on his written thoughts than on his teachings as disseminated by his disciples. The most celebrated of these was Thomas à Kempis (c. 1379–1471). His output was considerable and yet his most famous work has come down to us cloaked in mystery: arguments have long raged around *The Imitation of Christ*. Excellent studies have shown that Thomas à Kempis is undoubtedly the author.[5] The work is definitely based on earlier writings and may even reflect a very exact recollection of some treatise by Geert Groote: the creative process of the authors of the Devotio Moderna consisted in precisely this constant appeal to earlier writings, this reconstruction of new thought from a mosaic of textual fragments.

However that may be, the *Imitation*, even with its often pronounced incongruities, conveys to us the clearest, the most immediately and enduringly experienced message of the Devotio Moderna. There was a twofold lesson. Philosophical systems were rejected in favour of facts, those of the Gospel, meditation on which was constantly urged. Meditation on and imitation of Christ, these were the bases of the prayer which would open up a path to God through self-knowledge. Imitation of Christ did not, however, indicate a desire to rival God, for Jesus himself counsels renunciation of the self before the will of God. It means that the sinner must become aware of his shortcomings and rely utterly on the grace which alone can redeem him.

The *Imitation* enjoyed considerable and immediate success. The first part is known in a Latin manuscript of 1424 and we find a Dutch translation as early as 1428. The three other fragments appear in a manuscript of 1427. There was an enormous number of near-contemporary copies—at the present time, around 700 are known to be extant. The tradition was taken up, though only rather late, by printing.

We may justifiably wonder about the attitude of the thinkers of the Devotio Moderna towards art. It is a difficult question to answer. We should not attach too much importance to the fact that Geert Groote wrote a pamphlet *Contra turrim traiectensem*, against the building of the tower of Utrecht cathedral.[6] His protest is not against the work of art but against the financial burden of erecting such a monument. In this respect, paintings on wood remained a relatively 'cheap' art and could have been regarded favourably by him.

five nunneries, sixteen of them in the northern Netherlands. These were Marienborn near Arnhem and Nieuwlicht near Hoorn (1392), St. John the Evangelist near Amsterdam (1394–5), Mount St. Agnes near Zwolle (1398), Frenswegen (1400), Engelendaal near Leiden (1403), St. Elizabeth at Briel (1406), the Visitation at Haarlem, St. Saviour at Thabor (Friesland), Pieterswel and Sneek (1407), Amersfoort, Marienhof and Vrendendael near Utrecht (1417) and Marienhage near Eindhoven (1420). Still later came the incorporation in 1430 of five monasteries formerly dependent on the chapter of Neuss, then those of Beverwijck and Bethany near Arnhem (1431), St. Elizabeth near Roermond (1436), Angum in Friesland (1438–9), St. Jerome in Roermond (1444), Bergum near Leeuwarden and Marienburg at Nijmegen (1453), and finally Haske in Friesland (1464).

The Windesheim congregation played a crucial rôle in the spread of the spirituality of the Devotio Moderna. The major thinkers and writers were to be found in its monasteries. Their rule was not, however, original but borrowed from the Augustinians, and hence permitted their presence in the world. Their communal life was characterised by an application of the rule in a spirit of strict observance and by an extension of the monks' individual devotion by frequent meditations, which were regarded as having greater importance than a proliferation of ceremonial. A similar and parallel attempt is represented by the chapter of Sion, but the latter did not enjoy such a wide

40 *Portrait of David of Burgundy, bishop of Utrecht* (Recueil d'Arras)

41 Master of the Princely Portraits, *Louis de Gruuthuse*, Bruges

Neither Geert Groote nor Thomas à Kempis seems to have expressed a direct opinion on the function and value of art. Its practice was not neglected in the convents influenced by the Devotio Moderna: Henric Mande, who enjoyed a great reputation as an illuminator, is a significant example. We know that copies of works produced in the houses of the Windesheim congregation could be illuminated, even if such decoration was somewhat rough and ready.[7] Finally, we shall see that Dieric Bouts and Geertgen tot Sint Jans painted pictures for the convent of the Visitation at Haarlem, one of the congregation's most important centres.

It is quite possible that the rigour of the earliest thinkers of the Devotio Moderna could have turned them from art. Nevertheless, such was the expansion of the movement that the appearance of more flexible attitudes is understandable. In a sermon delivered at Haarlem and Leiden in 1451, Nicholas of Cues declared: 'All images are worthwhile: they are venerable in so far as they call to mind the saints and symbolise their lives'.[8]

This was a tactful warning against the cult of images and the danger of idolatry. But at the same time the legate welcomed works of art as a prop for that inner devotion, that imitative path which was the Devotio Moderna, and from which his own attitude did not significantly differ. It is noteworthy that he commissioned an altarpiece devoted to the Passion of Christ for the hospital of St. Nicholas at Bernkastel-Kues.[9] Such an outlook is probably very close to that of the world of the Devotio Moderna.

Nevertheless, the development of this movement should not blind us to the renewal of other forms of spirituality. The old monastic orders took on fresh vigour. The Carthusians, at the height of their activity, had three new foundations during the century. The Dominicans enjoyed the favour of John and Jacqueline of Bavaria, who chose to be buried in their church at The Hague. Shortly before 1456 a reform of the order developed in The Hague and Rotterdam, giving birth to the 'congregation of Holland', whose first chapter-general was held at Lille in

51

1464. As for the Franciscans, they saw a return to the strict observance which made its first appearance at Gouda in 1418, spreading to most of the friaries by 1439.

Certainly, this enthusiasm did not affect all religious foundations. A contradictory example was the rich and noble abbey of Egmont which, throughout the century, resisted all proposed attempts at reform. As for the chapters, still powerful and numerous, they were more often assemblies of aristocratic secular canons than of priests with profound spiritual yearnings. But each large church was served not only by several priests attached to the sanctuary itself, but also by those connected with the dedication of one altar or another. The frequency of such dedications and the great number of confraternities bears witness to the strength of a religious faith which remained loyal to the daily ritual.

In this period when art was essentially religious—especially when princely patronage was lacking—it could only benefit from such a notable expansion of religious observance, and the reconstruction of the very channels of this devotion was inevitably felt, directly or indirectly, by artists.

IV. The challenge of Flemish art
Guelders and the Haarlem School in the reign of Philip the Good

When Philip the Good took possession of the county of Holland and Zeeland, the scene was already set for what is conventionally referred to today as Flemish art. Jan van Eyck did not complete the *Mystic Lamb* until 1432, but there is every reason to think that this great polyptych had been started several years earlier.[1] The painter is mentioned in the service of the Duke of Burgundy since 1425 and his art had certainly already reached its maturity.

In 1430, the work of the Master of Flémalle must have been essentially complete—although his only dated painting, one of the wings of the *Werl Altarpiece*, is from 1438—but there is agreement on its being the latest of his surviving productions. His major compositions, the *Triptych of the Descent from the Cross*, the *Mérode Altarpiece*, the *Flémalle Panels* are probably all earlier.[2] As for Rogier van der Weyden, he was no doubt officially only an 'apprentice' of Robert Campin and it was not until 1432 that he was admitted to the Tournai guild. Nevertheless, it is probable that his style had already acquired considerable individuality and that he had assumed the rôle of foreman in his master's workshop.[3] From 1435 and perhaps even a little earlier, the town of Brussels honoured his talent by choosing him as its official painter.

Since the murder on the bridge of Montereau in 1419, the Duke of Burgundy had taken up residence in the southern Netherlands, dividing his time between his palaces in Lille, Brussels, Ghent and Bruges. A brilliant court gathered around him, clamouring for artists of renown to satisfy its artistic tastes. Moreover, the oligarchs of the Flemish cities had acquired such wealth in the preceding decades that they too competed in the employment of painters.

In the North, on the other hand, the only princely court active after 1424 (and that on a very modest scale) was that of the Duke of Guelders. The richest and most active regions, Holland and Zeeland, no longer had a resident prince. Did they, from then on, trail in the wake of Burgundy? Are there any signs of an increased emigration depriving these territories of their most brilliant artists to the advantage of their foreign overlord? It seems not, for no northern name appears among those of painters on the sovereign's rolls. Only Jan van Eyck, who could have become the great inspiration of the northern provinces, left one prince for the other and it was probably not until a little later that Dieric Bouts left Haarlem to settle in Louvain.

The art of the North could not, however, completely escape the influence of the South. The works of the great creative spirits were too powerful not to leave their mark on the northern artists, who must have known of their existence: the political and economic links between the two regions were sufficiently close to ensure the existence of artistic contacts.

The earliest expressions of northern painting in the reign of Philip the Good remain shrouded in obscurity. In Guelders or at Utrecht, it is one exceptional work, that of an illuminator, which confirms the existence of an original tradition of painting. In Holland, the evidence of the paintings must be reconciled with the remarks of Karel van Mander, and it is from their twin testimony that we can derive a more precise view of artistic activity.

The Master of Catherine of Cleves

Once again an illuminated book of hours must be studied as an important turning-point in north Netherlandish painting. This book of hours is less lavish than the *Turin-Milan Hours,* but nevertheless of unusual richness; and its history, though less complicated than that of the volume now in Turin, remains mysterious.

Only half of it was known—and that not well, since it was in a somewhat inaccessible collection—until 1963, when a volume of equal size turned up, belonging undoubtedly to the same original ensemble. The two fragments have now been brought together in the Pierpont Morgan Library and have been the subject of many studies and even of a complete colour facsimile which has enjoyed wide distribution.[4]

The origin of the volume remains partly obscure. It was certainly illustrated for the Duchess Catherine of Cleves who is depicted on the first page in an attitude of prayer at the feet of the Virgin. Her parents' and grandparents' arms decorate the borders.

However, when we try to pin down the date at which the manuscript could have been produced, the clues are lacking. The niece of Philip the Good through her mother, Mary of

42, 51 169, 181

42 *Hours of Catherine of Cleves.* The Virgin of the Immaculate Conception adored by Catherine of Cleves (*37-P 1*), New York, Pierpont Morgan Library

Burgundy, Catherine of Cleves was born on 25 May 1417 and betrothed at the age of seven to the young Arnold van Egmond, who had just been chosen as Duke of Guelders in succession to his great-uncle Reynald IV who had died without issue. The wedding was not celebrated until 1430 and the young bride not taken to join her husband for another year after that, on 4 February 1431. Two years later, at the age of 16, she gave birth to her first daughter and in 1439 to the third, who was also the last of her children. Shortly afterwards, relations between husband and wife worsened. In 1449–51 the duchess acted as regent while the duke made a pilgrimage to Rome and Jerusalem, but after his return she entered into open conflict with him with the support of her son Adolf. In 1461 the duke was even obliged to concede Lobith and Rozendaal to her as her personal property, and to acknowledge a debt to her of 17,000 Rhenish florins.

Was this sumptuous book of hours presented to the princess on the occasion of her wedding? It seems unlikely, since her portraits in the manuscript, though indistinct, seem to depict a young woman of more than fourteen years. But in that case, when could she have commissioned or received such a gift? Duke Arnold was engaged in a constant struggle against his rival Adolf van Berg, on whom the Emperor Sigismund had conferred the duchy, or against the towns; and in 1441 he was so short of money that he had to give in to the demands of the latter. Moreover, the book of hours is certainly the duchess's and the duke is not even portrayed in it, except perhaps in an illumination which characterises his face so little that it is not certain whether it was he the illuminator wished to depict. At the end of her life the duchess was leading an independent existence. Very early on, however, she disposed of funds of her own, as witness the sale by her in 1434 of a house, the 'Huis ter Kleef', which she had inherited at Haarlem.[5]

The manuscript itself offers some occasional dating clues, discovered by the astuteness of researchers like Friedrich Gorissen. A coin depicted in one of the margins was only minted from 1434 onwards. The style of the illuminations seems earlier than the manner evolved by the same master in the drawings which illustrate a bible in the Munich Library, which is dated 1439. In short, a date between 1435 and 1440 seems probable; at a time, in other words, when both Robert Campin — the Master of Flémalle — and Jan van Eyck were still active in the southern Netherlands.

180

52, 168

Acquaintance with these two masters, which is attested by some of the illuminations, should not mislead us, however: it is not sufficient to confirm the suggested dating. In 1435–40 it indicates not direct contacts but old links: of van Eyck there is no trace of the *Mystic Lamb*, for example, completed in 1432, but only of the *Turin-Milan* illuminations executed between 1424 and 1425. As for the Master of Flémalle, it is not his *Werl Altarpiece* whose resonances we sense, but those of much earlier works like the lost *Deposition from the Cross*.

The special appeal of this manuscript is precisely that we constantly find echoes of works from the Flemish territories or even from the Parisian court at the turn of the century, but translated into a rough, spontaneous language which recalls the style of the Dutch illuminators of the beginning of the century. In the richness of its content, the *Book of Hours of Catherine of Cleves* recalls the most magnificent works of the Duke of Berry. It even seems to rival them in the quantity of its illustration. But there is sparing use of the noble and expensive materials — gold and azure — employed lavishly by the painters of the French king's uncle. Instead of refined, mannered arabesques, the broadly decorated margins contain lush acanthus leaves or remarkable depictions of a whole naturalistic world: mussels, cages, arches, pretzels.

Can we see in this the work of a single master? Can we accept as a single whole a volume containing 157 illuminations, not

43 *Hours of Catherine of Cleves.* Death of a rich man (*37-P 41*), New York, Pierpont Morgan Library, enlarged approx. 1.6 ×

including numerous decorative designs and figures in the margin? The size of the task would certainly justify us in expecting a collaboration of several artists. And yet what strikes one immediately about the illustration is its remarkable unity. There is no sign here of the change of hand so frequent in the great princely manuscripts, of which the *Turin-Milan Hours* provide one of the most complex examples. The same harmony of colours, the same rhythm, the same style of background, are maintained from the first page to the last.

Nevertheless, this does not exclude the possibility that several hands may indeed be present. If one compares the full-page portrayal of the Trinity (Plummer 32) with the following scenes (Plummer 33, 34, 35), the diversity of styles becomes apparent. The faces in the large illumination are vigorously modelled with a strained, rather dramatic expression. Those in the three small

44 *Hours of Catherine of Cleves.* St. Cornelius and St. Cyprian (*37-P 121*), New York, Pierpont Morgan Library

scenes which follow are more impersonal, more elegant and less interesting. All the same, the overall conception of the large and small illuminations is very similar, the style of the drapery folds identical. The type of seat is the same, and the colouring is similar with only a few slight variations. The example cited here could be repeated throughout the volume. If it is possible to distinguish three or even four hands, they are so similar that it would be difficult not to link them very closely. They were undoubtedly different craftsmen of one workshop, inspired by a dominant personality who probably sketched all the scenes and executed the most important himself. It would not, therefore, be going too far to regard the entire volume as the expression of a single creative artist.

The diversity of the illustrations could, however, cast doubts on such homogeneity as is suggested by their execution. Sometimes very modern in conception, sometimes very traditional in techniques, they are often disconcerting. Many scenes are set against a decorative background, sometimes even like the 49, 173 *Entombment* (Plummer 30) against one of those chequered backcloths so dear to the thirteenth and fourteenth centuries. *Joachim and St. Anne* (Plummer 91) is even set against a gold 169 background. Above all, the illuminations are centred on the figures. It is they that take pride of place, appearing in the foreground and leaving all elements of the setting at the back. The choice of format for the scenes is in itself significant. Apart from the rare full pages, they are set in an almost square frame which scarcely allows the development of large landscapes or interiors. If we take the illuminations of the *Turin-Milan Hours* as our point of reference, it is certain that the Master of Catherine of Cleves is, in this respect, closer to Master H than to Jan van Eyck, whose revolutionary outlook he does not attempt to adopt.

In the full-page illuminations and sometimes even in the small pictures, the artist is fond of using an architectural frame to enclose the scene. It is not, however, that adopted by Rogier van der Weyden for the *Altarpiece of the Virgin* at Granada: it has neither the latter's Gothic elegance nor its subtle mediating rôle between the world of the painting and that of the spectator, between the time of the scene depicted and history. Rather, it seems to spring directly from the tradition of manuscript illumination and of architectural frameworks which begin to take shape as a convention in the thirteenth century. The bases of these frames never appear on the page, and they seem to float on the parchment. Moreover, the strapwork in the margins clings to their edges as if the illuminator had wanted to emphasise that they both had the same essentially decorative character. These arches open up on to a clearly defined space, a niche, a room or even the choir of a church, and their architecture usually blends in with the structures on to which they open out. In this there is a trend towards illusionism, which makes itself felt in these details and which, this time, is breaking new ground. In several cases the arch is drawn very flat, harking back almost to Romanesque forms, and its surface is shown as coinciding with that of the parchment, with the space containing the scene recessed behind it (Plummer 7, 19, 56, 59).

45 *Hours of Catherine of Cleves*. Three souls fed in Hell by an angel (*37-P 46*), New York, Pierpont Morgan Library

46 *Hours of Catherine of Cleves*. The Tree of Life growing from Adam's tomb (*37-P 82*), New York, Pierpont Morgan Library

An equally remarkable novelty is the importance accorded to the landscapes. The illuminator seems to seize every excuse for elaborating their elements, just as the mood takes him. Certainly, his view does not have the refinements of Jan van Eyck's art, nor even Master H's. It is much more spontaneous, a little uncouth even, but it attracts attention by the pursuit of effect at the expense of rigour or precision. A revealing instance is that of the page devoted to the scene of *Jesus in the Garden of Gethsemane* (Plummer 16). The composition is a very free interpretation of the picture by Master H in the *Turin-Milan Hours (27)*. Curiously, the landscape is in quite a different vein from that of its model. For the rather dry convention of round hills, the Master of Catherine of Cleves has substituted simpler distances with a completely empirical and foreshortened perspective. The white streak of a road links the main area with the lakes in the background, and rather than strive for minute exactness, the artist has tried to express some effects of light in a very painterly manner. The sky itself is suggested by a few whitish and silvery trails on a blue background, instead of Master H's fluffy clouds. This completely spontaneous evocation of the background is much closer to the spirit of Jan van Eyck's illuminations than to those of his collaborator or colleague whose composition inspired the arrangement of the scene. The effects of light in the background, the linking of the different areas by a path are visibly and directly inspired by the Eyckian technique, but in a manner which does not aim at the same minuteness.

Sometimes, especially when the subject does not lend itself to a great expansion of landscape, the artist nevertheless falls back on the convention of the round hills dear to Master H, as in the *Visitation* (Plummer 11) or even the background of the *Crucifixion* (Plummer 26). However, in most cases he prefers a more ambitious idea, like the curious and appealing half-mountain, half-marine landscape in the scene of *St. Peter giving the Grace of the Holy Ghost* (Plummer 59). It is quite possible that this aspect of the pictures was left to the initiative of each executant and that each of the two approaches corresponds to a different artist. The more elaborate style remains close to that of the large compositions and therefore probably belongs to the master of the workshop.

172

It is difficult not to acknowledge an unusually poetic imagination in the principal artist of this manuscript. His art is summed up in the baffling modernism of *The Tree of Life growing out of Adam's tomb* (Plummer 82), in which the tender growth of the new tree stands out, with a moving simplicity and effectiveness, against a dramatic sunset.

46

The sources of this complex art enable us to pin down the artist's personality better. In the first place there is the tradition of Parisian illumination of which the painter must have been aware. His manner of conceiving the architectural frame as a structure without foundations comes directly from the evolution of the frame of the picture in thirteenth- and fourteenth-century books. An obvious case of contact with a great Parisian artist is provided by the illustration of the pool of Bethesda (Plummer 86): this is an almost literal transposition of a drawing by the Master of the Rohan Hours now in the Brunswick Museum.[6] The illuminator has preserved the essence

47 *Hours of Catherine of Cleves.* The Holy Family (*37-P 93*), New York, Pierpont Morgan Library

of his model while simplifying it and copying very exactly the figure of the sick man on the right who is trying to raise himself by leaning on his stick.

Perhaps more surprising are the borrowings from the Master of Flémalle. Let us cite first of all the reworking, often mentioned since 1904, of the *Deposition from the Cross* which formed the centre of the altarpiece known to us through a copy in the Walker Art Gallery in Liverpool. The illumination (Plummer 28) simplifies the original a little, of course, but keeps its essential character. Here again, the former has introduced a landscape where the latter had a gold backdrop. The *Crucifixion* has also often been cited as a copy of a lost work by the Master of Flémalle (Plummer 26). Nevertheless, it is more probable that the illuminator has only reconstituted this scene from the same triptych to which the *Deposition from the Cross* belonged; the two thieves are mere variants of those from the wings of that ensemble, while the group of the Virgin and St. John, despite modifications of their poses, could have been based on the same model.

These are not the only imitations of paintings by the Tournai Master. The Master of Catherine of Cleves often draws inspiration from a layout or group chosen from a painting with a large number of figures, and extracts from it a highly personal interpretation which retains only the spirit of the model. Such is the leaf depicting the *Marriage of the Virgin* (Plummer 8), each of whose figures can be found in the Prado painting,[7] but several of them, particularly the High Priest, are dressed more simply and humbly than in the full-size model. Other leaves lead one to suppose that the illuminator could have drawn inspiration with

the same freedom from lost works by the same artist. Perhaps the most obvious case is that of the *Meeting at the Golden Gate* (Plummer 4), in which the characters themselves are not the standard types of the Master of Catherine of Cleves, but recall those in paintings like the *Nativity* in Dijon, of which the landscape is also reminiscent.

The *Turin-Milan Hours* are a no less evident source for the artist. We have already cited a direct re-interpretation, that of *Christ in the Garden of Gethsemane*, inspired by Master H. The scene of the *Carrying of the Cross* comes either directly from the original by van Eyck that we know through the version in Budapest, or from a variant of the same composition. Other instances are less obvious: the *Nativity of the Virgin* (Plummer 5), for example, has been conceived from a detail of the *Nativity of St. John the Baptist* in the Turin volume. Still further pictures could have been inspired by lost originals by Jan van Eyck: the elegance of *St. Hubert* (Plummer 124), with its rearing horse surrounded by lithe hounds, suggests such an origin by recalling the figures of the *Sovereign's Prayer*.

The Master of Catherine of Cleves finds an unusual source of inspiration in engravings. A number of the animals depicted at the foot of pages or in the margins recur in engravings by the Master of the Playing-Cards and the Master of the Berlin Passion. The engraver's work, however, seems earlier. This is one of the first examples of the use of engravings as models in the decoration of an illuminated book.[8]

Nevertheless, although the illuminator must have had direct acquaintance with such models, it remains improbable that he was trained in the workshop of the southern masters, since he never attempts direct imitation either of their colouring or even of their drawing. Between the duke of Bavaria's painters and the Master of Catherine of Cleves there must be some missing links. There are two artists whose style and technique suggest such a background. First of all there is Hulin de Loo's Master K, the 'continuator' of the *Turin Hours*. He could have played the rôle of intermediary since he had made the acquaintance, under the best conditions, of the volume on which Jan van Eyck and Master J had worked, and because he himself had tried to draw inspiration, in an equally rough technique, from the compositions of his elder. We may even presume that for certain pictures painted by him in the *Turin-Milan Hours,* he possessed a sketch by Jan van Eyck or Master H. This could be so for the lower margins of the calendar; and quite possibly also for the *Nailing to the Cross* (Durrieu, 1902R, pl. XIX), and definitely for the *Carrying of the Cross* (Durrieu, 1902R, pl. XVIII) which is a variant of the composition of the Budapest painting. This painter, in his uninhibited style, his love of the picturesque and the common touch, in his taste for landscape, has several things in common with the Master of Catherine of Cleves. Even the curious mannerism of indicating the eyes by such clearly defined strokes that they impart a sort of grimace to the face finds some analogy in the draughtsmanship of the illuminator of the New York volumes, especially in his large miniatures.[9]

The most immediate antecedents of the Master of Catherine of Cleves can be found, however, in the miniatures of the

169

171

181

172

Breviary referred to as Reynald IV's, now in the Pierpont Morgan Library in New York (MS 87).[10] Several scholars (Byvanck, Finke, Pieper) even attribute part of these illuminations to the Master of Catherine of Cleves himself.

If this breviary was produced for Duke Arnold, however, as there is now a tendency to believe,[11] it would date from 1425–35 and would just precede the *Hours of Catherine of Cleves*. One of the most novel aspects of its illustration is certainly the prominence of the landscapes: they can be seen, as it were, as free interpretations of Eyckian models, very painterly sketches which retain an interest in the rendering of light from Jan van Eyck. The landscapes by the Master of Catherine of Cleves are very much in the same spirit.

Nonetheless, the most remarkable originality of Catherine of Cleves' illuminator is that he married together two traditions: on the one hand the spontaneity and freshness, in both invention and technique, of Dutch illumination, on the other hand a certain elegance and pursuit of refinement in colouring which derive from court art, and in his particular case from the artists of John of Bavaria. The former has been demonstrated by Hoogewerff and Byvanck, and more recently and more precisely in Delaissé's analysis of the characteristics peculiar to the northern Netherlands.[12] The interest shown at the beginning of the twentieth century in Parisian and Burgundian court illumination, which seemed the most perfect and most significant aspect of this technique, had led art historians to neglect northern productions, which seemed somewhat heavy, even rustic, by comparison with the former. Modern sensibility, influenced by expressionist traditions which western countries are beginning to appreciate, is allowing us a better understanding of the true quality of this art. It is just this expressive force which is its most notable element. The crudeness is due in part to economic problems: the absence of wealthy patronage and the need for cheapness. But it was also a matter of principle, of preferring the spontaneity of a gesture, the immediacy of an expressive form, to exactness and minute description. Delaissé has rightly emphasised how much the Devotio Moderna movement, by rejecting the splendour and richness of princely art, could have contributed to such a trend.

Master K. strove to adapt this freedom of style to the world of van Eyck. After him, the Master of Catherine of Cleves adopted it with greater vigour. His colouring is based on much more refined harmonies than those used by some of his contemporaries like the Master of Otto of Moerdrecht. He is familiar with broken tints. He is conscious of the elegance of forms: the pictures of the saints provide a fine example. The drapery of the figures also recalls Eyckian models both by its simplicity and by its plastic quality. This marriage of the two tendencies was to recur several years later in the work of the Master of Evert van Soudenbalch.[13]

This does not, however, mean that this tradition is not original. The very fact that it is enlivened by a popular streak has given it its strength. If we add that the Master of Catherine of Cleves was evidently gifted with considerable individuality and an exceptional inventiveness, he becomes a crucial figure. The

48 *Hours of Catherine of Cleves*, Crucifixion (*37-P 96*), New York, Pierpont Morgan Library

greatest surprise, when the second fragment of the princess's book of hours turned up, was the presence of marginal decorations based on realistic depictions of everyday objects. The idea was known in Bruges at the end of the fifteenth century, but whatever date one accepts for the production of the book of hours, here it is particularly early and marked by a great freedom of imagination. The fish devouring each other around St. Laurence (Plummer 128), the caged birds around SS. Cornelius and Cyprian (Plummer 121), the open mussels and the crabs which so unexpectedly accompany St. Ambrose (Plummer 119), the butterflies of St. Vincent (Plummer 129), the pretzels of St. Bartholomew (Plummer 112), these are all extraordinary, and partake of a popular humour which finds its only equivalent in Pucelle's lower margins. Sometimes the attributes or legend of the saint suggest the motifs in these decorations: this is so with St. Sebastian surrounded by bows and arrows, and St. Cecilia, who is accompanied by bird-feathers (Plummer 151). This seems less frequent, however, than inventions justified solely by fantasy, unless the allusions are so subtle that their significance has so far escaped us, or relies on puns. (The birds of St. Cornelius justified by his name, for example—*corneille*, 'the crow'?)

This popular, fantastic imagination is also given its head in the treatment of evangelical or biblical scenes. One need only think of the table set up in the mouth of Hell so that three souls can savour the food brought to them by an angel (Plummer 47). The scenes of the childhood of Christ are in the same vein and

49 *Hours of Catherine of Cleves.* God the Father adored by the saints (*37-P 61*), New York, Pierpont Morgan Library

directly foreshadow seventeenth-century Dutch art or, at a lesser distance, the *Virgin with the Milk-pap* by Gerard David. Good old St. Joseph, sitting in an armchair made out of a barrel and doing his utmost to cool the Child's pap (Plummer 93), is inconceivable in a Parisian volume, let alone in a book of hours for the use of the Burgundian court.

The other works attributed to the Master of Catherine of Cleves have the same characteristics, but rarely the same spontaneity and imaginative vigour. The eight illuminations of the *Bible* dated 1439 in the Munich State Library[14] show forms seized by a turbulent emotion. The two volumes recently discovered, the *Book of Hours of Katharina van Lochorst* and the *Book of Hours* which probably belonged to the same Lochorst family before passing to the Sevichvelds,[15] even when they offer illuminations whose richness and elegance aim at the standards of court art, have, in spite of everything, some of the roughness of the Munich drawings. The first of these two volumes does not include any really new themes, except for a more elaborate interpretation of the *Taking of Christ,* enriched by a broad landscape but still based on van Eyck's illumination. The second, however, contains a *Last Judgment* in the formula which was to achieve wide currency in both the north and south Netherlands, and a curious depiction of the *Mass of St. Gregory,* in which the instruments of the Passion are arranged as a sort of trophy beside the altar. The device seems to have enjoyed some popularity: we find it notably in an altarpiece by the Master of the Morrison Triptych in the Church of San Salvador in Valladolid.[16] The master gave of his best, however, in the volume intended for Catherine of Cleves. This was an exceptional commission by reason of the large number of illuminations required and by the richness of the ornamentation desired. On this occasion he produced what was, perhaps, his masterpiece.

Who then was this unusual master? A Carthusian monk? It is unlikely. Even if the text of the volume had been transcribed in a monastery of the order, Nieuwlicht (Utrecht) or Monnickhuizen (Arnhem), that would not necessarily mean that the illuminations were also.[17] Rather, one is put in mind of those Utrecht craftsmen of whom we only know the names. The artist's work for members of the Lochorst family lends probability to this hypothesis.

Panel paintings contemporary with the Master of Catherine of Cleves

One would expect to find echoes of such an artist in the field of panel painting. But few works contemporary with his output have survived. The nearest is the altarpiece formerly in the church at Roermond, that is, in Guelders.[18] This panel (*38*), of popular inspiration brings together in three tiers eighteen scenes from the life of Christ. The formula itself suggests comparison with the illuminations. Much less skilfully than the Master of Catherine of Cleves, the painter depicts scenes inspired by similar models.

There is even a discreet architectural frame in some of the compositions to recall the common source. The date established by identification of the donor situates the work between 1430 and 1440, making it, in other words, almost contemporary with the *Hours of Catherine of Cleves*.

A later painting, apparently datable around 1450 through the identity of its donor, offers many points of similarity with the Master of Catherine of Cleves; but it comes from Dordrecht, that is, from Holland. This is a *St. Agnes with donor* in the possession of the Rijksmuseum (*40*). The depiction of the saint is very similar to that in the fragment of the book of hours in the Pierpont Morgan Library (Plummer 147): a notable example is the delightful sheep standing on its hind legs, with its forelegs resting against the saint. The manner is similarly unrefined and the draughtsmanship a little stiff. This is not the place to look for a profound renewal of painting in the northern Netherlands. It is none the less interesting to note that the panel, devised for a Dutchwoman and probably painted in Holland, was composed according to the same design as that of the Utrecht illuminator.

In contrast, the painting in Kranenberg church, published by F. Gorissen, belongs to the cruder tradition (*39*). From the art of the southern provinces, its author has scarcely learnt more than a technique of modelling which endows the figures with some plasticity, and a certain simplicity of shape and drapery. The work remains striking only by reason of the expressions of the faces, their dramatic aspect, and the austerity of the colour, with a red ground replacing the traditional gold backcloth.

51 *Hours of Catherine of Cleves.* Preparations for the Crucifixion (*37-P 25*), New York, Pierpont Morgan Library

50 *Hours of Catherine of Cleves.* The alms-giving (*37-P 57*), New York, Pierpont Morgan Library

These three works bear very modest witness to the persistence of the two trends and to their unification so perfectly achieved by the Master of Catherine of Cleves in his principal work. They certainly cannot in themselves be taken to prove that an important school of painting existed in the ecclesiastical principality of Utrecht or in Guelders. At the most, they suggest the survival of a tradition of which they are no more than the faint echo.

The Haarlem School

'Tradition asserts that the town of Haarlem, in Holland, possessed distinguished painters early on, indeed the best in the Netherlands, and the fact is confirmed by the existence of Albert van Ouwater and Geertgen tot Sint Jans, as well as Dieric of Haarlem, who was also a famous painter in those far-off times. The oldest painters are of the opinion that it was at Haarlem that the correct manner of treating landscape was first adopted'.[18]

These words of Karel van Mander have often been quoted and even more often criticised. Their tone of surprise has been casually ascribed to a literary conceit and their declarations written off as the unfounded invention of local patriotism. This is easily said, but deserves more careful examination. We must remember firstly that van Mander was only a citizen of Haarlem by adoption[19] and that such a determined desire to create a glorious past for the town would be, to say the least, odd. It would be even more surprising in view of the fact that in 1604, when our chronicler published his *Lives,* Haarlem was far from

52 MASTER OF CATHERINE OF CLEVES. *Death of Noah*, Munich, State Library (Cod. Germ. 1102 folio 15 v.)

playing a leading rôle in either the politics, economics or art of the northern Netherlands.

Let us suppose for a moment that Haarlem had become for Karel van Mander his true home. Why then did he not devise a richer, more appealing legend to justify his statements? If he had invented an artist, why did he only find a single painting to ascribe to him, and one, moreover, only known through a copy? To this mysterious Albert van Ouwater, could he only add this Dieric of Haarlem without even noticing that he was identical with the great artist of Louvain? He must have had a poor imagination if he could dream up nothing better in order to credit his home town with an important school of painting!

No, the simple-mindedness does not lie where one expects it; not among those who accept the chronicler's statements, but on the contrary among those who see them as the fruit of a patriotic imagination. To deny the problem is to leave all the riddles unexplained: the existence of a painting answering to the description of Albert van Ouwater's; the refined art of Geertgen tot Sint Jans, which one would then have to link up, with some difficulty, to southern art alone; the evidence of Bouts's origins in Haarlem.

The accounts of the town of Haarlem, and likewise those of the Church of St. Bavo, attest the existence of a great number of painters in the town during the fifteenth century.[20] Of course, like all such references, they are not explicit enough for us to be sure that they all concern artists in the true sense of the word, rather than simple craftsmen-painters. Only one of them, Vrederick Hoon, has been partially identified through an important work of which we have only sketchy indications. It is thus an argument of little weight in favour of van Mander's statements, but it would be just as irresponsible not to take it into account.

It would be more justifiable to ask how Haarlem could have become the centre of such great artistic activity in the fifteenth century. The answer to this, however, is clear. If we consult the known records, it seems that the city was at that time the second of the northern Netherlands, after Dordrecht and ahead of Leiden and Amsterdam. Although in 1515 it only came third for the number of hearths, with 2,714 against Leiden's 3,017 and Delft's 2,733,[21] during the fifteenth century it remained, in contrast, the most heavily taxed town when Dordrecht was not, and the second when Dordrecht was: in 1426 it paid 5,000 *écus* while Leiden and Delft only paid 3,500 each,[22] and in 1461 it was still taxed at the rate of 3,594 *écus* when Dordrecht paid 3,920, Delft and Leiden 3,375 each.[23]

Throughout the fifteenth century Haarlem seems to have been a rich and busy town. Its main activity was industry: the manufacture of linen-cloth, in which it was a by no means negligible rival of Leiden, and above all brewing, one of its vital resources.[24] Also a market town, it was the urban centre of an agricultural region which formed its hinterland.

By comparison with its neighbours, its history was relatively calm in the fifteenth century. It was only marked by two troubled periods. In 1444 it was the scene of a revival of the struggle between the *Kabeljauwen* and the *Hoeksen*. Violence broke out. With the people up in arms, several burgomasters were forced to resign. Order was quickly restored by the Duchess Isabella of Portugal, sent for this purpose by the duke. Haarlem experienced disturbances on one other ocasion, in 1492. This time they were caused by a peasant uprising and the principal victim was the bailiff (that is, the count's representative) Niclaas van Ruyven, who was lynched by the populace. This was one of the most violent incidents sparked off by the poverty from which the country was suffering as a result of the political struggles that had been raging for over ten years.

A further token of the city's wealth is the number of religious foundations. At the beginning of the century the only ones recorded were a Carmelite convent (founded in 1249), a Béguine nunnery (1262), a Dominican friary (1287), and the Commandery of the Order of St. John (1310). From 1400, foundations followed one another in quick succession: the canons regular of Windesheim established their monastery of the Visitation; the new convent (Nieuwe Klooster) founded by Willem van Egmont was short-lived; then came the convent of the Nuns of St. Michael in 1414. The movement was temporarily halted by an edict of 1426 forbidding the foundation of new religious houses. However, it resumed a little before the middle of the century and there appeared successively in 1445 the convent of St. Ursula, in 1446 that of St. Catherine, in 1449 that of St. Margaret, in 1456 the Minorite friary founded with the support of Philip the Good himself, a monastery of Bernardines in 1457, a convent of St. Clare in 1459, of Carmelites in 1465, of the Nuns of St. Cecilia in 1468, of the Virgin between 1468 and 1485, of the Sisters of Mary Magdalene in 1474, of St. Anne in 1485, an Augustinian priory in 1490 and a monastery of 'Cellebroers' in 1496.[25] The list is eloquent and probably incomplete. Need we also recall that the same century saw the erection of one of the largest, if not *the* largest, of Holland's parish churches, St. Bavo?[26]

All these facts do not, in themselves, establish the existence of a school of painting. But at least they guarantee that favourable circumstances existed to encourage its development and that, of all the towns of the northern Netherlands, Haarlem was probably the one which offered the most propitious conditions. We have here yet another reason for putting our faith in van Mander's statements.

Albert van Ouwater

To van Mander we owe the essence of what we know about Albert van Ouwater, and admittedly that is very little. According to van Mander he was a contemporary of Jan van Eyck and in confirmation he cites the testimony of an old painter whom he had just interviewed in 1604, Albert Simonsz.[27] Sixty years earlier, around 1544, the latter had been a pupil of Mostaert who claimed he was about seventy[28] and declared that he had never known either Geertgen tot Sint Jans or Albert van Ouwater. What can we deduce from this calculation? If we agree, as appears reasonable, that from the age of ten Mostaert could have known and remembered into his old age the famous painters of his home town, the death of Geertgen must have occurred before 1484. As we know that the latter lived for twenty-eight years, that would place his entry into the workshop of his master, Albert van Ouwater, thirteen years earlier at the latest, around 1470. But this will not suffice to establish that the first great painter of the Haarlem school was a contemporary of van Eyck, who died in 1441.

Most modern historians have pointed out the irrelevance of this calculation, often forgetting that the dates derived from it only constitute *termini ante quos*. The fact that Mostaert did not know Geertgen only means that the latter died around 1484 at the latest. Theoretically, there is no reason why he should not have died ten, twenty or thirty years earlier. Van Mander's assertion is therefore backed up only by a very rough estimate. It could just as easily be wrong as be a clumsy setting-out of more precise information provided by Albert Simonsz. Would the archives be more explicit? We might have believed so, along with van der Willigen, who published a text which he read as a payment for the burial of the artist's daughter in 1467.[29] Unfortunately, a check reveals a mistake in the reading and that the entry refers to a certain 'ouwe Claes'.[30]

All investigations have failed to find any trace of the painter in the archives. What conclusion should we draw from this? That the Haarlem master was a pure invention of van Mander? Once again, this seems unlikely when we think of how little the latter was able to say about him. Should we therefore assume that the artist was a citizen of Oudewater, as his name may indicate, and that he only worked at Haarlem from time to time? It is one of the possible hypotheses. The fact remains, however, that the mention of two important works, still known in Haarlem in the seventeenth century, suggests sufficient fame to render this solution improbable. There are also plenty of large gaps in the archives, but the gaps occur at widely spaced intervals throughout the century, so that it is difficult to explain by them alone the absence of any reference to our painter.[31]

What if the artist did appear in these archives, but under another name? After all, Albert Simonsz was already very old in 1604—he was eighty-one—when van Mander appealed to his memory, and, moreover, only had his information at second hand. Among the painters working at Haarlem in the fifteenth century there is no Albert—Albrecht—but there is a Lambrecht: the two Christian names sound similar and confusion could have arisen with the passage of time. There is no proof, however, that the two men were one and the same. Lambrecht is never called 'van Ouwater', but is nearly always mentioned as the son of Rutgen. Neither is his father, a painter before him, mentioned as coming from that town. No fifteenth century archives from Oudewater have survived which might help us find further clues. We are thus left with no more than a hypothesis. The fact remains that Lambert Rutgenszoon was a considerable painter, very active and frequently mentioned between 1428 and 1465. If we are satisfied with the dates currently accepted for the painter in recent literature, we should have to eliminate this possibility at once.

We must therefore resign ourselves to returning to van Mander's text and analysing his evidence in the hope of finding some indication which would enable us to date the artist's activity. The first work mentioned, although lost, deserves some attention: this 'Roman altar' was one of the altars standing against the pillars of the ambulatory in St. Bavo. It had been dedicated by the pilgrims to Rome. The pilgrimage to the pontifical city had been practically abandoned during the first half of the fifteenth century because of the great schism. It was on the occasion of the Jubilee of 1450, preached in 1449, that Pope Nicholas V succeeded in restoring it to its former status.[32] Such a commission should therefore be dated about 1450.[33]

The second painting is well known; it is the *Raising of Lazarus* (42) in the Berlin Museum. On the surface there is no indication of a date: no coat of arms reveals for whom it was painted, no inscription enlightens us. One single fact assists us in dating it: the common inspiration which seems to link it with the *Exhumation of St. Hubert* in the National Gallery in London.[34] Both scenes are set in the chancel of a church whose axis coincides exactly with that of the painting. In both panels the centre foreground contains the open tomb from which Lazarus steps in the one, and from which the saint's body is raised in the other. In both, the principal characters are huddled in two groups, one on each side of the tomb, the only difference being that Albert van Ouwater's St. Peter occupies the centre of the middle ground. The final shared motif is the popular touch of the bystanders who observe the miracles through the screen of the chancel.

It happens that the London painting has recently been dated with some certainty between 1437 and 1440–5.[35] If we grant it precedence, we cannot place Ouwater's before the fifth decade of the century. This question deserves closer examination. As Wolfgang Schöne has rightly noted,[36] both paintings are derived from the *Madonna of Canon van der Paele* by Jan van Eyck, which is dated 1436. The originality of the two works lies in their having adopted the idea of van Eyck's composition while

53–56

rejecting its horizontal format, no doubt dictated by its purpose, in favour of a vertical design, which is more suitable for showing off the structure of a church. The *Raising of Lazarus* is much closer to the van Eyck model; firstly in the style of the architecture, which is Romanesque in both cases, and secondly because both masters have placed, in defiance of all likelihood, columns of precious marble in the chancel. The similarities do not end there. Albert van Ouwater has also adopted, naturally with variations, the capitals of the Bruges painting while retaining the type of crockets created by van Eyck. Similarly he has kept the decorative capitals for the columns of the choir and adopted, for the pilasters in the ambulatory, figured capitals whose scenes emphasise, as in the van Eyck, the significance of the main scene.

In contrast, the artist of the London painting, whose relation to Rogier van der Weyden is evident and universally accepted,

follows his master in adopting a more down-to-earth realism. The fact that he prefers to depict a Gothic church rather than a Romanesque one could be explained by the subject, which quite obviously belongs in the Christian era. He gives the church a much more commonplace character, even a certain dryness: the columns are of stone as in all the churches of Brabant, while the foliage capitals and the strictness of the axial arrangement are slightly pedantic, and the light lacks the delicacy which characterises the Berlin painting. However, the design of the two works is so similar that one must be derived from the other. This analysis leads to the following vital conclusion: the *Raising of Lazarus* was painted after the *Madonna of Canon van der Paele*, i.e.

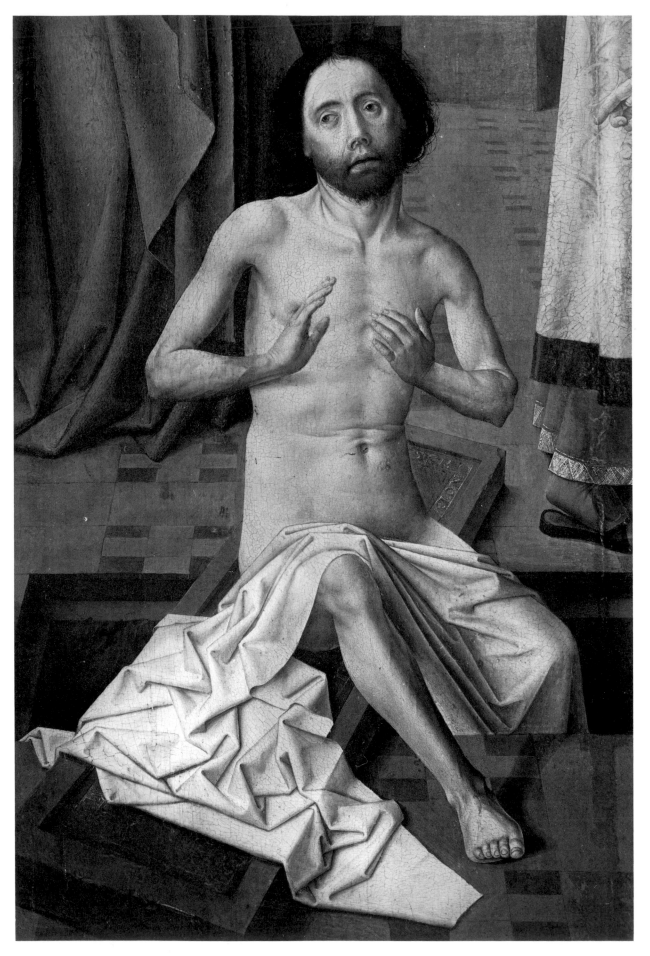

55 OUWATER. *Raising of Lazarus,* details of Lazarus, Berlin, Staatliche Museen (*42*)

56 OUWATER. *Raising of Lazarus,* detail, Christ and the Believers, Berlin, Staatliche Museen (*42*) ▷

after 1436, and before the *Exhumation of St. Hubert,* i.e. before 1437–45. To simplify matters, let us say that it must have been produced between 1435 and 1445.

The links between these three paintings also teach us another important fact: that the contacts between the Haarlem painter Albert van Ouwater and the southern artists of Bruges and Brussels were closer than we have dared to imagine. Indeed, the speed with which this model was transmitted from Bruges to Haarlem, then from Haarlem to Brussels, all in the space of about ten years is worthy of note. Moreover, the attention paid by a Haarlem artist like Albert van Ouwater to the work of Jan van Eyck is no less surprising. It suggests that we should not entirely exclude the possibility that the former had been trained by the latter. The fact that we can prove that Ouwater was already working around 1435–45 lends more credit to his hypothetical identification with Lambert Rutgenszoon.

In 1439 Lambert Rutgenszoon was paid for 'washing' (verwaschen) the backgrounds of six apostles depicted on the pillars of St. Bavo, a routine job, which was probably entrusted to him because he himself had painted these apostles. The murals have vanished today, but the remains of three of them were discovered in the mid-nineteenth century during the restoration of the church. Unfortunately, nothing has been preserved of them except some watercolours published in 1867 which are apparently not very accurate, and some large tracings. The latter confirm that the originals could not have been much earlier than 1439 and were therefore probably the work of this same Lambert Rutgenszoon. As far as one can judge, their style recalls that of the *Raising of Lazarus* in Berlin. The drapery transforms the bodies into heavy, powerful masses in a similar

184 manner. The *St. Paul* has an outline which resembles the St. Peter in the Berlin painting: the same fullness, the same outstretched arm lifting a broad expanse of cloak, the same stiffness of the fabric breaking off the curve of the folds. Here again it is difficult to be absolutely certain: the evidence remains too imprecise to guarantee that the hand was the same. It does not, however, refute the suggestion, and lends some support to the identification of Lambert Rutgenszoon with Albert van Ouwater.

Karel van Mander described the painter as 'very skilful in the painting of heads, extremities, draperies and landscapes'. His judgment is obviously that of a mannerist who gives prime importance to the evocation of characters by the quality of their anatomy and of the drawing of their clothes. Nevertheless, his remarks correspond very well with what we know from the works with which we are acquainted.

56 Albert van Ouwater's faces catch one's eye on a very first sight of the Berlin painting. In the circle of characters, he has skilfully given each a personality of his own. But the painter catches our attention most of all by the precision of the details of each physiognomy: wrinkles, skin colouration, eye shape, hair. On the other hand, the faces are virtually expressionless: each character is looking into empty space, and it is by the poses and gestures of the hands that the painter indicates their rôle and their significance. Here, as with Dieric Bouts, the governing

mood seems to be one of reserve and meditation. The drawing of these faces, however delicate, does not avoid the use of conventions, such as the curious manner of defining the opening of the eyelids by the arc of a circle when the eyes are cast down. Nor does the precision of detail exclude an impression of rounded form, often rather smooth, but always expressed by the play of light and shade.

The extremities—hands and feet— are just as remarkable for the same characteristics of precision and assurance in 55 modelling as much in the Berlin painting as in the Granada 59, 60 wings. The painter delights in the enumeration of details, going as far as to depict the lines on the palm of the hand (of St. Peter in the Berlin picture, for example), and he delineates very recognisable, very square fingernails with great minuteness. Generally, his hands are rather stumpy and lacking in elegance, perhaps because of this obsession with exactitude.

These characteristics of faces and hands, already noted by van Mander in the case of Albert van Ouwater, support, it seems to me, an attribution which may surprise, that of the *Man holding a Pink* (Berlin, Staatliche Museen; *41*) which for half a century has 57 desperately tried to find a place in van Eyck's œuvre. It certainly owes a great deal to Philip the Good's painter: its setting in the frame, its modelling by light and shade, the delicacy of its technique. However, it differs from him in its much more minute insistence on details like wrinkles or prominent veins, by a certain rigidity in the position of the hands, by the stare of the eyes. These wrinkles are those of the faces in the *Raising of* 53 *Lazarus;* these hands, whose fingernails are drawn so regularly, are those of St. Peter in the same painting. The colour harmony in which the finesse of the tone of the collar adds a kind of delicacy to a work of rough appearance is the same which gives the other painting in Berlin its almost feminine refinement.

What has made such a hypothesis impossible until now is the fact that Albert van Ouwater has always been seen as a painter who was only active in the second half of the fifteenth century. If he was already painting in 1428, the attribution becomes plausible. For the wearing of the Order of St. Anthony, the order of the house of Hainault-Bavaria, is only likely up until the early years of the third decade, while Jacqueline of Bavaria still held some vestige of sovereignty.

There remains, indeed, a portrait of Jacqueline of Bavaria (*49*) which copies a lost fifteenth-century original whose 185 characteristics are exactly those of the *Man holding a Pink:* the 57 same arm and hand behind the frame, the same presentation as a three-quarters view bust, the same lighting, the same exactness of detail, apparently a little blurred in the insufficiently sharp copy. This format is the one devised by Jan van Eyck at least as early as 1428 when he painted Isabella of Portugal in Lisbon[37]: the frame, whether it is painted, as in the van Eyck and in the *Man holding a Pink,* or solid, is an essential part of the conception, the realisation of a physical opening which locates the hands and thus the sitter in space in relation to it. But the mastery and

57 OUWATER. *The Man holding a Pink,* Berlin (*41*)   ▷

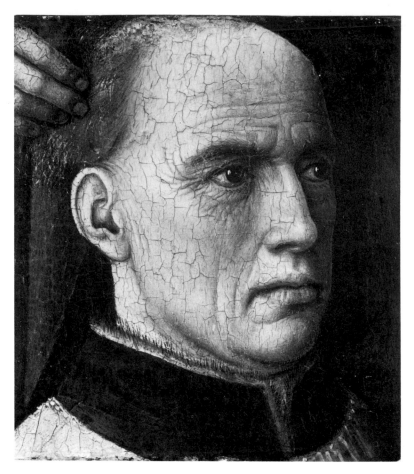

58 OUWATER. *Head of a donor* (a canon?), New York, Metropolitan Museum
(*43*)

nobility of the painter from Bruges give place, in these two
paintings, to a less acute observation.

Few other paintings can yet be included among the works of
Albert van Ouwater: two wings of a triptych identified by
stylistic attribution, *St. John the Baptist* and *St. Michael* (Granada,
Capilla Real, *44 and 45*) and a small fragment of a *Donor's head*
(New York, Metropolitan Museum, *43*). To this can be added a
drawing, *Jesus among the Doctors* (London, British Museum, *46*)
and two copies of lost works, one of which seems quite faithful,
the *Crucifixion* (Dresden, Print Room, *51*), the other probably
less accurate, the *Mission of the Apostles* (Aschaffenburg, Stifts-
kirche, *50*). Taken all together however, they enable us to pick
out the characteristics of a distinctive style.

To his admiration for the drawing of the extremities, Karel
van Mander adds that which he felt for the depiction of the
Lazarus in Berlin which 'for the period... deserved to be
considered a remarkable nude figure'. Such an opinion seems
fully justified, since Albert van Ouwater here displays a genuine
interest in strictly defined anatomy. Let us take as an example
the figure's right leg: it clearly reveals not only the lines of the
tibia and of the knee-cap beneath the skin, but also the veins and
tendons of the foot. One could make similar remarks about the
arms or the suggestion of the collar-bones. Here is a sense of
the nude which equals, in its concern with true anatomical
precision, the figure of Adam in the *Mystic Lamb*.[38] Only certain

figures of *Hell* by Bouts (Louvre, on loan to the Musée de Lille)
give such exact indications. In comparison, the nudes of Rogier
van der Weyden in the *Triptych of the Last Judgment* in the
Hôtel-Dieu at Beaune are much less assured, and it does not
seem possible to explain this difference by the damage they have
suffered through the centuries.[39]

The drapery also drew van Mander's admiration, which is
more surprising. Perhaps his praise was meant for the appearance of purely decorative bunched folds in Ouwater's work:
cases in point are the fabric surrounding the head of Mary
Magdalene in Berlin, the unfurling of Lazarus' shroud, the
movements of the doctor's robe in London or the spread of the
robe in Dresden. It is the decorative function of these draperies,
elaborated by the Master of Flémalle with the roughness typical
of his style, then developed with greater subtlety by Jan van
Eyck. In Ouwater's work it lies almost half-way between these
two great artists. The fabric never has the same softness as in
van Eyck, the folds proliferate rather in the manner of the
Master of Flémalle, but they are set out in a more harmonious
arrangement which derives from the example of the Bruges
master. The increased number of the folds accentuates their
purely decorative nature and, for that very reason, perhaps made
them more attractive to a Mannerist.

In other respects, however, the same draperies would rather
be liable to arouse the criticism of van Mander. Not that they
lack amplitude or that they do not reflect the structure of the
body, but they have a fondness for a long straight hang, clear-cut
and even stark, which tends to freeze the poses in strict
verticality. One could go on pointing out these heavy accents,
which hold the figures straight like so many props: the St. Peter
in Berlin or the right-hand doctor on the sheet in London are
good examples.

In extreme cases, the drapery completely envelops a figure,
which becomes almost abstract in its recreated structure. The
presentation then acquires a tinge of fantasy as in the mass of
brocade surmounted by a red hood which so curiously opens up
the group of Jews in the Berlin painting. Without the hand
behind the back and open towards us, it would seem inhuman.
Similarly there is the strange, revealing character, scarcely
misrepresented by the copy, of the St. Mary reduced to a mass of
mourning veils in the Dresden drawing. In this latter case,
though, we may recall the example of the *pleurants* in Burgundian sculpture since Sluter and, in the realm of painting, the
precedent of the corresponding figure in the *Pietà* by Master H
in the *Turin Hours* (*26*).

As for the last feature vaunted by van Mander, the landscape,
we must look for it in the works which have only a stylistic
attribution, the *St. John the Baptist* in Granada (*44*) and the drawn
copy of a *Crucifixion* (Dresden, Print Room, *51*). The common
spirit of the two works reinforces the attribution of them both,
which also finds confirmation in the close relationship to the
work of Geertgen. It is the latter who is immediately recalled by

59 OUWATER. *St. John the Baptist*, Granada, Capilla Real (*44*) ▷

one of the essential characteristics of the Granada painting: the precision and subtlety of the foliage. In the foreground, the painter delights in depicting each leaf individually, giving it an outline to gladden a botanist's heart. And yet this interest is accompanied by a desire to grasp the character of each frond and to suggest its structure both by an exact outline and by brush-strokes laid on in characteristic arcs which conjure up the branches lying on top of one another. At Granada the technique does not attain the realism that Geertgen was to impart to his best works: it is clearly preparing the way for it, while revealing the point of departure for such a device. It is difficult to imagine how such an interest could have arisen except through meditation and reflection in front of some works of van Eyck, perhaps even in front of the *Mystic Lamb*. The foliage in the foreground is a more commonplace rendition of the trees on the *Hermits* and *Pilgrims* wings in Ghent. As for the structure of the distant trees, it can be seen in embryo in the central panel of the *Lamb*, beside the group of Virgins.

The spatial conception of these works is immediately striking because of the attempt at defining the setting, not without difficulty, as a unity. The planes are separated from one another by rather artificial lines of hills like those favoured by Master H. Their progression, however, is distinctly suggested as a continuity and not as the sum of separate elements. This attempt is accompanied by a desire to create a deep space, so that the painter is forced to set up a sort of 'foreshortened perspective' to reconcile the irreconcilable: hence that touch which could draw accusations of clumsiness and which is rather excess of subtlety. On a first analysis, the space of these landscapes might seem governed by a steeply angled view from above, like that of Dieric Bouts. This is not the case, however, for the figures are surrounded by objects close at hand which contradict such a description of the angle of vision. It is the foreshortening between successive grounds which creates this impression.

It will also be noted, both in the Dresden drawing and the Granada painting, that picturesque rocks with elegant shapes are included: no doubt a survival of International Gothic, but absorbed into an Eyckian outlook which gives these forms body and substance and endows them with a new reality.[40] It is these same rocks which we find poorly rendered by a German artist and yet still recognisable in the *Mission of the Apostles* in the church at Aschaffenburg (*50*).

Finally, one cannot stress too much—although we only have one example to rely on, the *St. John the Baptist* (*44*)—the vital contribution of colour in these landscapes. Albert van Ouwater expresses depth not only by the layout of his planes, but also by colour which creates an atmospheric perspective. The greens of the trees in the foreground are shaded off towards the back into a greenish brown. The brown rock takes on a pinkish hue in the sunshine. The whole is composed as a set of variations on green, which thus forms a mount for the burst of carmine from St. John's cloak.

This sense of atmospheric perspective is noticeable not only in the Granada landscape: it has also often been pointed out in the *Raising of Lazarus* in Berlin (*42*). The quality of the light and its shadings on the stone support and develop the effect aimed at by the perspective of the setting. This return to the Berlin painting leads us also to note an aspect not commented on by van Mander: the actual quality of the perspective drawing (the chronicler was too shocked by 'the rather small columns' to appreciate it). What is immediately striking is that in the *Raising of Lazarus* and in the drawing of *Jesus among the Doctors* in London (*46*), the slope of the main ground is much less steep than in the œuvre of Bouts. The two works are constructed around the human groups which form a compact mass in the front: the space is organised behind them while seeming to enclose them. In both compositions, this latter effect is clearly sought both by the structure of the architecture which suggests its extension forwards, and by figures cut off by the edge of the frame. This technique also seems to derive from Jan van Eyck: the earliest example is found in the *Requiem Mass* in the *Milan-Turin Hours* (*19*).

All these features make Albert van Ouwater a highly original personality. The exceedingly small number of his surviving works makes it difficult to analyse the range of his interpretations of religious subjects. Nevertheless the *Raising of Lazarus* is sufficient testimony to his iconographic subtlety. The picture evidently refers to the resurrection of the soul, but also to faith. The participants are divided into two groups: the disciples, in other words the believers, on the left; the Jews, in other words the unbelievers, on the right. Between these two St. Peter, the founder of the Church, forms the link, attempting to convince the infidels by showing them the miracle. The theme is taken up and expanded in miniature by the figured pilaster capitals, which have recourse to the language of typology. Above Christ, the Sacrifice of Abraham prefigures his own future sacrifice. The next capital on the right, but still in the centre, also relates to Christ: to his sacrifice, with the scene of Moses and the Burning Bush, and to his divine message, with Moses receiving the tablets of the Law. The last capital on the right shows yet another scene borrowed from the story of Moses: this time the presentation of the tables of the Law, in which typology sees a foreshadowing of the gift of the Law to St. Peter: thus the saint's crucial rôle in the painting is emphasised. The last capital on the left is no less significant: it represents Hagar and Ishmael in the desert. This episode from the Bible occurs more rarely. Lost in the desert, they were saved by the appearance of a miraculous well through divine intervention (*Genesis* XXI: 14–19). Neither the tree beneath which Hagar had laid Ishmael nor the well is shown here, but the simple depiction of the fugitives no doubt suffices, in the painter's mind, to recall the divine aid granted to those who believe in God. This scene has been placed immediately above the group of Christ's followers.

Panofsky hopefully saw, in this painting, a true equivalent of a Last Judgment. For him the choice of Romanesque architecture, conjuring up both the earthly and the celestial Jerusalem, the leading part given to St. Peter, whom he sees separating the

60 OUWATER. *St. Michael*, Granada, Capilla Real (*45*) ▷

61 OUWATER.
Jesus among the Doctors,
London, British
Museum (*46*)

faithful from the unbelievers, the attitude of Lazarus which seems to him similar to that of current depictions of the risen dead on the Latter Day, and the symmetrical, hieratic composition itself, all are elements by which the painter strove to suggest to the spectator a parallel with the Last Judgment.[41] The idea is very attractive, but Albert van Ouwater has shown himself more precise by the choice of themes for the capitals. He follows the text of St. John closely, but also the commentary by Ludolph the Carthusian. That is why he reserves an important place for Mary kneeling in prayer, Mary who is the 'type of the contemplative life', and whom the commentator also likens to Mary Magdalene, in other words to the repentant sinner. In giving her this important rôle, the painter stresses the necessity of faith for the obtaining of grace. St. Peter by his appeal to the Jews, of whom, according to the Gospel 'many believed in Jesus', (*John* XI: 45), lays the accent on the same idea.

In this way, more than the Last Judgment properly so called, Albert van Ouwater's *Raising of Lazarus* exhibits the immortality of the believer's soul and perhaps more particularly the individual judgment that awaits each soul immediately after death. Was not the text of St. John the very one chosen by the Church to be read and meditated on during the Requiem Mass?

The *Raising of Lazarus* is therefore based on three themes: the redemptive rôle of Christ, which guarantees the survival of the soul; the rôle of St. Peter in the spread of the Faith, which corresponds here to a special devotion to the saint or to an evocation of the Church through its founder; finally the necessity of faith, which is perhaps the core of the message which the painter wanted to communicate. This complexity of thought certainly indicates a commission from a religious *milieu* of high culture and remarkable spirituality. However, the picture does not have a sufficiently distinctive character to be linked with a particular current of thought.

Dieric Bouts at Haarlem

Of the three artists connected with Haarlem—Dieric Bouts, Albert van Ouwater and Geertgen tot Sint Jans—the first is still the best-known, with the reservation that his Haarlem period is completely conjectural. We might even doubt that there ever was such a period, as some have wished to do, but the evidence is in favour of it.

That the artist was a native of Haarlem is confirmed by two fairly late but independent sources. First there is Karel van Mander, whose knowledge of Bouts seems patchy. He does not refer to him as Bouts, but simply as Dieric of Haarlem, relying on an earlier tradition, that of Lampsonius who, in his *Pictorum Effigies* of 1572, gave a portrait of 'Theodorus Harlemius' accompanied by a quatrain quoted by van Mander.[42] On the other hand, he knows the exact location of his house, 'in the Cruysstraet, near the orphanage, where one can see a gable with sculpted heads.' However, he knows that Bouts had lived at Louvain, because at the house of Jan Gerritsz Buyttewegh[43] he

has seen a triptych of Christ between St. Peter and St. Paul which bore the inscription 'in the year of grace 1462, Dieric who was born in Haarlem painted me at Louvain; may he enjoy eternal peace.' This last phrase is surprising, as its wording seems applicable to an epitaph painting. It was indeed hardly usual in the fifteenth century to invoke blessings on the painter unless he himself were the donor of the work. The Louvain chronicler, Molanus, mentions a painting in the Franciscan friary in the latter town[44] which could only have had this function. So in 1462, thirteen years before his death, did Dierik Bouts offer to some church or monastery in Holland—and most probably in Haarlem—a triptych to serve as his memorial at a future date? This is the most likely suggestion, though a surprising one; in 1475, in his will, he made no further reference to Haarlem, but he made a bequest to the Church of St. Lambert in Liège, with which he had no links known to us.[45]

Forty years or so before Karel van Mander, Lodovico Guicciardini spoke both of *Dirik da Lovano* and of *Dirick d'Haarlem*.[46] Moreover, in the French edition of the same work published at Arnhem in 1613, Pierre du Mont added this significant note:

> The fine painting, executed with great care, which was once in the Augustinian priory and which depicted the story of the life of Bavo, formerly patron of Ghent and Haarlem, and to which was also added the fair countryside around the town of Haarlem, the latter being reproduced to the life with the Augustinian priory, the houses of Cleef, the wood commonly called Aerden-Hout and the hollow tree once celebrated in that place, likewise the north side of the great cemetery of Haarlem; is today in the house of the lover of art Master T. Blin.[47]

Here we have, from a different source and apparently without reference to van Mander, an important assertion: that at Haarlem in the early seventeenth century there existed a work by Bouts from the Augustinian priory.

Two important points emerge from this curious text. The first is the actual description of the painting, which stresses the representational accuracy of the landscape and seems thus to illustrate Karel van Mander's comment (which does not, however, concern Bouts) on the birth of landscape art in this city. The second point is the provenance of the work: it belonged to the Augustinian priory, i.e. to the convent of the Visitation founded in 1406 by the Windesheim congregation. Our text confirms not only that Bouts had left some traces of his art in Haarlem, but also that he had worked there for the religious house connected with the most important spiritual movement of the time and the most active section of the Devotio Moderna.

We must therefore accept the evidence. Dieric Bouts was born in Haarlem and must have begun his career there and maintained contact with the town at least until 1462. We have no certain information on his activity before his first mention at Louvain in 1457; the documents relating to his private life show

62–63 BOUTS. *Triptych of the Virgin*, Annunciation and Visitation, Madrid, Prado (*52*)

that he must have started work much earlier, at least around 1445.[48] We might reasonably expect to find in the town archives some reference which would confirm this.

However, this is not the case. The name of *Bouts* does not appear once in the surviving documents, nor is there a record of the activity of any artist by the name of Dieric.[49] Could the situation be similar to that presumed in the case of Albert van Ouwater, i.e. a corruption of the name? The structure of the patronymic might suggest this since Bouts could be a contraction of Boutszoon (son of Bouts) or even, as van Even would have it, of Romboutszoon.[50] But this line of enquiry is no more profitable, for the name Rombout occurs at Louvain but not at Haarlem.

One possibility remains: that the name Bouts is a contraction of *Albout,* the name of an important family in Haarlem in the first half of the fifteenth century. The ending in *s* is not debarred for this form, as it occurs with two members of the family, Dirck Gheryt Alboutszoon and Claes Gheryt Alboutszoon, who both died in 1473. Perhaps it was used to denote natural children.[51]

This Albout family came from Utrecht and was probably descended from a junior branch of the Uten Goye, whose arms they bore with the addition of a label. Its first representative in Haarlem was Gheryt, alderman in 1390 and 1401 and burgomaster in 1412. He died in 1436 and is known to have had eight sons and four daughters. Hugo Albout was also burgo-

64   BOUTS. *Triptych of the Virgin*, Adoration of the
Magi Madrid, Prado (*52*)

master in 1417, then again from 1441 to 1444, when he was obliged to resign in the face of the popular uprising. He then had to move to Leiden. One of his sons was called Dieric, and it is tempting to see in him the Louvain painter; but in 1437 he was declared incompetent to manage his finances, and in 1439 he acquired an allowance from the town of Haarlem in respect of a daughter called Aechte, who is never mentioned in any documents concerning the painter. After 1441, all trace of him vanishes at Haarlem.[52]

The Albout theory does not yet enable us to pick up the trail of the young Bouts. Nevertheless, after the political events of 1444 which ruined Hugo Albout, no important member of the Albout family seems to have remained in Haarlem. Only the widow of Gheryt Albout Gherytszoon, Aechte, and her two children Dirck and Claes appear in the records after this date. The disturbances which led to the exile of most members of the Albout family could also explain the departure of the young painter. It was shortly afterwards that he must have married Catherine Mettengeld at Louvain, in 1448 at the latest.[53]

Unfortunately, we have no document concerning the Haarlem painters' guild before the sixteenth century which might confirm this hypothesis. If Bouts had worked for several years in his home town as a master, he must have been young and could not have hoped to supplant his elders quickly for commissions from the town or from St. Bavo, the only ones of which we have any trace. Supposing his departure to have occurred around 1444, his birth must be dated around 1420: with a mastership gained between the ages of twenty and twenty-two that would leave the possibility of two to four years' independent activity in Haarlem, enough time to establish himself and leave behind a reputation, especially if he maintained some personal links with the town.

In the *Triptych of the Last Supper* in St. Peter's at Louvain painted by Bouts between 1464 and 1468, two unusual subjects are treated; the Passover and the fall of manna from heaven. These same subjects are included in the *Hours of Catherine of Cleves* (Plummer 74 and 76), where they follow the same design. They are also found following the same scheme in the first woodcut editions of the *Speculum Humanae Salvationis*, which were certainly produced in Holland and probably in Haarlem.[54] But neither in the *Hours of Catherine of Cleves* nor in the *Speculum* is there any hint of a reworking of Bouts's painting. In both, a less inhibited energy and less formalised figure-types continue the traditions of northern manuscript illumination. Similarly, one might mention the martyrdom of St. Erasmus in the same *Hours* (Plummer 125): it could not be derived from Dieric Bouts's painting in Louvain, which in any case is certainly later,[55] but directly foreshadows it with its indulgence of artless sadism and its picturesque details. In other words, Bouts, settled in Louvain, still relied on formulae originating in his homeland and this not only testifies to his origin, but also to his probable training in his home town.

Nevertheless, to the difficult question whether we know any works belonging to this Dutch period of Bouts, we can only give a hypothetical answer. To recreate the career of Dieric Bouts we only have a few landmarks, those provided by the dates of his last works, the only ones attested: the *Ordeal by Fire* (Brussels, Musée des Beaux-Arts) of 1473, the *Last Supper* (St. Peter's, Louvain) of 1468, and a *Portrait of a Man* (London, National Gallery) dated 1462. Earlier works can only be placed by comparisons and stylistic analyses. They reveal two groups, one strongly influenced by Rogier van der Weyden and probably datable from the 1460s, and an earlier group, in which the same influence is combined with a stronger hint of Jan van Eyck. To this latter group belong the *Heaven* and *Hell* of the Lille Museum, which can be dated 1445–50 at the earliest.[56]

So if any 'Dutch' works by Bouts have come down to us, we must concede that they are earlier than the Lille panels and probably than the paintings which are comparable to them. Only a small group of panels seems to answer to this description: it consists of the *Triptych of the Virgin* (52) in the Prado and the Berlin Museums' *Meal in the House of Simon* (53), to which we may add the copy of a lost work, a *Virgin and Child* in the Metropolitan Museum (54). Rogier's influence is barely noticeable and, when it is present, only derives from his early works. Thus the idea of architectural surrounds may have been borrowed from the *Granada-Miraflores Altarpiece*, if it is certain that it was Rogier who introduced this motif into northern art. The *Visitation* of the Prado triptych (52) is also certainly reminiscent of the one in the Leipzig Museum; and yet it should be stressed that the presence of a similar composition in the *Hours of Catherine of Cleves*—the *Meeting at the Golden Gate* has an analogous theme (Plummer 4)—leaves open the possibility of a common archetype, perhaps by the Master of Flémalle. This is the limit of any borrowing from Rogier van der Weyden. Otherwise, these works put one in mind, more than anything, of an attempted imitation of Jan van Eyck. The special fondness for oval faces modelled by exact lighting seems derived from some schematisation—deliberate rather than unskilful—of the human types on the outer wings of the *Mystic Lamb*.

Stylistic criticism certainly gives us little alternative but to consider these works earlier than the Lille panels, in other words, to date them around 1445 or perhaps a little earlier. However, there is another clue worth adding: the Prado's *Triptych of the Virgin* sets the Visitation apart in such an unusual way that one wonders if it was not intended for the convent of the Visitation in Haarlem, for which we know that Dieric Bouts worked.

The dominant feature of these works is the imitation of Eyckian forms and motifs. The angels in the Prado triptych seem to be derived from the wings of the *Mystic Lamb*. Their large, richly-brocaded copes recall the splendour of the singers in the Ghent painting. Van Eyck's influence also reveals itself in a more subtle way: in the brilliance of the light, in the broad background landscapes linked to the foreground by winding paths, in the interior of the *Annunciation*, derived directly from the *Nativity of John the Baptist* in the *Milan-Turin Hours* (18) with its sidelong perspective.

The use of light in the *Meal in the House of Simon* (53) is also essentially Eyckian in its play of reflections on shiny surfaces

65   BOUTS. *The Meal in the House of Simon*. Berlin, Staatliche Museen (53)

and its proliferation of shadows. It reminds one, by its very systematic use, of a work by Rogier van der Weyden, but one of his earliest: the *Annunciation* in the Louvre. The painting dwells so much on Eyckian themes that perhaps there is no reason to stop short at this comparison; moreover, the characteristics of Rogier's painting which may have been imitated here are themselves a slightly pedantic imitation of the motifs of the Bruges master.

This does not mean that these three paintings are solely imitative. They possess highly individual characteristics which should also be emphasised. We have seen that the arches are possibly derived from acquaintance with Rogier's work. We should nevertheless note that they are treated with an attention to detail and decorative richness which we never find in Rogier. The motif of the medallions in the spandrels seems typically northern: it appears in embryonic form in the *Hours of Catherine*

of Cleves (Plummer 8),[57] and recurs right up to the beginning of the sixteenth century in the work of Jacob Cornelisz. Similarly, the idea of using a marble column to separate the scenes grouped together on the central panel of the Prado triptych shows the same care and, by the deliberate use of a costly material, reveals an Eyckian tendency.

More important is the organisation of space. The figures are brought forward into an area clearly defined by the points of reference around them. But in order to create a greater depth behind them, Bouts inclines the angle of vision considerably. Even in an interior like that of the *Arnolfini Wedding Portrait* (London, National Gallery), Jan van Eyck does not exaggerate the slope of the floor so much. In this we have a deliberate mannerism which links our painter with van Eyck's main collaborator in Holland, Master H.

An atmosphere of informality lends the scenes a more popular flavour than van Eyck's. In the Madrid triptych's *Adoration of the Magi*, St. Joseph is depicted in a pose of delightful   64

79

simplicity; with one hand he draws back his hood, while he stretches out the other to receive the second king's gift, as if he had been waiting for the offering before making his greeting. As for the table in the *Meal in the House of Simon* (*53*), it is laden with a descriptive detail which makes it one of the first 'arranged' still lifes in northern art. This immediacy is exactly what one finds in other northern works like the 'Dutch' illuminations; and the table in the Berlin painting is the more elaborate equivalent of the one set up in the jaws of Leviathan for three souls in the *Hours of Catherine of Cleves* (Plummer 47).

One can detect another, more typically Boutsian, touch in these paintings. It lies in the hieratic pose of the figures, which lends solemnity to all the scenes despite the freshness of the details. Perhaps we should see this as a sort of restraint on the part of the artist, or rather perhaps as a desire to encourage meditation by the contemplative attitude it suggests. One of the three works is particularly explicit in this respect: the *Meal in the House of Simon* (*53*). The principal characters are grouped around a table, as if frozen in amazement at Mary Magdalene's gesture. Only one stands out from among them, St. John the Evangelist who points out the deed to a Carthusian monk. The latter does not seem to see the scene, so lost in prayer is he. But his meditation is indeed directed by St. John, although John's text on the scene (XII: 3) is much less explicit than Luke's (VII: 37–50), who here counsels humility and faith before God. This attitude is very similar to that of the Devotio Moderna in its appeal to the Gospel for the guidance of one's own conduct, in its *Imitation of Christ* depicted here so literally. Doubtless it is this which gives the Boutsian hieratism its sense: it is a call to contemplation.

Karel van Mander declares that he was unable to discover who Dieric of Haarlem's master was. This is a pity, as the problem of Bouts's training is a difficult one. Unless one accepts the thesis that the artist had a longer life, i.e. that he was born around 1410 at the latest, it seems impossible to imagine direct contact—in Holland at least—with Jan van Eyck. Moreover, the work makes no clear suggestion of this, but is more indicative of indirect acquaintance. It seems necessary either to imagine that Jan van Eyck had left behind some collaborator or disciple, or to return to the hypothesis of training in the South. It remains probable that Jan van Eyck's stay in Holland had been sufficient to have a profound influence on the beginnings of northern painting, even if it were to turn out that this influence only resulted in inducing several young artists to leave for the South to follow in the footsteps of this famous artist who had graced the court of John of Bavaria.

The Master of the *Taking of Christ*

One might well believe that Bouts's stay in Holland had left no trace, for until now we have detected no evidence of his direct influence in Holland except in the work of the Master of the *Tiburtine Sibyl*, whom a recent study inclines to place, at least for part of his active life, in Louvain.[58]

One may of course cite the sculptured group of the *Meeting at the Golden Gate* in the Rijksmuseum in Amsterdam which seems a direct reflection of the painter's work.[59] Nevertheless, in this area caution should be observed. Could we not be misled by the tall, slender forms of the figures and the realistic precision of their features? Could we simply be looking at a type which is as characteristic of Rogier as of Bouts? The question is a reasonable one, although the very restraint of this fine group indicates a relatively close link with Bouts. From another point of view, the isolation of this work amidst an output in which similar characteristics do not recur makes any conclusion difficult to reach.

Nevertheless, among the paintings attributed to Bouts there is one group which can be associated with Holland. Firstly there are the two wings in Munich representing the *Taking of Christ* and the *Resurrection* (*55 A* and *B*). Most scholars agree that these do not fit in with the rest of the master's work. Karl Voll attributed them without hesitation to Albert van Ouwater, whereas Wolfgang Schöne connects with them a whole series of paintings in which he sees the work of an artist who may possibly be Dutch.

The history of the two panels may help to date them. They come from the church of St. Laurence in Cologne and it seems practically certain that they were painted for that very church. Indeed, before 1464, the Master of the Lyversberg Passion drew his inspiration directly from them for the painted panels which give him his name. As major building works were in progress at St. Laurence's until 1454, it is probable that both panels were painted between 1454 and 1464. Economic and religious links (it should be remembered that the diocese of Utrecht formed part of the archbishopric of Cologne) were much closer between Holland and Cologne than between Louvain and Cologne.

Could this anonymous painter have been a Dutchman trained by Bouts, either before or after his departure from Haarlem? It is a plausible theory, and is supported by two other facts. A second work can be attributed to the same artist, the *St. John on Patmos* in the Boymans Museum, Rotterdam (*57*). This painting is part of the bequest made by the founder of the museum: as Boymans seems to have built up his collection mainly from within his own country, it is more than likely that the painting in question also originated there. This is only a presumption, but one which should not be ignored.

Finally, one of the human types which recurs most frequently in the paintings of Geertgen tot Sint Jans, a bearded, long-haired man with an often rather haggard expression, is so similar to one of the most striking figures in the *Taking of Christ*, the apostle in the background of the group to the right of Christ between a torch and a halberd, that a borrowing by one master from the other seems undeniable.

Once again conclusive proof is lacking, but the theory is credible. Certainly the painter announces himself straight away

66 MASTER OF THE TAKING OF CHRIST. *Taking of Christ*, Munich, Alte Pinakothek (*55 A*) ▷

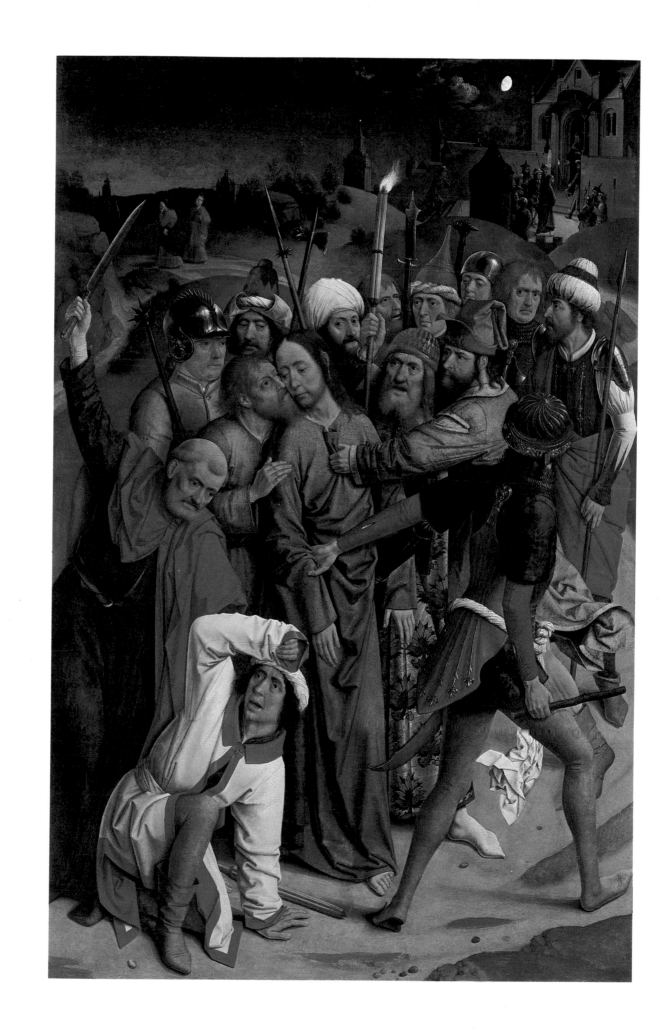

67 MASTER OF THE TAKING OF CHRIST. *Resurrection*, Munich, Alte Pinakothek (55 B)

68–69 MASTER OF THE TAKING OF CHRIST. *St. John the Baptist*, Cleveland Museum of Art, and *St. John the Evangelist*, Munich, Alte Pinakothek (*55 C & D*)

as a very close follower of Dieric Bouts: the adoption of the composition of the Resurrection in the triptych of the *Deposition from the Cross* in Granada bears this out. He also owes his conception of space to Bouts. The Master of the *Taking of Christ* nevertheless retains enough independence to display an individual style. In the Lyversberg panels, alongside free variations on the theme of his Munich paintings, we find a *Last Supper* which is also definitely borrowed from him. This is not based on the arrangement of Bouts's painting—which in any case had not yet been executed at that time, but which Bouts could already have worked up beforehand for another purpose. It adopts the general layout of a composition which we find again in the *Hours of Catherine of Cleves* (Plummer 77). In other words, the Master of the *Taking* draws direct inspiration from a north-Netherlandish scheme, no doubt giving it a new lease of

176

life with his sense of how to animate the scenes and with the quality of his technique.[60]

The *Taking of Christ* (*55 A*) is also a revealing example of his personality. Whereas for the *Resurrection* (*55 B*) we know that he used Bouts's work as a model, this is not the case here and it does not seem necessary to presume the existence of a lost painting which might have served as a model for the Munich painting. It is simpler to explain it as the creation of a new arrangement, developed from the Eyckian example in the *Turin Hours*. The very styles of armour are so similar to van Eyck's that the theory seems plausible. The distinction between the two compositions is that the second has tried, without complete success, to strike a monumental note and abandon the narrative air of the first. Then the second is primarily a remarkable grouping of heads surrounding Christ's face, so much so that one is reminded of

66
67

16

83

70 MASTER OF THE TAKING OF CHRIST. *St. John on Patmos*, Rotterdam, Boymans-van Beuningen Museum (*57*)

The Ars Moriendi

Alongside the series of drawings and paintings by Dieric Bouts, the Master of the *Taking of Christ* and Albert van Ouwater, we cannot ignore the woodcut illustrations which appeared around the same time. For a century they have been the subject of numerous controversies, which are not yet settled. Their place of origin is a matter for sometimes passionate argument; for a long time their date was difficult to pin down; and the identity of the artist who produced them remains elusive.

It seems agreed, however, that Haarlem must have been a production centre for books containing woodcuts. The question is complicated by the claims of the town to have been the birthplace of printing. The thorny question of the rôle of Laurens Janszoon Coster is too complex to be considered here,[61] but we must bear in mind Theodor Musper's interesting suggestion that Gutenberg's rival was, first and foremost, a publisher of woodcuts.[62] This theory is based essentially on the evidence of Petrus Scriverius (Pieter Schryver) who, in 1628, mentioned four works by this mysterious character: the *Biblia Pauperum*, the *Canticum Canticorum*, the *Ars Moriendi* and the *Speculum Humanae Salvationis*. In 1765 Meermann added the *Apocalypse* to this list. No incontrovertible proof has yet been discovered which might confirm that these five works originated in Haarlem. One may therefore doubt the good faith of Petrus Scriverius, who could have been influenced in his assertions by national pride. His testimony runs counter to his intention, however, since he is striving to give Coster the credit for inventing movable type, whereas it was not used for any of the four books he mentions, at least in their first editions.

It seems logical therefore to give credence to Scriverius's statements, and several definite facts point in the same direction. As Schretlen has pointed out,[63] a large number of the surviving copies come from Holland or are preserved in Holland. It is a minor argument, but not one to be overlooked. More telling is the re-use of the illustration blocks from the *Speculum Humanae Salvationis* in 1481 by the publisher Jan Veldener of Utrecht, and of some from the *Biblia Pauperum* and the *Canticum Canticorum* by Pieter van Os of Zwolle in 1487 and 1494. Finally, the most conclusive argument, but one which has too often left book historians unmoved: the style of the illustrations for these works is close to that of works produced in the northern Netherlands.

If we are to accept the recent studies by Allan Stevenson, the earliest of these volumes, the *Apocalypse,* should be dated 1451.[64] This dating is certainly much more plausible than the one of c. 1420 still being suggested recently by Theodor Musper.[65] The illustrations of this book, however, are difficult to study in the light of painted works of the same period. On one hand, the designer was very closely bound to the old models provided by manuscript illumination, which he has done his best to 'modernise', and on the other hand, he has adopted a purely linear technique, without shadows, which is rather different from that used in painting. In spite of this, one cannot fail to notice that the drapery, with its strong vertical lines, has

Bosch's famous *Carrying of the Cross* (Ghent Museum), without the visionary quality. Lastly, the painter has tried to isolate the character of Jesus, not only by contrasting the purity of his face with those around him, but also by setting his calm, entirely passive attitude against the two violent movements which frame him: that of St. Peter and the servant Malchus, and that of the soldier who prepares to drag him away.

One might add some features which are even more distinctively personal: a certain stiffness in the drapery folds, which have neither the weight of Bouts's, nor the jaggedness of Albert van Ouwater's, but rather a certain crudeness. This is particularly noticeable in the grisailles, and it lends a slightly naïve freshness to the *St. John on Patmos* in Rotterdam. Finally, an interest in landscape, closer to the style of Bouts himself than that of Albert van Ouwater, is evident in the three key paintings of the series. These characteristics, and above all that spontaneity which separates this artist from Bouts himself, the mature Bouts, are not incompatible, a priori, with a Dutch origin.

68, 69
70

71 MASTER F.V.B. *St. Michael*,
Vienna, Albertina

something in common with Albert van Ouwater's, and that the facial appearance assigned by the designer to the angels and St. John the Evangelist appears to be a kind of simplification of St. John the Evangelist's in the Berlin *Raising of Lazarus*. This volume is none the less the most difficult of the five to compare with any painted work.

With the *Biblia Pauperum* and the *Speculum Humanae Salvationis* we find ourselves back in a world much closer to that of the works created by craftsmen-illustrators in the northern Netherlands. The illustrators were guided by earlier models from the sphere of manuscript illumination. They even give the impression of being very well-acquainted with this technique. Some scenes, by virtue of certain details, occasionally recall figures by Albert van Ouwater. But the overall style, with its liveliness, its striving after expressive poses, its blunt realism, is much closer to illumination. On glancing through, one especially calls to mind the Master of Evert de Soudenbalch and his illustrations for the Vienna Bible done around 1465.[66] With both the illuminator and the engraver, we seem to have a popular version of the Haarlem style. Allan Stevenson would date the *Biblia Pauperum* 1465; this is perhaps a rather late date and could be pushed back a few years, but it takes account of the kinship of its style with that of the illuminator of the Vienna Bible.

72, 73
192
The *Ars Moriendi* (59) and the *Canticum Canticorum* (60), both dated 1466 by Stevenson, offer works by great artists who seem more familiar with contemporary painting. The problems of the geographical placing and of the authorship of the *Ars Moriendi* are, however, particularly complicated by the existence of a series of engravings by Master E. S. on the same themes. It now 190, 191 seems clear, though, that the engraver from the upper Rhine cannot be the author of the series of illustrations in the book of woodcuts. We also know that these are not a completely fresh invention. Some earlier illustrations were produced for the same text, of which an early fifteenth-century copy is preserved in a manuscript in the Wellcome Institute collection in London.[67] They imposed a rather restrictive model on the designer of the woodcuts. However, he makes a double contribution of his own. Firstly he managed to create drawings which were easy to render by means of the woodcut technique, either by inventing himself the pattern of simple hatching which has been used, or by producing a drawing sufficiently schematic to be transcribed without difficulty by a wood-engraver—in which case he was extremely skilful. However, what interests us most is that he recreates the scenes from his model in a very expressive idiom which organises the surface of the page like that of a painted panel.

The Master of the *Ars Moriendi* has, first of all, a conception of space which is very like that found in painting. Like all the painters who use the 'proscenium arch', he creates a frame, itself placed in perspective by discreet hatching, which locates and delimits the scene. Although he borrows the diagonal position of the dying man's bed from the archetype, he uses it very systematically to serve as a second point of reference in the space and to arrange all the characters around it. From these elements (which only mildly interest Master E. S., in whose

work the frame has disappeared) he creates a sharply plunging angle of vision reminiscent of Bouts and the Master of the *Taking of Christ*.

All the scenes have a strong vertical rhythm conveyed by several figures who are stiffened with an arrangement of drapery folds in the manner of Ouwater. However, the prominence of the vertical lines is accentuated here by a deliberate elongation of the figures, which has often led Rogier van der Weyden to be mentioned. Rather than attribute this feature to the influence of the Brussels painter, of whom we find here no other truly characteristic mannerism, we should think more in terms of Dieric Bouts or the Master of the *Taking of Christ*. This general peculiarity is accompanied by a striving for liveliness, revealed by bold gestures which are not merely due to the stiffness resulting from the process of engraving in a hard material. The finest illustration of all, and the most significant, is the *Temptation of Impatience*. The large female figure invests the 73 foreground with that imposing rigidity which first catches our eye, but behind her the violent gesture of the dying man has a picturesque verve. The composition is based on a reversal of the arrangement of the *Resurrection* by the Master of the *Taking of* 67 *Christ:* there the vertical is central and the movements marginal; here the vertical is marginal, with the movement cutting across it.

The *Ars Moriendi* indeed seems closest to the work of the Master of the *Taking of Christ*, in its compositions, its spatial arrangements, its movements, even its human types: the parallels are so close that I do not consider it impossible for the anonymous painter to have designed the woodcuts himself. However, the differences of technique make it difficult to assert this without reservations. The *Ars Moriendi* seems at least to have originated in the painter's *milieu*, in other words probably in Haarlem.[68]

Several scholars have attributed the *Canticum Canticorum* (60) 192 to the same artist as the *Ars Moriendi*. The style of the two works certainly seems very different at first glance, and the resemblance appears to lie above all in the engraving technique. But the designer's rôle in the two works was not the same. In the *Ars Moriendi* he had to adapt an existing scheme and rework it. In the *Canticum Canticorum* he could be original and was much less 192 restricted. The slenderness of the figures forms a sharp and deliberate contrast to the horizontals of the frame which surrounds them. This peculiarity seems absent from the *Ars Moriendi* and from the paintings of the Master of the *Taking of Christ;* but a more thorough analysis reveals it, at least in embryo. In the book of woodcuts all the small figures have this tendency, whereas the characters of normal size are filled out more, no doubt in accordance with the spirit of the prototype. The Master of the *Taking* displays a similar tendency, both in the angel of the *Resurrection* (55B) and in the grisailles on the two 67 panels of the St. Laurence altarpiece (55C and D). So an 68, 69 attribution of both works to the same artist does not seem impossible.

Another book of woodcuts has also been compared with the *Ars Moriendi*, the *Grotesque Alphabet* of 1464 (61). In this case, the

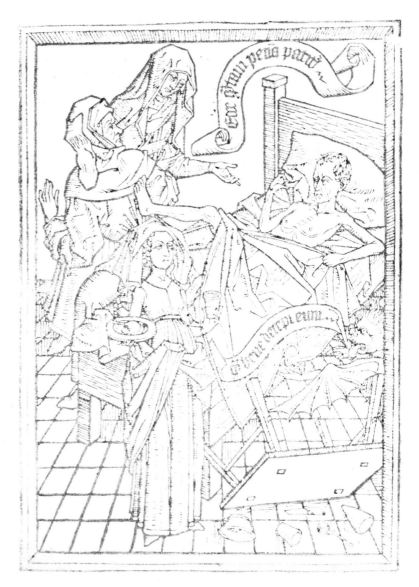

72 ARS MORIENDI. *Inspiration against vainglory*, London, British Museum (*59*)

73 ARS MORIENDI. *Temptation of impatience*, London, British Museum (*59*)

analysis is less rewarding where the problem of pictorial design is concerned; the artist had to treat an unusual theme, which forced him into deformations and complicated exercises in which his style is difficult to recognise. What is beyond doubt is that in both works one finds a similar use of the frame set in perspective, and such an identical style of hatching, that the engraving at least must be by the same hand. A comparison of the *Alphabet* with the *Ars Moriendi* has above all the merit of indicating a date for the latter, since the former is dated 1464. This indication is perfectly compatible with the work of the Master of the *Taking of Christ* and with the conclusions reached by Allan Stevenson, who gives the *Ars Moriendi* a date of 1466. I could easily accept the designs for the *Ars Moriendi* at least as being a little earlier—around 1460 at the latest, perhaps even around 1455–60. Indeed, it seems to me that the volume's imposing features reflect the influence of Albert van Ouwater, which must have been greater at that period. This, however, is the kind of hypothesis which is difficult to confirm.

The choice of the *Biblia Pauperum* and the *Speculum Humanae Salvationis* answered an immediate need—to supply preachers with convenient textbooks rounded off by illustrations; the *Canticum Canticorum* perhaps attempted to satisfy a predilection for the most poetic part of the Bible and the memories of courtly language, and its illustrations strive to recapture the spirit of these; but the choice of the *Ars Moriendi* is more unusual. It certainly responds to that fear of death which was so marked in the fifteenth century.[69] And yet, through the care it takes to summon Jesus and all the saints to attend the dying man, through its constant search for examples to encourage him towards the best manner of death, it also responds to the fundamental attitude of the Devotio Moderna. Even if the original text was not actually composed by a writer belonging to the movement,[70] it is difficult not to connect this text and its great success with the spirit of the Devotio Moderna.

One might hesitate to see the creator of this series of woodcuts as a painter, because of the sketchiness of the features;

192

74 After a Haarlem artist c.1440–1450. *Epitaph of Dirck van Wassenaar*, The Hague (*62*)

this is dictated by the material, which does not permit the subtlety of silverpoint to which artists had become accustomed. Copper-plate engraving is, in this respect, much closer to their current technique and much more comparable to painting. Amongst the anonymous works of the fifteenth century there is one more set of engravings which demands comparison with the probable Haarlem paintings. It is no longer possible to accept the old identification of the engraver who signs himself FVB with Franz von Bocholt, which would situate his activity in the duchy of Cleves. There have been no other clues to suggest different names or places, as there is no solid argument for locating him in Bruges.[71] On the other hand, the types and compositions reproduced by the engraver are very similar to the works of the Master of the *Taking of Christ*. The Boutsian mood is tempered by greater severity and by a tendency to make the faces more rudimentary. The engraving of *St. Michael* seems closely akin to the grisailles on the panels from St. Laurence's in Cologne and on the back of the *St. John on Patmos*. Perhaps this group of engravings should be seen as further evidence of Haarlem work, whether the engraver himself worked in the town or simply borrowed his models from its painters. It is a possibility, but the indications are as yet too slight to justify a confident assertion.

The genuine importance of this first generation of Haarlem painters is confirmed by a curious piece of evidence, unfortunately too imprecise to be placed exactly. A pen drawing made in 1660 reproduces a painting which certainly comes from Haarlem and which cannot be much later than 1450. It is the epitaph of a priest of St. Bavo who held his benefice in plurality with a canonry at Utrecht, Dierik van Wassenaer. The painting must have been famous in Haarlem, for Jacob Jansz drew inspiration from it several years later. Indeed, despite the inexactness of the drawing, we can make out the echo of a work of high quality. Unfortunately, it is impossible to know if the original could have been by one of the three great Haarlem masters. We do not find the severity of Albert van Ouwater or the delicacy of Bouts; all things considered, the painting seems least remote from the Master of the *Taking of Christ*: the steep tilt of the floor, the curly hairstyles which could be taken from pictures related to the *St. John on Patmos*, the broad expanse of drapery folds which spreads across the ground in rather jumbled shapes, all these support the comparison but cannot on their own guarantee that the lost painting was indeed by that artist. At least it provides us with further confirmation that there was in Haarlem an original movement in painting towards the middle of the fifteenth century.

The early masters of the Haarlem School and the northern Netherlands

It is not easy to detect signs of the influence of Bouts and Ouwater. This could be due to the disappearance of many of their works, but also to caution in acknowledging an influence which was not the only dominant one. When the *Gathering of the Manna* (*63A*) in the Douai Museum was examined for the first time (Valenciennes, 1918), the suggested attribution to a follower of Ouwater was not obvious. Not until the oeuvre of the Master of the *Manna* had been isolated by K. Boon in 1950 did it become clearer, and it only became established with the discovery, three years later, of the grisaille on the reverse of the painting in the Boymans Museum.

This is because the artist's work combines the influence of the Haarlem painters with other sources of inspiration. The Douai painting (*63A*) is immediately striking in its taste for anecdotal detail, in the variety of poses, and in its emphasis on the picturesque, even comic, aspect of these poses. There is a parallel tendency in the world created by the Master of the *Manna*: it leads him to contrive outlandish garb whenever the opportunity arises, in particular when he has Jews to depict, and it leads him to choose heavy, almost grotesque facial features. Today one would describe such art as 'expressionistic'. But this term would only be justified if the artist's choices were determined by the desire to express something. It is true that deliberate ugliness is often associated with the wicked or the unbelievers, but with an artist like the Master of the *Manna*, it is not restricted to these alone. Rather, he is displaying a fondness for a certain rusticity, similar to that already noticeable in Guelders at the beginning of the century. So it seems to me more apposite to term this approach 'the rustic tendency', a phrase implying neither disparagement nor deliberate expressiveness on the part of the artist.

It is immediately obvious that the 'rustic tendency' predominates in the art of the Master of the *Manna*. It relates his work to the illustrations of the *Speculum Humanae Salvationis*. The comparison gains further interest from the fact that the incunabulum contains an illustration of the *Gathering of the Manna*. There are correspondences, albeit few, between the details of the two versions. Even more important is their genuinely common spirit: both make the most of anecdotal details, seek out the picturesque pose and generally turn the miracle into a quaint and bizarre scene. The characters are rigid and frozen in their exertions. This resemblance occurs not only with the Douai painting, but also with the other panels of the same altarpiece (*63B and C*) and with the *Healing of the blind man of Jericho* (*64*). Even the artist's palette matches this narrative mood; there is hardly any harmonisation of tones—they are those of colouring rather than painting. Reds and yellows are given their maximum brilliance and inject a kind of gaiety into the story.

Nevertheless, closer analysis reveals meticulous brushwork often of extreme smoothness. The figure drawing, though strained in its deliberate use of exaggerated poses, is skilful and draws its inspiration from Haarlem examples. The drapery is particularly significant: it imitates that of Bouts, the Master of the *Taking of Christ* and Albert van Ouwater, but stiffens it. The Jewess in the foreground of the *Gathering of the Manna* (*63A*) could have stepped out of Ouwater's *Raising of Lazarus* (*42*). The kneeling man on the left is reminiscent of those in Bouts's Louvain Triptych. The monolithic silhouettes of the Jews in the *Offering* (*63C*), especially those seen from the rear, recall the group of Jews in the Berlin Museum's *Raising of Lazarus* (*42*).

The point is established even more clearly by an examination of the *St. Peter* in grisaille on the reverse of the painting in the Boymans Museum. E. Haverkamp Begemann has rightly compared it to the *St. John the Baptist* by the Master of the *Taking of Christ* (*55C*). He has drawn attention to the severe simplicity of the architecture in the two works, as well as to a similar use of shadow to suggest space and a very similar treatment of drapery folds.

This combination of two fundamentally conflicting tendencies is the most original characteristic of the Master of the *Manna*. His taste and temperament probably inclined him towards the 'rustic tendency', which sets the mood of his works, but he borrows his technique and his style of drawing from the Haarlem artists. In this way he shows that the influence of Haarlem had penetrated the art of the northern Netherlands more deeply than has generally been thought.

It is therefore tempting to locate the artist's activity in the same town as that of Albert van Ouwater, especially when we remember that the *Speculum Humanae Salvationis* was probably also produced there. We must not forget, however, that the Netherlands are not so extensive that the influence of these works could not have been felt in other towns. The Dutch towns of Delft and Leiden, for example, could have been acquainted with this art. Nor can we utterly exclude the possibility that the work originated in Utrecht, bearing in mind the strength of the 'rustic' movement in the episcopal scriptoria. There is no hard evidence for any particular locality. Neither do the close links with the illustrator of the *Speculum* justify the

75   MASTER OF THE MANNA. *Fall of the Manna*, Douai (*63 A*)

attribution of both the paintings and the engravings to the same artist. So I feel that it is not unreasonable to suggest that the work may have been produced in a Leiden workshop. The Master of the *Manna* seems to have found a successor in the Master of the Altarpiece of John the Baptist, indicated by all the evidence as Hugo Jacobsz (cf. p. 157); the story unfolds with the same spontaneity, the 'rustic tendency' is just as predominant, and even the palette is similar. The presence of St. Peter on the reverse of the Rotterdam panel lends further support to the idea, since the main church in Leiden was dedicated to him. This can only remain a hypothesis. It at least has the merit of showing that the Haarlem solution is not the only possible one.

Two other isolated paintings present similar cases. The *Epitaph of Raes van Haemstede* (*66*), which for historical reasons can be dated around 1440, should logically be attributed to a Dutch painter since it was commissioned by the family of the dead man, who was lord of one of the islands of Zeeland. But as to which town the artist could have come from—Gouda, as has been supposed without solid reasons by Hoogewerff, Dordrecht, Delft or Leiden—there is no clue available to set us on the right track. Here again, we cannot dismiss the possibility of its being by a Utrecht artist, especially if we remember that an artist called Sander van Heemstede worked in that city, although he could just as easily have come from the nearby town of Haarlem as from Zeeland. The unrefined appearance of the painting itself has definite echoes of Haarlem art. The figure of Christ must have been inspired by a famous model of which we find another replica in one of the *Turin Hours* illuminations by hand K, in other words by an artist from the northern Netherlands. Its stiffness and slight hardness, however, are much more reminiscent of Albert van Ouwater; in particular, we find the latter's fondness for giving drapery folds a very vertical hang.

195   Hoogewerff has rightly linked this *Epitaph* with the *Baptism of Christ* in the Twenthe Museum (*67*). Christ's body seems a direct echo of Albert van Ouwater's Lazarus, and it is hard to see who else but the Haarlem artist could have inspired a landscape so skilful in its arrangement (but not in its handling, which remains very hard). Here we are even worse off than with the *Epitaph*; there is no indication whatsoever of a particular provenance, leaving the field free for speculation.

These are scanty indications. Perhaps they only bear witness to the diffusion of the art of the great masters in Haarlem itself. Nevertheless, in so far as we can envisage other provenances for the paintings discussed above, we cannot dismiss the possibility that the influence of the Haarlem school extended over the whole of Holland, and even over the entire northern Netherlands.

The Haarlem School and the southern Netherlands

The close connection between the Master of the *Taking of Christ* and Dieric Bouts is obvious. On the other hand, the relationship between Albert van Ouwater and Dieric Bouts is less clear and has given rise to widely differing interpretations. In Friedländer's view Bouts was more a giver than a receiver. Panofsky was more inclined to see a parallel evolution of two artists belonging to the same generation. Finally, W. Schöne has no doubt that Dieric Bouts owed his formation essentially to his fellow-townsman.[72]

Re-examining the problem in the light of the conclusions presented here, it is clear that Friedländer's position is untenable and that only the other two can be considered. In default of new discoveries, it seems we can trace Dieric Bouts no further back than the fourth decade of the fifteenth century, whereas the *Raising of Lazarus* can date from the third. The dating of Bouts's works is too uncertain, however, to justify immediate rejection of the possibility of parallel development.

One hesitates to adopt W. Schöne's thesis because van Mander had obtained no evidence pointing in that direction. If the Louvain painter had indeed been the disciple of Albert van Ouwater, however, it would be very odd that the memory of this remarkable pupil had not continued to be linked with the name of his master until the beginning of the seventeenth century.

The oldest surviving works by Dieric Bouts, the *Triptych of the*   62–64 *Life of the Virgin* (*52*) and the *Meal in the House of Simon* (*53*),   65 cannot be understood by reference to the influence of Ouwater alone. The Prado triptych reflects a more direct acquaintance with the art of Jan van Eyck, perhaps even of the first glimmerings of Rogier van der Weyden's. There is no doubt that there is a kinship with Ouwater. The work of both artists gives the same impression of inner tension through the restraint of their effects and the meditative attitude of each character. It is remarkable that, in the *Raising of Lazarus,* only the unbelieving   54 and curious Jews look towards us, while the other characters, Jesus and all the faithful, look downwards at the ground or are lost in a meditation which prevents their eyes from meeting ours. So should Panofsky's idea of a parallel formation be preferred? Possibly, but with the proviso that we should grant Albert van Ouwater a precedence which enabled him to influence a younger man apprenticed to the same master as himself.

Both Dieric Bouts and Albert van Ouwater played their part in the diffusion of Eyckian art, so it is not surprising that people have tried to link them with Petrus Christus. In Panofsky's view, the latter was even Ouwater's master. W. Schöne thinks that Petrus Christus worked at Haarlem before acquiring citizenship in Bruges in 1444.[73] There do seem to have been links between Bouts and Christus, but at a fairly late stage in their careers: the *Lamentation* (Brussels Museum) by Petrus Christus seems to have been painted for the abbey of Tongerlo, for which Dieric Bouts executed an altarpiece containing the two panels now in Lille. It is possible to date the Brussels painting around 1449 because of its similarity to the *St. Eligius* (New York, Lehmann Collection, Metropolitan Museum) of the same year. I have been able to show that the Lille panels must have been painted c. 1445–50.[74] These facts point to the possible influence of Dieric Bouts on Petrus Christus when the latter had already been fully active for some years. The Brussels *Lamentation* is the very work in which W. Schöne saw a clear example of this stylistic affinity. One can also detect it in the Washington *Nativity,* dated with good reason around 1450 by C. Sterling.[75]

It seems that the problem has, in fact, been posed in a misleading way. Along with Dieric Bouts, Petrus Christus is the only artist to maintain van Eyck's mannerisms and technique in Flanders until late in the century. The difference between them, however, is that the art of the Louvain painter is more personal; he has absorbed certain elements of Rogier van der Weyden's style more completely and created a highly original manner of expression from them. The connection between Petrus Christus and the Haarlem School, however, is that the latter also arose directly from van Eyck's example. This is a crucial point and is too often overlooked. The inheritance of Jan van Eyck did not fall to Petrus Christus alone—and perhaps not by direct

76   MASTER OF THE MANNA. *The Offering of the Jews*, Rotterdam, Boymans-van Beuningen Museum (*63 C*)   ▷

descent, in any case—rather it was shared with Albert van Ouwater and Dieric Bouts, who both developed it in a much more idiosyncratic manner.

This is doubtless how the ambiguities have arisen. Christus may seem closer to Jan van Eyck because he is less inventive and more literally faithful. But Albert van Ouwater and Dieric Bouts harnessed what they had learnt from van Eyck to more profound ideas. It is perhaps their guiding religious thought which helps them to avoid total domination by van Eyck. In the latter, the glory of light is the ruling factor; it is an almost tangible expression of the divine presence, transforming all things into a purer reality.[76] For the Dutchmen, light is always present and retains its function of suggesting space. However, it has lost its immaterial quality. It has become more commonplace, more everyday. Our two painters bring us back to earth, whereas van Eyck drew us towards heaven. It is significant that Albert van Ouwater's key surviving painting should be an exaltation of faith: like Bouts, this master teaches us to find the way to God on earth. He does not seek communion with Him in the purity of a vision which uses light to transcend matter. Like Thomas à Kempis, he and Bouts demand meditation on the earthly life of Christ and the imitation of his acts.

V. Geertgen tot Sint Jans

Of all the fifteenth-century north Netherlandish painters, Geertgen tot Sint Jans is the only one so far to have won an international public.[1] The exhibitions of the Berlin Museum collections, just after the last war, made his remarkable *John the Baptist in the Wilderness* known and admired. Already, in 1936, the *Jeroen Bosch Noord-Nederlandsche Primitieven* exhibition had reserved an important position for him. The Amsterdam exhibition of 1958, *Middeleeuwse Kunst der Noordelijke Nederlanden,* gave him pride of place. And yet this fame has not led to any notable advances in our knowledge of his art, which remains cloaked in almost as much obscurity as when it was discovered at the beginning of this century.

The sources

For Geertgen tot Sint Jans, the indispensable document is still the testimony of Karel van Mander;[2] this fortunately contains a description of an easily identifiable work, the panels from the altarpiece of the Knights of St. John, now in Vienna.

Karel van Mander gives us important data about the artist's life. We learn that he was a pupil of Albert van Ouwater 'when still very young'.[3] He lived with the Knights of St. John, hence his surname, and yet 'he was not a member of the Order'. Finally, he died 'aged barely 28'. As for his dates, the chronicler simply informs us that Jan Mostaert never even knew him. This is little enough, but it contains some crucial points. The shortness of the artist's life must be borne in mind when dating and interpreting his work. We must never lose sight of the fact that Geertgen's active period could have lasted at the most ten years. 'At the most' means just what it says, for the artist would have had to be truly precocious to have enjoyed ten productive years: he would need to have been taught by Albert van Ouwater between the ages of 15 and 18, and to have worked independently from the age of 18 onwards. This does not seem impossible in the fifteenth century, but neither does it appear very frequent.[4]

His residence with the Knights of St. John should not surprise us; taking lodgings in a religious house was fairly common during the fifteenth century in the northern Netherlands. 'Maintenance' contracts could be made with a craftsman or layman who received board and lodging in return for money or for payment in kind, according to his capacity. The altarpiece painted by the artist for the commandery church could well have been part of the contract between him and the Knights; perhaps they undertook to lodge him for life in return for adorning their sanctuary with this work of art. (If so, the Knights had a bargain, as the painter's untimely death soon released them from their side of the agreement!)

Apart from the panel from this *Triptych of the Crucifixion,* easily identified with the two paintings in the Kunsthistorisches Museum, Vienna, Karel van Mander knows little of the artist's work. He mentions a *View of the Church of St. Bavo,* still preserved in that very sanctuary. Finally, he informs us that there were also 'several works by the painter' in the Augustinian priory. This is an important clue which so far has been overlooked by all historians: this priory is none other than the 'Convent onser Vrouwe Visitatie buyter de St. Janspoorte' (the convent of the Visitation of Our Lady outside the St. John's Gate), affiliated to the Windesheim congregation in 1406. In this way we learn that Geertgen too had direct contact with one of the most representative houses of the Devotio Moderna movement.

One last piece of information from van Mander has also given rise to much argument. According to him, 'when Albrecht Dürer came to Haarlem, the contemplation of the works of Geertgen tot Sint Jans drew this exclamation from the illustrious artist: "Truly, here is a man who was a painter from his cradle."' The Nuremberg artist's travel-journal, however, which records the journey he made between July 1520 and July 1521, makes no mention of Haarlem.[5] Consequently, one could accuse the chronicler of invention yet again. Some scholars — including Panofsky himself, who has no high regard for Karel van Mander's statements where Haarlem is concerned — have preferred to believe the chronicler. In that case, we must accept that Dürer visited Holland twice. This other visit — in fact the first in date — can only have taken place during his educational travels, the 'Wanderjahre' (1490–4), undertaken on his father's orders. There are many arguments to support this notion.[6]

Apart from van Mander's account, there is precious little additional information on Geertgen. An engraved reproduction

77 GEERTGEN TOT SINT JANS. Wings of the *Adoration of the Magi*, Prague, National Gallery (*68*)

of the *Lamentation* in Vienna was made by Theodore Matham between 1621 and 1630 and dedicated by Jacob Matham to Jacob van Campen.[7] Its legend complements van Mander's information on one point. It reads: 'Geradus Leydanus Pictor ad S. Io. Babt. Harlemi pinxit'. The Mathams, though from Haarlem, have no hesitation in describing this ornament of their town as a native of Leiden. For his part, van Mander certainly does not declare that he was not, but the name he gives the painter ('Gerard of Haarlem, called of St. John') suggests it. In fact, this is only a minor point since, after his apprenticeship to Albert van Ouwater, Geertgen must have settled in the town where he was to spend his entire career.[8]

The other known documents are hardly more than references to lost paintings. The most interesting one is that which accompanies a curious portrait drawing of the painter in the Haarlem City Archives.[9] The handwriting indicates that it could date from the seventeenth century. It testifies to the existence of a painting by Geertgen depicting the seven works of mercy and the Last Judgment in the Heilige Geesthuis in Haarlem.[10]

Principal theories about the artist's life

It is with the aid of such sparse information that art historians have tried to date Geertgen's work. Summarising the old research, which shows signs of superficiality, we find that most of the authors follow the conclusions offered by Max J. Friedländer in 1903. He takes into account van Mander's assertion that Mostaert did not know Geertgen, but considers that this means that the latter died shortly before the younger man became an independent master, that is, according to him around 1490. He therefore proposes to date Geertgen's birth c. 1460–5 and his death c. 1490–5.[11]

In 1909, Balet thought to find a firmer basis by examining the painting of the Church of St. Bavo which had been identified with the one mentioned by van Mander. He dated it c. 1480, because the lantern at the crossing was built in 1479 if we are to believe Georg Galland, a historian of the church. More recently, new studies have shown that the portrayal of the building cannot be earlier than 1514, and Ter Kuile has suggested an identification of the painting with 'a model' of the church executed in 1518 by a Haarlem painter named Pieter Gerritz.[12] It is easy to imagine a confusion arising after a century between a Gerrit and a Gerritz.[13] Besides, neither the quality nor the handling of the painting argues in favour of van Mander's attribution, and we must regretfully find him at fault here.

In short, none of the theories rests on solid foundations, and all are open to criticism.[14]

The Knights of St. John at Haarlem

The records of the Commandery of St. John are also at first sight silent on the subject of Geertgen tot Sint Jans. There is, however, a reference to him in a *Liber Memoriarum*[15] which informs us that he was called Gherijt Gheritsz, that he was buried in the convent courtyard near the gate, and that his *obit* was celebrated in July. Unfortunately, the book only records a few rare dates of death, and that of the painter is not among them.

The Haarlem commandery had been founded in 1310 by a canon of the Church of St. Mary in Utrecht, Gerard of Tetrode.[16] In 1316 the first church was built. Like the eleven other commanderies of the northern Netherlands, Haarlem's was subject to the monastery of St. Catherine in Utrecht, whose prior held the rank of bailiff, and was included in the German province, whose prior-general resided at Heitersheim in Breisgau.

There were at most ten brothers in the Haarlem house. At the time of a visitation in 1494 there were only five, while eight are mentioned in 1483. For nearly a century, from 1394 to 1489, the office of commander was held by members of the same family, the van Scotens. Two of them were especially distinguished by their stewardship. Gerrit, commander from 1427 to 1460, seems to have expanded the establishment considerably. On 10 April 1437, he decided on the endowment of an altar dedicated to the Virgin Mary, John the Baptist and Elizabeth the Widow. No doubt he intended to enlarge the commandery

78 GEERTGEN TOT SINT JANS. *Adoration of the Magi*, Prague, National Gallery (*68*) ▷

38

94

church, but it is not until ten years later, in 1446, that we have evidence of building works from another text.[17]

His successor, Pieter, at first encountered difficulties in having his election recognised: the bailiff in Utrecht wanted to promote the commander of Oudewater over his head. To make good his claims, Pieter escalated the conflict and did not give up the struggle until he had been granted complete independence from Utrecht, and the right for the Haarlem commandery to be thenceforward directly answerable to the prior-general of Germany. He obtained confirmation of this arrangement and the title of preceptor first from Charles the Bold in 1463, then from the pope in 1466, and finally from the prior-general of Germany on 18 April 1469.

This policy of aggrandisement seems to have gone hand in hand with an authoritarian and spendthrift rule. Consequently, at his death in 1472, the knights elected another Scoten, Niclaas, but forced him to accept a constitution which forbade him to take any decision of importance on his own. These vicissitudes throw some light on Geertgen's career: the commander was even forbidden to take sole responsibility for the presence in the convent of monks from outside the community ('fratres extraneos eiusdem ordinis non conventuales'), or to grant pensions for life ('solvere aliquas pensiones vitales').[18] This rule seems to have been observed scrupulously; in 1476 a contract for board and lodging was revoked with the consent of the community, and two similar agreements were terminated in the

79   GEERTGEN TOT SINT JANS.
Raising of Lazarus, Paris, Louvre (*69*)

same circumstances in 1483 and 1486.[19] Since there is no mention of Geertgen in the commandery's cartulary, he must have taken up residence at the latest during the rule of Pieter van Scoten, i.e. before 1472.

The portraits of the Hospitallers

88 We might hope to find some confirmation of this by analysing the portraits of the Hospitallers in the panel in Vienna devoted to the story of John the Baptist. It is obvious that the artist seized the pretext of depicting the saint's disciples to give them the features of the knights, and that the character who stands out at their head must be their chief. As it happens, the Haarlem Museum possesses a series of portraits of commanders which also comes from the Commandery of St. John.[20] A comparison is not, unfortunately, very instructive. The poor quality of this series of paintings prevents us from reaching a definite conclusion. The commander in the Vienna panel is perhaps

202 Pieter van Scoten, for in both portraits we find strong, arched eyebrows over deep sockets, a broad nose and a lantern jaw. Any dissimilarity can be put down to a difference of age: Pieter van Scoten died at the age of seventy-two, while the Haarlem portrait could be a free copy of an original dating from the early years of his rule. As for the second figure near the commander,[21] the one who in both groups holds the bones of the saint's forefinger, one wonders if he could be Pieter's successor,

203 Niclaas van Scoten. Again, a comparison does not justify a definite opinion: the Haarlem portrait is of an elderly man, whereas the Vienna panel shows a young man. In fact, the features of Niclaas are more recognisable in another knight from the Vienna painting, the one who receives a bone in the foreground of the main group and brings up the rear of the second group.

Geertgen tot Sint Jans and Pieter van Scoten

Geertgen must therefore have been a protégé of Pieter van Scoten and one of the instruments of his prestige policy. Perhaps the commander had had the opportunity to discover the young genius at Leiden itself, his home town, as records show that he transacted various business there after being a priest there from 1440 to 1454.[22]

During his rule, the dedication of the commandery church was altered. The charter signed by the Grand Master of the Order and recognising his election, dated 1469, no longer mentions St. Elizabeth in addition to God the Father, the Virgin Mary and St. John the Baptist as had been the case in 1437 when the principal altar was founded by Gerrit van Scoten.[23] Now St. Elizabeth was probably not depicted in Geertgen's painting, which must have been devised to match the new dedication.

It is also unlikely that Pieter van Scoten could have contemplated the commission of such a large altarpiece before obtaining formal recognition of his election, that is, before the end of 1469. If we calculate that at least three or four years were required to bring this great undertaking to fruition, it seems reasonable to assign it to somewhere between 1470 and 1475. In other words, the artist's working life must date from about 1465 to about 1475.

These dates are very different from those proposed by Friedländer. They correspond quite well with our present knowledge of Jan Mostaert; mentioned for the first time as a painter in 1498, he was probably already married at that time, and must have been born in 1473.[24] With this in mind, we can no longer date the death of the painter of the Hospitallers around 1493—his younger colleague would have been twenty

80 GEERTGEN TOT SINT JANS. *The Lamentation*, detail of the two Marys, Vienna, Kunsthistorisches Museum (*70*)

years old and would certainly have known him—but some time before 1480.

Geertgen's works

When the Rijksmuseum acquired the *Tree of Jesse* from the collection of Frau von Pannwitz, A. van Schendel attributed it without hesitation to Geertgen tot Sint Jans. Ten years later, his colleague K.G. Boon dissented and returned to the old attribution to Jan Mostaert. This example shows the uncertainty which can exist in the identification of the artist's works.

As early as 1937, Martin Davies published a very outspoken article in which he did not hesitate to cast doubts on the list then accepted. He drew attention to facts which are often overlooked: the artist's early death and the injuries his works have certainly suffered. We must not forget that two thirds of his principal work—a painting of large dimensions for its time—have disappeared: namely the central panel and one wing of the Hospitallers' altarpiece. His painting for the Heilige Geesthuis and those for the Augustinian priory have suffered the same fate. We cannot even believe that what we have of Geertgen's work was saved by the Hospitallers along with the wing of their altarpiece; for in the inventory of the commandery's property drawn up at the end of the siege, only two entries—unaccompanied by the artist's name, of course—could correspond with paintings attributed to him: an *Adoration of the Magi* and a *Tree of Jesse*.

Two works are so like the Vienna panels that they have retained their attribution to Geertgen without difficulty: the 79 *Raising of Lazarus* (Paris, Louvre, *69*), which has almost the same 90 composition, and the *St. John the Baptist* (Berlin, Staatliche 91 Museen, *72*), whose landscape is enlivened by the same type of foliage.

77, 78 On the other hand, the *Triptych of the Adoration of the Magi* (Prague, National Gallery, *68*), may give rise to hesitation. Nevertheless, at the Amsterdam exhibition in 1958 it stood up reasonably well to the juxtaposition; it has exactly the same 85 plastic qualities as the *Lamentation (70)*, and the Virgin Mary has a strong affinity with the female figures in that work. It is the mutilations suffered by the triptych, altering its overall balance, which are disconcerting and may have given rise to doubts.

90 The *John the Baptist* facilitates comparison with small-scale works and allows us to distinguish four of the same style: the 92 small *Virgin and Child* (Milan, Ambrosiana, *73*) of such unusual 93 vigour despite its small size, the *Nativity* (London, National Gallery, *74*), viewed too critically by Martin Davies, the *Man of* 95 *Sorrows* (Utrecht, Archiepiscopal Museum, *76*), very similar in 94 its modelling to the Berlin panel, and lastly the *Adoration of the Magi* (Cleveland Museum, *75*), unfortunately in a poor state of preservation.

There are thus only nine paintings—including the two panels in Vienna—which may reasonably be attributed to Geertgen alone, and not the fifteen or so ascribed to him at

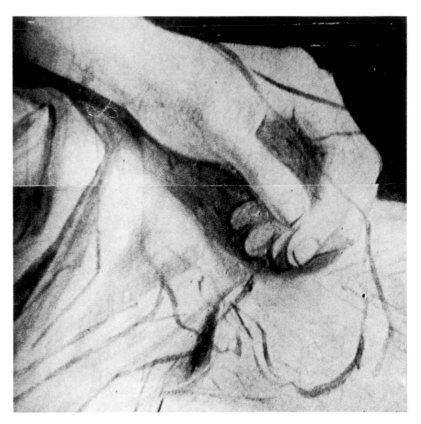

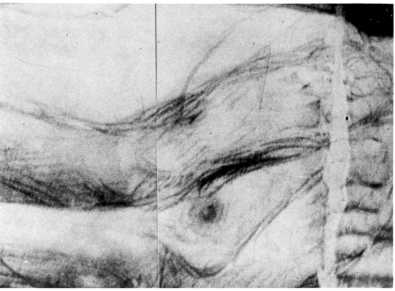

81–82 Infra-red reflectograph photographs of the left hand and feet of Christ in the *Lamentation (85)*, showing the original drawing. (J.R.J. van Asperen de Boer)

present. This misapprehension has also made it difficult for people to accept a dating earlier than Friedländer's.

The present confusion is due, in fact, to the attribution to Geertgen of the curious painting of the *Holy Kindred* in the 102 Rijksmuseum in Amsterdam (*81*). It has often given rise to hesitation, in any case. Without attaining the severity of Thoré-Bürger who considered it 'a wretched copy of some wretched painting or other', several scholars have had their doubts concerning it, notably Martin Davies. Any judgment is difficult, as the painting has been badly worn by over-drastic cleaning. The last restoration, completed a little before 1958, has given some unity to the work, but could not mitigate the effects of wear and tear. However, its condition is not enough to explain the work's weaknesses, and people are too readily captivated by the naïve charm which it radiates. The artist has not profited from the example of Albert van Ouwater, whom he evidently knows. He has attempted a composition which relies on the placing of the main characters off centre, as in the *Raising of Lazarus* in Berlin, but without realising that there the figure of St. Peter restored the balance.

Even more significant is the fact that some of the figures in this painting can be seen immediately to have a close affinity with those in the Vienna panels: compare Mary Salome with Mary Magdalene in the *Lamentation,* or even the face of St. Anne with that of the third Mary on the left in the same work. And yet the handling is stiffer and the modelling more perfunctory (even allowing for the wearing away of the surface layers, it is difficult to imagine that these faces ever had any finesse unless we can detect, in the now visible underdrawing, hints of a more delicate modelling). For these reasons most scholars see this as an early work. But how can types which were to be a feature of the artist's mature period appear in an identical form in a juvenile work? And how is one to explain that they do not recur in the *Adoration of the Magi* in Prague, which is also thought to be earlier than the altarpiece of the Hospitallers? It is a clear case of imitation of the forms of Geertgen's maturity by an artist who lacks the same quality of technique.

With the elimination of this painting, Geertgen's oeuvre regains its coherence, for reference to this fundamentally debatable work is nearly always the main argument for other attributions. It would surely never have been possible to attribute the *Tree of Jesse* (Rijksmuseum, Amsterdam, *93*) to Geertgen if the *Holy Kindred* had not been brought into the discussion (although to my mind it does not serve as sufficient justification in itself). The artist of the *Holy Kindred* is certainly very close to Geertgen, but tries to imitate him without the benefit of the same training.

The altarpiece of the Hospitallers— Reconstruction

Geertgen's magnum opus therefore remains the altarpiece which he painted for the Hospitallers of Haarlem. Given its size, it must have occupied him for several years. At a reasonable guess, its production must have taken up a very large part of his short active life, probably nearly half of it.[25] The ensemble formed a triptych of considerable size. When open, it must have had a width of more than six metres. Two comparisons will show how large it was. The *Portinari Altarpiece* (Florence, Galleria degli Uffizi), completed by Hugo van der Goes around 1476, is scarcely wider; when open, it measures six metres 45 cm. across (with the frame) but its panels are 75 cm. taller (250 cm.). The *Triptych of the Last Supper* (Louvain, Saint-Pierre),

finished by Dieric Bouts in 1468, has very slightly taller panels (180 cm. at Louvain against 175 cm. in Vienna), but they are much narrower since the painting opens out to a mere three metres 30 cm. with its frame, i.e. barely more than half the width of the Haarlem altarpiece.

This exceptional size is surprising, as the altarpiece was intended for a chapel of modest proportions. It must have been designed virtually to fill the chancel newly built by Commander Gerrit van Scoten; a comparison of the dimensions confirms this. In 1495, the order's Visitor found that the church was of 'indifferent beauty', by comparison with the conventual buildings.[26] He was probably struck by the simplicity of the architecture and by the use of simple, plaster-covered brick, and had not appreciated the extravagance represented by a painting of this size, which was intended to take the place of decoration and furnishings. We may be surprised that it did not occur to the commander, having a painter at his disposal, to cover the walls of the chapel with a series of murals. Perhaps it is not too far-fetched to suggest that this represents a deliberate choice, corresponding to an evolution of taste. Admittedly, there is no documentary evidence for such a claim, but one only has to recall what Jodocus Vyd did when he acquired a chapel in the church of St. John the Baptist (now St. Bavo) in Ghent. His idea was not for mural decoration, but, on the contrary, for an altarpiece on panels which was quite deliberately out of proportion with the available space, as if to emphasise the magnificence of the donor. The pretensions of the Scotens were probably no humbler than those of the alderman of Ghent.

As this work must have been one of the greatest paintings, if not the greatest, of its day in the northern Netherlands, one would like to know what it originally looked like. This is not beyond the bounds of possibility; such a major work must have been imitated, and it is feasible, through surviving versions of it, to reconstruct at least its main outlines.

One triptych in particular must have recaptured the essential structure of Geertgen's, the one by the Master of Aix-la-Chapelle (Aix-la-Chapelle, Cathedral Treasury).[27] It may well seem odd to go looking for this evidence in the work of an artist working in Cologne for the Carmelite monastery. But the prior who commissioned the triptych, Theodoricus de Gouda, was himself Dutch by birth and could have known the Haarlem painting and demanded an imitation of it.

The right-hand panel of the Aix-la-Chapelle altarpiece brings out this connection. The Cologne painter did not follow his model literally (he has moved some of the characters such as Mary Magdalene and Nicodemus), but he has preserved its basic composition: the group set out in such a clearly defined oblique line, and the strengthening of the right-hand side by means of a standing figure (now one of the Virgin's sisters rather than Mary Magdalene).

Of course, the liberties taken with the original mean that we cannot expect to find the details of Geertgen's painting, but only a common theme and a similar structure. Thus the slanting line of the right-hand panel is balanced by a slanting line on the left-hand one, both braced, as it were, against the sides of the

99

83–84   GEERTGEN TOT SINT JANS. *Burning of the bones of St. John the Baptist*, Vienna, Kunsthistorisches Museum (*71*), details

two triangles of the central panel; these are joined at the base, leaving a broad V-shaped opening in the centre, which is occupied by the cross. Such a strongly articulated composition allows scenes and groups to be arranged clearly on the long central panel without their profusion creating too great an impression of disorder. This characteristic is already noticeable in the *Lamentation,* and must have impressed other artists by its technical mastery.

The choice of subjects may seem odd. On the central panel we certainly expect a Crucifixion, which van Mander has in any case mentioned. But on the left-hand panel we might have

expected a Carrying of the Cross rather than an Ecce Homo. And yet we find precisely the same subject (that is, the *Ecce Homo*) in the triptych by the Master of Delft (*143*) (who has replaced the Lamentation by the Deposition, although his work also betrays links with Geertgen's). The *Ecce Homo* of the Master of Aix-la-Chapelle is a composition on which works were based by two great masters: the painting by Bosch in the Frankfurt Museum and Dürer's engraving in the *Great Passion* series.

132
234

85   GEERTGEN TOT SINT JANS. *The Lamentation*, Vienna, Kunsthistorisches Museum (*70*)   ▷

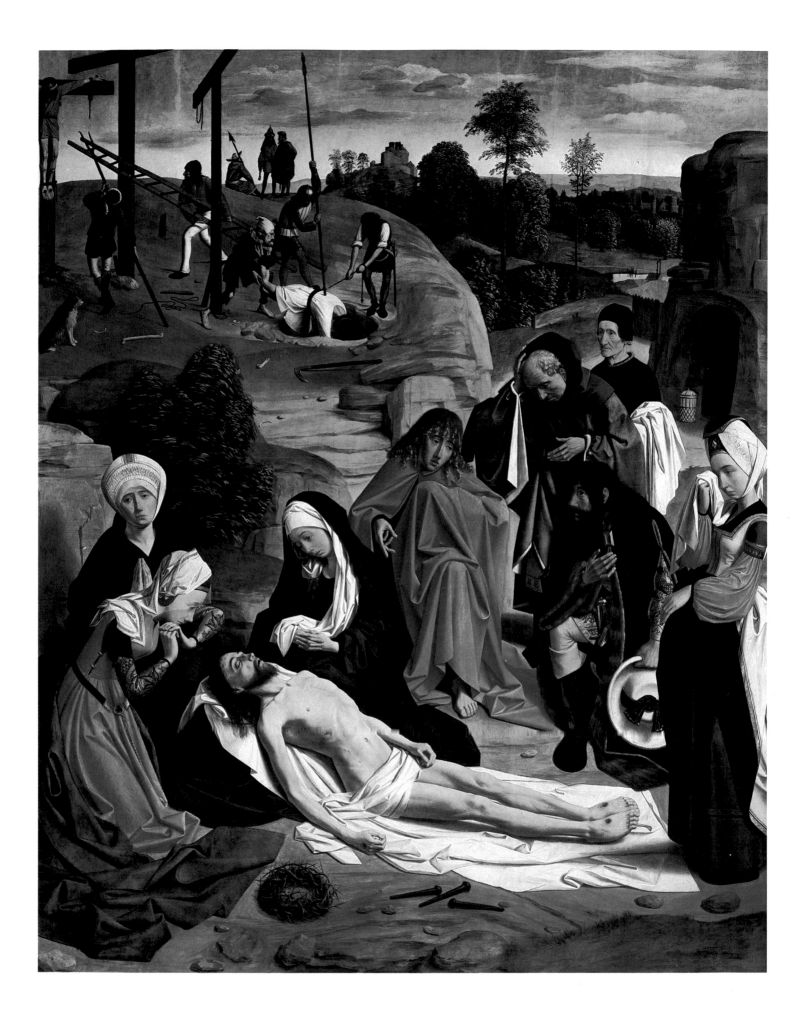

86 GEERTGEN TOT SINT JANS. *Burning of the bones of St. John the Baptist*, Vienna, Kunsthistorisches Museum (*71*), detail of the presumed self-portrait

Despite the differences between the three interpretations, there are so many similarities that the theory of a common archetype, probably by Geertgen, is easy to accept. The arrangement of the groups is similar. In a raised position on the left there is the presentation of Christ by Pilate; Jesus is shown with his hands tied (except by Dürer) and his head bowed, clothed in a large piece of fabric, serving as the purple cloak, which another character lifts up behind him to reveal his scourged body. On the right is the crowd of Jews, waving their hands in the air, in the midst of whom stands a figure who seems derived in all three cases from a common model: a large man with a full, heavy-jowled face. Even the motif of the child playing in the foreground (omitted by Bosch) could well be derived from an idea of the Haarlem master, in whose work children's faces often play an important rôle.

Now the meaning of the inside face of the triptych of the Hospitallers can be analysed more precisely. The Lamentation differs from the Pietà in that it combines the grief of the Virgin

with that of her companions, Mary Salome, Mary Cleophas and Mary Magdalene, and also the devotion of Nicodemus and Joseph of Arimathaea. Geertgen's composition emphasises 85 these figures: it draws attention to the homage of the two men, who are shown here in the company of a priest, probably an Augustinian. John the Evangelist shows them the dead Christ, before whom they bare their heads and kneel. In this, Geertgen has closely followed Ludolph the Carthusian on the scenes which followed the death of Christ.

'After arriving at the place of crucifixion', he writes, 'Joseph and Nicodemus went down on both knees to adore the divine Master'. The artist has slightly postponed the episode, which Ludolph placed before the deposition, but this does not alter its meaning.

The same author significantly stresses what these two characters stand for. 'Joseph here represents anyone who, progressing in virtue, requests the Lord's body when he prays to God before receiving the Eucharist.' The artist has clearly understood this indication, which throws light on Joseph's connection with Mary Magdalene: both are sinners, both are believers. More curious is the function attributed to Nicodemus: 'an educated man, he represents the truly good teacher, whose knowledge drawn from the Scriptures is like an excellent blend of perfumes for anointing the mystical body of Jesus Christ in order to save his spiritual limbs from corruption.' Here again, the Gospel commentator illuminates our understanding of the painting; he explains why the canon who figures in the work as a 87 donor is placed directly behind Nicodemus, who is, as it were, his precursor at the time of the Crucifixion.

If we try to summarise the essential significance of this *Lamentation* in Geertgen's mind, Ludolph the Carthusian comes to our aid again. 'When they took Our Lord down from the cross', he says, 'they caused Him no suffering since His body was lifeless, but neither did they show Him any disrespect, since this act was performed not by enemies or executioners, but by friends and faithful servants who wanted thus to display their loving devotion; and so the Jews were outraged to see all the honours rendered to Him after His death.'

In other words, the *Lamentation* is the homage of the Faithful to Christ, who has sacrificed himself. This immediately explains its juxtaposition with the *Ecce Homo*, in other words with the refusal to acknowledge Jesus as the Son of God. On one side the Unbelievers, on the other the Faithful, and in the middle the sacrifice: this programme stresses Christ's Eucharistic rôle, but also faith and its necessity, and the understanding and imitation of Jesus. Meditation on the Passion in all its aspects, including its cruelty, was one of the favourite themes of the Devotio Moderna. This is what St. John the Evangelist is suggesting to us when he points out the dead body of Christ to Joseph of Arimathaea and Nicodemus, who typify two categories of believers. He might well be saying, like Thomas à Kempis in the *Imitation of Christ*:

87 GEERTGEN TOT SINT JANS. *The Lamentation*, Vienna, Kunsthistorisches Museum (*70*), detail, Nicodemus and a canon (?) ▷

Many follow Jesus to the Breaking of the Bread, but few to the drinking of the Cup of His Passion. Many admire His miracles, but few follow Him in the humiliation of His Cross.' (Book II, Ch. 11).

This appeal to Faith is presented less as a need to mourn for the death of Jesus as a need to share in it oneself, an attitude which, directly or indirectly, must have its origins in the meditations of practitioners of the Devotio Moderna.

The subject on the back of the triptych's wings

In comparison with the high-mindedness expressed by the subjects of the inside faces of the altarpiece, the reverse of the surviving wing seems an almost trivial conception. To the world of the new devotion it appears to contrast the traditions of an aging religion, burdened down with relics and the sale of indulgences. Rather than the life of a saint, it apparently tells of the discovery of his relics and in so doing glorifies the Hospitallers as an order. The description of the fate of the bones of John the Baptist is based here on the account by Rufinus[28] or the virtually verbatim transcription of it in the *Golden Legend*.[29] Julian the Apostate, surrounded by his court, is shown giving the order to burn the saint's bones, which had been working miracles. The executioners remove them from the tomb at Sebaste, between those of Elisha and Obadiah. Monks from Jerusalem, portrayed here as Hospitallers, retrieve some of the bones and take them to Jerusalem to the Bishop or Abbot Philip. Meanwhile, Herodias buries the Baptist's head in another place.

All this follows Rufinus and the *Golden Legend* faithfully, but neither justifies the substitution of Hospitallers for the monks of Jerusalem. On the contrary, according to Jacobus de Voragine, the relics saved in this way were taken to Alexandria, then to Antioch, where they were kept in a former temple of Serapis converted into a basilica, before being brought to Genoa. We must refer to another source, more recent and closer to the Netherlands, for an explanation of this intervention by the Hospitallers. This source is the *Dialogue of Miracles* (Dialogus Miraculorum) by the monk Caesarius of Heisterbach who was writing early in the thirteenth century. According to him, the Knights of St. John owned a relic of their patron while they were still based in the Holy Land. However, it was stolen by a Dutch merchant who brought it to Groningen.[30] In the fifteenth century, this celebrated relic was still preserved in the Church of St. Martin in Groningen, which featured the saint's head on its seal until the sixteenth century.[31]

This enlargement upon the episode of the relics on the panel of the Haarlem commandery's altarpiece was therefore intended to recall the part played by the Knights of St. John in saving these relics, which at that time were improperly held in Friesland. We might even go further and imagine that Pieter van Scoten cherished the hope of securing the return or purchase of these venerable remains of his order's patron saint. It is a possibility, but there is no indication in the surviving documents of any such steps being taken.[32] By a curious coincidence, though, a few years later in 1484 Pierre d'Aubusson, Grand Master of the Order, received an arm of the saint from Sultan Bayezid. But this cannot be the one alluded to in Geertgen's painting; it was an arm still covered in flesh and was taken from the saint's tomb by St. Luke and his disciples and carried to Antioch![33] So the triptych of the Haarlem Hospitallers must be dated earlier than 1484, as the story it describes would have cast doubt on the authenticity of the relic received in that year by the Grand Master of the Order.[34]

Viewed correctly, however, the main theme of the Vienna panel is not the story of the relics, which occupies the background, but the burning of the bones of John the Baptist; in other words an episode directly connected with the saint's life and not simply with the cult of his relics. On the authority of Eusebius, the *Golden Legend* claims that this event occurred on 29 August—the same date as the saint's beheading—and that it was 'as it were a second martyrdom suffered by St. John, since he was burned in his bones'.[35] From this it is easy to deduce that the possible theme of the reverse of the left panel was the first martyrdom, in other words the beheading of John the Baptist. The altarpiece when closed must thus have shown the two incidents commemorated on 29 August, the principal feast of the patron saint of the Order.[36]

There may even be an echo of this lost panel in an engraving by Israel van Meckenem[37] which depicts two episodes from the martyrdom of the saint in the flesh, his execution and the presentation of his head to Herodias. The engraver, faithful to his own style, has probably given more elegant outlines to some of the figures, such as the trumpeters on the right. The female characters, by contrast, like the almost rigid Salome presenting the head and Herodias, who faces her, may reflect something of Geertgen's figures. The engraving, however, can only reproduce the main part of the lost panel, not its overall composition. If these two scenes had filled the panel on their own, the figures in them would have been much larger than those in the Vienna panel. So we must suppose that Geertgen had depicted Herod's palace as a 'country house' set in a landscape which may have served as a setting for other incidents such as the Baptism of Christ. In any case, we can easily imagine some such arrangement which would match the number and diversity of the incidents on the panel depicting the *Burning of the bones of St. John*. The last prophet thus serves to prepare the way for Christ's sacrifice and the expansion of the Faith, but he displays the same self-effacement with which he stepped aside in favour of the Messiah he had announced. His beheading reflects his self-abasement and his sacrifice, thus forming a parallel with the *Ecce Homo,* a mock glorification of the kingship of Jesus and a forewarning of his condemnation. The burning of the saint's

88 GEERTGEN TOT SINT JANS. *Burning of the bones of St. John the Baptist*, Vienna, Kunsthistorisches Museum (*71*) ▷

104

bones stresses his abasement even more by its contrast with the *Lamentation,* which speaks of the veneration of the faithful for the body of the dead Christ.

Although the story of the relics is only a secondary episode, the fact that it was used is indicative of the outlook we might well impute to the van Scotens: a pride which found its main outlet in the enlargement of a church already quite adequate for a small community like the one in Haarlem, and in the commissioning of an altarpiece of exceptional size. At the same time, however, we may well wonder if Geertgen's programme was not directed by two separate mentors. One was certainly Pieter van Scoten, who insisted on the splendour of the work and on his own proud appearance in the miraculous story; but there may also have been a priest, with a completely different outlook, who laid down the guidelines and marked the altarpiece with the deep spirituality that pervades the *Lamentation.* It would be foolhardy to try to name him, but we might well discern him in the solemn old man, whose drawn features are the outward sign of his inner life, praying behind Nicodemus.

87 He is not a Hospitaller, since he is not wearing the cape embroidered with a cross. His dark clothes, his collar trimmed with fur and the white surplice over his arm could mark him as an Augustinian; at Haarlem, this would mean a canon of the Windesheim congregation from the convent of the Visitation,
39 of which Jan à Kempis, Thomas's brother, was the first prior.[38]

The style of the Vienna panels

The two sides of the right-hand panel, now in Vienna, may at first seem strikingly disparate in style. The inside face, the
85 *Lamentation,* is notable for its monumental effect. The foreground is filled by a small number of figures, who are grouped along the sides of a right-angled triangle and frozen in their grief
88 or their devotion. By contrast, the *Burning of the bones of St. John the Baptist* on the reverse has a large cast of characters performing on several different stages. Despite its firm structure, it still creates a first impression of disunity, leaving the spectator to scan the various parts in search of a thread to link the episodes of the story. This marked difference between the two treatments is partly determined by the subjects. For a main altar, the inside face, 'die Feiertagsseite' or face exposed on Sundays and feast days, must be designed with the solemnity of the most important ceremonies in mind. Its devotional aspect is therefore much more prominent.

Nevertheless, one should not lay too much stress on the differences between the two sides of the panel, as they do not preclude composition based on exactly the same principles. Each side is arranged around a strong slanting line which is not quite parallel with the true diagonal of the panel. These lines of force break up the space in a way which is especially suitable for the disposition of many different incidents. This arrangement is similar to the one often used in south Netherlandish manuscript illumination towards the middle of the century; Simon Marmion's illustrations for Jean Mansel's *Fleur des Histoires* are a

notable case in point.[39] But in the hands of Geertgen it acquires the plasticity which alone enables it to be adapted to painting. This comparison also highlights another special feature of the composition of the Vienna panels. Whereas Marmion juxtaposes the various settings with minimal links between them, the painter imposes a unity on each face of his panel. The breaks indicated by lines of rocks or undulations of the land are no more than devices for splitting up a single site whose coherence is strongly emphasised by paths, lines of foliage and even expanses of water. Deliberately breaking with the rigorous logic of realism, Geertgen combines unity of place with plurality of time. The unity of place is so evident in the surviving panels that one wonders if it did not extend from one panel to another, using a single broad landscape as a setting for scenes from the Passion, from the *Ecce Homo* to the *Lamentation,* and for episodes from the life of John the Baptist, from the Baptism of Christ to the fate of his relics.

This conception of space highlights the poetic aspect of the landscape and its crucial rôle in the composition. This is one of the most original features of Geertgen's art, but it will be brought out more clearly by a study of the entire corpus of his work than by the analysis of a single painting. We must be content simply to draw attention to it here.

People have often remarked on the rather unsophisticated charm of these stiff figures, boldly modelled by a light which acts as if on wooden forms rough-hewn into smooth, clean-cut surfaces. Such are the characters of the *Lamentation,* particularly the three Marys and Mary Magdalene; their oval faces, their delicate hands hardened in their pose and the folds of their garments petrified in their various movements have all been considered the artist's trademark.

However, it would be wrong to generalise too hastily. Geertgen uses two modes of expression for his figures, and although they are related they are not identical. The first, and better-known, is the one analysed above. But its characteristics are evident neither in the figures of the reverse nor in those of the burial of the Good Thief. These generally have much more flexible poses—they are often depicted in movement, and always with lively gestures. A popular appeal is never far below the surface, whether in the human types chosen or in the presentation. In these cases the faces are much more closely scanned, and analysed with realistic precision; this approach is applied just as much to the caricatures of Julian the Apostate, the executioners and the Jews as to the intentional portraits of the Hospitallers and their friends. By tiny but expressive touches, the artist recaptures the inventive energy of the north Netherlandish illuminators. Cases in point are the executioners burying the thief, the witty portrayal of the three Jews chattering on Golgotha and silhouetted against the sky, and the delightful 83, 85 Herodias burying St. John's head.

The artist relates these two modes of expression to the particular purpose of his work. The first mode is naturally

89 GEERTGEN TOT SINT JANS. *Burning of the bones of St. John the Baptist,* Vienna (71), detail of the group of Hospitallers and their friends ▷

reserved for devotional subjects. Alongside or around these, the second mode brings in a more popular touch, which links these incidents to everyday life. In such cases, a note of humour or sympathetic observation is not out of place.

Finally, if all these figures strike us as peculiarly mute, we should not forget that they were less so for contemporaries. Their hands speak a language which is sometimes quite explicit; in other cases, consideration and imagination are needed to reconstruct what the artist wanted them to say. Conventions of this sort existed, but their keys appear to have been lost.[40] The use of this sign language was quite widespread in the fifteenth century, but it was practised very consistently by two Haarlem painters, Albert van Ouwater and Dieric Bouts.

Geertgen handles all these elements with a remarkable technique: he creates an extremely smooth surface on which the brushstrokes only become noticeable in the middle and backgrounds. The very firm modelling which makes the forms seem somewhat impenetrable is also in the Eyckian tradition as handed down by Albert van Ouwater. This technique has a close affinity with that of Dieric Bouts, but is immediately distinguishable by its greater restraint. So the brocades which play such an important part in defining the rhythms of compositions by Jan van Eyck or Dieric Bouts hardly make any appearance, being merely glimpsed in one or two scenes.

This severity is reflected both by the major figures and, in a sense, by the palette. It is not dull, but its flashes of brilliance are kept within strict limits. Both sides of the panel are built up on a basic harmony of two related colours: an olive-green with hints of brown, diffused by the vegetation, and a brown of wide-ranging intensity, principally used for earth and rocks. The figures are woven into this texture with hues which are often related to the basic tone—greens, blacks, and browns. Lastly, adding emphasis and spice and signalling the points of interest, there come some touches of red, which are picked up by others of pure white, singling out the dramatic centres: Christ on his shroud surrounded by the veils of the Marys, and the group comprising the emperor and his counsellor, with the ermine of the one and the gown of the other corresponding to the shirts of the executioners. Such a range of colours is austere in the extreme, and itself serves the purpose of communicating the subjects.

Works antedating the altarpiece of the Hospitallers

Of the seven paintings whose attribution to Geertgen tot Sint Jans can still be accepted, two are definitely earlier than the Haarlem altarpiece: the triptych of the *Adoration of the Magi* in the Prague Museum (*68*) and the *Raising of Lazarus* in the Louvre (*69*). The former differs distinctly from the Haarlem triptych in its character and in its uncertain handling. The latter is much closer to it, but does not have the same power either of composition, or of interpretation, or of execution.

The gulf which separates the *Adoration of the Magi* from the altarpiece of the Hospitallers is understandable in the case of a youthful work, full of uncertainty and revealing the debts owed to formative influences. Predominant is the influence of Albert van Ouwater, an influence which itself bears the imprint of Jan van Eyck. This debt to van Ouwater is evident mainly in the imitation of his human types. Geertgen's Virgin is an almost exact copy of the face of Mary Magdalene in the Berlin *Raising of Lazarus*. In the handling, however, the mannerism of suggesting downcast eyes by a U-shaped line has been abandoned. The most notable contrast with the Berlin Magdalen is the Virgin Mary's rounder face; this is the motif which was to be developed on the Vienna panel to create the characteristic appearance of the female faces.

But it is in the actual composition that Albert van Ouwater's influence is most noticeable. The arrangement of the triptych is partly suggested by the subject, but it is quite different from that of Geertgen's other paintings. All the main characters occupy a limited space in the foreground and are on a fairly large scale in relation to the total area of the painting (they fill slightly less than half of it). The background—as far as we can judge from the central panel, which alone survives—contains only small figures. This is the same arrangement as in the *Raising of Lazarus*, where the onlookers behind the choir-screen seem to have been half-hidden to reduce their importance.

Albert van Ouwater also acted as an intermediary between his pupil and the art of van Eyck, into which he had initiated him. The richness of the brocades in the costumes of the Magi, the highlighting of the scene by articles of gold and other precious metals which throw back scintillating reflections, the play of light on armour (Balthasar can be seen reflected in St. George's breastplate) are all motifs of unmistakable origin. Perhaps Geertgen was even responsible for a more specific borrowing: the features of this Melchior could easily be a variation on those of Chancellor Rolin, but one cannot be categorical because of the alterations. Similarly, the depiction of Jerusalem is not a copy but a reworking of the study of the Holy City in the *Carrying of the Cross* (*22*).

Nevertheless, we can still make out the first stirrings of a highly original style. The landscape background, with the Three Kings' lively and picturesque entourage, is not very well integrated into the composition. It uses an arrangement which recalls both Jan van Eyck's *Rolin Madonna* and Rogier van der Weyden's *Virgin and St. Luke*, but it enhances the importance of the secondary theme. By means of the procession, which begins behind Balthasar, the artist has tried to stress the unity of place, even at the expense of exaggerating the progressive diminution of the figures towards the rear. This is surely an early attempt at the arrangement of several scenes in one landscape, as it was to be developed in the Vienna panels.

In the actual interpretation of the subject, Geertgen is less original. The placing of the characters and their gestures seem to owe a great deal to a model by the Master of Flémalle, now lost but known through a drawing in the Frankfurt Museum and a painting in Berlin.[41] Here, however, there is no sign of Joseph,

90   GEERTGEN TOT SINT JANS.
St. John the Baptist in the Wilderness,
Berlin, Staatliche Museen (*72*)

who receives Balthasar's offering in the version by the Tournai Master. He may have appeared on the left, behind or beside the Virgin, in the missing part of the work; this layout would have been similar to that later adopted by the Master of the Brunswick *Diptych* in his version (*86*). On the other hand, Geertgen may have decided to turn his back on artistic tradition and follow Ludolph the Carthusian, who writes:

> Joseph is not mentioned here because, according to St. John Chrysostom, we are not yet discussing the functions of the foster-father. Or, according to St. Hilary and Rabanus Maurus, God wanted Joseph to be absent at that moment, lest the Three Kings should have reason to think that he was the Child's father and that this Child, to whom they had come with their gifts and adoration, was not God.[42]

Nevertheless, there are two innovations in the scene. The first involves Caspar, who is depicted holding out his reliquary in his left hand and placing his right on his breast in a gesture of greeting or rather of homage. This is probably the first appearance of this motif in northern painting.[43] The second novelty is the portrayal of Balthasar as a negro. Even so, on this point Geertgen is following Johannes von Hildesheim, according to whom Balthasar was 'the greatest of the three' and 'an Ethiopian negro, without the slightest doubt'.[44] In this he is imitating examples which had already appeared, in particular in works of the Cologne school.[45]

This analysis brings out the hesitant, youthful aspects of the Prague triptych. Unfortunately, the mutilation of the panels has led to the loss of the upper parts, which probably contained the donors' arms. The couple's patron saints are insufficiently characterised for any identification. A likely date can only be established through hypotheses relating to the altarpiece of the Hospitallers. If the latter was produced during the final years of Pieter van Scoten's rule, distinguished by his formal appointment as preceptor in 1469, the Prague triptych could have been painted around 1465. This is a perfectly possible date, as the sole objection to it is the style of the costumes. But we have no dated documentary evidence for rejecting such a date for these; so we should argue the other way round and take the view that Geertgen's painting contains the first known depiction of certain styles of clothing.[46]

There is a great difference between the *Adoration of the Magi* and the *Raising of Lazarus* in the Louvre (*69*). Between them there probably lies a large gap in Geertgen's surviving works, since the latter painting displays almost the style and qualities of the Vienna panels. The figures are in the 'narrative mode' of the Hospitallers' altarpiece, that used in the *Burning of the bones of St. John the Baptist;* in other words they differ even more from those of the Prague triptych, which were in the same vein as those of the *Lamentation*. In the *Raising of Lazarus,* the protagonists are given much less rigid poses, sometimes even suggesting movement, as in the case of St. Peter, for example.

The artist's relationship to his master, Albert van Ouwater, is easy to study here because they have both depicted the same subject. Geertgen is remarkable for the freedom with which he has treated his model. His borrowings are limited to the figure-type of Christ, his gesture of benediction and beckoning and his general stance; the motif of a Jewish character, clad in brocade and seen from behind, also reappears.

The young artist has rejected the unusual but symbolic staging inside a church in favour of the more traditional and canonical approach which sets the scene in the open air. By so doing, he seems to draw his inspiration, even for the arrangement of the scene, from the woodcuts in the *Biblia Pauperum* and the *Speculum Humanae Salvationis*. The placing of Christ in relation to the tomb and the figure of Lazarus sitting in his sarcophagus, still partly wrapped in his shroud, seem to be derived from this image, which must have achieved popularity very rapidly. Most notably, Geertgen has rejected the symmetry of grouping conceived by his master and charged with significance. In this painting, the faithful form a rough circle set between two groups of Jews. St. Peter no longer links the groups by appealing from one to the other, as he does in the Berlin painting, but adopts a more commonplace pose of astonishment and admiration before the miracle.

The painting's fundamental novelty, which explains its meaning, lies in the composition of the main group, which is set out along the sides of a triangle, one apex of which is the head of Jesus. On the right, Christ is linked to the figure of the praying Mary; she is more isolated than in the Berlin painting, no doubt because she alone must stand for the necessity of Faith. On the left, the eye glances from Christ to Lazarus via the figure of Peter and is drawn down to the kneeling 'donor'. The allusion is clear: the praying man is likened to Lazarus—he is dead, but has sure and certain hope of his resurrection. The painting is his epitaph. Praying behind Mary, and a little further away, is another small female figure, clad entirely in black. This may be the daughter or the wife of the dead man. It is hard to know whether to account for her small size merely by the effect of perspective, or to take it literally and see her as a very young woman. Once again, there is no coat of arms to identify the donor, indicate his dates or clarify his relationship with the young woman.

This interpretation partly explains Geertgen's alterations to Albert van Ouwater's composition. He had to honour a male figure whom he could not assimilate to any of Christ's followers. There is also the fact, however, that he has deliberately chosen to sacrifice a large part of the allegorical programme and replace it by a narrative. Instead of the figured capitals and their typological language, we have the scene of Jesus being welcomed at the gates of Bethany by Martha and Mary. This was probably a conscious choice on the part of the artist or his theological adviser.

Picturesque touches abound: the naturalistic poses of the Jews, the child standing by them, the spectators in the background, and the delightful and characteristic detail of the

91 GEERTGEN TOT SINT JANS. *St. John the Baptist in the Wilderness*, Berlin, Staatliche Museen (*72*), detail of landscape ▷

Evangelist: 'He must increase, but I must decrease' (John, III:30). The landscape in its summer splendour foretells the degeneration of nature, just as it recalls the prophet's birth at the summer solstice. According to Panofsky the saint is meditating on the necessity of repentance, since St. Luke wrote in his gospel: '...the word of God came unto John the son of Zacharias in the wilderness. And he came into all the country about Jordan, preaching the baptism of repentance for the remission of sins' (III: 2–3).[48]

Both theories have an immediate appeal and both are completely justifiable. Therefore they can both be accepted, since Geert Groote, the founder of the Devotio Moderna, said of meditation on sacred texts: 'In them, I myself find several mystical senses together; one leads me on insensibly to another, so that I never feel any boredom during the reading, and I should like to be able to linger over these sweet reflections.'[49] This idea could have been applied just as easily to painting by a contemporary influenced by the spirituality of the Devotio Moderna. But at the risk of seeming prosaic, it should be pointed out that the main source for this masterly work is much more straightforward. From Ludolph the Carthusian, once again, Geertgen drew precise indications which determined his interpretation.

The Strasbourg monk makes great play of the prophet's stay in the wilderness, much more so than any of the evangelists. 'John lived in the wilderness,' he writes, 'where the air is purer and the horizon broader, where God communicates more readily with man... He therefore sets himself apart from the crowd and the tumult, so as not to dim the shining glory of his conduct and his reputation...' He does not conceive of the desert in the ecological sense of modern geography, but simply as a lonely place far from the town (hence the presence of a city on the horizon in Geertgen's painting). His authority for this is St. Peter Chrysologus, particularly in the following passage which he quotes: 'The caves of the mountains, the trees of the forest and the depths of the valleys served as a shelter and abode for this infant patriarch.'[50] Hence, in the same author's opinion, 'through the amazing life of which he offers the first example, he becomes the model of the monks, the prince of anchorites and the cornerstone of every religious institution'. And according to St. John Chrysostom, 'he leads the monastic life in the midst of the wilderness, which provides him with all his sustenance'.

So in the eyes of the Carthusian, sure in the knowledge of the authorities he can quote, St. John the Baptist is the first eremitic monk. He specifies what he means by this: 'The monk should therefore understand the meaning of the name he bears. The word "monk", in Latin *monachus*, comes from the Greek *monos*, which means "alone" and *achos* which means "sad". The monk should remain in salutary sadness and solitude, concerned entirely with his own duty and not involving himself in outside functions'.[51] So we see before us the first monk, taking solitude and melancholy upon himself. His solitude, however, is a lush countryside in full bloom perhaps because St. Jerome, also quoted by Ludolph the Carthusian, said that 'for me the world is but a prison, and seclusion a paradise'. The artist felt it natural

and necessary to depict the wilderness as an earthly paradise. The identification of the prophet with the first monk is emphasised by the costume Geertgen has given him: instead of the more usual animal skin, he has painted the hermit's sackcloth.

In this work the artist has once again broken new ground in iconography. The fact that he has adhered to the text of Ludolph's *Vita Christi* does not lessen his worth. For although he has indeed represented the Hospitallers' patron as the first monk, he has also placed near him the Lamb of God; in so doing he opens up other perspectives, recalling John's rôle as prophet of the coming of Christ, and highlighting all the interpretations of John's meditations in the wilderness, of his destiny linked with that of Jesus, or of the destiny of man.

Works postdating the Vienna panels

Three paintings reveal a slightly different handling from that of the *St. John the Baptist,* despite their similar dimensions. The execution is less polished, tending to simplify shapes by suggesting them with brushwork which is less determinedly discreet. These are the *Nativity* in the National Gallery in London (*74*), the *Adoration of the Magi* in the Cleveland Museum (*75*), and the *Man of Sorrows* in the Archiepiscopal Museum in Utrecht (*76*).

Closest in its handling to the Vienna panels is the *Nativity* in the National Gallery in London (*74*). The face of the Virgin is similar in character to those of the *Lamentation* and the small *Virgin and Child* in the Ambrosiana Library. But here form is suggested at the expense of detail. There are two possible and probably complementary reasons. The aim of depicting a light shining in the darkness may have led Geertgen, like Georges de La Tour two centuries later, to take account of the simplification of volumes caused by such a light. On the other hand, this tendency towards more schematic modelling becomes even more noticeable in the other two works, and may represent a deliberate technique in the artist's last paintings.

Once again, Geertgen breaks new ground in iconography. Not, however, in his choice of subject; Master Francke had long before depicted the supernatural glow of the Christ-child on the night of His birth, this detail being borrowed from the revelations of St. Bridget. His personal contribution lies in the realistic treatment of this vision.[52] The child glows with a light which might be that of a torch and which does not penetrate beyond the faces of Mary and the angels. He becomes more prominent as the scene is enveloped in darkness. That side of the artist's temperament which one might almost describe as materialist finds expression here, in its preference for lifelike lighting over a more immaterial brilliance.

The *Adoration of the Magi* in the Cleveland Museum (*75*) is unfortunately very badly damaged; even its original composition is difficult to reconstruct. Nevertheless, it still has some

94 GEERTGEN TOT SINT JANS. *Adoration of the Magi*, Cleveland, Museum of Art (*75*) ▷

114

very fine parts like the striking head of Balthasar and the beautiful portrayal of the Child. What sets it apart from the first version of the subject—in the Prague Museum—is the pose of the Three Kings. Their rather stiff solemnity in the Prague painting gives place to dramatic tension, compassionate in Melchior, theatrical in Caspar.

In a work so ravaged by time it is difficult to judge the original technique. It can be seen, however, that St. Joseph is depicted with a few brisk strokes which suggest more than they define; a few dabs of colour in a summary treatment which cannot on its own justify the character's place in the painting; the background figures of the Vienna panels never suggest such rapid execution and yet they are less easy to make out. These are the first stirrings of a move towards a simpler technique.

95   With the *Man of Sorrows* in the Archiepiscopal Museum in Utrecht (*76*), Geertgen adopts a very original approach towards an iconographic type which had enjoyed a fairly wide vogue since the fourteenth century, especially in Germany. To the *Man of Sorrows*, as seen on the altar in St. Gregory's vision, emerging from his tomb with all the marks of his agony, he has added the witnesses of his Passion: the Virgin Mary, St. John the Evangelist, Mary Magdalene and angels bearing the instruments of his Passion. Here the artist aimed at depicting both Christ's Passion, which he does with remarkable concision, and the Virgin's grief—a notable instance of that double devotion whose development has been described by Emile Mâle.[53]

94   The drama of the Cleveland *Adoration of the Magi* is here pushed even further. The bold arrangement of the composition itself makes the dreadful apparition of the bloodstained Christ stand out. Geertgen has striven to capture the imagination, and has not eschewed distortion or an unusual degree of violence. Christ's right hand is deliberately enlarged, the better to surround the wound in his side; the anatomy is suggested, but without straining after absolute accuracy—compare this nude to the Lazarus in the Louvre or the Christ in Vienna—and the drops of blood are over-abundant. The atmosphere created by this violence had occurred earlier in the work of certain Dutch illuminators: the mystic wine-press in the manuscript of Dieric van Delft's *Table of the Christian Faith* now in the Pierpont Morgan Library is no less cruel or exaggerated in its use of a realism which verges on what today would be called expressionism.[54]

It would seem that this was the direction in which Geertgen was moving in these three works, probably his last: expressiveness even at the expense of the literal realism which had been his starting-point, as if to recapture the inspiration which powers all Dutch manuscript illumination and which has been so ably analysed by Delaissé.[55]

Landscape

An examination of Geertgen's work gives its full force to van Mander's remark about the Haarlem painters' skill as landscapists. What could be glimpsed in the work of Albert van Ouwater, for instance in the *St. John the Baptist* in Granada, becomes with Geertgen one of the essential ingredients of a powerful style.

In his earliest work, the *Adoration of the Magi*, the countryside seems secondary. We must remember, however, that we have lost the tops of the panels, which must have contained important elements of it. The development of the vegetation, with close attention to the foliage, is nevertheless significant. It is worth adding that from this very first work Geertgen reveals his Dutch temperament; he cannot imagine an outdoor setting without an expanse of water, placid water which conjures up the lakes and canals that were more widespread then than now in Holland. This aqueous mirror, which distributes the light and lends itself to reflections, is a mainstay of his style.

In the major works, the *Raising of Lazarus,* the Vienna panels 79
and the *St. John the Baptist,* the landscape is almost the principal 90
element. It gives the incidents not a backdrop but a setting, and asserts a unity of place in that setting. One's reading of the scene is guided by clear articulations, formed by the lie of the land and the layout of trees and bushes. The source is obvious: through his master Albert van Ouwater, Geertgen has acquired the techniques of van Eyck as they were developed in such a modern way in the *Carrying of the Cross (22)*.

Trees and grass play a crucial rôle in the poetry of such works. However, we do not find the carpets of flowers so beloved by Bouts, imitating Jan van Eyck. The ground is basically grass-covered, then broken up by plants of an almost filigree delicacy which themselves help to suggest space.

In his depiction of the various species, Geertgen displays dazzling skill. His foliage technique is, to a certain extent, 91
governed by a system (which was itself widely imitated). But in his work, artistic sensibility avoids the pitfall of mechanical repetition and submits to an understanding of tree species worthy of a botanist. His objective is to particularise both the general outline and the density of the internal structure of the trees. To this end he is quite ready to enumerate the leaves in detail in the foreground and arrange them according to the layers of branches. Then, as the trees recede into the distance, so their portrayal becomes more artificial until we reach those 91
curving strokes, one on top of the other, which are so characteristic of the artist's manner but also particularly suggestive of foliage.

The system is very original in the subtlety of its application. But it would be a mistake to think it unique. Even before the precedent set by Albert van Ouwater, it can be seen in embryonic form in the *Mystic Lamb*, especially in the central panel above the procession of the Virgins. In manuscript illumination it was being developed at the same time, but with much less sensitivity, by the Master of Girard of Roussillon (Dreux Jean?), notably in the Vienna manuscript which gives the artist his name.[56] The technique probably spread from

95   GEERTGEN TOT SINT JANS. *Man of Sorrows*, Utrecht, Archepiscopal Museum (*76*)   ▷

Haarlem, via Cologne, into Germany, where it was frequently employed.[57]

The under-drawing

Landscape does not necessarily require adherence to an under-drawing, although in Geertgen's work all the rocky elements have a clearly discernible linear structure. The figures, however, which are at one and the same time both hieratic and strictly realistic, must first have been drawn. Modern scientific methods, in particular infra-red reflectography, reveal the artist's original drawing. Some recent photographs of the *Lamentation* taken by J.R.J. van Asperen de Boer using this method, which he himself has perfected, show a sinewy, spontaneous drawing which does not fix the position of every shape, but freely and frankly casts about for it. The lines cross over one another, altering the position of parts of the body in a very modern manner. This is quite different from the technique of Dieric Bouts, who usually sets out the main elements of his compositions in a very precise under-drawing.

Nevertheless, like his contemporaries, Geertgen must have relied for inspiration on extremely detailed preliminary drawings. Three sheets, probably from the same sketchbook, can in my opinion be attributed to him (*77–79*). Hand studies are grouped together on two sides. Their finesse indicates a meticulous study from life. Yet this delicate though masculine hand appears different from those in the known paintings with their gnarled joints and dried-out flesh. This is precisely where the painter's work can be appreciated. For, as J.Q. van Regteren Altena has rightly pointed out to me, all these hand movements

have been studied from a single model, the painter's own left hand. (In the Vienna sheet the hand is seen in a mirror and may thus appear to be the right.) Once the structure has been analysed in this way, the artist transposes it to the painted work and endows it with the necessary character. The left hand of the *Virgin and Child* in Milan seems to have been based on one of the studies on the sheet in the Louvre, changing from masculine to feminine.

The three head studies on the same sheets can also be related to the paintings. They should be seen as analyses whose components were later to provide the painter with inspiration. Two of them were probably studied from the same model, an old man with deep-set eyes and hollow cheeks. This type has close affinities with that represented by the priest in the Vienna *Lamentation,* without being identical to it. He probably remembered it when he had to draw the portrait of that noble old man. The other face, also of an old man, bears a strong resemblance to that of the second figure from the right in the group of Hospitallers in the Vienna panel. In this case the similarity is so great that the models probably were one and the same.

Geertgen tot Sint Jans and Hugo van der Goes

Ever since a memorable article published by Adolph Goldschmidt in 1915, Geertgen has been seen as a follower of Hugo van der Goes and the opinion has prevailed that the Vienna *Lamentation* cannot be earlier than the *Monforte Altarpiece* (Berlin, Staatliche Museen).[59] In fact, the Ghent painter is first

96–98 GEERTGEN TOT SINT JANS. Studies for heads and hands, Paris, Louvre (*77–78*)

99–100 GEERTGEN TOT SINT JANS.
Studies for a head and hands, Vienna (*79*)

mentioned on 5 May 1467 on the occasion of being received master by the Guild of St. Luke. If Geertgen's active period must be situated between 1465 and 1475, the relationship between the two artists can no longer be viewed as that between a younger and a much older man, but as that between two contemporaries whose age difference must have been minimal.

How, under these circumstances, are we to account for the similarity between the poses of the second King in the *Monforte Altarpiece* and Joseph of Arimathaea in the Vienna *Lamentation,* which was Adolph Goldschmidt's principal argument? Let us first be clear that the resemblance is merely formal, since the two gestures have different meanings: the King kneels in homage, but points with his right hand to the gift which his page hands to him; Joseph of Arimathaea, on the other hand, brings his hand to his breast in order to complete the homage of his genuflexion. Geertgen is introducing a new gesture which he had, in fact, already used for a king in the Prague triptych; Hugo van der Goes is only enlarging, with an extra narrative touch, upon the theme of the offering of the Kings' gifts.

In fact, there is no doubt that both figures are derived from a common model. As far back as 1464, that is at about the same time as the *Monforte Altarpiece,* the Master of the Lyversberg Passion gave one of his Kings a comparable pose,[60] which was probably borrowed by all three artists from Dieric Bouts; the latter used it for one of the Israelites in the *Gathering of the Manna* from the *Last Supper Triptych* (1464–8) and perhaps for other figures in works now lost.[61]

This does not mean that there was no relationship between Geertgen and van der Goes, but that it was of a different order. A *Pietà* (Granada, Gomez Moreno Foundation) by van der Goes has the same grouping of the Virgin and Christ as the Vienna *Lamentation.* But it owes so much to Dieric Bouts's *Pietà* in the Louvre[62] that one can only see it as a youthful effort by Hugo van der Goes, whose apprenticeship to Dieric Bouts remains the most likely theory.[63] Now we can begin to grasp the connection between the two artists: it must have been established under the aegis of the Louvain master, during their formative years, before 1467. There is nothing improbable about the notion of the young Geertgen being sent by his master Albert van Ouwater to complete his training with his celebrated compatriot; the *Virgin and Child* in the Ambrosiana Library proves that he was acquainted with the latter's art.

This analysis confirms the chronology suggested above. If we suppose that this meeting with Hugo van der Goes took place under the auspices of Dieric Bouts before 1467, this would tend to date the altarpiece of the Hospitallers shortly afterwards— between 1468 and 1475 approximately, i.e. at the end of Pieter van Scoten's rule and perhaps not reaching completion until the beginning of Niclaas's. The Prague triptych, since it may be earlier, could then certainly be dated around 1465.

The originality of Geertgen tot Sint Jans

These conclusions certainly demand radical changes in the hitherto accepted outlook. Geertgen no longer appears as an out-of-date follower, reviving some of the spirit of van Eyck at the end of the fifteenth century. He takes his place as one of the formative influences of the generation to which Justus of Ghent belonged.

There is nothing surprising in this; it was clear that Geertgen's clearly-defined personality was constricted by the traditional view. His art could not be explained by the influence of van der Goes alone. As a figure of the close of the century he displayed incomprehensible archaism in his conception of forms. This had to be put down to provincialism, and even that did not account intelligibly for the components of his style.

Of all the aspects of his art, the most surprising is perhaps its Eyckian quality. The latter is not patently obvious and takes the form of borrowed methods, not copied motifs. The affinity between Jan van Eyck and Geertgen tot Sint Jans exists at a very deep level. The nature of Geertgen's realism is remarkably close to that of his older colleague; one can cite the emergence of landscape, the vigorous analysis of facial features, the naturalness of the poses, even the touch of humour so important in the artist who painted Canon van der Paele. What separates the two artists is a religious attitude. In place of the almost mystical spirit which informs not only Jan van Eyck's share in the *Mystic Lamb* but all his other work, Geertgen reveals a more human passion. His characters are more concerned to urge meditation than to portray an event. The pageant of saints converging on the Lamb in the St. Bavo polyptych is part of a great heavenly festival. The Hospitallers are dreaming of the burning of the bones rather than taking part in the scene; they are not so much living it as pointing it out to spectators. And this is not only true of this borderline case, in which contemporary personalities are associated with a sacred story; it is just as true of the *Lamentation* which St. John the Evangelist indicates to Joseph of Arimathaea and Nicodemus, and to ourselves.

This religious inspiration alone could justify the presence of the Hospitallers and of a priest within the sacred stories of the Vienna panels. Of course, the portraits of the Hospitallers are also the expression of a pride quite at odds on the surface with the humility of the followers of the Devotio Moderna. However, their group presentation diminishes the importance of each individual and integrates them more fully into the action. Here Riegl rightly saw the archetype of the guild portraits which were to celebrate the vanity of members of the Dutch bourgeoisie from the next century onwards.[64] The Hospitallers are depicted performing together an act which links them with their Order. They are brought together in a group and yet strongly characterised. Their integration into a religious scene, however, is the mark of an age which placed religious devotion at the very heart of human experience. Despite appearances, the Hospitallers are in this instance more modest than Jodocus Vyd, who had himself painted alone in a niche, even though this was on the reverse (the weekday face) of the panels of the altarpiece which he commissioned.

So there is nothing fanciful in seeing in the midst of the group a young face—solemn and lost in meditation like those of his companions—which is probably that of Geertgen himself. That he appears here is not necessarily ostentation, but rather a declaration of faith and of a deep devotion which drives him to live what he paints.[65] It is one more testimony of religious feeling.

VI. The workshops of Haarlem in the last third of the fifteenth century

It must be borne in mind that the late fifteenth century does not seem to have been an age that was economically and politically favourable to artistic production. The disturbances that broke out on the death of Charles the Bold in 1477 have been mentioned. Haarlem seems to have escaped these at first, but in 1492 it was the scene of violent incidents culminating in the lynching of bailiff Niclaas van Ruyven. Although violence only occurred at this late stage, the town seems none the less to have been hit by the grave economic recession. The drop in beer production—one of the main indicators of urban activity—was spectacular from 1480 onwards, and recovery was not under way until 1499.[1]

However, the crisis does not seem to have affected work in progress. The building of the nave of St. Bavo went on. In 1485 several of the town's artists were commissioned to paint panels for the high altar. This fact, which may seem surprising at first sight, illustrates how difficult it is to relate an economic situation to artistic activity. It is probable that the church fabric fund had accumulated a sufficient surplus in the preceding years to permit work to continue uninterrupted even in times of crisis. However, the period must have been less favourable for independent commissions from burghers for their own foundations.

Artists known from public records

For this period the town records and those of St. Bavo's church give us a great deal of information about the artists. They do not enable us to isolate clearly the activity of any single one, but they do provide us with plenty of names. Two generations of painters had a share in the work, one appearing around 1465, the other between 1470 and 1480.

The first must have been contemporary with Geertgen tot Sint Jans and is distinguished by two names, Vrederic Hoon and Jan Aerntsz. The former receives his first mention in 1463 for some minor work on the organ-case in St. Bavo. He was buried in 1505. His most important commission came in 1465, the painting of the organ shutters. These have unfortunately disappeared, although they survived the upheavals of the Reformation. They are reproduced on an interior view of

St. Bavo painted by Saenredam (Rijksmuseum, Amsterdam) and in a seventeenth-century drawing which shows them closed (Haarlem archives). This is not much on which to base any ideas about a painter's art, but nevertheless these visual documents are not to be despised.

At any rate, Hoon had no fear of huge surfaces. The inner face of the right shutter, the only one visible in Saenredam's painting, showed the *Resurrection of Christ* (*80*) and naturally invites comparison with the work by the Master of the *Taking of Christ*. The resemblance between the two works is closer than it might seem. The only essential difference is that in Hoon's painting Christ stands astride the tomb, as in the triptych by the Master of Flémalle in the Seilern collection, instead of standing before the sarcophagus as in the Munich painting; but this is only a variation of design, implying no change in the iconography.[2] The spirit of the two works is in fact very similar, especially in the way they place the figure of Christ in the centre of the picture and arrange the sleeping soldiers in the foreground in poses which are very similar in the two paintings. It is impossible to be sure about the identity of the two painters with our present knowledge, especially as the drawing which shows the reverse of the shutters seems to indicate cruder work, closer to that of the Master of the *Holy Kindred*. Certainty is even less possible given that Vrederick Hoon seems to have had the assistance of Jan Aerntsz in this work and that the two sides were perhaps by different hands.

Apart from this, Hoon is mentioned only for more modest tasks, such as the painting of numerous coats of arms. We know scarcely more about his contemporary Jan Aerntsz. Apart from his collaboration on the organ shutters, we find him still mentioned for day-to-day work until 1472. It is perhaps also he whom we find taxed at the rate of 1/100th in 1493–4, 1495–6 and 1499–1500.

The second generation is more numerous. Its senior member is Jacob Willemsz, whose career we can follow from 1470 to 1490. In 1485 he had received a commission for the high altar of St. Bavo, but it was withdrawn because the materials supplied were judged to be of inferior quality. He had engaged the collaboration of two brothers, no doubt younger than he, who were awarded the contract to continue the work on their own.

These were Mouwerijn and Claes Simonsz van Waterlandt, both sons of a Haarlem painter mentioned between 1428 and 1463. They had presumably not been trained by their father, since their names do not occur until 1473 in the case of Mouwerijn, certainly the elder, and 1485 in the case of Claes. The former was active for a long time in the town; he is recorded there until 1509, the date of his death. Little is known of Claes, on the other hand, whose name does not appear after 1490.

Alongside these artists one must mention two painters about whom we have little information, despite a career spread over several decades. Cornelis Willemsz (we have no evidence as to whether he was the brother of Jacob Willemsz, or the son of another Willem) appears in 1481 and can be traced until 1523 working on small tasks. His contemporary Jacob Jansz is mentioned for the first time in 1483 and must have died in 1509, the year in which a bequest made by him to the church was registered. And yet the references to him in public records alone are rare, so it would be difficult to discern the nature of his work if we did not know through an eighteenth-century document that he was responsible for the Porters' altarpiece and was the master of Jan Mostaert.

The Master of the *Holy Kindred* of Amsterdam

The *Holy Kindred* in the Rijksmuseum (*81*) displays, as we have seen, the art of an imitator who borrows both character types and mannerisms from both Geertgen and Albert van Ouwater. With this work one can easily associate several paintings of the same character.

The *Adoration of the Magi* in the Reinhart collection (*82*) is composed, like the *Holy Kindred,* principally from borrowings. The second Wise Man is an exact copy of Joseph of Arimathaea in the Vienna *Lamentation,* a copy so faithful that the folds of the breeches are identical in the two paintings. The background owes a number of its figures to the Prague triptych. The artist also drew inspiration from that same painting to depict St. Bavo in a badly damaged panel in the Hermitage, probably a fragment of a triptych panel (*83*).

So scrupulous an imitation could not be the work of a master as gifted as Geertgen copying himself. It is surely the product of an imitator, no doubt very close to his model and seeking to plagiarise him in order to profit from his success. Nevertheless, he tends to simplify effects: his figures are not so much stiff as rigid, their gestures are not so much hanging in mid-air as frozen into puppet-like poses, and the female faces not only have evenly curved eyebrows, but are consistently given an almost artificially ovoid structure.

From these very simplifications the Amsterdam painting derives a sort of naïve grace, to which it owes it popularity. But

101 SAENREDAM. *View of St. Bavo's, Haarlem,* Amsterdam, detail showing the organ shutter painted by Vrederick Hoon (*80*)

102   MASTER OF THE AMSTERDAM HOLY KINDRED. *Holy Kindred,* Amsterdam, Rijksmuseum (*81*)

107 JACOB JANSZ. *St. Bavo* (outer wing of the *Diptych of the St. Anne Trinity*), Brunswick (*90*)

the structure of the landscape, but without conveying any real sense of depth.

In this work too, Jacob Jansz draws inspiration from his elders: the *Taking of Christ* is a transposition into an anecdotal

66   idiom of the work by the Master of the *Taking of Christ* in Munich. But he probably also borrows from Geertgen: the turbaned, smiling figure behind Christ is almost identical to the one on the sheet of drawings in the Louvre; Jacob Jansz

128

108   *Engraved portrait of Jacob Jansz* (de Jongh's edition of van Mander, 1764)

probably knew it through some painting, perhaps the *Ecce Homo* from the Hospitallers' triptych.

A *St. Jerome* (De Boer Foundation, Amsterdam, *91*) which has   211 recently been rediscovered and attributed too hastily to Geertgen should also be ascribed to the hand of Jacob Jansz. Here we find a facial type similar to that engraved by de Jongh, and the disproportionately large and rather shapeless feet which can also be seen in the two panels in the Brussels Museum.

But above all we should attribute to him the delightful *Tree of*   106, 109 *Jesse* (*93*) in the Rijksmuseum in Amsterdam, in connection with which the names of both Jan Mostaert and Geertgen tot Sint Jans have been mentioned. Unlike the previous work it is remarkably well-preserved, and the colour range alone shows at once that it cannot be from the hand of Geertgen. It could be entitled 'Harmony in white and pink', and this in itself would almost suffice to confirm the attribution. The composition possesses the naïve charm of all those known to us from the hand of the painter of the Brunswick *Diptych*. The strange   109 contortions in which these Kings of Judaea indulge are an elegant invention despite their incongruity. The space is rather clumsily rendered, and the buildings which can be seen through the foliage stand awkwardly.

In his long analysis of the painting, A. van Schendel has revealed many links with the *Holy Kindred* in Amsterdam. And   102 yet the difference in handling between the two works is so obvious that one cannot possibly attribute them to the same artist. But the debt of the latter painter to the former seems to confirm a vital point: the artist did not himself know Geertgen tot Sint Jans and was more influenced by the style of one of his

109   JACOB JANSZ. *Tree of Jesse*, Amsterdam, Rijksmuseum (*93*), detail   ▷

110–111 JACOB JANSZ.
Taking and Entombment of Christ,
Brussels, Musées Royaux des Beaux-Arts (*92*)

imitators, borrowing only elements of composition from the painter of the Hospitallers. One may even wonder if they were not master and pupil. The awkwardness of the latter's compositions may result from the former's example; he also arranges figures in space without being able to link them together clearly. Similarly, the imitations of profiles, as pointed out by A. van Schendel between two of the Kings in the *Tree of Jesse* and the left-hand Child in the *Holy Kindred*, are acquired better in a workshop than by mere imitation.[7]

106
102

Another work, also one of the artist's latest, is only known through a nineteenth-century drawing, fortunately very exact,

though one hopes that the original will come to light one day: a triptych of the *Last Judgment*. K. Boon published this document in 1966 and attributed the lost original, like the *Tree of Jesse*, to Jan Mostaert. It is certainly difficult to distinguish between the early works of Margaret of Austria's painter and those of his master; we lack hard evidence to elucidate the problem. Nevertheless, what we know to be by the latter—such as the *Speyart van Woerden Triptych* (Amsterdam, Rijksmuseum), the

113

112 JACOB JANSZ. *The Meal of the Holy Family*, Cologne, Wallraf-Richartz Museum (*95*)

▷

113 Copy of JACOB JANSZ. *The van Scoten Triptych*, Amsterdam, Rijksmuseum (*97*)

portrait of *Jacob Jansz van der Meer* (Copenhagen, National Museum) painted before 1510,[8] the *van Noordwijk Triptych* (Bonn, Rheinisches Landesmuseum), datable between 1512 and 1514, the *Portrait of Abel van den Coulster* (Brussels) from around 1512—seems to indicate a rapid evolution towards a freer technique than that of Jacob Jansz, less meticulous, towards more 'modern' forms, i.e., at that period, more mannerist. The lost painting, on the other hand, displays a very traditional art, and that type of rather flat face in which the pupils seem to form clearly defined round holes which are highly characteristic of the Master of the Brunswick *Diptych* and which Mostaert soon abandoned. The depiction of Gheryt van Scoten and his family allows us to date this painting fairly exactly around 1497.

This van Scoten triptych is remarkably faithful to the fifteenth-century style. In fact, it is based on the panels by Dieric Bouts in the Musée de Lille. The entire group of the elect on the left of the central panel is a very careful plagiarism from the *Paradise*. The depiction of the Heavenly Garden and of Hell on the central panel and on the wings is derived from the same

source: we find the elect climbing from the earthly to the heavenly paradise and the damned being flung into the abyss of Hell. The style that emerges from the drawn copy seems imbued with the rigidity of composition and forms which marks the artist's entire work. If we compare the portraits of the van Scotens to those of the Speyart van Woerdens, we notice that in the former the entire foreground is filled by Jacob Jansz's costume accessories and sharp-edged, gratuitous drapery folds. On the other hand, Mostaert's panels reserve an empty space in the foreground and avoid all unnecessary drapery folds.

One last painting also poses a problem of distinction between master and pupil, namely the *Holy Family* in Cologne (*95*). Two elements may be taken into consideration in forming a judgment: the forms and the spirit. The Virgin's face, almond-shaped and almost devoid of modelling, is certainly redolent of the stock of the master of the diptych. Similarly, although the Child Jesus has a head less out of proportion with his body than in the artist's other works, he still has the characteristic face with the snub nose. So if this was a work by Mostaert, we would need to assume that it was executed under the very direct influence of his master. But this familiar, almost trivial realism, similar to that of the *Virgin with the Milk-pap* by Gerard David, surely belongs

112

to the fifteenth century rather than to the new generation. It is the same naturalism which is evident in the *Hours of Catherine of Cleves*, and which governs the still life in Dieric Bouts's *Meal in the House of Simon* (*53*). Mostaert offers no other examples of it in the later development of his career. If we add that all the surfaces of the panel have been worn away by over-drastic cleaning, and that the harmony between the green of Joseph's robe and the lilac of the Virgin's provides a matching of tones very similar to that of the Brunswick *Diptych*, then the attribution to Jan Mostaert's master will at last seem more likely.

Jacob Jansz seems to have been brought up in the spirit of the fifteenth century amongst the followers of Geertgen tot Sint Jans, but with a close acquaintance with the art of Dieric Bouts. It is from the latter that he derived the technique of his extremely finished execution. His sense of composition and form nevertheless remains imbued with a simplicity and even a naïveté which contrasts strongly with Geertgen's plastic vigour. However, it is clear that he remained faithful during the whole of his active life to the forms of his youth, and that during the first decade of the sixteenth century he expressed himself in a spirit closer to that of the middle of the preceding century than to that of his pupil.

The Master of the Antwerp *Triptych*

This artist has been isolated by W. Cohen,[9] who attributed only three paintings to him: the *Triptych of the Virgin and Child* in the Antwerp Museum from which he draws his name (*101*), the *Virgin and Child with a donor presented by St. Michael* in the Staatliche Museen in Berlin (*100*), and an *Assumption with a pair of donors* in the Bonn Museum (*102*). All three display very close links with one another, and yet each one represents a very different stage in the development of a single style. The Berlin painting is the one which shows the clearest connection with Geertgen tot Sint Jans. The Virgin's face seems to have been imitated from those by him, and the drapery still has numerous folds, though here they are more gratuitous than in their model. A taste for contrived poses is also apparent, a clear sign of the first stirrings of northern mannerism.

This last characteristic is also present in the work which gives the painter his name (*101*), and to which too little importance has been attached, no doubt as a result of the unsatisfactory state in which it has appeared for several decades. Its appearance is partly distorted by an uneven yellow varnish and some unfortunate overpainting, especially on the Virgin's face. The execution is nevertheless of excellent quality, but the mannerist tendency is even more pronounced than in the Berlin painting. To this we owe the strange acrobatics of the flying putti and the angel musicians, who no longer have anything in common with van Eyck's in the *Mystic Lamb*. It is the same tendency which makes the artist extend the outline of his St. George by a bizarre transparent drapery creating fantastic shapes against the sky.

And yet the composition of the triptych follows traditional formulae closely. The central panel, with the Virgin seated on a throne of exotic architecture under a canopy, adopts a motif of Tournai art from the first half of the fifteenth century.[10] The sky background is a simple 'modernisation' of the archaic golden backcloth, but its broad expanse indicates an unwillingness to evoke a specific site.

Nevertheless, the work can only date from the last decade of the fifteenth century or the first decade of the sixteenth. The extravagant architecture of the throne and the mannerism of the poses indicate this. Yet another argument can be brought into play: the putti on the back of the throne, holding garlands in the form of rosaries, are a motif of Italian origin introduced into northern art by Memling (*Triptych* in the Kunsthistorisches Museum in Vienna) and Gerard David (*Justice Panels*, Bruges, Groeninge Museum).

All these features recur in the last picture attributed by Cohen (*102*), even though an initial examination may suggest that this work is less mannered than the preceding ones. The explanation of this difference in spirit is not hard to find: for in the *Assumption* the artist is following a model by the Bruges Master of *St. Lucy*,[11] which dictates a calmer overall structure. But in the detail, and especially in his treatment of the folds of the robes and of the angels' cloaks, he recaptures the imaginative drawing which characterises his two other works. The donors of this painting have been identified by E. Peilinck with a pair of Amsterdam worthies, Jan Dircs Cill and his wife Lysbeth Hugensdochter, but this clue does not permit a definitive dating of the picture; the beginning of the sixteenth century is only probable, as on 10 December 1513 Jan Dircs endowed a curacy on the altar of Our Lady in a chapel of the Nieuwe Kerk in Amsterdam.[12]

Restricted to Cohen's attributions, the work of the Master of the Antwerp *Triptych* would seem to be datable mainly to the opening years of the sixteenth century. Nevertheless, the Berlin painting has features which indicate familiarity with Geertgen's work, just as the Antwerp *Triptych* displays archaisms. The artist's personality reveals itself perhaps more clearly if we are willing to add to the same group two other attributions which to me seem essential. The first should be associated directly with the Berlin painting. This is a lost painting devoted to the *Institution of the Rosary* and known by two old copies, which bear witness to its popularity (*98*). If we compare the group of the Virgin and St. Dominic and the Berlin painting, the unity of conception will be apparent. Whether in the face of the Virgin, or in the type or pose of the Child, or even in the type of the angels, the similarity of spirit is obvious. And yet the painting represents an earlier stage in the painter's career, when he had not yet submitted to manneristic stylisation. It is composed with a simplicity and rigour still redolent of the fifteenth-century spirit and the works of Geertgen or his followers. If we remember that the Dominicans of Haarlem founded the first Congregation of the Rosary in Holland in 1478, and that the painting can therefore be dated around 1480 at the earliest, we shall be able to understand the difference in style.

114 MASTER OF THE ANTWERP TRIPTYCH.
Virgin and Child (centrepiece of the triptych),
Antwerp, Musée des Beaux-Arts (*101*)

The second work is more prestigious: it is a diptych, now divided between the Boymans Museum in Rotterdam and the National Gallery of Scotland in Edinburgh, representing on one side a *Crucifixion with St. Jerome*, on the other a *Maria in Sole* (*99*). Discovered first, the picture of the Virgin was quick to arouse interest and delighted excitement. The depiction of the divine group against a background of angel musicians dimly perceived, submerged in the radiance of the Virgin's glory, had a certain charm and an attribution to Geertgen tot Sint Jans seemed only natural. When, in 1959, S. Sulzberger and J.Q. van Regteren Altena joined forces to allow the work's other panel to be identified, the latter author was quick to state: 'The discovery

117, 115

threatens us with a disappointment: that of seeing a painting believed to be by Geertgen consigned to the fringes of his workshop.'[13] How could one accept that this artist could have produced such an awkward composition as the Edinburgh *Crucifixion* with its proliferation of secondary scenes? How could one imagine that the creator of the Vienna *Lamentation* could have re-used its composition with so little vitality and without grasping its monumentality in the background of this painting?

85

115 MASTER OF THE ANTWERP TRIPTYCH. *Maria in Sole*, Rotterdam, Boymans-van Beuningen Museum (*99 A*)

▷

There is, however, a simple solution. We should compare the *Virgin and Child* in the Ambrosiana, the Rotterdam *Maria in Sole* and the Antwerp *Triptych*. It will then be quite clear that the artist of the Rotterdam painting cannot be that of the Milan picture. The latter shows a clear ability, even on a small scale, to draw hands which are more than merely suggested, and to depict a child's body not jointed like a puppet. But in the Antwerp painting we find just such a child, so characteristic with its odd setting of the head on the shoulders, the same stiff gestures, the same strangely-constructed feet. The Edinburgh painting confirms the attribution by depicting a St. Jerome who is the blood-brother of the St. Dominic from the *Legend of the Rosary*.

In addition, the engaging charm of the Rotterdam *Maria in Sole* (*99A*) reveals its limitations when compared with the Edinburgh painting. All the poetry which surprises us comes from a technique derived from manuscript illumination and used particularly for manuscripts painted on a black ground, like the *Vienna Book of Hours* said to be of Galeazzo Maria Sforza.[14] The performance, however, does not match the conception. The figures of the angels are no better outlined than those of the background of the *Crucifixion*.

Defined in this way, the oeuvre of the Master of the Antwerp *Triptych* consists of work spanning several decades. The two last-mentioned paintings, the *Legend of the Rosary* and the *Diptych*, could date from as far back as the 1480s, perhaps even the

closing years of the preceding decade. The Berlin painting dates perhaps from a little before 1500, while the *Triptych* and the *Assumption* in Bonn probably belong to the first decade of the sixteenth century. The artist can thus be seen passing from a narrative style which owes much to the example of Geertgen to a kind of mannerism usually associated with Antwerp.

The Master of the *Figdor Deposition*

This artist was isolated by Valentiner in 1914. It has been possible to reconstruct his oeuvre from two panels of the same size, probably coming from the same altarpiece: the *Deposition from the Cross* formerly in the Figdor collection (*105*) and the *Martyrdom of St. Lucy* in the Rijksmuseum in Amsterdam (*106*). It is interesting to note that the work in question was a triptych whose composition must have been directly inspired by the altarpiece of the Haarlem Hospitallers. The *Martyrdom of St. Lucy* presents a series of episodes from the saint's life dotted across a landscape broken up by rocks similar to those in the *Burning of the bones of St. John the Baptist*. From this same painting the artist has also borrowed the saint's executioners, interpreting them freely. Like the Hospitallers' altarpiece, this work must have carried on its inner faces scenes from the life of Christ, probably the Carrying of the Cross, the Crucifixion and the Deposition—the last being the only one known to us.

As far as we can judge from these two panels, this artist's style seems very close to that of the Master of the Antwerp *Triptych*. Like him, he has a fondness for rather slender figures and delights in enlarging on anecdotal subjects. Also like him, in his early period, he has a predilection for a human type derived from Geertgen with a very oval, smoothly-textured face. Again like him, he displays a tendency to contrive distraught poses and indulges a taste for purely decorative drapery volutes. The miniaturist aspect, however, is more pronounced with him than with his contemporary. His figures have a delicate, doll-like fragility, full of charm and even more so of naïveté.

To these two works Valentiner added the *Crucifixion* in the Rijksmuseum in Amsterdam (*107*), whose handling is identical to that of the two preceding works. We have seen that this painting was probably directly inspired by the lost central panel of the Hospitallers' altarpiece. But the most notable feature is the presence in the background of the silhouette of Utrecht Cathedral, which clearly indicates that the work was intended for that town. This is corroborated by the existence of an almost exact copy, now in the Utrecht Museum, which originally came from a church within the diocese, St. Vitus in Naarden. Nevertheless, the hallmark of the Haarlem school is undeniable. This evidence therefore seems to suggest that the popularity of Haarlem artists led to their receiving commissions from neighbouring areas that were under a different jurisdiction.

To this nucleus, accepted by Friedländer, three minor works can be added. Two panels in the Rijksmuseum depict *St. Valerian* and *St. Cecilia* (*103*). They are usually attributed to the Master of

118 MASTER OF THE FIGDOR DEPOSITION. *Deposition from the Cross* (destroyed), formerly in Berlin (*105*)

the Brunswick *Diptych*, but do not have the quality of his draughtsmanship. The precision of their outlines and their delicate handling are much more in the manner of the Master of the *Figdor Deposition*. To him also can be ascribed a *Glorification of the Virgin* in Pretoria City Hall (*104*) and a recently discovered painting of the *Family of the Virgin* in the Bührle collection in Zurich (*108*). However, these works do not add much to our idea of a likable artist whose narrative style is but a one-finger melody in comparison with his models, the works of Geertgen tot Sint Jans.

The Master of the *Figdor Deposition* is nevertheless an important figure in the development of the Haarlem school. As long ago as 1914 Valentiner had drawn attention to the surprising similarity between his work and that of Cornelisz van

Oostsanen. In 1937, Baldass and especially Schretlen had no doubt that the two artists were one and the same; in their eyes, the first was no more than the early period of the second. Irene Kunze protested against this assertion, and rightly so, in 1939. The resemblance between the two artists is obvious, but it bears witness to two fairly distinct temperaments. The two *Crucifixions* by the Amsterdam artist (Rijksmuseum, Amsterdam, and Bowes Museum, Barnard Castle) were directly inspired by that of the Master of the *Figdor Deposition*, but they have a much more developed sense of space and composition which cannot be explained simply by the progress of an artist in the course of his evolution. At this point, a theory put forward in 1914 by Valentiner acquires new interest: for him the relationship between the two artists was one of master and pupil. It remains to discover who could have been the master of Cornelisz van Oostsanen, a subject on which Karel van Mander offers no information. But Valentiner has rightly pointed out that a young painter from Oostsanen would normally have had to seek a master in Haarlem, the most important centre of artistic production, and that it was natural that he should present himself to compatriots from the Waterlandt: and as it happens, Mouwerijn and Claes Simonsz were sufficiently well-known towards the end of the fifteenth century for young apprentices to be entrusted to their care.

Mouwerijn and Claes Simonsz van Waterlandt

Valentiner's theory may seem unfounded, yet it has considerable interest. The first step of a young artist or of his parents, when seeking a master to train him, is naturally to apply to fellow-countrymen. It is quite probable that Mouwerijn and Claes Simonsz had left Waterlandt long before. Their father Simon is mentioned as a painter at Haarlem between 1428 and 1463, but he may have retained interests in his district of origin. Above all, almost all the public records which mention his sons refer to them by the name of their locality, 'van Waterlandt'. This means that they were generally known by this title, which could have sufficed to attract young artists from that region to them.

We should add that their fame must have been considerable in Haarlem at the end of the fifteenth century. One recalls that in 1485 they won the contract for continuing work on the panels for the high altar of St. Bavo; these had been begun by Jacob Willemsz, who had been unable to satisfy the churchwardens' requirements. For five years they worked for the church and thus attained a position of prominence.

Nevertheless, here we have two brothers. Supposing that the Master of the *Figdor Deposition* was in fact one of them, which one was he and who was his brother? This may seem an idle question, unlikely to find any answer. However, analysis of the style of Jacob Cornelisz's probable master has shown that it was very similar to that of the Master of the Antwerp *Triptych*. Now

119   MASTER OF THE FIGDOR DEPOSITION. *Martyrdom of St. Lucy* (106), Amsterdam, Rijksmuseum

the work of the Amsterdam painter contains traces of acquaintance with the works of the latter artist, and a very close acquaintance at that. In a painting like the *Nativity of Dirck van Boschuysen*, dated 1512 (Naples, Museo Nazionale di Capodimonte), we find putti which strongly resemble his or even the Child Jesus in his Berlin painting. Both artists also use the same technique for depicting curly hair. Similarly, the Virgins of Jacob Cornelisz's early works, particularly that of the Naples painting or in the *Virgin and Child surrounded by Angels* in the Staatliche Museen, Berlin, have strong affinities with the one in the Triptych Master's Berlin painting. The connection is close enough for us to assume fairly direct links between the two artists.

So it is not impossible to advance the following theory: Mouwerijn and Claes Simonsz are none other than the Master of the Antwerp *Triptych* and the Master of the *Figdor Deposition*. If the theory could be fleshed out, it would even be easy to distinguish them. Mouwerijn was the elder; he is known from 1473 onwards and died in 1509. This period of activity would correspond better with the first of the two artists, whose earliest works may date from around 1480. Claes is first mentioned in 1485 and I know of no documents concerning him later than 1490. Did he die young? Did he move to another town? We do not know. But his later start, from 1485 onwards, would correspond better with the style of the Master of the *Figdor Deposition*, who, in the rare works known to be by him, already displays a more mannerist tendency despite his attachment to models by Geertgen.

It is still impossible to offer this identification as an established fact.[15] We should notice, however, that the work of these two artists tallies with that of a generation which began work in the closing decades of the fifteenth century and was still productive at the beginning of the sixteenth. An output like that of the Master of the Antwerp *Triptych*, with several early works probably dating from around the 80s, then with later paintings dating from after 1500, even agrees with the working conditions suggested by contemporary events. The outbreak in 1492 of the crisis which had been brewing at Haarlem for several years and was already causing havoc in many Dutch towns must have resulted in a several years' halt in the flow of large artistic commissions. Such a break in an artist's output could easily result in a distinct change of style when work is resumed.

The Master of the *Tiburtine Sibyl*

It would, however, be too hasty to conclude that artistic production in Haarlem at the end of the fifteenth century was restricted to the work of these four artists—the Master of the Amsterdam *Holy Kindred*, the Master of the Brunswick *Diptych*, the Master of the Antwerp *Triptych* and the Master of the *Figdor Deposition*—who were Geertgen's spiritual descendants. Geertgen's was not the only influence at work during this period, and it could be combined with others. The Master of the *Tiburtine Sibyl*, first isolated by Valentiner in 1914, demonstrates this. In Valentiner's view the artist's oeuvre included the eponymous picture in the Frankfurt Museum (Staedelsches Kunstinstitut, *114*), a *Raising of Lazarus* (Mexico, Museum of Fine Arts, *109*) and the *Marriage of the Virgin* (Johnson collection, Philadelphia, *112*). Since then the following additions have been made to the list: the *Crucifixion* in the Detroit Museum (*111*), which has the same dimensions as the Philadelphia painting, the *St. Anne Trinity* in Baron van der Elst's collection (*113*) and the *Virgin and Child* in the Twenthe Museum in Zwolle (*110*), seen by Hoogewerff as no more than a product of the artist's workshop or following.[16]

In these works the overriding influence is the style of Dieric Bouts. For this reason some scholars, like Hoogewerff and Wolfgang Schöne, have immediately concluded that the artist had come from Louvain to Haarlem. His links with the latter town are certainly undeniable. The Mexico *Raising of Lazarus* borrows from the versions of both Albert van Ouwater and Geertgen. In the *Marriage of the Virgin* in Philadelphia the young man on the far left is patently imitated from Geertgen's figures, borrowing not only the typical hose which end in rounded shoes but also the clothing and stance. Most importantly, he has been

120   MASTER OF THE TIBURTINE SIBYL. *Crucifixion*, Detroit, Institute of Arts (*111*)

121   MASTER OF THE TIBURTINE SIBYL. *Marriage of the Virgin*, Philadelphia, Johnson collection (*112*)   ▷

122 MASTER OF THE TIBURTINE SIBYL. *Augustus and the Tiburtine Sibyl,*
Frankfurt, Staedelsches Kunstinstitut (*114*)

identified as the illustrator who worked between 1484 and 1486
for the printer Jacob Bellaert in Haarlem. The lively style of his
illustrations, which were his own invention, well matches the
mood of the secondary scenes in his paintings, and Valentiner
has discovered numerous details that the two groups of works
have in common.

However, our man was probably a travelling artist. In 1960,
James Snyder demonstrated that the painting of *Augustus and the*
122 *Tiburtine Sibyl* should be linked with the town of Louvain. In the
left-hand group we see doctors wearing the robes of that town's
university. On the far right, the young nobleman wearing the
collar of the Golden Fleece has been identified as Engelbert II of
Nassau, who was made a knight of the order in 1473 and was, as

lieutenant-general of Brabant, a faithful protector of the
university. The painting's theme seems to be a kind of
justification of the Latin studies which shed light on Christianity, like the Sibyl announcing the coming of Christ to Augustus.
This ingenious and plausible interpretation confirms that the
artist must have worked at Louvain.

Nevertheless, on close examination we cannot but notice that
the influence of Bouts on this artist is less deep and less evident
than it may seem. To the Louvain painter he is indebted for
some human types, for a tendency to elongate his bodies, and for
a few faces. But he did not learn design from him. He juxtaposes
his figures without managing to impose a solid structure on his
groups. He is happy to leave large areas of open space, and
indulges in a proliferation of secondary scenes—as in the
Marriage of the Virgin—to an extent which jeopardises the 121
coherence of the whole.

142

His book illustrations are notable for the still wholly Gothic elegance of the outlines, and this could be largely due to the influence of Dieric Bouts. And yet one thinks even more of possible contacts with south Netherlandish illuminators like Loyset Liedet. Even so, the Master of the *Tiburtine Sibyl* displays a highly individual personality, a spontaneity of gestures and poses combined with a direct and familiar realism. It is this latter feature that gives force to illustrations like those of the *Livre de la Propriété des Choses* of 1485.

The paintings, besides their borrowings from Dieric Bouts, Albert van Ouwater and Geertgen, are also marked by a realism verging on caricature. In the Mexico *Raising of Lazarus* (*109*), the rings round the eyes are so prominent that they somehow turn the expressions into grimaces. Figures like the High Priest in the *Marriage of the Virgin* or the two men behind him to the left have a hard, deeply lined appearance which recurs with the same harshness in the *Crucifixion*, even if only in the faces of St. John and Mary Magdalene. This is a tendency which we have not yet noticed in the Haarlem sphere of influence.

The artist can thus be seen as an eclectic drawing the elements of his style from different traditions. The remarkable fact is that, in the 1480s, he borrowed to only a limited extent from Geertgen. His landscapes owe nothing to him. They have neither the artist's characteristic foliage nor the organised structure of the Vienna panels. They seem more like variations on motifs of Dieric Bouts with their jagged rocks, more Gothic than Geertgen's, their sparser vegetation and their stronger impression of distance. The setting of the Detroit *Crucifixion* is similar to both that of the *Elijah in the Wilderness* from Bouts's *Last Supper Triptych* and to that of his *Lamentation* in the Louvre.

The artist's presence first at Haarlem and then at Louvain may justify hopes of finding his name in the public records.

There is only one published reference which could concern the painter in question. In 1487, at Louvain, an artist from Haarlem named Joes Wilen Valcx, the son of Wilen Valcx, was murdered. And yet neither father nor son seems to occur in the Haarlem archives, unless the latter can be identified with one Jan Valls (?) who was paid for banners by the town in 1480.[17] The coincidence of the date of the murder at Louvain with the cessation of the activity of Jacob Bellaert's engraver is remarkable, but one wonders if it is enough to justify our declaring the two men identical. One would like at least to discover some traces of this Joes Wilen Valcx's activity at Haarlem.

The 'rustic' tendency

Alongside these two major artistic traditions, which can be distinguished quite well, there must have existed a third tendency. We are assured of its existence by a small painting which can only have come from Haarlem. This is a *Christ before Pilate*, now in the Frederiks collection in The Hague (*116*). Schretlen, its former owner, had pointed out that the building in the background was none other than Haarlem town hall. He also believed it possible to identify the artist with the engraver who worked for the printer Bellaert. Such a conclusion might be suggested by the cursory definition of the figures and the scale of the characters. And yet we find none of the engraver's elegance and delicacy here. On the contrary, the work displays a kind of wilful roughness, both in the handling, which is deliberately coarse, and in the choice of human types, which verge on caricature. One of the executioners leading Christ offers a remarkable profile with an exaggerated Jewish nose. Christ himself is shown covered with bruises, his body stiffened by suffering.

The mood here seems popular. But in the northern Netherlands one cannot guarantee this as an accurate description, since this 'popular mood' can be found in works which were evidently not intended for humble circles, such as the *Turin-Milan Hours* or the *Hours of Catherine of Cleves*. It is the same spirit as occurs in the works of the Master of the *Manna*, which I have linked to a 'rustic' tendency.

The fact that a painting like this *Christ before Pilate* originated in Haarlem opens up important perspectives. It could account for the undercurrent so clearly present in the style of the Master of the *Tiburtine Sibyl*, and which cannot be explained by the other sources of his style. The art of Geertgen himself is marked by this rustic tendency, though it is better integrated into an overall style than in the work of the Master of the *Tiburtine Sibyl*.

No doubt other works of the same tendency must have been painted at Haarlem. However, we lack the data which would entitle us to locate others at Haarlem with certainty. We can thus only proceed by hypothesis. A *Crowning with Thorns* (*118*), in a private Dutch collection, is in a style very similar to that of *Christ before Pilate* and could be from Haarlem. It is even more violent, and its handling even freer. Nevertheless, the group of Jews has some affinity with those depicted by Albert van Ouwater and Geertgen tot Sint Jans.

A kindred spirit can also be found in a curious little painting in the Chicago Museum (*117*), quite wrongly attributed to the Master of the *Virgo inter Virgines*. In it, the *Ecce Homo* is depicted rather differently from the way it was in Geertgen's lost painting. The Jews are in the foreground and are overlooked by the flight of steps on which Christ is presented. The work's handling is much lighter than that of the two paintings mentioned previously. However, we find the same near-caricature of the faces and the simple narrative touch in the grouping of the characters.

These three paintings have only been brought together in an attempt to outline how this tendency may have expressed itself at Haarlem. As it also occurs in other Netherlandish workshops, it is still difficult to distinguish what belongs particularly to Haarlem from the more general characteristics of north Netherlandish work.

The Haarlem painters in the fifteenth century: school or workshops?

An analysis of the fifteenth-century paintings whose origins can be traced to Haarlem does not indicate a very close relationship between the development of the town's workshops and the historical situation in the county of Holland and in Haarlem itself. Doubtless the greatest development of painting took place during the most favourable period, the reigns of Philip the Good and Charles the Bold. Albert van Ouwater, the Master of the *Taking of Christ* (probably) and Geertgen tot Sint Jans all came into the limelight during this period, not to mention Dieric Bouts who, however, left his homeland early on. At the same time, the work of these artists is closer to the style of the southern masters than that of any others working in the northern Netherlands during the fifteenth century.

The traceable links between one or other of these painters and their southern contemporaries do not, however, imply any direct affiliations. When Albert van Ouwater or Geertgen borrow from southern artists, the borrowings are only very limited ones and do not affect their style. What we seem to have, in fact, is an independent tradition springing from the legacy of van Eyck in Holland; in other words, an art of southern origin but, as it were, imported directly into Holland and developed on the spot. Geertgen owes more to his master Albert van Ouwater than to Hugo van der Goes. Albert van Ouwater himself learnt little from Rogier van der Weyden and owes the essence of his style to Jan van Eyck (the early works rather than the mature ones).

After Geertgen's death (c. 1475–80), the workshops appear to have carried on under their own momentum. The works that can be dated to the last quarter of the fifteenth century are relatively numerous, so much so that one might think that artistic activity had not been affected by the political and economic crisis which shook the region between 1480 and 1495. It is probable, though, that a large proportion of the known paintings should be dated before or after this period. The work of the Master of the *Holy Kindred* surely belongs mainly to the period before 1480–5. That of artists like the Master of the Antwerp *Triptych* or the Master of the *Figdor Deposition* must date from after 1495, even though the former may have been active around 1480. Only Jacob Jansz seems to have been working more regularly during the troubled times. If we must date the triptych painted for Gheryt van Scoten around 1497, it seems difficult to place all the rest of his work between then and the date of his death, twelve years later.

The first 'mannerist' tendencies probably appeared after the political and economic crisis. They became even more strongly marked with painters of the new generation, like the Master of

Alkmaar or the artists working for the Abbey of Egmont in the first quarter of the sixteenth century,[18] although they did not hold absolute sway: Jan Mostaert was little influenced by them, and, to a certain extent, remained more faithful to the fifteenth-century tradition.

The question is, however, whether these artists form a school or whether the links between them are only limited. It is not easy to give an answer; it rather depends on what one means by 'a school'. It is undeniable that there is an easily discernible continuity from Ouwater to the Master of the *Figdor Deposition*. Geertgen owes more to Ouwater than to any other artist. The Master of the *Holy Family*, Jacob Jansz, the Master of the Antwerp *Triptych* and the Master of the *Figdor Deposition* are indebted to Geertgen, from whom they borrow their types, their conventions and even their general inspiration. If it is true that the Master of the *Taking of Christ* was from Haarlem, that would suffice to explain the 'Boutsian' aspect of the work of the Master of the *Tiburtine Sibyl*, who also owes much to Geertgen. This continuity of tradition and orientation meets the definition of a school. Not one of the great 'schools' which define the culture of a large region, such as 'Early Flemish', but a provincial school which corresponds to the maintenance of a tradition through several generations of local artists.

In so far as this tradition originates with van Eyck, its work draws its guiding principles from and has its source in the art of the 'Early Flemish School'. With this it shares a fundamental realism based on observation of everyday life, and a taste for smooth, precise handling which conceals the brush-strokes. It is thus a branch of a much larger school. It is nevertheless distinguished from south Netherlandish painting above all by the unimportance of Rogier van der Weyden's influence, by a more plastic conception of form—arising once again from the Eyckian tradition—and by a sort of internal tension in the figures which seems to fix them in a solemn attitude while yet revealing an undercurrent of deep feeling.

The art of this school does not reign unchallenged, however. The faint signs of a rustic tradition at Haarlem are significant. They reveal the presence of another current, at first sight more 'popular'. They also explain the similar touches noticeable in the works of the Haarlem school (and which are almost entirely absent from south Netherlandish works). In this respect, the art of Haarlem stands apart from developments in the south, but also allies itself to other manners of artistic expression that can be seen in the northern Netherlands.

VII. Workshops outside Haarlem
Delft, Leiden, Gouda, Utrecht

The fact that, of all the Dutch towns, Haarlem was the best placed to experience important artistic developments in the fifteenth century does not mean that no studios were set up or expanded in other towns. The conditions of 'patronage', or rather the size of the 'clientèle', were different. Leiden had periods of prosperity and its cloth trade must have led to the growth of large fortunes. Delft was in a similar position. On the other hand, Amsterdam had not yet fully established its economic power as it was to do in the following century. Moreover, Holland bordered on the city of Utrecht, strife-torn but still rich and powerful and open on to the Germanic world.

Van Mander, the first historian of Dutch painting did not speak of these towns, and the chroniclers prove no more communicative. The name of only one artist from outside Haarlem has been passed on to us, and even then he owes this posthumous celebrity more to his son's fame than to his own; this is Hugo Jacobsz, the father of Lucas van Leyden. The public records tell us little more. At Delft, Leiden, Utrecht and other towns they provide us with the names of several painters, associating them generally with minor work. They give us too little information, however, to distinguish the artists from the artisans, or to make connections between these references and surviving works. Beyond Haarlem the period is cloaked in obscurity. From the darkness emerge some personalities whom one can only identify for the time being by an arbitrary title. Nevertheless, some figures stand out clearly enough to merit detailed examination. At Delft there is the Master of the *Virgo inter Virgines*, the most remarkable of all, followed by the Master of Delft, whose career extends beyond the period covered by this book. The Master of the *St. John* panels, who can only be Hugo Jacobsz, probably worked at Leiden; Utrecht can only offer artists of lesser rank—the Master of Evert van Soudenbalch, and the painter whom Boon linked with the Buukerk, where he executed a mural.[1]

Delft as a centre for painting

At the beginning of the fifteenth century, Delft had been the centre of activity for an artist who seems to have been fairly well known, Dirc de Maelre.[2] Unfortunately, it has not been possible to identify his work. Several other names emerge from the town archives of the fifteenth century, but there is none whose personality takes on definite shape. What kind of artist was Jan Isbrantsz, known between 1446 and 1448, or Pieter, who appears between 1450 and 1495, or Dirc Jansz who comes on to the scene in 1474 and disappears after 1495, not to mention those of whom we know almost nothing, like Mester Craut (1447) or Staes (1495)?[3] The crop of names is particularly poor in this town, and sheds no light on the relative importance of these artists. At least we know that they existed, even if we have no idea of the nature of their work.

One might think that manuscript illumination could throw light on painters' studios in the town; a manuscript now in the Bibliothèque Royale in Brussels[4] contains a colophon noting that it was written and illuminated at the convent of the Augustinian canonesses of St. Agnes, near Delft. However, this reference to the illumination may only concern the decoration of the margins and initials, which is modest enough. The book contains 22 full-page miniatures, but they have been painted on separate sheets inserted into the body of the manuscript. They could thus be the work of artists from outside the convent, priests or laymen, and come from Delft or some other town.

Nevertheless, these illuminations deserve some study. They belong to a genre which enjoyed a significant increase in popularity towards the middle of the fifteenth century, namely grisaille. There were probably two reasons for the passion for this technique: one purely aesthetic, the method having established itself in favour by the example of Parisian illumination, but also as a result of the increased use of grisaille for the reverse of paintings; the other reason was quite simply financial, grisaille miniatures costing less than those requiring a large range of often expensive colours (notably lapis lazuli).

The Brussels manuscript manages to exhibit all the tendencies of this genre. It contains two groups of illustrations. Some are very refined, depicting figures and compositions which still draw on the conventions current at the beginning of the century. They are a legacy of court art. But alongside these appear coarser illustrations, with a propensity for giving their characters ugly, sometimes grimacing faces;[5] they are yet another expression of the 'rustic tendency', which became very widespread in the sphere of grisaille. It is notably present in the *Livre d'Heures de Kaetzaert de Zaers* (Leiden University Library, MS B.P.L.224), in which leaves in this style are found alongside pages decorated by the Master of Catherine of Cleves or a close follower of his.[6] It is also clearly recognisable in a *Book of Hours* in the Bodleian Library in Oxford (MS Douce 248) which once more was produced at the convent of St. Agnes at Delft.[7]

It is very tempting to say that all this work was produced at Delft, but not possible to give in to that temptation completely. To take just one of the examples given, the *Livre d'Heures de Kaetzaert de Zaers* seems to have been produced at Utrecht, as the calendar mentions the death of a Carthusian of that town. Moreover, these illuminations were mass-produced and were thus the work not of a single master but of a workshop, or even of several workshops copying from one another. Thus the scene of the *Circumcision* in the Oxford *Book of Hours* is an exact copy of the formula found in the *Livre de Kaetzaert de Zaers*, and dozens of similar examples could be cited. One can at least assert that this unrefined art must have been known at Delft, even if it did not originate there.

Similarly, the existence of a scriptorium at the convent of St. Agnes must be considered an important fact. Certainly, the illuminations that Byvanck found attributable wholly to this convent are late and mediocre.[8] All the same, the nuns' work must have led to exchanges with other studios—as witness the insertion of grisaille leaves in several of their productions—and thus stimulated fruitful competition among local artists.

The Master of the *Virgo inter Virgines*

The importance of these grisaille illuminations for the Delft studios becomes apparent when we consider the woodcuts produced between 1483 and 1498 by a designer working for various publishers in Delft.[9] There is a striking similarity between the ones and the others. The engraver who illustrated the *Evangelien ende Epistelen*, published in 1486, is primarily in search of effect. He is not very concerned to suggest space accurately or to introduce refinements in the arrangement of his figures, provided that the protagonists stand out and have eye-catching expressions. And, perhaps to heighten the effect or perhaps simply to follow a well-established tradition, he prefers bucolic, often ugly faces, always with very prominent features, in the manner of the grisaille illuminations.

Like most engravers, perhaps in order to meet the demands of printers, he has no qualms about copying the work of other artists (this is the case with the *Historie van die seven wise mannen*, which copies the illustrations for the same text published the previous year at Gouda). But when he undertakes this task, he does so with the freedom and energy of a highly individual designer. It is unlikely that he cut the blocks himself, as there are very noticeable differences between the cut of his first book and that of the *Passionael* (Delft, 1487), and even more from the 1488 edition of Ludolph the Carthusian. Nevertheless, despite the diversity of the executants, the same sinewy style is recognisable from one volume to the next.

123   MASTER OF THE VIRGO INTER VIRGINES. *Annunciation*, outer wings of a triptych, Aix-la-Chapelle, Suermondt Museum (*119*)

Whatever may be said of his facility, the designer does not always seem to take a great deal of care over his works. He often falls back on stereotyped poses which recur in one picture after another; hence the large number of men planted squarely on both legs, one of which is stretched out in front at an angle. This does not detract, though, from the quality of his compositions, which display a perfect understanding of the possibilities of the woodcut. He knows how to arrange the components of his design clearly, though to the detriment of a satisfying perspective. Above all, he knows how to avoid a clutter of inessential details in order to make the main theme easier to follow.

In 1910, Friedländer compared some of these illustrations with the paintings of an artist whom he had provisionally baptised the Master of the *Virgo inter Virgines*. The comparison is important, firstly because it gives new depth to the painter by revealing another aspect of his art, and secondly because it enables us to locate his workshop. There can hardly be any doubt that he worked at Delft, since his designs were used successively by three of the town's printers: Jacob van der Meer, Christiaan Snellaert and Eckert van Homburch.[10] This location

124   MASTER OF THE VIRGO INTER VIRGINES. *Adoration of the Shepherds*, Vienna. Kunsthistorisches Museum (*122*)   ▷

146

125 MASTER OF THE VIRGO INTER VIRGINES. *Adoration of the Magi*, Berlin, Staatliche Museen (*123*)

maintained close links with the monastery of Sint Bartholomeusdal, near Delft, founded in 1470 by monks from Herne. In 1482 one of the founder monks, Gaspar van der Stock, went back to Herne to become prior. One is tempted to connect this return with the presence in Brabant of a work by the Delft artist. If we accept K.G. Boon's suggestion to link the execution of the work to the appointment of the prior, the date confirms those provided by the book illustrations.

The artist therefore most probably flourished during the last quarter of the fifteenth century. During this period the archives of Delft mention the work of two artists. The first, Pieter die Maelre or die Scilder, must already have been advanced in years by 1475. His name appears as early as 1450 in connection with a rent derived from his house, and the text refers to him as 'meester'. He was still alive in 1495, however, when he was paid for some minor work at the Oude Kerk. The second is Dirc

126 MASTER OF THE VIRGO INTER VIRGINES. The *Virgo inter Virgines*, Amsterdam, Rijksmuseum (*125*)

is also confirmed by the presence, on one of the artist's best paintings, the *Annunciation* (*124*), of a coat of arms of the van der Bergh family, several of whose members undertook administrative responsibilities at Delft at the end of the fifteenth century and the beginning of the sixteenth.[11]

The dates of the artist's career can be determined without great difficulty; minimum limits are provided by his production of illustrations, between 1483 and 1498. The paintings contain hardly any clues which might confirm or contradict these data. The arms in the *Annunciation* in the Boymans Museum have not been identified with sufficient exactness to be taken into consideration. Only the provenance of the Enghien painting may supply some indication, as Boon has shown.[12] This *Lamentation* comes from the Charterhouse of Herne, which

127 MASTER OF THE VIRGO INTER VIRGINES. *Adoration of the Magi*, centrepiece of a triptych, Salzburg, Carolino Augusteum Museum (*126*)

Jansz, who first appears only in 1474 when he was paid for the tomb of Hans Sluyters' wife. He reappears in 1495, but the references are very brief, and rendered even less significant by the rarity of the surviving entries.[13] It is difficult to suggest an identity for the artist on the strength of such vague indications. We may simply note that the latter artist corresponds better to one's idea of the Master of the *Virgo inter Virgines*, who is unlikely to have been active around 1450 and thus born about 1430 at the latest.

The known work suggests a division into three periods. The early paintings, which have a hesitant feeling, are a *Triptych of the Lamentation* split up between the Prado and the Suermondt Museum in Aachen (*119*), a *Nativity* in a private German collection (*120*) and the Princeton Museum's *Virgin and Child* (*121*). A fact that tends to confirm that these are youthful works is their fairly close similarity to the grisaille illuminations of the preceding decades. There is the same emphasis on the figures, which take pride of place at the expense of the setting, the same simplicity of modelling, reduced to broad surfaces, and the same faces verging on caricature. To this group we should perhaps add the *Adoration of the Shepherds* in the Kunsthistorisches

223, 224
123
225
124

Museum, Vienna (*122*). The attribution of this painting may seem doubtful. There are curious details which do not recur elsewhere, particularly the little figures with rounded heads in the middle ground. Above all, the effects which seem rather clumsy and hesitant in the other paintings of the same group lend the composition a monumental aspect. Perhaps it was just a particularly successful work by the master, though its fullness may also put one in mind of an artist like Hugo Jacobsz.

These paintings in the first style indicate no more than a very distant acquaintance with the painters of the south. The *Nativity* in the German collection (*120*) may recall the centre of the *Portinari Triptych* by Hugo van der Goes; it is a distant recollection which may rely on no more than a drawing in which the composition had been clumsily copied.[14]

225

In the artist's middle period, motifs borrowed from southern works are frequent. And yet they are never copied literally, but are always interpreted with great individuality in a composition in which they become almost imperceptible. The artist's technique now acquires genuine virtuosity. The modelling loses the harshness of the early works, and gains relative sensitivity. The range of colours, though muted, nevertheless attains real refinement: browns and greys in all their variety form the basis for all the painter's harmonies. Touches of dark red and green give life to this rather subdued palette.

128 MASTER OF THE VIRGO INTER VIRGINES. *Massacre of the Innocents*, panel of the triptych of the Adoration of the Magi, Salzburg, Carolino Augusteum Museum (*126*)

This is the artist's most fruitful period, that of the Enghien 125 *Lamentation (128)*, the *Adoration of the Magi* in Berlin (*123*) and 130, 230 the *Triptych* at Barnard Castle (*130*). By reason of its size, the last painting is the most important. It is also the most unusual by reason of the profusion of participants, their disturbing faces and their contorted poses. We may well wonder if the artist was not somehow trying, in this huge work for its time, to emulate Geertgen's triptych for the Hospitallers—unless he was fulfilling the special requirements of an Italian client. Geertgen's work was by no means unknown to the Master of the *Virgo inter Virgines*, who borrows from him as often as he does from

southern artists. The Enghien *Lamentation* can only be understood in this light. The *Adoration of the Magi* in Berlin probably 125 owes more to the same artist's *Prague Triptych (68)* than to the 78 *Monforte Altarpiece* by Hugo van der Goes. As for the work from 198 which the artist derives his name, it borrows as much from the Master of the *Tiburtine Sibyl* as from van der Goes.

Of the painter's last style we shall mention only two pictures which, as it happens, may come from the same ensemble. These are the *Crucifixion* in the Uffizi (*132*) and the *Entombment* in St. Louis (*133*). In both works, the dramatic tension of the forms increases to impose strange contortions on the figures. The grandeur of the compositions of the middle period now disappears in favour of an emotion expressed more spontaneously, with wilful violence and excess. The date of these works may be suggested by a comparison between the crucified Christ in the Uffizi painting and the one in the *Crucifixion* engraving from the *Missale Trajectense* printed at Delft in 1495.

We may look for confirmation of this chronology in the evolution of a face that reappears in many paintings and is too individual not to be based on a living face (fig. 232). We find it in 232 the shepherd who puts his head through a window in the *Adoration of the Magi* in Berlin. There his features are young, but 125 already distinctive. He becomes St. John the Evangelist in the *Crucifixion* in the Lebel collection, in which his features show the first signs of aging. In the Barnard Castle triptych he is oddly inserted between the two arms of the Cross in the scene depicting the Carrying of the Cross, forming a sort of agonised counterpoint to the face of Christ. His cheeks have hollowed, his eyes become more sunken. The expression is all the more painful in that the character is uttering a cry of protest and grief, while uncovering his head just as in his very first portrayal, in the Berlin painting. The same face occurs yet again as St. John in the *Entombment* in Liverpool. Less hemmed in than in the 129 previous paintings, the character presents a strange swollen head with a sharp profile and heavy eyes. The last known picture we have of it is probably in the St. Louis painting. There the face seems almost relaxed, though the effects of aging are now more marked by a coarsening of the features, which were previously more tautly modelled. What can we make of this remarkable series? None of these figures is posed in a manner suitable for an artist painting his own portrait from a mirror. And yet the keenness of the expression leaves us in no doubt as to the importance attached by the artist to these features. It is also significant that the character is twice shown uncovering his head. The painter's imaginative talent would, it seems, justify our taking this as a sort of freely interpreted self-portrait, or more exactly as a sort of signature within the painting itself, in the form of free variations on the artist's own features.

The originality of such an artist is unmistakable and reveals itself, upon analysis, in many areas. It is noteworthy that the iconographic sources of his compositions are a mixture of

129 MASTER OF THE VIRGO INTER VIRGINES. *Entombment*, Liverpool, Walker Art Gallery (*129*) ▷

archaic or unusual elements and the novelties of southern art. Twice in his work we see, in an *Annunciation* scene, a child descending towards the Virgin, a very popular motif at the very beginning of the fifteenth century. Alongside this, the same artist is able to develop the theme of the Lamentation, which is relatively new in northern art. He can even break new ground with sometimes remarkable imagination; thus in the Zagreb painting (*131*) he adds to the 'Throne of Grace' not only the angels carrying the instruments of the Passion, but also the protagonists of a Pietà.

More generally, the Master of the *Virgo inter Virgines* is a story-teller. He likes his main themes to be accompanied by secondary scenes, often taken from everyday life, even if they are not directly suggested by any of the commentaries on the Gospel. Thus he depicts the departure of Joseph and Mary in the background of the *Nativity* (private collection, Germany), or, in the same work, the shepherds performing a bizarre dance as a sign of their joy, or again the men carrying ladders who appear again and again in the different versions of the *Lamentation* and in the *Entombment* in Liverpool. Several details of the large triptych at Barnard Castle can probably be set down to this imaginative faculty. It is just this sort of inventiveness that has given a black skin to the soldier carrying the sponge. We know of no other examples. The negro here is probably taken as evil by reason of the very colour of his skin. But this is giving black men a very different rôle from that played by the character that first inspired their portrayal in western painting; the Wise Man Balthasar never has such a negative significance. Also in this painting, the same zest is responsible for the rare depiction of Judas hanged and of the curious scene, so difficult to interpret, of a couple seated at table in front of a house in the background.

This lively fancy in the invention of details finds a counterpart in the unconventional arrangement of the altarpieces themselves, such as four-panel triptychs, the centre being composed of two, of the same size as each of the wings. There are three similar ensembles extant, and two others seem to have existed: one consisted of two panels now lost, the Berlin *Adoration of the Magi* and the Rotterdam *Annunciation;* the other included the Uffizi *Crucifixion* and the St. Louis *Entombment.* Certainly, the idea was not new and copied that of Dieric Bouts's Marian Triptych. It is nevertheless indicative of the painter's underlying tendencies; by eliminating the predominance of the central panel, it effectively emphasises the narrative aspect of the ensemble.

The oddness of these arrangements is matched by the strangeness of the composition of the scenes themselves. In this respect, the large Salzburg Triptych (*126*), which combines both features, is very significant. Here the central component *is* given the advantage of size. Indeed, the artist has gone to the other

231

225

129
230

125
131

127, 128

130   MASTER OF THE VIRGO INTER VIRGINES. *Carrying of the Cross*, left wing of the triptych of the Crucifixion, Barnard Castle, Bowes Museum (*130*)

131   MASTER OF THE VIRGO INTER VIRGINES. *Entombment*, St. Louis, City Art Gallery (*133*)

▷

extreme, for the wings are divided into two panels which have now become very narrow. The painter has thus been constrained to diminish the central theme so as not to overwhelm the wing scenes by its mass, and to introduce at both its edges secondary scenes pushed into the background by way of transitional elements. Even more surprising is the arrangement of the scene in the artist's second version of the *Entombment*, the one now in St. Louis (*133*). Here, the main theme, that of Christ carried by Nicodemus, Joseph of Arimathaea and Mary Magdalene has almost become the secondary element, and is certainly given no greater prominence than that of the cortège of mourners consisting of the Virgin, St. John the Evangelist and two Marys.

    This original treatment of the scenes is matched by the eccentricity of the world created by the painter's stock characters. Like the grisaille illuminations, his work contains men with disturbing physiognomies, strongly chiselled profiles and sunken eyes which bring a note of drama to the scenes. The women are never graceful, however richly bedecked, and display bony faces, with broad, bulging foreheads, oddly attached to long, slender necks. If the character whose frequent appearance has been noted is indeed a more or less idealised portrait of the artist himself, we surely have a perfectly natural explanation of this bizarre world: it becomes a projection of the artist himself.

    The grotesqueness of these faces is one of the essential elements of the dramatic atmosphere created by the artist. It is combined, however, with other expressive factors. It is remarkable that he strives to keep his figures in the static poses that we have noticed in Haarlem work, and of which Geertgen provides the best example. Nevertheless, the agitated rhythms of the drapery folds and the gestures of the hands counterbalance this tendency to a certain degree, and emphasise the repressed turmoil which is written on the faces by means of their deformed features.

    These characteristics recur in other artistic media of the northern Netherlands and have had attention drawn to them by Delaissé's analysis of the illuminations.[15] A contempt for conventional beauty, a predilection for rough, coarse faces, a taste for story-telling and dramatic expression are all part of these common tendencies. One may wonder, though, if the use of these techniques to create such an intensely dramatic climate is a tendency peculiar to the Master of the *Virgo inter Virgines* or if he was influenced by Hieronymus Bosch. The two artists must have been very much contemporaries. If Bosch was indeed born in 1453, as a relatively recent but unconfirmed discovery shows, he could have begun working around 1470–5—in other words, around the time when the Master of the *Virgo inter Virgines* must have produced his own first works.

    The problem is all the more difficult to analyse as the precise points of contact between the two artists are hard to pin down. The *Nativity* in the Kunsthistorisches Museum, Vienna, has an undeniable affinity with Bosch's painting of the same subject now in the Wallraf-Richartz Museum in Cologne. It could not be said that one was copied from the other, as the precise

arrangements are different. But the general approach is identical: both compositions have half-length figures, a stone manger in the foreground which serves as an improvised cradle for the Child, and the same prominence given to the ox, also placed in the foreground. However, they are early works of both artists and, as we have seen, it is possible to doubt the attribution of this painting to the Master of the *Virgo inter Virgines*. A common source seems more plausible, and perhaps one should look for this in van der Goes or one of his followers. There are virtually no other exact points of contact to be found. One should, however, mention the striking profile of the shouting woman (St. Anne?) in the right foreground of the *Trinity* by the Master of the *Virgo inter Virgines* in Zagreb. This is a motif which is very Boschian in spirit, and remarkably reminiscent of the small fragment now in the Boymans Museum in Rotterdam.[17] This is one of those rare instances where similarity goes beyond the spirit of influence to attain a true community of motif. But as this is an isolated example in the work of the Master of the *Virgo inter Virgines* he is probably indebted for it to Bosch. These two exact correspondences are thus too isolated to justify a general conclusion. We must rest content with seeing a simple parallelism in the two artists' inspiration rather than assuming the dependence of one on the other, except in secondary instances.

    As a colourist, the Master of the *Virgo inter Virgines* is scarcely less original than as an inventor of forms. He has a fondness for a very narrow range of colours, within which he devises delicate modulations. His landscapes, of great simplicity, are handled in a variety of browns barely set off with a few greens, giving them a very austere character. One can hardly fail to be struck by this characteristic tendency towards monochromy; it would be reasonable to see this as a direct legacy from the grisaille illuminations. The flesh of the figures is also restricted to tones which are often surprisingly pallid and recall the similar effects sought after by Hugo van der Goes. But we do not need to bring the latter in by way of explanation. Once again, the same illuminations could have led the artist to acquire this very noticeable taste. Such a technique also reflects the vogue, current throughout northern Europe in the last quarter of the fifteenth century, for flesh of alabaster hue. There were probably many reasons for this obsession. Firstly there was the development of painted grisailles, so frequently used for the reverse of panels. There was also the realistic development of stained glass, which nevertheless continued to model flesh in very light harmonies. In this respect, the work of Hugo van der Goes is probably less an innovation than the most dazzlingly successful expression of a much broader trend.[18]

    Less profound and less fine than Geertgen tot Sint Jans, the Master of the *Virgo inter Virgines* still takes his place with him as one of the most notable masters of the northern Netherlands. Above all, by comparison with Geertgen, his art shows less of the influence of the great southern masters. When he borrows from them, which he not uncommonly does, it is to integrate into his personal style, by means of an unfettered imagination, some motif or detail which becomes virtually unrecognisable beneath his brush. In this, he belongs to the 'rustic tendency' of the northern Netherlands.

The circle of the Master of the *Virgo inter Virgines*

On the other hand, it would be a mistake to see this artist as an isolated master. A large number of works has been attributed to him or compared to his style, and this indicates the presence round him of a group of artists working in his manner. We may wonder if they were collaborators from his own workshop or simply independent painters working under his influence. A wide variety of hands can be made out in the paintings associated with the master. It would be hard to reduce them to the output of one or two collaborators, and tempting to see them as scattered remnants of a genuine 'school'. It is not only the quality of execution which eliminates them from the catalogue of the Master's work, but also a different approach. The *Annunciation with the Duke of Alba* (*136*) is certainly a work of rather hurried execution, but it is also more traditional, at least on the side depicting the Annunciation. The *Marriage of the Virgin*, in the Johnson collection (*137*), has a stiffness and severity in its composition which suggests some influence from the Master of the *Tiburtine Sibyl*. On the other hand, the *Crucifixion* in the Thyssen-Bornemisza collection (*138*), although one of the first paintings to serve as a touchstone for the identification of this artist's oeuvre, must probably be excluded from it by reason of the highly original development of devices which only appear in the Master's last works.

One is inclined to see all these as products of artists from Delft. It is the most plausible hypothesis in so far as it accounts adequately for the extent of the influence of the Master of the *Virgo inter Virgines*. But we cannot exclude the possibility that such artists may have worked elsewhere, possibly even in Haarlem.

The Master of Delft

Alongside the Master of the *Virgo inter Virgines* we must place a second painter whose studio may well also have been situated in Delft, namely the Master of Delft. However, the major part of his career seems to have occupied the first two decades of the sixteenth century, and his style was very quickly affected by the artistic changes of the beginning of the new century. A good part of his work therefore falls outside the scope of this book.

Two things help to locate him. The first is the fact that he painted a triptych for a burgomaster of Delft, Dirck van Beest (J.P.R. de Nerée van Babberich collection). The second is the depiction, in the background of the central panel of the London triptych, of the tower of the Nieuwe Kerk at Delft. These are seemingly weak arguments, but strong enough to establish the conclusion as virtually certain.

The artist's earliest work is also the best of his known paintings; this is the *Triptych of the Crucifixion* in the National Gallery in London (*143*). It is the only one which can be said to display the style described in this book. It was probably painted for one of the Carthusians of the Abbey of St. Bartholomeusdal near Delft.

The ensemble contains three scenes—the Ecce Homo, the Crucifixion and the Deposition—which, following Geertgen and the Master of the *Virgo inter Virgines,* are accompanied by secondary themes. The Ecce Homo is matched with a curious scene, the departure of the Two Thieves for Golgotha. It is hard to decide whether the artist saw this as a later scene, linking the wing to the central panel, or whether he imagined Christ's companions in misfortune as being led to the place of execution before Him. In the central panel the secondary episodes are arranged without any logical connection between them. On the left we find the Carrying of the Cross alongside the suicide of Judas and a weeping Virgin attended by St. John the Evangelist and two women. On the right we see Jesus in the Garden of Gethsemane and the approach of the soldiers coming to arrest Him.

The composition is involved, and there is such a proliferation of characters that one has difficulty identifying them all. St. John the Evangelist and two female saints, presumably the two Marys, cluster round the Virgin Mary in the central panel. The young woman at the foot of the Cross is probably Mary Magdalene, but who is the other mourner kneeling in the foreground? Is it St. Anne? In the *Ecce Homo* there is a woman with two small children; her identity is also difficult to grasp. Sometimes the artist tries to co-ordinate the scenes of his three paintings, while at other times he does not trouble to do so. Thus the two principal horsemen in the centre have the same faces and clothes as the two characters who appear in the palace in the *Ecce Homo,* and must be intended as Pilate and Caiaphas. On the other hand, the female saints surrounding the Virgin in the *Deposition* have neither the same features nor the same costumes as those in the central panel. This capriciousness is one of the few characteristics the artist shares with his predecessor, the Master of the *Virgo inter Virgines.*

In fact, this painting is more reminiscent of the Haarlem School, by reason both of the plasticity of the figures and of their thick-set shapes. The women with their oval faces put one in mind of Geertgen. However, the painting recalls the work of Joos van Kalkar even more strongly. The simplicity of the landscape with its sparse, almost leafless trees spreading isolated branches against the sky, the styles of costume and the figures themselves, all these features are very similar to those in the altarpiece at Kalkar. It would therefore be perfectly justifiable to see this painting as a product of the early years of the sixteenth century.

In the artist's other works the character of the northern Renaissance emerges even more strongly. This evolution is clearly signposted by the architectural elements in the *Triptych of the Deipara Virgo* in Amsterdam [19] and by those in *Christ's farewell to His mother* [20] in the former Katz collection. At the same

132 MASTER OF DELFT. *Crucifixion*, central panel of a triptych, London,
National Gallery (*143*)

time, the characters lose the plasticity of the artist's early figures and become more gaunt. The drapery becomes thinner and more complex, acquiring a rhythm like that of the Antwerp mannerists.

It is therefore difficult to talk here of a continuation of the Delft school. The characteristics of the London triptych bear witness rather to a mixture of the styles of various towns, to a common evolution in Holland at least, if not throughout the whole of the northern Netherlands.

Leiden and Hugo Jacobsz, the Master of the St. John Altarpiece

The case of Hugo Jacobsz is a good illustration of the difficulties that can arise when one tries to match the information from public records with that from the works of art themselves. This painter's life is fairly well-known; from 1480 he appears quite frequently in the Leiden archives. Twice married—the first time a little before 1489, then again around 1494—he had five children, the eldest of whom, Lucas van Leyden, was to distinguish himself so brilliantly that he put his father in the shade. And yet he survived his famous son who, on his death in 1533, left him half his property.

If we are to believe Opmeer, Hugo Jacobsz also worked at Gouda. Marc van Vaernewijk asserts that one of his paintings hung in the Church of St. Peter in Ghent, while de Jongh says that in the same church there was also stained glass designed by him.[21] Of the few paintings mentioned as being by him, none has survived.

It needed the boldness and perceptiveness of J. Q. van Regteren Altena to link this celebrated name with a group of paintings from an altarpiece dedicated to St. John the Baptist and brought together under a provisional name by D. Hannema in 1936. One can well imagine that such an ensemble could have come from Gouda, which had the largest church in Holland dedicated to that saint; destroyed by fire in 1438, it was rebuilt between 1485 and 1493.[22] Its high altar must have been given a large altarpiece. As Hugo Jacobsz seems to have worked at Gouda,[23] the task could have been entrusted to him.

The links are fragile; nothing is established beyond doubt. There is no documentary evidence that the panels of the Life of St. John came from Gouda, and we know no more than what Opmeer tells us about the activity of Hugo Jacobsz in that town. And yet this house of cards seems credible enough.

The best test is an examination of the work of the artist's son; however talented he was, he must inevitably have retained some features of his father's art which will betray the relationship. And there are indeed several similarities between the panels of the altarpiece and Lucas van Leyden's earliest engravings.

134 The Eve in the *Original Sin,* with her heavy body and particularly her strange head, with flattened face and forehead, recalls the women in the *Birth of St. John the Baptist (147 A).* The drawing of the hands also has the softness of those of

St. Elizabeth in the *Flight (147 B).* The men are no less similar; 133 glancing from the paintings to the engravings, we find the same heavy features and the same stocky bodies. The seated pilgrim in the well-known engraving could easily come from the group of Jews in the *Birth of St. John (147 A).* Many similar examples 134 could be cited.

However, the shared features of the two series can best be seen at the level of expressive techniques. In the *Birth of St. John* as 134 in the *Meeting of St. John and Christ (147 C),* one cannot fail to be 135 struck by the figures seen from behind, enveloped in very simple drapery which gives them a monumental character. A similar technique recurs constantly in the engravings of Lucas. The same characters are modelled by the contrast of large, brightly lit surfaces with deep shadows which make the outlines stand out starkly. This technique was also used extensively by Lucas, but with more subtlety and more successful results. The comparison is nevertheless striking.

Even the arrangement of the planes of recession lends some credibility to the theory. There is a remarkable similarity between the empty foregrounds, broken up only by a few scattered plants, of the *Flight of St. Elizabeth (147 B)* and the 133 *Meeting of St. John and Christ (147 C)* and those of Lucas's earliest 135 engravings between 1508 and 1515. In these first sheets the artist reserves all the foregrounds, which remain very bare, for the figures and only depicts more detailed landscapes in the distant views which can be made out behind several trees enclosing the nearer area. Exactly the same technique is found in panel paintings by the Master of the St. John Altarpiece.

There would, therefore, seem to be some substance to J. Q. van Regteren Altena's hypothesis, bold as it may seem, and the Master of the St. John Altarpiece is very probably Hugo Jacobsz. However, there are still some formidable hindrances to its complete acceptance. The most important is that the painter had a long life—he is known from 1480 to at least 1534—and that the panels of the St. John Altarpiece only display a late fifteenth-century style. How did this father of an outstandingly talented son react to the development of the latter's art, and why have we no trace of his late works? J. Q. van Regteren Altena has proposed a bold solution to this problem too, by attributing to the Master a small triptych of the *Adoration of the Magi,* now in a Swiss collection *(150).* 239

His arguments have met with widespread scepticism; and it must be admitted that in the 1958 Amsterdam exhibition, where it was displayed alongside the panels of the St. John Altarpiece, the painting seemed to be by a different hand altogether. All the same, before discarding the theory, we should take into account two points which are not immediately obvious: the considerable difference in size between the two works—the Swiss panels form a small portable altarpiece only 35 cm. high—and the probable difference in date. The first point accounts for the miniature quality, surprising at first, but contradicted by effects as powerful as that of the large figure of a soldier seen from behind in the foreground of the wing showing the *Massacre of the Innocents.* The second point may justify the complete difference in handling, which could result from the artist's trying to 'get up to

133 HUGO JACOBSZ (?). *Flight of St. Elizabeth*, Rotterdam, Boymans-van Beuningen Museum (*147 B*)

date'. The sombre tonality, with its rather murky colours, may be derived from imitation of certain paintings by Lucas van Leyden or his contemporaries. But other features of the work look to the past: the *Adoration of the Magi* is a direct descendant of fifteenth-century designs, and the *Massacre of the Innocents* adopts the formula used by the Master of the *Virgo inter Virgines* in his Salzburg altarpiece and in a woodcut illustration. J. Q. van Regteren Altena has also shown how similar are the landscape elements in this triptych to the engravings of Lucas van Leyden, thereby indicating an imitation of the son by the father rather than the reverse. The attribution may be doubtful, but it has more arguments in its favour than are immediately apparent.

If one tries to define the Master's style on the strength of the four panels of the St. John Altarpiece, one is immediately struck by his attempts to give his forms greater volume. The effect is obtained by the simplification of drapery folds and facial details. It is also achieved by the structure of the surfaces and the planes, which stretch away in broad, bare zones and provide a background which is appropriate to the amplitude of the figures. In this respect the effect is different, but the technique is similar to the practice of the Master of the *Virgo inter Virgines*. The kinship of the two artists hardly makes itself felt on a first examination; the Master of the St. John Altarpiece does not make a point of portraying coarse features or violent poses. The kinship nevertheless probably exists, at least in the spirit of their compositions.

Violence, however, is not altogether absent from the works of the Master of the St. John Altarpiece. It is there in the background of the *Flight of St. Elizabeth*, where the Massacre of the Innocents is shown with quiet horror. For me, this aspect fully justifies the attribution to this artist of the *Carrying of the Cross* in the Frederiks collection (*146*) and the *Entombment* in the Budapest Museum (*148*). In these two works we find a larger number of rustic faces, and a tendency to distort the shape of heads, which is much less noticeable in the panels of the St. John Altarpiece, but which is not completely absent (notably in the detail of the Massacre of the Innocents). In this respect the artist is yet another follower of the Dutch 'rustic' tradition, in company with the Master of the *Virgo inter Virgines*.

The works of Hugo Jacobsz are much closer to the early paintings of the latter artist. The *Triptych of the Lamentation* (*119*), of which the centre panel is now in the Prado, shows the same urge towards a simplified modelling and those strongly defined forms which are the trademarks of the Leiden master. In the particular case of the *Nativity* in the Kunsthistorisches Museum in Vienna (*122*), one may find it hard to decide between the two artists. If the singing angels and the type of the Child seem to belong to the repertoire of the Delft painter, the Virgin and St. Joseph have features closer to those of the characters in the St. John Altarpiece. As for the round-headed shepherds, they appear to be related to all those figures with geometrically simplified heads. We may therefore wonder whether the two artists were not formed side by side in the same circle.

Hugo Jacobsz's use of colour, however, is very different from that of his contemporary from Delft. While his backgrounds are restrained and keep within an austere range, his characters' costumes employ a much richer palette, in which glow dark reds, greens, yellows and even violets. He lays his colours on without matching the shades, showing himself in this respect less sophisticated than his contemporary.

Although this artist's work seems at first sight rather isolated, it nevertheless belongs to a clear tradition. He is a descendant of that somewhat 'popular' approach which sprang from the art of Dieric Bouts and which is known to us through the work of the Master of the *Manna*. The latter's paintings already contain human types similar to his, and a hint of the stylisation of volumes which was to become firmly established in the work of the Leiden painter. The resemblance is evident when one compares the panels of the St. John Altarpiece with the *Healing of the blind man at Jericho* in the Kleiweg de Zwaan collection (*64*).

134 HUGO JACOBSZ (?). *Birth of St. John the Baptist*, Rotterdam, Boymans-van Beuningen Museum (*147 A*) ▷

135 HUGO JACOBSZ (?). *Meeting of St. John the Baptist and Christ*, Philadelphia, Johnson collection (*147 C*)

136 HUGO JACOBSZ (?). *St. Anne Trinity*, Amsterdam, Rijksmuseum (*149*)

Even the arrangement of the landscape is similar, and the treatment of drapery folds is a first step towards a simplification of outline. If the Master of the *Manna* could be identified with a Leiden painter, his connection with Hugo Jacobsz could easily be explained. But he has strong links with the art of Bouts, with the Haarlem studios and with the Utrecht illuminators. In other words, the interdependence of these artists and artistic traditions compounds the difficulty of assigning each of them to a particular town with any assurance.

The illustrators of Gouda and Schiedam

The complexity of the situation in Holland is thrown into relief by the problem posed by the origin of the exceptional illustrations for two books, one published at Gouda around

1486, the other at Schiedam in 1498. The first is probably the first edition of a romance by Olivier de la Marche, *Le Chevalier Délibéré*, of which another edition, unconnected with the first, appeared in Paris in 1488 (*154*). Its sixteen plates stand out sharply from other works of the period. The hardness of some of the faces is faintly reminiscent of the Master of Delft, to whom Friedländer wanted to attribute them in 1932, after attempting a comparison between the ample modelling of the figures and the handling of the painting by the Master of the St. John Altarpiece in Philadelphia. Schretlen, on the other hand, discerned in this remarkable work an early production of Jacob Cornelisz van Amsterdam. The surprising diversity of these three hypotheses illustrates the difficulty of finding anything genuinely comparable with these unusual images in Netherlandish work.

To understand the nature of the problem, we must take into account the personality of the author of the romance and the nature of his text. Olivier de la Marche had no connection with the northern Netherlands. He was attached to the court of Charles the Bold, then to that of Mary of Burgundy. In 1483 he wrote this allegorical romance, which is very similar in inspiration to that by King René, the *Cuer d'Amours Espris*. Both works belong to that category of stories which set in motion personifications of virtues and vices which involve a knight in picturesque adventures. The manuscript of *Le Chevalier Délibéré* now in the Bibliothèque Nationale contains notes by the author

137 HUGO JACOBSZ (?). *Entombment*, Budapest, Museum of Fine Arts (*148*) ▷

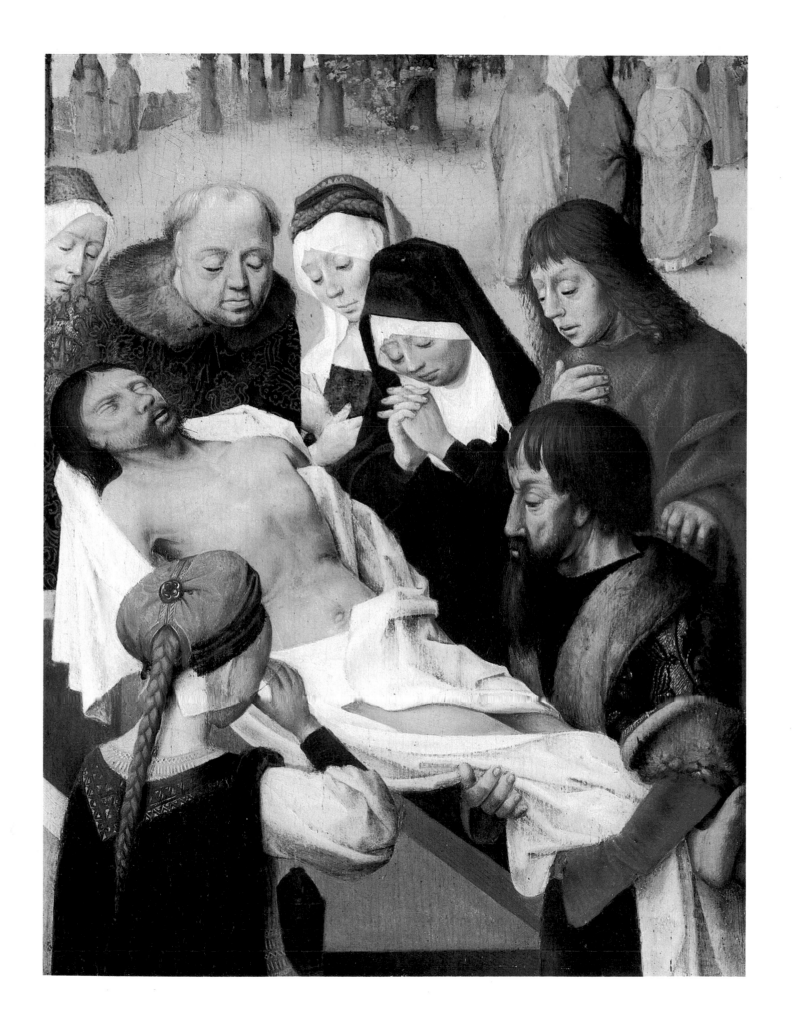

138 Illustration from *Le Chevalier Délibéré*, published at Gouda *c*.1486–8. *Combat between the Actor and Age* (154)

139 Illustration from *Le Chevalier Délibéré*, published at Gouda *c*.1486–8. *Combat between Philip the Good and Sir Feeble* (154)

giving the illustrator very precise guidance on the scenes to be depicted and even on the colours to be used for each detail.[24] The illustrator was therefore obliged to follow precise instructions, which considerably restricted his freedom of imagination.

I feel that *Le Chevalier Délibéré* is one of those books which can only be explained by the collaboration of several artists. The illustrations certainly possess features which link them with north Netherlandish work: a certain harshness in the faces, some stiffness in the poses, and a fondness for figures seen from behind whose clothes are modelled by bold highlights. In this respect, they undeniably have some features in common with the work of Hugo Jacobsz. On the other hand, other characteristics have no counterpart in north Netherlandish art: the importance accorded to the figures, which sometimes fill the entire composition, the conception of the landscape, which is

quite secondary and nevertheless contributes decisively to the atmosphere of the scenes. We cannot exclude the possibility that the author may have sent the printer, along with his text, drawings by a painter or artist of his entourage whose inspiration he had been able to guide directly.

Hind had a similar feeling when he wrote, 'We might have expected that he would have turned to some artist of the southern Netherlands, and in some respects I feel a nearer relation in these designs to French art than in any other woodcuts'.[25] This connection with French art does seem very noticeable to me. But we can be more specific: it should be drawn with the collaborators of King René, and particularly the illustrator of his similar romance. It is quite probable that Olivier de la Marche knew the king's book and drew his inspiration from it, as some picturesque details occur in both texts, for instance, the hermit. But we may even believe that he must also have known the illustrations for the manuscript now in Vienna, whose main original feature was the pride of place accorded to the figures in a very comparable manner to that found in these woodcuts. Amongst Netherlandish productions, the work which resembles the Gouda volume most closely, without being attributable to the same artist, is the illustration of the 1476 *Boccaccio,* in which I feel it possible to recognise the work of a French painter, Philippe de Mazerolles.[26] Did the illustrator of Olivier de la Marche have access to some models by one of the followers of this artist, who died in 1479? Or was the Dutch designer content to follow the author's indications very closely, perhaps drawing his inspiration from some French work he may have seen? It is an open question. But whatever the possible connection between these remarkable woodcuts and the art of Hugo Jacobsz, one cannot bring oneself to accept them as entirely by him.

The second artist, the illustrator of the *History of St. Lydwine* (*155*), has been arbitrarily linked with the first. If he is indeed the only great illustrator of the northern Netherlands at the end of the fifteenth century, he shows precious little connection with the author of the illustrations for *Le Chevalier Délibéré.* Neither the figures nor the landscapes of the *History of St. Lydwine* are in any way comparable with the others. Through their narrative energy, these sketches achieve a mood similar to that of the north Netherlandish manuscript illuminations. It is more understandable that they should have been seen as the first stirrings of the art of Jacob Cornelisz van Amsterdam.

If it seems quite impossible to follow Friedländer's proposed attribution of *Le Chevalier Délibéré* woodcuts to the Master of Delft, it seems more plausible to credit him with the designs for the *History of St. Lydwine.* Schiedam is not far from Delft, and there would be nothing odd in a publisher of the latter town employing to an artist of the former. Certain distinctive features of the designs resemble the painter's mannerisms: for example, a certain fondness for rather pointed profiles, the curious swing of the hips noticeable in many of the figures standing with legs apart, and hair tumbling over shoulders in distinct locks. If one were to settle for an attribution of these designs to the Master of Delft, they would be dated between the triptych in the National Gallery, London, and that in the Rijksmuseum, Amsterdam. In fact, the forms and human types of the woodcuts are closer to the second painting than to the former. This would make it necessary to date the first painting to the fifteenth century. But it does not seem impossible to think in terms of an artist close to and contemporary with the Master of Delft.

Whatever the truth may be, the woodcuts of the Schiedam volume are a perfect summation of fifteenth-century conventions and also herald the illustrations of the sixteenth century. It is characteristic that we should find here the 'dividing' arches so beloved of north Netherlandish painting and which had already appeared in the illustrations for the *Speculum Humanae Salvationis.* The popular, good-natured mood of the story-telling follows the tradition of the same work. But from another point of view, the more flexible understanding of space and the simplification of drapery directly foreshadow sixteenth-century ideas.

Artistic activity in the county of Holland

One may be surprised by the relative extent of artistic activity in the county of Holland in the last quarter of the fifteenth century when one thinks of the current political and economic difficulties. Haarlem has already surprised us in this respect, even if some gaps can be discerned in the work of certain artists.

In fact, the history of the towns perhaps accounts for the localisation of known activity. After Haarlem, Delft seems to be the town whose workshops were the largest and most productive; it is also the one which seems to have been least affected by the disturbances arising after the death of Charles the Bold. It experienced no major upheaval, not even an uprising along the lines of Haarlem's in 1492.

On the other hand, Leiden fell victim to often violent conflicts. It underwent a siege in 1479; taken by the *Hoeksen* in 1481, it was then retaken by Maximilian's troops, only to be severely condemned to a fine of 50,000 *livres* and the loss of its privileges. This would seem to be the very moment at which Hugo Jacobsz settled in Gouda. This town suffered some hardships, though they were not of any gravity. The *Hoeksen* laid siege to it unsuccessfully in 1489. We may therefore wonder whether the relative calm of this town did not encourage a regrouping of certain artists within its walls. The building of the chancel of the Church of St. John the Baptist could also have attracted them with the hope of worthwhile commissions. It is remarkable that Gouda should have witnessed the foundation in 1487 of one of the first guilds of St. Luke mentioned in Holland. This company brought together painters, sculptors, glass-makers and printers at the very moment when illustrated books were being published in the town.[27] Was this creation the result of a shrewd policy of a city which wanted to encourage the development of this nascent artistic activity and to offer protection to newcomers? Perhaps that is the best explanation of this surprising gesture in such troubled times, and of the appearance of a sizeable artistic activity in a town which, though admittedly of secondary importance, was relatively sheltered from the struggles of the time.

The fact remains, however, that the disorders of the age are perhaps not unconnected with the peculiar mood emanating from these works. The violence so often present in the paintings of the Master of the *Virgo inter Virgines,* and which is not altogether missing from those of Hugo Jacobsz or from the woodcuts of *Le Chevalier Délibéré,* must correspond to something in the artists' temperament. Is it too fanciful to think that this tendency must at least have been aggravated by the political and social climate of the times? The artists were hemmed in on every side by armed conflicts, murders, sackings of towns and ravaging of the countryside, and constant uncertainty about the future. Such conditions are not conducive to optimistic art, but rather to one with a tragic and bitter outlook—the same which made the Master of the *Virgo inter Virgines* the most inspired commentator on this age.

The problem of the importance of the Utrecht workshops

Utrecht, the bishop's see and the heart of the episcopal principality, would seem naturally destined to witness the activity of large painting workshops. This assumption seems to be confirmed by the list of Masters of the Saddlers' Guild (to which the painters belonged), which has survived in its entirety for the fifteenth century.[28] The installation of an illegitimate son of Philip the Good, David of Burgundy, as bishop in 1460 may also have favoured the development of the arts in both the city and the diocese.

These points are counterbalanced, however, by as many adverse circumstances. We have seen that the political situation between 1460 and 1500 was far from stable. Apart from a short period of calm between 1470 and 1477, during which the bishop harshly imposed his authority, the diocese was a constant prey to factional strife. As for David of Burgundy, the fact that he belonged to the ducal family did not necessarily make him a patron of the arts. We know that he liked a certain amount of luxury, and the château of Wijk bij Duurstede was enlarged and embellished by him.[29]. And yet no major painting commissioned by him has survived.[30] Moreover, a prince raised at the court of Philip the Good would have been inclined to show preference for the artists of the southern Netherlands.

The existence of an active and strongly organized painters' guild is not necessarily a factor of progress and intense artistic activity. It could well have encouraged the development of a conservatism echoed by the taste of the cathedral chapter. In this connection, we should remember that in the first half of the century the principality was distinguished above all by reason of its manuscript illuminations, and that these may have helped to give the painting of the diocese its direction.

The Master of Evert van Soudenbalch

In fact, very few panel paintings have survived and no major work stands out among them. On the other hand, from amidst a large output of illuminations of extremely variable quality there emerges one exceptional personality, the Master of Evert van Soudenbalch, whose art blossomed in the illuminations for the Book of Hours of Jan van Amerongen, dated 1460 (156).

In this book, now in the Bibliothèque Royale in Brussels, the artist executed 12 full-page illuminations which were inserted into the volume on separate sheets. In them his sources stand clearly revealed, for one can identify borrowings from two important ensembles: the Turin-Milan Hours and the Hours of Catherine of Cleves. From the first comes the composition of the scene showing the Taking of Christ, from the second Christ before Pilate and, more freely adapted, the Crowning with Thorns. But the borrowing is not restricted to the re-use of motifs. An analysis of the 12 illuminations reveals that the artist's formation was dominated by these two works. The illuminator owes a great deal to the Master of Catherine of Cleves, and it is conceivable that he was his pupil. In the miniatures for which no exact model can be cited, he displays above all a fondness for anecdote, which leads him to multiply the characters and give them highly individualised features and often very expressive poses. His figures, moreover, have the thick-set look and lively attitudes of the Master of Catherine of Cleves.

Yet although the painter's basic training was certainly due to the creator of the Hours of Catherine of Cleves, the Turin-Milan Hours, or more exactly a circle strongly influenced by van Eyck, was just as decisive a factor. The Master of Evert van Soudenbalch surpasses his first mentor above all in his search for a certain elegance of forms. A comparison of their two versions of Jesus before Pilate is significant in this context. With the older artist we find rather heavy figures, arranged in a somewhat chaotic rhythm; the characters of the younger artist, on the other hand, possess a more serene harmony, and the elegance of each shape seems to emulate that of the Birth of St. John the Baptist from the Milan-Turin Hours.

The difference is most noticeable in the sphere of colour and light. The light, lively but sometimes rather harsh tones of the first master contrast with the fine, often precious and always subtly harmonised shades of the second. An absence of real effects of light is answered by an organization of the scenes under a coherent light which plays over all the shiny surfaces.

We must also add a major contribution of the Master of Evert van Soudenbalch: the development of landscape. To trace the origin of this it is not enough to refer to van Eyck, even though the indication of the planes by means of figures advancing along a sunken path in the Deposition is directly reminiscent of both the Crucifixion from the Milan-Turin Hours and the Carrying of the Cross in Budapest.

It is clear that the Master must at least have seen drawn copies of some of the illuminations in the Turin-Milan Hours, as only this could explain such an exact plagiarism of the Taking of Christ; but it is not impossible that he acquired his mastery of Eyckian techniques from an intermediate artist. Although it is difficult to prove, one may wonder if this rôle was not played by Albert van Ouwater. The illuminator could have been guided by landscapes similar to those in the St. John the Baptist in Granada. And it is worth noting that the illuminator's palette includes lilacs and violets—quite rare in Netherlandish painting, but present in the Raising of Lazarus in the Staatliche Museen in Berlin.

Apart from this prestigious book of hours, the known work of the Soudenbalch illuminator is shared between three other volumes: a book of hours in Liège University Library which only contains two pages from his hand, a book of hours that has recently emerged on the international market, and above all the Bible written for Evert van Soudenbalch and now in the

140   MASTER OF EVERT VAN SOUDENBALCH. *Taking of Christ* (illumination from the Book of Hours of Jan van Amerongen), Brussels, Bibliothèque Royale, enlarged approx. 1.3 × (156)

141 MASTER OF EVERT VAN SOUDENBALCH. *Last Judgment* (illumination from the Book of Hours of Jan van Amerongen), Brussels, Bibliothèque Royale (*156*)

airiness to his backgrounds, despite their miniaturisation. One of the most significant illuminations, in all three respects, is that of *Moses on Mount Sinai* (folio *129 v.*).

No other north Netherlandish illuminator testifies more clearly to the persistence of the Eyckian tradition. But as the works of the Master of Evert van Soudenbalch only appear around the 1460s, it is clearly necessary to postulate an intermediary between Jan van Eyck and himself. The idea that such techniques may have been transmitted by Albert van Ouwater remains one of the most plausible possibilities: it would prove that the artists of Utrecht did not remain enclosed and isolated in the cathedral city or the principality, and that they had contacts with the art of the other towns.

Paintings from Utrecht

Compared with the exceptional quality of the manuscript illuminations of the Master of Evert van Soudenbalch, the few known paintings which can be firmly identified as coming from Utrecht have far less artistic impact. Two of them, however, can be directly related to the work of the illuminators of the *Book of Hours of Jan van Amerongen.*

The *Triptych of the Crucifixion* in the Centraal Museum in Utrecht (*157*) has for a long time been known to have come from that city: it contains in the background a view of the Cathedral so precise in its detail that it has been established as representing the appearance of the building in the years 1460–67. The central panel is an almost literal reproduction of the *Crucifixion* from the *Book of Hours of Jan van Amerongen.* 247, 248 However, there is no question of the painting and the illumination being by the same hand. In the painting there is a stylisation of the poses and facial expressions of the figures which is never present in the work of the illuminator. In point of fact, the illumination is clearly the earlier work. It is far closer to the miniature in the *Turin-Milan Hours* painted by Master H 163 after a design by Jan van Eyck, which it follows in both spirit and proportion, while the painter of the triptych imitates him in the liberties taken with the original.

The difference in character between the two artists is more striking still when we examine the wings of the painting: there we find a sense of disorder and a jerkiness and hardness of outline. It has nothing in common with the work of the Master of Evert van Soudenbalch; on the contrary, we see here the reappearance of that 'rustic' tendency found in the art of the northern Netherlands.

A similar problem is posed by a *Crucifixion* in the Museum at Providence (*158*). The similarity of the painting's composition 250 to that of folio 54v of the *Book of Hours of Jan van Amerongen* is 246 such that one might imagine that they were produced in the same workshop. But here also both derive from an Eyckian

National Library in Vienna. It is in this last work that one can best appreciate the variety of the artist's talent. The illustrations do not have the outstanding character of the Brussels book of hours. They are completely integrated into the book and their rôle is not of such prime importance, since they are restricted to vignettes of small dimensions in a large-format work. The illuminator is thus freer and allows himself to be guided by his narrative talent, which comes close to rivalling that of his predecessor, the Master of Catherine of Cleves. However, his qualities as a painter reveal themselves in three different ways: firstly by the subtle harmony of his tones, which are skilfully matched and are restricted to a very individual range in which violet often occurs; then by his skill in arranging the space to be decorated, frequently introducing elements of landscape to divide the space or to emphasise the main point; and finally by his feeling for landscape, which makes him give a peculiar

142 Utrecht artist, last quarter of the fifteenth century, *Mystic Marriage of St. Agnes,* Esztergom, Christian Museum (*163*) ▷

166

model—the *Crucifixion* of the diptych in New York (*20*)—and again the illuminator displays a better knowledge of his model and follows it more faithfully. The rotunda of the Holy Sepulchre is placed in the illumination exactly as it is in the painting in New York, while the painter of the Providence panel has entirely rearranged the disposition of the buildings in the view of Jerusalem. The illuminator reproduces almost literally (in reverse) the horsemen of the New York painting while the painter makes his own changes in this group with the result that the proportion of the horsemen to their mounts is unsatisfactory.

In this case, as in the preceding one, the two works are very different in spirit. In the painting, the artist has emphasised the theme of the wounds inflicted on the thief by showing very clearly a soldier, sword in hand, about to strike. In the illumination, the same figure is present, but inactive and almost hidden behind Christ's cross. This taste for violence is accompanied by a fondness for heavy and slightly vulgar human figures which are at odds with the courtly world reflected in the Book of Hours.

It was probably the same artist, as Boon has pointed out, who painted both the Providence panel and a fresco of the *Tree of Jesse* in the Buukerk in Utrecht (*160*). Unfortunately the latter work is very damaged and difficult to make out in detail, but it would seem to contain the same human types as the painting. Moreover, it can be dated around 1453. Can it be by *Hilbrandt die maelre*, who is known to have worked in the church between 1456 and 1465? It is possible, and this idea is of especial interest since the painter can be securely identified with Hillebrant van Reuwich, who was dean of the guild in 1470 and who was probably the father of the Erhard van Reuwich who accompanied Bernhard de Breydenbach to the Holy Land and illustrated the account of their journey with a series of remarkable woodcuts.[31]

A group of similar works probably painted a little later have been localized in Utrecht by Grete Ring and Karel Boon.[32] These panels too are weak in pictorial quality, but share a particular style. Three of them probably came from the same workshop: *The Mystic Marriage of St. Agnes* (*161*), *The Virgin and Child with St. Anne* (Archiepiscopal Museum, Utrecht; *162*), and another version of *The Mystic Marriage of St. Agnes* in the Museum at Esztergom (*163*). They all contain half-length female figures, rather graceless in appearance, but apparently deriving from those of Dieric Bouts. They have been justly associated with the earliest works of the Master of *St. Bartholomew*, who seems to have worked in Utrecht or at least appears to have been very familiar with artistic developments in the city. A triptych preserved in the Church of Djursdala in Sweden and also representing the *Mystic Marriage of St. Agnes* is painted in a closely related style. The artist of this work is probably not the same painter, but he reproduces the same details and similar human types, notably in the angels supporting the draperies behind the sacred figures.

Two further paintings, very similar in character, both represent *The Virgin and Child surrounded by angel musicians* (Berlin-Dahlem; *164*; and private collection, U.S.A.; *165*). The figures with their characteristically long, flat faces are closely related to those in the preceding group. On the other hand, the technique is different and is distinguished by the unusual manner of treating the hair in individual strands. Here again, however, we are not dealing with innovatory works, for both figures and compositions derive directly from the school of Dieric Bouts.

What emerges from this brief account is that among the works which in all likelihood can be localised in Utrecht, none displays a style of great originality. Indeed they all reveal the influence of workshops outside the principality, and in this way demonstrate the artificiality of political divisions in the realm of art. If there were no convincing arguments locating these works in the capital of the bishopric, one might be tempted to associate them with some Dutch centre in more or less direct contact with Haarlem.

In fact the only works of any quality which have been associated with Utrecht are those of a master who is normally considered as an emigrant, the Master of *St. Bartholomew*. However, although we can identify features in his paintings and illuminations which seem to belong to the art of Utrecht, the evidence suggests that he came in fact from Guelders, probably Arnhem.

The Master IAM van Zwolle

The complexity of the artistic situation in the ecclesiastical principality of Utrecht during the second half of the fifteenth century is further illustrated by the work of the engraver who signs himself "Zwoll" followed by a burnisher and, less often, with the letters and marks IAM or I̧AM. There seems little doubt that the first word refers to the place in which he worked, the town of Zwolle, in the northern province of the principality.[3] We can therefore consider the 29 works catalogued by Lehrs as evidence of an artistic tradition which flourished in this region, even if the engravings were in the first place destined, as seems likely, for export.

However, a study of the works of this artist reveals a complete lack of homogeneity. There is little in common, apart from their technique, between a print like *The Adoration of the Magi* and *The Lamentation* (Lehrs 7) or between *The Taking of Christ* (Lehrs 4) and *The Lactation of St. Bernard* (Lehrs 15). As far as pure style is concerned, we can distinguish four groups, each of which has its own unity, but which have few characteristics in common.

The most archaic style to be found in these engravings is marked by the influence of Dieric Bouts. It is present in several representations of the Virgin and Child (Lehrs 9, 10, 11, 12), *The St. Anne Trinity* (Lehrs 13) and *Christ in Benediction* (Lehrs 8). In each of these we encounter a similar feminine type, with an oval face and head of strongly three-dimensional quality, directly recalling the figures of Bouts and his school. Many other details reminiscent of this painter could be cited—for example, the figures of children, the sober yet extravagantly swathed draperies, or indeed the composition of *The Virgin with cherries* (Lehrs 9), which is very close to that of Bouts's *Virgin and Child* in the National Gallery, London.

The second group is made up of the two versions of *The Crucifixion* (Lehrs 5, 6), *The Adoration of the Magi* (Lehrs 1) and *St. George* (Lehrs 17). The plasticity of the figures is here more evident than in the first group. The human types are different, more thick-set and with less idealised features. There is a general tendency to simplify the forms, which has the effect of emphasising volume. From this point of view, these prints seem similar to the panels of the altar of St. John the Baptist at Gouda by Hugo Jacobsz.

The third group is the most curious and the furthest in style from the others. It includes the *Christ at Gethsemane* (Lehrs 3), *The Taking of Christ* (Lehrs 4), *The Last Supper* (Lehrs 2) and *Saint Christopher* (Lehrs 16). All these prints belong to what has been described as a 'rustic' tendency in Dutch painting. The faces are grimacing or caricatural, violence is present throughout, the twisting of the bodies is emphasised by the fall of the robes in exaggeratedly agitated folds. The compositions are crowded and tend to give an impression of confusion. It is difficult to relate these prints to surviving paintings. They are fairly close, however, to two particular paintings, a *Carrying of the Cross* in the Museum at Brussels (*166*) and a *Crucifixion* in the Capilla Real, Granada. (*167*).

The fourth group contains *The Lactation of St. Bernard* (Lehrs 15), the different versions of *The Mass of St. Gregory* (Lehrs 18, 19, 20, 21), *St. Augustine* (Lehrs 14), the *Memento Mori* (Lehrs 22), and *The Crossing of the Ways* (Lehrs 24). This series is marked by a preoccupation with the rendering of space and in particular with architectural space. The church interior of *The Lactation of St. Bernard* is very close to that in *The Mystic Marriage of St. Agnes* in the Museum at Utrecht. The figures show a greater realism, with meticulous attention paid to wrinkles and other details of the face as well as to the clenched hands. In all the work of the engraver, he here comes closest to the style of the Master of St. Bartholomew.

There is one engraving which has no obvious connection with any of the others, *The Lamentation* (Lehrs 7). An attempt has been made to connect it with the art of Rogier van der Weyden. However, the pathos evident in this work is very different from that of the Brussels painter, in whose works we find neither the figures nor the draperies. It seems to me that this is not the first, but rather the last work of this artist. The interpretation of the subject and the treatment of the figures seem to me to derive from the early works of Quentin Metsys and I would not be surprised to discover that the engraving was directly inspired by a drawing or painting by that artist.

What emerges most strongly from this analysis is the variety of the engraver's sources. If one element is common to all these groups, it is fragments of architectural decoration which display fantastic and elaborate scroll-work in the manner of the ornamental prints of this period. Yet apart from the two engravings of ornamental designs (Lehrs 25, 26), the artist

143 MASTER IAM VAN ZWOLLE. *Crucifixion*, Vienna, Albertina

seems to have been inspired for the most part not by decorative styles such as those employed by goldsmiths, but by simpler styles seen in paintings. On the other hand it is all too easy to identify a particular tendency with a tradition conveniently localised in the ecclesiastical principality, while exiling all others to the frontiers of the State.

In the light of this analysis, the proposal to identify the engraver with Jan van den Mijnnesten[35] takes on another character. This artist came originally from Schüttorf and is recorded for the first time in Zwolle in 1462, at which date he acquired citizenship of the town. He died in 1504. All the documents which mention him describe him as a painter, and several of them concern the commission of important paintings. This might lead us to doubt the identification, for it hardly seems likely that the work of a master painter in the fifteenth century would display stylistic changes so abrupt as to account for the distinct groups which have been isolated within the engraved work. However, one argument difficult to refute has

While it seems unlikely that the same artist was responsible for all the different engraved compositions, it may be that the artist from Zwolle was the head of a workshop and acted as the publisher of engravings which were not all taken from his own work. The presence beside his monogram of a burnisher might indicate that the engraving was made under his surveillance by a goldsmith who was a member of his workshop. This hypothesis would explain the diversity of style to be found in the engravings.[37]

Of all the styles represented in the art of the engraver, only one corresponds to any degree with that of an artist of the generation of Jan van den Mijnnesten. If the latter was first recorded in 1462, he must have been born about 1430 or 1435,[37] and so is unlikely to have adopted the premanneristic tendencies of the end of the century so apparent in the work of the 'Utrecht' group, for example. On the other hand, the first style, so directly influenced by Dieric Bouts, could very well correspond to the work of a man of that generation. This theory is based on the idea that there existed in Zwolle traces of an art which we would more readily associate with Louvain or Haarlem.

145 MASTER IAM VAN ZWOLLE. *Taking of Christ*, Vienna, Albertina

144 MASTER IAM VAN ZWOLLE. *St. Anne Trinity*, Vienna, Albertina

been advanced by B. Dubbe in favour of this identification: the son of Jan van den Mijnnesten adopted as his own the mark in the form of a stylized house which appears in several of the engraver's signatures.

Can we then distinguish the works signed IAM from those which carry the mark IAM? This seems very unlikely. In fact all the former belong to the 'Boutsian' group (Lehrs 10, 12, 17 and 26), but the second mark appears on other engravings in the same style (Lehrs 8, 9, 13). We must therefore conclude that Jan van den Mijnnesten's mark changed and that the IAM is the earlier version.[36] But what the two scholars who have made a study of this problem have forgotten is that there is yet another mark: the burnisher. It is remarkable to discover that this mark appears on all the signed works, even where the initials are absent. This instrument has never been associated with the art of painting and indeed probably had no connection with it, for it is a tool commonly used by an engraver or a goldsmith.

Therefore, if we accept that the IAM is the mark of Jan van den Mijnnesten, we must try to define the position of the painter in relation to the other artisans' crafts of the fifteenth century.

The Ecclesiastical Principality

During the last third of the fifteenth century, few paintings would seem to have been produced in the ecclesiastical principality of Utrecht. It was, however, at this time that Adrien van Wesel emerged as one of the leading sculptors of the northern Netherlands.[39] In fact, the arts of sculpture and painting were more closely related than has generally been imagined. The identity of the 'Master of the Angels', as van Wesel was at first described, was established by a commission given by the Brotherhood of Our Lady of 's Hertogenbosch, a town which lay outside the boundaries of the ecclesiastical principality and even beyond the jurisdiction of the diocese. Indeed, this is the most important of the artist's commissions known to us. Nevertheless it would be surprising if the sculptor did not receive important commissions within the principality itself.

The lack of evidence about the artistic situation in Utrecht has suggested another hypothesis. It is possible to imagine that the relatively unimportant works which have survived are the feebler examples of a production decimated by the iconoclasts and successive wars. This theory has been put forward by several historians, although there is no firm evidence to support it. The numerous documentary mentions of painters do not distinguish the artisans from the masters, or the illuminators from the painters.

Historical circumstances would seem to favour the first hypothesis, which views Utrecht and the principality as barren as far as painting is concerned. The eventual emergence of David of Burgundy as enthusiastic patron remains, as we have seen, hard to judge. It would seem that his commissions were limited to the decoration of his own residence at Wijk bij Duurstede and did not extend, as has been thought, to the religious foundations under his jurisdiction. His influence can therefore be judged as essentially modest.

The character of the surviving works deserves to be examined. This is not a very original art; rather it depends heavily on those artists who worked in the county of Holland: Jan van Eyck, on the one hand, but also Dieric Bouts and the painters of his school (that is, the Master of the Taking of Christ and the Master of the Tiburtine Sibyl) and Albert van Ouwater. However, in addition to these borrowings, we must not neglect the fact that the paintings created in Utrecht belong to the 'rustic' tradition, in their taste for anecdote, their predilection for thick-set grotesque or violent human types. In this way the ecclesiastical principality can be seen to belong to the same cultural *milieu* as the county of Holland: there is no fundamental difference between the paintings made in Utrecht and those created in Haarlem or Delft, except for a lower level of quality.

Paintings which cannot be localized

From the preceding analyses, it emerges clearly that works which cannot be firmly localized must be dealt with in a different manner. This is the case with two paintings which are certainly by the same hand: a *Carrying of the Cross* in the Museum at Brussels (*166*) and a *Crucifixion* in the Capilla Real at Granada (*167*). The style of the two compositions is directly related to that of the third group of engravings by Master IAM van Zwolle. The contortions of the bodies, the angry faces often shown in profile, the over-elaborate draperies, the very density of the compositions can be found in both groups. But the engraver, as has just been established, appears to have borrowed from works made outside the diocese, which may also have been the source of the painter's inspiration.

Moreover, the two paintings are executed with a smoothness of technique and a richness of detail which relates them to the the work of the school of Haarlem. *The Carrying of the Cross* (*166*) is also inspired by an Eyckian original, from which it takes the group of figures which precedes Christ and includes the two thieves making their way along a sunken path. In both works the landscape is far more convincingly rendered than it is in a painting such as *The Crucifixion* in the Museum at Utrecht (*157*). The recession is not treated with the skill of a Geertgen tot Sint Jans, but it does show a real interest in the representation of space. It seems, then, very possible that this was painted in the ecclesiastical principality, but there is no evidence to confirm this and we cannot rule out the possibility that the painter was from Holland.

We could just as easily take the opposite view: it is possible to relate to the school of Haarlem two paintings in the Johnson collection at the Philadelphia Museum, a *Saint Martin* (*168*) and the *Portrait of Petrus Veenlant* dated 1489 (*169*). The two paintings are extremely close in technique and may well be by the same artist. Veenlant is described as the burgomaster of Schiedam; the painter of the portrait may also have come from that town. However, he may just as easily have come from Delft or Leiden, both closer than Haarlem. Even the ecclasiastical principality itself cannot be entirely excluded, for its frontiers were close by and Utrecht itself is no further than Haarlem from Schiedam. The style alone gives us an indication, though not a conclusive one. The similarities with the school of Haarlem are essentially superficial. There is in both paintings some imitation of the attitudes and draperies of the figures of Geertgen tot Sint Jans. However, the precisely painted flowers on the ground, in the *Saint Martin*, belong to a broader Eyckian tradition, which could have been known at first hand or in the form of works of the Boutsian school. The first possibility is the more likely, for the saint's horse is a copy of that in the *Sovereign Prayer* in the *Turin Hours* (*14*). In both cases, however, we are dealing with poor, clearly provincial imitations.

A very similar problem is posed by two panels which unquestionably come from the same altarpiece. One shows the *Ecce Homo*, the other must have been one of a pair of panels together illustrating the *Adoration of the Magi* (*170*). The faces of the figures are strongly caricatured, with heads too heavy for the small bodies. The compositions are well-defined: the emphasis is on the figures, the setting being treated very summarily and the space largely limited to the action. In the plasticity of the bodies,

146
252
145

146
162

248

253
254

253

14

146 North Netherlandish artist of the last quarter of the fifteenth century. *Carrying of the Cross*, Brussels, Musées Royaux des Beaux-Arts (*166*)

these paintings remind us a little of the works of Hugo Jacobsz, but the style remains difficult to place. Here again, though we might reasonably assign them to the northern Netherlands, it is virtually impossible to be more precise about their origin.

256   A final example of the problems posed by paintings of this type is provided by a *Crucifixion* in the Museum of Fine Arts in Budapest (*171*). The harshness of the faces and the violence of the gestures in this painting belong to the 'rustic' tradition. However, the costumes, in which much use is made of brocade, and the finish of the work seem closer to the school of Haarlem. The landscape with its background scenes recalls the work of the imitators of Geertgen tot Sint Jans. In addition, there is in the panorama of the city of Jerusalem a tower of the Brabantine type very similar to one which figures in a large number of paintings by the Master of the *Virgo inter Virgines*. In other words, the borrowings are so complex that it is impossible to localize the painting more precisely than in the north Netherlands.

To these four examples, it is possible to add a number of other paintings of second rank. The dissemination of styles and of individual motifs throughout the various administrative regions of the northern Netherlands at the end of the fifteenth century is too certain a fact for us to be able to pinpoint the origin of such works.

Painters from the northern Netherlands working abroad

Any study of the painters of the northern Netherlands must take account of the fact that many of them went to seek their fortune elsewhere during the fifteenth century. Such emigration was quite usual at the time and does not imply the radical cutting of

147 GERARD DAVID. *Nailing to the Cross*, London, National Gallery

all ties which it has meant in the nineteenth and twentieth centuries. The attachment to one's native land—not to mention national pride, which was to a large extent non-existent—was too little developed to provoke any real sense of loss. However, when a fully trained artist became an emigrant, he carried with him an artistic heritage which was rarely entirely replaced by the culture of his country of adoption.

The activity of painters of the northern Netherlands outside their own country can today be felt better than it can be fully described. Numerous mentions attest their presence practically all over Europe, while several unidentified painters reveal in their work characteristics which leave very little doubt about their country of origin; in fact, several of the great figures of Western painting have their roots in that cultural *milieu*. A long and methodical enquiry still needs to be made if we are to assess more precisely the pattern of this emigration.

The southern Netherlands were, of course, the most popular destination for painters from the North: the splendid court of their common sovereign, the Duke of Burgundy, and their cities' reputation for great wealth were enough in themselves to justify such movements. The position occupied by a Dieric Bouts at Louvain is significant, but, curiously, few Northerners seem to have followed him there and we know of no other

Dutchmen in Louvain, except for Joes Wilen Valcx, who was killed there in 1487.[40]

Antwerp certainly welcomed many northern artists. Its rapid expansion and its close proximity account for the massive influx which would seem to have taken place.[41] For this reason it is tempting to follow Valentiner in his identification of the Master of the Morrison *Triptych* with Simon van Herlam, many of whose pensive female figures call to mind the work of Geertgen tot Sint Jans.[42] Julius Held is equally convincing when he suggests that Hendrick van Wueluwe is in fact the powerful Master of Frankfurt who in placing a view of the tower at Utrecht in the background of a *Crucifixion* (Frankfurt, Staedelsches Kunstinstitut), seems to be remembering his native town.[43] And the relationship between the figures of the Master of Hoogstraeten and those of Jacob Jansz is so clear that his identification as a northern master working in Antwerp or a nearby town is readily apparent.[44]

Ghent and Brussels seem to have attracted fewer northern painters[45] and although some northern names appear in the lists of the Tournai guild, they cannot be linked with any particular work.[46]

Many illuminators from Utrecht[47] settled in Bruges, which seems to have contained a small northern colony. Indeed, Holland gave to the city one of its last great masters of the fifteenth century, Gerard David. He became a master in the

148 GERARD DAVID. *Nativity*, Budapest, Museum of Fine Arts

they be described as actual migrations or seen rather as simple artistic exchanges, born of geographical proximity? It is not possible to give a precise answer to this question without much further research. Moreover, it is difficult to trace the artistic frontier between the two regions. The example of sculpture demonstrates this. A certain Adrien van Wesel, who came from the duchy of Cleves, is regarded as the most brilliant sculptor of the northern Netherlands, and the entire sculptural production of Kalkar is so close to that of the northern Netherlands that it is difficult to make a division between them.

There are many artistic links between the painters of Westphalia and those of the northern Netherlands. For example, the entire oeuvre of the Master of Liesborn displays a direct

149 GERARD DAVID. *Landscape*, outer wings of a triptych, The Hague, Mauritshuis

guild in 1484 at which time he described himself as a native of Oudewater, although he does not seem to have known his compatriot Albert van Ouwater. His early works make us think of the paintings of Jacob Jansz rather than of those of his great predecessors. In his work, and in that of many of his compatriots, we can detect a familiarity with the Dutch works of Jan van Eyck.[48] Such compositional devices as the unusual

147 perspective in *Christ Nailed to the Cross* (London, National
51 Gallery) have their equivalents, notably in *The Hours of Catherine of Cleves*. His taste for a down-to-earth realism, of which the *Virgin with the Milk-pap* is the best and most popular example,
112 can also be seen in Jacob Jansz (*The Meal of the Holy Family*) or in
45 the Master of Catherine of Cleves (*Souls in Hell fed by angels*). A final but no less significant reminder of Haarlem is the leafiness
149 of his trees; the two wings in the Mauritshuis (The Hague), which are entirely devoted to landscape, seem like details taken from the Altarpiece of the Hospitallers by Geertgen tot Sint Jans.

There are very close links between the northern Netherlands and northern Germany, especially Westphalia. The precise nature of these links, however, is difficult to determine. Should

174

150 ERHART REUWICH (?). *Carrying of the Cross*, Amsterdam, Rijksmuseum

knowledge of the style of Bouts or of the Master of the *Taking of Christ*.[49] A generation later, Dieric Baegert was to develop a very similar manner which presented a strikingly Dutch aspect.[50] The Master of 1473 so closely recalls the work of Jacob Jansz, although in fact he seems to have been the elder, that we might imagine that the two shared a workshop, perhaps in Haarlem.[51] A *Nativity* by the Master of Schöpfingen has so much in common with that of Hugo Jacobsz in the Brussels Museum that we must imagine either that the latter borrowed from the former or that both painters followed a common model.[52]

A similar relationship existed with the workshops of the Hanseatic towns. The *Triptych of Djursdala* which has been attributed in turn to the school of Utrecht, to Bernt Notke[53] and to Heinrich Funhof of Hamburg, recalls both the work of the Master of the *Tiburtine Sibyl* and that of Geertgen tot Sint Jans.[54]

In other parts of Germany, it is less easy to identify the presence of artists from the northern Netherlands. We can presume that they were in Nuremberg[55]; it has been established that they were in Nördlingen[56]; but their greatest impact was in the Rhineland, in the work of two great artists. In Cologne, the Master of *St. Bartholomew* is recognised as having come from Utrecht or Guelders, where two of his most important works originate: *The Book of Hours of Sofia van Bylant* (Cologne, Wallraf-Richartz Museum), whose first owner belonged to a family living near Arnhem, and the triptych, now dismembered, from the St. Catharina Gasthuis in Arnhem (the central panel is today in the Louvre). His violence derives from the 'rustic' tradition, his manner is Netherlandish and it is possible to identify features in his work which point to a probable apprenticeship in Utrecht.[57]

As for Erhart Reuwich, there is no doubt that he belonged to the family of painters of the same name who are mentioned in Utrecht. If we could attribute to him no more than the woodcut illustrations to the account of the pilgrimage to the Holy Land undertaken by Bernhard de Breydenbach, published in Mainz in 1486, he would be an important artist. There are now grounds for believing, however, that he is identical with the Master of the Book of Reason,[58] all of whose work displays an essentially

150

Dutch character. It has a lighter side reminiscent of the illustrations of the *Hours of Catherine of Cleves*. It may be that this artist's engravings were not executed in Mainz, but rather in the Netherlands.

Fewer north Netherlandish artists moved to France, but perhaps it is here that we can solve the mystery of the identity of two major artists: the Master of the Aix *Annunciation* may have been Arnould de Cats from the diocese of Utrecht,[59] and the surname of Jean Hay may indicate that his home town was The Hague.

In Italy, as in Spain and Portugal, the style of various works points to the probable Netherlandish origin of their creators, but here again more research is needed to determine the extent and importance of this emigration.[60] It was perhaps in Portugal that the Netherlandish immigrants exerted the most influence. The painter Vasco Fernandez in his *Altarpiece of the Se de Viseu* seems to employ Dutch compositional schemes and a technique which recalls that of Hugo Jacobsz. As for the *St. John on Patmos* from Lorinha (Misericordia), it is difficult to understand outside the context of a northern tradition.[61]

42–51

VIII. The originality and the limitations of painting in the northern Netherlands

From a study of the surviving northern Netherlandish paintings, one clear fact emerges: the region possessed an artistic unity, even though it is possible to distinguish two traditions, that of Holland and Zeeland, which includes the work of artists living in and around Haarlem, and secondly, that of Utrecht and Guelders. It is true that these areas are not the whole of the modern Netherlands: we know very little about artistic activity in Friesland or even in the northern part of the ecclesiastical principality, Overijssel. This also excludes northern Brabant, which was annexed by the United Provinces in 1629 and confirmed as part of their territory in the treaties of 1648.

This last omission would be of little significance—it only concerns a very small part of the Netherlands—if it did not also involve the neglect of a great town, 's Hertogenbosch, and a great artist of the period under discussion, Hieronymus Bosch. Should we not abandon the territorial borders of the fifteenth century and adopt those of our own time, as Luttervelt[1] had no hesitation in doing? There is unfortunately no simple answer.

The city of 's Hertogenbosch was the fourth in order of importance in Brabant, coming after Brussels, Antwerp and Louvain, but its population outnumbered that of Haarlem at the end of the fifteenth century.[2] Primarily a market town, it was nevertheless the scene of intense religious and intellectual activity throughout the fifteenth and into the early sixteenth century. One need only recall the importance of the Brethren of the Common Life who settled there in 1424 at the invitation of the municipality itself. We know that the young Erasmus received his education in one of their houses.[3] However, it is difficult to substantiate any marked orientation in the city towards the north. The fact that the powerful confraternity of Our Lady chose to commission a sculpted altarpiece from an Utrecht artist, Adrien van Wesel, is not sufficient to prove the existence of links as strong as those which exist today. The evidence would suggest that 's Hertogenbosch developed at the same time as Antwerp. The Confraternity's commission simply tells us that relations with the ecclesiastical principality of Utrecht, and perhaps Holland, existed alongside those with the towns of Brabant, which came about as a consequence of territorial divisions.

The complicated artistic situation of 's Hertogenbosch is reflected in the career of its most illustrious painter, Hieronymus Bosch. There is no historical proof of his links with the northern Netherlands beyond the commission, which has just been mentioned in connection with the town, for an altarpiece to be made by Adrien van Wesel. It was Bosch's father, Anthonis van Aken, accompanied by his son, probably Hieronymus himself, who negotiated in 1475–6 with the Utrecht sculptor about this work, which was to be sent to him to be painted in polychrome.[5]

The works themselves are scarcely more explicit. It is clear that in common with many other northern painters, Bosch was familiar with the early works of Jan van Eyck and borrowed from them freely.[6] The few connections with the art of Dutch painters which can be established would appear to be of little importance were it not that there are even fewer with that of the painters of the south.[7] However, it does seem that Bosch knew the works of Geertgen. We have already noted that the *Ecce Homo* at Frankfurt (Staedelsches Kunstinstitut) was probably inspired by the left wing of the altarpiece of the Hospitallers.[8] So it is not surprising to discover that the executioner who points out the fire to the Emperor in the *Burning of the bones of St. John the Baptist* is to be found copied almost literally in the *Crowning with Thorns* in London (National Gallery) by the painter from 's Hertogenbosch. Clearer still is the dependence of the *St. Antony* in the Prado on the Haarlem artist's *St. John the Baptist*. Not only is the theme of a monk in solitary meditation identical[9], but there are other characteristics which confirm the close relationship between the two works. The foliage, which is rare in the work of Bosch, is very like that of Geertgen, as is the landscape which recedes, though less convincingly, in clearly defined planes. 151, 90

It would be possible to take this argument further. One could claim that the world of Hieronymus Bosch, peopled as it is with beggars, caricatured Jews, grimacing peasants and, most strikingly, with vividly imagined monsters, represents a very personal development of the types which appear in the paintings of the 'rustic' tendency. The work of the Master of the *Virgo inter Virgines*, the production of the grisaille illuminators of Delft, the popular art of the Master of Catherine of Cleves

all display undeniable affinities with the creations of the 's Hertogenbosch painter.

On the other hand, Bosch is not only to be understood in the context of the art of the northern Netherlands. An essential aspect of his art—his tone of sarcasm, his black humour in representing the sins of mankind—has no equivalent in the northern provinces, where only a few of the expressive techniques used by Bosch can be found.[10] His possible links with the Brabant chambers of rhetoric, whose character is epitomized by the famous *Den Spiegel der Selicheyt van Elkerlyck*, performed in Antwerp in 1485, best clarify this aspect of the Boschian spirit.[11] However, without wishing to evade this issue, it must be said that the personality of the artist resists pigeon-holing. So it is neither legitimate nor necessary to refuse to take account in his honour of the territorial boundaries of the fifteenth century, even though one ought to bear in mind the extent of his debt to the art of the northern Netherlands.

The question which remains is that of the existence of an independent artistic tradition in the northern Netherlands comparable to that of the south. In the latter, after the death in 1441 of Jan van Eyck, who left few followers, painting remained strongly influenced, until the end of the century, by Rogier van der Weyden and the Gothic rhythms which he reintroduced into realistic figure painting. Dieric Bouts, working in Brabant, was profoundly influenced by this style, while Memling adopted it in a more graceful manner.

It is interesting to note how little van der Weyden's art influenced the painters of the northern Netherlands. When they follow southern models, they tend to be Eyckian. One of the most striking characteristics of these painters, their mastery of landscape, developed from the work of Jan van Eyck, who brought to the court of John of Bavaria one of the most original visions of the time.

The 'rustic' tendency which also appeared to originate in the northern Netherlands is similarly not without its counterparts in the south. However, its affinities lie only with the developments which seem to have been eclipsed by the dominance of Rogier van der Weyden, that is, the first examples of Flemish realism such as the *Cy nous dit* in the Bibliothèque Nationale in Paris,[12] and the art of Campin. Can we see here an art rejected by an urban and princely civilisation as too popular, even vulgar? This seems unlikely, however, since it was undoubtedly admired and appreciated in the Dutch cities which were dominated by a rich *bourgeoisie*. Perhaps it would be more accurate to consider this art, in Holland as well as in the Hainault of Robert Campin, as the survival of a mode of artistic expression which developed in a country whose origin was more agricultural than urban and commercial.

At first sight the paintings of the northern Netherlands can scarcely be distinguished, as far as their subject-matter is concerned, from those of the south. However, the manner of interpretation betrays a profound debt to the Devotio Moderna which has no strict equivalent in the south, unless it is to be found in the work of Hugo van der Goes, itself close to that of Geertgen.[13] The widespread influence of the *Vita Christi* of Ludolph the Carthusian also served to give a distinctive character to all these works.

The art of the northern Netherlands is no less realistic than that of the south, whose example it follows. However, it is caught between a severe restraint—that above all of the painters of Haarlem—and the roughness of a rusticity often close to ugliness, which is not merely adopted but deliberately sought out.

All these characteristics would seem to entitle us to distinguish the northern Netherlands, and especially Holland, as a region which possessed in the fifteenth century a coherent artistic personality, in spite of its close links with the south, and to set the 'Dutch primitives' apart from those of Flanders.

◁ 151   HIERONYMUS BOSCH. *St. Antony*, Madrid, Prado

Notes

Notes to the introduction

1 Friedländer, in his summary of existing scholarship in 1916, then in his studies and catalogues published between 1924 and 1937. Charles de Tolnay principally in his book of 1939 and Panofsky in his summary of existing scholarship in 1953.

2 Hoogewerff has tried to link all forms of pictorial expression: manuscript illumination, frescoes and panel paintings. It does not seem possible to accept his approach. Dutch manuscript illumination, though remarkably sophisticated, usually differs from panel painting in its visual approach and only those examples which bear the closest resemblance have been considered. The rare examples of fresco have mostly survived in such a fragmentary condition that an analysis of them is difficult. It should be added that frescoes seem to be more strongly influenced by their function and their particular location, and thus constitute a different mode of expression from panel painting.

3 Byvanck and Hoogewerff, 1926 and Byvanck, 1937.

4 Delaissé, 1968.

5 It is significant that the studies in the *Algemene Geschiedenis der Nederlanden* have generally taken this division between the northern and southern Netherlands into account.

6 Huizinga, 1930–1.

7 The idea had also been developed in a more speculative way by Zimmermann (1917) and Dvořák (1918) followed by Charles de Tolnay (1939), on the strength of the definitions of Dutch painting given by Karel van Mander. An unfounded attribution of part of the *Turin-Milan Hours* illuminations to Ouwater was arrived at in this way.

8 [Transl. into French by Hymans 1884, I, p. 87.]

9 The term 'Dutch' is no more restrictive than 'Flemish', and should be understood in the sense given it by Huizinga in 1930–1 (p. 172) when he said that 'it will be used to describe everything relating either to the county of Holland in the Middle Ages or to the United Provinces or the modern Kingdom of the Netherlands'.

Notes to chapter I

1 Charles V was first cousin to William VI and married his son John of Touraine to Jacqueline of Bavaria, the count's daughter and heiress.

2 On the historical problems of this period, cf. especially Block, I, 1892; Pirenne, II, 1903; *Alg. Geschiedenis*, III, 1951.

3 I use here the title proper to the county of Holland. One should bear in mind, however, that the same nobleman may be referred to as William II in his capacity as Count of Hainault.

4 This interpretation has been doubted by Pirenne (II, 1912, pp. 165–7). However, it seems difficult not to acknowledge the decisive part played by the bourgeoisie in the *Kabeljauwen* faction.

5 For the *Devotio Moderna* see Chapter III below; reference may also be made to Hyma 1924, Debongnie, 1954 and R. Post, 1968.

6 There is a plentiful literature on Master Theodorik. Cf. especially the fullest and most recent work by Antonin Friedl, 1948.

7 In particular Sterling, 1938, p. 25, and Panofsky, 1953, p. 36.

8 Hulin de Loo, 1911, pl. XII.

9 The importance of the Liège circle at the end of the fourteenth century is proved by two works of high quality: the *Antependium* in the Musée des Beaux-Arts in Brussels and the *Portable Triptych* in the Boymans-van Beuningen Museum in Rotterdam.

10 Byvanck, 1937, fig. 101.

11 Cf. especially Panofsky, 1953 B, Lieftinck, 1959, Hoogewerff, 1961 and Fincke, 1963.

12 G. van Klaveren, 1935 and Hoogewerff, 1961, p. 26.

13 Lieftinck, 1959, p. 201.

14 Byvanck, 1937, p. 120.

15 Byvanck, 1937, p. 156.

16 For this artist, cf. especially Rickert, 1949.

17 An inscription appearing on folio 410 of the manuscript states that it was completed by Brother Helmich die Lewe, canon regular of the Marienborn convent, in 1415.

18 For an analysis of the style of these illuminators, see especially Delaissé's work of 1968.

19 Boon, 1958, p. 18.

20 Hoogewerff, 1961 and Fincke, 1963.

21 Gorissen, 1954 and 1957.

22 Italian borrowings by the Limbourgs are mentioned by nearly all authors: cf. in particular Winkler 1930. For the Limbourgs, cf. M. Meiss, 1974, and its review, by F. Avril, 1975.

23 Gorissen, 1954, pp. 191–8.

24 Reynaud, 1961, followed by Sterling-Adhémar, 1965.

25 Gorissen, 1954, p. 199 (47).

26 Gorissen, 1954, p. 200 (53).

27 Gorissen, 1954, p. 202 (67).

28 Monget, I, 1898, pp. 194–5.

29 Monget, III, 1898, p. 83. The paintings of Carle van Loo are now in the Musée des Beaux-Arts, Dijon.

30 Sterling-Adhémar, 1965, no. 14, pp. 6–7; now on loan to the Dijon Museum.

31 It is very difficult to adduce conclusive proofs concerning the execution of pictures painted from the top to the bottom. The technique of Malouel's period, and even more so that of the following century, required a gradual completion through the application of successive layers of paint. However, the finishing touches do seem to have been applied from top to bottom. Two examples may be cited. In the second Justice panel commissioned from Dieric Bouts, the only parts reasonably close to the Master's style are situated in the upper half. In the *Last Supper* in Urbino, left unfinished for unknown reasons by Justus of Ghent,

only the two angels in the upper half have been completed with Flemish modelling and material.

32 For the *Large Tondo*, cf. esp. Sterling-Adhémar, 1965, no. 8, p. 4, which gives the essential bibliography.

33 For Jean de Beaumetz, see Sterling, 1955.

34 For the Master of Dirc van Delft, cf. Rickert, 1949.

35 On this subject one should refer to the excellent and sensitive analyses by Delaissé, 1968.

36 Painting on wood, 25 × 19, from the Figdor collection (cat. III, no. 34). Cf. especially Panofsky, 1953, p. 94 and pp. 159 and 164, fig. 110.

37 Martens, 1929, pp. 184–92.

38 Especially by Reincke, 1958, who insists on the identification of the monk 'Francone Zutfanico' with the son of a shoemaker from Zutphen mentioned at Hamburg from 1373 to 1404. Also Reincke, 1959, and Rensing, 1967. Summary of the question by H. Grohn in Hamburg, 1969, pp. 17–21.

39 Published by Reincke, 1959, pp. 23–6 and by Grohn in Hamburg, 1969, p. 19.

40 The argument is not quite conclusive. On the one hand, the commission for the Hamburg Altarpiece dates from 1424 and the reference to a Dominican friar from 1429, so that it is not impossible for the painter to have been professed in the interim. On the other hand, the 1429 text is only known to us through an eighteenth-century note, which may have simplified the reference in transcribing it.

41 Bella Martens (1929) and Reincke (1958 and 1959) also incline towards this view in so far as they take Francone Zutfanico to be the son of Nicolaus of Zutphen.

42 Reynaud, 1970.

43 The problem of the chronology of the works, also posed by Nicole Reynaud, is just as complex. I feel that Reynaud was right to point out the close links between the Hamburg *Man of Sorrows* and the *St. Barbara Altarpiece*. On the other hand, it seems less certain that this group would be dated later than the St. Thomas Altarpiece, i.e. 1435. At this date, the art of the *St. Barbara Altarpiece* and the *Man of Sorrows* would have been very old-fashioned. It is difficult to see in which workshops the Master could have been attracted by conventions of the first decade of the century. It seems to me more logical to see these two works as representing the early style of an artist formed in circles close to Parisian workshops in the years 1415–20. The St. Thomas Altarpiece, commissioned in 1424, and the *Man of Sorrows* in Leipzig could rather indicate a more monumental art under the combined influence of the Master of Flémalle and the artists of Lower Germany whose influence has been painstakingly analysed by P. Pieper (Hamburg, 1969, pp. 34–41). In this case, it would only be necessary to rectify the currently accepted chronology by an earlier dating of the Hamburg *Man of Sorrows*.

44 Weale, 1872–3, pp. 238–9.

45 Porcher's suggestion (1961) that he was Aragonese is attractive, but has no other basis than the nationality of the wife of Louis II of Anjou. Too little is as yet known about Aragonese manuscript illumination of this period to confirm this idea. The comparison cited here, on the contrary, is a disconcerting one and Porcher has offered none so evident.

Notes to chapter II

1 The references to painters found in the inventories of Albert of Bavaria by Mme Toth-Ubbens (1963) are so insignificant that there is no reason to take them into consideration here.

2 On this subject, cf. Schneider, 1913, and especially the estates of the duke's servants in 1417 (pp. 199–236).

3 It should be remembered that Dirc de Maelre, known at that time only from his work in the Nieuwe Kerk, had been identified by Goffin (1907) with the young Dieric Bouts; this theory can no longer be upheld if one takes into account all the known documents.

4 Pinchart in the Italian edition annotated by Crowe and Cavalcaselle, 1899, pp. 42–3, note 2. Mande's work as an illuminator after his admission to the monastery in 1395 is mentioned by the chronicle of Busch (Grube, 1886). Cf. also Visser, 1899.

5 Mentioned especially by Denuit (n.d.), p. 34.

6 State Archives, The Hague, Grafeligkleidsreken-kamer van Holland, Rekeningen, no. 168, folio 34 *r.* and *v.*, 43 *v.* and 44 *r.*

7 This idea seems to have been first put forward by Delaissé in a paper read at the annual Congress of German Art Historians at Münster in 1966.

8 There is no reason to go into further discussion here about the place of birth of the van Eycks, usually supposed to be Maaseyck, but which F. Lyna in particular preferred to place at Maastricht: both towns belonged to the ecclesiastical principality of Liège. For the van Eycks at the court of John of Bavaria in Liège, cf. Schneider, 1913, p. 225.

9 The problem of Jan van Eyck's early career is too complex to be tackled here. The theory of a Parisian training, in contact with the Limbourg brothers and the Boucicaut Master, seems quite plausible.

10 Cf. the documents published by Weale, 1908.

11 The idea was put forward by Crowe and Cavalcaselle (1899, p. 43) almost as a matter of established fact, and has been accepted as such by many later authors.

12 On this subject, cf. Châtelet, 1956, 1957 and 1967. I shall return to the question in the near future and try to refute Marrow's criticisms (1968) of my publication of 1967, in the introduction to the facsimile edition of the *Milan-Turin Hours* to be published by Electa of Milan in 1981.

13 Paris. Bibliothèque Nationale, Lat. 1804, folio 106 *r.*; cf. Meiss, 1967, fig. 117.

14 The Emperor was preceded by soldiers with drawn and raised swords. The Emperor Sigismund had conferred suzerainty over Hainault, Holland and Zeeland on John of Bavaria, as he confirmed in a letter of 28 March 1418 addressed to John of Brabant (cf. Schneider, 1913, pp. 89–91.

15 Lyna, 1955; Sterling, 1978, pp. 15–18.

16 Dynter (ed. de Ram, III, 1854–60, pp. 810–11) only states that John of Bavaria made his way from Dordrecht to Woodrichem by boat when the negotiations were concluded. Löher (I, 1869, p. 393) goes further and says that he was welcomed by Philip, Count of Charolais, and John of Brabant. It is possible that he simply deduced this plausible circumstance from the texts, as I have found no mention of it in the sources cited by him. The presence of Philip, Count of Charolais, is at least attested by Mieris (IV, 1756, pp. 525–6).

17 Bibliothèque Royale de Belgique, MS. II. 1862, folio II. Cf. Brussels, 1977.

18 For the hats adopted by the *Kabeljauwen*, cf. Löher, 1869, pp. 88–9.

19 The painting in the Musée de Versailles known as the *Fête at the Burgundian Court* (Inventory V. 144) also links hunting and fishing, while one of the main groups (slightly left of centre) clearly indicates the theme of marriage by showing a princess pushing a young woman towards a young man who has taken her right arm. In the tapestries featuring hunting and fishing, the figures often walk in pairs. I have not been able to find the source of this relationship, which nevertheless seems probable.

20 In 1956 I suggested that this latter artist—hand K in Hulin de Loo's classification—might have been an illuminator from Brabant. In fact, this theory was principally based on the fact that the painter had included this duchy's standard among those of the troops of the king of France in the illumination of folio 77 in Turin. However, I have since ascertained that this illumination should be grouped with the illustrations produced for John of Bavaria. Furthermore, the Dutch origins of hand K have since been proved by the discovery of other illuminations from this hand in a book of hours produced for a Dutch family. See catalogue entry on the *Turin-Milan Hours*.

21 Tolnay, 1939, pp. 28–30.

22 On folios 14 (pl. XIII in Durrieu) and 60 (pl. XXVIII in Durrieu).

23 Particular mention should be made of MS 10.174 in the Walters Art Gallery, in which the illumination of folio 79 *v.* uses the composition of the *Finding of the Cross*. The *Hours of Catherine of Cleves* provide many similar examples.

Notes to chapter III

1 For this period, cf. *Alg. Geschiedenis*, III and IV (1951–2), also P.J. Blok, 1884 and 1893 and Pirenne, II and III (1903 and 1904). For Burgundian rule, R. van Marle, 1908.

2 Cf. Chastellain, ed. Kervyn de Lettenhove, III, chapter XV. The detailed account (The Hague, Alg. Rijksarchief, III, chap. XV) only concerns the appointments of the Palace, which were of no great importance.

3 The *Devotio Moderna* is the subject of an extensive literature, indexed in 1941 by J. M. F. Dols. Special mention should be made of Albert Hyma's book of 1924, the article by Fr. Debongnie in the *Dictionnaire de la Spiritualité*, III, Paris, 1954, col. 727–47, and R. R. Post's recent work, 1968, which however treats the topic rather too much from the purely historical point of view.

4 R. R. Post has attempted to define and clarify the rôle of the Brethren in teaching, especially in his book of 1968, chapter IX.

5 The two studies, parallel but conducted along different lines, by Delaissé, 1956, and by Huyben and Debongnie, 1957, leave no doubt, in my opinion, despite the reservations stated in a work like that by G. Epiney-Burgard, 1970, pp. 306–16.

6 R. R. Post, 1967.

7 Cf. Lieftinck, 1959, who has devoted himself to identifying the volumes produced in the convents of the Windesheim congregation. The importance accorded by Delaissé, 1968, to the influence of the *Devotio Moderna* on Dutch manuscript illumination should be understood in the same way as for painting: it is not a question of attributing the decoration of the books to convents of the congregation or of other orders affected by the movement, but of bringing out the influence of the spirit of the *Devotio Moderna* on the approach adopted by book illustrations.

8 Vansteenberghe, 1921, p. 98.

9 A work by the Cologne Master of the *Life of Mary*, cf. especially Stange, 1967, no. 159.

Notes to chapter IV

1 If one accepts the existence of Hubert van Eyck and his share in the work—and I am among those who feel unable to reject the evidence of the inscription and the archive entries concerning Hubert—one must concede that the *Mystic Lamb* was begun before 1426. Jodocus Vyd had acquired a chapel in the Church of St. John the Baptist (now St. Bavo) in 1420. The commission must therefore have been given between these two dates. Vyd may have wanted to create a stir by the splendour of this commission, and it is interesting to note that he became burgomaster the year after the work was completed (1433).

2 The chronology of the Master of Flémalle has been most convincingly established by Tolnay (1939).

3 I have shown elsewhere that the apprenticeship of Rogier van der Weyden was probably a legal formula and that the artist's formation must already have been complete (cf. Châtelet, 1966 and 1974).

4 Plummer, 1966. For the bibliography on the Master of Catherine of Cleves, cf. catalogue entry.

5 Allan, II, 1870–83, pp. 76–7.

6 Cf. Grete Ring, 1949, no. 90, pl. 36.

7 The *Marriage of the Virgin* by the Master of Flémalle, wing of a triptych, Prado Museum, Tolnay, 1939, no. 2.

8 Gorissen, 1973, pp. 1083–96, has traced the engravings from which they were derived. Cf. the general study by Calkins, 1978. For a similar use of engravings as models, cf. James Marrow, 1978.

9 Master K has attracted little study since Hulin de Loo's publication of 1911. One may, however, consult the study by Schilling (1961), who made known a hitherto unpublished book of hours, probably from the hand of this master, and Delaissé, 1968, pp. 76–7.

10 For the *Breviary of Reynald IV*, cf. Byvanck, 1937, pp. 28 and 66, Panofsky, 1953, pp. 102–4; Hoogewerff, 1961; Fincke, 1963; Delaissé, 1968, pp. 22–4, Keller, 1969.

11 Fincke, 1963 and Pieper, 1966, p. 98. The arms featured on folio 428 of the book could just as easily be those of Reynald IV as those of Arnold. Surprise has been registered at the fact that the donor should only have been shown on folio 324, kneeling before St. Nicholas. This would be explained if the volume had been a gift from the town of Nijmegen to the duke, as the Confraternity of St. Nicholas played the dominant rôle in that city.

12 Delaissé, 1968.

13 For this Master, cf. Delaissé, 1949 and Chapter VII below.

14 Byvanck, 1937, p. 148.

15 For these volumes, cf. Boon, 1964, The Hague, 1965 Vermeeren and Pieper, 1966.

16 Bruges exhibition, 1958, nos. 24–7. The attribution of this painting to the Master of the Morrison Triptych has been disputed; if it has to be abandoned, the artist will no doubt have to be seen as a native of the northern Netherlands.

17 The relatively large number of 'verlichter' illuminators mentioned among the Loughmen of Utrecht may even lead one to wonder if the books written by monks such as the Carthusians were not subsequently entrusted to lay illuminators for decoration, especially in the case of large and expensive commissions.

18 Van Mander-Hymans, 1884, I, pp. 93 and 87–8.

19 Born in the vicinity of Kortrijk in Flanders and trained in Ghent at the workshop of Lucas de Heere, Karel van Mander only settled at Haarlem in 1583, at the age of 25, and left for Amsterdam in 1604.

20 Van der Willigen, 1866 and 1870. More methodical searches have enabled me to trace some additional information, which is made use of in this book.

21 Orlers, 1641, p. 33, and van Marle, 1908, p. 19.

22 Amsterdam, 1663, p. 111.

23 Van Marle, 1908, p. 19.

24 For the Haarlem brewery, cf. van Loenen, 1950.

25 Cf. Ampzing, 1628, and Allan, 1870–83.

26 St. Bavo was begun about 1400, from the east end. Work started on the transepts in 1445 and on the nave in 1483. There is at the moment no authoritative study of this important church. Cf. Cuypers and Gonnet, 1894, and Stuffers, 1915.

27 De Jongh (I, 1764, p. 44) states that he was born at Haarlem in 1523 and was a history painter. He gives a portrait of him on plate KK 2.

28 The first known reference to Jan Mostaert as a painter is in 1498 (Dolleman, 1963).

29 Van der Willigen, 1866, p. 47, 1870, p. 49.

30 Châtelet, 1960, p. 73. A brewer, according to Dolleman.

31 The municipal accounts are missing for the years 1423–5, 1443, 1446, 1449–50, 1452, 1459, 1469, 1483 and 1489. Apart from Lambert Rutgensz, the painters mentioned before 1470 are: Zweder, who seems to have played a leading rôle, but who is only cited between 1420 and 1437, and Symon van Waterlant, whose career can be followed from 1428 to 1463, the year of his death. The name of the latter could also have caused confusion with that of Ouwater, but his death in 1463 is rather early if we suppose him to have been the master of Geertgen tot Sint Jans. Moreover, his sons were still active during the youth of Mostaert, who would surely have mentioned this connection to Albert Simonsz.

32 Cf. Aubenas and Ricard, 1951, p. 20; the *Coronation of the Virgin* by Enguerrand Quarton, commissioned in 1453, was another consequence of this renewal of the pilgrimage to Rome.

33 I had suggested (Châtelet, 1960, p. 74) that the painting must have been completed before the construction of the transepts of St. Bavo, which were begun in 1445, because this enterprise must have demanded the concentration of all funds and efforts. As the initiative for the paintings was in fact taken by a confraternity, the work could have been executed while construction was in progress.

34 Already noted by Kurt Steinbart, Thieme and Becker, XXVI, 1932.

35 Davies, 1954, pp. 184–5. The date of 1437 is that of the foundation of the chapel for which the painting was intended. That of 1440–5 is more hypothetical: it rests only on the supposition put forward by Davies that the commission for the painting must have followed closely on the foundation of the chapel; this seems to be confirmed by the style of the costumes.

36 Schöne, 1942, p. 12.

37 Cf. Bauch, 1962 and Châtelet, 1979 B.

38 I should like to thank Dr Henri Blum for giving me his views on this subject.

39 It should be remembered that the figures of the risen dead in the Beaune *Triptych* had been 'clothed' in

the nineteenth century, and that this has caused a certain amount of damage.

40 Similar rocks are found in the work of Dieric Bouts, especially in the wings of the *Last Supper* in Louvain (*The Gathering of the Manna* and *Elijah and the Angel*), and in that of the Master of the *Taking of Christ*.

41 Panofsky, 1953, pp. 320–1.

42 Lampsonius, 1572. Cf. also Lampson, 1956.

43 The painter. It is noteworthy that several paintings saved from churches after the ravages of the Reformation had been preserved by artists whose own styles were quite different from those of the works they saved.

44 Published in Molanus, Brussels, 1861, p. 610; cf. also Schöne, 1938, p. 249, Dok. 92. The painting was a portrait of Dieric Bouts and his two sons then in the Franciscan friary in Louvain, where the artist must have requested to be buried alongside his first wife.

45 Archives of the chapter of St. Peter, Louvain, General Archives of the Kingdom of Belgium, litt. A. no. 228; text principally in Schöne, 1938, pp. 230–2, Dok. 17.

46 Guicciardini, 1567, pp. 128 and 129, text reprinted in Schöne, 1938, pp. 248–9, Dok. 86.

47 Guicciardini, 1613, p. 125, text reprinted in Schöne, 1938, pp. 247–8, Dok. 86.

48 Cf. the text of 15 January 1474 (Schöne, 1938, p. 230, Dok. 14) which enables us to deduce that the artist must have married at Louvain in 1448 at the latest.

49 To be exact, it should be mentioned that a 'meester Dirck' of unspecified profession appears in the accounts between 1447 and 1456 (1447 folio 41; 1448 folio 50; 1451 folio 41; 1454 folio 15 *v.*; 1455 folio 11*v.*; 1456 folio 12 *v.*). This cannot be Bouts, for he is mentioned as having a son called Adrian and lived on the south side, whereas the Cruystr. is on the north.

50 Van Even, 1870, p. 169, note 2. The confusion which arose in the fifteenth century itself between Dieric Bouts and the Louvain painter Hubert Stuerbout is significant: it clearly indicates that for copyists of the time Bouts must have been an abbreviation. They name Stuerbout 'Bouts' in several texts: cf. Schöne, 1938, p. 228, Dok. 5 and 6.

51 A suggestion of Michel Thierry de Bye Dolleman, who has a superbly detailed knowledge of the Haarlem archives and to whom I owe most of the information on the Albout family.

52 Haarlem archives I 1073, folio 16.

53 This at least is the usual interpretation of the document dated 15 January 1474 (cf. Schöne, 1938, p. 230). Dieric Bouts the younger is there described as 'prior emancipatus', which would suggest that, according to Louvain law, he was at least 25. However, this text is hardly compatible with that of 30 September 1473 (Schöne, 1938, p. 229) in which Bouts declares all his children, Dieric, Albert and Catherine, to be of age;

the last two being nevertheless declared 'annis minores' in 1474.
In a paper on Bouts read at Brussels in 1956, Frans Baudoin had already suggested that the disturbances of 1444 might have led to the painter's departure. Valentin Denis (1957, p. 6) takes up the idea without mentioning its source.

54 The *Speculum Humanae Salvationis* is mentioned as a Haarlem production by Petrus Scriverius as early as 1628. See below for other reasons for locating its execution at Haarlem.

55 It should be remembered that the curious date 'MCCC 4 XVIII' which appears on the frame of the painting and has puzzled many historians seems to be the work of a restorer in 1889 (cf. van Even, 1895, p. 329). An identical inscription also appeared on the frame of the *Last Supper* until 1918 (cf. Schöne, 1938, p. 85). It is quite probable that the 1889 restorer, on the advice of a historian, wanted to give both works the known date of the *Last Supper*, viz. 1468: not being familiar with Roman numerals, he changed the L of 50 into an Arabic 4.

56 Châtelet, 1965. See this study for a chronology of Bouts's work based on stylistic analysis.

57 Also in Baltimore, MS 174, cf. Delaissé, 1968, p. 34.

58 Snyder, 1960. Cf. Chapter VI below.

59 Bouvy, 1947, p. 79, fig. 82; Timmers, 1949, pp. 59–60, pl. 103. Amsterdam Rijksmuseum, 1973 (Leeuwenberg) no. 43, p. 75.

60 K. G. Boon (1947) had thought that the original of this composition could have been the work of Albert van Ouwater. The theory is not necessarily to be rejected, but proof is lacking.

61 Cf. especially the diametrically opposed views adopted by Zedler, 1923 and Scholderer, 1940. Also Portenaar, 1947.

62 Musper, 1938.

63 Schretlen, 1925, reprinted 1969, p. 12.

64 Stevenson, 1966 B. This author's method of dating is both precise and debatable. The date of the various watermarks is obtained from their appearance in the municipal registers of their place of origin. But it is hard to be sure that, in the fifteenth century, papers of the year were always used. Besides, the surviving woodcut publications are so few that we cannot be certain that we have the first printings. Stevenson's dates must therefore be taken as points of reference, from which it is possible to gauge variations.

65 Musper, 1961.

66 Vienna, National Library, MS 2771–2. Cf. Byvanck, 1937, pp. 85–8, pl. LIV and LXIV, and Delaissé, 1968, pp. 42–4, figs. 91–8. Cf. also the catalogue entry concerning this Master. Koch (1977) proposes that the production of the *Speculum Humanae Salvationis* should be located at Utrecht because he has found copies of certain illustrations in the illuminations for the *Book of Hours of Mary van Vronensteyn*.

67 Saxl, 1942 and Zerner, 1971.

68 In suggesting Cologne, 1971, p. 17, Henri Zerner has adopted a related idea, since he is thinking of the Cologne masters influenced by the Master of the *Taking of Christ*, particularly the Master of the *Life of Mary*. I feel, nevertheless, that he has been so impressed by the similarity between the female types of the *Canticum Canticorum* and those of the latter artist that he is ignoring the rather different characteristics of the *Ars Moriendi*. Even the spatial conception of the scenes in the *Canticum Canticorum* barely corresponds with the style of the Cologne artists.

69 Cf. Huizinga, 1919 and Tenenti, 1952.

70 For an examination of the text and its sources, cf. O'Connor, 1942.

71 For FVB, cf. Lehrs VII, 1930, pp. 102–5 and Hollstein XII, n.d., pp. 140–67. The sole basis for an identification with Franz von Bocholt is an untrustworthy account by Quadt von Kingelbach published at Cologne in 1609 (*Teutscher Nation Herligkeit*), which stated that the earliest known engraver was a shepherd from near Berg called Franz von Bocholt. Lehrs has suggested that he was one Franz van Brugge, solely on account of the initials and certain stylistic affinities with Memling that he believes can be observed, but which are hard to discern.

72 Friedländer, II, pp. 58–9; Panofsky, 1953, p. 322; Schöne, 1942, pp. 35–8.

73 Panofsky, 1953, p. 322; Schöne, 1938, pp. 23–8 and 1942, pp. 27–35.

74 Châtelet, 1965.

75 Sterling, 1971. In Charles Sterling's view, Christus was active as early as 1435–40, a period during which he completed the *Crucifixion* in Dessau, the *Lamentation* in New York, the *Ecce Homo* in Birmingham and the *Pietà* in the Louvre: i. e. works similar to those of van Eyck's circle and especially to those of Master H.

76 For the meaning of light in the work of Jan van Eyck, cf. Tolnay, 1939, pp. 28–31 and Châtelet-Faggin, 1969, pp. 8–9.

Notes to chapter V

1 Literally 'Little Gerard of St. John'. For bibliography, see catalogue.

2 Van Mander-Hymans, 1884, pp. 90–1.

3 Diane Scillia (1978B) has shown that the term *discipel* used by van Mander indicates a relationship less close than that between apprentice and master and corresponds more to our use of 'follower'. If it is correct that the word is generally used in this sense, the actual words of Geertgen's biography assume a different meaning. 'Geertgen is *noch jongh* een Discipel geweest van den voorighen Ouwater', it reads; as it is unlikely that a stylistic link would have been established in early youth, it must in fact be an apprenticeship which is referred to here.

4 It is very difficult to establish the age at which a young artist might be admitted as a master in the

fifteenth century. The example of Rogier van der Weyden, declared master at Tournai at the age of 32, is deceptive as it probably relates to a special legal situation (on this question, cf. Châtelet, 1966, pp. 24–5). A century later, the examples become more precise: Rubens was admitted as a master at the age of 21, van Dyck at 19.

5 Dürer, I, 1956.

6 Panofsky, 1945, pp. 23–4 and in particular Schürer, 1937. Also Châtelet, 1975.

7 Hoogewerff, II, 1937, pp. 138–9 has established the date of this engraving by using the date of Jacob van Campen's return from Italy as a *terminus post quem*.

8 This has not prevented Dülberg (1899) from seeing Geertgen as the first great representative of the Leiden school, in particular by trying to show the possible debt to him of Cornelis Engelbrechtsz.

9 Haarlem Archives no. P V-IV 19a. Pen drawing with brown wash on light brown paper (16 × 10.4). On the back is written:
'Het Schilderij voor de Schoorsteen van de Eetzaal in t'heijligs Geest of weeshuijs te haarlem verbeeld de 7 werken van barmhertigheijd in den voorbelde is het laatste Oordeel die is geschilderd door Geertgen tot st Jan daar zijn portreet in is op die wijs als deze Tekening die hier agter op getekend is.'

10 The reference to works by 'Gerardo de Olanda' by Marc Antonio Michiel (Frimmel, 1888, p. 104) could just as easily concern Gerard David. As for the 'stukje van Gerritje Jans' sold on 4 April 1634 (Willigen, 1870, p. 14), even if it does concern our painter, it tells us no more about him.

11 Balet, 1909, pp. 6–7, lists the various theories put forward from the beginning of the nineteenth century until 1909.

12 The complementary argument based on the history of costume, in particular of shoes, carries little weight. The type of round-ended boots believed by Friedländer to date from the 1490s were worn mostly by common people and are already found in the *Hours of Catherine of Cleves* (particularly Plummer, 23 and 24). Israel van Meckenem reserves them for his figures of poor people, in contrast to the *poulaines* (already out of fashion in his time, in fact), which he uses for persons of consequence.

13 Balet, 1909, pp. 9–10; Kessler, 1933, Ter Kuile, 1933 and Gratama, 1933. The confusion appears even more likely when one realises that Geertgen tot Sint Jans was called Gerrijt Gerritsz.

14 The identification of Geertgen tot Sint Jans with the *Gheerkin de Hollandere*, taken on as an apprentice at Bruges in 1475–6 by Jean Guillebert, (Koch, 1951) is without foundation: Jean Guillebert was only a bookbinder and would not have been competent to train a painter as well as an illuminator.

15 *Liber Memoriarum domus Hospitalis S. Ioannis Hierosolimitani in Haarlem* (Haarlem Archives, L 43a). The original binding bears a date of 1570. This appears to be also the date of the handwriting in the book, which was no doubt a copy of an older document. Only a few names have been inserted into the unbroken text and they can be dated to around 1570. The reference to

Geertgen tot Sint Jans appears on folio 35 *v*. The book had been lost in 1950, when I began my searches of the records, and I was not able to consult it until 1972.

16 Cf. particularly Allan, II, 1870, and Beresteyn, 1934, for the history of the commandery.

17 Cartulary vol. 2, no. 482, folio 208: Dirc van Assendelft agreed that the Mass he had founded at the altar of St. Margaret should be transferred to the high altar, because the church was under construction.

18 Cartulary 1095: publ. in Allan, II, 1870, pp. 292–4.

19 Cartulary nos. 835, 341 and 343.

20 Catalogue no. 345. The panels are considerably overpainted: all the inscriptions have been rewritten over an earlier text which shows through the new layer of paint, the backgrounds have been cut down and the figures appear to have been repainted to a large extent. It is possible that the series was begun under the rule of Johann Willem Janszoon, since the handling is uniform as far as his portrait but varies from the likeness of his successor Symon van Zanen onwards. However, X-ray photographs taken at my request and by courtesy of the director of the museum reveal no noticeable alteration of the shapes of the faces caused by the overpainting.

21 In 1951 I suggested that the second portrait could be that of Pieter van Scoten, the first thus being of Gerrit. The prominence accorded to him could have been justified by the title of coadjutor, which he received in 1460. In fact, this nomination, which was unusual at Haarlem, contrary to what Panofsky says (1953, p. 496, notes 327–6), must have had the same purpose as that of Willem van Scoten in 1399, to provide a deputy for a sick commander.

22 Leiden, Archives, Church Archives. 103: acquisition of a rent by Pieter van Scoten; 151: same reference to the rent; 153: 18 March 1443, sale of a parcel of land belonging to the capellany of P v S.; 168: 25 April 1444, surrenders the enjoyment of a house; 172: sells a house on 23 March 1445; 241 and 242: 1 July 1455, buys a plot of land; 243: 17 July 1455, rents a house; 661: 1 March 1454, sells a rent. Church Archives no. 298: Pieter van Scoten, commander, sells a plot of land belonging to the Haarlem commandery on 15 November 1467; Convent Archives: 1351, 1354 and 1471: sale of a plot of land by the commander dated 7 February 1466.

23 Allan, II 1870, pp. 271 and 285.

24 Dolleman, 1963.

25 I.e. three to four years. Such a length of time seems reasonable for a work of this size. However, we lack definite points of comparison. We realise the difficulty of specifying the actual time spent by the van Eycks on the *Mystic Lamb*. A rare instance of exactness is that of the *Last Supper* by Dieric Bouts, commissioned in 1464 and completed in 1468. But even in this case, we have no guarantee that the artist was not simultaneously maintaining a considerable output, which would have slowed down the completion of the commission from the Confraternity of the Holy Sacrament.

26 Wiersum and Cosquino de Bussy, 1927, p. 208:

'habet ecclesiam mediocrem pulchram ad latus ipsius domus...'

27 Cologne, 1961, no. 41.

28 Migne, XXI, cols. 536–7; Pardiac, 1886, p. 46.

29 Roze, II, p. 156.

30 Caesarius (ed. Stange), 1851 Bk. VII ch. IV, pp. 125–6. Mechel (1781) asserts that the painting commemorates the translation of the relics of St. John to Acre in 1252. I have been able to find no reference to any such event.

31 The relic is mentioned in the documents published by Driessen (1822–30) and dating from 1360 (I, no. LXV, pp. 225–9) and in a *vidimus* of 1477 of a bull of 1399 (II, pp. 815–20).

32 Emile Mâle (1958, p. 46) noted the importance accorded to the history of the relics by mentioning, in a quite different context, that the Haarlem commandery itself owned such relics.

33 The justification of the authenticity of the relics gathered by the Hospitallers in 1484 was published in a book by Caoursin in 1496. It was based on a story in Theodorus Daphonapata, according to which St. Luke and his disciples stole the saint's right arm from his tomb in Samaria and took it to Antioch.

34 H. van de Waal, in a paper read to the Society of Dutch Art Historians, had proposed the opposite view: that Geertgen's painting could not antedate the acquisition of the relics of St. John by the Hospitallers in 1484 (quoted in Amsterdam, 1958, p. 18). But he had not realised that the scene depicted in the painting was incompatible with the authenticity of the relics from Rhodes. Nevertheless, I am indebted to him for guiding my research on this point.

35 Roze, II, p. 156.

36 The *Breviarium Romanum* had already omitted the second martyrdom, that of the bones. It may seem surprising that the Hospitallers did not choose the theme of their patron saint's second feast, his nativity (24 June): but it would have been out of place, by reason of its joyful character, in an atmosphere of the Passion.

37 Lehrs no. 366; Geisberg, 1903, no. 299.

38 It should be noted that the face of this canon is remarkably similar to the portrait of Thomas à Kempis now in the Historical Museum in Zwolle (pl. 39). Both have the same eyes set deep in broad sockets, the same long, straight nose curving downward slightly at the tip, the same fairly pointed chin. The most notable difference lies in the lips, which are full in the Zwolle portrait whereas the Vienna painting depicts those of a toothless old man. It would be theoretically possible to imagine that Geertgen depicted the author of the *Imitation* shortly before his death in 1471 at the age of 91. To lend weight to this hypothesis, however, we should have to establish the existence of links between the canon of Agnietenberg and the commandery of St. John at Haarlem. As there is no trace of such links, it is more likely that the resemblances between the two portraits are purely coincidental.

39   Bibliothèque Royale, Brussels, MS. 9232. If links must be established between Geertgen and manuscript illumination, it will be from observations like this and not from the false assertion that the Milan painting was executed on parchment.

40   A manual on the use of just such a language of the hands was published in Italy as late as the seventeenth century (Bonifacio, 1616).

41   Winkler, 1960.

42   Ed. Brocquin, I, p. 203.

43   This gesture of homage is apparently shown in a fresco by Benozzo Gozzoli in the Campo Santo at Pisa, but oddly using the left hand. It is used again by Ghirlandaio in a painting in the Uffizi dated 1487.

44   Johannes von Hildesheim, Chapter 21 (Christern, 1963, p. 38). It is worth noting that in this text the author names the third king Caspar and the second Balthasar.

45   It is not yet certain where the negro King first appeared. The sculpted portal of the Church of St. Thibault in Thann is still cited, but the head of the Wise Man with negroid features seems to be a nineteenth-century restoration. Amongst paintings of the Cologne school, the panels in Linz by the Master of the Lyversberg *Passion*, dated 1463, should be singled out for special mention (Stange, V, fig. 84). It is significant that the following year, in the panel of the altarpiece from which he takes his name (Nuremberg, Germanisches Museum, Stange, V, fig. 91), the same master reverts to a white Balthasar: the tradition was not yet firmly established.

46   For the dating of the costumes, cf. catalogue entry.

47   Cf. W. Krönig, 1950. Engravings by the Master of *St. John the Baptist* (Lehrs 77) and by Master E.S. (Lehrs 149).

48   Krönig, 1950, pp. 197–8; Panofsky, 1953, p. 328.

49   Saintyves (*Vie de Gérard le Grand*, ch. XII) t. VII, p. 209.

50   Note that on this point—placing St. John's stay in the wilderness during his childhood—Geertgen does not follow St. Peter Chrysologus.

51   Ed. Brocquin, I, pp. 284–6. It goes without saying that this etymology of 'monachus' is pure fiction.

52   There is no reason to credit Hugo van der Goes with the invention of the formula: there are none of the characteristics of his work in the London painting. This is, however, the position adopted by Winkler, 1964, p. 148, following Baldass (1919).

53   Mâle, 1905, esp. pp. 122–3.

54   MS. 691. Byvanck, 1937, pl. IX, fig. 16.

55   Delaissé, 1968.

56   Cf. esp. Winkler, 1925, pl. 15.

57   It is found in the Cologne school (Master of the

Lyversberg *Passion*, Master of the *Holy Kindred*) as well as in the Nuremberg school (Pleydenwurff, Wolgemut).

58   Cf. esp. Albert and Paul Philippot, 1958, and van Schoute, 1970.

59   With the exception of Oettinger (1938), who has a less dogmatic view and prefers to see a parallel evolution of the two artists.

60   Germanisches National Museum in Nuremberg, *Adoration of the Magi* from the Lyversberg altarpiece.

61   As the pose of the Israelite in the *Gathering of the Manna* does not correspond exactly with that of van der Goes's Wise Man and Geertgen's Joseph of Arimathaea, it is plausible to suggest that there was another model, now lost.

62   Van der Goes has copied the posture of Christ's left arm and hand exactly, also the entire structure of the chest, with a somewhat inaccurate arrangement of the collar-bones.

63   The fact that Hugo van der Goes was asked to complete the *St. Hippolytus Triptych* and to appraise Bouts's Justice panel, left unfinished at his death, indicates that he was known to have close connections with the Louvain Master.

64   Riegl, 1902, pp. 75–87.

65   This identification has already been contemplated by Hoogewerff (ms. letter) and put forward by James Snyder (1960, p. 127). Moreover, it draws support from a comparison with the mediocre drawing in the Haarlem archives (pl. 196): although the two sets of features are not absolutely identical (in particular, the draughtsman has given the artist a squint and an absurdly large nose), the tilt of the head is so similar that the drawing might almost be a fanciful copy of the Vienna painting.

Notes to chapter VI

1   Between 1463 and 1480 production fluctuated between 2,250 and 2,500 brews. In 1480 it fell to 1,493, then remained between 1,300 and 1,600 until 1499. The worst year was naturally 1492–3, in which only 1,205 brews were recorded. Production took off again in 1499 with 4,383 brews. Cf. van Loenen, 1950.

2   Bruyn, 1963, who published these documents, drew from them the conclusion that Vrederic Hoon was an archaising artist. Such a deduction is all the more misguided as it can be easily shown that both conventions were being used concurrently in Westphalia at that same period. The Schöpfingen altarpiece, probably executed between 1453 and 1457 (Münster, 1952, nos. 24–8) depicts Christ standing outside the tomb, while Johann Koerbecke shows Him astride the sarcophagus in the Langenhorst altarpiece (*ib.* nos. 49–50). In his altarpiece of the *Resurrection* (*ib.* nos. 128–30), the Master of Liesborn also adopts the 'standing astride' pose; but an artist of his circle, perhaps even of his workshop, the painter of the Vellern altarpiece (*ib.* nos. 173–82), prefers the 'outside the tomb' stance.

3   Kramm (II, 1859, p. 788), in his entry on Jacob Janszoon, followed the quotation from van Mander by the date 1474 in brackets. This is repeated without comment by Hoogewerff (II, 1937, p. 220), who takes it to be the date of the Porters' painting. In fact, Kramm relies solely on van Mander and his commentator de Jongh, neither of whom gives any such date. Moreover, the dates in brackets in all Kramm's entries refer to the publication dates of the texts quoted; here it should be that of van Mander's, 1604. The mistake is not rectified in the errata. However, one can understand how it may have occurred; owing to a mistaken transcription of notes, the generally accepted date of birth of Jan Mostaert, mentioned two lines above in the same sentence, was inadvertently substituted for that of the publication date of van Mander's book.

4   Cf. de Jongh, 1764, pp. 162–3. The commentator states that the artist portrayed himself in the guise of St. John the Evangelist in the Porters' painting. It seems to me rather unusual for an artist to choose so important a character to bear his own features. The paintings in which one can plausibly discern artists' self-portraits, in the northern Netherlands, indicate that they were relegated to secondary characters. It is therefore probable that the 'self-portraiture' of the engraving given by de Jongh was largely due to wishful thinking on his part.

5   The whole composition is only known through a copy formerly in the Müller collection in Berlin (Schöne, 1938, pl. 87d), but two fragments of a version by a follower of Bouts are now in the Louvre and at Berlin (*ib.* pl. 86).

6   Jean Gerson, *Consideration of St. Joseph*, quoted by Schapiro, 1945, p. 185.

7   The only difficulty in accepting that the Master of the Brunswick *Diptych* was trained by the Master of the *Holy Kindred* lies in his delicate, smooth technique, which the latter never seems to have possessed.

8   Boon, 1966, p. 63.

9   Cohen, 1914.

10   The theme of the Virgin beneath a canopy in the work of the Tournai school has been studied particularly by Rolland, 1932.

11   Kress collection, Washington, National Gallery.

12   Regteren Altena, 1966, p. 77, note 6; cf. also Catalogue, below.

13   Regteren Altena, 1959, p. 172.

14   Cf. Winkler, 1925, pp. 79–82 and Smital's facsimile, 1930.

15   It is difficult to follow J. Q. van Regteren Altena's suggestion (1974) that the work of Mouwerijn and Claes should be seen in a *Tree of Jesse* in the Twenthe Rijksmuseum; the format of the painting seems to be too high for the predella of the retable of the high altar of St. Bavo, and the style of the painting seems closer to Cornelys Buys, and to belong to a later generation than that of Mouwerijn and Claes.

16   Hoogewerff, II, 1937, pp. 78–81. Schöne's attributions (1937, p. 175, note 5) are unacceptable. Similarly, the *Virgin and Child* in the Howard Heath

collection, already associated with the Master of the *Tiburtine Sibyl* by Valentiner in 1914, is too like Dieric Bouts to be by him.

17 Accounts of the town for 1480, folio 165 *v.* Another tempting identification is with Jacob Willemsz, mentioned in 1470 (register of movements no. 348, folio 105 *v.*), 1482 (town accounts folio 49) and in 1483 (*ib.* folio 51, payment of taxes in the name of himself, his wife and child); in 1485 he received a commission for the first panel of the high altar of St. Bavo (van der Willigen 1866, p. 49), which did not satisfy the churchwardens. After this setback, a departure for Louvain would be plausible. But in 1490 a Jacob Willemsz drew interest on a rent, and his widow and daughter are mentioned in 1493 (town register folio 231). In the same year Jacquet Englebert, who had begun his apprenticeship with him, was taken on in Tournai by Philippe Truffin (Renders, 1931, p. 133). Jacob Willemsz thus seems to have died in 1493, and not in 1487 like 'Joes Wilen Valcx'. The text concerning the latter is the deed registered on folios 199 and 200 of register 7774 of the municipal archives of Louvain (*Greffes scabinaux*) published by van Even, 1867, pp. 457–8.

18 It did not seem worthwhile, in the context of the present work, to analyse the works of the Master of Alkmaar. His earliest work is dated 1504, but already shows new features. Cf. Hoogewerff, II, 1937, pp. 346–88. J. Bruyn (1966) has produced an important study of commissions from the Abbey of Egmont at the beginning of the sixteenth century.

Notes to chapter VII

1 The only overall study of the problem is that in Hoogewerff, II, 1937, and the brief remarks found in Gerson, 1950, and van Gelder, 1946.

2 Cf. Chapter I, B.

3 The usable sources consist mainly of a very incomplete series of account books of the Oude Kerk, now in the municipal archives.

4 Book of Hours in Latin MS 21.696 Byvanck, 1937, p. 124.

5 For the Brussels Book of Hours, cf. Byvanck, 1937, p. 74.

6 Byvanck, 1937, pp. 142–3.

7 Byvanck, 1937, p. 152.

8 Byvanck, 1937, pp. 99–103.

9 For the woodcut illustrations by the Master of the *Virgo inter Virgines*, cf. Schretlen, 1925, pp. 38–42, and Boon, 1963, who lists the books.

10 The engravings produced at Antwerp for Gerard Leu, thought by Schretlen (1925, p. 36) to be by the Master of the *Virgo inter Virgines*, are more likely to be the work of an imitator (Boon, 1963, p. 13).

11 Luttervelt, 1952.

12 Boon, 1963, pp. 18–21.

13 Pieter de Maelre: Haarlem, episcopal archives, 590, folio 17 *v.*; Delft, Oude Kerk 559 folio 77 (1467) and 561 folio 217 (1495). Dirc Jansz: Oude Kerk 560 folio 16 (1474), 561, folio 216 *v.*, 217, 218, 219, 220 and 221 (1495). Could Dirc Jansz be the same as the Diric Jan mentioned at Haarlem in 1471 (municipal accounts, 1471, folio 41)?

14 Nevertheless, this would confirm a fairly late dating for the earliest known works, since the *Portinari Triptych* was executed around 1470 (Panofsky, I, 1953, note 333, p. 499).

15 Delaissé, 1968.

16 Mosmans is supposed to have discovered that the date of Bosch's birth could be fixed exactly as 2 October 1453 (Cf. *Gazette des Beaux-Arts* 1959, *Chronique des Arts*, p. 13). His arguments seem to be very weak, however, and based solely on the interpretation of a doubtful inscription on a painting in a private collection in Zurich (Gerlach, 1968, p. 110).

17 Tolnay, 1965, p. 348.

18 One may also cite the Master of Moulins, who is by no means proved to have borrowed this treatment of flesh from van der Goes. (Cf. Châtelet, 1962).

19 Friedländer, X, 1932.

20 Friedländer, X, 1932.

21 Opmeer, 1611, folio 406 *v.*; van Vaernewijk, 1568, p. 119; de Jongh, 1764, p. 72.

22 Walvis, II, 1714, pp. 9, 19 and 23.

23 It is a little surprising, however, to come across a reference in 1515, at Gouda, to 'Jacob Hugensz de scilder', dean of the Guild of St. Luke. One can imagine a copyist's error, transposing the two Christian names. But we cannot exclude the possibility of the reverse: a confusion on Opmeer's part, due to the proximity of the two names.

24 Lippmann, 1898.

25 Hind, II, 1953, p. 590.

26 For the attribution of the Boccaccio engravings to Philippe de Mazerolles, cf. Châtelet, 1963.

27 Obreen, III, 1877–90, pp. 1–2.

28 Muller, 1880, and Swillens, 1925.

29 He had acquired it for life in 1459 from Jacob van Gaesbeck. It is now a ruin and the documents on its original condition are few and imprecise.

30 For the patronage of David of Burgundy, cf. Zilverberg, 1951, who is nevertheless very brief on the topic.

31 Boon, 1961.

32 Ring, 1939, and Boon, 1940.

33 Cf. the similar case of Alart du Hamel, who signed his engravings 'bosche' for 's Hertogenbosch.

34 It is surprising that nothing has been made of the diversity of the engravings and that recent authors (de Vries, Dubbe) have tried to identify the engraver without taking this into account.

35 Cf. de Vries, 1954 and 1958, and Dubbe, 1970.

36 Could the A be the initial letter of his father's Christian name?

37 The theory can draw some support from the fact that Jan van den Mijnnesten seems, from entries in the archives, to have been a man of consequence who enjoyed a certain amount of authority. It should also be noted that one of his sons was a goldsmith.

38 It is pointless to assume a date of birth in 1425 as suggested by de Vries.

39 For Adrien van Wesel, see Swillens, 1948, and Leeuwenberg, 1948.

40 Cf. Chapter VI above.

41 The Ghent illuminator, Lievin van Lathem, settled in Antwerp in 1462 and married the daughter of Jacob Meyster, a native of Amsterdam (Schryver, 1969, p. 43, nos. 60 and 61; Rombouts and Lerius, I, 1872, p. 11). Jorys Jan Jansson de Hollandere is mentioned there in 1461 and 1473 (Lavalleye, 1936, pp. 32–3).

42 Valentiner, 1955. Criticisms have been offered with little justification by Martin Davies (London, National Gallery, 1955) and Wittmann, 1955.

43 Hypothesis suggested by word of mouth to A. Delen (Antwerp, Musée Royal des Beaux-Arts 1948, p. 168), who subsequently developed it himself (1955). P. Vanaise (1966) has proposed, apparently correctly, that the production of two different artists should be distinguished in the work brought together under the name of this master.

44 V. N. Volskaja, 1960 has suggested an identification of this painter with Passcier van der Mersch, apprenticed to Memling in 1483.

45 The possible stay of Hugo Jacobsz at Ghent should, however, be borne in mind (cf. VII above).

46 Arnoul de Cats in 1424, Philippe Truffin of Utrecht in 1495 and Jacquet Englebert of Haarlem in 1493, cf. Renders, I, 1931, p. 152.

47 The Utrecht origin of Willem Vrelant is perhaps not as certain as has been believed. But there are Warenbout van Hutrecht (1477), Robout van Utrecht (1475–81), Cornelis Rineltou (1477–88), Jacob van Huten Broucke (1463–83). Cf. Weale, 1872–3, pp. 267–317.

48 The *Crucifixion* in New York and the *Carrying of the Cross* in Budapest.

49 Münster, 1952 and Stange, VI, 1954.

50 Münster, 1937 (Niessen).

51 Münster, 1952; debatable interpretation by Schabacker, 1975.

52 Münster, 1952 no. 28.

53 Ring, 1939, pp. 30–1 (Utrecht); Busch, 1939 and 1940, no. 40 (Notke).

54 Busch, 1940, pp. 77–8 and Stange, VI, 1954, pp. 83–6.

55 Cf. Châtelet, 1975.

56 The paintings discovered recently on the back of the chest of the high altar are in a typically Dutch style, even though the artist was second-rate.

57 Exhibition catalogue 1961 with earlier bibliography.

58 Pitt, 1891 and Solms-Laubach, 1935–6. Theory opposed by Hotz, 1953 and 1956, who suggests an identification with Nicolas Nievergalt of Worms, rightly criticised by Stange, 1958, pp. 44–5 no. 3. Strocka, 1970 proposes the name of Wolfgang Peurer, which appears on a drawing which must have belonged to Dürer; but this work, while similar to that of the master, lacks its force. It could be a copy of one of his creations or the work of one of his followers.

59 Châtelet-Thuillier, 1963, p. 38. Arnoul de Cats is only known up to 1434, and not 1458 as I wrote in 1963, repeating an error of Canon Requin's (cf. Sterling, 1966). But this, in my opinion, does not exclude the possibility of his being identified with the Master of the *Annunciation* of Aix-la-Chapelle as the altarpiece seems to have been begun for a donor other than Corpici and may well have been essentially complete before 1440 (cf. Grete Ring, 1949, nos 91, p. 205, who points out the presence of the arms of the de Maillé family.)

60 In Italy, the altarpiece of *St. John the Baptist* (Genoa, Palazzo Bianco) and that of the *Annunciation* (Milan, Museo Poldi Pezzoli), cf. Friedländer, 1927–8; perhaps also the Master of the *Adoration of the Magi* in Turin (*ib.*). In Spain, the painter of the Triptych of the *Disputacion Provincial* at Avila (Boon, 1968), the altarpieces of Palencia and Burgos attributed to Joest van Calcar (Friedländer, IX, 1935, pp. 10–11 and Chandler R. Post, 1942). In Portugal, the great altarpiece of the Se d'Evora, attributed to a follower of Gerard David, could be by a Dutchman (Friedländer, 1935; Reis Santos, 1953, pp. 67–72; Friedländer, IVa, 1969, add. 146).

61 Reynaldo dos Santos, 1957, p. 57 and pl. LX.

Notes to chapter VIII

1 Amsterdam, 1958, p. 12 and p. 8 of the English translation of the prefaces.

2 Cf. Pirenne's article in the catalogue of the 1967 's Hertogenbosch exhibition (Bijdragen, pp. 42–7). At present there is no general survey of 's Hertogenbosch in the fifteenth century.

3 Cf. Post, 1968, esp. pp. 369–70, 391–8 and 592–6.

4 Cf. Swillens, 1948 and Leeuwenberg, 1967.

5 Leeuwenberg, 1967.

6 The *Adoration of the Magi* in the Johnson collection (Philadelphia Museum of Art) is inspired by a drawing in Berlin (*35*), and a group of figures in the *Haywain* triptych (Madrid, Prado and Escurial) adopts the types found in the *Carrying of the Cross* in Budapest (*22*).

7 Particularly remarkable is the absence of any borrowing from Rogier van der Weyden. In fact, apart from the use of a figure from the *Garden of Love* by Master ES to create the unforgettable beggar on the reverse of the wings of the *Haywain* and the painting in the Boymans Museum, and some possible borrowings from the engravings of the *Ars Moriendi* for the *Seven Deadly Sins* in the Prado, there is hardly anything worth mentioning apart from the inspiration for the paintings of Heaven and Hell (Venice, Doge's Palace) among the paintings of Bosch (Châtelet, 1965).

8 Cf. V above.

9 Cf. V above.

10 Bosch's technique aims at neither the finish nor the delicacy of south Netherlandish painters, and is much closer, by reason of its expressiveness, to the manner of the painters of the 'rustic' tradition, e.g. the Master of the *Virgo inter Virgines*.

11 Unfortunately, little is known about the activities of chambers of rhetoric in the fifteenth century, but five are mentioned as existing in 's Hertogenbosch alone. Only M. Gauffreteau-Sévy (1965) has considered the possibility of links between Bosch and these societies, just as she has rightly stressed the connection between Bosch and the *Devotio Moderna* movement, another feature shared with the northern Netherlands. For *Elkerlyck*, cf. Endepols, 1932.

12 Cf. Lyna, 1946–7 and Panofsky, 1953, pp. 91–129.

13 The importance of the writings of Ludolph the Carthusian for an understanding of Hugo van der Goes has not yet been pointed out, to my knowledge. Nevertheless, the commentaries on the *Nativity* and the *Adoration of the Shepherds* are of particular help in clarifying the conception of the *Portinari Triptych*, not only as regards the choice of certain details but also as regards its underlying significance. I hope to be able to devote a study to this topic.

Catalogue

This catalogue does not claim to be exhaustive and is not intended as a list of all known fifteenth-century paintings from the northern Netherlands. It has been devised principally to facilitate the reading of the main text by bringing together all complementary information on the works examined, wherever that information was not relevant to the general argument. It also seemed useful to include here some elements foreign to the northern Netherlands, wherever acquaintance with and understanding of them were necessary for a grasp of the arguments put forward (particularly the work attributable to Master H).

Dimensions are given in centimetres, the first figure denoting the height, the second the width.

Painter working at Utrecht *c.* 1363

1 Epitaph of Canon Hendrik van Rijn
Antwerp, Musée Royal des Beaux-Arts (Pl. 1)

At the bottom of the panel is an inscription which mentions the date of death of the canon depicted in prayer at the foot of the Cross (1363). As there is no discernible trace that this text has been overpainted, or added within a space left for this purpose, we may take it as contemporary with, or very slightly later than, the death of the man who commissioned it. The work thus constitutes one of the earliest examples of Netherlandish painting (from the north or the south), being earlier than the *Altarpiece of the Tanners* (Bruges, Church of Saint-Sauveur) and the *Scenes from the life of the Virgin* (Brussels, Musée Royal des Beaux-Arts). For this very reason it is difficult to situate and interpret. The representation of the sun and the moon on either side of the Cross seems quite rare in works of this period; it appears in the Duke of Berry's *Belles Heures de Notre Dame* (Paris, Bibliothèque Nationale, MS. Lat. 3093, p. 209). The Virgin carrying a book at the foot of the Cross is also an unusual theme, of which an example,

slightly later, can be cited in the Crucifixion from the *Friedberg Altarpiece* (middle Rhine) in the Darmstadt Museum. The nailing of Christ's feet side by side with two nails also occurs in the picture by Master Theodoric at Karlstein and in the *Holy Trinity of Vratislav*.

Dimensions:	Wood. 150 × 146.
Inscription:	'Anno domini M° CCC° LXIII° in crastino sancti Bonifacii et socior (um) eius, obiit dominus Henricus de Reno, hui (us) eccl (es) ie prepositus et archidiaconus istiusque altaris fundator. Orate pro eo.'
Provenance:	Church of St. John at Utrecht (and not the cathedral, as Panofsky states incorrectly); collection of the Chevalier van Ertborn (bequeathed to the city of Antwerp in 1841).
Catalogue:	Antwerp, 1948 (Delen) no. 519.
Literature:	Hoogewerff, I, 1936, p. 98–102; Sterling, 1938, p. 25 and fig. 15; Gerson, 1950, p. 7–8; Panofsky, 1953, p. 36.

Utrecht painter (?), *c.* 1375–80

2 Epitaph of the lords of Montfoort (Pl. 2)
Amsterdam, Rijksmuseum

The inscription along the bottom of the panel only concerns the first three lords, killed in 1345 during an expedition against the Frisians.

The blank line was probably intended to receive the obit of the last. The first three donors are Jan I, burgrave of Montfoort, Roelof de Rover, lord of Heulensteyn, great-uncle of the preceding, and Willem de Rover de Montfoort, his uncle. Obreen (1877–90) established that the fourth was probably Hendrick de Rover van Montfoort Willemsz, i.e. the son of the third and the cousin of the first, who is mentioned between 1375 an 1377. This identification draws support from the fact that the artist has placed the last two lords in such a way as to bring them together, and that they have facial resemblances which are noticeable even in the present condition of the painting. The epitaph must have been commissioned by the youngest of the Montfoorts; it is thus hardly possible to date it 1375–80 at the earliest. The youthful appearance of the donor prevents us from bringing this date forward much more: his father having died in 1345, Hendrick de Rover van Montfoort was by that time already 30 years old. An analysis of such a work must take account of the

considerable wear suffered by the original materials and of the extent of retouching, which has certainly dulled the execution.

Dimensions:	Wood. 69 × 142.
Inscription:	Along the bottom of the painting: 'Int jaer ons heeren dusent drie hondert vijf en veertich op sante cosmas en damianus dach doe bleven doot op die vriezen bij grave willem van heynegouwen van hollant van zelant en heer van vrieslant heer jan van montfoorde met veel hare magen vrienden en onderhebben den.', followed by a later reference to a restoration 'bidt voor haer allen zielen dit is verlicht anno 1608'. A similar reference also appears on the steps of the Virgin's throne: 'voor de derde maal verlicht 1770'.
Provenance:	altarpiece of the Virgin from the Sint-Janskerk at Linschoten; found in the farm at Heulesteyn between Linschoten and Montfoort; bequeathed to the Rijksmuseum in 1884 by Dr. H. van der Lee.
Exhibition:	Amsterdam, 1958, n° I.
Literature:	Obreen, 1877–90, VI, p. 57–81; Hoogewerff, I, 1936, p. 92; Panofsky, 1953, p. 93.

Utrecht painter, *c.* 1410 (?)

3 Christ on the Cross, with the Virgin, St. John the Evangelist and St. Margaret (Pl. 3)
Utrecht, cathedral, second chapel of the north aisle (known as the chapel of Guy of Avesnes)

Placed beneath a Gothic arcade, creating the illusion of a recess, the ensemble probably originally adorned an altar. According to Haslinghuis and Peeters (1965, p. 258) this chapel contained altars dedicated to St. Laurence, St. Barbara and St. Margaret (mentioned for the first time in the known documents in 1438). The ensemble contains not only the scene of the Crucifixion, but also six figures of saints on the soffit of the arch (two bishops, two female saints, a young mounted saint, a sixth unidentifiable); they are too badly worn to be identified with precision, but have very elegant outlines still marked by the International style. The main fresco is itself often misted over, and there is no indication on photographs that behind the figures are mountains

152

which, as it were, define the space in the lower part of the red background.

The date of *c.* 1430–40, suggested by Hoogewerff, seems to me to be clearly too late; and the attribution to the miniaturist known as the Master of Zweder van Culemborgh, due to Byvanck, seems unfounded. The style of the figures—the manner in which they are drawn out and curved—is still so influenced by the fourteenth century that it is difficult to date the execution much later than the first years of the fifteenth century. The fillet around St. Margaret's head might suggest a later date, but an example from as early as 1401–2 can be cited from a Parisian illumination (Paris, Bibliothèque Nationale, MS. Fr. 12.420; Meiss, 1967, fig. 287). The tautness of the arms of the Crucified Christ and the tilt of his head towards the left have an equivalent—in a completely different technique—in the *Wildungen Altarpiece* by Conrad of Soest, dated 1404. All things considered, a date of *c.* 1410 does not seem improbable.

Fresco: Arch, 160 × 165.
Literature: Por, 1929; Byvanck, 1930, p. 139, note 3; Hoogewerff, I, 1936, p. 349–54; Ozinga, 1953, p. 27 and pl. 8 and 9; Haslinghuis and Peeters, 1965, p. 258 and 347–348.

Painter working in Guelders, first quarter of the fifteenth century

4   Altarpiece
Zutphen, Church of St. Walburga

153

In the middle of the altarpiece there must have been a carved crucifix, probably in wood, standing in the case which survives and is closed by two shutters. On the inside of this case are painted the figures of the Virgin and St. John the Evangelist. On the shutters are Mary Magdalene and Mary Cleophas (or Mary Salome), who rarely appear like this as isolated characters complementing a Crucifixion scene.

The figure types show a direct link with the International style. Hoogewerff compared them with a Cologne altarpiece in the Wallraf-Richartz Museum in Cologne, but many other comparisons could be suggested. One thinks especially of the *Three Marys at the Tomb* attributed to Hubert van Eyck (Rotterdam, Boymans-van Beuningen Museum), in which the female figures have similar proportions (with heads which are remarkably small and delicate for their bodies) and also outlines comparable in the abundance of their drapery, with a strong vertical rhythm. The handling seems very coarse, however, even allowing for the overpainting, which seems to have been extensive. This altarpiece should thus probably be seen as a reflection of more important and original creations, executed rather mechanically in a provincial workshop.

The Church of St. Walburga in Zutphen also contains a large set of frescoes, now unfortunately badly damaged. Some of them, as Hoogewerff has already rightly pointed out, have an obvious affinity with the altarpiece. Three inscriptions give *termini post* and *ante quos* for one of them, depicting four saints, which is in a style relatively close to that of the work under discussion (Hoogewerff, I, fig. 85); they are funerary inscriptions relating to three different persons, probably those who commissioned the work. The earliest inscription dates from 1405, the latest from 1432. The altarpiece should probably also be dated within these limits.

Dimensions: Wood (oak). Centrepanel 210 × 92; shutters 210 × 89.
History: on loan for a time to the Rijksmuseum, Amsterdam.
Literature: Dülberg, 1929, p. 17; Hoogewerff, I, 1936, p. 189–93 and 197.

Jean Malouel

Born at Nijmegen (?) *c.* 1365–70, died at Dijon 12 (?) March 1415

Known in France from 1396, Jean Malouel is certainly identical with Jean, the son of Willem Maelwael, who in 1387 at Nijmegen received a payment due to his father. His career at the court of the dukes of Burgundy, from 1397 onwards, did not cause him to abandon his interests at Nijmegen; he returned there as late as 1413, between 1 September and 5 December, to settle problems of inheritance. He took an interest in the training of his nephews, Herman and Jacquemin of Limburg, whom he placed with a goldsmith in Paris in 1400.

Literature: Dehaisnes, 1886; Monget, 1896–1905; Gorissen, 1954 (transcribes all known archive references) and 1957; Sterling, 1959.

5   Quadriptych of the Life of Jesus (Pls. 8–13)
Antwerp, Mayer van den Bergh Museum, and Baltimore, Walters Art Gallery

The belief that this quadriptych, now split up, came from the Chartreuse of Champmol rests only on presumptions and oral tradition. The known inventories make no mention of it, nor has any documentary reference to it been discovered. The Antwerp panels were acquired at the Bartholomey sale by the Parisian collector Micheli. In the catalogue of this sale, in 1849, they appear under a single number (73) with no mention of provenance, but many items from this collection are known to have come from the Charterhouse. As for the Baltimore panels, when selling them to Henry Walters in 1919, Arnold Seligman—assured him that they had been in the Dijon monastery. According to him, Louis XV had authorised his chaplain, Cardinal Charles-Antoine de la Roche-Aymon, to remove them from the Charterhouse. The cardinal allegedly kept them at his château of Champigny-les-Vitraux (Indre et Loire) and bequeathed them to Charles-Guillaume de la Roche Aymon (d. 1861). They then passed into the Cuvillier collection in Niort. Such exact information is difficult to invent.

The small dimensions of the quadriptych indicate that it was either intended as a portable altarpiece or as decoration for a small oratory, like that of the dukes at the Charterhouse of Champmol. The unusual four-part construction has suggested a set of shutters for enclosing a sculpture. However, the reconstruction of the original state, grouping from left to right on the open quadriptych the *Annunciation*, the *Nativity*, the *Crucifixion* and the *Resurrection*—established by Panofsky (Spencer, 1940)— is most satisfactory. It is confirmed by the symmetrical composition of the inner panels, which each have the same segmental view into heaven in the upper part.

Panofsky (1953) has shown that the scenes were chosen to create a 'contrasting correlation' between the episodes of the Childhood and of the Passion. This idea is further supported by the presence on the two outer panels of God the Father carrying a book with the inscription 'alpha and omega'. The parallelism is emphasised by the confrontation of the *Annunciation* and the *Resurrection*, representing the descent from and ascent to heaven, and of the *Nativity* and the *Crucifixion*, linking the two limits of Christ's human existence. Philippe Verdier (Baltimore, 1962) has attempted to explain the choice and association of the *Baptism of Christ* and the *St. Christopher* on the reverse of the panels. In his view, St. Christopher is taken as a symbol of the baptism of the New Testament, whereas St. John the Baptist, seen as the last prophet, represents the Old Law. Nevertheless, the baptism scene may simply have been chosen to depict the patron saint of John the Fearless. In this case the presence of St. Christopher may reflect a special devotion of the duke's or a cult established in one of his residences for which the altarpiece was originally intended. In the 1404 inventory of Philip the Bold (Dehaisnes, 1886, II, p. 840) mention is made of 'ung autre grant tableau de bois long, sur le carré à ung saint Christofle').

Panofsky has pointed out the uncommonness, at this date in the North, and the Italian origins of the Virgin of the Annunciation with her hands crossed on her breast. He has also pointed out that it was rare for depictions of the Crucifixion to evoke the despair of Christ abandoned by God (the phylactery bears the inscription 'eloy lamazabatani'). This detail reveals a deliberate insistence on the theme of Christ taking on the burden of humanity and reacting on the Cross like a suffering man. Human concerns are also stressed, not without a certain humour, by the trivial details of the Nativity: the servant-girl wearing an apron, the table with the pottery utensils, and above all St. Joseph cutting up his hose to make breeches for Jesus (J. de Coo, 1958, 1960, 1965 and 1965 B has identified and studied this curious scene, connected with the veneration of the relics

190

known as 'the breeches of St. Joseph' at Aix-la-Chapelle). Such spontaneous picturesqueness, also evident in the rivers of the *Baptism of Christ* and of the *St. Christopher* with all their fauna, is found only in the northern Netherlands and has scarcely a more noticeable equivalent than in the *Hours of Catherine of Cleves.*

By comparison with the *Martyrdom of St. Denis* and even with the *Small Tondo*, the modelling in these compositions may seem surprisingly soft. This can be explained partly by the size of the panels and partly by the adoption of a Gothic manner, which does not recur with this artist: it is an imitation of the style of Jean de Beaumetz, discovered by Charles Sterling (1955). The Baltimore *Christ on the Cross* immediately recalls that of the painting now in the Louvre. The outlines of the Virgin and St. John also imitate the flowing rhythm of those in the paintings from the cells of the Carthusians. One may even wonder if the rare Italianate traces in the quadriptych, noted by Panofsky, do not reflect an Avignon influence, but one transmitted by the work of Beaumetz and already less directly Italian.

Dimensions: Each panel with original frame 38 × 26.5 (painted area about 33 × 21).
Provenance: Antwerp: Bartholomey collection, sold Paris 15 March 1849, lot 73; Micheli collection: acquired from the latter by Mayer van den Bergh. Baltimore: Charterhouse of Champmol; passed into the collection of Charles-Antoine de la Roche-Aymon, cardinal from 1772, by the gift of Louis XV; kept at the château of Champigny-les-Vitraux; collection of Charles-Guillaume de la Roche-Aymon; Cuvillier collection, Niort; Arnold Seligman, New York; acquired from the latter in 1919 by the Walters Art Gallery.
Exhibitions: Antwerp: Antwerp (Sterling), 1930, no. 31; London, 1932, no. 17; Paris, 1937, no. 6; Paris, 1950, no. 10; Dijon, 1951, no. 2; Amsterdam, 1951, no. 28; Brussels, 1951, no. 2; Vienna, 1962, no. 12 (Heinz). Baltimore: Paris, 1904 (not in catalogue); Detroit, 1960, no. 2 (Folie); Baltimore, 1962, no. 24 (Verdier).
Literature: Bouchot, 1905, no. XX; de Mont, 1905, p. 15–16; Reinach, 1907, p. 66, 85, 492 and 599; Conway, 1921, p. 113; Michel, 1924, p. 41–2 and 58; Fierens-Gevaert, 1927, p. 32 (studio of Broederlam); Weese, 1927, p. 93 (Broederlam); Lemoisne, 1931, p. 52 (Franco-Burgundian); Schrade, 1932, p. 190–3; Baldass, 1934, p. 379 (studio of Broederlam); Dupont, 1937, p. 14; Dimier, 1938, p. 173 (rejects attribution to Broederlam); Réau, 1939, p. 12 (Franco-Flemish at Paris); Spencer, 1940, p. 30 (Panofsky's reconstruction); Sterling-Jacques, 1942, p. 24 and no. A 26, p. 6 (Hainault studio); Ring, 1949, nos. 19 and 20 (more Flemish than Franco-Flemish); Schaefer, 1949, p. 30–1 (close to Broederlam); Panofsky, 1953, p. 93–5, 97 and 127 (Guelders); Axters, III, 1956, p. 404–5; de Coo,

1958, p. 186–98; de Coo, 1960, p. 222–8; Roques, 1963, p. 46, 56, 61–2; de Coo, 1965, p. 144–84; de Coo, 1965, p. 362, no. 283; Antwerp, Mayer van den Bergh, 1966, no. 374, p. 110–5 (de Coo).

6   Christ on the Cross and the Martyrdom of St. Denis (Pls. 4 & 5)
Paris, Musée du Louvre

154

The problem of Malouel's share in the execution of the work has been examined above (p. 15). The altarpiece was intended for one of the six altars consecrated in March 1389 at the Charterhouse of Champmol (Monget 1896–1905, I, p. 194–5). It was thus one of the five altarpieces commissioned from Malouel in 1398 (id. I, p. 295; Gorissen, 1954, p. 199). Subsequently it must have been transferred to one of the two altars of the lay-brothers' choir, the other receiving the painting now in the Louvre, *Christ on the Cross with the Martyrdom of St. George*, with a similar scheme. Both were replaced in the eighteenth century by two paintings by Carle van Loo with the same subjects, now in the Dijon Museum (Monget, 1896–1905, III, p. 83). This explains why neither is mentioned in the Revolutionary inventory. There is nothing surprising in the fact that the *Martyrdom of St. Denis* had still not been completed 17 years after being commissioned. The accounts show that Malouel was constantly occupied on other tasks—painting of the *Well of Moses*, painting of the monastery parlour, etc.—and could thus only make slow progress. The gold necessary for the background was only obtained in 1402 (Dehaisnes, 1886, II, p. 787; Gorissen, 1954, no. 82) and was used by Herman de Couloingne, 'peintre et ouvrier de dorer à plat', both for Sluter's *Crucifixion* and the altarpieces. Philip the Bold died in 1404: Malouel does not seem to have resumed work at the Charterhouse until 1406 at the earliest. In 1410 he was engaged on the tomb of Philip the Bold. It is not until 1411 that a text, by mentioning the 'grands et notables ouvraiges mis sus et ordonnés estre fais en l'église des Chartreux de Champmol' (Monget, 1898, II, p. 4; Gorissen, 1954, no. 96), makes a possible fresh reference to work on the altarpieces.

Moreover, the texts of 1402–3 concerning the gilding are essential to an understanding of the work. The methods of fifteenth-century painters required that the general plan of the composition should be sketched out before the application of gilding to the background, all the areas that were to be painted being left blank. In the case of the *Martyrdom of St. Denis*, the entire composition must be considered as invented by Malouel around 1402. The intervention of Bellechose to 'complete' the

painting in 1416, even allowing that the work had not progressed far, can thus only have altered the handling, modelling or palette.

Dimensions: Wood transferred to canvas in 1852, 166 × 211.
Provenance: Charterhouse of Champmol; Bartholomey collection, Dijon, sold Paris 15 December 1849, lot 1 (as Simone Memmi!); acquired by Frédéric Reiset and presented by him to the Louvre in 1863.
Exhibition: Paris, 1904, no. 16.
Literature: Prost 1891, p. 25; Champeaux 1898, p. 130–6; Bouchot, 1904, p. 155–61; Bouchot, 1905, B, no. XIII; Durrieu, 1907, p. 148–9 and 154; Lemoisne, 1929, p. 8; Lemoisne, 1931, p. 42; Dimier, 1936, p. 208–10; Sterling, 1938, p. 38–9 and notes 41–2 (Bellechose); Ring, 1949, no. 54, p. 198–9 (Bellechose); Panofsky, 1953, p. 83–4 (Malouel completed by Bellechose); Sterling, 1955, p. 62–8; Reynaud, 1961; Laclotte 1961, p. 287–8; Châtelet-Thuillier, 1963, p. 15 and 18 (Malouel); Sterling-Adhémar, 1965, no. 11 (Bellechose).

7   Pietà known as the Small Tondo (Pl. 7)
Paris, Musée du Louvre

There is no documentary evidence for the Burgundian provenance of this panel, whose history remains unknown before its appearance on the Parisian market at the beginning of this century. It has thus sometimes been ascribed to the Champmol workshops, and sometimes to those of the capital.

An important element in its appreciation is provided by a painting formerly in the Berstl collection and now in the Brussels Museum. Charles Sterling (1941) and Georg Troescher (1966) have both seen this work as the source of the one in the Louvre. It seems difficult, however, not to reverse the relationship. The style of the Brussels painting is indeed clumsy, both in the uncertain balancing of the masses and in the extraordinary and unjustifiable diversity in the proportions of the figures. The elements which recur in the *Small Tondo*, the heads of St. John the Evangelist, Nicodemus and Joseph of Arimathaea, are handled heavily and with a superficial realism closer to the spirit of the *St. George Altarpiece* (Sterling-Adhémar, 1965, no. 14). On the other hand, all the other components of the painting can be found in the Louvre's: the Virgin, Mary Magdalene (whose face has been copied in reverse), even Christ himself. The Brussels painter has even oddly borrowed the style of Joseph of Arimathaea's cloak from the *Small Tondo*—in which it looks like a fur-lined coat—for the garments of the angels and of Mary Magdalene, for which it is inappropriate.

The Brussels painting, as Charles Sterling has remarked (1942, p. 79–80, note 32), could come from the Charterhouse of Champmol as it includes a kneeling Carthusian donor, like the *St. George Altarpiece* and the two known paintings by Jean de Beaumetz (Sterling, 1955). The correspondences between the two works, though not justifying a categorical assertion, thus make it probable that the *Small Tondo* had a Burgundian origin and was perhaps even in the Charterhouse of Champmol.

Dimensions:	Wood (walnut?). Frame and panel are of a piece and cut from a single block. Diameter: 22.8 (painted area 17). On the reverse are painted the three nails and the crown of thorns on a red ground.
Ownership:	Camille Benoit collection; presented by M. Fenaille in 1918.
Exhibitions:	Paris, 1950, no. 12; Amsterdam, 1951, no. 291; Brussels, 1951, no. 4; Vienna, 1962, no. 18; Hamburg, 1969, no. 5.
Literature:	Durrieu, 1918–19, p. 63; Brière, 1919, p. 232; Fierens-Gevaert, 1927, p. 33; Lemoisne, 1929, p. 5 (Paris); Lemoisne, 1931, p. 58 (id.); Sterling, 1938, p. 58 (close to the *Martyrdom of St. Denis*); Sterling-Jacques, 1942, no. A, no. 29, p. 27 (Dijon workshop); Ring, 1949, no. 8 (French school); Panofsky, 1953, p. 85–6 (Paris); Porcher, 1961, p. 148–9 (similarities with the Bedford master); Sterling-Adhémar, 1965, no. 7 (Dijonnais or Parisian?); Troescher, 1966, p. 62 (Arnoul Picornet).

8 Virgin and Child with Butterflies (Pl. 6)
On loan to the Staatliche Museen, Berlin

This is surely the right wing of a diptych. This is indicated by the composition's being very slightly weighted towards the left, and also by the attitude of the Virgin looking towards the left. The Child's gesture could be interpreted as an attempt to grasp the red flower held out by an angel, but it is more probable that the artist wanted to depict Him making a sort of gesture of welcome to the donor. Millard Meiss and Colin Eisler have picked up a trace of the missing panel in a drawing from a volume in the Burgundy collection at the Bibliothèque Nationale, reproducing a portrait of John the Fearless in prayer. The identification is confirmed by the presence of the same oriental embroidery forming the arc of a circle at the bottom of both compositions. The reversal of the drawing (the donor is looking towards the left, whereas the Berlin painting would require him to be looking towards the right) need not be a serious objection as it seems frequent in old copies. The function of the embroidered drapery is perhaps not only to establish a link between the outside world and that of the painting. It may also separate two spaces, isolating celestial space from the earthly world of the spectator. The butterflies could symbolise souls (cf. Ferguson, 1957, p. 27–40). In this case the diptych would take on a funerary significance. This theory seems to be confirmed by the inscription on the phylactery in the copy of the portrait of John the Fearless, 'Domine Jesu accipe spiritum meum et... statuas... hoc...' (text deciphered and quoted only by Troescher, 1966, p. 386, note 98). It also explains why the duke is represented behind the drapery, i.e. in the celestial space, since he is depicted as dead.
This interpretation would logically suggest that the work postdates the murder at Montereau in 1419, which would exclude Malouel. The style, however, argues an earlier date. Besides, it is quite possible to imagine an epitaph diptych commissioned during the duke's lifetime to be placed in one of the ducal chapels, perhaps even the one in the Charterhouse of Champmol. This idea of a funerary diptych recurs about 50 years later, in a similar composition, with the paintings

155

Portrait of John the Fearless, reversed copy of the left wing of the diptych of the *Virgin with the butterflies* by Malouel.

commissioned from Jean Fouquet by Etienne Chevalier for the church of Notre-Dame at Melun.
Contrary to the statements of Millard Meiss and Colin Eisler, the painting is not on its original support, but has been transferred from wood to canvas (one can still make out, by careful scrutiny, the traces of the joints between the original boards). It even has the smooth surface common to many paintings which have been smoothed down too vigorously in the course of this operation. Nevertheless, a skilful restoration, no doubt during the last century, has concealed the defects, but has not disguised a number of worn areas. A comparison of the angels with those of the *Martyrdom of St. Denis* is very striking. Especially if one compares the angel on the left, behind Christ, with the one on the left of the lowest row in the Berlin painting, one cannot fail to note the similarity of types. However, although the drawing of the faces seems almost identical in the two works, one is all sweetness while the other remains tense; the one has a smooth and delicate face, the other is vigorously modelled. Here is a further proof that a second artist completed the painting in the Louvre, from a drawing that he could not alter.

Dimensions:	Wood transferred to canvas. 107 × 81.
Provenance:	presented to a church in Berlin in the latter half of the nineteenth century; on loan to the Staatliche Museen, Berlin, since 1959.
Literature:	Winkler, 1959; Meiss & Eisler, 1960; Laclotte, 1961, p. 287; Troescher, 1966, p. 77–8, fig. 55, pl. 17.

Attributed to Malouel

9 Presumed portrait of Wenceslas of Brabant
Lugano, Thyssen collection

This painting has been made known and studied by Charles Sterling (1959). The identification of the subject is based on an old inscription which appeared on the picture before it was transferred to canvas. Charles Sterling has shown, however, that it is difficult to see the same person in the painting and in the two drawings from the *Recueil d'Arras* and the *Recueil Succa*. One may follow Sterling in preferring the evidence of the inscription, but it is also possible to consider it mistaken. If the panel belonged at some time to a series, a confusion may have arisen between two neighbouring

portraits such as those of two dukes of Brabant. The *Recueil Succa* has a copy of a portrait of Philippe of Saint Pol (1404–30) which, despite the different angle, shows certain similarities to the painting in the Thyssen collection: the short face, the prominent ear, the pronounced curve of the lower jaw all appear in both portraits.
The attribution of the painting to Jean Malouel, suggested by Charles Sterling, is based mainly on historical reasons: the dating of the portrait *c.* 1405–10 and the attribution to the Burgundian court, which would guide one towards the name of Malouel. The idea is plausible, but requires this to be seen as a retrospective portrait. The style, allowing for the wear suffered by the surface layers, is not incompatible with Malouel's as shown in the *Martyrdom of St. Denis*.
Nevertheless, one cannot fail to be surprised at the liveliness of the upward gaze and by the prominence given to the face. The abrupt cutting-off of the headgear by the edge of the painting certainly has an immediate precedent in the *Portrait of Louis II d'Anjou* in the Bibliothèque Nationale. However, the costume is modelled by skilfully emphasised folds which push the profile towards the back of the picture. The painting thus seems closer to portraits by the Master of Flémalle (without being otherwise comparable to them) than to faces in the paintings of Malouel. One may therefore wonder if an attribution to an artist working at the court of Brabant at a later date, *c.*1425–30, is not more probable.

Dimensions:	Wood transferred to canvas, 34.4 × 25.4.
Inscription:	The reverse of the panel bore the inscription 'Wenchcaius dux Brabanciae in antiquitate 34 tum annorum'.
Provenance:	Schloss Seebenstein (Austria), property of the Princes of Liechtenstein; acquired from them in 1941 for the Hammel collection.
Exhibition:	Vienna, 1962 (Heinz), no. 17.
Literature:	Sterling, 1959; Meiss & Eisler, 1960, p. 234; Laclotte, 1961, p. 287; Troescher, 1966, p. 108–9.

After Malouel

10 Portrait of Philip the Bold

There is no documentary evidence that Malouel ever had to paint a portrait of the first of the dukes of

156

192

Burgundy by whom he was employed. Nevertheless, such a commission would be likely and, as Charles Sterling has rightly pointed out (1959, p. 304), the surviving copies of portraits of Philip the Bold seem to depict the duke towards the end of his life; this would make it possible for the original to have been executed between 1397 and 1404, when Malouel was in his service. To this one can add the style of the composition and the modelling which, as far as can be made out from the copies, appear similar to those found in the portrait of John the Fearless (cf. no. 11 below).

Known copies:
Musée National de Versailles.

Dimensions: Wood. 42 × 30.
Inscription: (above) 'PHILIPPE LE HARDY F̄IX DV ROY JEAN DVC DE BŌGN̄E'.

Sixteenth-century copy?

Cincinnati Museum.
Wood.
Same inscription as at Versailles, but arranged differently.
No hand.

Dijon Museum.

Dimensions: Wood. 42 × 38.
A second version of the portrait of Philip the Bold, known through two drawings (Prost, 1902–13, pl. III and Troescher, 1966, pl. 19, nos. 65 and 66), displays very different characteristics, and it is more difficult to assert that this is a copy of Malouel.
Literature: Prost, 1902–13, I, p. 630; Sterling, 1959, p. 295–6; Troescher, 1966, p. 80–1.
Exhibition: Paris, 1904, no. 361.

In 1904 (Paris, 1904, no. 361) Bouchot listed four other copies, one of them possibly that now in the Cincinnati Museum:
collection of Mme Vaucheret, Paris;
collection of M. Georges de Monbrison;
two copies in Italy.

11 Portrait of John the Fearless

Documents quoted by Charles Sterling (1959, p. 302–4) show that a portrait of Duke John the Fearless was commissioned from Jean Malouel before 1413, to be sent to the king of Portugal. Naturally, these documents do not exclude the possibility of other portraits of the same sitter by Malouel.
Among the known likenesses of the duke of Burgundy, only two can be considered to date from the fifteenth century. That in the Louvre, studied by Mme Adhémar (1961), symbolises his taking possession of the duchy of Burgundy. The graceful, unemphatic style makes attribution to Malouel difficult, although the circumstances of the work's execution put one in mind of him. As the painting principally depicts him taking possession of the duchy of Burgundy, the commission may have been given by the abbots of Saint-Bénigne at Dijon, who were the official keepers of the symbolic ring represented, or by some notable of the duchy. The second

copy, that in the Antwerp museum, appears slightly later. The quality of its workmanship is remarkable and has suggested the names of Hubert and Jan van Eyck or Rogier van der Weyden (cf. esp. Panofsky, 1953, p. 171). The fine, delicate and meticulous handling seems far removed from one's idea of Malouel's portrait style. Among the known copies should be remembered the drawing in the Bibliothèque Nationale, mentioned above (no. 8), which is probably a reversed reproduction of the other wing of the *Virgin with the Butterflies* diptych. The same type seems to have given rise to another profile portrait of which there are several known replicas dating from the end of the fifteenth century or the beginning of the sixteenth. The similarity of the two representations should not, however, lead us to exclude the possibility of a second original by Malouel; the artist could have reworked the profile conceived for the first painting and adapted it for a new commission.
This double version of the duke's portrait is the one which seems closest to the style of Malouel. The precision of the profile is very much in the tradition of royal and princely likenesses, whose earliest example is that said to be of John the Good (Louvre). The hypothesis draws strength from the minute, meticulous detailing of the profile and from the vigorous modelling with which it seems possible to credit the original through an examination of the copies.

Surviving copies:
Chantilly, Musée Condé.

Dimensions: Wood. 24 × 26.
Inscription: (above) '1419 JEAN DVC DE BŌGNE FVC OCCIS A MŌTEREAV'.
Versailles, Musée National.
Wood. 42 × 30.

Semur-en-Auxois, Museum.
35 × 31 (No. 112 in the 1855 cat.).
Cincinnati Museum.
Sold, Galerie Charpentier, 6 June 1958, no. 6 (pl. III).

Literature: Sterling, 1959, p. 295–6; Troescher, 1966, p. 82; Châtelet, 1970, no. 5.

Workshop of Malouel

12 The Entombment
Paris, Musée du Louvre

This panel is generally associated with the *Pietà* in Troyes and the *Small round Pietà*. The three works are indeed very similar in style, but here one notes a certain stiffness in the handling and even some hesitations in the spatial arrangement. The figures are not all to the same scale: Nicodemus, in the foreground, is distinctly smaller than the other figures, whereas the head of St. John the Evangelist gives the impression of being abnormally large between those of the Virgin and a female saint. The features of the male figures are marked by wrinkles executed rather mechanically. The composition itself is not very balanced (it was perhaps the left-hand wing of a triptych, which would explain the accentuation of the diagonal). All this indicates not a work by the master himself, but by an artist very close to him, from his own workshop.
The identity of the donor remains unknown. Bouchot considered him to be a pope on account of his skullcap.

He seems more likely to have been a member of some religious order. It is also difficult to make out what he is carrying in his right hand.

Dimensions: Wood. 32.8 × 21.3.
Provenance: Nolivos collection; acquired by the Louvre in 1869.
Exhibited: Paris, 1904, no. 4 (Jean d'Orléans?).
Literature: Champeaux, 1898, p. 130; Bouchot, 1905, pl. VIII; Durrieu, 1907, p. 50; Durrieu, 1918–19, p. 85; Brière, 1919, p. 249; Fierens Gevaert, 1927, p. 33; Lemoisne 1929, p. 5; Dupont, 1937, p. 14; Sterling, 1938, p. 58; Sterling-Jacques, 1941, no. A 28, p. 9; Ring, 1949, no. 9; Panofsky, 1953, p. 85–6 (Paris school); Laclotte, 1961, p. 288 (Bellechose); Sterling-Adhémar, 1965, no. 6 (Dijonnais or Parisian workshop); Troescher, 1966, p. 62–4 (Arnoul Picornet).

13 Pietà
Troyes, Musée des Beaux-Arts

Despite its small size, this panel was originally an object of considerable splendour; its original frame still bears traces of the chasing for the precious stones which adorned it. It was thus a devotional work intended for some great lord.

157

At first sight, the theme of the painting seems to be the Deposition from the Cross rather than of the Pietà in the strict sense. The body of Christ is held upright by St. John the Evangelist and the Virgin, as if it had just been taken down. At the same time, however, it is offered for the devotion of the faithful by its prominence in the composition, and thus the concept of a Pietà re-emerges. The style and the figure-types recall the *Small Tondo* and, like the latter, the upper part of the *Martyrdom of St. Denis*. Especially comparable are the angels supporting Christ in the Troyes panel and the heads forming an aureole in the Louvre altarpiece. However, both invention and execution lack sufficient strength for this painting to be attributed to the master himself.

Dimensions: Wood. 39 × 26.
Provenance: Flechey collection.

Exhibitions: Paris, 1904, no. 14; Paris, 1950, no. 14; Dijon, 1951, no. 4.

Literature: Bouchot, 1905, pl. XIV; Sterling, 1938, p. 58 (Dijonnais workshop?); Sterling-Jacques, 1941, no. A 33, p. 10 (affinities with the *Martyrdom of St. Denis*); Ring, 1949, no. 52 (Malouel or Bellechose); Laclotte, 1961, p. 288 (Bellechose?); Troescher, 1966, p. 65–6.

The Turin-Milan Hours

The original manuscript contained all the four fragments known at present: the *Très Belles Heures de Notre Dame* (Paris, Bibliothèque Nationale, new acq. Lat. 3093), the *Turin Hours* (Turin, Biblioteca Nazionale; destroyed by the fire of 25 January 1904), the *Milan-Turin Hours* (Turin, Museo Civico, before 1935 in the Trivulzio collection, Milan) and five isolated leaves (Paris, Musée du Louvre, Cabinet des Dessins, RF 2022-2025).

Written for a prince of the French royal house (Duke Louis II of Bourbon?), who commissioned the first illustrations, these Hours belonged to Duke John of Berry, who continued the programme of illumination. But in 1412–13 he gave them, still incomplete, to Robinet d'Etampes, his 'keeper of the jewels'. It was the latter who made the first division of the volume, keeping for himself the fragment now in the Bibliothèque Nationale.

The programme of illumination for John of Bavaria

The other three fragments (Turin, Milan-Turin, pages in the Louvre) then came into the hands of John of Bavaria, Count of Holland. He resumed the work of illumination, no doubt entrusting it to the direction of Jan van Eyck, who was in his service in Holland between 1422 and 1424. On his death the manuscript seems to have remained in the northern Netherlands: the final illustrations, executed a little later, *c.* 1450 (?), are from the hand of a northern artist, another specimen of whose work has recently been identified: part of the illumination of the *Llangattock Hours* (Schilling, 1961), on which he worked with Vreelant.

The 'Eyckian' workshop

The apparent dispersion of the Eyckian illuminations (those by Jan van Eyck and the artists who worked with him) within the manuscript has caused surprise. It has even been used as an argument against any attribution to Jan van Eyck. However, a reconstruction of the original state of the manuscript and a codicological analysis has revealed a certain logic in the organisation of the task.

Van Eyck's team included the artists that Hulin de Loo has designated by the letters G (Jan van Eyck), H (an important illuminator, close to but distinct from Jan), F3, I and J. It can then be seen that these various masters mostly worked on the sections begun and left unfinished in the course of earlier programmes. The most important illuminations are reserved for Master G—Jan van Eyck—and Master H. Their distribution in the programme is fairly clear. One should not be misled by the rather isolated position of the only two surviving miniatures by Jan van Eyck; they both corresponded to illustrations which were particularly dear to the heart of Duke John of Bavaria. The *Birth of John the Baptist* depicted his patron saint, and the *Requiem Mass*, by its display of heraldry and rich hangings, served as a reminder of the power and splendour of his house. It was this same love of display which led to the

duke's own painter being entrusted with the *Sovereign's Prayer*, a leaf now destroyed. No doubt he would also himself have decorated the series of prayers to be said during Mass, a series in which he would have been able to depict the prince on each leaf, if only he had had time (they were illuminated after the death of John of Bavaria by painter K who, for this purpose, probably followed, though unskilfully, sketches by Jan van Eyck himself).

Masters G and H

On the reasons for not identifying Master H with Jan van Eyck, cf. above. Many scholars (esp. Friedländer and Panofsky) have thought that the work of Master H is that of an artist working *c.* 1445, long after the intervention of Jan van Eyck. On the contrary, the portrayal, on one of the pages decorated by this artist, of a donor identifiable with the prince in the *Sovereign Prince's Prayer* confirms that the two artists were working at the same time.

A facsimile edition of the *Milan–Turin Hours*, to be published by Electa (Milan) in 1981, will contain, under my signature, a more detailed study of the problems posed by the manuscript and its illuminations.

The reference RD followed by a figure refers to the reconstruction of the original manuscript and its illustrations by Durrieu (1910).

Bibliography for the *Turin–Milan Hours*

Delisle, 1884 (first mention) p. 290–1; Durrieu, 1901 (first attribution to the van Eycks); Durrieu, 1902 (facsimile of *Turin*, reprinted 1967); Hulin de Loo, 1902 (attribution to the van Eycks); Durrieu, 1903 (development of the Eyckian attribution); De Jongh, 1903 (first formulation of the Ouwater theory); Haseloff, 1903 (attribution of the leaves by hand G to Jan van Eyck); Six, 1904 (theory of the marriage of Jacqueline of Bavaria to the Dauphin); Woestijne, 1904 (study of the lower page-borders); Heins, 1906 (attempt at identifying the Ghent settings); Durrieu, 1910 (reconstruction of the original manuscript); Durrieu, 1910B (identification of the characters in the *Sovereign's Prayer*); Hulin de Loo, 1911 (facsimile of *Milan–Turin*, fundamental study of the hands); Hulin de Loo, 1911B (criticism of Durrieu's identification of the characters); Six, 1911 (attempt at identifying the settings); Friedländer, 1916 (G = Jan van Eyck, H = imitator of *c.* 1440); Dvořák, 1918, p. 51 (Dutch theory); Post, 1919 (rejection of early dating on the strength of a study of the costumes); Durrieu, 1922 (facsimile of *Paris*, repeat of reconstruction of original manuscript); Six, 1922 (predominance of Hubert van Eyck's rôle); Winkler, 1924, p. 35–46 (follows Durrieu and Hulin de Loo); Friedländer, I, 1924 (maintaining his thesis of 1916); Winkler, 1925, p. 15–23 (maintaining his earlier ideas, attribution of the Frontispiece of Chevrot's *Augustinus* to a 'continuator' of the *Hours*); Maeterlinck, 1925, p. 51–3 (arbitrary attribution to Lievin van Clite); Johannsen, 1932 (definition of a 'Master of the small hands' identified with G and H); Hulin de Loo, 1932 (identification of the journeys of Jan van Eyck); Tolnay, 1932 (works of G and H only inspired by Jan van Eyck); Lyna, 1933 (G and H dated *c.*1445); Renders, 1933 (repeating Freidländer's theses); Beenken, 1934, p. 176–232 (p. 202 quotes Jolles' theory that the *Sovereign's Prayer* commemorates the triumph of Albert of Bavaria over the Frisians in 1398); Kerber, 1937, (G = Hubert van Eyck); Hoogewerff, II, 1937, p. 5–15 (G = Jan van Eyck, H = Petrus Christus); Tolnay, 1939,

p. 35–7 (G = Albert van Ouwater); Beenken, 1941, p. 3–10 (follows Durrieu and Hulin de Loo); Lavalleye, 1947, p. 104 (G style of van Eyck, H = follower of *c.*1435); Sulzberger, 1951; Sulzberger, 1952 (Lombard model for the *Virgin among the Virgins*); Sulzberger, 1952B (influence on Pinturicchio); Baldass, 1952, p. 30–3 and 90–4 (after Jan van Eyck: *Crucifixion* and *Garden of Gethsemane*, principal master working *c.*1430–40); Panofsky, 1953, p. 232–46 (G = Jan van Eyck, H = imitator of *c.*1435–40); Garas, 1954 (Dutch master, prob. Ouwater); Held, 1955, p. 222–3 (G = Hubert van Eyck, except for the *Finding of the Cross*); Lyna, 1955 (reversal of the *Sovereign's Prayer*); Pächt, 1956, p. 272–4 (suggests possibility of an attribution to Hubert van Eyck); Châtelet, 1956 and 1957 (studies of the stages in the illumination, Eyckian hands: G = Jan van Eyck, H = collaborator of Jan van Eyck between 1422 and 1424); Delaissé, 1959, p. 116–9 (suggesting attribution of illuminations by hand G to the master of the frontispiece of Chevrot's *Augustinus*); Lyna, 1961 (hypothesis of commission by Elizabeth of Görlitz); Lyna, 1962 (influence of the illuminations by hands G and H); Delaissé, 1963, p. 133–9 (theory of an earlier owner than John of Berry, doubt concerning the homogeneity of the volume as reconstructed by Durrieu); Marrow, 1966; Châtelet, 1967 (summary of earlier theories, bibliography); Meiss, 1967, esp. p. 107–33 (studies of the first illuminations, revival of identification of hand A with the Master of the *Parement de Narbonne*); Marrow, 1968 (hypercritical of Châtelet, 1967, rejecting all research based on historical elements); Lejeune, 1968 (arbitrary hypotheses and unfounded attempt at identifying the settings); Spencer, 1969 (Charles V as the volume's first owner); Marijnissen, 1969 (infra-red photograph of the *Nativity of St. John the Baptist*); Meiss, 1971, p. 229–30 (listed in the duke's inventories in 1405–6, presented to Robinet by 1412 at the latest); Delaissé, 1972 (produced between 1436 and 1445 by partisans of Jacqueline of Bavaria); Sterling, 1978 (hand H later than intervention of Jan van Eyck); Châtelet 1979 B.

Jan van Eyck

14 The Prayer of a Sovereign Prince (Pls. 14 and 20)
Turin Hours, folio 69 *v.*, RD 38

For the interpretation of this scene, which has been at the heart of the debate on Jan van Eyck's share in the decoration of the manuscript, cf. above. In spite of Sterling's criticisms (1978), Lyna's theory, that this illumination is a reversed reproduction of an earlier composition, still retains some interest. Some details indicate, if not necessarily a reversal, at least the modification of a different picture: the clouds surrounding the apparition of God the Father partly mask the town in the background, the prince's gesture of prayer does not match the tension of his horse's reins, which ought to be firmly held by one of his hands. This does not mean, however, that this was merely the work of an executant of the second rank. The workmanship, very noticeable in the surviving photographs, displays a stunning mastery of technique. This is Jan van Eyck copying himself, probably on the instructions of John of Bavaria, who commissioned the work.

Taken as a whole, the composition has no known precedent. For certain details, however, characteristic borrowings can be cited. Bella Martens (1929, p. 174–5) has seen the prince's horse as a version of one belonging to one of the Magi in an illumination from the *Wonders of the World* by the Boucicaut Master (Paris, B.N., MS. Fr. 2810, folio 11 *v.*). But this horse is itself an adaptation of that from the famous *Medal of Constantine* (cf. Meiss, 1967, fig. 462) which belonged to the Duke of Berry. Jan van Eyck seems to have known both works: that of the illuminator, from which he borrows the new pose of the horse, and that of the goldsmith, whose modelling (which the Boucicaut Master had ignored) he has tried to imitate in paint.

Another horse repays examination, the one which is ridden by the young lord following the prince on the left and which is rearing. The rarity of such exact depictions at the beginning of the fifteenth century justifies our looking for its source. The posture of the horse is almost identical with that of the mount of one of the Wise Men's attendants in the central lunette of the altarpiece by Gentile da Fabriano (Florence, Uffizi), and the neighing head seems to be a copy of the one on the right in the same altarpiece. The Uffizi picture is dated May 1423. Jan van Eyck, who is mentioned at The Hague between 1422 and 1424, could have known it; a work of such size must have been begun at least a year before, and if he went to Italy shortly before entering the service of John of Bavaria, he could have seen it in Gentile's workshop.

It should be noted that Jan van Eyck re-uses many elements of this composition in the panel of the *Honest Judges* on the Ghent altarpiece. Suzanne Sulzberger (1952 B) also thought that Pinturicchio had drawn inspiration from the *Sovereign's Prayer* for one of his frescoes in the Libreria Piccolomini at Siena; the idea is attractive but not altogether convincing.

15   The Taking of Christ (Pl. 16)
Turin, folio 24 *r.*, RD 51

Inserted as an illustration of the prayer at matins for the Lamentations of the Virgin on the Passion, the picture depicts the Taking of Christ and is based on the account of the synoptic gospels (*Mark 14, 43–52, Matthew 26, 47–56, Luke 23, 47–53*). The components of the scene are very similar to those used by Master A of the *Très Belles Heures de Notre Dame* to depict the same subject at the beginning of the *Hours of the Passion* (Paris, p. 181). To be noted in van Eyck's version are the discreet addition in the left background of two fleeing apostles and, more curiously, the presence of a dog in the foreground; as a symbol of fidelity it is surprising to find it in a scene where Judas plays the leading rôle, but it must be connected with the gesture of St. Peter, contrasted with his denial illustrated in the lower margin.

Whereas Master A gives space only to the figures, which practically fill the entire area, Jan van Eyck reduces the scale of the actors in order to place them in an extensive landscape, which brings in the theme of Jerusalem. The entire upper half of the picture is devoted to it; the city is shown as Westerners might have imagined it, like a fortified Flemish town but dominated by a massive religious building of circular plan (a purely theoretical representation of the mosque of Omar).

The main novelty of this page is its evocation of night. It had been preceded by the purely symbolic depictions of the late fourteenth century and by the celebrated page in the *Très Riches Heures du duc de Berry* (folio 142 *r.*). In the latter the Limbourgs were mainly attracted by the theme of the starry night and by a vision of grey shapes in the darkness. For this purpose they adapted the technique of grisaille. Jan van Eyck, on the other hand, is less concerned to express the darkness than the light

in the darkness. He gives us the dull glow of a sky covered with clouds that have turned greyish in the dusk, the miraculous rays of Christ's cruciform halo, and the reflections which, even in the dark, appear wraith-like on breastplates and helmets. An enlargement of the surviving photographs reveals, on the helmet of the soldier nearest Christ, tiny reflections of the shadows of St. Peter, Christ and Judas—forerunners as it were of the reflections on the breastplate of St. George in the *Virgin with Canon van der Paele*. Here the Eyckian theme of light finds one of its most remarkable expressions for the period.

One might also note the artist's delight in the soldiers' ugliness and in the flamboyant, glittering cuirasses; these are points which link this picture to the *Carrying of the Cross* in Budapest.

Initial and lower margin

The lower margin, representing the denial of St. Peter, has few Eyckian features. The outlines are those of Hulin de Loo's Master A bis, but the landscape in which they move has been amplified and enriched in details. It is not impossible that some figures may have been slightly touched up on the surface: the photographs do not permit us to state this with assurance.

The initial, however, is entirely the work of Jan van Eyck. It is one of the most remarkable inventions in the volume: the anguish of *Christ in the Garden of Gethsemane* is expressed only by a strange prostrate form, modelled by half-light. All the difference between Master H and Master G is strikingly epitomised by a comparison between this moving composition and the precise, clear and yet somehow dry version in the *Milan–Turin Hours* (*26*).

16   The Intercession of Christ and the Virgin
Paris, Louvre, Cabinet des Dessins, Rf 2025, RD 65

It may cause surprise to find this illumination mentioned among those by Jan van Eyck. Hulin de Loo attributed it to hand K. A careful examination reveals a work which has suffered considerably but which has also not been finished off: the Virgin's face, the hands and above all the legs of Christ are hazily defined and contrast with the other parts of the bodies, which are better modelled. The figure-drawing reveals Jan van Eyck's characteristic manner, creating delicate forms which are still distinct and substantial. There are weaknesses at certain points, especially in the handling of the ground in a very rough imitation of Jan van Eyck's manner; this no doubt indicates a clumsy

158

attempt at completion by hand K, whose means of expression were much less forceful.

The Virgin's mantle must have been finished off with the characteristic medium employed by Jan van Eyck in his illuminations; it has a luminous quality which distinguishes it from the rest of the leaf.

17   The Voyage of St. Julian and St. Martha
(Pl. 22)
Turin, folio 55 *v.*, RD 67

The prayer illustrated by this picture oddly links St. Julian the Hospitaller and St. Martha, 'for those who have to travel'. St. Martha is invoked because of the voyage in a boat without sails or oars which took her with her brother Lazarus and her sister Mary Magdalene from Galilee to Marseille. She is quite unconnected with St. Julian, but this has not prevented illustrators from putting them in the same boat (cf. esp. the *Petites Heures* of the Duke of Berry, B.N., MS. Fr. 18.014, folio 181 *v.*; Meiss, 1967, fig. 151).

The *Golden Legend's* version of the story of St. Julian the Hospitaller has also been altered. After his involuntary parricide, the saint indeed became a ferryman on a river; but the mysterious traveller whom he ferried presented himself in the form of a 'man dying of cold', and when he had been cared for and warmed in Julian's bed, 'rose up as white as snow to heaven' (ed. Roze, I, 1967, p. 171). He has here been replaced by Christ himself.

The subject has received an essentially realistic rendering. The chosen setting shows a fast-flowing, choppy river in a deep valley. It is reminiscent of the Meuse as it passes through the Ardennes (around Dinant, for example) or of the Rhine. Recent researchers have even tried to identify it with a precise location, but apparently without advancing serious arguments (Lejeune, 1968). At first sight, the castle overlooking the town seems sufficiently well characterised to be an exact portrayal. But we must take into account our artist's powers of invention.

In the *Hours of Charles the Bold* (sold at Christie's in London 26 May 1965, lot 195), the 25th illumination is a clumsy copy of the illustration by Jan van Eyck; it confirms how difficult it was for illuminators to imitate van Eyck's exceptional technique.

18   The Nativity of St. John the Baptist (Pls. 15 and 17)
Milan–Turin, folio 93 *v.*, RD 83

Marijnissen (1969) has published an infra-red photograph of this page, which reveals, beneath the visible image, the outline of an arch with spandrels pierced by oculi. This was obviously not an original intention of Jan van Eyck's, but a frame similar to those found in several illuminations by hand C (*Turin*: folio 58, RD 34, pl. XXXIII; *Louvre*, RF 2023, RD 35; and *Turin*, folio 80 *v.*, RD 47, pl. XLV). Jan van Eyck thus reworked an illumination which had only been sketched out by Master C, who had been responsible for the immediately preceding illumination in the original volume (*Milan–Turin*, folio 90, the *Last Supper*).

In his interpretation of the theme, Jan van Eyck was inspired both by St. Luke (*I. 57–66*) and by Ludolph the Carthusian (Broquin, I, p. 106–13). The Virgin Mary is present, as indicated by Ludolph; she can be recognised in the young woman in blue approaching from the right. She carries a flask and a small basin, no doubt for washing the new-born child; here these objects acquire a significance symbolic of his future rôle. In the right background is an old man with a book in his hand: this must be Zacharias holding the 'tablets' on which he wrote the name of John at God's behest (*Luke I. 63*). The artist has embroidered freely on these basic facts. He has added the motif of a young woman and her child visiting the mother in her confinement, illustrating the visits from relatives and neighbours apparently suggested by Ludolph. Above all, Jan van Eyck has taken advantage of a theme less restricted by iconographic traditions than the Nativity of Christ to give the subject an everyday setting. With loving detail he depicts the bedroom, its simple furniture and all the household utensils: glasses, jugs, candlesticks and dishes—none of which have any obvious symbolic significance. In the foreground he has placed a dog gnawing a bone and a cat in front of its bowl. Are these household pets intended as the equivalents of the ox and ass of Christ's Nativity? Does the dog, the image of fidelity, symbolise the saint's disciples while the cat, usually considered to be an instrument of the Devil, represents his persecutors? Even if this interpretation does perhaps correspond with the artist's intentions, it can only do so at a deeper level of interpretation. There can de no doubt that, at the same time, Jan van Eyck wanted to draw our attention, by means of this trivial detail right in the foreground, to the very ordinariness of the setting for the saint's birth. It is a note of whimsical humour very indicative of his own temperament.

The Baptism of Christ (Pl. 17)

The initial, depicting God the Father, is here skilfully linked to the lower margin both iconographically and formally. It should be noted that Panofsky (1953, p. 244–5) has explained the landscape's surprisingly low horizon, which has no contemporary equivalent either in painting or in illumination, as an inspired interpretation of the traditional lower margin conceived in silhouette, and thus requiring a very low horizon.

19 Requiem Mass (Pl. 21)
Milan–Turin, folio 116 r., RD 91

The Requiem Mass is a fairly frequent theme in early fifteenth-century manuscripts (cf. Meiss, 1968 B). It is more often illustrated by the lying-in-state than the Mass itself. Nevertheless, no earlier illumination attains such unity in the representation of space and figures. The church is presented here not as an abstract contruction, guided by a regular plan and perfect symmetry, but as a real building with its variations of plan: thus the elevation of the apse differs from that of the chancel bays. The same points can be made with regard to the *Virgin in the Church* in the Staatliche Museen, Berlin, which has undeniable affinities with this illumination.

Durrieu asserted that the arms on the catafalque in this illumination were those of the house of Hainault-Bavaria, whereas Hulin de Loo stated that it was difficult to make them out. With a magnifying-glass one can discern, running round the bottom edge of the catafalque, a quartered scutcheon (whose figures are represented only by small blotches of colour, which nevertheless convey an overall impression of the arms of Hainault-Bavaria) alternating with a scutcheon having a field *or* with a charge *sable* which seems to be a lion (and thus corresponds to the arms of Hainault). On the sloping sides of the catafalque, all the scutcheons are the same and also have a field *or* with vague traces of black, once again corresponding to the arms of Hainault. But there is a definite heraldic link between this illumination and the *Sovereign's Prayer*; note the prominence of the colours blue (the catafalque) and red (the cloth covering the coffin), which corresponds with the systematic use of the colours of the tinctures in the arms of the dukes of Bavaria, as in the various portrayals of the sovereign prince.

A Burial (Pl. 25)
Milan–Turin, folio 116 r., lower page-border, RD 91

The lower margin of the *Requiem Mass* belongs to the most frequent tradition of the genre: the figures move along a narrow strip of ground and are silhouetted against the bare parchment above a very low horizon. The scene is the same as that shown in the lower page-border of the illustration of the *Vigil for the Dead* (Paris, p. 104, RD 10). But Jan van Eyck has enriched it with his gift for observing attitudes, by his skilful grouping of the participants—suggesting the movement of a cortège—by his mastery of modelling, by the colours, and by the light which imparts a highly realistic aspect to the scene. One may feel that the arrangement of the figures into groups could have been suggested to the artist by the Weepers of the Burgundian tombs. The connection is not direct enough to be considered definite, but is worth pointing out.

20 Diptych: The Crucifixion—The Last Judgment (Pl. 23)
New York, Metropolitan Museum

Published by Passavant in 1841, these two panels have given rise to much controversy. They have been variously attributed to Hubert or Jan van Eyck, to a Dutch master, perhaps even Albert van Ouwater, or to a follower of Jan van Eyck. I myself had ascribed them to Master H (1958 and in the first typescript of the present work), only to re-attribute them now to Jan van Eyck.

According to Passavant, these panels formed the wings of a triptych whose centrepiece depicted the Adoration of the Magi. The latter was stolen from its owner (Prince Tatistscheff, the Russian ambassador at Vienna) a little before 1841. Many authors have pointed out the obvious iconographic incoherence of such an association. One may therefore wonder if this was not merely a later assemblage of heterogeneous panels to make up a triptych. The grisailles which were formerly on the reverse of the panels, but which disappeared during their transfer to canvas in Russia, may also have dated from this time. Also unlikely is Kern's theory (1926–7) that the centrepiece was a Carrying of the Cross; Panofsky has provided a decisive and definitive refutation of this (1927–8). Although we cannot absolutely exclude the possibility of an original triptych, we can take the idea of a diptych as being more plausible. Durrieu (1920) noted that a similar ensemble, with the same subjects, was mentioned in the collections of the Duke of Berry. Peters' theory (1968) that the two panels were the doors of a tabernacle is attractive, plausible, but hard to confirm. It amounts to denying that there was a central panel and maintaining the idea of a diptych, while accounting for the lack of coherence between the two panels, which were intended to be separated by the tabernacle.

Unfortunately, there is no sure indication of the origin of the New York diptych. Of the princes shown among the blessed, not one has features which are properly individualised and recognisable. Panofsky has rejected, no doubt rightly, the identification of a horseman beneath the cross of the Bad Thief with Philip the Good (1953, p. 454, note 238–42). This figure, like its neighbour, is on a larger scale than those which surround it. It appears that both are interpolations in the original composition. Perhaps after all they are two portraits, although their placing in the midst of the crowd of unbelievers is surprising; we cannot tell whether it was the whim of an ill-educated nobleman or a solecism on the part of a misinformed painter.

There is just one clue: here we find yet another of those burghers' straw hats like those in the *Sovereign's Prayer* or in its lower margin. It is worn by a bearded horseman whose profile appears on the right between the heads of two other riders with their backs to us. If this is indeed the hat of the *Kabeljauwen*, this would again indicate that the panel could have been painted for John of Bavaria, Count of Holland.

159

The two panels do not display the same quality of execution. The *Crucifixion* reveals exceptional mastery in its organisation of space, while the *Last Judgment* is less skilful and less well handled; it could be the work of a collaborator of Jan van Eyck working under the latter's direction, perhaps Master H, or more probably hand I of the *Turin–Milan Hours*.

In the *Crucifixion*, the group in the foreground may seem surprising; there is no known equivalent among the paintings that can be attributed with certainty to Jan van Eyck. None deals with such a dramatic subject. However, the very restraint with which it is treated here argues in favour of its attribution to the painter himself, contrary to what I have previously maintained.

Charles Sterling (1978) has shown how difficult it is to understand the nature of the landscape without assuming knowledge of the Alps, and from this has deduced that the master had made a voyage to Italy. Moreover, certain iconographic details, such as the portrayal of Longinus assisted by another soldier who guides his lance, or compositional devices like the linking of the two groups by figures seen from the rear, also seem to presuppose an acquaintance with Italian works, especially Altichiero's *Crucifixion* in the oratory of San Giorgio in Padua (Châtelet 1980).

Dimensions:	Wood transferred to canvas. Each 56.5 × 19.7.
History:	Unidentified Spanish convent; collection of Prince D. Tatistscheff, Russian ambassador at Vienna; acquired *c.* 1845 by Tsar Nicholas I; Hermitage Museum, Leningrad, un-

til 1933; Knoedler, New York; acquired in 1933 through the Fletcher Fund.

Literature:
Passavant, 1841 (first publication); Waagen, 1864, p. 116 (Petrus Christus, close to Hubert van Eyck); Kämmerer, 1898, p. 52 (either Jan as a young man or his sister Margaret); Crowe and Cavalcaselle, 1899, p. 163–4 (Petrus Christus); Voll, 1900, p. 107 and 132 (school of Jan van Eyck); Durrieu, 1903, p. 11, 18, 108 (similar to the *Mystic Lamb*); Dvořák, 1904, p. 177 and 228 (Jan van Eyck before 1425); Voll, 1906, p. 269, 1923 ed., p. 245–6 (Dutch artist *c* 1450); Weale, 1908, p. 146–50 (Dutch artist, perhaps collaborator on the *Milan–Turin Hours*); Durand Gréville, 1910, p. 95 (Hubert van Eyck); Hulin de Loo, 1911, p. 33–5 (Hubert van Eyck, Master G of the *Milan Hours*); Schmidt-Degener, 1911 (Amsterdam drawing based on the centrepiece of the triptych); Maeterlinck, 1913, p. 62 and 119 (Ghent artist contemporary with Hubert van Eyck); Zimmerman, 1917 (Ouwater *c.* 1440); Dvořák, 1918, p. 66 (Master of the *Turin Hours*, perhaps Ouwater); Durrieu, 1920 (Hubert and Jan van Eyck, diptych belonging to the Duke of Berry); Conway, 1921, p. 60 (Hubert van Eyck); Friedländer I, 1924, p. 49 and 76 (Hubert or a early work by Jan); Winkler, 1924, p. 49 (Hubert); Kern, 1926–7 (wings of a triptych of the *Carrying of the Cross*); Panofsky, 1927–8 (criticising Kern, drawing attention to the Berlin drawing); Tolnay, 1939, p. 37, 53, 64 and 79 (Ouwater *c.* 1420–30); Beenken, 1941, p. 10–12 (Hubert van Eyck); New York, Metropolitan (Wehle-Salinger), 1947, p. 1–12 (Hubert van Eyck); Baldass, 1952, p. 95–6 and no. 62, p. 287 (principal Master of the *Turin Hours*); Panofsky, 1953, p. 237–40 (Hubert van Eyck); Châtelet, 1958, p. 160 (attribution to Master H); Peters, 1968; Chatelet–Faggin, 1969, nos. 3 & 4, p. 88; Sterling, 1978, p. 46–8 (*c.* 1426); Châtelet, 1980.

After Jan van Eyck

21 Allegorical depiction of the Conference at Biervliet
Paris, Louvre, Cabinet des Dessins, inv. 20 674

Otto Kurz believes that this drawing can be identified with that listed as no. 7 in the inventory of the Imperial collections in Vienna by Christian de Mechel (1784, no. 7). However, Charles Sterling (orally) has rightly pointed out that the drawing in the Louvre corresponds to the description quoted in all but one vital point: all its elements are reversed. This observation leads to the conclusion that there were at least two drawings, one being a reversed copy of the other. The theory is

160

confirmed by the origin of the watercolour in the Louvre: it came from the Brunswick collections through the Napoleonic conquests of 1806, and is therefore unlikely to be identical with the version mentioned at Vienna in 1784.

Nor is it possible to follow Kurz or Luttervelt in their identification of the characters. Kurz's starting-point is the identification of the fourth man from the centre, the one with a long nose seen in profile, with John of Bavaria, and of the man wearing a garter in the foreground with William VI of Holland. Kurz sees this garter as one of the insignia of the English order, conferred on the duke during his visit to England. But this honour is blue and is worn on the left knee; in the Louvre drawing it is brown and, if this is not the original version, should be shown on the right knee. Moreover, several of the figures in the drawing are wearing the collar of the Order of St. Anthony, of which William was the legitimate head during his lifetime. Is it conceivable that he should be depicted wearing another order of chivalry beside knights of his own order? It seems unlikely.

For the identification of the characters and the significance of the scene, see p. 28 above.

The identification of the main character as John of Bavaria is also confirmed by the presence, in the background of the male group, of a man wearing a grey hat (whom Luttervelt oddly wanted to identify with Louis the Roman, despite the modesty of his dress); this hat is almost identical with that held by the peasant in the *Sovereign's Prayer* and worn by the horsemen in the lower margin of that illumination, i.e., in all probability the hat of Duke John's supporters, the *Kabeljauwen*.

Otto Kurz has rightly observed that the original scene was in the form of a diptych. Perhaps they were two illuminated pages intended to face one another in a book, the frontispiece of a de luxe edition of the treaty of Biervliet or of a chronicle of John of Bavaria. It could

161

Portrait of John of Brabant, Recueil Succa, Brussels, Bibliothèque Royale.

also have been a small diptych on wood; it is difficult to decide. It should be noted, however, that the Emperor Matthias's inventory of 1619 mentions the Vienna version as 'ein taffel von miniatur'.

It was O. Kurz once again who noticed that the landscape in the Louvre version has sixteenth-century characteristics, and is in a style which he considers close to that of Hans Bol. J. G. van Gelder, arguing from the style of the inscription, thinks that Hoefnagel could have been responsible for the retouching of the drawing. It seems difficult to follow Kurz in asserting that the drawing could be a fifteenth-century original, left unfinished and completed in the sixteenth century.

If the format of the original compositions was identical to that of the version in the Louvre, we should perhaps not exclude the possibility of their being the work of Master H. The space reserved for the landscape seems rather scanty in relation to the figures for a composition by van Eyck.

Watercolour and ink on two sheets of paper glued side by side on wood. Inv. 20 674 (N III 14 540; Morel d'Arleux 12 023).

Provenance:
ducal collection of Brunswick; conquest of 1806.

Literature:
Popham, 1926, p. 145; Winkler, 1927, p. 91; Kurz, 1956; Luttervelt, 1957; Delaissé, 1968, p. 21; Lugt, 1968, no. 16, p. 5–6.

22 The Carrying of the Cross
Budapest, Museum of Fine Art

Often taken for a sixteenth-century copy, the Budapest painting could well date from the fifteenth century, as Klara Garas (1954) has already supposed. Its handling corresponds to this period better, but it cannot be an original. This is clearly indicated by the clumsy execution of certain details such as the backgrounds. The model copied by the artist may have been smaller than the copy, and the awkwardness may be partly explained by the enlargement. Three other partial copies of the same composition confirm the existence of a common model. A drawing in the Brunswick Museum, probably dating from the beginning of the fifteenth century (Baldass, 1960, no. 80), reproduces the group of horsemen on the right very exactly. A freer version occurs in the manuscript of the *Milan-Turin Hours* (Turin folio 31 v., RD 54, Durrieu, pl. XVIII): this is the work of hand K, i.e. of a Dutch artist working around the middle of the century, but probably completing an illumination begun by a miniaturist of the Eyckian workshop (hand I?), as indicated by the figure of Christ, which is much more skilful than the rest of the composition. Finally, a fairly free illumination from the *Hours of Catherine of Cleves* (Guennol fragment folio 63 v., Plummer no. 24) reproduces the central group. This last variant proves that the original was known in the northern Netherlands *c.*1435–40.

There also exists a second series of interpretations, which can be grouped around a drawing in the Albertina, Vienna (*34*); we shall see later on that this must have been a slightly different composition conceived by Master H. Winkler (1916) must take the credit for comparing the Budapest picture to the works of van Eyck. His conclusion is rightly based on comparisons with the illuminations of the *Milan-Turin Hours* by hand G, with the *Mystic Lamb* and the New York diptych. These comparisons range from details

162

(view of Jerusalem as in the Turin *Taking of Christ*, similarity of the armour in the same illumination, horses comparable with those of the *Knights of Christ* from the *Mystic Lamb*) to the conception of the landscape and the integration of the figures into the space, which has no equivalent but in the illuminations by Jan van Eyck.

An iconographic analysis of the Budapest painting is no less revealing of its essential contribution. Saxl (1926) has shown that the composition implies acquaintance with an Italian work similar to the *Carrying of the Cross* by Andrea da Firenze in the Spanish Chapel in Santa Maria Novella in Florence. The works have in common the themes of the crowd, of the procession headed and rounded off by horsemen, the departure from Jerusalem and the climb to Golgotha: all features which have no equivalent in northern painting before the van Eycks. However, Andrea da Firenze retains an episode from the apocryphal gospels which is taken up in the *Meditations* of the pseudo-Bonaventure: the Virgin, accompanied by St. John, watches the procession pass by and is pushed aside by a soldier — a theme also found in fourteenth-century northern illumination.

Curiously, however, this group of the Virgin and St. John has been omitted from the Budapest painting. This can doubtless be explained by the presence of Simon of Cyrene, who does not appear in the Florentine fresco; the intervention of this character comes after the meeting of Christ and his mother in the narrative of Ludolph the Carthusian. The omission is also significant in other respects: it rejects all reference to the compassion of the faithful and lays stress only on the Jews and the onlookers. Whereas the Florentine fresco clearly indicates the presence of Roman soldiers by means of a banner bearing the initials S.P.Q.R., here the proliferation of pointed, fanciful hats emphasises the Jews much more. One can see here the influence of Ludolph the Carthusian, who stresses their responsibility for the Crucifixion, taking as his text *Luke 23.25* 'but (Pilate) delivered Jesus to their will' (Ludolph, Chapter LXII, Broquin, VI p. 341–3). It is thus probably no exaggeration to say that the painting reflects the anti-Semitic climate of the late Middle Ages, which was particularly strong in the Netherlands (cf. Stengers, 1949, p. 52–9). Hence the possibility of seeing historical personages among the riders, as suggested by A. Pigler (1950–1), is remote. Even if we recognise the centurion Longinus among the horsemen, it is very hard to accept that this character was intended to represent the Emperor Sigismund, even more so if the others are chief priests and leaders of the Jews.

Dimensions: Wood. 97.5 × 129.5.
Provenance: acquired in 1904 from the Péteri collection (Ignuz Pfeffer).

Catalogue: Budapest, Museum der Bildenden Künste, 1968 (Pigler) no. 2531.
Literature: Grisebach, 1912, p. 265 (Dutch, fifteenth century); Winkler, 1916, p. 288–9 (after van Eyck); Zimmerman, 1917, p. 15–18 (copy of Ouwater by the Brunswick Monogrammist); Dvořák, 1918, p. 66 (copy of an original by the Master of the *Turin Hours*); Baldass, 1919, p. 14 (copy of Ouwater); Winkler, 1924, p. 49 (copy of Hubert van Eyck); Friedländer, I, 1924, p. 121 (copy of an Eyckian painting of *c*.1420); Saxl, 1926, p. 142 (iconographic sources); Winkler, 1927, p. 100 (notes old replicas); Kern, 1926–7; Panofsky, 1927–8; Hoogewerff I, 1936, p. 505–9 and II, 1937, p. 67 (Master of *St. Elizabeth*); Tolnay, 1939, p. 37, 53 and 80 (copy of Ouwater); Pigler, 1950–1; Baldass, 1952, no. 63, p. 287–8 (copy after the principal Master of the *Turin Hours*); Garas, 1957, p. 237–43 (after a Dutch Master, probably Ouwater); Pigler, 1954; Châtelet, 1980.

Master H

Master H was first accorded a distinct identity in 1911 by Hulin de Loo, though at that time the latter took him to be Jan van Eyck. Through all the vicissitudes of the study of the *Turin-Milan Hours*, one constant has stood out: the personality of Master H, defined through his collaboration on the illumination of that book.

Many authors, however, see this artist as a late imitator of Jan van Eyck working around the 1440s. I have shown (1956–7) that his illustrations for the celebrated volume belonged to the same programme of illumination as those of Jan van Eyck. I have also proposed that he should be credited with a series of small paintings usually attributed to one or other of the artists of the *Mystic Lamb* (1957).

These theories seem to have been greeted with caution by most critics. Such a suggestion seems to lead to the construction of a sort of 'amico di Giovanni' along the lines of Berenson's famous 'amico di Sandro'. It may thus appear to be both a facile solution and a gratuitous invention. We should remember, however, that the rare data on Jan van Eyck indicate the existence of a large workshop associated with him. In this context, there is nothing improbable in the idea of a collaborator with a sufficiently individual style to be recognised and identified.

This possibility is confirmed by the starting-point for the reconstruction of the Master's work, his collaboration on the *Turin-Milan Hours*. These illustrations reveal his peculiar qualities: an illuminator's technique, a love of anecdote, deliberate expressiveness of the faces and precision of detail. They are also a sure sign of close contacts with Jan van Eyck and of sufficient humility towards him to inspire actual plagiarism, even copying, as in the flagrant instance of the *Crucifixion*.

All the other evidence on the painter remains in the realm of supposition, more or less. The use of the layout of the Turin *Pietà* by Petrus Christus in the painting from the former Schloss collection (Louvre) indicates a fairly long activity after the collaboration on the Book of Hours. This seems to be confirmed by the attribution of the *St. Jerome* in Detroit, dated 1442.

With many reservations, I have suggested the identification of this master with Jan Coene. The latter is mentioned at Bruges between 1424 and 1450. He is cited as an illuminator but also seems to have worked as a painter; indeed, he was admitted to the Painters' Guild before it made any systematic attempts to recruit workers in the book trade. He was also paid for paintings he made for the city of Bruges (Duverger, 1955, p. 113–14). He was a full member of the guild and even dean twice, in 1426–7 and 1436–7. His name suggests that he may have been a son or relative of Jacob Coene the miniaturist, who was sufficiently celebrated to be summoned from Paris to work at Milan cathedral. This means that our artist was probably trained in the workshop of a fourteenth-century illuminator. If these data correspond with our ideas about the artist, Jan Coene's apparent fame, on the contrary, may be considered less compatible with Master H's evident subordination to Jan van Eyck. Even so, we may still imagine that the Painters' Guild, by electing him dean twice, wanted to guarantee through him the support of the painter of the Duke of Burgundy. However this may be, the clues which suggest an identification do not justify its being proposed with any certainty.

Literature: Hulin de Loo, 1911 (for the illuminations); Châtelet, 1957; Châtelet, 1979 B; Châtelet, 1980.

23 The Virgin among the Virgins (Pl. 29)
Turin, folio 59 *r.*, RD 37

This illumination was ascribed by Hulin de Loo (1911) to group G. In 1918, however, Dvořák deemed it necessary to detach it from this group, as also the *Finding of the Cross* (1925 ed., p. 265). In 1957, I in my turn suggested its attribution to Master H.

All the space in the composition is given over to the figures, with no attempt to locate them in space, in contrast to all Jan van Eyck's illuminations. The female faces lack elegance and have an undeniable affinity with those of the *Pietà*; in several female saints we find the same prominent lower jaw, slightly swollen cheeks and very deep-set eyes of Mary Magdalene. The spread of the drapery folds across the ground is of equal extent in both pictures. Here, however, there is a greater striving for elegance, noticeable in the pointed ends of these folds and in the prominence given to the graceful form of the saint on the right.

On the surviving photographs one can clearly distinguish the use of coloured stippling to modify the basic tone and indicate shadows, which is peculiar to the works of Master H.

The elegance which gives this work the stamp of International Gothic and which may raise doubts about its being by hand H can perhaps be explained by its sources. Suzanne Sulzberger (1952 B) has shown that the Turin illumination draws its inspiration from the frontispiece of the *Panegyric of Gian Galeazzo Visconti* (Paris, Bibliothèque Nationale, Lat. MS. 5888, folio 1), executed shortly after 1404. It would be natural for Master H to have retained a little of the actual style of this Lombard miniature, a typical expression of the International Gothic.

A second surprising point is the exuberant marginal decoration of this page. It has been very skilfully substituted for the original decoration, which has been partly scraped off and partly overpainted, as can be clearly seen at the edges of the lower border. Its style has long seemed very late to historians of illumination. Since examination of the *Hours of Catherine of Cleves*, it no longer seems impossible to locate its execution in the northern Netherlands between 1430 and around 1450. It is unlikely to be contemporary with the illumination. The trumpet-playing angel on the right, entwined by tendrils, is certainly the work of Master H, whose technique can be clearly made out in the photographs. But it seems to have been incorporated into the arabesque rather than created with it. This last observation may offer the key to this curious decoration. The fact that it occurs on this page alone in the whole volume indicates that something required concealing, or that some unsightly scratchings-out needed to be masked by a new decoration. The angel, by sounding his trumpet, draws our attention towards the margin. He is somewhat similar to the one on folio 14 of *Turin* who points at the owner depicted in the initial. The two illuminations were probably similar; so the last owner, by ordering a new marginal decoration, must have wanted to remove the portrait of some lady shown praying in the margin, like the lord on folio 87 *r.* of *Milan-Turin*. Perhaps this was Elizabeth of Görlitz, the wife of John of Bavaria, and the saint greeted by the Virgin could be her patroness; the garland she holds in her hand could be a garland of flowers, a variation of one of St. Elizabeth's most frequent attributes.

The representation of the Holy Ghost hovering above the group of saints like a dove in full flight, seen head-on and diffusing golden rays, is identical to that in the polyptych of the *Mystic Lamb*. This detail would not be important if the subject were not unusual in such an iconographic context and if the lower scene of the same leaf (see below) did not also recall the same painting. One could use this to attribute a late date to the illumination. But both borrowings are made from the central panel of the *Mystic Lamb*, the panel which, according to all the evidence, was produced first. Unless we refuse to attach any importance to the altarpiece's famous inscription and deny the worth of the archive entries which have been connected with Hubert van Eyck, we must accept that the Ghent altarpiece was begun between 1420 (date of the acquisition of a chapel in St. Bavo by Jodocus Vyd) and 1426 (date of Hubert's death); some of its features could therefore have been known to Masters H and I between 1422 and 1424.

Lower Scene

The adoration of the Mystic Lamb by the Virgins is inspired by the central panel of the Ghent altarpiece. The clumsy composition and the rather dry precision of the drawing indicate the work not of Master H, but of a more modest collaborator of the Eyckian workshop, the artist whom Hulin de Loo designated by the letter I. Lucien Fourez (1949) and Frédéric Lyna (1955) have pointed out that the hills in this landscape were identical to those of the frontispiece of Chevrot's *Augustinus* (Brussels, Bibliothèque Royale, MS. 9015, folio 1); this is not surprising as the two illuminations were probably executed by the same artist at several years' interval.

24 St. Thomas in his cell (Pl. 28)
Turin, folio 73 *v.*, RD 41

Concerning this illumination, Durrieu (1910, p. 259) writes: 'The head of the saint must have been very fine and his hand is perfectly drawn; but the surface has suffered badly.' Hulin de Loo (1911, p. 48) also remarks that 'the picture, now destroyed, was already very badly damaged when I was able to see it. The saint's head,

especially, was in very poor condition.' What worried both these authors is indeed noticeable in the photographs. One may wonder, however, if this is really due to wear or to incompleteness. The saint's head, in particular, seems to have had its contours and masses defined, but not to have received the touches of colour which would have modelled it. It is also noticeable that the paint of the back wall, behind the chair, is so light that the letters written on the reverse show through it. This also tends to prove that this area of the composition had only received its first coat, and was awaiting further touches.

Durrieu ascribed this illustration to the programme of illumination undertaken for the house of Hainault-Bavaria. Hulin de Loo hesitated, and suggested an attribution to hand I. In my opinion we have here a work by hand H, left unfinished. The style may certainly appear rather disconcerting, given its subject, which makes it difficult to compare with other works by the same artist. One detail, however, is fairly significant: the saint's hand has the same proportions and is drawn in the same way as that of *Jesus in the Garden of Gethsemane* (*Milan-Turin*, C 26). The manner in which the saint's head is enfolded by his hood is also reminiscent of St. Peter on the same leaf. Finally, the delicate, linear outlining of the facial details, which was only just begun here (or has partly vanished), displays the same technique as can still be seen on that page and makes the faces so expressive.

This poses the problem of the connection between this illumination and the painting of *St. Jerome* in the Detroit Museum (no. 33 below). Most authors take the illumination as a free interpretation of the panel. If the illumination copied the painting, it is difficult to understand why it offers such a different and much less suggestive interpretation of perspective. In the panel, the objects are interconnected with more skill, the removal of the table towards the side allows greater prominence to the figure, and the placing of the chair at an angle gives the impression of a deeper space. The difference between the two works is most noticeable in the treatment of the table. In the illumination the artist has combined a level view with a slightly tilted one, so as to give a clearer view of the objects thus spread out on a broader surface. This splitting of the view in the organisation of objects recalls that employed by the Master of Flémalle in his *Annunciation* in the Cloisters Museum. In the Detroit painting, on the other hand, the side and top of the table are both drawn in the same perspective, and the objects have been arranged near the edge so that they can be shown in better detail. There has been a development from one to the other, and I therefore feel it is logical to reverse the generally accepted relation between the two works.

The subject of the illumination is not new. It belongs to a tradition of portrayal of Doctors of the Church writing or reading which goes back at least to the fourteenth century (cf. Strümpell, 1925–6). Originating in Italy, the idea was known in Paris in the first decade of the fifteenth century. A drawing of it is known, attributed to the circle of the Limbourgs (Bibliothèque Nationale, Fr. MS. 166; cf. Strümpell, 1925–6, pl. XLIa and Ring, 1949, fig. 13), and above all an illumination by the Master of the *Boucicaut Hours* (Meiss, 1968, pl. 42). This latter work is probably the source of the *Turin* composition. The artificial setting imitated from Italian conventions is here replaced by the depiction of a monastic cell and its study corner. Nevertheless, the elements of the composition are very similar, and the outlines of the saints in the two pictures are so alike as to suggest a direct connection. This last observation indicates that it is perhaps unnecessary to suppose the existence of an 'Eyckian' archetype. Master H displays

sufficient inventive capacity to have been able to produce an 'updating' of the Parisian illumination on his own.

25 God the Father enthroned and pavilioned (Pl. 30)
Turin, folio 14 *r.*, RD 49

This picture illustrates the diverse sources of the style of Master H. As Panofsky (1953, p. 235) has rightly noted, the pavilion motif originated in Tournai. However, to the examples drawn from the work of the Master of Flémalle (the *Trinity* in Leningrad and the drawing of the *Sacra Conversazione* in the Louvre) should be added those offered by funerary sculpture. The motif of flying angels supporting the pavilion only occurs in sculpture, and even then they are shown holding up a piece of drapery. This is especially the case in the *Epitaph of Jean Gervais* (d. 1400) and his wife Marie Follette (d. 1438) in Tournai Cathedral, and also in an anonymous carved epitaph depicting the *Nativity*.

Similarly, the nimbus is conceived here as an open cloud bordered by smaller fan-shaped clouds, following a convention found also in the Master of Flémalle's small panel of the *Virgin in Glory* in the museum at Aix-en-Provence. However, alongside apparent borrowings from Tournai, one cannot fail to notice reflections of Jan van Eyck. The angel musicians of the lower margin, although displaying no direct link with those of the *Mystic Lamb*, inevitably recall the theme developed in the Ghent altarpiece. But it is above all the figure of God the Father, seated on his throne and making a gesture of benediction, which invites comparison with the divine figure in the centre panel of the upper register of the polyptych. It is probable that the motif used in the Ghent altarpiece had already taken shape between 1422 and 1424, either through the panel being started or through similar compositions being worked up in the Eyckian workshop (or workshops). What is most surprising is that the very meaning of the picture seems to take on the same complexity as the Eyckian portrayal in the Ghent altarpiece. God the Father is identifiable here both by his elderly appearance and by his orb. We cannot reject the possibility, however, that the artist may have wanted to depict the Trinity in one person; the two angels standing either side of Him hold the lily and the sword, attributes of Christ the Judge. This iconographical hint reveals the originality of the theological thinking that inspired the *milieu* of Master H and Master G.

26 Pietà (Pl. 31)
Turin, folio 49 *v.*, RD 66

The choice of subject here is rather curious. The prayer is addressed to the Holy Cross, and one would sooner have expected a Crucifixion or the Cross on its own. In the *Grandes Heures* of the Duke of Berry, the same prayer is illustrated by a nobleman kneeling before an altar on which stands a Crucifix. The preference for a *Pietà* was probably imposed by the volume's owner and may reflect a personal devotion.

The composition is very characteristic of Master H. It uses only two planes. The first is reserved for the figures, which occupy most of the space. Behind is the landscape, which serves as a backdrop; it is not directly linked to the foreground and has little depth, its structure being essentially vertical. It is thus a conception quite different from Jan van Eyck's. On the other hand, it is from him that Master H borrows the idea of cutting off figures by the frame in order to suggest a greater space. The use of the technique is less subtle here, however, and the result is less suggestive.

The main group, that of the Virgin holding the body of Christ, forms such a striking plastic unity that it is reminiscent of a sculptural group. The position of Christ's head and legs, so closely matched with the Virgin's all-enveloping garments, might reflect a sculptor's attempt to create forms from a single block of wood or stone. The style of the draperies, with their multiple folds falling in cascades, is characteristic of that which became popular in northern sculpture during the first half of the fifteenth century. The *Pietà* in the church of Saint-Jacques in Liège has a sufficiently similar structure to suggest a sculpted model common to both works.

Rogier van der Weyden may have borrowed some elements of his *Pietà* in the Altarpiece of the Virgin (Granada) from Master H. But it was Petrus Christus who reproduced it most faithfully in a painting, unfortunately very worn, now in the Louvre. Nevertheless, its interpretation does not exclude acquaintance with the works of Rogier van der Weyden and inspiration by them for certain variations. In the central group, the Virgin hugs the body of Christ as in the Granada painting, although the general structure remains more faithful to the illumination. But he has chosen a stiffening of the legs in preference to the curious twisting that Master H probably inherited from his sculpted model. The kneeling Mary disappears and her gesture of grief is transferred to Mary Magdalene. As for the third Mary, her profile, so striking in the Turin picture, is retained but muted by alterations to her veil.

27 Jesus in the Garden of Gethsemane (Pl. 32)
Milan-Turin, folio 30 *v.*, RD 75

This page is one of those which, at first sight, best justified the identification of Master H with Jan van Eyck, championed by Hulin de Loo. The ample forms, the simple draperies, with broken folds gathered only on the ground, even some of the faces, are reminiscent of the reverse panels of the *Mystic Lamb*. The effects aimed at, however, are very different. In the Ghent altarpiece the forms are modelled by the light so as to take their place in niches or interiors. Here they are arbitrarily situated in a schematic landscape to which they are not organically bound. In the *Mystic Lamb* the monumentality fulfilled a function; here, it is unnecessary and assumes an aspect more fictitious than real.

In the illumination the figures are arranged in two registers, one above the other, occupying nearly the entire surface. This therefore represents a return to fourteenth-century principles, which sought to fill all the available space with figures. The two registers are treated in isolation, without any formal link between them. Rather than being connected, in fact, they are separated by the groups of rocks continued by a line of hills. In a general way, the space is divided abruptly by closely-packed, rounded hills, with only two clumps of trees to confer some semblance of reality on them. In the upper right-hand corner is a glimpse of a distant landscape which has more delicacy and atmosphere than all the rest of the composition. This is the only point at which Master H seems to have drawn any inspiration from Jan van Eyck. The colour harmony also remains linked to the principles of the preceding century. Far from being based on a blending of colours around a single dominant one, it is distinguished by

very assertive local tones, even at the expense of the subject. Thus the bright red of the robe of St. John Evangelist draws our attention even more to the foreground and away from the praying figure of Christ, whose violet-blue robe is too pale to balance its brightness.

The most important element of the scene is the group of three sleeping apostles. The artist has lavished meticulous detail on the relaxed pose of St. John and the heavy sprawling of St. Peter, whose snores can almost be heard. Lastly, the anecdotal aspect is extended to the faces, which are minutely described by pen or fine brush marks on the basic tone. This meticulousness tends to harden the expressions until they seem almost forced. The passion for an elaborate miniaturisation of details is also noticeable in the hair of St. Peter and St. John, each curl being individually represented.

28 The Crucifixion
Milan-Turin, folio 48 *v.*, RD 77

The execution of this picture shows it to be wholly by Master H. The almost grimacing faces, the overall colour harmony in which the greens of the ground and the reds of a few garments dominate by their harshness, and the stippling technique used for modulating the tone of the earth, are all indubitable trademarks of the illuminator.

On the other hand, the composition itself is surprising and runs counter to the rest of Master H's work. Here the relationship between the figures and the landscape is fundamentally different from that in *Jesus in the Garden of Gethsemane* for example: the protagonists are integrated into the landscape and, with due allowance made for the distance between the two groups, are on the same scale as the secondary figures in the middle ground. The structure of the landscape itself is conceived as a continuum whose articulations are clearly marked: the troop of horsemen indicates the line of a downhill path which ends at the city gates; and the ramparts effect a junction between this middle ground and the far distance.

All these are characteristics of compositions by Master G, i.e. Jan van Eyck, copied here by Master H. Later on we shall see Master H's second version, less close to its original model, in the panel in the Ca' d'Oro (*32*).

163

29 The Finding of the True Cross (Pl. 33)
Milan-Turin, folio 118, RD 92

This illumination had been attributed by Hulin de Loo to Master G. Dvořák (1919, 1925 ed. p. 247) wrote that it seemed to him to be by another hand. I have shown

(1958, p. 156) that it should be attributed to hand H. This last attribution is based mainly on the technique, which uses the characteristic stippling for modulation of the basic tones, especially in the treatment of the ground. It is confirmed by the structure of the landscape, which forms a backdrop and not a setting to embrace the figures, and which is divided by the typical round hills, stacked together in alternation. The association of a touch of coarseness (the servants digging the ground) with the elegance of the figures in the group including St. Helena is also significant: it recurs notably in the Turin *Pietà*.

However, the overall colour harmony is much more balanced than in the other leaves decorated by Master H. There are fewer of those harsh tones which prevent any accord. This may be so because certain parts (especially St. Helena's blue dress) show signs of having been repainted in a different technique, which gives the paint surface a slightly glossy appearance, i.e. the technique found in the leaves by Jan van Eyck, who probably retouched the illumination conceived and executed by his collaborator.

The Gothic elegance of the figures, similar to that of the *Virgin among the Virgins* (*23*), stems from the same source. Here also we can cite a Lombard model for the composition; we find a version of it by Michelino da Besozzo in the *Bodmer Book of Hours* (New York, Pierpont Morgan Library, MS. 449, cf. Castelfranchi Vergas, 1975), which can be dated *c*.1405.

The artist has not followed the *Golden Legend* exactly. Here, the Jew Judas points to the place where the servants are unearthing the crosses, instead of doing the digging himself, as in the legend. Moreover, St. Helena is surrounded by numerous characters whom the artist seems to have intended as Jews, judging by the pointed hats he has given them. As two of them are carrying sceptres, it would seem difficult to identify them with the Jewish scholars summoned by the empress to inform her of the location of the True Cross. The legend has thus been adapted here, unless the picture is based on a literary text as yet unidentified.

However that may be, it seems impossible to take the figures of the empress's suite as portraits, as has been suggested by A. Pigler (1950–1) and again by F. Lyna (1961). An artist would not have been able to give the features of influential people of his own time to figures of Jews. The face of St. Helena also seems too conventional to be claimed as a portrait of a particular person.

30 St. Francis receiving the Stigmata (Pl. 34)

Philadelphia, Johnson collection.

The 'manuscript illumination' quality of this painting — meaning a small-format picture, rich in very minutely depicted details — is not found elsewhere in the works of Jan van Eyck, even those of small format; in the *Virgin in the Church* (Berlin, Staatliche Museen) or in the *Virgin by the Fountain* (Antwerp, Musée Royal des Beaux-Arts) he works much more in the manner of a panel painter, synthesising his elements more fully. An attribution to Master H, whose qualities and training as an illuminator have been pointed out, therefore seemed unavoidable (1958). This seems to be confirmed by certain features of the execution: the craggy, deeply-cleft rocks, the characteristic shapes of the small cumulus clouds, the elongated hands and delicate wrists, and the bushy trees. Over all, the painting exhibits close parallels with the *Jesus in the Garden of Gethsemane* from *Milan-Turin* (*27*): the same structure of the landscape, the same manner of placing the figures, and the similarity of the silhouettes, whether of Christ and St. Francis or of the sleeping apostles and the Franciscan friar.

There is a larger version of the same composition in the Turin Museum. The condition of its paint surface is somewhat unsatisfactory and makes it difficult to assess. It seems unlikely, however, that it could be an original by Jan van Eyck, as suggested once again by Charles Sterling (1978, p. 53–4); it is not only the execution of the Philadelphia painting which is not Eyckian, it is the very nature of the composition.

Weale (1908) proposed to identify these two panels with those mentioned in a clause of the will of Anselme Adorno (1424–83) initialled 10 February 1470: to each of his two daughters who had entered convents, he bequeathed a small painting (*tavereele*) of St. Francis by the hand of Master Jan van Eyck (*van meester Jans handt van Eyck ghemaect staet*). The idea deserves more interest than has been shown to it. At least one of the paintings comes from Italy, where Adorno's daughters were in convents. The theme is more Italian than northern. Lastly, if Adorno commissioned the paintings himself, he could not have done so from Jan van Eyck, since he was only 17 at the time of the artist's death. Now in the fifteenth century, as in the sixteenth and seventeenth centuries, the responsibility for a work of art was not as strictly bound to execution by the artist in person as it would be today. Hence, if Master H was still painting after the death of Jan van Eyck, as seems certain, he could well have guaranteed to continue his master's work by invoking his possession of 'patterns' from the latter's hand. Thus the paintings now in Philadelphia and Turin could well be those bequeathed by Anselme Adorno, without in fact being by Jan van Eyck.

Philadelphia

Dimensions:	Wood (oak). 12.5 × 14.5.
History:	Acquired in 1830 by Lord Heytesbury from a Lisbon physician; acquired in 1890 by Mr. Johnson.
Exhibitions:	London, 1865, no. 41; London, 1886, no. 198.

Turin

Dimensions:	Wood (oak). 29.5 × 33.7.
History:	coll. of a monk at Casale (Piedmont), early nineteenth century: coll. of Prof. Bonzani, Casale; coll. of Luigi Fascio, Mayor of Feletto in Canarese, sold by him in 1866 to the Royal Gallery in Turin.
Exhibitions:	Antwerp, 1930, no. 132; Florence, 1948, no. 1.
Literature:	Waagen, 1863, p. 389 (Philadelphia: van Eyck); Phillips, 1886 (doubting Philadelphia attribution); Conway, 1887, p. 147 (Philadelphia replica of Turin); Hymans, 1888 (Turin, van Eyck); Jacobsen, 1897, p. 208 (Turin replica of Philadelphia); Voll, 1900, p. 109 (rejecting Turin as a later work); Dvořák, 1904 (Turin and Philadelphia Eyckian originals); Mather, 1906 (Philadelphia, van Eyck); Weale, 1908, p. 130–5 (Philadelphia and Turin by van Eyck, provenance from Adorno); Lane, 1908; Friedländer, I, 1924, p. 101–4; Mayer, 1926; De Poorter, 1931 (Adorno's will); Hoogewerff, 1935 (work by Christus); Tolnay, 1939, p. 68, no. 11 (Philadelphia original,

Turin copy, Jan van Eyck *c.*1438–9); Beenken, 1941 p. 23–5, (Philadelphia original, Turin later original replica, between 1426–9) Baldass, 1950 (Philadelphia overpainted?); Baldass, 1952, p. 29–30 and p. 276–7, no. 6 (Philadelphia by van Eyck before 1430, Turin old copy); Aru-Gerardon, 1952, p. 5–13 (Philadelphia and Turin originals by Jan van Eyck); Panofsky, 1953, p. 432, note 192–1 (doubting attribution to van Eyck); Châtelet, 1958, p. 161 (attribution to Master H); Châtelet-Faggin, 1969, p. 89, no. 5; Sterling, 1978, p. 29 and 53–6 (Philadelphia van Eyck).

31 The Crucifixion
Berlin, Staatliche Museen

164

This *Crucifixion*, the attribution of which to Jan van Eyck has often called forth reservations, takes its place more easily among the works of Master H. Its figures are inspired by the compositions of Jan van Eyck (New York and *Hours of Milan*), but the artist displays his originality in the way in which he fits the figures into the landscape: skilful as it is, the landscape here is a backdrop and not a setting as in the illumination of *Jesus in the Garden of Gethsemane*. The enlargement of the silhouettes by amplification of the draperies is another sign of the master working more freely.

Dimensions:	Canvas (transferred from wood). 43 × 26.
Provenance:	Acquired in 1897 from an English dealer, Mr. Buttery.
Literature:	Tschudi, 1898, p. 202–5 (J. van Eyck); Seek, 1899, p. 5–13 (not by the van Eycks); Voll, 1906, p. 48 (2nd half fifteenth century); Weale, 1908, p. 151–2 (J. van Eyck); Friedländer, I, 1924, p. 178 (J. van Eyck); Tolnay, 1939, p. 80 no. 2 (attribution to Ouwater); Beenken, 1941, p. 12–13 (Hubert van Eyck), Musper, 1948, p. 107 (Jan van Eyck *c.*1430–2); Baldass, 1952, p. 95 and no. 61 (principal master of the *Turin-Milan Hours*); Panofsky, 1953,

p. 236–7 (Pastiche); Sterling, 1976, p. 48–9 (J. van Eyck after 1426); Châtelet, 1980.

32 The Crucifixion (Pl. 35)
Venice, Ca' d'Oro

The restoration of this painting, long neglected by critics, has confirmed it as a fifteenth-century work but has also shown that it cannot be by Jan van Eyck, whose technical qualities it does not display. Hence, the attribution proposed by myself (1958) to Master H seems now even more plausible.

The painting adopts the composition of the *Milan-Turin* illumination (folio 48, cat. *28*) almost literally, at least for the foreground. However, neither work is a copy of the other, but both are clearly derived from a common model: in the illumination, the miniaturist has even oddly deprived one of the right-hand horsemen of his interlocutor while leaving him in a conversational attitude. The original group of horsemen is no doubt to be found in the painting, but in it the view of Jerusalem takes on another character and constitutes a new interpretation of the original.

The Venice panel comes from a very old Paduan family, the Dondi dall'Orologio. Italian versions dating from as far back as the fifteenth century give us reason to think that the work was known by the middle of the century in the north of Italy, where it may even have been produced, as suggested by several 'southern' details of the townscape (Châtelet, 1980). This version is thus probably the one that was known to Mantegna and was his inspiration for the central panel of the predella of the altar of San Zeno in Verona.

Dimensions:	Wood. 46 × 31 (painting 45 × 29.8). Reverse painted in red and black marbling. Unidentified wax seal (nineteenth century?).
Provenance:	Dondi dall'Orologio collection, Padua; Giorgio Franchetti collection (presented to the nation in 1916).
Exhibition:	Florence, 1947, no. 3.
Catalogues:	Ca' d'Oro, 1946, no. 37 (manner of the van Eycks); Ca' d'Oro, 1950, p. 15 (id.).
Literature:	Bodenhausen, 1905; Gamba, 1916, p. 333; Friedländer, I, 1924, p. 81 (copy); Wescher, 1936, p. 34 (seems to be an original); van Gelder, 1951, p. 324–7 (Hubert van Eyck); Baldass, 1952, p. 32 and no. 34, p. 283 (after Jan van Eyck); Panofsky, 1953, p. 235 (copy of an Eyckian original); Châtelet, 1958, p. 161 (Master H); Châtelet-Faggin, 1969, no. 8, p. 89; Sterling, 1978, p. 50–2 (copy of van Eyck); Châtelet, 1980 (Master H, *c.*1442).

33 St. Jerome (Pl. 36)
Detroit, The Detroit Institute of Arts

Only discovered in 1925, this painting has been the subject of numerous studies. As soon as it came to light, it was thought possible to identify it with a panel listed in 1492 in the collection of Lorenzo de' Medici and described as 'a St. Jerome at work, with a cupboard in perspective and a lion at his feet' (*uno San Girolamo a studio chon uno amarietto di prospettiva e uno lione a piedi*). The identification seems all the more probable as the fresco of the same subject by Ghirlandaio in the Church of Ognissanti in Florence, painted in 1482, appears to be inspired by it.

The doubts expressed recently about the work's authenticity (Marijnissen, 1978) seem baseless: they rest on insufficiently weighty scientific arguments (unusual transposition of the panel, analysis of paint specimens), details of which are in any case not given. It is true that the paint has deteriorated considerably, but it would be too hasty to cast doubt at once on the originality of the panel itself.

The date 1442 and the inscription that can be made out on a paper on the table were only discovered in 1936 and 1954 respectively, and are hence difficult to attribute to a forger, who would have sought to make them known at the time of the sale. The date excludes an execution by Jan van Eyck, the inscription, first discussed by Panofsky (1954), informs us that the painting was made for Cardinal Albergati.

This last piece of information has been analysed again by Edwin C. Hall in two articles (1968 and 1971). He thinks it possible to return to an attribution to Jan van Eyck and to imagine that the panel was commissioned by Philip the Good in 1435, during the Congress of Arras, as a gift for the cardinal legate, who took part in the diplomatic negotiations. Attractive as it is, this theory is unacceptable in that it supposes completion of the panel within two months—probably too short a time for van Eyck's technique, which required time for drying—and too early a date to be compatible with that of the painting.

It is more plausible to regard the Detroit *St. Jerome* as an original variant by Master H of the formula created for the *St. Thomas* page in the *Turin Hours* (*24*). I have suggested that the execution could have been completed in Italy like that of the *Crucifixion* in the Ca' d'Oro (Châtelet, 1980).

Dimensions:	Wood. 20 × 13.
History:	Collection of a north German noble family, which believed that the picture had come from Italy; Paul Bottenwieser, dealer in Berlin and New York; acquired in 1925 by the Detroit Institute of Arts.
Exhibitions:	London, 1927, no. 14; Chicago, 1933, no. 35; Toledo, 1935, no. 5; Cleveland, 1936, no. 186; Worcester-Philadelphia, 1939, no. 2; New York, 1939, no. 114; Bruges, 1960, no. 3 (cat. entry by H. Pauwels); Detroit, 1960, no. 5 (cat. entry by Jacqueline Folie).
Literature:	M. J. Friedländer, 1925 (first publication, attribution to Christus); W. R. Valentiner, 1925 (Christus); Strümpell, 1925–6, p. 196–200 (iconographic study); Winkler, 1927 (id. after Jan van Eyck); Baldass, 1927 (Jan van Eyck before the *Mystic Lamb*); Richardson, 1936; Tolnay, 1939, p. 76 (Christus after van Eyck); Baldass, 1952, p. 25–6 and no. 5, p. 276 (Jan van Eyck, *c*.1425); Bazin, 1952, p. 202–6 (Christus); Panofsky, 1953 (van Eyck, completed by Christus for Albergati); Panofsky, 1954 (general study); E. P. Richardson, 1956 (van Eyck, account of the restoration); Châtelet,

1958, p. 160–2 (attribution to Master H); Edwin C. Hall, 1968 (Jan van Eyck commissioned by Philip the Good, portrait of Albergati); Edwin C. Hall, 1971; Marijnissen, 1978 (forgery?); Châtelet, 1980.

After Master H

34 The Carrying of the Cross
Vienna, Albertina

It is fairly obvious that this drawing is inspired, in its overall conception, by the same original as the *Carrying of the Cross* in Budapest (*22*). Nevertheless, the differences between the two compositions are too great for this to be seen as a simple replica. Besides, the very limited nature of the gaps in the drawing indicates a meticulous copy of some model, no doubt painted, but excludes the possibility that this was a sketch. The figure-types and the spirit of the work make it clear that this is not a copy of a second version of the theme by Jan van Eyck; rather, they point to his collaborator, Master H. The drawing invites comparison especially with the *Jesus in the Garden of Gethsemane* from *Milan-Turin* (*27*).

Baudoin (Brussels cat. 1957) and Winkler (1958) attribute the drawing itself to Brueghel, an attractive and plausible theory, but one that does not affect the identification of the original model. Hieronymus Bosch probably knew the original or a copy of it; he re-uses the motif of the man and child in the centre of the drawing in the left foreground of the *Hay-wain* in the Prado.

165

Dimensions:	Pen, brown-olive ink, over traces of a preparatory drawing in black chalk, on white paper. 20.4 × 27.6.
Literature:	Schönbrunner-Meder, 1896, no. 1021 (anonymous Netherlandish); Winkler, 1916, p. 292 (after an Eyckian composition); Dvořák, 1918, p. 66 (after a Dutch work, perhaps by Ouwater); Winkler, 1924, p. 48 (after Hubert van Eyck); Benesch, 1925, p. 181 (original Dutch fifteenth-century drawing, like the *Fall of the Damned* in the Louvre); Saxl, 1926, p. 139–54 (iconographic study); Benesch, 1928, no. 22 (Dutch master *c*.1450–60); Baudoin in Brussels-Delft cat., 1957–8, p. 150 (Brueghel); Winkler, 1958 (copy by Brueghel of an Eyckian original); Berlin, 1975, no. 178; Châtelet, 1980.

North Netherlandish painter or illuminator
c.1422–30

35 The Adoration of the Magi
Berlin, Staatliche Museen, Kupferstichkabinett

This delightful drawing was considered very early on as a copy of a lost work by Hubert or Jan van Eyck. Schmidt-Degener (1910), followed by many authors, thought that it represented the panel stolen from Ambassador Tatistscheff which formed the centrepiece of a triptych whose wings consisted of the New York *Diptych*. Panofsky (1953) has shown the deficiencies of this theory (cf. *20*). The attribution to the van Eycks was mainly based on comparisons with the illuminations by hand G in the *Turin-Milan Hours*.

The figures indeed display an elegance and delicacy of outline which suggest a link with the miniatures. And yet here these characteristics become slenderness and excessive delicacy. A comparison between the figure of Melchior in the drawing and that of the peasant in the *Sovereign's Prayer* (*14*) is revealing: the pose of the two men is almost identical, and their faces have similar features. The peasant is caught in mid-movement, however, while Melchior is motionless; the peasant gives the impression of a normally built body, while Melchior is just a pleasing outline.

Taking up the remarks of Winkler (1927), who had discovered a certain number of imitations of this composition in north Netherlandish illumination, Ulrich Finke (1965) wanted to make the drawing the last link in the evolution of a formula. It is true that there are versions of an *Adoration of the Magi* similar to the drawing and earlier than the probable date of its production. The illumination in the *Missal of the Teutonic Order* in the Zwolle Museum (Finke, 1965, fig. 1) and that in the *Missal of Zweder van Culemborgh* at the seminary of Bressanone (Finke, 1965, fig. 2) are of this type. But they should be connected to a Parisian model known through the *Breviary of John the Fearless*, as has been shown by Bella Martens (1929, p. 201–3). However, it is no longer possible to follow Finke in making the illuminated versions from the Book of Hours formerly in the Blum collection at Kottbus (his fig. 3) and from the Book of Hours dated 1438 in the Meermanno-Westremianum Museum (his fig. 4) simply variations on the first formula. These two works assume an acquaintance with the Berlin drawing (or, of course, the illuminated or painted version of the same composition). Both contain a figure of Caspar which must be a more or less happy imitation of the drawing; they give him the same pose (the same, indeed, as in the *Breviary of John the Fearless*, but strained and mannered), and even copy the details of the costumes, the curious

166

fur hat and the heavy greatcoat. Melchior also has the same pose as in the drawing, which is itself indebted to the Eyckian example in the *Turin Hours*. Finally, the Kottbus illumination, crude as it is, contains a landscape forming a strip above the crib, as in the Berlin drawing, with a village in the same position and above all—betraying the copy—a hollow lane with no *raison d'être*, since no figures emerge from it.

The Berlin drawing, like the first two illuminations cited, is inspired by the illumination in the *Breviary of John the Fearless*, but also by the *Turin-Milan Hours*. On the other hand, the two later illuminations (of which one has been dated *c.*1420–30, the other 1438) are indebted to the version known through the drawing. But the drawing in the Rijksmuseum in Amsterdam (Baldass, 1952, no. 78, pl. 167), which has been associated with this group, offers a very different variant of the scene and owes nothing to the Berlin drawing and relatively little to the *Breviary*. It could be the work of a southern artist.

In conclusion, the Berlin drawing represents an imitation of Jan van Eyck and not a copy of him. Its composition was an important landmark in the development of the theme in the northern Netherlands, and was very well-known in its time. Its wide diffusion implies that a painted or illuminated version must have existed. Nevertheless, the quality of the drawing leaves open the possibility that it may be from the hand of the creator of the formula himself. If it is only a copy, at least it appears to be a contemporary copy from the early decades of the fifteenth century.

Dimensions:	Pen on parchment. 14.3 × 12.5.
Inscription:	At the bottom on the left, later inscription 'A. Thurer'.
Provenance:	Collection of J.C. Robinson (marks, Lugt, 1433); acquired in 1902.
Exhibitions:	Amsterdam, 1958, no. 172; Vienna, 1962, no. 247.
Catalogues:	Berlin, Kupferstichkabinett, 1918 (Lippmann), II, no. 214; Berlin, Kupferstichkabinett, 1930 (Bock), no. 4244.
Literature:	Schmidt-Degener, 1910; Winkler, 1915 (Dutch variants); Friedländer, I, 1924, p. 125; Winkler, 1927, p. 98–102; Panofsky, 1927–8, p. 74; Martens, 1929, p. 201–3; Byvanck, 1930, p. 133; Byvanck, 1931, p. 37; Hoogewerff, I, 1936, p. 461; Kerber, 1937, p. 19–80 (Hubert van Eyck); Tolnay, 1939, p. 37 (Ouwater); Hulin de Loo, 1943–4, p. 11; Musper, 1948, p. 88 (Jan van Eyck); Baldass, 1952, p. 95 and no. 77, p. 290 (principal master of the *Turin Hours*); Panofsky, 1953, p. 237 (copy of Jan van Eyck); Finke, 1965 (Dutch *c.*1440); Kerber, 1968 (criticising Finke, reaffirming attribution to Hubert).

Artist working in Holland *c.*1430

36 Portrait of Lysbeth van Duvenvoorde
The Hague, Mauritshuis

This charming portrait must have been painted around 1430, on the occasion of Lysbeth van Duvenvoorde's marriage. The phylactery bears the inscription 'Mi verdriet lange te hopen, wie is hi die zijn hert hout

167

open'—'I have long yearned with hope, who is he that will open his heart?'

Hoogewerff has rightly pointed out that the shape of the phylactery itself answers the question by describing an S, the first letter of the Christian name of Simon van Adrichem, the young woman's husband. There was indeed a pendant to this portrait; it appeared in a sale in the Netherlands at the beginning of this century, but has since been lost sight of. The young man also carried a phylactery with an inscription in the same style: 'Mi banget seret, wi is hi die met minne eeret', i.e. 'I am greatly troubled, who is she who will honour me with her love?'

The work is not of exceptional quality, however; the handling is wooden and the colours murky. The face, fleshy and too big for the body, gives a fair idea of the true quality of this work. Rather than a production of the International Gothic style, it should be seen as an imitation of that style. It is surprising that the left-hand panel of the diptych should have been allotted to the woman. Fifteenth-century tradition usually reserved this side for the man. We thus cannot exclude the possibility of a reproduction by tracing, leading to a reversal of poses and positions. The comparison, proposed by Karel Boon (Amsterdam, 1958, notice 171), between this painting and a drawing in Uppsala Museum is not completely convincing. The latter work displays the grand manner of the International Gothic style, not the imitation of it as here. The Adrichem family came from Beverwijk and played an important rôle in the neighbouring town of Haarlem. This picture therefore takes us to Holland. The work's reflection of the International Gothic style could be a consequence of Jan van Eyck's stay at The Hague.

Dimensions:	Parchment. 32.5 × 20.5.
Inscription:	The impaled arms of Duvenvoorde and Adrichem seem to be a later addition. Inscription on the reverse, also later: 'Afbeeltsel van Juffer Lijsbeth van Duvoorde, Heer Dircks dochter. Dij troude den 19 Meert anno 1430 aen Symon van Adrichem, Ridder, Heer Floris soon, en sterf op Ons Heeren Hemelvaerts Avond anno 1472, en is begraven in de Bewerwijck int Reguliers-convent voor het H.Cruys Autaer dat hy hadde doen maehen' (Hoogewerff, II, 1937, p. 51).
Provenance:	Coll. of H.Hetuysen, Haarlem, 1910; Jhr H. Texeira de Mattos, Vogelenzang; P. van Son, Aerdenhout;

acquired at a sale by F. Muller, Amsterdam, 1944.

Exhibitions:	Haarlem, 1915, no. 348; The Hague, 1945, no. 3; Amsterdam, 1958, no. 3; Vienna, 1962, no. 75; Hamburg, 1969, no. 21.
Literature:	N. Nahuys, 1877; Obreen, 1903; Gratama, 1915, p. 78; Huizinga, 1919 (Eng. ed. 1924); Hoogewerff, II, 1937, p. 50–4; Gerson, 1950, p. 8; Panofsky, 1953, p. 92; Boon, Amsterdam, 1958, notice 171.

The Master of Catherine of Cleves

In 1937 Byvanck tried to establish the work of this illuminator, but the many discoveries in recent decades have completely changed our view of him. Of Byvanck's attributions we can retain the seven pen drawings in a *Bible* in the Munich Library (cod. Germ. 1102). The idea of seeing the artist's beginnings in the so-called *Breviary of Reynald IV* (New York, Pierpont Morgan Library, MS. 87) also still holds good, despite the reservations expressed in most recent writings.

These have since been joined by the second fragment of the *Hours of Catherine of Cleves*, which joined the first in the Pierpont Morgan Library in 1963, and also the *Book of Hours of Derich van Sevichveld* (The Hague, 1965) and the *Book of Hours of Catherine van Lochorst* (Pieper, 1966). Taking into consideration the dates suggested or established for these various manuscripts, the illuminator must have been active between 1435 and 1455 approximately, or as early as 1430 if we accept his participation in the so-called *Breviary of Reynald IV*. He probably worked at Utrecht, but may well have also resided in Guelders.

It does not seem necessary to give a complete description of his works here, and only remarks on the *Book of Hours of Catherine of Cleves* will be given. This is the most important of all his known productions, and the one whose illustrations come closest to painting.

Literature:	essential: Beissel, 1904 (first publication of the illuminations of the *Hours of Catherine of Cleves*); Hoogewerff, I, 1936, p. 447–71 (the master is named 'Pelagius'); Byvanck, 1937, p. 65–70 (study of the œuvre); Panofsky, 1953, p. 103, 122 and 170; Plummer, 1964 (first publication of the second fragment of the *Hours of Catherine of Cleves* and reconstruction of the original arrangement of the volume); Boon, 1964 (publication of the *Book of Hours* in The Hague); The Hague, 1965 (exhibition centred on the *Book of Hours*); Plummer, 1966 (facsimile of the illuminations of the *Hours of Catherine of Cleves*); Pieper, 1966 (publication of the Münster *Book of Hours* and general study); Gorissen, 1967 (general critical study of the *Hours of Catherine of Cleves*); Delaissé, 1968, p. 37–40 and 81–6; Gorissen, 1973 (crucial study, though often debatable); Lane, 1973 B; Calkins, 1979. (The doctoral thesis of Robert G. Calkins, presented at Harvard University in 1967, has not been published)

37 The Hours of Catherine of Cleves

New York, Pierpont Morgan Library. The illuminations are designated by the number allotted to them by John Plummer in his reconstruction of the illustrative scheme of the original manuscript (Plummer, 1964 and 1966). These numbers are preceded by the letter P.

The content of these *Hours* is very comprehensive: it combines the Hours of the Virgin, of the Cross, of the Trinity, of the Dead, of the Holy Ghost, of All the Saints, of the Holy Sacrament, of the Lamentation over Christ, and also the Masses for the Dead, the Holy Ghost, All Saints, the Holy Sacrament, the Cross and the Virgin, and even the Penitential Psalms and the Invocations of the saints. Taking into consideration a number of missing folios, the original volume must have contained 369 folios. The pages measure 192 × 130 mm. There are 157 illuminations, of which 25 are full page. The borders are extensively decorated with grotesques and arabesques, even on the leaves without illuminations.

There is no doubt about the identification of the owner as Catherine of Cleves, despite some anomalies in the coats of arms on the first two folios (P. 1 and 2, cf. Pieper, 1966 and Gorissen, 1973). On the illumination of the Crucifixion (P. 96) the donor is only wearing a light veil over her hair. F. Gorissen (1965) states that this type of head-dress can only be that of a young unmarried woman. He thus saw her first (1965) as Catherine of Cleves before her marriage, while P. Pieper (1966, p. 141–2) preferred to see her as the duchess's eldest daughter, Marie, born in 1433. Finally, F. Gorissen imagined that she was a young woman of the Lochorst family to whom the duchess had given the manuscript before its completion (1967, p. 15–16, and 1973). This theory is based on the presence, in illumination P. 97, of cushions whose embroidery can be taken as a depiction of the Lochorst arms, and on the rather arbitrary interpretation of the initials ED in illumination P. 116 as an abbreviation of Ermengard. It seems difficult to accept such speculations, despite their ingenuity; the identification of Ermengard van Lochorst is too tenuously supported. In fact, it is probably a false problem: F. Gorissen has never proved that custom absolutely forbade a young married woman to wear only a single veil over her hair. Plummer (1968, p. 20) has tried to show, with some possibly disputable examples, that this alleged rule was not observed, but he was probably on the right track: the young woman in the *Crucifixion* is indeed Catherine of Cleves.

Similarly, the complex analysis of the illumination of the *Adoration of the Trinity* (P. 40), also proposed by F. Gorissen (1968 and 1973), must be rejected. It is not necessary to the see the emperor depicted as Frederick III (crowned in 1442); it could be Albert II (1438–41), whose brief reign did not permit a wide distribution of his portrait. To see two popes in the illumination smacks of gratuitous speculation; even in a time of

schism, an illuminator would not have depicted more than one pope, namely the one recognised by his clients. There are thus only two elements which can serve to date the manuscript: the coins shown in the border of the page featuring St. Gregory (P. 117), which set a *terminus post quem* of 1434 (Plummer, 1966 and Gorissen, 1973) and the dating of the manuscript relative to the illuminator's other works. The drawings of the Munich Bible dated 1439 seem to belong to a later development. The *St. Michael* of the manuscript dated 1438 in the Meermanno-Westreemianum Museum, corresponding to illumination P. 101, certainly displays a more advanced handling if it is indeed by the same artist; but there is a fluidity which assorts uneasily with the work of the Master of Catherine of Cleves, and suggests execution by another illuminator from a common model (perhaps by Jan van Eyck?). One is thus led to conclude an execution before 1439 and after 1434; this can be simplified to 1435–40.

The tendency to argue for a date later than 1440 (Finke, 1964, Gorissen, 1973) seems unjustified.

The illuminations

P. 1 The Virgin of the Immaculate Conception adored by Catherine of Cleves (Pl. 42)

Borders with coats of arms: bottom centre, the princess's (Cleves and Guelders impaled); above, Cleves and Mark; below, Bavaria and Brieg.

The framing of the picture by a moulding which is transformed into the columns of an architectural niche is an archaistic device which can be traced back to the fourteenth century.

P. 2 The Angel's Message to Joachim

The coats of arms in the borders — France and Flanders above, Juliers and Berg below — complement those on the preceding page, opposite, to represent the houses of the princess's eight great-grandparents.

The landscape is perhaps devised from a very freely interpreted recollection of the illumination *Jesus in the Garden of Gethsemane* by Master H in the *Milan-Turin Hours* (27).

P. 3 Angels singing

Borders with realistic decoration: open pods with golden peas inside. According to Plummer (1964, p. 26) they accompanied a lost illumination, a pendant to this one, showing the Angel's Message to St. Anne, and represented fertility.

P. 4 The Meeting at the Golden Gate

Full page. Interpretation of a lost composition by the Master of Flémalle?

P. 5 The Nativity of the Virgin

Inspired by the background of Jan van Eyck's illumination, *The Nativity of St. John the Baptist*, in the *Milan-Turin Hours* (18). Gorissen (1968, p. 20, and 1973, p. 265) sees the two beehives in the border as a symbol derived from a vision of St. Bridget, to whom the Virgin had appeared with a beehive to symbolise the union of soul and body in the mother's womb.

P. 6 The Presentation at the Temple

Full page. Free transposition of the *Purification* from the *Très Riches Heures du duc de Berry* (folio 54 v.), itself inspired by the *Presentation at the Temple* by Taddeo Gaddi (fresco in Santa Croce, Florence).

P. 7 The Choice of Joseph

First page with an architectural frame. According to Panofsky (in Plummer 1964, p. 10) the device is derived from the Master of the Boucicaut Hours, but it could just as easily have been borrowed from other illuminations like those by Master B in the *Milan-Turin Hours*. It is interpreted in a completely individual manner which was to enjoy great success in the northern Netherlands: the extrados of the arch is bare or slightly hollowed, while the soffit may be discreetly moulded.

P. 8 The Marriage of the Virgin

Full page. Free transposition of the main group from the *Marriage of the Virgin* by the Master of Flémalle (Madrid, Prado).

P. 9 God sends the angel of the Annunciation

The depiction of God is inspired by the *God the Father giving benediction* from the *Turin Hours* (folio 75 v.) by illuminator J, or by the variants occurring on other pages of the manuscript; the motif itself is an interpretation of the Almighty from the *Mystic Lamb*.

P. 10 The Annunciation

Full page. The arrangement and pose of the figures are versions of those in the painting in the Musées Royaux, Brussels, which is itself a variant of the *Mérode Triptych*. On the other hand, the scene is set in an oratory. The two shields hanging from the keystones of the building correspond to the arms of St. George; their presence can hardly be explained except by a whim of the illuminator.

P. 11 The Visitation

The picture does not seem to be based on a model by another master. The illumination in the lower margin shows the Child Jesus and St. John the Baptist playing at catching birds — no doubt an allegory of the catching of souls.

P. 12 The Nativity

Full page. Free interpretation of the *Nativity* by the Master of Flémalle (Dijon, Musée des Beaux-Arts).

P. 13 The Flight into Egypt

Scene of the main picture depicted very simply. In the border, at the lower right-hand corner, a woman churning milk: this is doubtless a purely realistic motif, with no allegorical significance.

P. 14 The Death of the Virgin

Composition fairly similar to the painting in the National Gallery, London, considered to be a copy of a lost original by the Master of Flémalle.

P. 15 The Assumption

Naïve composition, rather weakly handled

168

The Vengeance of Lamech, Munich, Cod. Germ. 1102 folio 11 v.

169

P. 16   Jesus in the Garden of Gethsemane

Full page. Free interpretation of the composition by Master H in the *Milan-Turin Hours* (*27*).

P. 17   The Taking of Christ

Could be an interpretation of the illuminated page from the *Turin Hours* (*15*) or of an intermediate composition inspired by it.

P. 18   Jesus before Caiaphas

Full page. Skilful composition, which seems to owe nothing either to the Master of Flémalle or to Eyckian models.

P. 19   The Mocking of Christ

Similar layout in the *Book of Hours of John the Fearless* (Paris, Bibliothèque Nationale, Lat. MS. new acq. 3055, cf. Panofsky, 1953, fig. 184).

P. 20   Jesus before Pilate

Full page. Composition akin to that of P. 18. In the border, a figure gives a comic illustration of the theme of the washing of the hands in the central scene. The two facing cocks at the bottom of the page seem to have no allegorical significance.

P. 21   Jesus before Herod

Simple composition, probably without direct model.

P. 22   The Scourging

Full page. No doubt inspired directly by a lost painting, as indicated by the curious moulding at the bottom, designed to reduce the picture's size in order to adapt it to the proportions of the model. This could have been another work by the Master of Flémalle.

The same composition is re-used in the *Book of Hours written by Aetzart van Zaers* (Leiden, University Library) and more freely in the *Book of Hours of Catherine van Lochorst* (Münster, cf. Pieper, 1966, p. 8).

170

P. 23   The Crowning with Thorns

Layout perhaps inspired by that of the *Mocking of Christ* (P. 19).

P. 24   The Carrying of the Cross

Uses the central group from the Eyckian *Carrying of the Cross* known through the copy in Budapest (*22*), reproduced in reverse.

171

P. 25   Preparations for the Crucifixion (Pl. 51)

Association of the theme of Christ awaiting execution with a more picturesque study of the carpenters completing work on the cross.

P. 26   The Crucifixion

Rather than a copy of a lost work by the Master of Flémalle, this should be seen as an original work conceived from elements of the latter's *Triptych of the Descent from the Cross* (fragment in Frankfurt, copy in Liverpool). Gerard David adopted the same composition in his early work (Lugano, Thyssen collection).

172

P. 27   Joseph of Arimathaea before Pilate

Variant of the layout for *Christ before Pilate* (P. 20). The hunting scene at the foot of the page, which probably has no allegorical overtones, is very similar to the one in the *Rhymed Bible* by Jacob van Maerlant (Groningen, University Library, folio 9; Hoogewerff, 1922–5, pl. 22).

P. 28   The Deposition from the Cross

Directly inspired by the lost panel by the Master of Flémalle (copy in the Walker Art Gallery, Liverpool).

P. 29   The Lamentation over Christ

Probably there was no direct model for this composition.

P. 30   The Entombment

Development of a motif in northern illumination known through an illumination in a Book of Hours from the S. Cockerell collection, Cambridge (Byvanck, 1938, fig. 98).

P. 31   The Resurrection

Interpretation of a layout developed in north Germany: cf. the painting by the Master of St. Laurence (Cologne, Wallraf-Richartz Museum; Stange, III, fig. 74).

P. 32–6   Depictions of the Persons of the Trinity

Five variations on the depiction of one or more divine Persons seated on a throne, perhaps inspired by examples in the *Turin-Milan Hours*.

P. 37   God the Father sends Jesus down to earth

Isolated treatment of a motif more usually associated with the Annunciation (esp. in the *Mérode Triptych*). The realistic scene in the lower margin, in spite of its everyday atmosphere, is an allegory of Christ's fishing for souls.

P. 38   The Throne of Grace

Variant of the layout used notably by the Master of Flémalle.

P. 39   The Trinity

Composition akin to P. 32–6.

P. 40   The Adoration of the Trinity

It is impossible to follow Gorissen in his historical interpretations of the characters (1973, p. 699–706). It is not pope and antipope who are depicted here, but the pope on the left accompanied by two cardinal legates and a bishop on the right (despite the illuminator's whim of reversing the colours of the ribbons on the tiara and the mitre). The presence of the Emperor beside the bishop and not behind the pope is unusual, but is probably of no more significance than the reversal of the colours of the ribbons. The stag grazing at the foot of the page is a reproduction of a model by the Master of the Playing-Cards (stags on cards 3, 4, 6 and 7, Lehrs 75–8). The owl occurs in the engraving of the fifth day of creation by the Master of the Banderoles (Lehrs 2), perhaps itself copied from a lost engraving by the Master of the Berlin Passion.

173

P. 41   The Death of a rich man (Pl. 43).

Full page. With its down-to-earth realism, this illumination is a predecessor both of the engravings in the *Ars Moriendi* and of the *Death of the Miser* by Bosch (Washington, National Gallery).

P. 42   Souls of the Damned in Hell
The similarity of the pose of the young woman raising her arms in horror to a figure from the *Damned* by Dieric Bouts (Lille, Musée des Beaux-Arts) may indicate a common model for both works. Gorissen (1973, p. 1006–8) suggests, without much reason, that this is a reflection of the lost predella of the *Mystic Lamb*.

P. 43–8   Illustrations of the Prayers for the Dead (Pl. 45)
Unusual sequence: preparation of the corpse, vigil, interment, requiem, three souls fed in Hell by an angel, some of the damned rescued from Hell.

174

P. 49   The Last Judgment
Full page. One of the most elaborate illuminations. Development of a layout very popular in the northern Netherlands (cf. esp. *Breviary of Mary of Guelders*, Berlin, MS. Ger. Q 42, folio 18 *v.*; Byvanck, 1938, fig. 33).

P. 50   St. Michael weighing souls
First example of the device adopted throughout the rest of the book for the depiction of saints: on a narrow strip of ground in front of a ceremonial hanging.
The heron at the bottom of the page is borrowed from an engraving by the Master of the Playing-Cards (Lehrs 61).

P. 51   Pentecost
Probably an 'updating' of an older layout known through the illumination from the *Missal of Zweder van Culemborgh* (Bressanone, MS. C 20, folio 173 *v.*; Byvanck, 1938, fig. 103).

P. 52   The Judgment of Solomon
One of the illuminations closest to the illustrations of the Munich *Bible*, both in the complexity of the draperies and in the attempt to secure the effect of movement.
The heron in the border is once again copied from the Master of the Playing-Cards (Lehrs 61).

P. 53   Solomon prays for the gift of understanding

P. 54   Solomon in council

P. 55   Jacob and the angel

P. 56   Master and pupils
A group of illuminations probably not based on models, and with a passion for everyday detail. The two herons at the foot of P. 53 and P. 54 are very similar, but not identical, to the two examples by the Master of the Playing-Cards.

P. 57   Alms-Giving (Pl. 50)
The young woman is probably intended to represent Catherine of Cleves, as Plummer and Gorissen have noted. One of the Master's most remarkable personal compositions by its vigorous characterisations.

P. 58   The Fear of God
Plummer sees the praying man as a portrait of Duke Arnold, the husband of Catherine of Cleves, a plausible suggestion though not confirmed by any attribute.

P. 59   St. Peter gives the blessing of the Holy Ghost
Full page. The architectural setting seems inspired by that first used by Rogier van der Weyden in the *Miraflores Triptych* (rather than by that of the *Maelbecke Madonna* by van Eyck, as suggested by Gorissen [1973, p. 470]).

P. 60   Simon Magus and St. Peter
Probably an original composition.

P. 61   God the Father receiving the prayers of the saints (Pl. 49)
Full page. The motif of the throne floating in the air may be borrowed from the Master of Flémalle.

P. 62 to P. 67   Illustration of the prayers of all the saints
Variation on the theme of illumination P. 61, with the exception of P. 62, which depicts the Virgin interceding with Christ.

P. 68   St. Michael fighting the Demon
The elegance of the outline suggests a model from the circle of the Limbourgs.

P. 69   St. Peter, St. John the Baptist and St. Martin

P. 70   Solomon distributing the bread

P. 71   Moses and St. John the Evangelist before a monstrance

P. 72   Communion

P. 73   Isaiah, Aaron, Paul and Luke praying before a monstrance
Group of illuminations probably not based on any models.

P. 74   The Fall of the Manna
Similar interpretations of this theme, inspired perhaps by an earlier Netherlandish version, occur with some variations in the *Speculum Humanae Salvationis*, in the painting by the Master of the *Manna* and in the *Last Supper Triptych* by Bouts.

P. 75   The Supper at Emmaus
Probably an original composition.

P. 76   The Passover
This representation was foreshadowed by the one in the so-called *Breviary of Reynald IV* (folio 195 *r.*) and is a direct forerunner of the one by Bouts in the *Last Supper Triptych*.

175

P. 77   The Last Supper
Full page. The similarity of this interpretation of the subject to that by the Master of the Lyversberg Passion (Cologne, Wallraf-Richartz Museum, cf. Stange, V, fig. 85) proves that the formula must have been adopted in the circle of Dieric Bouts, probably by the Master of the *Taking of Christ*. The composition exists in embryonic form in an illumination from the manuscript by Dirc van Delft in the British Museum (Add. MS. 22.288, folio 156).

176

P. 78   Moses and St. Paul at a Mass
Composition similar to those of illuminations P. 71–3.

P. 79–85   Story of the wood of the True Cross (Pl. 46)
Very rare subjects, known in the Netherlands at least through the Chronicle of Jean d'Outremeuse, as Gorissen has shown (1973, p. 494–505). The themes are interpreted with a freshness that is disconcerting in its homeliness. In several pages, the common touch is emphasised by the popular appeal of the scenes illustrated at the foot of the page.

P. 86   The Pool of Bethesda
This scene, which belongs to the 'wood of the True Cross' group, is a free variation on a composition known through a drawing in the Brunswick Museum attributed to the Master of the Rohan Hours (Ring, 1949, fig. 36).

P. 87   The Man of Sorrows
At the bottom of the page is the mystic winepress, a motif already present in the *Treatise* by Dirc van Delft (New York, Pierpont Morgan Library, MS. 691, folio 5; Byvanck, 1938, fig. 16).

P. 88   The Creation of Eve
Full page. Probably inspired by a lost painting (by a member of the van Eyck circle?). A variant of the same composition can be found in the Vienna *Bible* (MS. 2771, folio 10; Delaissé, 1968, fig. 94). Barbara Lane (1973 B) has shown that illuminations P. 88 to P. 97, which illustrate the Hours of the Virgin for Saturday, constitute a cycle on the theme of the Immaculate Conception.

P. 89   Eve and the Virgin Mary

P. 90   The Tree of Jesse

P. 91   Joachim and St. Anne
Probably not based on a model.

P. 92 and P. 93   The Holy Family (Pl. 47)
Notable for the domestic intimacy, which develops the formula of the *Mérode Triptych* with a rather spontaneous fancifulness.

P. 94   Christ appearing to the Virgin Mary
Rendering of a subject suggested by depictions of the Ascension.

P. 95   The Burial of the Virgin Mary
A rare theme which appears in northern Germany in the sculpted part of the *St. Barbara Altarpiece*, whose wings are by Master Francke (Helsinki, National Museum).

P. 96   The Crucifixion with the Virgin interceding and Catherine of Cleves presented by a saintly abbot (St. Bernard?) (Pl. 48)
The iconography of this curious page has been scrupulously analysed by Barbara G. Lane (1973): the princess prays to the Virgin, who intercedes with Christ, who Himself appeals to God the Father.
The geometrical motifs in the border may reflect acquaintance with the pavement mosaics of northern Italy—such as that in St. Mark's, Venice—rather than with Moorish designs.

P. 97   The Virgin and Child in an arbour
Gorissen has rightly pointed out the similarity of the Virgin's pose to that in the Annunciation from the *Mérode Triptych* (1967, p. 49). The subject is akin to that of the 'Virgin with the rose-bush' so dear to German art.

P. 98   The Man of Sorrows adored by penitents
Variation on the theme of the *Vision of St. Gregory*.

P. 99   Hell
Full page. Similar to illuminations P. 42, 47 and 48, but on a larger scale.

P. 100   Absolution
Composition inspired by the traditional illustrations for the Office of the Dead (cf. Meiss, 1968 B).

P. 101   St. Michael (ill. 178)
Composition re-used with variations in manuscript 10 E 1 in the Meermanno-Westremianum Museum at The Hague, dated 1438 (ill. 177). Inspired by an Eyckian painting?

177

Illumination in a Book of Hours dated 1438, The Hague, Meermanno-Westremianum Museum

178

P. 102   Angel and demon fighting over a soul
In some respects a trivial variant of the illumination in the *Rohan Hours*, 'The dead man before his judge'. It is not impossible that these two works, albeit so different, were inspired by a common model.

P. 103–115   St. John the Baptist and the Apostles
St. John the Baptist and St. James the Greater (P. 107) are set in a landscape, the other saints stand on a narrow strip of tiling in front of a ceremonial hanging.
The border decorations often pose problems. In several cases the motifs chosen have a fairly obvious connection with the saint: fish for St. Peter, the former fisherman (P. 104), St. John's martyrdom beneath his portrait (P. 108), the Mayday drinking scene for St. James the Less, whose feast falls on 1 May (P. 110), the decoration imitating a carved wooden frame for St. Matthew, patron saint of woodworkers (P. 113), fishing nets for St. Simon the fisherman (P. 114), the cross formed from four axes (and not a swastika) for Matthias, whose emblem is an axe (P. 115). In other cases, the connection between the scenes or motifs in the borders and the principal character is doubtful: David and the lion with St. Paul (P. 105), a wild man killing a swan for St. Andrew (P. 106), a widow or nun giving alms to a monk (for a pilgrimage?) with St. James the Greater (P. 107), a female heretic (the placards she wears on her head and breast probably designate her as such) under St. Thomas (perhaps through confusion

with St. Thomas Aquinas?) (P. 109), the preparation of bread with St. Philip (P. 111), the 'pretzels' and biscuits for St. Bartholomew (P. 112). Should they simply be taken as fanciful decorations or as references to cults peculiar to a region and now forgotten? I incline towards the former view.

P. 116   The Adoration of the Magi
A similar composition to that of the Eyckian drawing in Berlin (35), but not directly derived from it. The choice of a coral rosary as a marginal decoration is difficult to explain.

179

P. 117–123   Various Saints (Pl. 44)
As with the preceding series, the problems mainly concern the decoration of the borders: coins hardly represent St. Gregory's rôle as a church administrator, as Gorissen supposes (1967, p. 55–P. 117); the banner can be made to fit St. Jerome as a prince of the church but would be suitable for plenty of other saints (P. 118), mussels and crabs have no particular connection with St. Ambrose (P. 119); the pierced hearts are the emblem of St. Augustine (P. 120); the cages of birds recall the fact that the feast of SS. Cornelius and Cyprian (14 September) marked the opening of the season for goldfinches, and arrows and crossbows are natural attributes for St. Sebastian (P. 123).

180

P. 124 The Conversion of St. Hubert
Perhaps inspired by a model from the Parisian studios. The doe in the illumination in the lower margin is very similar to those by the Master of the Playing-Cards.

181

P. 125 The Martyrdom of St. Erasmus
A depiction which foreshadows that by Dieric Bouts in his Louvain triptych.

P. 126 The Martyrdom of the Ten Thousand and St. Achatius
Composition imitated very closely in the *Montfoort Book of Hours* (Vienna, Cod. ser. no. 12.878, folio 135 *v.*; Byvanck, 1938, fig. 151; Pächt and Jenni, 1975, pl. III and p. 31–2).

P. 127 to 130 Various Saints
The chained dogs on the background tapestry and the monkey flushing out birds in the initial appear to have no connection with any of St. Blaise's characteristics (P. 127); the fishes have no connection with St. Laurence, unless some confusion has arisen with another deacon saint, St. Vincent, whose body was fished out of the sea (P. 128), the butterflies have even less to do with St. Vincent (P. 129), or dragonflies with St. Valentine (P. 130).

P. 131 The Stoning of St. Stephen
Conception and graphic style very close to the drawings in the Munich Bible.

P. 132 St. George
Similar interpretation to that on folio 23 of the *Hours of Marshal Boucicaut* (Meiss, 1968, fig. 10), but the idea may have been known through an Eyckian version of the theme.

P. 133 St. Christopher
Variation on an iconographic design very popular in the north and south Netherlands, examples of which are an Eyckian drawing in the Louvre and the wing of the *Pearl of Brabant Triptych* (Munich, Alte Pinakothek).

P. 134 St. Adrian
Illumination from the series of saints, without special features.

P. 135 St. Martin
As Gorissen has noted (1973, p. 955–6), the saint's horse is borrowed from the *Sovereign's Prayer* in the *Turin Hours* (*14*). The composition is also similar to the earlier version in the so-called *Breviary of Reynald IV* (Pierpont Morgan Library, MS. 87, folio 410 *v.*; Delaissé, 1968, fig. 25).

P. 136–157 Various Saints
The remarkable sky revealed through a gap in the clouds and the groups of three monsters yoked together have no connection with St. Nicholas (P. 136); on the other hand, St. Maurus rescuing a drowning man (*Golden Legend*, Roze ed., I, p. 238–9) is indeed a subsidiary episode of the legend of St. Benedict (P. 137); St. Alexis is shown under his staircase (P. 142); the Tree of Jesse is naturally suitable for St. Anne, but the bizarre insertion of a dog in one branch of the line is still unexplained (P. 143); the monkey has little to do with St. Catherine (P. 145), likewise the porcupine with St. Barbara (P. 146); the pearls may be a reference to the story of the suitor who actually promised diamonds to St. Agnes (P. 147; *Golden Legend*, Roze ed., I, p. 141); the angel musicians in a garden ornamented with a fountain in the form of a castle seem to have no special connection with St. Dorothy; jewels and caskets can hardly be said to suit St. Agatha, unless a pun on her name was intended (P. 150); a falcon and feathers seem rare attributes for St. Cecilia (P. 151); the demon tempting a man does not occur in the legend of St. Gertrude (P. 154); the woman spinning only suits St. Martha in her capacity of housewife.
The figure of St. Mary Magdalene (P. 144) imitates the outline and pose of one of the Marys in the painting attributed to Hubert van Eyck in the Boymans-van Beuningen Museum in Rotterdam.

Provenance:	1) Guennol volume: Jacques Joseph Techener, bookseller, Paris (cf. *Bulletin du Bibliophile*, 12th series, 1856); collection of the Duke of Arenberg; Guennol collection, New York; acquired in 1971 by the Pierpont Morgan Library;
	2) Morgan volume: European private collection; acquired in 1963 from a New York dealer by the Pierpont Morgan Library.
Exhibitions:	Düsseldorf, 1904, no. 564 (Guennol vol.); Amsterdam, 1958, no. 157 (Guennol vol.); New York, 1964 (both volumes).
Literature:	Beisel, 1904; Hulin de Loo, 1911 B (*c.*1430); Byvanck, 1923; Byvanck, 1931 (*c.*1440); Hoogewerff, I, 1936, p. 447–56 (*c.*1435–40); de Wit, 1937 (*c.*1430); Byvanck, 1937, p. 65–6 and 117–8; Boon, 1947, p. 36 and 38; Panofsky, 1953, p. 103, 122 and 176 (*c.*1435); Gorissen, 1958 (*c.*1431); Plummer, 1964 (1435); Finke, 1963, p. 61 (1445); Boon, 1964 (*c.*1440–5); Gorissen, 1965 (after 1428); Pieper, 1965 (*c.*1440); Plummer, 1966 (facsimile of the whole work, *c.*1440–5); Pieper, 1966, p. 128–45 (*c.*1440–5); Gorissen, 1967 (1442–5); Delaissé, 1968, p. 37–40 and 81–6 (*c.*1440); Gorissen, 1973; Lane, 1973; Lane, 1973 B; Scillia, 1978; Calkins, 1979.

Artist working in Guelders *c.*1440

38 The Roermond Altarpiece
Amsterdam, Rijksmuseum

From the Church of St. Mary, Roermond, in Guelders. Hoogewerff (I, 1936, p. 180–1) has identified the donor as Bela van Mirlaer, the daughter of Jan van Mirlaer, Lord of Milendonck, and of Bela Sheiffart van Merode-Hemmersbach, who in 1447 became abbess of a convent of noble nuns in Roermond. As she is shown in the painting without an abbess's insignia, the work must have been commissioned before 1447.

182

Dimensions:	Wood. 103 × 167.
Provenance:	Church of St. Mary, Roermond: acquired in 1889.
Exhibitions:	The Hague, 1945, no. 2; Amsterdam, 1958, no. 4.
Literature:	Winkler, 1923, p. 139; Winkler, 1924, p. 67; Friedländer, III, 1926, p. 63, no. 39; Hoogewerff, I, 1936, p. 177–88; Gerson, 1950, p. 8.

Artist working in Guelders *c.*1430–40

39 The Crucifixion
Kranenburg, Church of St. Peter and St. Paul

Either side of the cross are shown the Virgin Mary and St. John the Evangelist, St. Antony and St. Catherine and two donors kneeling at the feet of the latter two saints. Gorissen (1954) identified these figures with Count Adolf II of Cleves and his mother Margaret of Berg (in preference to the count's second wife, Mary of Burgundy). But there are no distinctive clues to justify this theory.
The attribution of the painting to Malouel is no better based and was rejected in the catalogue for the Amsterdam exhibition of 1958. The costume of the donors suggests a date of *c.*1430–40. The depiction of the Crucifixion is fairly similar to that in the *Roermond Altarpiece* (*38*). The work gives the impression of being a provincial production marked by archaisms.

Dimensions:	Wood. 100 × 135.
Exhibition:	Amsterdam, 1958, no. 2.
Literature:	Clemen, 1892, p. 129; Gorissen, 1953, p. XXIII; Gorissen, 1954, pl. and note between pages 180 and 181.

Artist working in Holland *c.*1450–60

40 St. Agnes and Geertruy Haeck
Amsterdam, Rijksmuseum

The donor of this painting has been identified by Luttervelt (Amsterdam, 1958, no. 5) as Geertruy Haeck, née van Slingelandt and married to a prominent citizen of Dordrecht, Adriaen Haeck, who assumed various municipal duties between 1436 and 1449. Four members of his family entered the convent of St. Agnes at Dordrecht between 1450 and 1477.

The painted architectural setting has a column on the left, but the arcade finishes in a respond on the right. In other words, the painting seems designed to be continued on the left by one or several other panels. The present panel may have been complemented by one depicting a saint and Adriaen Haeck in prayer. However, the column suggests a larger ensemble, which may have been a non-closing triptych, including a central scene—*Virgin and Child* or *Crucifixion*—and a left-hand wing with the donor and his patron saint. This formula would probably correspond better to the fact that the surviving portrait is heavily weighted towards the right, which would be less necessary in a diptych.

The depiction of St. Agnes with a lamb leaning against her must have been very popular in the northern Netherlands. It occurs in the *Hours of Catherine of Cleves* (P. 147). The modelling is fairly heavy, the perspective quite empirical and clumsy, the poses stiff and stereotyped.

Dimensions: Wood. 60.5 × 46.4.
Provenance: English private collection: sold at Christie's, London, 17 May 1957, lot 107 (Bruges school); acquired from an English dealer.
Exhibition: Amsterdam, 1958, no. 5.

Albert van Ouwater

(Lambrecht Rutgenssoen? active from 1428 to 1465)

Our entire knowledge of Albert van Ouwater still depends on what Karel van Mander (1604) tells us about him. No reference in public records, not even the one that van der Willigen believed he had found, can possibly relate to the artist under the name given him by the seventeenth-century historian.

None of the theories put forward concerning him can be allowed to stand (Châtelet, 1960). Karl Simon (1905) identified him with a 'weltberimte Mahler' Albert, artist of an altarpiece in Glogau Cathedral dated 1476. Dvořák (1919) and Charles de Tolnay (1939), rejecting the identification of the Berlin painting, preferred to see him as Master G of the *Turin–Milan Hours*. Valentiner (1943) wanted to credit him with the entire output of the Master of the *Tiburtine Sibyl* and the Master of Bolloour Finally, K G P sss tried to discover traces of his influence in fifteenth-century Netherlandish painting (1947). Donat de Chapeaurouge (1977) imagines contacts in Burgundy with the artist identified with Henri Vulcop. The list of works proposed here reveals a style strongly influenced by Jan van Eyck, but also highly individual.

Literature: van Mander, 1604 (ed. Hymans, p. 87–8); Friedländer, III, 1925, p. 56–63); Schöne, 1942; Boon, 1947; Panofsky, 1953, p. 319–24; Châtelet, 1960; Snyder, 1960; Donat de Chapeaurouge, 1977; Châtelet, 1979, p. 179–81.

41   The Man holding a Pink (ill. 57)
Berlin, Staatliche Museen

This famous painting, initially attributed to Hubert or Jan van Eyck, has for several decades been considered by critics to be only the work of an imitator of Jan. The sitter has not been identified. The collar of the Order of St. Anthony of the house of Hainault suggests a date before the death of Jacqueline of Bavaria (1436).

The work has an odd feature: the portrait is surrounded by a painted frame, which seems original on three sides (the top part has been restored, according to information kindly given by Dr. Rainald Grosshans). It is even more remarkable that the sitter's right hand casts a shadow across this fictive frame, to show that it is above it.

The Master of Aix-la-Chapelle has given this sitter's face to Melchior in an *Adoration of the Magi* (Cologne, 1961, no. 36). This is a further interesting hint in favour of a Dutch origin for the painting; the Cologne artist shows familiarity with the Netherlandish world. Moreover, the earliest known owner of the painting was the count of Landsberg, whose houses at Velen and Gemen, in the ecclesiastical principality of Münster, are very close to Dutch territory.

Dimensions: Wood (oak). 41.5 × 31.5.
Provenance: coll. of Philip Engels (sold at Cologne, 16 May 1867, lot 17) (Hubert van Eyck); acquired by Suermondt, Aix-la-Chapelle; acquired in 1874 by the Staatliche Museen with a large part of the collection.
Exhibition: Bruges, 1867, no. 3.
Literature: Galichon, 1867 (Jan van Eyck); Brüger, 1869 (J. van Eyck, between 1432 and 1436, engraving by Guillard); Kaemerer, 1898 (J. van Eyck, c.1433); Seek, 1899 (Hubert van Eyck, before 1422); Voll, 1900, p. 113–9 (not J. van Eyck); Voll, 1906, p. 45–6 (late fifteenth-early sixteenth c.); Weale, 1908, p. 122–4 (Hubert or Jan); Weale-Brockwell, 1912 (*id.*); Friedländer, I, 1924, p. 93 (J. van Eyck, c.1422–5); Burroughs, 1938, p. 236 (handling not Eyckian); Tolnay, 1939, p. 77, no. 3 (attribution doubtful); Beenken, 1941, p. 57 note (not by van Eyck, c.1440); Cornette, 1947; Musper, 1948, p. 104 (J. van Eyck 1430–2); Ring, 1949, p. 216, no. 144 (J. van Eyck); Baldass, 1952, p. 289 (follower of J. van Eyck); Panofsky, 1953, p. 201 and 438 (not first half of fifteenth century); Winkler, 1959 B, p. 202–4 (Mostaert); Bauch, 1962, p. 110 (early sixteenth-century copy of an early work by J. van Eyck); Châtelet-Faggin, 1969, p. 94 (attribution to J. van Eyck, c.1435); Grosshans in Berlin, 1975 (follower of J. van Eyck).

42   The Raising of Lazarus (Pls. 53 to 56)
Berlin, Staatliche Museen

The identification of the painting is based on the description given by van Mander: 'There existed, by van Ouwater, a painting of medium height. It depicted the Raising of Lazarus. For the period when this work was produced, the figure of Lazarus deserved to be considered a very remarkable nude. In the same painting could be seen a fine temple, with columns which were unfortunately rather small. On one side were the apostles, on the other the Jews. There were also some good female figures, and in the background people watching the scene through the pillars of the choir.'

This description is too precise in its details, especially the reference to the figures watching the scene from the ambulatory, for the identification with the Berlin painting to be doubted, as it has been by Dvořák (1918) and Tolnay (1939).

For the iconographic elements of the scene, cf. Chapter IV above. It is very probable that the painting was the epitaph of a young woman shown in the guise of Mary; this figure, by reason of its prominence, its costume, which seems more contemporary than that of the other characters, and its face, may well be considered a portrait.

The interpretation by Donat de Chapeaurouge (1977), who sees the prominence of St. Peter as an allusion to the assertion of papal supremacy as expressed in the bull *Execrabilis* of Pius II (1460), does not take sufficient account of the significance of the scenes on the capitals. It also ignores the formal links with the painting by the Master of the *Exhumation of St. Hubert* and prefers, oddly, to compare it with the *Raising of Lazarus* in the Louvre attributed to Henri Vulcop (but, in my opinion, by Pierre Coustain), which does not have a single feature in common with Ouwater's painting and can in no way be its source of inspiration.

The suggestion by Leurs (1954) that the choir shown is that of St. Donatian in Bruges seems open to a multitude of objections and is inadequately supported.

Dimensions: Wood (oak). 122 × 92.
                The picture seems to have been cut down slightly on the right. On the other sides the uncovered edges of the prepared surface are clearly visible, confirming that the composition is complete.
Provenance: Balbi family of Genoa (according to family tradition it was a gift to one of its members from Philip II); inherited by the Marchese Mamelli; acquired from him, in 1889, by the Berlin Museum.
Literature: Bode, 1880, p. 35; Durant-Gréville, 1904, p. 251–6; Friedländer, III, 1925, p. 57–60 and no. 34, p. 113; Hoogewerff, II, 1937, p. 56–65; Schöne, 1942, p. 6–12; Panofsky, 1953, p. 320–3; Leurs, 1954; Snyder, 1960, p. 40–3; Châtelet, 1960; Donat de Chapeaurouge, 1977; Châtelet, 1979, p. 180.

43   Head of a donor (a canon?) (Pl. 58)
New York, Metropolitan Museum

This fragment has been attributed to Albert van Ouwater by Friedländer (III, 1926, p. 61), who has been followed by most authors. It goes without saying that such a small fragment is hard to ascribe conclusively. Nevertheless, it has characteristics in common with the *Raising of Lazarus*, such as the minute depiction of the wrinkles, the small, curved folds at the corners of the eyes, the clear indication of a point of light on the pupil, and the finely-modelled fingers with square fingernails.

Dimensions: Wood. 9.8 × 8.9.
Provenance: Thomas Howard, Duke of Norfolk and Earl of Arundel, 1655 (cf. Cox, 1911, p. 284); Howard coll., Grey-

stoke Castle, Penrith, Cumberland; acquired by J.Pierpont Morgan, New York, in 1909 and presented by him to the Metropolitan Museum in 1917.

Exhibitions: London, 1858, no. 125; London, 1906, no. 6.
Engraving: Hollar (with alterations to turn it into a portrait of Thomas Becket).
Literature: Kämmerer, 1898, p. 56 (van Eyck); Weale, 1904, p. 244; Friedländer, 1906 B, p. 574 (rejecting attribution to van Eyck); Weale, 1908, p. 171 (van Eyck); Weale, 1910, p. 177; Weale-Brockwell, 1912, p. 184; Friedländer, III, 1925, p. 61 and 112, no. 35; Schöne, 1938, p. 23; Schöne, 1942, p. 12–13; Wehle-Salinger, 1947, p. 50–2; Châtelet, 1960, p. 66–7.

44 St. John the Baptist (Pl. 59)
Granada, Capilla Real

Old inventories of the Capilla Real at Granada mention this picture as one wing of a triptych of which the central piece consisted of a *Virgin and Child*, painted on parchment stuck to wood, and the other wing of a *St. Michael* (*45*) (Gomez Moreno, 1908, p. 289). The central panel seems to have been lost. In any case, it seems unlikely that the juxtaposition of the three panels constituted the original arrangement: the difference of technique between the centre and the wings suggests a later montage.

The depiction of St. John the Baptist in hermit's garb, carrying a book and the Lamb, made its appearance in the Netherlands very early in the fifteenth century. An example is an illumination in a Book of Hours in the Pierpont Morgan Library (MS. 439, Panofsky, 1953, fig. 192) dating from 1430 at the latest. The theme was adopted successively by Jan van Eyck and the Master of Flémalle in two works which must both have influenced the Granada version. On the reverse of the *Mystic Lamb*, the saint is shown in grisaille in imitation of a statue. Only a single detail links this representation with the one in Granada: the gesture of the right hand pointing to the Lamb, with the forefinger half-straightened and the other fingers clenched.

In the wing of the *Werl Altarpiece* (Madrid, Prado), by the Master of Flémalle and dated 1438, the donor is presented by St. John the Baptist. The latter is clothed as in the Granada painting: a hermit's sackcloth tunic covered by a large drapery. All this material still leaves the saint's legs bare almost up to the knees. Whereas the Master of Flémalle, influenced by the style of van Eyck or of his disciple Rogier van der Weyden, softens the modelling of the forms and tries to set them in space by effects of light, Ouwater hardens the folds, stiffens the pose and lingers over anatomical details—for example, in the right leg, the bulge of a vein and the shape of the kneecap.

In the Granada painting the saint is shown in the wilderness to which he had retired. His sackcloth tunic recalls his rôle as the first hermit, which Ludolph the Carthusian pointed out (ed. Broquin, p. 284). This conception must have been widespread in the North during the fifteenth century. Two main variants can be cited. In 1489, an artist from the circle of the Master of Liesborn shows the saint thus in the *Noli me tangere Altarpiece* in Münster (Münster, 1952, no. 151). In the *Pearl of Brabant* (Munich, Alte Pinakothek), Dieric Bouts

the Younger (?) uses the same idea in the left-hand wing, giving the saint only a slightly different pose.

Dimensions: Wood. 70 × 31.
Literature: Gomez-Moreno, 1908, p. 289; Gallego y Burin, 1931, p. 166–9; Wescher, 1942, p. 65–71; Châtelet, 1960; van Schoute, 1963, p. 15–22; Châtelet, 1979, p. 181.

45 St. Michael (Pl. 60)
Granada, Capilla Real

This panel was a pendant to the foregoing (*St. John the Baptist*) in an ensemble which it seems impossible to reconstitute (cf. *44*). At first sight the composition is rather disconcerting and has even led Wescher (1942) to dissociate the picture from its pendant. However, once the first impression, due mainly to the difference of themes, has been overcome, identical characteristics can be found in both works. The influence of van Eyck is even more apparent here: it is revealed in the passion for shiny surfaces, in the play of reflections (especially on the shield) and in the sumptuousness of the brocades.

The depiction of the saint is, moreover, partly inspired by a model by Jan van Eyck or one of his followers: the archangel in the panel of the Last Judgment from the New York *Diptych* (*20*). In the Granada panel he stands on the demons as he stands on Death in the New York work. His arms have been modified but contain similar details: the shields are of similar shape, the breastplates are decorated with a similar double arabesque. The diadem surmounted by a cross is identical in the two panels.

The saint is represented attacking the demon with a processional cross, a very rare iconographic motif. There is a precedent, however, in the *Hours of Catherine of Cleves* (*37*, P. 68) in an illumination whose style suggests a copy of an original dating from the early years of the fifteenth century. The same motif is adopted later by Gerard David in a triptych in the Kunsthistorisches Museum in Vienna.

It is possible that the astonishing demons were also partly inspired by details of the panel of the New York *Diptych* (*20*): several of the demons' heads show similarities. However, Ouwater seems to have allowed his imagination a fair amount of freedom in the grouping and the movement.

Bartolomeo Bermejo drew his inspiration from this panel for the *St. Michael* in Tous, which has been dated c.1474 (Gudiol Ricart, 1955). This fact makes the two Granada panels earlier than that date, but also suggests their presence in Spain as early as 1474; which is by no means impossible, since they perhaps formed part of the gift of Isabella the Catholic to the Capilla Real in Granada.

Dimensions: Wood. 70 × 31.
Literature: Gomez Moreno, 1908, p. 289; Gallego y Burin, 1931, p. 166–9; Châtelet, 1960; van Schoute, 1963, p. 15–22; Châtelet, 1979, p. 181.

46 Jesus amongst the Doctors (Pl. 61)
On the reverse is a drapery study
London, British Museum, Department of Prints and Drawings

Waagen (MS. note) had attributed this drawing to Geertgen tot Sint Jans; Popham believed it to be Dutch, but dated it between 1490 and 1500. In fact, there seems to be hardly any doubt in my opinion that this work is by Albert van Ouwater. His style can be seen notably in the characteristic drapery with its large flat expanses and in the figure types, like the doctor in the left foreground who bears a strong resemblance to one of the apostles in the *Raising of Lazarus* in Berlin. The composition itself, with the main character off-centre and the protagonists linked together by their gestures, is very indicative of Albert van Ouwater.

The drawing gives the impression of a very advanced study for a composition. The figures have been placed and the setting defined. One of the figures has already received its final touches. At all events, the incompleteness of the work seems to exclude the possibility of its being a copy of a lost composition, and indicates rather a working drawing by an extremely self-confident artist.

Dimensions: Brush and brown wash drawing on paper (Watermark: dog's head surmounted by a crown, similar to Briquet no. 14.236). 28.5 × 21.2. On the reverse, drapery sketches in black chalk, very faint.
Provenance: acquired in 1854 by the British Museum (no. 6–8–24).
Literature: Popham, 1926, p. 28 and pl. 34; Popham, 1932, no. 70, p. 81–2.

47 Drapery study
Haarlem, Teyler Foundation

The attribution of this drawing, due to J.Q. van Regteren Altena, is most convincing. Apart from the drapery style, which is reminiscent of the *Raising of Lazarus*, the technique of hatching by small, fine strokes is the same as in the London drawing (*46*). The pattern of the hairnet is similar to that of Jacqueline of Bavaria in the Copenhagen portrait (*49*).

183

Dimensions: Pen and grey ink, brush and touches of watercolour. 15 × 6.4. Folded double. On the lower margin, inscription 'Olanda'.
Provenance: J. von Sandrart; Christina of Sweden; Azzolino; Odescalchi; dukes of

210

Bracciano; acquired in 1790 by the Teyler Foundation.

Exhibition: Paris, 1972, no. 49.

After Ouwater

48 Three Figures of Apostles

Amsterdam, Koninklijk Oudheidkundig Genootschap

184

Tracings of frescoes discovered towards the middle of the nineteenth century on the piers of the Church of St. Bavo in Haarlem. St. Peter and St. Paul were together on the same pier, the third apostle being on the next. The originals certainly dated from before 1439, when their backgrounds were 'washed' by Lambert Rutgensz.

Literature: van der Kellen, 1861, pl. II, column 2; Hoogewerff, II, 1937, p. 117–21 (Albert van Ouwater?).

49 Portrait of Jacqueline of Bavaria

Copenhagen, Royal Museum of Fine Art

185

The Copenhagen portrait has been identified with a portrait of the princess by Mostaert that Karel van Mander mentions seeing at the house of a descendant of the artist. The mediocre portrait now in the town hall of St. Maartensdijck (Hoogewerff, II, 1937, p. 50, fig. 21) is probably a copy of the same original. On the other hand, both the drawing in the *Recueil d'Arras* and the one in the *Memorials* by Antoine de Succa (Brussels, Bibliothèque Royale) correspond to different likenesses.

Dimensions: Wood. 61 × 42.5.
Provenance: sold by Otto Thott, 1787, no. 188 (Jan van Eyck) acquired at Copenhagen between 1787 and 1807.
Catalogue: Spengler, 1827, no. 161 (Jan van Eyck); 1904, no. 105 (copy by Mostaert after Jan van Eyck); 1951 (Mostaert).
Literature: Dollmayer, 1894 (Mostaert, after Jan van Eyck); Gluck, 1903, p. 68 (*id.*); Madsen, 1903; Weale, 1908, p. 181–2 (sixteenth-century copy after Jan van Eyck); Friedländer, X, 1932, p. 15 and 124, no. 40 (Mostaert); Hoogewerff, II, 1937, p. 488–9 (Mostaert); Winkler, 1959 B, p. 196–200 (Mostaert after Jan van Eyck).

50 The Mission of the Apostles

Aschaffenburg, Stiftkirche (loan from the Bavarian State collections).

186

Gerstenberg (1936) has rightly compared this composition with the description of the altarpiece of the pilgrims to Rome given by van Mander, 'a curious landscape in which were shown pilgrims, some on their way, others resting, eating and drinking'. It is more likely that the scene thus described was in fact an illustration of the Mission of the Apostles. To liken pilgrims to the apostles, to represent them as propagators of the faith, would accord well with the ideal of the *Devotio Moderna* which advocates the imitation of Christ and the saints in every man's life.

Gerstenberg's argument seems to be confirmed when one compares the figures of the Aschaffenburg painting, and especially the manner in which they stand and are draped, with those in the *Raising of Lazarus (42)*. The structure of the landscape, with its closely interlocking hillocks, is slightly reminiscent of that in the Granada *St. John the Baptist (44)* and foreshadows those of landscapes by Geertgen tot Sint Jans. During a recent

restoration the tree in the right backgro foliage, which was an addition to the origi sition.

Dimensions: Wood. 146 × 153.
Provenance: City of Nuremberg; collection of the Bavarian State; exhibited successively at the Pinakothek in Munich, at the Schleissheim Gallery (1920–8), in the Germanisches Nationalmuseum in Nuremberg (1928–36), at Rothenburg, and finally at Aschaffenburg.
Literature: Gerstenberg, 1936; Katzenellenbogen, 1949, p. 96; Stange, IX, 1958, p. 191 (Bamberg Master of the *St Claire Altarpiece*); Châtelet, 1960, p. 72.

51 The Crucifixion

Dresden, Kupferstichkabinett

The credit must go to Friedländer (III, 1926, p. 60) for recognising this drawing as an interpretation of a lost work by Albert van Ouwater. This attribution has since found general acceptance and may easily be confirmed by comparison with the *Raising of Lazarus (42)* for the figures and the *St. John the Baptist* in Granada *(44)* for the landscape. Comparison of this drawing with the one in London — *Christ amongst the Doctors (46)* — suggests that it is perhaps a copy, not of a painting, but of an original drawing. The sheet in Dresden displays a style of shading similar to that in the study in London, but rendered lifeless and mechanical by the hand of a copyist.

187

Dimensions: Pen on paper. 36.4 × 27.6.
Provenance: acquired before 1765 for the Dresden collections.
Literature: Woermann, 1896, vol. I, pl. IV; Friedländer, III, 1926, p. 60 and no. 4; Hoogewerff, II, 1937, p. 69–70; Schöne, 1942, p. 17; Snyder, 1960, p. 45; Châtelet, 1960, p. 67 and 72.

Dieric Bouts

(Haarlem *c.* 1420 (?)—Louvain 1475)

The reconstruction of the career of Dieric Bouts is still highly problematical. Hulin de Loo (1926) had imagined a short journey to the south around 1447, on the occasion of his marriage to Catherine van der Bruggen, then a long stay in Haarlem from 1447 to about 1457 before settling in Louvain. This view no longer seems tenable, because no trace of the artist can be found at Haarlem during this period. Moreover, the *Crucifixion* in Berlin, which served the author's argument because it has a depiction of Brussels in the background, can no longer be accepted as by the artist himself and may be an early work by Albert Bouts.

One therefore wonders whether the artist did not move to another town in the south before finally settling in Louvain. As the Lille panels come from the Abbey of Tongerloo, for which they had probably been painted, the idea of a residence in the nearby city of Antwerp during the 1450s can be put forward as a hypothesis. In 1453, the year of the foundation of the Guild of Painters in Antwerp, mention is made of a 'Dieric de verlichtere' (Rombouts-Lerius)—apparently a reference to an illuminator, but which may possibly designate the painter. Quite recently, Antoine de Schryver was wondering if the influence of Bouts 'did not, for one reason or another, manifest itself particularly at Antwerp', pointing out how much is owed to him by both Lievin van Lathem and Justus of Ghent (1969, p. 139). The idea can therefore be cautiously accepted as a working hypothesis.

Essential
literature: van Even, 1870; Heiland, 1903; Friedländer, III, 1925; Hulin de Loo, 1926; Pächt, 1927; Schöne, 1938; Schretlen, n.d., 1946; Denis, 1957; Baudoin, 1958; Châtelet, 1965; Louvain, 1975.

52 Triptych of the Virgin (Pls. 62 to 64)
Madrid, Prado Museum

This triptych would be more accurately entitled 'of the Virgin Mother of God'. The choice of episodes is centred on her maternity and on recognition of the Child's divine nature: designation and conception on the left-hand wing, recognition of the Child by Elizabeth and St. John the Baptist in the middle, adoration of the Child by the Virgin Mary and the angels at the Nativity, and recognition by the Magi, i.e. by the whole world, on the right-hand wing.

The secondary scenes on the extrados of the arches complement the meaning of the main scenes. Scenes of the original sin (creation of woman, God the Father, and the first man and woman before the Tree of the Knowledge of Good and Evil—temptation—Adam and Eve driven from Eden—Adam delving—Cain killing Abel) correspond to the *Annunciation*: the Virgin is thus seen as the new Eve who will redeem the sins of the first. The two scenes of the central panel are matched by episodes of the Passion, from the betrayal by Judas to the Resurrection, which emphasise the redeeming rôle of the Child. Finally, the *Adoration of the Magi* is linked with manifestations of the divinity of Christ after His death (*Noli me tangere*—the Supper at Emmaus—Appearance at Lake Tiberias—the Unbelief of St. Thomas—Ascension—Pentecost) developing the theme of recognition of His divine nature.

Such a conception also turns the Virgin into a symbol of the Church, while Joseph, at her side, as Ludolph the Carthusian points out, 'represents the bishop who wears the ring as a husband of the Church' (Broquin I, p. 154); this explains why he adores the Child with the

Virgin Mary and receives the gifts of the Magi, placing them on a table which symbolises the altar.

Apart from several borrowings from Rogier van der Weyden, such as the device of the architectural frames with sculpted extrados, or the design of the *Visitation* which recalls the painting now in Leipzig, the predominant influence here is still that of Jan van Eyck. Friedländer and Schöne have rightly pointed out the damage suffered by the central panels, which are quite badly rubbed and partly repainted, and the excellent state of preservation of the wings.

Dimensions: Wood. Centre 80 × 105. Wings 80 × 56.
History: Escorial collection, where it is first mentioned in 1584.
Literature: Passavant, 1853, p. 129 (Christus); Friedländer, III, 1925, p. 34–6 and no. 1, p. 105; Winkler, 1924, p. 92–3; Baldass, 1932, p. 79–81; Schöne, 1938, p. 23–8 and no. 1, p. 75–7.

53 The Meal in the House of Simon (Pl. 65)
Berlin, Staatliche Museen

This theme enjoyed great popularity in the Netherlands, especially in the north—partly, perhaps, because of its presence in both the *Biblia Pauperum* and in the *Speculum Humanae Salvationis*. It also took on this importance through the double lesson which emerges from it: 'This woman who was a sinner, prostrating herself at the feet of Jesus Christ,' says Ludolph the Carthusian (Broquin, III, p. 243), 'represents everyone truly contrite for his sins', but at the same time she obtains remission of her sins: 'Thy sins are forgiven', says Jesus to her (*Luke 7. 48*).

The painting is very similar in style to the *Triptych of the Virgin* in the Prado: it has the same figure types with oval faces, the same 'Eyckian' love of detail (marble colonnettes in the left-hand opening, the same precision of form), but above all the same use of light modelling the forms in simple planes. But here one notes an almost pedantic insistence on multiplying the cast shadows (especially through the introduction of the two wall-chandeliers).

Dimensions: Wood (oak). 40.5 × 61.
Provenance: Turin collection in the nineteenth century; collection of A. Thiem of San Remo, from which it was acquired.
Exhibition: Bruges, 1902, no. 39; Brussels-Delft, 1957–8, no. 25.
Literature: Hulin de Loo, 1902, no. 39; Heiland, 1903, p. 155 (Master of the *Pearl of Brabant*); Voll, 1906, p. 125 (Master of the *Pearl of Brabant*); Winkler, 1924, p. 99 (Bouts), Friedländer, III, 1925, p. 45 and no. 16, p. 108 (Bouts); Baldass, 1932, p. 104–7 (Bouts); Schöne, 1938, p. 48 and no. 68, p. 181–2 (Master of the *Pearl of Brabant*); Schretlen, n.d., 1946, p. 28–9 (Bouts).

After Dieric Bouts

54 Virgin and Child
New York, Metropolitan Museum

Winkler has rightly seen this work, sometimes attributed to Albert van Ouwater, as a copy of a lost original by Dieric Bouts from his early period. The often clumsy execution (cf. especially the Virgin's hands and the Child's head), like the handling of the landscape, which indicates a later date towards the beginning of the sixteenth century, are conclusive arguments for seeing this merely as a copy. The formula of this painting must have been quite popular, as the Correr Museum in Venice possesses another fairly mediocre replica by an Austrian painter, perhaps the Habsburg Master (Schöne, pl. 50 a).

Dimensions: Wood. 39.7 × 30.8.
Provenance: Coll. of James Broughton Hillary Place, Leeds (c.1887); Thomas Grosvenor, London; Durlacher Bros., New York; acquired in 1922 through the Pulitzer Fund.
Catalogue: Wehle-Salinger, 1947, no. 22–96, p. 52–3 (follower of Albert van Ouwater).
Literature: Conway, 1922, p. 120 (Ouwater); Pächt, 1921–2, p. 820 (Master of the Prado Triptych, Bouts?); Friedländer, III, 1925, p. 61 and no. 36, p. 112 (follower of Bouts); Winkler, 1926, p. 47–50 (copy of an early Bouts); Baldass, 1932, p. 80 and 114 (copy of a painting by Bouts dating from before 1450); Schöne, 1938, p. 23, 25, 30 and no. 22, p. 136–8 (copy of Bouts).

Master of the *Taking of Christ*

The first doubts on the correctness of the attribution to Dieric Bouts of the panels from the Lorenzkirche in Cologne were expressed in 1906 by Voll, who proposed an attribution to Albert van Ouwater. In 1938, W. Schöne took up this criticism again and offered a reconstitution of the work of a separate artist, similar to but different from Bouts, perhaps Dutch.

The list of attributions proposed by Schöne is extremely debatable. He himself later partly retracted his thesis by admitting (p. 37, note 1) that he had been too generous. It is impossible to follow him in ascribing to the same artist the *Martyrdom of St. Hippolytus* (Bruges, St. Sauveur), whose anecdotal character, like the structure of the forms, bears no relation to the paintings which form the core of the group. It is the same for the *Coronation of the Virgin* (Vienna, Academy of Fine Arts), also a work typical of Dieric Bouts.

Alongside these important paintings, Schöne also set some works of inferior quality which seem rather to be the products of a workshop or of other masters influenced by Bouts: such is the case of the *Annunciation* (Cracow, Czartoryski Museum), graceful, but weakly drawn and composed; the *St. Christopher* (Philadelphia, Johnson collection), a fairly mediocre replica of a lost original from Bouts's most Eyckian period, that of the *Ecce Agnus Dei*; the *Virgins* in Frankfurt and in the Strauss collection, New York, are probably products of Bouts's circle, but are also very strongly influenced by the workshop of Rogier van der Weyden; as for the *Portrait of a Man* in the Brown collection in London, it seems very late, perhaps even early sixteenth century.

Schöne's most plausible attributions are those of the *Annunciation* in the Gulbenkian collection and the *Virgin and Child* in the former Gutekunst collection, on which notices will be found below. To them should perhaps be added the *Fragment of a Nativity* in the Johnson collection, Philadelphia, and the *Portrait of a Man* in the Metropolitan Museum, New York. Schöne had also drawn up a second grouping based on the *St. John on Patmos* in Rotterdam, in which I see the hand of the Master of the *Taking of Christ*. I have not been able to see either of the two paintings associated by the same author with the one in Rotterdam. That in the former Brockhaus collection in Leipzig seems a very late work from the very end of the fifteenth century, drawn and executed rather weakly and certainly very different from the group's cardinal work. As for the *St Luke* in the collection of Lord Penrhyn, I should be inclined to attribute it to the Master of the *Pearl of Brabant*.

Judging from his works, the Master of the *Taking of Christ* seems to have been active between 1455 and *c*.1475. One may thus imagine a Haarlem painter, trained by Bouts in the southern Netherlands (at Antwerp?), working for a time in Cologne around 1460 (Lorenzkirche altarpiece), then returning to his homeland, where he provided drawings for woodcuts and painted the *St. John on Patmos*. Could he be identified with Vrederick Hoon, who is mentioned from 1463 to 1505, with commissions between 1463 and 1477? Or rather with Jan Arntszn, whose career can be followed from 1465 to 1495?

Literature: Voll, 1906; Schöne, 1938; Châtelet, 1965 and most of the works on Bouts which examine at least the major works of the Master.

55   Wings of the altarpiece from the Lorenz-kirche, Cologne
Munich, Alte Pinakothek, and
Cleveland, Museum of Fine Arts

A reconstruction of the original form of the altarpiece can only be conjectural. One may envisage a triptych consisting of the *Taking of Christ* as the left wing, the *Resurrection* as the right wing, and in the centre a *Crucifixion* which could have been either a panel or a sculptured ensemble. Schöne (1938, p. 164) supposed that the two surviving panels might have belonged to a larger ensemble, similar in arrangement to the *Lyversberg Passion* (Cologne, Wallraf-Richartz Museum; Stange, V, pl. 85–6), i.e. that they might have formed part of wings consisting each of four similar panels. It .... very great size, measuring about 226 cm high (105 × 2 + 2 widths of frame calculated at 8 cm) and 320 wide (68 × 4 + 6 widths of 8 cm frame), which would be quite exceptional. Such a reconstruction is contradicted above all by an examination of the grisailles on the reverse; these are clearly conceived as pendants, because they represent the two Saint Johns. In an arrangement of panels like that of the Lyversberg wings, the two figures would have been set apart from one another. The first solution, therefore, that of a simple triptych, remains the most probable.

55 A   The Taking of Christ (Pl. 66)

The composition is derived from that in the illumination in the *Turin Hours* (*15*). It is nevertheless still probable that there was an intermediate stage between Jan van Eyck's design and the painter's, perhaps in Dutch manuscript illumination. This can be seen by comparing the Munich panel with the one by Johann

Koerbecke (private collection; Münster, 1952, no. 59) painted *c*.1456 and with the illumination in the *Hours of Jan van Amerongen* (Brussels, Bibliothèque Royale, MS. II, 7619; Delaissé, 1968, pl. 104). The two latter versions are derived from a single design, which is itself closer to van Eyck's version than the Munich panel.

The Munich *Taking of Christ* is today the oldest surviving painting in which the *nocturne* effect of van Eyck's illumination is taken up and developed. But Jan van Eyck had shown, above the main group, a cloudy sky lit by the moon, which certainly gave the scene as a whole a unity of atmosphere and lighting. Here, on the other hand, the artist has preferred to contrast a dark, inky blue sky with a foreground illuminated by a torch. However, he has been unable to represent the effect of a light emanating from this single source. Thus the scene would appear to be taking place in broad daylight if he had not had resort to this dark sky. It is only in the small secondary scenes that he has been more successful in representing moonlight on groups of figures.

The background shows Jesus before Pilate and the flight of St. John and St. James (the latter incident being, strictly speaking, simultaneous with the main subject). The locations of the various incidents are linked together by the design of the setting; this device was never used by Dieric Bouts himself, but was to be adopted by Geertgen tot Sint Jans.

55 B   The Resurrection of Christ (Pl. 67)

The composition is based directly on that of the right-hand wing of the *Triptych of the Deposition from the Cross* by Dieric Bouts in the Capilla Real, Granada. The artist's alterations to his model are fairly significant. Bouts had opposed the three sleeping soldiers, forming an arc in the left foreground, to the two verticals of Christ and the Angel. The Master of the *Taking of Christ* has arranged the three soldiers around Christ and developed the theme of wonder and bedazzlement by means of the figure lying on his back, who takes on a greater importance here, and his crouching companion, who this time faces the spectator. The anecdotal aspect is thus strongly emphasised, whereas the Granada panel is dominated by the austere and mysterious figure of Christ.

The same importance was accorded to the soldiers in the foreground on the organ-shutter in St. Bavo's painted by Vrederick Hoon (*80*). There, however, Christ stood astride the tomb instead of standing in f.... .. it .. .. the ...... by D... ... that by the Master of Munich. This fact does not make an identification of the two artists impossible; such a motif, the archaism of which has been pointed out by Josua Bruyn (1963), could well have been demanded by one of the priests of St. Bavo. For the rest, it should be noted that Hoon introduces the same details as Bouts and his imitator: Christ's robe, cross and pennon, the gesture of benediction, a similar grouping of the soldiers, and secondary scenes in the background.

55 C and D   Grisailles: St. John the Baptist and St. John the Evangelist (Pls. 68 & 69)

The trompe-l'œil effect is deliberately enhanced by the choice of a deep niche and by the meticulous rendering of the shadows. The shadow of the lower edge, also that of the pedestals, differs slightly from one painting to the other; the painter's concern for realism made him broaden the band of shadow slightly on the left-hand panel since the light falls from the right.

The drawing is rather unsubtle and the figures display a stiffness which could not come from Dieric Bouts. And yet what may seem a defect gives the figures a certain charm, tinged with naïveté. It is also remarkable that the architecture of the niches has no Gothic features like those favoured by Rogier van der Weyden at the same period, but displays a surprising sobriety and only angular forms which seem almost ahead of contemporary architecture, though the Master of Flémalle had provided an example in painting (reverse of the *Marriage of the Virgin*, Madrid, Prado).

Dimensions: Wood. Each panel measures 105 × 66.

Provenance: Altarpiece from the Lorenzkirche in Cologne; at the beginning of the nineteenth century in the collection of Rector Fochem.
a) *The Resurrection* and *St. John the Evangelist*:
acquired in 1812 by the Boisserée brothers: nos. 44 and 45 in their sale in 1827; acquired at that sale for the Nuremberg Museum; transferred in 1911 to Munich.
b) *The Taking of Christ*:
acquired in 1822 from Rector Fochem by the dealer Schreiber on behalf of the Alte Pinakothek, Munich.
c) *St. John the Baptist*:
acquired from Rector Fochem by H. W. Campe, Leipzig; 'Gotisches Haus' in Wörlitz (Dessau); Goudstikker, Amsterdam, catalogue, 1928, no. 5; acquired from the latter for the Thyssen collection (Schloss Rohoncz); presented by the Hanna Fund in 1951 to the Cleveland Museum of Art.

Exhibitions: Bruges, 1902 (*St. John the Baptist*); Brussels-Delft, 1957–8, nos. 3 and 4 (*Taking of Christ* and *Resurrection*).

Literature: Heiland, 1903, p. 63–85; Voll, 1906, p. 156–8 (Ouwater?); Valentiner, 1914, p. 40 (Bouts); Winkler, 1924, p. 92 (Bouts); Friedländer, III, 1925, p. 37 and no. 20, p. 109 (Bouts); Pächt, 1927, p. 46 (Bouts); Baldass, 1932, p. 88–9 (completed by collaborators); Schöne, 1938, p. 31–42 and no. 45, p. 163–5 (Master of the *Taking of Christ*); Panofsky, 1953, p. 315 and 491, note 4 (Bouts).

56   The Annunciation
Lisbon, Gulbenkian Foundation

In my 1965 article, I believed it possible to reintegrate this painting into the corpus of Bouts's original work and to date it to his first period. However, at that time I paid too little attention to the figure types and the character of the faces, which are very different from those found in the *Triptych of the Virgin* and the *Meal in the House of Simon*. Nor did I take into account the colour harmony, especially of the flesh, which is treated in a more whitish range. It therefore seems necessary to abandon this view and revert to Schöne's, who saw this as a work by the Master of the *Taking of Christ*. The head of the angel, with its very rounded face and straight hair, is indeed much closer to that of the Munich *Resurrection* (*55 B*). The face of the Virgin, so curiously flattened, bears a marked resemblance to that of the St. Agnes on the reverse of the *St. John on Patmos* in Rotterdam (*57*). The drapery, with its straight hang and stiff appearance, is also very similar to that on the Munich panels.

Dimensions:	Wood transferred to canvas in 1889. 27.3 × 34.
Provenance:	Collection of the Hermitage, Leningrad; acquired from there in 1929 by Mr. Gulbenkian.
Exhibitions:	on loan to the National Gallery in London from 1936 to 1950 and to the National Gallery in Washington from 1950 to around 1960.
Literature:	Friedländer, III, 1925, no. 28, p. 110 (Bouts); Pächt, 1927, p. 47–8 (not by Bouts, master influenced by Rogier van der Weyden); Baldass, 1932, p. 112 (not by Bouts); Schöne, 1938, p. 41–2 and no. 42, p. 161–2 (Master of the *Taking of Christ*); Châtelet, 1965, p. 36–7 (Bouts, first period); Gottlieb, 1977.

57 St. John on Patmos (Pl. 70)
Rotterdam, Boymans-van Beuningen Museum

In most descriptions of this work, it is said to have had a strip 10 to 12 cm wide cut off the top. This assertion is based on the fact that the reverse displays a St. Agnes in a niche of which the top of the arch is cut off. A careful examination of the picture reveals, however, that on both faces the painted area has a 'burr' round all the edges. The cutting-off of the grisaille arch is thus an intentional effect and not the result of a mutilation. In his review of Friedländer's third volume, Otto Pächt devoted much attention to this painting (1927). He showed that it lacked unity and contained obvious borrowings from the work of Dieric Bouts. In his view, the foreground is imitated from the left-hand panel of the *Pearl of Brabant* (Munich, Alte Pinakothek). This observation is certainly basically justified, but not correct in detail. In fact, this flower-sprinkled ground does not only occur in the Munich painting, which in any case is probably contemporary with or later than the Rotterdam panel. It was used most of all by Bouts during the period when the influence of van Eyck on him was at its peak. It occurs mainly in two surviving works: the *Ecce Agnus Dei* (Munich, Prince of Bavaria's collection) and the *Paradise* (Lille, Museum). It was probably the latter work which served as a model for the *St. John on Patmos*; we find not only the same flower-sprinkled ground, but also the same river flowing over precious stones (which is virtually meaningless in the context of the island of Patmos) and even

a bird similar to those which surround the river in the Lille painting.

Similarly, Otto Pächt has shown—and this time quite rightly—that the upper right-hand side of the painting, with the path winding amongst the rocks, is taken almost literally from the panel of the *Last Supper Triptych* in Louvain depicting *Elijah in the Wilderness*. Also correctly, he pointed out that the third sector of the landscape, on the left, no longer reflects the influence of Bouts, but shows some affinity with the backgrounds of works by Geertgen. Indeed, this plain in which water introduces an area of brightness and reflections is a typical theme with Bouts and even more so with his followers.

Dirk de Vos's proposal (1976) to see this type of landscape as the trademark of the Master of the *Legend of St. Lucy* is unconvincing: it is in fact the only respect in which the two artists are comparable—the work of the anonymous artist from Bruges reveals neither the characteristic handling of the Master of the *Taking of Christ* nor the borrowings from Bouts, which are quite absent from his other paintings. Even if the reconstruction of the coat of arms on the reverse is correct and it must be taken as that of the van der Lende family of Bruges, that alone would not preclude execution by a Haarlem artist who could quite easily have worked for a Fleming after working at Cologne.

The date of the painting can be established fairly exactly. We have already seen that it is later than 1468. But we also find a very free interpretation of the work's composition, though sufficiently faithful for the dependence to be evident, in a panel from the Rohrdorf altarpiece (Stuttgart, Staatsgalerie; cf. Stange, VIII, p. 229), dated 1485. The Rotterdam panel must therefore have been produced between 1470 and 1485. I feel 1470–75 to be a probable date. It would indicate this as a late work by the Master of the *Taking of Christ*, in which he is trying to 'update' himself somewhat by borrowing from his younger colleague Geertgen while remaining faithful to Boutsian models.

Dimensions:	Wood. 69.8 × 65.
Provenance:	Boymans bequest, 1847.
Exhibition:	Brussels-Delft, 1957–8, no. 69.
Literature:	Voll, 1906, p. 116–7 (late Master); Winkler, 1924, p. 99 (Bouts); Friedländer, III, 1925, no. 6, p. 106 (hesitant about the attribution); Pächt, 1927, p. 42–5 (not by Bouts); Baldass, 1932, p. 112 (not by Bouts); Schöne, 1938, p. 50 and no. 132, p. 208 (by a Master of *St. John*, perhaps identical with Bouts); Schretlen, n.d., 1946), p. 24 (Bouts); van Gelder, 1972; de Vos, 1976,

58 Virgin and Child in a Landscape
England, B.S. Barlow collection

This delightful picture has been put together from a variety of sources, like many of the works by the Master of the *Taking of Christ*. The Child is similar to the one in the *Adoration of the Magi* from the *Triptych of the Virgin* by Dieric Bouts in the Prado (*52*). The Virgin's head, on the other hand, with its ovoid shape, has clearly been influenced by the manner of Rogier van der Weyden and resembles the one from the *Annunciation* in the Gulbenkian Foundation (*56*). The landscape in the background is treated in a miniaturistic style very similar to that of the preceding work. The heaviness of the Virgin's hands and her downcast eyes, forming narrow crescent shapes, are other details of handling

189

fairly typical of the Master of the *Taking of Christ*. The device of the Virgin seated in a landscape on the low wall of a small garden seems to have been quite popular in Holland, where it was adopted by the Master of the *Tiburtine Sibyl* (*110*).

Dimensions:	Wood. 33 × 25.
Provenance:	Coll. of R. A. Ogilvy; coll. of O. Gutekunst.
Exhibitions:	London, 1927, no. 57; Antwerp, 1930, no. 26; London, 1953–4, no. 7; Bruges, 1956, no. 9.
Literature:	Friedländer, III, 1925, no. 89, p. 125 (fine work by a close imitator); Friedländer, 1927, p. 210–1 (possibly by Bouts); Baldass, 1932, p. 112 (follower of Bouts); Schöne, 1938, no. 46, p. 165 (Master of the *Taking of Christ*, similar to the *Annunciation* in the Gulbenkian Foundation).

Master of the *Ars Moriendi*
(Master of the *Taking of Christ*?)

59 Illustrations for the woodcut edition of the *Ars Moriendi* (Pls. 72 & 73)

190

MASTER E.S., *Inspiration against Avarice*, Oxford, Ashmolean Museum

Content of the Ars Moriendi

The text of the *Ars Moriendi* must have originated around the beginning of the fifteenth century. According to the study by Sister Mary Catharine O'Connor (1942), there were two versions, one more fully developed than the other. It was the short text which was used for the woodcut edition of the work, no doubt after having served for an illustrated manuscript version. The work is intended to offer advice for a good death by drawing the attention of the dying to the temptations which lie in wait for them. An introduction is followed, in the manner of diptychs, by five temptations and five inspirations for resisting them (unbelief, despair, impatience, vainglory, avarice) and a conclusion.

Woodcut editions

Schreiber (IV, 1891–1911) distinguishes 13 successive editions of the illustrated volume. The first edition is known through two copies in Latin, one in the British Museum (former Weigel collection) and an incomplete copy in the possession of the Earl of Pembroke, and through a French edition (Count van der Cruyse of Waziers, Zerner, 1971). The copy in the British Museum is reproduced here.

Drawn or illuminated archetype

In 1942, F. Saxl published a series of watercolour drawings inserted into a manuscript in the Wellcome Institute for the History of Medicine (also reproduced in Zerner, 1971). The weakness of the handling marks them as copies. Nevertheless, the style of the compositions also reveals them as replicas of a work antedating the woodcut editions. The woodcut illustrations follow those in the Wellcome Institute manuscript very closely, at least in their elements if not in their handling.

Theme of the illustrations

In each composition, the dying man appears in his bed, which is arranged slantwise across the scene. He is surrounded by figures which have a more or less direct bearing on the printed text facing the woodcut in each case.

Relationship to the archetype

A careful comparison of the illustrations of the Wellcome Institute manuscript with the woodcuts shows that the latter are very faithful to the details of their model. All the compositions are reversed in relation to the manuscript; this reversal may be due to the engraver or to the copyist who has preserved the spirit of the archetype for us; no conclusion can therefore be drawn from the fact. Otherwise, the designer of the woodcut edition faithfully retains not only the figures used, but even their grouping and more often than not their poses. However, he arranges them in a new way in a space which he strives to define, and gives them new personalities. Thus the scenes seem very faithful to the archetype, while yet becoming quite new and individual. The woodcuts devoted to *Impatience* are, in this respect, very significant. The motif of the temptation is probably the one in which the designer has achieved the most striking composition, but also the only one in which he takes greater liberties with his model, by giving the friends a new position and giving the woman a new rôle. On the other hand, in the scene of the *Inspiration against Impatience* he follows his model very exactly. The figures are arranged in an identical way in the two compositions; but in the woodcut they are grouped with an impressiveness which gives the theme quite a different spirit.

The noticeable differences between the scenes in the Wellcome Institute manuscript and the woodcut edition are minimal. The following may be cited as examples: in the temptation of unbelief there are two Jews instead of three in the woodcut; in the inspiration against despair, there are several saints behind St. Peter and St. Mary Magdalene, etc. The only one of slightly more consequence is the omission of the dove of the Holy Ghost in the woodcut version of the temptation of vainglory.

Relationship to the engravings of Master E.S.

This question has given rise to heated arguments and still sets book historians against engraving experts. It should be noted at the outset, however, that the attribution to Master E.S. of the original conception of the scenes in the series of engravings (complete series in the Ashmolean Museum, Oxford; Lehrs, II, p. 170–8 and III, 223–31 and 337–41) is an unusual idea in that examination of the engraver's output shows that he mostly based his work on an earlier drawn or painted model.

191

The most recent suggestion is H. Zerner's (1971) that there were two intermediate stages between the archetype and the woodcut version, the second being the common source of Master E.S.'s engravings and of the woodcuts in the book. However, the first intermediate stage assumed by Zerner seems redundant: the engravings that he proposes to derive from it—those by the Master of the Flowery Borders and the Master of the Dutuit *Garden of Gethsemane*—in fact follow the main lines of the woodcut version, with some simplifications, and the variations may be due to the engravers, who may also have been acquainted with a variant of the archetype. The argument for a common source of the series by Master E.S. and the woodcut book does not really bear scrutiny. The compositions are so similar that one would need to assume a model followed very closely by both artists. If Zerner means that Master E.S. had access to the original drawings for the woodcuts or to a first series of woodcuts of which no copies have survived, that is a possibility—but one which does nothing to alter the conclusion: the woodcuts constitute the best example and the most faithful interpretation of the designs of an artist who reworked the illustrations of the archetype to give them new expressiveness.

In fact, Master E.S. follows the compositions known through the woodcut book very closely. When he does depart from it, he does so because he has not had a clear view of the print; either because the copy to hand was faulty, or because he had made too rapid a sketch of a composition which he did not have in front of him while engraving his plate: in the *Inspiration against Despair*, he has left out the claws of the cock on the bed-frame, and in the *Inspiration against Impatience* he transforms St. Stephen's three stones into curious folds. Only once does he introduce a variation which indicates acquaintance with another version: in the *Inspiration against Vainglory*, the angel at the head of the bed flourishes a large sheet of paper. This is a detail derived from the archetype, suppressed by the book designer in favour of a phylactery.

One final detail clearly shows that Master E.S. depended on the woodcut book or its original drawings. His plates consistently reproduce the odd difference in the hair which in four scenes from the book, for no apparent reason, gives the dying man long, curly hair,

while the other plates show him with short, straight hair. There is nothing in the text to justify this variation in the main character, which seems to be due to a 'continuity' error. An explanation of this can be found for the woodcut book (see below, hands and style) but not for Master E.S., who must therefore be copying this series.

Hands and style

Are all eleven plates of the woodcut edition by the same hand? One's initial reaction would be to answer in the affirmative, going by the impression of homogeneity in the overall conception of the scenes. Nevertheless, one detail demands deeper investigation. In four scenes (2. *Inspiration against Unbelief*, 8. *Inspiration against Impatience*, 9. *Temptation of Avarice*, 11. *Conclusion*) the dying man is depicted with hair of a different type from that in the other plates. In one of these compositions—the *Inspiration against Impatience*—there also appear angels of a different type from those in the other illustrations: rounder faces, more strongly indicated eyes and curly hair. These types have an affinity with the figures in the edition of the *Apocalypse*.

These four plates are also those whose spatial composition is the least happy. The forms are heaped up and crowded together rather confusedly. In the *Temptation of Avarice* in particular, the designer shows how embarrassed he is by the necessity of putting an entire house in the foreground. It is thus probable that there were at least two designers, doubtless from the same circle but working in parallel. The difference could perhaps be explained even more simply. It is quite probable that the plates are the work of a designer and an engraver, as was the usual practice later. One might then assume the existence of a designer for the whole series and two engravers: one following his model as closely as possible, the other interpreting it and introducing variations derived from his own practice. It would be this second engraver who worked on the four 'curly hair' blocks. This is the most satisfactory theory; it has the advantage of explaining the simultaneous presence in the *Inspiration against Vainglory* of two angels with curly hair, akin to the style of the *Apocalypse* engravings, and a third, on the left, more like the types in the rest of the volume. For the first two the engraver must have followed his own usual practice, for the third he must have stayed more faithful to his model.

Literature: Facsimile: Weigel, 1869; Rylands, 1881.
Study of the text: O'Connor, 1942.
Engravings by Master E.S.:
Cust, 1898; Lehrs, II (1910) and III (1915); Geisberg, 1925; Shestack, 1967.
On the archetype: Saxl, 1942.
Principal studies: Lehrs, 1890; Schmarzow, 1899 and 1900; Schreiber, IV, 1891–1911; Delen, 1924, p. 73–6; Schretlen, 1925, p. 16–17; Hind, 1935, p. 224–30; Musper, 1950; Fischel, 1952, p. 44–8; Stevenson, 1966 and 1966 B; Zerner, 1971.

60 Canticum Canticorum

Copies of the first edition in Manchester, Paris, Rome and Munich

Rather than a proper woodcut book, this is a small volume of illustrations. The text is reduced to the

215

192

contents of the phylacteries. The book contains 32 compositions, two by two on a page. In the second edition, a title in Flemish was added to the first plate: 'Dit is die voersienicheit vā mariē der mod'godes en is gehetē in latȳ cantice'. The work is cited by Petrus Scriverius in 1628 as a Haarlem production. Its style relates it particularly to the *Ars Moriendi*, although many authors prefer to compare it with the *Speculum Humanae Salvationis*. According to Stevenson, the watermarks of the first edition indicate a date of 1466; Schreiber had already dated it *c.*1465 (IV, 1902, p. 151). The style of the figures, especially in their drapery, shows an even greater affinity with painting than the other books which are known to have come from Haarlem. The frequency of very long and rather slim female shapes, associated with certain arrangements of the scenes in which the figures are set against a blank background on a narrow strip of ground—as if the artist had wanted to translate the device of a gold backdrop into the idiom of book illustration—may doubtless put one in mind of paintings by the Cologne Master of the *Life of Mary*. It seems, however, that this connection is more likely to be due to their having a common source: the work of the Master of the *Taking of Christ*.

Literature: Schreiber, IV, 1902, p. 151; Delen, 1924, p. 69–70; Schretlen, 1925, p. 21; Hind, 1935, p. 243–5; Musper, 1938; Stevenson, 1966.

Facsimile: Berjeau, 1860 (London copy); Clemen, 1910 (Munich copy); *Canticum Canticorum* (1921–2).

61 Grotesque Alphabet of 1464
Complete series in the Dyson Perrins collection, Malvern, and an incomplete series in the British Museum, London

The grotesque alphabet consists of a series of 24 woodcut compositions which were probably originally arranged in three blocks. The letter A bears the inscription 'mine lxxiiii', which in the Basle copy is corrected to 'MCCCC–LXIIII', also adopted in the variant by the Master of the Banderoles. It thus seems that the date 1464 can be accepted.
The style of this series is difficult to analyse; the designer had to comply with a formula in which the letters of the alphabet were made up of groups of people or animals. This imposed many deliberate deformations and accentuations of line, making the artist's handling more difficult to discern. Nevertheless, it will be noted that the artist uses a frame for which the perspective is indicated by hatched shading, as in the *Ars Moriendi*. Generally speaking, the woodcut technique appears

very similar to that of the latter work, with its use of little parallel hatchings which leave the blank areas with an essential rôle. It would also be easy to compare the predominant verticality of the drapery folds to the style of the *Ars Moriendi*, but it must be admitted that in this instance the technique is dictated by the subject-matter.
The presence of a rebus in French in the letter K (mon Ꝺaues) does not seem a serious argument against a Haarlem origin. It should be remembered that French was the official language of the Burgundian court until 1467, and that the publisher may have wanted to ensure sales in the southern Netherlands.
A second version, slightly later than the original and known through a copy in Basle, is sometimes taken to be the first edition (Musper, 1938). It has also been reworked by the Master of the Banderoles, in three plates (complete series at Bologna and Munich).

Literature: Facsimile: Dogson, 1899. Schreiber, IV, 1902; no. 1998; Dogson, 1910; Hind, 1935, p. 147–52; Musper, 1938 B.

After a Haarlem artist, *c.*1440–50

62 Epitaph of Dirc van Wassenaer (Pl. 74)
The Hague, Hoge Raad van Adel

This curious drawing, included in a genealogy, reproduces a painting which formed part of the Cottereau collection in Antwerp in 1659. It was the epitaph of Canon Dirc van Wassenaer, priest of St. Bavo from 1418, a benefice he later held in plurality with a canonry at Utrecht. On his death in 1465 he was buried in St. John's Church, Utrecht; another drawing (folio 30 of the same manuscript) shows the original appearance of his tomb, of which only fragments remain.
The epitaph reproduced was certainly intended for Haarlem, because of the inclusion of St. Bavo. The priest is depicted with much younger features than on his effigy. The painting must therefore date back to at least *c.*1450 or even *c.*1440. The seventeenth-century artist's interpretation of his model makes it difficult to analyse the style of the original, which must nevertheless have been by an important master.

Dimensions: Pen on paper. Folio 28 of MS. 540. ('Corte genealogicque. Beschrijvinge van den Ouden Edelen ende Doorluchtigen Stamme van Wassenaer... door D.J.H(agens)', completed in 1660). On folio 30, drawing of the tomb in Utrecht.

Master of the *Manna*

The isolation of this artist's work is due to K.G. Boon (1950). Hoogewerff (I, 1936) saw the hand of the illuminator known as the Master of Evert van Soudenbalch (christened Zeno by him) in the Douai painting. For his part, Haverkamp Begemann located the artist in Haarlem because of the connection he saw with the illustrations of the *Biblia Pauperum*.
If the links with Leiden suggested here are accepted, the Master of the *Manna* could be identified with Jacob Clementsz, whose period of greatest activity lay between 1460 and 1467, or perhaps Simon Jansz, known between 1435 and 1475.

All the known paintings could be dated to the 1460s, which would make them contemporary with both the illuminations of the Master of Evert van Soudenbalch and the illustrations of the *Biblia Pauperum*.

Literature: Hoogewerff, I, 1936, p. 552–8; Boon, 1950; Haverkamp Begemann, 1951.

63 Eucharistic altarpiece

Three of the known paintings by the Master of the *Manna* come from the same altarpiece, as is indicated by their noticeably similar dimensions (they have been cut down slightly) of around 70 × 54 cm. Their subject-matter makes it difficult to reconstruct the original arrangement of the altarpiece. Two of them, the *Gathering of the Manna* and the *Offering of the Jews*, were painted on both sides and thus constituted shutters. The third panel, depicting the *Crucifixion*, could have been placed alongside the *Offering of the Jews*, seen as its prefiguration (though I can cite no other instance of such a juxtaposition). The *Gathering of the Manna* was no doubt matched by a depiction of the *Last Supper* as in the *Speculum Humanae Salvationis* and the *Biblia Pauperum*. Hence we can imagine a closing quadriptych whose centre consisted of two equal panels representing the *Last Supper* and the *Crucifixion*. The theme would thus have been essentially eucharistic.
There is no precise indication of provenance through which the original ensemble can be localised. In the old descriptions of St. Peter's in Leiden (van Mieris, 1762, p. 29–30), one notes the presence of an altar of the Holy Cross and the existence of a Brotherhood of the Holy Cross, founded in 1411, which could have commissioned such an altarpiece. Certainly, in this case one would have expected an ensemble of which the *Crucifixion* was the centre. And yet one can imagine that they may have wanted to stress the actual significance of the *Crucifixion* by setting it alongside the *Last Supper*. Moreover, the unusual depiction of St. Peter with his cross (Haverkamp Begemann, 1953, p. 11) could be explained if the commission had come from this brotherhood. However, this is no more than a hypothesis and guideline for future research.

63 A The Gathering of the Manna (Pl. 75)
Douai, Musée des Beaux-Arts

The artist, like the designer of the *Speculum Humanae Salvationis*, does not follow the Biblical text on the Gathering of the Manna; the Bible does not speak of Manna falling from the sky, but describes the appearance, in the morning, of dew which turned into manna as it dried (*Exodus*, 16 : 14–15). Both artists are probably following the same example: the verses in the *Speculum* describing the fall from the sky.
The links between the two illustrations do not end there. Although it is not possible to point to direct borrowings from one by the other, they are at least both derived from the same design: both have figures standing up and bending down, the latter in the centre, the former at the sides. The painting is naturally richer in details, with a greater variety of poses, and contains an extra group which breaks up the arrangement of the engraving, that of the three figures trying to seize the manna in mid-air. It will be noted that the use of an architectural frame creates another parallel with the *Speculum*, in which it also occurs.

The Douai painting is unfortunately less well preserved than the other two. It is very worn and has been retouched, especially on the arch. It was probably the left wing of the polyptych.

Dimensions: Wood. 66.5 × 51.
Traces of cutting down along the edges.
Traces of paintings on the reverse.
Provenance: Holland, Musée Napoléon; lent by the Louvre before 1869.
Exhibitions: Valenciennes, 1918, no. 420; London, 1927, no. 26; Paris, 1956, no. 21; Amsterdam, 1958, no. 8.
Literature: Waagen, 1839, p. 451; Baldass, 1919, p. 9 (Ouwater); Dülberg, 1929, p. 76; Friedländer, III, 1924, p. 61, no. 37; Hoogewerff, I, 1936, p. 552 (Master Zeno); Friedländer, XIV, 1937, p. 97 (follower of Geertgen); Boon, 1950, p. 207; Haverkamp Begemann, 1951, p. 52.

63 B   The Crucifixion
Saint-Germain-en-Laye, private collection

This work was made known by K. Boon (1950, fig. 3), but has unfortunately never been exhibited. That it belonged to the same altarpiece as the *Gathering of the Manna* and the *Offering of the Jews* hardly seems to be in doubt. This panel has an architectural frame similar to those on the other two panels, but of a slightly different design with less prominence given to the spandrels. The dimensions are very similar, the height being almost exactly the same as that of the painting in the Boymans Museum, which is more intact than the Douai panel (70 against 69.5 cm). On the other hand, the width is slightly greater (54 cm against 51.4); this difference, however, strengthens the argument presented above for a triptych with two scenes on the central panel. If these two scenes were originally painted on a single panel (of which we only possess half), this panel would have had to be wider than the two wings to allow for the width of the two uprights of the frames of the wings when they met in the centre. This is the design of the *Triptych of the Virgin* by Dieric Bouts (*52*).
The treatment of the subject is surprising, in that Christ on the Cross is only shown amidst those who do not recognise his divinity, ie. Jews and Roman soldiers.
The high priest, identified by a fanciful mitre and by an inscription in a script intended as an imitation of Hebrew, is given a prominent place in the left foreground. Though this device succeeds in unifying the ensemble — by creating a continuity with the wing depicting the *Offering of the Jews* — it emphasises the negative aspect of the Israelites, who are shown as the predecessors of Christianity but above all as its opponents. The altarpiece as a whole must therefore have been clearly anti-Semitic in tone.

Dimensions: Wood. 70 × 54.
Literature: Boon, 1950, p. 210–211; Haverkamp Begemann, 1951.

63 C   The Offering of the Jews (Pl. 76)
(on the reverse, grisaille of *St. Peter*)
Rotterdam, Boymans-van Beuningen Museum

The subject of this painting was at first incorrectly identified as the Passover. It is in fact the *Offering of the Jews* in a version which in its essentials seems to follow the text of *Exodus 13:10–12*. Although this subject does not occur in the typological series, it is possible to conceive of a sacrifice as a parallel to the Crucifixion. The presence on the Jewish altar of a relief representing Cain killing Abel, often considered as prefiguring the Crucifixion (especially in the *Glossa Ordinaria*) would tend to confirm this view.
The colour harmony shows a fondness for bright tones, here yellow and red. Judging by the way in which the figure on the reverse is facing, this must have been the right hand wing of the original ensemble.

193

Dimensions: Wood. 69.5 × 51.4.
False signature of a later date at bottom left, 'Israhel van Meckenem'.
Provenance: Collection of the Earl of Mount Edgcumbe; acquired in 1951 from Duits Ltd. of London.
Exhibition: Amsterdam, 1958, no. 9.
Literature: Boon, 1950, p. 208; Haverkamp Begemann, 1951; Haverkamp Begemann, 1953.

64   The Healing of the Blind Man of Jericho
Blaricum, Kleiweg de Zwaan-Vellema collection

Here the artist follows St. Mark (*10:46–52*), as Hoogewerff has pointed out; he depicts a single blind man and not the two mentioned by Matthew (*20:29–34*). From the Gospel story he has taken three successive incidents which he places in different areas of the picture: the departure of Jesus from Jericho, Bartimaeus rebuked and, in the foreground, Bartimaeus healed.
The composition, weighted heavily towards the bottom left, gives the impression that it was not devised to hang in isolation, but to form part of an ensemble such as a diptych or better still a triptych. The subject only occurs rarely. It may have been chosen for an altarpiece intended for a hospice or one of the charitable institutions founded in large numbers in Dutch towns during the fifteenth century. To this end it may have been juxtaposed with another of Christ's miracles.
The style gives a good indication of the different tendencies which converge in this artist. Christ is taken almost straight from the *Raising of Lazarus* by Albert van Ouwater (*42*). By reason of their picturesqueness, the coarseness of their features, and the theatricality of

their clothes, the figures belong to the 'rustic tendency' in northern art. The construction of the landscape, with its large massings, recalls the wings of the *Hospitallers' Altarpiece* by Geertgen tot Sint Jans (*70* and *71*), which would indicate a fairly late date, unless the conception had already been used by Ouwater.

194

Dimensions: Wood. 89.3 × 75.
Provenance: Schlosse collection, Ypres, Albert Cels, Brussels.
Exhibitions: Ghent, 1913, no. 1666; Rotterdam, 1930, no. 1; Rotterdam, 1936, no. 16; Rotterdam, 1955, no. 16; Amsterdam, 1958, no. 10.
Literature: Hoogewerff, I, 1936, p. 552–8; Friedländer, XIV, 1937, p. 97; Boon, 1950, p. 208 (rejecting attribution to the Master of the *Manna*); Haverkamp Begemann, 1951, p. 53.

Attributed to the Master of the *Manna*

65   St. Antony leaving the Monastery
Haarlem, Archiepiscopal Museum

The tau cross on the cape of the main figure doubtless identifies him as St. Antony himself. The scene therefore probably represents his departure from the monastery for his hermitage. On the reverse of the panel, the remains of a grisaille seem to show a female saint or a Virgin of the Annunciation. The picture is probably a wing of a triptych dedicated to St. Antony.
The attribution to the Master of the *Manna*, suggested by K. Boon, is no longer found convincing by its own author. Although there is some similarity between the figure types of the Haarlem painting and those of the eucharistic altarpiece, the modelling seems freer here. In the composition itself, the artist aims at a more monumental organisation of mass, which has no equivalent in the known works of the Master of the *Manna*. This work is therefore perhaps the work of another artist from a similar background.

Dimensions: Wood.
Provenance: Poeldijk Church (Westland): transferred to the Archiepiscopal Museum in 1880.
Literature: Boon, 1950, p. 212–5.

Dutch (?) painter c.1440 (?)

66 Epitaph of Raes van Haemstede
Utrecht, Centraal Museum

The principal figure in this family epitaph, Raes van Haemstede, died at the Battle of Brouwershaven in 1426, as indicated in an inscription on the modern frame, probably copying an earlier inscription. The work should therefore be dated to the years following, but the style seems to suggest a later date, around 1440.

As the subject was a lord of Haemstede (on the island of Zeeland), it is logical to suppose that the family of the deceased called on the services of an artist from a nearby town in either Zeeland or Holland. Without offering any evidence, Hoogewerff suggested Gouda, which is relatively far away. Nevertheless, the artist may have come from further away; a painter named Sander van Heemstede is mentioned at Utrecht between 1420 and 1439. His name may mark him as a native of the same island as the nobleman (unless it refers to Heemstede near Haarlem), and this may have prompted the family of the lords of Haemstede to employ him. The style of the work does not admit of an exact localisation. The figure of Christ is probably inspired by a lost original of which another interpretation occurs in a page from the *Turin Hours* illuminated by hand K (Durrieu, 1904, pl. XXV). On the other hand, the very full shapes and the straight hang of the draperies recall the style of Albert van Ouwater, though with a tendency to schematisation.

According to local historical investigations, the persons depicted are Raes van Haemstede on the left and, behind him, his son-in-law Lodewijk Bloys van Tres-long and his daughter Maria van Haemstede; on the right are Agnes de Vriese van Oostende, wife of Raes van Haemstede, and probably two of their daughters, unidentified.

Dimensions:	Wood. 63.5 × 78.
	Inscription (on the frame): 'Anno CIC CCCC XXVI op sinte pontiaensdag wort verslagen Heer Raes van Haemstede in den strijt voor Brouwershaven ende leit begraven te Bethlehem in...'.
Provenance:	in 1783, coll. of Cornelis Citters, Bruelis; 1838, coll. of Jhr G.J. Beels-nijder van Voshol, Utrecht; presented by the latter's son-in-law, J. des Tombe, to the Museum Kunst-liefde in Utrecht; acquired in 1918 by the Centraal Museum.
Literature:	Nagtglas, 1878, p. 216; Moes, 1897, p. 399; Martin and Moes, 1912, pl. 37 and accompanying text; Fried-länder, III, 1924, p. 63 and 113; Dülberg, 1929, p. 77; Hoogewerff, II, 1937, p. 23–9 (Master of Gouda).
Catalogue:	Utrecht, Centraal Museum, 1952, no. 1162, p. 395–6.

Dutch (?) painter c.1440–50 (?)

67 The Baptism of Christ
Enschede, Rijksmuseum Twenthe

This picture has been compared by Hoogewerff, I feel rightly, to the *Epitaph of Raes van Haemstede*. One notices the same imitation of Haarlem conventions in a more schematic handling. However, a comparison with the *Baptism of Christ* (153) in Copenhagen reveals that both paintings are indebted to the same model (probably followed more faithfully by the latter), which could well have been by Albert van Ouwater or an artist very close to him.

195

Dimensions:	Wood. 48 × 36.
Provenance:	acquired in 1935.
Literature:	Hoogewerff, II, 1937, p. 29–32 (Gouda artist).

Geertgen tot Sint Jans

(Leiden c.1445–50—Haarlem c.1475)

Apart from the paintings listed here, Friedländer attributed to Geertgen the *Holy Kindred* (Master of the *Holy Kindred*) and the *Adoration of the Magi* in the Rijksmuseum, Amsterdam (Master of the Brunswick *Diptych*), the *Adoration of the Magi* in the Reinhart collection at Winterthur (Master of the *Holy Kindred*), the *Virgin and Child* (*Hollitscher Madonna*) in the Staatliche Museen, Berlin (Master of the *Holy Kindred*), the *St. Bavo* in the Hermitage, Leningrad (Master of the *Holy Kindred*), the *Legend of the Rosary*, known through two old copies (Master of the Antwerp *Triptych*). He also made known (1949) the *Madonna in Sole* in

196

Portrait of Geertgen tot Sint Jans, Haarlem, Archives.

Rotterdam (Master of the Antwerp *Triptych*). Recently, the following works were still attributed to the artist: the *Tree of Jesse* in the Rijksmuseum, Amsterdam (Master of the Brunswick *Diptych*), the *Crucifixion with St. Dominic* in Edinburgh (Master of the Antwerp *Triptych*) and the *St. Jerome* in the Boer Foundation (Master of the Brunswick *Diptych*).

Kneeling man by Bouts (*Fall of the Manna*, Louvain), the Master of the Lyversberg *Passion* (Nuremberg) and van der Goes (*Monforte Altarpiece*)

197

Literature:	Friedländer, 1903; Durand Gréville, 1904; Balet, 1909 (important bibliography for pre-1900 publications); Baldass, 1921; Friedländer, V, 1927 (fundamental work with a catalogue of works); Kessler, 1930; Hooge-werff, II, 1937, p. 138–91; Davies, 1937 (major article criticising Friedländer's catalogue); Oettinger, 1938, p. 68–73 (attempt at parallel interpretation with the work of van der Goes); Boon, 1939; Vogelsang, 1942; Châtelet, 1951; Koch, 1951 (groundless theory of the artist's having been trained at Bruges in 1475–6); Panofsky, 1953, p. 324-30; Snyder, 1960, p. 113–32; Boon, 1967 (excellent little monograph, but taking the traditional view of the artist); Châtelet, 1979, p. 181–9.

68 The Adoration of the Magi (Pls. 77 & 78)
Triptych: on the left wing, donor presented by St. Bavo, on the right wing, female donor presented by St. Adrian; on the reverse, grisaille of the *Annunciation*. Prague, National Gallery.

This triptych has been badly mutilated. A band about 40 cm wide, which probably bore the donors' arms, has been cut off the top of the wings. The central panel has itself been cut down on both sides; it now measures 69 cm wide as against 89 cm or so originally (twice the width of a wing, 38.5 cm × 2, and two widths of frame in the centre, i.e. around 6 cm × 2). On the left-hand side the missing strip is probably larger and perhaps corresponded to the position of St. Joseph, who does not appear in the composition in its present state.

The doubt cast on the attribution of the triptych by Balet (1909), or only on the wings by M. Davies (1937), followed by Panofsky (1953, note p. 327–2) is unwarrantable. The panels display a clear unity of execution and their style is already very close to that of the Vienna panels.

In the absence of coats of arms, it is very difficult to attempt an identification of the donors. However, the choice of St. Adrian to present the young woman is most unusual; since the Christian name Adriane is even rarer than Adrian, we may well wonder if this was not her husband's patron saint, he himself being protected by St. Bavo, to whom the main church in Haarlem was dedicated. As it happens, a person of some consequence bore this Christian name: Adrian van Bakenesse, who married, doubtless around 1467 (according to information given by Mr. Thierry de Bye Dolleman), Margriet Pieter Roepersdochter. He was born c.1430–40, which would make him between 27 and 37 in 1467. The date of the marriage of Adrian van Bakenesse may correspond to that of the execution of the Prague triptych, but the hypothesis can only be confirmed by the discovery of new documents.

The long robe worn by the man was in fashion at the same period as the short doublet, and seems to have been the distinctive wear of the burghers. Hair was worn long more often in Germany than in the southern Netherlands. It is thus possible that in this respect Holland followed the German rather than the French fashion. I can cite no examples of wimples like that worn by the women from c.1465 in the northern Netherlands. But similar ones are worn by the female donors on the wings painted by the Master of the *Legend of St. George* before 1473 (cf. Stange, V, fig. 31–2 and p. 21–2). The fanciful costumes of the characters in the *Adoration of the Magi* prevent one from dating them exactly. The dress of the page, with his short, striped breeches and plumed hat, may appear rather later. In fact it occurs, with variations, in German art at dates almost as early, especially in the work of the Cologne Master of the *Holy Kindred*.

198

VAN DER GOES, *Monforte Altarpiece*, Berlin, Staatliche Museen

Dimensions: Wood (oak). Centre 111 × 69; wings 71 × 38.5 each.
Provenance: Prague Castle, where it is mentioned from 1797.
Exhibitions: London, 1929, no. 6; Rotterdam 1936, no. 2; Amsterdam, 1958, no. 22.
Literature: Friedländer, 1903, p. 68; Durand Gréville, 1904, p. 373–7; Balet, 1909, p. 32–3 (rejecting the attribution); Friedländer, V. 1927, p. 33 and no. 4; Kessler, 1930, p. 36; Davies, 1937, p. 3 (doubting attribution of wings); Oettinger, 1938, p. 66; Vogelsang, 1942, p. 48; Panofsky, 1953, p. 327; Snyder, 1960, p. 121; Sip, 1963 (monograph on the painting with reproductions of numerous details); Boon, 1967, p. 8.

69 The Raising of Lazarus (Pl. 79)
Paris, Musée du Louvre

Only Martin Davies has expressed serious reservations about the authenticity of this work, because of the condition of the painting; he thought that it might be merely a copy. Any examination must indeed take into account the unsatisfactory state of preservation. Considerable retouching, especially on the figures of Christ and St. John, has spoilt several of the figures. Moreover, an uneven, yellowing varnish has endowed the whole work with a softness of volume quite foreign to the artist's style.

The position of the donor kneeling in prayer below Lazarus, on an extension of the line joining Lazarus to Christ, gives a clear indication of the work's purpose as an epitaph. The female donor, placed behind Mary, seems to join in her prayer. She wears black veils, which could be a sign of mourning, but it is hard to make out if she should be taken as the donor's wife or daughter. Two details are difficult to explain: the black object in the donor's clasped hands and the dog in the centre foreground (did he carry a coat of arms which has since been scraped off or painted over?).

Dimensions: Wood, cradled (oak). 127 × 97.
Provenance: Acquired in Spain by Jules Renouvier; collection of Baron d'Albenas; acquired from him in 1902.
Exhibitions: Amsterdam, 1898; Rotterdam, 1936, no. 5; Amsterdam, 1958, no. 17.
Literature: Renouvier, 1857; Friedländer, 1903, p. 62 and 67; Durand Gréville, 1904, p. 381–4; Balet, 1909, p. 62–6; Friedländer, V, 1927, p. 27 and no. 5; Kessler, 1930, p. 37; Hoogewerff, II, 1937, p. 156; Oettinger, 1938, p. 66; Vogelsang, 1942, p. 50; Michel, 1944, p. 30–1 and 66–7; Panofsky, 1953, p. 327; Snyder, 1960, p. 117–18; Boon, 1967, p. 9.

70 The Lamentation (Pls. 80–82, 85–87)
Vienna, Kunsthistorisches Museum

This composition seems to have enjoyed great popularity even before the destruction — or disappearance — of the other fragments of the altarpiece. Indeed, it was copied several times, notably by Jan Mostaert. If this wing was rescued by the knights of St. John from the siege of Haarlem, it was probably because of the interest attaching to this scene. The painting is one of the earliest known examples in the Netherlands of the depiction of the *Lamentation*, which, unlike the *Pietà*, restricted to two or at the most four figures, introduces

a large number of characters around the Virgin. In the left background is the rarely depicted Burial of the Two Thieves.

The figure of Mary Salome, in the left foreground, is probably inspired by a model by Rogier van der Weyden; it may be a free interpretation of the Mary Magdalene from the *Deposition* in the Prado or an exact copy of the same character in the composition known through a painting by the Master of Frankfurt (Naples, Capodimonte), if this work indeed echoes an original by Rogier.

Dimensions: Wood (oak). 175 × 139.
Provenance: High altar of the Hospitallers' Church, Haarlem; deposited in October 1573 with Jhr. Wittenham of Utrecht as a precaution against the dangers of war; mentioned in 1606 at the Convent of the Hospitallers (the panel had by that time already been sawn in two); became the property of the town of Haarlem in 1625 on the death of the last Commander; sold by the town to a group of artists, who sold it in their turn to the States General (Bruyn-Millar, 1962); presented by the latter to Charles I of England in 1636; appears in the inventory of Leopold Wilhelm, Archduke of Austria, in 1659 (no. 224); Austrian Imperial collections.

200

VAN DER GOES, *Lamentation*, Granada, Gomez Moreno Foundation

MASTER OF AIX-LA-CHAPELLE. *Aix-la-Chapelle Triptych* (free interpretation of the Hospitallers' altarpiece by Geertgen tot Sint Jans?), Aix-la-Chapelle, Treasury

199

202

203

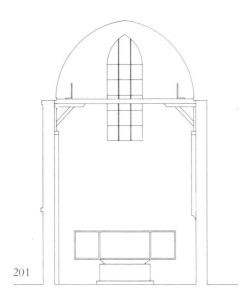

201

Section through the chapel of the Commandery of St. John at Haarlem with the altarpiece by Geertgen tot Sint Jans

Engraving: by Matham (copies in the Gemeente Archief in Haarlem, at the Albertina in Vienna and at the Staedel Institute in Frankfurt).

Copies: by Mostaert (Rijksmuseum, Amsterdam, on loan to the Frans Hals Museum, Haarlem); by a sixteenth-century Dutch artist in the museum of Princeton University (Mather, 1928); sixteenth-century (?) copy formerly in the Mestrallet collection in Paris.

Literature: von Mechel, 1781, p. 153; Friedländer, 1903, p. 64; Durand Gréville, 1904, p. 259–62; Balet, 1909, p. 77–83 and 99–108; Goldschmidt, 1915, p. 227–30; Friedländer, V, 1927, p. 16–19 and no. 6A; Kessler, 1930, p. 32–6; Hoogewerff, II, 1937, p. 148–52; Vogelsang, 1942, p. 24–6; Panofsky, 1953, p. 327–30; Snyder, 1960, p. 113–15; Boon, 1967, p. 5–6; Châtelet, 1979, p. 187–9.

71 The Burning of the bones of St. John the Baptist (Pls. 83, 84, 86, 88-9)
Vienna, Kunsthistorisches Museum

The main theme of the composition is the Burning of the bones of St. John the Baptist in 362 under Julian the Apostate. It is clear that the Hospitallers are intended as portraits of the Haarlem knights. The Commander must be the figure at the head of the second group and on the far left of the first. Comparison with portraits of the Commanders in the museum at Haarlem does not, however, enable him to be identified conclusively. We can confidently exclude Willem Janszoon, who should be portrayed if we adhere to the traditional dating. Of all the portraits which can be taken into consideration, that of Pieter van Scoten still bears the closest resemblance to the figure in the Vienna panel.

It will be noticed that the knights of St. John are five in number. There are two possible explanations for this. Either the total number of brethren, originally intended

Portraits of the Preceptors Pieter van Scoten and Niclaas van Scoten, Haarlem, Frans Hals Museum

to be ten, had at that time fallen to five, or the only ones portrayed were those who held some office (commander, prior, cellarer, vesterer and secretary). But we cannot identify the six laymen shown with them. They may be familiars of the convent, or benefactors. The fourth from the left is clad in comfortable middle-class style, which could mark him as a benefactor of the knights, perhaps even in the commissioning of the altarpiece. This could be Symon van Noirtich, 'rent-meester' of the convent under Pieter van Scoten. There has been a somewhat romantic suggestion that the bearded young man (third from the right) is the artist himself. J. Snyder, taking up an unpublished suggestion of Hoogewerff's, has rightly pointed out that it is more plausible to identify him with the clean-shaven young man, first on the right. The argument is supported by a comparison with a seventeenth-century (?) drawing which reproduces a portrait of the artist included in his painting, now lost, devoted to the works of mercy. There is not an absolute identity; but the drawing is fairly rough and ready, and may simply be a bad likeness.

Dimensions: Wood (oak). 172 × 139. A small strip has been cut off the upper edge. Inscription on the reverse: 'This is the second piece beinge one of the 5th pictures wich was presented tot the Kinge at St. James by the states huis Imbassadeur'.

Provenance: cf. above; no. 224 in the 1659 inventory of the collections of the Archduke Leopold Wilhelm.

Exhibition: Amsterdam, 1958, no. 18.

Literature: Dülberg, 1899, p. 25; Riegl, 1902, p. 75–87 (study of the portraits as forerunners of Dutch group por-

traits); Friedländer, 1903, p. 64; Durand Gréville, 1904, p. 259–62; Balet, 1909, p. 77–98; Friedländer, V, 1927, p. 14–19 and no. 6B; Kessler, 1930, p. 17; Beresteyn, 1935, p. 56–7; Hoogewerff, II, 1937, p. 141–7; Vogelsang, 1942, p. 26–8; Châtelet, 1951; Panofsky, 1953, p. 327–8; Snyder, 1960, p. 127–8; Boon, 1967, p. 6.

72 St. John the Baptist in the Wilderness
(Pls. 90-1)
Berlin, Staatliche Museen

Panofsky (1953, p. 328) has pointed out the profound influence this composition had on Albrecht Dürer, who drew inspiration from it for his engraving of *Melancholy*, after copying its landscape almost literally in an early drawing of the *Holy Family* (Berlin, Kupferstichkabinett).

Dimensions: Wood (oak). 42 × 28.

Provenance: Coll. of the English artist W. Cope; coll. P. Marquoid, London; acquired from this, in 1902, by the Kaiser Friedrich Museum.

Exhibitions: Bruges, 1902, no. 34; Masterpieces of the Berlin Museums, Washington (1948), New York, Philadelphia, Amsterdam, Brussels, Paris, Amsterdam, 1958, no. 19.

Literature: Weale, 1903, p. 329; Friedländer, 1903; Durand Gréville, 1904, p. 380; Balet, 1909, p. 109–14; Friedländer, V, 1927, p. 24 and no. 12; Kessler, 1930, p. 31; Hoogewerff, II, 1937, p. 158–62; Oettinger, 1938, p. 66; Boon, 1939, p. 335; Vogelsang, 1942, p. 55; Krönig, 1950 (important iconological study); Panofsky, 1953, p. 327–8; Snyder, 1960, p. 128; Boon, 1967, p. 10; Reuterswärd, 1971, p. 86; Châtelet, 1979, p. 187.

73 Virgin and Child (Pl. 92)
Milan, Pinacoteca Ambrosiana

204

BOUTS. *Virgin and Child*, London, National Gallery

It is inaccurate to call this little painting a miniature. It is not painted on parchment but on a small wooden panel, and still has the typical edges of a painting executed within a frame. Its present frame, which seems to date from the seventeenth century, has two small shutters, which give it the appearance of a triptych. This cannot be seen as an early work, as suggested by R. Koch; the meticulous handling, lending depth and solidity to the figures, is the same as in *St. John the Baptist in the Wilderness* and the Vienna panels.

Dimensions:	Wood (oak). 11 × 8 (painted area); 11.8 × 8.7 (panel).
Exhibition:	Amsterdam, 1958, no. 20.
Literature:	Dülberg, 1903, p. 68; Durand Gréville, 1904, p. 386; Balet, 1909, p. 32 (not accepted as a work by Geertgen); Friedländer, V, 1927, p. 37 and no. 9; Oettinger, 1938, p. 68; Hoogewerff, II, 1937, p. 164–5; Vogelsang, 1942, p. 55; Koch, 1951; Panofsky, 1953, p. 326; Snyder, 1960, p. 120; Boon, 1967, p. 7.

74   The Nativity (Pl. 93)
London, National Gallery

The original panel has been cut down by a narrow strip all round; this is confirmed by an early sixteenth-century copy by a Spanish artist (Barcelona, Museum of Fine Art, cf. Davies, 1937). Gerard David imported this interpretation of the subject into the southern Netherlands. The painting by him in Vienna has direct links with Geertgen's (although the composition is reversed), and one notes in particular that the St. Joseph adopts the figure type of its model. It was through this work that the motif achieved such a wide distribution, even reaching Italy, perhaps through the variant by Horenbout which appears in the *Grimani Breviary*.

The reservations on the work's authenticity, expressed by Martin Davies (1937), seem unfounded. The handling is the same as in the Vienna panels, softened here to serve a more deeply felt and spontaneous expression.

Dimensions:	Wood (oak). 34 × 25.
Provenance:	acquired in Paris by Richard Kaufmann (Kaufmann, cat., 1901, no. 32); Kaufmann sale, Berlin 1 December 1917, no. 100; Owlies coll., Nijenrode; sold at Amsterdam 10 July 1923, no. 6; Hans Tietje coll., Amsterdam; acquired from Cassirer in 1925 by the National Gallery.
Copies:	Sixteenth-century Spanish artist, painting from the Monastery of Pedralbes in the diocesan museum in Barcelona.
Exhibitions:	Utrecht, 1913, no. 26; Amsterdam, 1958, no. 21.
Literature:	Goldschmidt, 1902, p. 23; Friedländer, 1903, p. 68; Durand Gréville, 1904, p. 386–7; Balet, 1909, p. 64–76; Baldass, 1919 (study of the distribution of the motif, whose original is attributed to van der Goes); Friedländer, V, 1927, p. 31 and no. 1; Davies, 1937; Hoogewerff, II, 1937, p. 176–9; Oettinger, 1938, p. 67; Boon, 1939, p. 334; Vogelsang, 1942, p. 51; Davies, 1945, p. 37;

Panofsky, 1953, p. 323; Snyder, 1960, p. 124–5; Winkler, 1964, p. 148–9; Boon, 1967, p. 8–9.

75   The Adoration of the Magi (Pl. 94)
Cleveland, Museum of Art

This recently-discovered work is unfortunately in poor condition. The panel has probably been cut down on all sides. The figure of the black king, which is handled with a completely different technique, seems to be an overpainting. Originally, the third king was no doubt a little more to the right in a part of the composition now lost. Finally, the Virgin's face and hands and part of the figure of the Child are badly worn.

This painting may come from the commandery of the knights of St. John in Haarlem; an inventory of 1573 mentions 'een tafereel van de drie Coningen' (Allan, II, 1870, p. 354), which is more likely to be the Cleveland painting than the one in Prague, whose wings would have been mentioned.

Dimensions:	Wood. 29 × 18.5.
Provenance:	English coll.; Rosenberg-Stiebel, New York (1950); acquired from them by the Cleveland Museum (presented by the Hanna Fund, 1951).
Literature:	Friedländer, 1950; Francis, 1952; Boon, 1967, p. 9.

76   The Man of Sorrows (Pl. 95)
Utrecht, Archiepiscopal Museum

This panel also seems to have suffered damage. It seems to have been cut down on all four sides, and the gold background is not original; slight flakings reveal a colour which could be that of a marbled surface.

Dimensions:	Wood (oak). 24.5 × 24.
Provenance:	former Church of St. Willibrod, Utrecht.
Exhibitions:	Utrecht, 1913, no. 27; Rotterdam, 1936, no. 3; The Hague, 1945, no. 51; London, 1952, no. 3; Antwerp, 1954, no. 36; Amsterdam, 1958, no. 23.
Literature:	Dülberg, 1903, p. 6; Friedländer, 1903, p. 67; Durand Gréville, 1904, p. 383; Durand Gréville, 1909, p. 157; Panofsky, 1927, p. 261; Friedländer, V, 1927, p. 35 and no. 7; Kessler, 1930, p. 7 (oddly considered to be a copy); Hoogewerff, II, 1937, p. 179–86; Davies, 1937, p. 91 (authenticity doubted); Oettinger, 1938, p. 66; Vogelsang, 1942, p. 52; Panofsky, 1953, p. 323; Snyder, 1960, p. 123–4; Boon, 1967, p. 9.

77   Head and hand studies (Pls. 96-7)
Recto: head study
Verso: hand studies
Paris, Musée du Louvre, Cabinet des Dessins

This sheet, like the three following ones, has been attributed to Gerard David rather hastily. Its resemblance to certain works by David is in fact restricted to

a similarity of technique and to a similar size of paper. But the drawing style has none of the softness sought after by the Bruges painter; on the contrary, it is clear-cut and emphatic.

The study of the head (oddly considered by Lugt, 1968, to be a woman's) has no direct equivalent in Geertgen's known work. At the most, one can point to a similarity of overall structure to the head of Nicodemus in the *Lamentation* in Vienna.

The smiling face shown with the hand scratching the nose was probably used by the artist; a variant of it occurs with the Master of the Brunswick *Diptych* in his panel of the *Taking of Christ* in Brussels (*92*). It was probably intended for one of the Jews in the *Ecce Homo* of the Hospitallers' altarpiece. The fully-extended hand on the left was used, with the necessary stylisation, for the *Virgin and Child* in the Pinacoteca Ambrosiana (*73*).

Dimensions:	Silverpoint on prepared white paper. 9.4 × 6.65. Inv. 20.652.
Provenance:	Emigrés (Bourgeois Vialard de St.-Maurice coll.?)
Exhibition:	Paris, 1935, no. 187.
Literature:	Reiset, 1878, no. 633 (Flemish school, fifteenth century); Popham, 1926, no. 29; Lugt, 1968, no. 58 (Gerard David); Châtelet, 1973.

78   Head of an old man (Pl. 98)
Paris, Musée du Louvre, Cabinet des Dessins

The deeply-lined face of this old man bears a striking resemblance in some respects with that of the canon in the Vienna *Lamentation*. Several details, however, show that this is not the same person: the old man in the Vienna painting does not have the peculiar domed cranium of the one in the Paris drawing, his nose is broader and more curved, his lips—those of a toothless man—are even more pinched, and the eyes even more deep-set. The connection is so surprisingly close, however, that one may well imagine that the artist remembered this study when he came to paint his picture.

Dimensions:	Silverpoint on prepared white paper. The hair has been worked over with a brush. The slight touches of red on the lips and nose are probably later additions. 9.1 × 6.7.
Provenance:	Emigrés (Bourgeois Vialard de St.-Maurice coll.?).
Literature:	Reiset, 1878, no. 633 (Flemish school, fifteenth century); Popham, 1926, no. 29 (Gerard David; unconvincing comparison with a painting in the National Gallery, London, *Three saints and a kneeling donor*); Besançon, 1951, p. 43 (G. David); Lugt, 1968, no. 59; Châtelet, 1973.

79   Head in profile and hand studies
(Pls. 99-100)
Recto: head of a man, left profile
Verso: hand studies
Vienna, Albertina

The study on the recto shows a face which is probably the profile of the model who posed for the drawing now in the Louvre. It depicts a less aged character than the latter, and the artist may, in the other work, have deliberately exaggerated the marks of old age for some specific purpose.

The two upper hand studies could have been for a Virgin offering the Child an apple or an ear of corn. The half-clenched hand at the bottom left is very similar to that of the second Jew from the left in the *Raising of Lazarus* in the Louvre.

Dimensions: Silverpoint with highlights in brush on prepared white paper. 9.3 × 6.7.
Literature: Woltmann, 1866 (Holbein the Elder); Baldass, 1928, p. 175 (Holbein); Tietze-Conrat, 1931; Lugt, 1968, no. 59 (pointing out links with drawing in Louvre); Châtelet, 1973.

Vrederick Hoon

The artist is known to have been active between 1463 and 1505 through various texts published by Vente in 1961 and by van der Willigen. In 1463 he painted the consoles supporting the organ in St. Bavo's. In 1464 he undertook several tasks on the organ (painting and gilding), and in 1465 the shutters. In 1465 he painted a cock and keys at the north door, also some heraldry and a lion, in 1468 statues, niches and a coat of arms, and in 1477 some coats of arms. The other references only concern his payment of taxes. In 1505 the opening of his tomb is noted.

Literature: Willigen, 1866; Vente, 1961; Bruyn, 1963.

After Vrederick Hoon

80 Shutters of the Organ of St. Bavo's
(Pl. 101)

Inside of the shutters:
Only the right-hand shutter, depicting the Resurrection, is known from the painting by Saenredam of the interior of St. Bavo's in the Rijksmuseum, Amsterdam, and from a preparatory drawing, dated 1635, for this same painting in the possession of the Department of Drawings of the Staatliche Museen, Berlin.
Amsterdam, Rijksmuseum cat. 2096.

Dimensions: Wood. 95.5 × 57. Signed and dated 1636.

Outside of the shutters:
Saenredam also depicted the organ with the shutters closed, but in his painting and drawing of them only the bottom right-hand corner of the right-hand shutter can be made out (drawing in the collection of the Institut Néerlandais in Paris, painting in the possession of the Marquis of Bute, another version in the National Museum, Warsaw). An anonymous drawing gives a clearer idea of the two wings, which represented Judith and the choir of women (*Judith XVI*). It is probable that the right-hand wing represented the musician saints gathered around St. Cecilia. Haarlem, Archives (Gemente-archief), Portfolio 15/2.

Literature: Bruyn, 1963.

205

Master of the Amsterdam *Holy Kindred*

The designation of this Master is presented here for the first time. However, once the exclusion of the Amsterdam painting from Geertgen's oeuvre has been accepted—a rejection that has been considered by many authors, especially Davies (1937) and Oettinger (1938)—it soon becomes convincing.

The artist appears to have been uninventive, content to borrow both composition and figure types. Nevertheless, he must be granted, as well as smooth but somewhat unpoetical technique (clearly visible in a well-preserved work like the *Virgin and Child* in Berlin and in the better-preserved areas of damaged paintings), an inclination and aptitude for story-telling, and for finding simple, telling gestures.

As he also borrows from Albert van Ouwater, it is conceivable that he belonged to Geertgen's generation. The names of Vrederick Hoon or of Jan Arntszn may suggest themselves if they are not to be identified with the Master of the *Taking of Christ*, or perhaps that of Jacob Willemsz (active from 1470 to 1493).

Literature: There is obviously no study of the Master as such, but most of the works published on Geertgen tot Sint Jans describe or refer to his paintings.

81 The Holy Kindred (Pl. 102)
Amsterdam, Rijksmuseum

The subject of the kindred of St. Anne, very popular in the Rhineland during the fifteenth century, is derived from apocryphal tales taken up particularly by the *Golden Legend* (ed. Roze, II, p. 172–3). The favour it enjoyed in the fifteenth century was perhaps encouraged by the vision of the Blessed Colette Boilet, to whom St. Anne appeared, surrounded by her descendants, in 1406. St. Anne can be easily identified in the left foreground, reading a book; beside her is the Virgin Mary holding the Child on her knee. Joachim and Joseph, with the flowering branch of his marriage in his hand, stand behind their wives. The small child entering in front of them could be St. James the Less with his fuller's staff. Opposite, on the right, sits St. Elizabeth—not often associated with this subject—carrying the infant John the Baptist, who stretches out towards Jesus. The two women behind her are presumably the Virgin's two sisters, Mary Cleophas and Mary Salome.

In the middle, three children sit playing on the ground: St. John the Evangelist with his chalice, St. James the Greater with his cask and St. Simon with his knife.

According to Panofsky, the altar-boy snuffing out the candles is St. Jude, the snuffer possibly being a fanciful but familiar equivalent of his traditional emblem, a capital gamma. The two old men silhouetted against the doors of the choir-screen must be St. Anne's second and third husbands, Cleophas and Salome, in conversation with three people, two of them being young men, no doubt their sons-in-law Alphaeus and Zebedee.

Oddly, the artist has omitted the fourth child of Mary Cleophas, Joseph the Just; Panofsky explains this by the fact that he was the only descendant of St. Anne not to have been an apostle. Also odd is the apparent absence of Zacharias, unless, as suggested by Snyder, we see him in the third person talking with Cleophas and Salome; but even the one with his back to the spectator, on the left, seems very much younger than the appropriate age for the husband of St. Elizabeth.

The scenes shown on the figure-capitals of the columns go hand in hand with the main purport of the picture. On the left, above the Virgin, her prefiguration Judith is followed by a scene which is hard to identify but is probably of a Marian antetype. This is followed on the same side by two prefigurations of Christ: Cain and Abel foreshadowing the *Taking*, and the *Judgment of Solomon*, which announces Christ's rôle as Judge. On the right, the capitals prefigure the New Law with Moses and the brazen serpent, baptism with Moses making water gush forth from the rock, and finish with the recognition of Christ's divinity in the Adoration of the Magi. The programme is thus a little incoherent.

The unusual importance accorded in the scene to St. Elizabeth has led Panofsky, James Snyder and Karel Boon to think that the painting may have been intended for the Commandery of the Hospitallers at Haarlem. But it is mentioned in neither of the two known inventories. Besides, it should be remembered that a 'St. Elizabeth Gasthuis' had been founded in 1460 and had been granted privileges by Philip the Good (Ampzing, 1628, p. 84–6); it could just as easily have been the recipient of the painting, if not more so.

The centre panel of an altarpiece of 1473, now in the church at Soest (Münster cat. 1952, no. 221–35) also has a Holy Kindred set in a church interior. But the group of St. Anne, the Virgin and the Child is located in its more traditional position in the centre, in place of the altar. Several details, such as a certain similarity of costume and the depiction of a child stretching out towards Jesus (at Soest it is St. John the Evangelist) lead one to suppose a connection between the two works. Following Paul Pieper and Harald Busch, Peter Schabacker (1975) assumes a common model. The idea is a plausible one, and one may imagine a work conceived in the circle of Dieric Bouts, perhaps even by the Master of the *Taking of Christ*.

Dimensions: Wood (oak). 137.5 × 105.
Provenance: acquired at the G. van der Pot sale, Rotterdam, 6 June 1808 (described as 'Gothic temple with figures' by van Eyck).
Exhibition: Amsterdam, 1958, no. 15.
Literature: Alberding Thijm, 1881, f 21; Dülberg, 1899, p. 31; Friedländer, 1903, p. 67; Durand Gréville, 1904, p. 378; Balet, 1909, p. 37–53; Friedländer, V, 1927, p. 29 and no. 10; Hoogewerff, II, 1937, p. 165–70; Davies, 1937, p. 91; Oettinger, 1938, p. 66; Vogelsang, 1942, p. 37–42; Busch, 1943, p. 94; Panofsky, 1953, p. 327 and p. 495–6, note I; Snyder, 1957, p. 92–4; Snyder, 1960, p. 128–9; Boon, 1967, p. 8; Schabacker, 1975.

82 The Adoration of the Magi
Winterthur, Oskar Reinhart Foundation

206

At the beginning of this century, this picture was disfigured by overpainting on a large scale (photograph before restoration at the R.K.D. in The Hague). The original paint surface has been uncovered, but the work had been much damaged previously; it therefore requires careful interpretation.
The composition is clearly inspired by Geertgen's *Prague Triptych* (*68*) and adopts the latter's overall arrangement. The absence of Joseph suggests that he was not portrayed in the central panel in Prague, even before its mutilation. Also borrowed are the page and the dog from the Vienna panels. Geertgen's technique is also imitated, especially in the foliage of the trees, though this remains heavier and less lively.

Dimensions:	Wood. 133 × 108.
History:	C.J. Bordes coll., Netherlands; N. Beets, Amsterdam; acquired from the latter in 1923.
Exhibition:	Utrecht, 1913, no. 31 (as 'school of Geertgen tot Sint Jans', before the removal of the overpainting).
Literature:	Friedländer, 1923, p. 103; Friedländer, V, 1927, p. 33 and no. 3; Davies, 1937, p. 91; Hoogewerff, II, 1937, p. 171–2; Oettinger, 1938, p. 68, no. 20; Vogelsang, 1942, p. 43–4; Snyder, 1960, p. 121; Boon, 1967, p. 9.

83 St. Bavo
Leningrad, Hermitage Museum

This panel is probably a fragment of a larger composition, perhaps the left-hand wing of a triptych, as appears to be suggested by the saint's clearly facing right. It has not only been cut down along the edges, but also damaged and worn and largely overpainted. The convent depicted in the background bears some resemblance to the one in the *St. Jerome* by the Master of the Brunswick *Diptych* (*91*). Although the church, with its single nave, may recall that of the Hospitallers of Haarlem, the arrangement of the conventual buildings in relation to the sanctuary is not identical to that of the convent in which Geertgen lived. It may represent one of the many religious houses in the Haarlem area, or perhaps be no more than imaginary.

Dimensions:	Wood. 36.6 × 30.
Provenance:	acquired in 1923.
Literature:	Friedländer, XIV, 1937, p. 97.

84 Virgin and Child ('Hollitscher Madonna')
(Pl. 103)
Berlin, Staatliche Museen

The composition probably represents a fusion of elements borrowed from the little panel by Geertgen in the Pinacoteca Ambrosiana (*73*) and from the *Virgin and Child* by Dieric Bouts in the National Gallery. From the first the artist has taken the figure types, the general arrangement and the hand of the Virgin, albeit enlarged. From the latter he has taken the window and the brocades. These large moon faces are highly characteristic of an uninventive master who has here developed on too large a scale the types he had created for the *Holy Kindred*, taking his inspiration from Geertgen.

207

Dimensions:	Wood (oak). 81 × 52.
Provenance:	Lafitte coll., Madrid (1910); J. Boehler, Munich; Hollitscher coll., Berlin; acquired by the Kaiser Friedrich Museum in 1919.
Exhibitions:	*Masterpieces from the Berlin Museums*, at Washington, (1948), New York, Philadelphia, Amsterdam, Brussels, Paris.
Literature:	Friedländer, V, 1927, p. 36 and no. 0; Hoogewerff, II, 1937, p. 162–4; Davies, 1937, p. 91; Oettinger, 1938, p. 66; Vogelsang, 1942, p. 53–5; Panofsky, 1953, p. 326; Snyder, 1960, p. 119; Boon, 1967, p. 8.

85 The Raising of Lazarus
Berlin, Staatliche Museen, Kupferstichkabinett

Alongside obvious borrowings from Albert van Ouwater's painting in Berlin (for example, the figures of St. Peter and Martha), one can make out imitations of Geertgen (such as Jesus) and motifs of the Master of the *Holy Kindred* (the child seen from behind in the background), to whom this work should be attributed: we find the stiffness of his draughtsmanship in the drapery folds, his lack of imagination, which leads to

208

borrowings left and right, and his lack of skill, which forces him to drape Lazarus in a shroud to avoid the necessity of painting a nude; but we also see his fondness for anecdote, which leads him to invent the gesture of St. Peter tugging at the arm of one of the Jews. Lastly, we have one of this master's trademarks in the window opening on to the background, cut sharply out of the wall and with embrasures drawn in an exaggerated perspective, which, as in the *Adoration of the Magi* in Winterthur, gives on to a townscape (but with figures leaning on a balustrade, recalling the *Rolin Madonna* by Jan van Eyck).
Schöne has suggested (1942) a reconstruction of the original composition which, according to him, was set in a vaulted interior, of which the entire upper part is missing. The theory is plausible but not absolutely necessary, as the composition is balanced in the drawing's rectangular format.

Dimensions:	Ink on paper. 28 × 40.5.
Literature:	Friedländer, III, 1926, p. 122 and no. 4; Hoogewerff, II, 1937, p. 68–9; Schöne, 1942, p. 13–5; Châtelet, 1960, p. 67.

Jacob Jansz (Master of the Brunswick *Diptych*)

Known to have been active from 1483; died in 1509

The grouping of this artist's works under the provisional name of the Master of the Brunswick *Diptych* is due to Friedländer, who followed Balet in excluding the artist's eponymous painting from the œuvre of Geertgen tot Sint Jans.
The painter is easily distinguished from Geertgen by the greater clarity of his handling and by his light palette. In his narrative sense he comes close to the Master of the Amsterdam *Holy Kindred* but he also differs from him in the refinement of his technique. A long-standing confusion has grown up between the work of Jacob Jansz and that of his disciple Jan Mostaert. It has been notably revived in an article by Friedrich Winkler (1959). The identification of the anonymous master had been proposed in 1958 by Karel Boon (Amsterdam cat. 1958), then oddly abandoned by the same author in 1966 (p. 64, note 9).

Literature:	Friedländer, V, 1927, p. 52–4; Hoogewerff, II, 1937, p. 194–202; Amsterdam cat. 1958, no. 25–31.

86 The Adoration of the Magi (Pl. 105)
Amsterdam, Rijksmuseum

The attribution of this work to Geertgen has been doubted successively by Balet (1909), Martin Davies (1937) and K. Oettinger (1938, p. 68). The latter attributed it to the Master of the Brunswick *Diptych*. Analysis of the painting reveals it as a free interpretation of the *Adoration of the Magi* by Geertgen (*68*) and of that by Hugo van der Goes (*Monforte Altarpiece*, Berlin, Staatliche Museen). The general layout copies that of the Prague painting, reversed with slight variations, such as placing Balthasar in the foreground and pushing Caspar back into the middle ground. The figure of Caspar is taken from the Berlin painting.
This may have been the centrepiece of a triptych whose wings consisted of the following *Annunciation*, *Nativity* and *Presentation in the Temple*, and perhaps a lost *Adoration of the Shepherds*.

Dimensions: Wood (oak). 90 × 70.
Provenance: sold by W. Hekking Jr., Amsterdam, 20 April 1904, lot 7; acquired at this sale.
Exhibitions: London, 1929, no. 10; Rotterdam, 1936, no. 4; Brussels, 1946, no. 32; Amsterdam, 1958, no. 16.
Literature: Durand Gréville, 1904, p. 379–80; Balet, 1909, p. 32; Friedländer, V, 1927, p. 32–3 and no. 2; Kessler, 1930, p. 28; Hoogewerff, II, 1937, p. 170; Davies, 1937, p. 91; Oettinger, 1938, p. 68; Vogelsang, 1942, p. 47; Panofsky, 1953, p. 329; Snyder, 1960, p. 121; Boon, 1967, p. 9.

87 The Annunciation
Glasgow Art Gallery

The attribution of this work to the Master of the Brunswick *Diptych* is due to Friedländer (1927), who also assumed, apparently correctly, that the panel came from the same ensemble as the two following paintings. The composition is a distant descendant of one by Rogier van der Weyden (*Ferry de Clugny Annunciation*, New York, Metropolitan Museum), but known through intermediate works perhaps from the circle of Bouts (*Annunciation* in Cracow) (Cf. V).

Dimensions: Wood. 44.5 × 36.
Provenance: W. M. Burrell coll. (London); bequest.
Literature: Friedländer, V, 1927, p. 52–3 and no. 17; Hoogewerff, II, 1937, p. 197–8.

88 The Nativity
Amsterdam, Rijksmuseum

The composition draws its inspiration from a model by Dieric Bouts or an artist of his circle which is itself only known through replicas (cf. Schöne, 1938, pl. 88 B and C). However, the artist has not followed his model literally and has even simplified the iconography: he has omitted the candle held by St. Joseph, which symbolised, by its contrast, the light of day shining out miraculously on Christmas night.

209

Dimensions: Wood. 46 × 35.
Provenance: Hoogendijk coll.: presented by him to the museum in 1912.
Exhibition: Amsterdam, 1958, no. 25.
Literature: Friedländer, V, 1927, p. 51 and no. 20; Kessler, 1930, p. 28; Hoogewerff, II, 1937, p. 197–8; Vogelsang, 1942, p. 56.

89 The Presentation in the Temple
Minneapolis, The Minneapolis Institute

This work has deteriorated badly, and the unsatisfactory condition of the surface has weakened the effect of the modelling and highlighted the naïveté of the composition.
The figure of a priest in the right foreground could be that of the donor, as he is wearing contemporary ecclesiastical costume. A similarity has been pointed out (Amsterdam cat., 1958, no. 26) between the face of a young man in the right background and the drawing in the Haarlem archives which is supposedly a copy of a portrait of Geertgen tot Sint Jans (ill. 196). The resemblance is vague, but close enough to leave open the possibility of this being a free copy by Jacob Jansz of a detail from a lost work by Geertgen.

210

Dimensions: Wood. 46 × 35.
Provenance: J. Normand coll., Paris (sold Paris, 7 March 1923, lot 13); Herschell V. Jones coll., Minneapolis.
Exhibition: Amsterdam, 1958, no. 26.

Literature: Friedländer, V, 1927, p. 53 and no. 19; Kessler, 1930, p. 8; Hoogewerff, II, 1937, p. 197; Vogelsang, 1942, p. 56.

90 Diptych of St. Anne with the Virgin and Child (Pl. 104)
Left wing: St. Anne, the Virgin Mary and the Child Jesus
Right wing: Carthusian donor presented by St. Barbara
Reverse: St. Bavo
Brunswick, Herzog Anton Ulrich Museum

Luttervelt has assumed that the donor was Hendrik van Haarlem, prior of the Charterhouse of Amsterdam and then of Geertruidenberg from 1490 until his death in 1506. The theory is plausible, but difficult to confirm. The presence of St. Bavo on the reverse does indeed suggest that the donor came from Haarlem. On the other hand, there is nothing to indicate that the monk holds the office of prior. We know too little about the buildings of the Amsterdam Charterhouse to be able to say that they are depicted here. Luttervelt's theory explains neither the choice of St. Barbara as the monk's patron, nor even the choice of the central theme. The figure of St. Bavo is inspired by that in the lost votive painting of Dieric van Wassenaar, known through an old drawing (*62*).

Dimensions: Wood. Each panel: 35 × 23.
Exhibitions: Utrecht, 1913, no. 28; Rotterdam, 1936, no. 6; Amsterdam, 1958, no. 29.
Literature: Friedländer, 1903, p. 68 (Geertgen); Dülberg, 1903, p. 6; Durand Gréville, 1904, p. 266; K. Voll, 1906, p. 327; Balet, 1909, p. 152 (not by Geertgen); Friedländer, V, 1927, p. 51 and no. 16; Kessler, 1930, p. 16; Hoogewerff, II, 1937, p. 194; Vogelsang, 1942, p. 56; van Luttervelt, 1951, p. 75–80.

91 St. Jerome in the Desert
Amsterdam, De Boer Foundation

211

This painting, which has recently come to light, has been attributed to Geertgen tot Sint Jans. Nevertheless, the comparisons invoked are with debatable works. Here we find two elements characteristic of Jacob

Jansz: the facial type of the saint, and the sharp folds which do not correspond with the body structure covered by them. J.Q. van Regteren Altena has rightly compared this panel to a *St. Jerome* attributed to Memling (Basle, Kunstmuseum), which is probably its inspiration.

The painting was discovered set in a Venetian frame. It was thus tempting to see it as one of the works of 'Girardo da Ollanda' mentioned in 1521 in the collections of Cardinal Grimani. The evidence for this is very slight. It should not be forgotten, moreover, that Marc Antonio Michiel's descriptions are not infallible where northern works are concerned; so that even if it could be proved that the painting did indeed come from the prestigious Venetian collection, that in itself would still not prove that it was by Geertgen.

Dimensions.   Wood. 42 × 28.5
Exhibition: Laren, 1966, no. 84.
Literature: Van Regteren Altena, 1966; Boon, 1967, p. 9.

92 Two altarpiece wings: The Taking of Christ and the Entombment (Pls. 110-11)
Brussels, Musées Royaux des Beaux-Arts

These two panels, listed by Friedländer (1927) among the works of the Master of the Brunswick *Diptych*, are, in all likelihood, the wings of a triptych whose centrepiece, now lost or unidentified, painted or sculpted, must have been a *Crucifixion*. It has often been assumed that the two panels of similar dimensions on which are depicted St. Cecilia and St. Valerian (Rijksmuseum, Amsterdam) were the reverse of these. Friedländer, however, expressed doubts on this matter, pointing out a clear difference of quality between the two works. This difference is, in my opinion, very noticeable, and the Amsterdam paintings should be grouped with the work of the Master of the *Figdor Deposition*. Nevertheless, this does not exclude the possibility of a common origin; it could even reflect a collaboration on the part of the two artists.

Basing his argument on the unity of the Brussels and Amsterdam ensembles, Luttervelt (1951) thought it possible to deduce that the original ensemble was intended for the convent of St. Cecilia in Amsterdam. However, there is very little evidence for this theory. Firstly, the common provenance of the four wings is not established; and besides, there was another convent dedicated to St. Cecilia in Haarlem, which had been founded in 1468. The argument by which an Amsterdam provenance would explain the master's influence on Cornelis van Oostsanen is also open to dispute; for the young artist could just as easily have completed his training in Haarlem.

Dimensions: Wood. Each panel: 62.5 × 22.
Provenance: Bequest of Countess Valencia de Don Juan, 1919.
Exhibitions: Rotterdam, 1936, no. 7; Amsterdam, 1958, no. 27.
Literature: J.O. Krönig, 1909, p. 4; Friedländer, V, 1927, p. 53 and no. 20; Kessler, 1930, p. 13; Hoogewerff, II, 1937, p. 200; Vogelsang, 1942, p. 56.

93 The Tree of Jesse (Pls. 106, 109)
Amsterdam, Rijksmuseum

The attribution of this charming work has given rise to much debate. The name of Mostaert, almost universally accepted from the time of Friedländer until 1957, has been put forward yet again (Winkler, 1959; Boon, 1966). On the other hand, the former attribution to Geertgen has attracted new supporters and is the one which has been adopted by the Rijksmuseum in Amsterdam. The palette clearly indicates the hand of the Master of the Brunswick *Diptych*, who strangely has not yet been considered by any author. The moon-like faces with their round, dark eyes are also characteristic of this artist's style, as is the attempt, unsuccessful here, at creating a background by the device of buildings in light-coloured brick. We thus come back to the hypothesis suggested by Friedländer in 1927 that the painting should be attributed to Mostaert's master, Jacob of Haarlem, though he did not realise his identity with the Master of the *Diptych*.

James Snyder (1957), in an interesting analysis, has pointed out the connection between the iconography of this work and the development of the cult of the rosary in the Netherlands. We cannot, however, conclude that the painting was commissioned by one of the brotherhoods created at the end of the fifteenth century. The cult of the rosary was spread by the Dominicans, but not only by encouraging the institution of such associations. Luttervelt (1948) had in any case assumed, with some plausibility, that the nun donor could have belonged to the Order of Mary Magdalene, a convent of which had been founded at Haarlem in 1474.

Dimensions: Wood. 89 × 59.
Provenance: Kvocinsky coll., St. Petersburg (mid-nineteenth century); E. Meazza coll., Milan (sold Milan, 15 April 1884); acquired at this sale by Count G. Stroganoff, Rome; von Pannwitz coll. (acquired c.1923–24); acquired by the Rijksmuseum with the assistance of the Rembrandt Association in 1956.
Exhibitions: London, 1929, no. 14; Rotterdam, 1936, no. 40; Amsterdam, 1958, no. 24.
Literature: J. Burckhardt, 1898, p. 98 (Geertgen); Friedländer, 1903, p. 66 (not Geertgen); Durand Gréville, 1904, p. 377; Dülberg, 1907, p. 6–9 (workshop of Geertgen); Friedländer, XIII, 1926, no. 24 (Jacob of Haarlem?); Friedländer, X, 1932, no. 14 (Mostaert?); Hoogewerff, II, 1937, p. 456 (Mostaert); Davies, 1937, p. 91 (similar to Geertgen but not by him); van Schendel, 1957 (Geertgen); Snyder, 1957; Winkler, 1959 B, p. 179–83 (Mostaert); Boon, 1966 (Mostaert); Snyder, 1971.

94 Portrait of a Man with a Stick
Cologne, Wallraf-Richartz Museum

It seems possible to propose the attribution of this 'portrait' to the Master of the Brunswick *Diptych*. In the facial expression, as in the treatment of depth, there is that simplicity and also that material delicacy which are both characteristic of the artist. Much more unusual is the iconography. The kind of stick that the man is holding has sometimes been identified as a gun; it seems difficult to accept this notion when we observe that the gentleman is holding this supposed weapon by the barrel. Could it not simply be some attribute of a minor saint, and may this not be a fragment of a wing of

212

an altarpiece? The panel must have been cut down in the bottom half, and the original composition probably showed the figure full-length; his thoughtful expression would also correspond better with this interpretation.

Dimensions: Wood. 36 × 27.
Provenance: Van Diemen, Amsterdam (c.1926); Neuerberg collection, Hamburg; acquired in 1940 by the museum in Cologne.
Exhibitions: Amsterdam, 1958, no. 35 (follower of Geertgen, c.1525).
Literature: Friedländer, V, 1927, no. 31, p. 136 (follower of Geertgen); Winkler, 1959 B, p. 192 (Mostaert).

95 The Meal of the Holy Family (Pl. 112)
Cologne, Wallraf–Richartz Museum

Like the *Tree of Jesse*, this delightful painting has been variously attributed. Friedländer, in 1927, saw it as a work by a follower of Geertgen; but in 1937 he decided that in fact it was an early work by Mostaert, an opinion held subsequently by Winkler. Hoogewerff, in 1937, justifiably attributed it to the Master of the Brunswick *Diptych*, and was followed for a time by K.G. Boon.

Dimensions: Wood. 37 × 24.
Exhibitions: Rotterdam, 1936, no. 39; Amsterdam, 1958, no. 30.
Literature: Winkler, 1924, p. 236; Friedländer, V, 1927, p. 58 and no. 33; Friedländer, X, 1932, p. 27 and no. 20; Hoogewerff, II, 1937, p. 202; Winkler, 1959 B, p. 192–4; Boon, 1966, p. 64, note 9; Snyder, 1971.

Attributed to Jacob Jansz

96 The Annunciation
Paris, Musée du Louvre, Cabinet des Dessins

The attribution of this drawing to the Master of the Brunswick *Diptych* is attractive but not altogether convincing. Frits Lugt has rightly pointed out how the richness of the architecture contrasts with the usual plainness of the buildings depicted by the artist. The figure-types themselves are not quite those of the

Haarlem artist: they are less modelled by light and shade, more elegant in build, have more elongated faces and narrower eyes. This may therefore only be a drawing by a disciple of Jacob Jansz. The richness of the architectural décor suggests an artist working at Antwerp, notably the Master of the Morrison *Triptych*.

Dimensions:	Pen and brown ink on white paper. 28.1 × 18.6.
Provenance:	confiscation of emigré property.
Exhibitions:	London, 1929, no. 505; Paris, 1935, no. 189; Rotterdam, 1936, no. 6; Brussels, 1937–8, no. 1; Amsterdam, 1958, no. 179.
Literature:	Winkler, 1922, p. 61 (Master of the *St. Anne with the Virgin and Child* in the Louvre); Demonts, 1926, p. 16, note I (circle of Geertgen tot Sint Jans); Baldass, 1937, p. 21; Lugt, 1968, no. 63.

After Jacob Jansz

97   The van Scoten Triptych (Pl. 113)
Copy (drawing) in the Rijksmuseum, Amsterdam
Centrepiece: The Last Judgment
Left wing: The Ascent of the Blessed to Paradise, Jacob van Scoten, his wife and his son Willem
Right wing: The Fall of the Damned, Gheryt van Scoten and his wife Luytgard van Swieten
Reverse: Arms of Gheryt van Scoten and his wife

This lost painting, of which the very exact copy drawing (perhaps produced by tracing) was published by Karel Boon (1966), is of considerable interest in being approximately datable through the persons portrayed. On the right-hand wing are Gheryt van Scoten and his wife, Luytgard van Swieten, whose arms are also depicted on the reverse of the wings. The left-hand wing only features deceased members of Gheryt's family: his father Jacob, his mother, née van Adrichem, identifiable by her coat of arms, and his brother, Master Willem van Scoten, a monk, who died in 1496. The child is probably another of his brothers who died young (these identifications are due to Mr. Thierry de Bye Dolleman and rectify those proposed in 1966 by Karel Boon without taking account of the coats of arms on the left wing). The triptych must therefore have been painted shortly after the death of Master Willem, i.e. *c.*1497.
The style is obviously very similar to that of the *Tree of Jesse*, but also characteristic of the Master of the Brunswick *Diptych*: the faces of the central panel, as far as can be made out from the reproduction alone, seem to be of the very round type so beloved of this artist. Similarly, in the foreground of the wings, the donors' draperies are spread out on the ground in sharp folds in a style still very close to that of the fifteenth century. The composition of the central panel is a direct forerunner of that of the *Memorial painting of the van Noordwijk Family* (Bonn, Landesmuseum) and of the *Last Judgment* of Christian II of Denmark (Copenhagen, Nationalmuseum), both by Mostaert, as Karel Boon has rightly pointed out.
The house of Paradise, perched atop a lofty, precipitous crag on the central panel, bears an odd resemblance to the one that can be made out on Saenredam's copy of the organ-shutter in St. Bavo's in Haarlem by Vrederick Hoon. The similarity may be purely coincidental; but the rarity of buildings in such elevated situations lends some credence to the idea of a possible connection between the two works (impossible to examine more thoroughly, for lack of greater precision in the illustration of Hoon's picture).

Dimensions:	Pen on paper. Central panel 46 × 35.2; inner wings, each 46 × 15.5; outer wings, each 46 × 16.5.
Provenance:	Amersfoort, private collection; acquired in 1971.
Literature:	Boon, 1966; Snyder, 1971.

Master of the Antwerp *Triptych*

(Mouwerijn van Waterlandt?, known to have been active between 1473 and 1509)

To the paintings grouped together under this name by W. Cohen, three important works should be added: a copy of a lost original, the *Institution of the Rosary* (Leipzig, Museum of Fine Arts and an English private collection), a diptych consisting of the *Maria in Sole* in the Boymans Museum, Rotterdam and the *Crucifixion* in Edinburgh. This artist's style is marked by a fondness for movement and for broken folds which break up the continuity of the lines of the composition. This tendency is less noticeable in the three works whose attribution is suggested here for the first time, but it is there in embryonic form.

Literature:	W. Cohen, 1914; Friedländer, V, 1927, p. 54–5; Hoogewerff, II, 1937, p. 206–10.

98   The Institution of the Rosary (Pl. 116)
Copy of the whole in the Museum of Fine Arts, Leipzig, copy of the right-hand part in a private collection in England.

213

When featured in the exhibition of 'Early Flemish Painters' in Bruges, the Leipzig painting was naturally associated with the work of Geertgen tot Sint Jans on account of the type of the female faces. This conclusion has not been questioned until now. The theme is the Institution of the Rosary, according to the legend related by Alanus de Rupe (Van Os, 1964). On one side, St. Dominic has his vision of the Virgin and the Child, who presents him with a rosary. On the other side, the saint gives a rosary to the childless Blanche of Castile, who has come to plead with him to intercede on her behalf. Finally, in the background, St. Dominic advocates the use of the rosary by his preaching.

The style of the painting is less mature than that of the Antwerp *Triptych*. The figures still have simple, rather stiff poses like those in the works of the Master of the *Holy Kindred*. Also noteworthy is the fondness for secondary scenes, in imitation of Geertgen tot Sint Jans; but here they are allowed to proliferate without any care for the structure of the work. The painting could have been commissioned by the Brotherhood of the Rosary founded at Haarlem in 1478 at the instigation of Jacobus Weijts, prior of the Dominican friary and a disciple of Alanus de Rupe. This would indicate a date of around 1480, which corresponds well with the style of the work.

Dimensions:	Leipzig: Canvas (transferred from wood?). 42 × 28.
Provenance:	of the Leipzig painting: coll. of Sir Ch. Turner, London (sold by Lepke, Berlin, 7 November 1908); coll. of Dr. U. Thieme.
Exhibition:	Bruges, 1902, no. 256.
Literature:	Durand Gréville, 1904, p. 389–90 (follower of Geertgen); Conway, 1921, p. 277; Friedländer, V, 1927, p. 38–9 and no. 13 (copy of Geertgen); van den Oudendijk Pieterse, 1939, p. 292–3; Ring, 1952 (publication of English copy); Snyder, 1960, p. 131; van Os, 1964, p. 32–6.

99 A   Maria in Sole (Pl. 115)
Rotterdam, Boymans–van Beuningen Museum

The iconography of this painting has been studied several times (Hoffmann, 1950; Snyder, 1960; Engelbracht, 1963; van Os, 1964). Its basic motif is a representation of the Virgin of the 'Maria in Sole' type, as in the vision in the *Apocalypse* (12:1–3): she appears 'clothed with the sun' and with the moon under her feet, trampling the Demon. Her solar corona is formed by the three uppermost hierarchies of angels: seraphim, cherubim and thrones. The cherubim carry the instruments of the Passion, and three of them hold banderoles bearing the inscription 'Sanctus'; they thus symbolise Christ the Redeemer. The thrones play music on instruments of every possible kind, glorifying the Virgin. The vision in the *Apocalypse* is interpreted as an allegory of the Immaculate Conception. In the Rotterdam painting the Virgin's crown has a circlet of roses, an allusion to the rosary.
At one time, J. Q. van Regteren Altena (1959) suggested that a third panel was missing from the ensemble, but this seems unlikely. Certainly, the two compositions do not complement each other very well to twentieth-century eyes—or even to the more sensitive eyes of an artist like Geertgen—but such groupings seem quite frequent in the fifteenth century.

Dimensions:	Wood. 25.5 × 18.
Provenance:	coll. of Cardinal Fesch (sold at Rome, March-April 1845, lot 264); V. Spark, New York; Wildenstein, New York; acquired by Mr. van Beuningen in 1952; acquired with the van Beuningen collection in 1961.
Exhibitions:	Amsterdam, 1951, no. 43; Paris, 1952, no. 49; Rotterdam, 1955, no. 10; Amsterdam, 1958, no. 14; The Hague, 1966, no. 5; Paris, 1966, no. 4.

Literature: Friedländer, 1949; Hoffman, 1950; Grete Ring, 1952, p. 147; Panofsky, 1953, p. 495; Sulzberger, 1959; van Regteren Altena, 1959; Snyder, 1960, p. 131–2; Engelbracht, 1963; Van Os, 1964; van Regteren Altena, 1966; Boon, 1967, p. 9.

99 B The Crucifixion with St. Jerome and St. Dominic (Pl. 117)
Edinburgh, National Gallery of Scotland.

Originally a pendant to the Rotterdam *Maria in Sole*. Here the composition is much less successful, and the hand of the Master of the Antwerp *Triptych* is more easily discernible. The figure of St. Dominic is very similar to that in the left background of the *Institution of the Rosary* in Leipzig.

The iconographic programme of the work is strange in its complexity. The principal motif is that of the Crucifixion, shown as Christ's act of redemption by its association with the cries of the souls in Purgatory and the corpse of Adam (formerly concealed by an over-painting, which has recently been removed). In the background, the story of the Passion is narrated in a remarkable series of little scenes: Pilate washing his hands, the Ecce Homo, Christ at the scourging-column, the Crowning with Thorns, Christ in Gethsemane, the Ascent of Calvary with the sudary of St. Veronica, Christ mocked and despoiled of his garments, the Nailing to the Cross and the Lamentation. The artist has not troubled to place the incidents in rigorously chronological order, but has preferred to turn the landscape background to the best possible account. Finally, at the foot of the Cross, are St. Jerome imposing penance on himself and St. Dominic displaying a rosary that he wears as a belt. The diptych should thus be seen in connection with the cult of the rosary, with St. Dominic and with the eremitical life (represented by St. Jerome). Hence it may have been intended for the Dominican friary in Haarlem, which was a house of strict observance attached to the congregation of Holland, and of which the prior appointed in 1478, Jacobus Weijts, was to assist the development of the cult of the rosary.

Dimensions: Wood. 25.5 × 18.
Provenance: coll. of Cardinal Fesch (sold at Rome, March–April 1845, lot 264); English private collection.
Literature: Sulzberger, 1959; van Regteren Altena, 1959; van Regteren Altena, 1966.

100 Virgin and Child with a Donor presented by St. Michael
Berlin, Staatliche Museen

For the gesture of the Child, leaning forward and holding out his arms to the donor, who holds one of his hands, the artist probably drew his inspiration from some *Adoration of the Magi*. Of all the artist's pictures, this is the closest to the two newly attributed works, the *Institution of the Rosary* and the Dominican diptych.

Dimensions: Wood, 82.5 × 75.5.
Provenance: von Haxthausen coll. (Westphalia); von Arnswaldt coll. (Rostock); presented to the museums by Wilhelm von Bode in 1908.

Exhibitions: Utrecht, 1913, no. 176; Amsterdam, 1958, no. 37.
Literature: Cohen, 1914, p. 26–8; Valentiner, 1914, p. 74; Friedländer, V, 1927, p. 54 and no. 24; Kessler, 1930, p. 50; Hoogewerff, II, 1937, p. 208.

214

101 Triptych of the Virgin and Child (Pl. 114)
Left wing: St. Christopher
Right wing: St. George
Antwerp, Musée Royal des Beaux-Arts

If there is still an echo of Geertgen's style in this painting, it is very faint. The sharply-broken folds and the fabric lying crumpled on the ground are more in the manner of the Master of the *Holy Kindred*. By its ornamentation, typical of northern late Gothic, the Virgin's throne suggests a date very late in the fifteenth century or, more likely, in the early years of the sixteenth.

Dimensions: Wood. Centrepiece: 67 × 51; wings, 67 × 21 each.
Provenance: Van Ertborn coll., Antwerp (bequeathed to the museum in 1841).
Exhibitions: Utrecht, 1913; Amsterdam, 1958, no. 38.
Literature: Cohen, 1914, p. 26–8; Valentiner, 1914, p. 74 and 201; Friedländer, V, 1927, p. 54–5 and no. 23; Kessler, 1930, p. 50; Hoogewerff, II, 1937, p. 208.

102 The Assumption and two donors
Bonn, Rheinisches Landesmuseum

The composition is inspired by a painting by the Master of the *Legend of St. Lucy* (Washington, National Gallery, on loan from the Kress Foundation) or by the latter's model, which could be by a more important artist (Memling?). The artist has transposed it into his own style, however, giving the draperies a jerky rhythm and stiffening the figures.

Jan Dircs Cill, the painting's donor, endowed a curacy on the altar of Our Lady of the Seven Dolours in a chapel near the sacristy of the Nieuwe Kerk in Amsterdam on 10 December 1513. But it is unlikely that the picture was intended for this altar, as its subject has no direct connection with the altar's dedication. It may rather have been an epitaph commissioned for the same chapel.

Dimensions: Wood. 115 × 95.
Provenance: acquired in 1906 from a collection in the Rhineland.
Exhibition: Utrecht, 1913, no. 30.
Literature: Cohen, 1914, p. 26; Friedländer, V, 1927, p. 55 and no. 25; Hoogewerff, II, 1937, p. 209–10; van Regteren Altena, 1966, p. 77.

Master of the *Figdor Deposition*

(Claes van Waterlandt? known to have been active between 1485 and 1490)

The first listing of this artist's works was presented in 1914 by Valentiner, under the name of the 'Master of *St. Lucy*' and was accepted by Friedländer in 1927. Hoogewerff (1937) preferred the more poetic name of 'Master of the Page beneath the Cross' to that chosen by Friedländer, which has been retained here.

Valentiner (1914) tried to identify this Master. He assumed with some justification, that the young Cornelis van Oostsanen, who hailed from a small town in Waterlandt, must have been inclined to apprentice himself to a fellow-countryman, namely one of the Simonsz van Waterlandt brothers, Mouwerijn or Claes. This suggestion is at least better supported than Hoogewerff's, who proposed without any justification that the artist should be identified with a painter about whom very little is known, Jan Gerritsz Swegher.

Literature: Valentiner, 1914; Friedländer, V, 1927, p. 56–7; Hoogewerff, II, 1937, p. 211–20; Baldass, 1937, p. 119–20; Schretlen, 1938; Kunze, 1939.

103 St. Valerian and St. Cecilia
Amsterdam, Rijksmuseum

These panels may be the original reverse of the two panels by Jacob Jansz in Brussels (*92*). They are in a much less satisfactory state of preservation, however, which is hardly surprising in the case of the outer faces of a triptych. The wearing away of the paint surface over the whole picture emphasises the stylistic differences between the two works even more. The figure of St. Valerian is a sort of paraphrase of St. Bavo from the Brunswick *Diptych* (*90*).

Dimensions: Wood. Each panel 62 × 23.5.
Provenance: English private coll.; on the Amsterdam art market; Kessler coll.; presented to the Rijksmuseum by Mr. and Mrs. Kessler-Hülsmann in 1940.
Exhibitions: London, 1929, nos. 4 and 5; Rotterdam, 1936, nos. 8 and 9; The Hague, 1945, no. 19.
Literature: Friedländer, V, 1927, p. 54 and no. 21 (Master of the Brunswick *Diptych*?); Borenius, 1929, p. 134; Kessler, 1930, p. 29 (Geertgen); Hoogewerff, II, 1937, p. 200 (Master of the Brunswick *Diptych*), Vogelsang, 1942, p. 56 (*id.*); Lutterwelt, 1951, p. 81–3 (suggesting commission for the Convent of St. Cecilia in Amsterdam).

104 Maria in Sole crowned by two Angels
Pretoria, City Hall

This picture, which made its first appearance at the Amsterdam exhibition in 1958, was compared by J.Q. van Regteren Altena to the *Maria in Sole* diptych in Rotterdam (*99*). But although the two works have a similar theme, they differ in handling and figure-types. The style here can be said to resemble that of the Master of the *Figdor Deposition*: the same rounded face for the Virgin, the same lifeless folds, the same clumsy hands a little too large for the body. The simplicity and calm of the composition suggest that this is one of the artist's early works, close in date to the two figures of saints in the Rijksmuseum.

Dimensions:	Wood. 42.2 × 31.5. Inscribed on the reverse: 'Joanes obt 1579'.
Exhibitions:	Amsterdam, 1958, no. 31 (as by the Master of the Brunswick *Diptych*).
Literature:	Van Regteren Altena, 1959, p. 173 (School of Geertgen tot Sint Jans).

105 The Deposition from the Cross (Pl. 118)
Formerly in the Staatliche Museen, Berlin (destroyed or lost in 1944–5)

Irene Kunze has stated that this panel was a wing of a triptych of which the reverse was formed by the *Martyrdom of St. Lucy* (*106*). Her arguments are not, in actual fact, completely convincing. The two panels do seem to have been sawn in half through their thickness; but Irene Kunze's assertion does not seem to be based on an exact comparison of the way the backs of the panels match one another. The boards of which each is composed are not, in fact, arranged identically. Moreover, the *St. Lucy* painting has a clear orientation towards the right and was thus probably the outer face of a left-hand wing. The Berlin painting, on the other hand, had a clear orientation towards the left and adopted the overall composition of Geertgen's *Lamentation*; it must therefore have been the inside right-hand wing of some ensemble.

The original triptych thus probably consisted of a centrepiece depicting the Crucifixion, a left wing with the Carrying of the Cross (or with the Ecce Homo, as in the *Hospitallers' Altarpiece*), and a right wing with the Deposition. A comparison between this painting and a woodcut by Jacob Cornelisz van Oostsanen of the *Crucifixion* (Steinbart, 1937, no. 19) led Schretlen to suggest that the painter should be identified with that artist in his early years. However, although the woodcut adopts several features of the painting (the poses of the Thieves, the figure-type of the Virgin, for example), it is executed with a sureness in composition, a firm and generous design and a sense of space which a master would be unlikely to have learnt except in his maturity, and which were completely lacking in the Berlin painting.

Dimensions:	Wood. 131 × 102.
Provenance:	Schloss Schönau bei Vorlau (Austria) *c.*1896; Figdor collection; sold Berlin Cassirer-Helbing, 29–30 September 1930, III, IX, XVI; acquired at this sale.
Literature:	Frimmel, 1896, p. 9; Friedländer, 1903, p. 66; Valentiner, 1914, p. 70–1; Friedländer, V, 1927, p. 56–7 and no. 28; Hoogewerff, II, 1937, p. 215–16; Schretlen, 1938; Kunze, 1939, p. 9–10.

106 The Martyrdom of St. Lucy (Pl. 119)
Amsterdam, Rijksmuseum

This panel may have been the reverse of the left-hand wing of the triptych whose inner right-hand face was the *Deposition from the Cross* (cf. *105*).
The influence of Geertgen is even more noticeable here than in the Berlin painting. The artist follows the *Golden Legend* story (Roze ed., I, p. 54–57) very closely. We see the first attempt, by human force, at dragging the saint to a brothel; the artist has slightly exceeded the text in order to show the house. In the far background is the second attempt to move the saint, this time with the help of oxen. In the foreground is the scene of the martyrdom and, a little further back on the right, the saint's communion before her death. Finally, the artist has included a depiction of the execution of the Consul Paschasius at Rome.

Dimensions:	Wood. 152.5 × 101.5
Provenance:	F. Engert coll., Vienna, F. Lippmann coll., Vienna; acquired in Vienna by the Rijksmuseum in 1897 with the assistance of the Rembrandt Society.
Exhibition:	Amsterdam, 1958, no. 32.
Literature:	Friedländer, 1903, p. 66; Durand Gréville, 1904, p. 388–9; Valentiner, 1914, p. 69; Friedländer, V, 1927, p. 56–7; Steinbart, 1929, p. 217; Hoogewerff, II, 1937, p. 216–17; Schretlen, 1938, p. 149; Kunze, 1939, p. 8.

107 The Crucifixion
Amsterdam, Rijksmuseum

215

This work resembles the preceding panels in its sketchily modelled faces with black dots for eyes, in the stiff elegance of the poses, in the amiable appearance of the characters, and in the ample but crudely-folded drapery. Doubts have been expressed, however, on whether this work belongs to the same group as the *Deposition from the Cross*. Certainly, the violence of the latter is as yet hardly noticeable here; but there are intimations of it. We have seen that the composition of the painting is probably directly inspired by the lost centrepanel of Geertgen's *Hospitallers' Altarpiece*. Nevertheless, one notices the curious addition in the left background of two shepherds, probably borrowed from some scene of the Nativity or of the Angel's Tidings to the Shepherds.

Copy in the Archiepiscopal Museum, Utrecht, from the Church of St. Vitus in Naarden.

Dimensions:	Wood. 103 × 85.
Provenance:	coll. of Sir Henry H. Howorth; acquired from him in 1905.
Literature:	Valentiner, 1914, p. 69–70; Friedländer, 1927, p. 57 and no. 28; Kessler, 1930, p. 54; Hoogewerff, II, 1937, p. 211–14; Snyder, 1960, p. 126–7.

108 The Holy Kindred
Zurich, Bührle collection

This recently discovered work has been made known under the name of the Master of the Brunswick *Diptych*. Such an attribution is unacceptable, considering the stiffness of the figures and the clumsiness of the composition. But it shares many features of works by the Master of the *Figdor Deposition*: the same faces, the same stiff drapery, and the same hesitant composition. The picture takes the theme of the Holy Kindred and gives it a more down-to-earth setting. The apple-picking in which Joachim and Joseph are engaged symbolises fecundity. In the background are the Virgin's half-sisters, the two Marys, and their children.

216

Dimensions:	Wood. 43.5 × 35.5.
Provenance:	English collection; acquired in 1954 on the British art market.
Exhibition:	Zurich, 1958, no. 52.
Literature:	Fries, 1956.

Master of the *Tiburtine Sibyl*

(Joes Wilen Valcx? *d.*1487)

The credit for isolating this artist's work must go to Valentiner (1914). In a much later study (1943), he has notably advanced our knowledge of the artist by proposing, apparently with good reason, to attribute to him the work of the illustrator who worked in Haarlem for the publisher Jacob Bellaert. Unfortunately, he has also undermined the validity of his conclusions by proposing to identify the painter with Albert van Ouwater; the differences between the *Raising of Lazarus* in Berlin (*42*) and the paintings and engravings grouped under the above provisional name are so profound that no credence can be given to this theory.

It does not seem necessary to accept any of the paintings that W. Schöne has proposed to add to Friedländer's list (1937). They all belong to different stylistic groups, without any direct connection with this artist.

Literature: Valentiner, 1914, p. 44–52; Friedländer, III, 1925, p. 70–3; Glück, 1931; Schöne, 1937, p. 175; Schöne, 1942, p. 38, Valentiner, 1943; Snyder, 1960, p. 49–55.

109   The Raising of Lazarus
Mexico, Instituto Nacional de Bellas Artes

James Snyder (1960, p. 53) has rightly pointed out that in this composition the artist was borrowing from Albert van Ouwater as well as from Geertgen. From the former he has taken the figures of Christ, St. Peter and Martha; from the latter he has adopted the open-air setting and the figures which link the foreground to the background. The portrayal of Lazarus is midway between the two other versions, but copies Geertgen's larger expanse of drapery, thus partially avoiding the necessity for a depiction of the nude. The landscape, however, owes nothing to either of these Haarlem painters of the previous generation, but seems to be an imitation of the backgrounds of Bouts or, even more so, of those by the Master of the *Taking of Christ*.

The book *Epistelen en Evangelien*, printed in Haarlem by Jacob Bellaert in 1486, features a *Raising of Lazarus* which is very similar (Schretlen, 1925, pl. 30D). It is not a copy of the painting, however, but a variant which may be by the master himself or by a similar artist from the same workshop. It copies some elements almost exactly, but improves the overall arrangement in adapting it to the space available in the book.

217

Dimensions: Wood. 80 × 40.
Exhibitions: Brussels-Delft, 1957-8, not in cat.; Amsterdam, 1958, no. 13.
Literature: Valentiner, 1914, p. 46–7; Friedländer, III, 1924, p. 71 and no. 76; Hoogewerff, II, 1937, p. 78; Schretlen, 1946, p. 57; Gerson, 1950, p. 15; Snyder, 1960, p. 53.

110   Virgin and Child
Enschede, Rijksmuseum Twenthe

218

Hoogewerff saw this painting as a work of the Master's circle. It seems, however, that we can take it as by the Master himself. The Child's face is of a surprisingly elongated type; but it recurs in the Mexico painting, though it is less noticeable there by reason of the small scale of the figures. This may, like the *Raising of Lazarus* (*109*), be one of the artist's early works.

Dimensions: Wood (oak). 40 × 29.
Literature: Hoogewerff, II, 1937, p. 80; Snyder, 1960, p. 49.

111   The Crucifixion (Pl. 120)
Detroit, The Detroit Institute of Arts

On the left-hand side of the picture — on Christ's right — around the Virgin stand St. John the Evangelist, the Virgin's sisters, the two Marys, Mary Magdalene and a fifth woman (Ecclesia or a Sibyl?).

On the other side are three Jews and a soldier. The placing of the figures is thus based on a clear distinction between the side of the bad and that of the good. James Snyder (1960) has shown that the same division appears in the landscape: on the right, behind the Jews, the large crag bears only a dead tree and gives an impression of drought and desolation. The feeling is heightened by the presence of several snakes and a kind of dragon, symbols of evil, at the foot of the cliff. In contrast, behind the Virgin, the steep bluff is covered by abundant vegetation, a symbol of fertility.

Snyder has also noted that the composition is largely inspired by a lost *Crucifixion* by an artist of Dieric Bouts's circle, whose overall effect may be reflected in a painting from the Rhineland (Schöne, 1938, pl. 75C). The group of Jews also bears a strong resemblance to the 'executioner-princes' invented by this artist (*Triptych of St. Hippolytus*, *Triptych of St. Erasmus*). The composition of the Detroit painting has a certain grandeur, imposed by the calm rhythm of the tall figures. Yet the detail reveals a noticeable clumsiness in the rather awkward poses of the characters. The faces often verge on caricature. The landscape is not composed in Geertgen's manner; its successive lines of trees, all leading off to the horizon, are derived from Boutsian examples. Valentiner (1943) has shown that the curious shape of the overhanging rock on the right is found in the engravings of the *Historie van Troyen* published by Jacob Bellaert at Haarlem in 1485 (Schretlen, 1925, pl. 24a).

Dimensions: Wood. 144 × 103.
Provenance: Crombez coll., Paris; Harriman coll., New York; coll. of Mr & Mrs E.B. Whitcomb, Detroit; presented to the museum in 1941.
Exhibitions: Brussels-Delft, 1957–8, no. 50; Amsterdam, 1958, no. 12.
Literature: Friedländer, III, 1924, p. 81 and no. 77; Hoogewerff, II, 1937, p. 78; Valentiner, 1943, p. 79; Boon, 1947, p. 35; Richardson, 1954, p. 26–7; Gerson, 1950, p. 15; Snyder, 1960, p. 52.

112   The Marriage of the Virgin (Pl. 121)
Philadelphia, Johnson collection, Museum of Art

This painting has exactly the same measurements as the Detroit *Crucifixion*. It is unlikely, however, that the two works come from the same ensemble. This one appears to have quite a precise function. Behind the Virgin, one of her companions points out the group of bridegrooms to a young woman who is urged forward by a young man standing behind her. On the far side of the picture, behind Joseph, stands a young man, richly clad in what appears to be contemporary fashion, who seems to be looking at the young woman. These two figures are given considerable prominence and are probably portraits. The first impression is thus one of a painting commemorating a marriage.

The middle ground, however, indicates something slightly different. It recounts the story of Joachim and St. Anne in five episodes: Joachim driven from the Temple, the Angel's Message to Joachim, the Meeting at the Golden Gate, the Nativity of the Virgin and the Presentation in the Temple. The fruitfulness of St. Anne is heavily emphasised by the presence of six rabbits, classic symbols of that quality. Hence, this may either be a commemoration of a marriage accompanied by a vow or, strictly speaking, an ex-voto offered by a young couple anxious to be blessed with a family. The arrangement of the secondary scenes suffers from a certain clumsiness. The locations are not juxtaposed in chronological order and have no structural links. The artist has simply assembled the scenes in the manner of an illustrator bringing together several vignettes.

Dimensions: Wood. 145 × 103.
Literature: Valentiner, 1914, p. 50–2; Friedländer, III, 1924, p. 71, and no. 75; Hoogewerff, II, 1937, p. 78–9; Valentiner, 1943, p. 79–82; Schretlen, 1946, p. 59; Snyder, 1960, p. 53.

113   St. Anne with the Virgin and Child
Bruges, collection of Baron van der Elst

This delightful painting was added to the list of the works of the Master of the *Tiburtine Sibyl* by Glück (1931). Frans Baudoin has rightly remarked that an almost identical group of the Virgin and Child can be found in a small panel by the school of Bouts in the Correr Museum (Brussels-Delft, 1957–8), and that this fact probably indicates a common model from the hand of Bouts himself.

To the theme of the St. Anne Trinity, the artist has here adapted the motif of the Virgin on a grassy bank, which also derives from Dieric Bouts or his circle. He nevertheless gives it a highly individual interpretation by introducing a background wall of pink bricks, whose delicate colouring affects the whole picture and foreshadows certain trends in seventeenth-century Dutch painting. The two peacocks in the background may well be symbolic of immortality rather than purely decorative.

Dimensions: Wood. 37 × 23.
Provenance: Czeczowicka coll., Vienna; sold by Graupe, Berlin, 12 May 1930, no. 26 (as A. Bouts).
Exhibitions: Brussels, 1935, no. 81; Brussels-Delft, 1957-8, no. 49.
Literature: Glück, 1931; Friedländer, XIV, 1937, p. 76–8; Schöne, 1938, p. 188, no. 79c; Snyder, 1960, p. 49.

114 Augustus and the Tiburtine Sibyl (Pl. 122)
Frankfurt, Staedel Institut

Of all the artist's works, this is without doubt the best known. In its arrangement and in the poses of the characters it achieves a kind of equilibrium which endows it with a certain elegance. James Snyder, observing the strong influence of Bouts here, saw this work as the artist's earliest. One may well wonder if its very quality does not point to the opposite conclusion. It is noteworthy that the facial contortions have now disappeared, and have given way to a kind of serenity. For the painting's allegorical significance, analysed by James Snyder (1960), cf. Chapter VI above.

Dimensions: Wood. 69 × 85.
Literature: Valentiner, 1914, p. 47–9; Friedländer, III, 1924, p. 70–1, no. 74; Hoogewerff, II, 1938, p. 76–8; Valentiner, 1943, p. 79–82; Schretlen, 1946, p. 57–8; Snyder, 1960, p. 50–1.

Dutch (Haarlem?) artist, last quarter of the fifteenth century

115 The Crucifixion
San Francisco, M.H. de Young Memorial Museum

This curious painting offers a close combination of echoes of works by both Geertgen and the Master of the *Tiburtine Sibyl*. The whole of the right-hand group (Jews and soldier) is taken directly from the latter, as are some details of the landscape. The Jew in the right foreground is an almost exact copy of the one in the Detroit *Crucifixion* (111) by the same artist. The dragon on the standard in the San Francisco panel may also be taken from the same work, in which it assumes a symbolic significance. On the other hand, the group of the Virgin and the holy women is a clumsy interpretation of figures by Geertgen, of which the shapes and poses can still be discerned. It is also probable that Christ and the angels have been borrowed from Geertgen. James Snyder (1960) has rightly assumed that these figures had been copied from the retable of the high altar of the Haarlem commandery. The similarity between the crucified Christ of this work and the one by the Master of the *Figdor Deposition* (107) renders this theory very plausible. Unfortunately, the clumsiness of this version can give us no more than a very faint echo of the original composition. If the donor is indeed a Carthu-

sian, it is possible that the work was not painted at Haarlem, since there was never a charterhouse in that town.

219

Dimensions: Wood. 72.4 × 47.
Provenance: coll. of J.P. Weyer, Cologne (1862); Dr. Bock, Aix-la-Chapelle; Prince of Hohenzollern-Sigmaringen, Sigmaringen; sold by Kleinberger, New York, 18 November 1932, no. 25; coll. Henry P. McIlhenny, Philadelphia.
Literature: Boon, 1947, p. 35; Snyder, 1960, p. 52–3 and 127.

Haarlem artist, last third of the fifteenth century

116 Christ before Pilate
The Hague, collection of Dr. J. Frederiks (on loan to the Boymans-van Beuningen Museum, Rotterdam)

220

This painting must be considered as a Haarlem product because the building in the background is Haarlem town hall (Schretlen, 1930). All the same, it cannot be linked with the engravings of Jacob Bellaert's illustrator, as has been suggested by its former owner, J. Schretlen, since the latter are characterised by an elegance which is quite absent here.

The subject is fairly rare: it is not the classic scene of the Ecce Homo, but the episode that precedes it, the presentation of Christ, scourged and crowned with thorns, to Pilate. This can no doubt be explained by the panel's belonging to a series depicting various stages of the Passion.
The handling is very spontaneous. The artist is less concerned with organisation than in bringing his figures to life; their faces verge on deliberate caricature.

Dimensions: Wood. 38 × 25.
Provenance: Galerie Doria, Rome; Schretlen coll.
Exhibitions: Rotterdam, 1936, no. 13; Laren, 1961, no. 64.
Literature: Schretlen, 1930; Hoogewerff, II, 1937, p. 225–6.

Haarlem (?) artist, last third of the fifteenth century

117 Ecce Homo
Chicago, The Art Institute

221

There is no justification whatever for the attribution of this curious painting to the Master of the *Virgo inter Virgines*, as it represents neither his figure-types nor his handling.
The work is typical of the more 'popular' trend which predominates so clearly in Dutch miniatures. The spontaneity of the gestures, the over-indulgence in expressive hands and the caricatured faces are characteristic of this trend. The group of Jews in the foreground, both by the placing of the various figures and by their garments, is reminiscent of Albert van Ouwater and Geertgen. The connection is not very close, but it nevertheless exists.
In the absence of any firm clue which would enable us to localise the work plausibly, we may argue from this fact for a hypothetical attribution to the Haarlem workshops.

Dimensions: Wood. 52 × 35.
Provenance: Contini collection, Rome; New York, sold by Roerich, 27 March 1930, no. 64; Ryerson collection; presented with the latter to the museum.
Literature: Friedländer, V, 1927, p. 73 and no. 53 (Master of the *Virgo*); Boon, 1963, p. 14.

118 The Crowning with Thorns
Holland, private collection

This painting is related in its inspiration and handling to the *Christ before Pilate* and the *Ecce Homo* (cf. *116* and *117*). There is the same fondness for movement, facial caricature and unaffected composition. The figure of the high priest and that of Pilate on the right, however, have an affinity with those of Geertgen, at least remotely. As a hypothesis, the work may be localised at Haarlem. The donors, two monks and two nuns, have not been identified.

222

Dimensions: Wood. 41 × 38.
Provenance: Hulsemann coll.; Jansenius de Vries coll., Warffum.
Exhibition: Laren, 1961, no. 93.

Master of the *Virgo inter Virgines*

The first attempt at isolating this artist's oeuvre was made by Friedländer on the occasion of the Bruges exhibition of 1902, and this listing was confirmed by the Utrecht exhibition of 1913. Apart from Friedländer's writings, there has only been one other attempt at a monograph, that of K.G. Boon in 1963.
A comparison of the paintings with the book illustrations produced at Delft between 1483 and 1498 suggests the identification of the artist with Dirc Jansz, who is known to have been active in Delft between 1474 and 1495; unfortunately, there is no conclusive evidence for this theory.

Literature: Friedländer, 1903 B; Friedländer, 1906 B; Friedländer, 1910; Schretlen, 1925, p. 38–42; Friedländer, V, 1927, p. 65–78; Hoogewerff, II, 1937, p. 240–82; Baldass, 1937, p. 118; Boon, 1963; Châtelet, 1979, p. 190–1.

119 Triptych of the Lamentation

A The Annunciation (Pl. 123)
Aix-la-Chapelle, Suermondt Museum

Now forming a single panel, this picture was originally the reverse of the following two wings.
The interpretation of the subject follows the formula of the left wing of the *St. Columba Altarpiece* (Munich, Alte Pinakothek) by Rogier van der Weyden, of which the main elements are used here, but reversed. This is not a copy, however, but a very free interpretation of van der Weyden's arrangement. Thus, for example, the room is just sketched in without any detailed depiction of the interior.
The features of the artist's style are visible here, but are still linked to a laborious handling somewhat lacking in vigour. The faces are sharp, but not to the extreme degree of the mature works. The drapery folds billow out in a fussy rhythm.

Dimensions: Wood. 85 × 69.
History: collection of Dr. F. de Bock.
Exhibition: Rotterdam, 1936, no. 20.
Literature: Scheibler, 1903, p. 30, no. 15; Friedländer, 1910, p. 65 (Master of the *Virgo*); Friedländer, V, 1927, no. 61; Hoogewerff, II, 1937, p. 268.

B and C Inner faces of wings
Left: Joseph of Arimathaea and Nicodemus
Right: Mary Magdalene and another holy woman
Aix-la-Chapelle, Suermondt Museum

The artist has, oddly and unusually, spread this *Lamentation* across the three inside panels of the triptych. The figures thus isolated on the wings take on the aspect of weepers. The faces have the features characteristic of the master, but are conveyed in broad, simple lines without any refinement of modelling. The layout itself is different in character from the mature works: it devotes most of the surface to the figures, placing them in a very sketchily defined setting.

Dimensions: Wood. 85 × 34.5.
History
and Literature: cf. *119 A*.

D The Lamentation
Madrid, Prado

This was probably the original centrepiece of the triptych whose wings were formed by the panels in Aix-la-Chapelle. The different measurements — the Madrid panel is slightly wider than the ones at Aix — can be explained by subsequent mutilations and the disappearance of the original frame.
The interpretation seems to be derived, very freely, from Geertgen's version. The rigidity of Christ's body is emphasised here because it is lying wholly on the ground, without the torso being propped up on the Virgin's knees, but the idea is the same. The relationship

224

between the Virgin and the body of Christ bears some resemblance to the arrangement of the Vienna panel. The holy woman assumes the pose of the one placed by Geertgen immediately behind Christ's head. Even the depiction of Golgotha with the empty Cross in the background seems to be derived from the same source.

Dimensions: Wood. 84 × 78.
Provenance: acquired by the nation in 1928.
Literature: Friedländer, XIV, 1937, no. 123; Bermejo, 1955, p. 262–3.

120 The Nativity
Germany, private collection

Although the connection between the two works is not obvious, this interpretation of the subject should probably be compared with the *Portinari Triptych* (Florence, Uffizi Gallery) by Hugo van der Goes. The ring of kneeling figures around the naked Child, lying directly on the ground, immediately puts one in mind of this well-known picture. It goes without saying, though, that the interpretation is very free.
The artist complements the main scene with secondary ones by means of a device probably borrowed from the Haarlem school (Geertgen or the Master of the *Tiburtine Sibyl*). The style can be compared to the *Annunciation* in

223

225

Aix-la-Chapelle (*119 A*): the use of space has the same hesitancy which makes the figures appear to float slightly, and the figure-types are very similar. There is a strong resemblance between the two Virgins, but neither yet has such a high forehead as the one in the *Annunciation* in the Boymans Museum.

Dimensions: Wood. 96 × 78.
Provenance: English collection; Kaufmann collection, Berlin (sold Berlin, 1917, no. 107); O. Henkell collection, Wiesbaden.
Exhibition: Amsterdam, 1958, no. 53.
Literature: Friedländer, 1906, p. 36; Friedländer, 1910, p. 66; Friedländer, V, 1927, no. 46; Hoogewerff, II, 1937, p. 248–9; Boon, 1963, p. 18.

121   Virgin and Child
Princeton (N.J.), The Art Museum

This painting, whose surface layers are fairly worn, nevertheless seems characteristic of the Master of the *Virgo inter Virgines* in his early works. He conveys shapes by broad strokes, without refinements of modelling. The figure-types are very similar to those found both in the *Nativity* from the Henkell collection (*120*) and in that of the Kunsthistorisches Museum, Vienna (*122*).

Dimensions: Wood. 41.5 × 27.5.
Provenance: Cassirer, Berlin (in 1928–9); Tillmann collection, Amsterdam; acquired in 1949 by the Princeton Museum.
Exhibition: Rotterdam, 1936, no. 19.
Literature: Friedländer, XIV, 1937, no. 125.

122   The Adoration of the Shepherds (Pl. 124)
Vienna, Kunsthistorisches Museum

The attribution of this painting to the Master of the *Virgo inter Virgines* is less convincing than one may think. In the relative size of the figures, the composition is comparable to the Prado *Lamentation*. And yet the almost spherical heads of the shepherds do not recur in other works by the same artist. Similarly, although the head of the Virgin closely resembles the type regularly used by the artist, it is nevertheless more delicate than in his other works. It is also surprising that St. Joseph should be depicted here as a young man, in the manner of Jacob Jansz, whereas the Master of the *Virgo inter Virgines* had shown him as a bearded old man in the *Nativity* from the former Henkell collection (*120*). Like Hieronymus Bosch in the *Adoration of the Shepherds* in the Wallraf-Richartz Museum, Cologne, the Master of the *Virgo inter Virgines* draws his inspiration from a composition by van der Goes or his circle: the *Adoration of the Shepherds* in Wilton House (Winkler, 1964, p. 213), which may echo a lost original by the Ghent Master or itself be the creation of a painter closely associated with him. However, the paintings by Bosch and the Master of the *Virgo inter Virgines* have at least one more point in common: the unusual prominence given to the ox and the ass. As the Master of the *Virgo inter Virgines* differs less from the picture at Wilton, from which he even borrows some figure-types (especially angels), we cannot exclude the possibility that Bosch drew his inspiration from him.

Dimensions: Wood. 90.5 × 68.
Provenance: Somzée coll., Paris (sold Paris, 1904, no. 637).
Exhibition: Rotterdam, 1936, no. 22.
Literature: Freidländer, V, 1927, no. 47; Hoogewerff, II, 1937, p. 249–52; Boon, 1963, p. 18.

123   The Adoration of the Magi (Pl. 125)
Berlin, Staatliche Museen

Whatever may have been said about it, it is unlikely that this work was composed from echoes of the *Monforte Altarpiece* (Berlin, Staatliche Museen) by Hugo van der Goes. The entire scene is arranged differently, and the face of Melchior in this picture bears little resemblance to its alleged model. It was Geertgen's *Triptych*, now in Prague (*68*), that the Master of the *Virgo inter Virgines* principally had in mind. In that work, the Virgin presents the Child with the same hieratic gesture, the general arrangement is similar, and Balthasar is also a negro carrying a precious vase in the shape of a globe; the horsemen of the Kings' retinue can also be seen in the background. The head of Melchior is probably taken from one of the Jews in the *Ecce Homo* which probably occupied the left-hand wing of the Hospitallers' Altarpiece in Haarlem. The artist has given Melchior and Caspar a gesture which is difficult to interpret: does it signify admiration, astonishment or homage? The young man whose head and shoulders are framed by a window must be a shepherd, as is indicated by the two figures behind him.

Dimensions: Wood (oak). 63 × 48.
Provenance: Seligmann collection: presented by him to the Berlin Museum in 1910.
Exhibitions: Amsterdam and Brussels, 1950; Paris, 1951, no. 26; Amsterdam, 1958, no. 52.
Literature: Friedländer, 1906, p. 40; Friedländer, 1910, p. 66; Friedländer, V, 1927, p. 76; Hoogewerff, II, 1937, p. 252–3; Boon, 1963, p. 17.

124   The Annunciation
Rotterdam, Boymans-van Beuningen Museum

The depiction of the preformed Child descending towards the Virgin is a kind of iconographic archaism since the motif occurs at the beginning of the century. Particularly disconcerting is the architectural element which divides the scene into two: is it to be understood as a pillar to support the new church? Should we see the empty pedestal as intended for the new incarnation of God? Such a heavily-marked division is no less surprising from a formal point of view; it may have reflected a similar division in a panel placed symmetrically (a Presentation in the Temple, with a pillar dividing the architectural space?) Or should we simply lay the idea to the account of the artist's odd choice of motifs?
The panel has the same width as the *Adoration of the Magi* in Berlin, and a difference of only six centimetres in the height. It is thus possible that they both belonged to the same ensemble (assuming that the Rotterdam panel has had its height slightly reduced): perhaps a triptych with a centre consisting of four panels.

Dimensions: Wood. 57 × 48.
Provenance: Schöneberg coll., Berlin; coll. of Stefan von Auspitz, Vienna; coll. of D.G. van Beuningen, Vierhouten.
Exhibitions: London, 1929, no. 9; Rotterdam, 1936, no. 21; The Hague, 1945, no. 30; Rotterdam, 1949, no. 22; Paris, 1952, no. 60; Amsterdam, 1958, no. 50.
Literature: Friedländer, V, 1927, p. 69 and no. 45; Hoogewerff, II, 1937, p. 265–8; Gerson, 1936, p. 136; Gerson, 1950, p. 19; Luttervelt, 1952, p. 57; Boon, 1963, p. 17.

125   Virgo inter Virgines (Pl. 126)
Amsterdam, Rijksmuseum

Hugo van der Goes must have painted, around 1480 at the latest, a picture on the theme of the Virgo inter Virgines; the Master of 1499 has probably given us the most faithful imitation of this to date (Winkler, 1964, fig. 125, Richmond). Subsequently, a variant of the same formula was evolved at Bruges, incorporating the motif of the mystic marriage of St. Catherine. It is to this second formula, especially to the version by the Master of the *Legend of St. Lucy* now in Detroit and certainly dating from before 1483 (Detroit, 1960, no. 41), that the Master of the *Virgo inter Virgines* is indebted. But in accordance with his usual practice, he has not copied his model slavishly.
The buildings which flank the garden, the courtyard closed off by a monumental gateway and the figures conversing in the background appear to be derived from the repertoire of the Master of the *Tiburtine Sibyl*.
The Master of the *Virgo inter Virgines* seems to be the originator of the unusual motif of the saints wearing their emblems as items of jewellery. The four principal saints can thus be identified immediately: Catherine and Cecilia on the left, Ursula and Barbara on the right. The two figures in the right background wear similar jewels, but these are less easily discernible: one appears to be wearing a bird, the other two birds. Certainly neither is Mary Magdalene, as oddly stated by Smits (1933, p. 153–4).
A stranger feature of this concourse of virgins is the presence of two men, on the left. Smits (1933, p. 153–4) sees them, apparently without evidence, as St. James and St. John the Evangelist. The elder is very probably Joseph, whose presence here would be understandable. The younger man, with his long hair, certainly recalls the figure-type most favoured for St. John the Evangelist, but his presence would be inexplicable.
Arguing from the subject and from the prominent position of St. Ursula in the foreground, Luttervelt has assumed that the painting came from the convent of noblewomen at Koningsveld, near Delft, which was dedicated to that saint.

Dimensions: Wood. 123 × 102.
Provenance: convent of noblewomen, Koningsveld, near Delft (?); National Museum of The Hague, in 1801; transferred to the Royal Museum, Amsterdam, in 1808 (as J. van Eyck).
Exhibitions: Utrecht, 1913; Amsterdam, 1958, no. 54.

Literature: Friedländer, 1903, p. 108; Friedländer, 1906, p. 39; Friedländer, 1910, p. 66; N. Beets, 1914, p. 42; Friedländer, V, 1927, p. 65, 70 and 76, no. 63; Smits, 1933, p. 153–4; Hoogewerff, II, 1937, p. 241–3; Luttervelt, 1952, p. 59; Panofsky, 1953, p. 323; Winkler, 1964, p. 176–8; Boon, 1963, p. 21.

126 Triptych of the Adoration of the Magi
(Pls. 127-8)

Central panel: The Adoration of the Magi
Left-hand wings: The Annunciation; The Visitation
Right-hand wings: The Presentation in the Temple; The Massacre of the Innocents
Reverse of the wings: the four Evangelists in grisaille—John and Luke on the left, Mark and Matthew on the right
Salzburg, Museum Carolino Augusteum

226

The central panel is a variation on themes by Hugo van der Goes. One's thoughts turn first to the *Monforte Altarpiece* (Berlin) for the general layout. The stable with its ruined architecture seems to be borrowed from it; the ideas of the horsemen and of the figures looking through the window are also developed from motifs in the same picture. The arrangement of the Three Kings is more or less reminiscent of the same model. The pose of Caspar, however, is a reversed transposition of that of one of the shepherds from the *Adoration of the Shepherds* in Berlin, also by Hugo van der Goes. A similar borrowing occurs in the panel of the *Presentation in the Temple*, which seems to be inspired by the lost wing of the *Monforte Altarpiece* known through a variant by the Master of Frankfurt (Antwerp, Musée des Beaux-Arts; Winkler, 1964, fig. 3). In particular, we find the figure of the Virgin handled in the same way as that of St. Anne in the Antwerp painting, i.e. an outline seen in profile and completely enveloped by drapery, which endows her with a very monumental appearance.
Alongside subjects dealing with the recognition of the Virgin as the mother of God and the divine nature of the Child, the inclusion of the Massacre of the Innocents is unusual; even if we see it as an allegory of the impossibility of depriving the believer of Jesus

(Ludolph the Carthusian, ed. Broquin, I, p. 276), its connection with the other scenes is not self-evident. G. Heinz (1960) has written a long analysis of the iconography of the panel of the *Annunciation*; its recent restoration has revealed a Child descending towards the Virgin above the original dove of the Holy Ghost, as in the painting in the Boymans Museum, Rotterdam.
The comparison suggested by Schretlen between the panel of the Massacre of the Innocents and an engraving in the *Epistelen en Evangelien*, published at Delft in 1486, is not very conclusive: the only virtually identical detail is that of the infant impaled on the broad sword of one of the soldiers. It is difficult to base any argument on this, however, even for the date of the work; for the priority of the engraving, though probable, cannot be categorically asserted.

Dimensions: Wood. Central panel: 96.5 × 18.25; Wings, 96.5 × 36.5 each.
Provenance: Salzburg Cathedral; chapel of the Hallein salt-works; acquired by the museum in 1874.
Exhibition: Amsterdam, 1958, no. 51 (only the Visitation wing).
Literature: Friedländer, 1906–7, p. 79; Hermann Voss, 1909, p. 101–4; K. von Radinger, 1910–11, p. 114; Friedländer, 1910, p. 64; H. Tietze, 1919, p. 157; Friedländer, V, 1927, p. 76, no. 51; Hoogewerff, II, 1937, p. 253–7; Heinz, 1960; Boon, 1963, p. 22.

127 Triptych of the Passion

The catalogue of the Amsterdam exhibition of 1958 (nos. 59 and 60) had already stated that the three paintings belonging respectively to the Lebel collection in Paris, the Metropolitan Museum in New York and the Rijksmuseum in Amsterdam must have formed part of the same ensemble. The discovery of the grisaille of a saint on the reverse of the Resurrection panel in the Rijksmuseum indicates that this was an outer wing. Hence, we can imagine the original ensemble as a triptych whose centre consisted of two equal-sized panels. The subject of the missing left-hand wing was probably a Carrying of the Cross (or possibly an Ecce Homo), making the general theme that of the Passion.
The three known panels display the same restraint and the same sober harmony based on ochres and light greens. There is no sign of the direct influence of van der Goes.

A The Crucifixion
Paris, Robert Lebel collection

The simplicity of this composition with its small number of figures, and the extent of the background landscape, recall Albert van Ouwater's lost painting known through a drawing in Dresden. The character in armour on the far right—the good centurion?—contrasts strongly in dress with his neighbours, who wear the fanciful headgear traditionally allotted to the Jews. He may be an 'in character' portrait of a donor, as has already been remarked in the catalogue for the 1958 Amsterdam exhibition.
There is no particular connection here with the work of van der Goes. On the contrary, the second Mary, on the

227

far left, puts one in mind of the work of Petrus Christus both by her type and by the way she is modelled in large, simple areas; she is especially comparable with the woman in the painting of *St. Eligius* in the Lehmann collection (New York, Metropolitan Museum) and with the St. Catherine from the panel formerly in the Staatliche Museen, Berlin, but now destroyed.
The silhouette of the church which reappears in various pictures is very unusual. With its flying buttresses and large pierced bays it corresponds to a Brabantine type, and is slightly reminiscent of the tower of the main church of Breda, or at least its older part (its upper storey was rebuilt after the fire, in 1694, which destroyed the original spire). The curious motif of the half-tower also recurs in many other works.

Dimensions: Wood. 85 × 52.
Exhibition: Amsterdam, 1958, no. 59.
Literature: Friedländer, V, 1927, no. 57; Boon, 1963, p. 22.

B The Lamentation
New York, Metropolitan Museum

The theme is handled in an original manner which seems to be without direct precedent. The body of Christ rests on the Virgin's knees, as in the picture by Bouts (Louvre), but does not have the same rigidity. Moreover, Mary Magdalene intervenes by taking hold of His left arm. The Virgin's gesture is less one of grief than one of surprise, presumably at the behaviour of Mary Magdalene.

228

Dimensions:	Wood. 88.6 × 51.
Provenance:	Spain; coll. of Ulrich Thieme, Leipzig; Paul Bottenwieser, Berlin; acquired by the museum in 1926 through the Rogers Fund.
Literature:	Friedländer, 1903, p. 168; Durand Gréville, 1906, p. 55; Friedländer, 1910, p. 66, no. 14; W. Bürger, 1925, p. 93; Friedländer, V, 1927, p. 71 and 141, no. 59; Dülberg, 1929, p. 105; Hoogewerff, II, 1937, p. 270; Wehle-Salinger, 1947, p. 82–4; Boon, 1963, p. 22.

C   The Resurrection

On reverse, a bishop saint in grisaille (damaged)
Amsterdam, Rijksmuseum

229

The Master of the *Virgo inter Virgines* depicts the Resurrection by adopting the motif which J. Bruyn (1963) considered to be already archaic for the 1470s, i.e. representing Christ in the act of stepping out of the tomb.

Dimensions:	Wood. 87.5 × 51.
Provenance:	coll. of J. Goudstikker, Amsterdam; loaned by the department for the recovery of works of art in 1948.
Exhibitions:	Rotterdam, 1936, no. 23; Amsterdam, 1958, no. 60.
Literature:	Friedländer, XIV, 1937, p. 98; Hoogewerff, II, 1937, p. 272; Boon, 1963, p. 22.

128   The Lamentation

Enghien, Hôpital Saint-Nicolas

This work must have been particularly popular, as we know of three replicas of it, some of which may be autographs. The composition is inspired by Geertgen's picture (*70*). It is probable, however, that this version was conceived to stand alone, which has led to a redistribution of the masses. Moreover, following his usual practice, the Master of the *Virgo inter Virgines* does not copy, but draws inspiration from some of the elements of his model. Into his variant he also clearly introduces a note of pathos and violence which corresponds to his own temperament. The background incidents are not simultaneous with the main scene as

in the painting by Geertgen; they are the Deposition, the arrival—or departure—of the workmen with a ladder, and the Entombment. Only the group of Nicodemus and Joseph of Arimathaea can be considered simultaneous with the main scene.

Dimensions:	Wood. 77 × 63.5.
Provenance:	Charterhouse of L'Herne; after the closure of the convent in 1783, in the keeping of a local family; presented in 1820 to the Hôpital Saint-Nicolas.
Literature:	P. Landelin-Hoffmans, 1947; P. Rolland, 1949, p. 90; Leeuwenberg, 1950; Boon, 1963, p. 18–21; Friedländer, Va, 1969, p. 98 and 105 (note 139).

Variants:

Paris, collection of Mme Marquet de Vasselot

Dimensions:	Wood. 78 × 64.5.
Provenance:	Martin le Roy collection, Paris.
Exhibition:	Bruges, 1902, no. 245.
Literature:	Friedländer, V, 1927, no. 60.

Madrid, collection of Princess von Hohenlohe

Dimensions:	Wood.
Provenance:	collection of the Duchess of Parcent, Madrid.
Literature:	Bermejo, 1955.

Ghent, Hemptinne collection

| Literature: | Friedländer, Va, 1969, p. 93. |

129   The Entombment (Pl. 129)

Liverpool, The Walker Art Gallery

The Liverpool painting is one of the most elaborate by the Master of the *Virgo inter Virgines*. The composition is simple in conception, and not overloaded with figures. The palette displays the Master's usual austerity, making a few reds stand out against blue-grey and ochre backgrounds. This serenity would link the work with the *Adoration of the Magi* in Berlin, if the figure-types had not acquired here a delicacy of shape and greater sharpness of expression which testified to a development between the two works.

Several similarities link this composition to the *Entombment* illustrating the book *Ons Heeren Passie*, published at Delft in 1487 (Schretlen, 1925, pl. 58 B): the type of Christ and the position of his head in relation to his body is fairly similar in the two works.

Dimensions:	Wood. 54.5 × 54.5.
Provenance:	Count Truchsess von Waldburg in 1806; William Roscoe of Liverpool in 1816 (as van Eyck); acquired by Mr. Nason and presented by him to the museum.
Exhibitions:	Manchester, 1857, p. 443; Utrecht, 1913, no. 193; London, 1929, no. 11; Rotterdam, 1936, no. 17; London, 1952, no. 13; Bruges, 1956, no. 18; Amsterdam, 1958, no. 49.

| Literature: | Waagen, 1838, III, p. 234; Friedländer, 1903, p. 168; Friedländer, 1906, p. 39; Conway, 1921, p. 212; Winkler, 1924, p. 152; Friedländer, V, 1927, p. 66, no. 58; Hoogewerff, II, 1937, p. 268–70; Panofsky, 1953, p. 323; Fastnedge, 1954, p. 437; Boon, 1963, p. 20; Châtelet, 1979, p. 191. |

130   Triptych of the Crucifixion (Pl. 130)

Centre: The Crucifixion
Left wing: The Carrying of the Cross
Right wing: The Deposition from the Cross
Reverse of the wings: The Annunciation, in grisaille
Barnard Castle, The Bowes Museum

230

This triptych comes from the collection of the Duke of Lucca and is reputed to have hung formerly in a church in Lucca. The format of the work is similar to that of Italian altarpieces. It thus could well have been originally painted for an Italian church, like the *Portinari Altarpiece*. Certain curious details are worthy of remark. It is very surprising to find the soldier who offers Christ the sponge soaked in vinegar depicted as a negro. It is also strange to find, in the midst of the troop of horsemen beneath the Cross, a young man in white carrying a bow and a quiver. His head-dress and serrated collar resemble those found in princely fashions of the beginning of the century. His features are similar to those of John IV of Brabant as known to us through the drawing in the *Recueil Succa* (Brussels, Bibliothèque Royale). Is this a borrowing from an old portrait, as would appear on first examination? Does this figure have any special significance? (Could the picture have been donated by an association of archers, for example?). These questions remain unanswered.

The theme of the Thieves writhing on their crosses seems to have been very popular in the northern Netherlands; witness notably the engraving by Master IAM van Zwolle, dated 1480, which also contains a rear view of the Good Thief. Certain details in the central panel may be borrowed from the lost panel painted by Geertgen for the Hospitallers of Haarlem; in the Triptych by the Master of Aix-la-Chapelle, significantly, we find in the left foreground a holy woman on her knees and leaning towards the Virgin. Her shape appears very close to the effect sought by the Master of the *Virgo inter Virgines* with a similar figure; the common model for both artists must have been the lost picture by Geertgen.

On the other hand, the holy woman on the far left of the panel, behind the Virgin's group, is reminiscent, by her type and modelling, of a figure by Petrus Christus. And yet her gesture and her placing in the group link her directly with one of the main characters in the *Justice of Otto* by Dieric Bouts (Brussels, Musées Royaux des Beaux-Arts). The style of the panel seems to place it somewhere between the more relaxed works, like those in Berlin and Liverpool, and the supposedly late compositions (Florence and St. Louis), in which the shapes tend towards a new sinuosity.

Dimensions: Wood. Centre: 221 × 196; wings: 221 × 93 each.
Provenance: collection of the Duke of Lucca; acquired from him by John Bowes c.1840.
Exhibitions: London, 1906, no. 11; London, 1929, no. 7; London, 1952, no. 30; Bruges, 1956, nos. 19–20 (wings only); Amsterdam, 1958, no. 57.
Literature: Friedländer, 1906, p. 56; Durand Gréville, 1906, p. 56; Friedländer, 1910, p. 64; Friedländer, V, 1927, p. 75, no. 55; Hoogewerff, II, 1937, p. 258–60; Waterhouse, 1953, p. 120; Boon, 1963, p. 31.

131 The Trinity
Zagreb, Yugoslav Academy of Arts and Sciences.

This picture is a curious combination of the theme of the Trinity, in the formula known as the Throne of Grace, and accompanied by angels bearing the instruments of the Passion, with the characters of a Lamentation. To the Virgin and St. John the Evangelist the artist has added the two Marys, probably recognisable in the two women standing on the right and the left, hands crossed and clasped respectively: Mary Magdalene, who is presumably the heavily-veiled mourner on the right; and an old woman kneeling on the right who should probably be identified as St. Anne.
The decorative motifs of the throne would seem to indicate a fairly late date, not earlier than c.1485. They are comparable to the borders of the engraving of *Christ in the Garden of Gethsemane* by Master IAM van Zwolle. The disordered drapery folds are similar to those in the Barnard Castle *Triptych* (130) and foreshadow those of the Florence painting (132).

231

Dimensions: Wood. 126 × 127.
Provenance: acquired in 1883 for Bishop Strossmayer of Zagreb.

Exhibitions: Rotterdam, 1936, no. 18; Amsterdam, 1958, no. 58.
Literature: G. von Terey, 1927, p. 297; Friedländer, V, p. 76, no. 62; Hoogewerff, II, 1937, p. 272–4; Luttervelt, 1952, p. 68; Boon, 1963, p. 31.

132 The Crucifixion
Florence, Uffizi Gallery

This painting has the same measurements as the one in St. Louis and may come from the same ensemble: this would have been, once again, either a non-closing polyptych or a triptych whose centre was formed by two panels of equal size.
The pathos of this work is less pronounced than that of the preceding ones, but it is accompanied by very manneristic distortions, which can best be seen in the remarkably sinuous body of the Virgin and in the amazing contortions imposed on Mary Magdalene. In comparison with the *Crucifixions* in the Lebel collection (127 A) and the Bowes Museum (130), this one appears more restrained. Above all, it dramatises the face of Christ by plunging it into shadow and by cutting it off from the sky by the hang of His hair. A similar effect is aimed for in the very fine woodcut in the *Missale Trajectense* printed at Delft in 1495 (Schretlen, p. 64).

Dimensions: Wood. 57 × 47.
Provenance: Villa di Poggio a Caiano in 1792.
Exhibitions: Florence, 1947; Amsterdam, 1958, no. 48.
Literature: Friedländer, 1903, p. 168; Friedländer, 1906, p. 40; Dülberg, 1907, p. 9; N. Beets, 1914, p. 45; Friedländer, V, 1927, p. 74, no. 54; Hoogewerff, II, 1937, p. 262–4; Boon, 1963, p. 17.

133 The Entombment (Pl. 131)
St. Louis, City Art Museum

The subject is the same as in the Liverpool painting, but it has been given greater narrative power. In place of a meditation on the dead Christ, a sort of variant of the Lamentation, we find here the funeral cortège making its way across the landscape of Golgotha. In this version of the theme, the Virgin becomes the principal character while the body of Christ and its bearers form a group of lesser importance. In this picture, as in the one in Florence, the severity of the landscape of the central zone seems to yield before a relatively abundant vegetation, at least on the right-hand side. Should this distinction between the arid hills and the tree-covered slopes be seen as having a symbolic significance, contrasting the infertility of Golgotha, where Christ died, to the luxuriance of the land which received His mortal remains? Such an interpretation may seem logical, but against it is the fact that the Golgotha of the Florence panel is depicted with profuse vegetation.

Dimensions: Wood. 58.5 × 46.5.
Provenance: Cassirer, Berlin; acquired in 1935 by the museum.
Literature: Wescher, 1930, p. 573 and 578; Rogers, 1935; Hoogewerff, II, 1937, p. 270; Friedländer, XIV, 1937, p. 98; Boon, 1963, p. 31.

232

MASTER OF THE VIRGO INTER VIRGINES. Details of heads, free interpretations of the artist's own face? (from 123, 127 A, 129, 130)

Circle of the Master of the *Virgo inter Virgines*

134 The Deposition from the Cross
Present whereabouts unknown, formerly on the Paris market

The photograph of this painting published by Friedländer is hardly adequate for establishing a firm idea of the work. It does not seem to be in a very satisfactory condition and it is difficult to make out the quality of the execution. The unusual composition, which cuts off the figures at an arbitrary point, has affinities with that of the Vienna *Nativity*. The modelling by large areas and even the figure-types also display a similarity with the same work. Nevertheless, it is difficult to decide whether this is an original work by the Master of the *Virgo inter Virgines* or merely one by an artist of his circle, as the obvious weakness of the modelling would seem to indicate.

Dimensions: Wood. 80 × 62.
Provenance: Parisian art market in 1912.
Literature: Friedländer, V, 1927, no. 57; Boon, 1963, p. 31, no. 14.

135 Soldiers of the Three Kings' retinue
Philadelphia, Philadelphia Museum of Art (Johnson collection)

This curious scene, probably a wing of a triptych whose centre depicted the Adoration of the Magi, contains figure-types which are rather different from those of the Master of the *Virgo inter Virgines*. The modelling is also softer.

235

Dimensions:	Wood. 77 × 39.5.
Provenance:	H. Schwarz sale, Berlin, 8 November 1910, no. 25.
Literature:	Valentiner, 1913, no. 347; Friedländer, V, 1927, no. 52.

136 The Annunciation with a Donor
Reverse: The Adoration of the Magi
Madrid, collection of the Duke of Alba

The traditional identification of the kneeling donor as Don Garcia Alvarez de Toledo, the first Duke of Alba, appears to be confirmed by the coat of arms which is that of Toledo. The work is unfortunately in a very poor state of preservation; the reverse, the inner face of a wing of a triptych, is in an even worse condition. Nevertheless, the quality of the drawing and the weakness of the conception hardly support an attribution to the Master of the *Virgo inter Virgines* himself, as proposed by Angulo Iniguez (1925). Although the picture on the reverse is faintly reminiscent of the *Adoration of the Shepherds* in Vienna, it is none the less too poor to have ever constituted its pendant in a triptych, as suggested by the same author.
The panel must therefore be relegated to a follower of the Master of the *Virgo inter Virgines* who was not necessarily from Delft.

Dimensions:	Wood. 94 × 71.
Provenance:	collection of D. Valentin Carderera (*d.*1880); acquired from him by Don Carlos Maria Fitzjames Stuart y Portocarrero, 16th Duke of Alba.
Exhibition:	Amsterdam, 1958, no. 56.
Literature:	Carderera, 1887, I, no. 2; Barcia, 1911, no. 1; Angulo Iniguez, 1925; Boon, 1963, p. 32, no. 1 (circle of the Master of the *Virgo inter Virgines*); Friedländer, Va, 1969, p. 92, Add. 143.

137 The Marriage of the Virgin
Philadelphia, Philadelphia Museum of Art (Johnson collection)

This painting, a wing of a triptych or polyptych, has suffered badly as a result of its transfer from wood to canvas. In its present condition, it seems too weak in conception and execution to be attributed to the Master of the *Virgo inter Virgines* himself; but it is not beyond the bounds of possibility that this judgment is the result of the damage suffered by the painting. K.G. Boon thinks it may be the work of the same artist who painted the replica of the *Lamentation* in the collection of Princess von Hohenlohe (*128*) and the *Last Supper* (*141*).

Dimensions:	Wood transferred to canvas. 107 × 40.
Literature:	Valentiner, 1913, no. 349; Friedländer, V, 1927, no. 44; Boon, 1963, p. 25 and 32, no. 2 (circle of the Master of the *Virgo inter Virgines*).

138 The Crucifixion
Lugano, Villa Castagnola

Although this picture is one of those which served as a starting point for the reconstitution of the oeuvre of the

233

Master of the *Virgo inter Virgines*, I do not feel that it can still be included in the artist's work. The figure-types are not those regularly found in his paintings. The tonality is also much darker than his usual palette. This is a painting by an imitator whose inspiration comes from the latest style of the Master of the *Virgo inter Virgines*, that of the Florence and St. Louis panels (*132–133*).

Dimensions:	Wood. 78 × 58.
Provenance:	Glitza collection, Hamburg; Hauser Gallery, Lucerne; Heinemann collection, Munich.
Exhibitions:	Bruges, 1902, no. 255; Munich, 1930, no. 217.
Literature:	Friedländer, 1903, p. 168; Durand Gréville, 1906, p. 290; Friedländer, V, 1927, p. 66 and no. 56; Hoogewerff, II, 1937, p. 264–5; Boon, 1963, p. 31, no. (10 Master of the *Virgo inter Virgines*).

139 Triptych of the Adoration of the Magi
Left wing: The Vision of St. Bernard
Right wing: St. Jerome in the desert
Reverse of the wings: The Annunciation, in grisaille
Amersfoort, Museum Flehite

Although retained by Friedländer as a work by the Master of the *Virgo inter Virgines*, this triptych displays a very different and probably later style, and even seems to reflect some influence of Jacob Cornelisz van Amsterdam. The date of 1526, mentioned in the epitaph along the bottom of the frame, should not necessarily be discounted for the execution of this work, in which the echoes of the Master of the *Virgo inter Virgines* are only faint.

Dimensions:	Wood. Centre: 69 × 71; wings: 67 × 27.7 each.
Inscription (at foot of frame):	'In't jaer ons heren dusent Vc ende 26 op den XXV dach in Mey sterft den eerwerdigen heer Thoms van Snoel hier op Sintte Petrus' Kerchhof oender die grote Kerk begraven. Bit voer die syel'.

Literature:	Friedländer V, 1927, p. 69 and no. 50; Hoogewerff, II, 1937, p. 257; Boon, 1963, p. 32, no. 4 (circle of the Master of the *Virgo inter Virgines*).

140 The Adoration of the Magi
Milan, Pinacoteca di Brera

Retained by Friedländer as a work of the Master of the *Virgo inter Virgines*, this painting, in a poor state of preservation, displays figure-types very similar to that artist's. However, in both the palette and in certain distinctive features of the figures, a different spirit emerges. This is probably the work of an imitator working at the very end of the fifteenth century, or even the beginning of the sixteenth.

Dimensions:	Wood. 126 × 96.
Literature:	Friedländer, V, 1927, no. 48.

141 The Last Supper
Present whereabouts unknown, British art market in 1959

This painting, a wing of a triptych or polyptych, has only a fairly distant connection with the Master of the *Virgo inter Virgines*. Only the slight element of caricature in the features of the figures and a tendency to gesticulation recall some of his works. But the slightness of the figures, who seem to float in space, has no counterpart in his oeuvre. Boon's suggested comparison of this picture with the *Marriage of the Virgin* in the Johnson collection (*137*) and the replica of the *Lamentation* in the collection of Princess von Hohenlohe (*128*) is interesting, but not absolutely convincing on the strength of the photographs alone.

Dimensions:	Wood. Dimensions unknown.
Literature:	Boon, 1963, p. 25 and 32, no. 3 (circle of the Master of the *Virgo inter Virgines*); Friedländer, Va, 1969, add. 144.

Artist working at Delft *c.*1490

142 Portrait of Canon Hugo de Groot (Delft 1451–1509)
New York, Wildenstein & Co.

The identification of the sitter is due to D.P. Osterbaan (1956). It is based on the inscription discovered on the reverse, which reads:
'Hoc tumulo situs est Hugo cognomine Magnus,
Optatus Delphis Pastor in aede nova,
Consulis officio dignum quem Curia sumsit;
Hagia Canonicum templa habuere pium
Quem Geervlietensis tenuit sacer ordo Decanum.
Dic, Lector, superum sorte beatus est.
8 mai 1509'
The apparent age of the sitter, born in 1451, indicates a date for the painting of *c.*1490.
Before this identification, the painting had been attributed by Friedländer to Simon Marmion (report dated 14 September 1946). Boon subsequently attributed it to the Master of the *Virgo inter Virgines*. The thin, dry modelling and lifeless handling, however, are not in the least reminiscent of that artist's style. The portrait

seemed out of place amongst his works in the 1958 exhibition. It is in any case of only mediocre quality, and should be regarded as the work of an unknown painter.

Dimensions: Wood. 37.5 × 26.
Provenance: mentioned at the beginning of the eighteenth century in the collection of Franz van Overschie of Delft; English collection.
Exhibitions: Houston, 1952, no. 26; Amsterdam, 1958, no. 55.
Literature: Riemer, 1730, I, p. 250; Oosterbaan, 1956; Boon, 1963, p. 14–17.

The Master of Delft

In 1913, Friedländer grouped four paintings under this name and expanded this first list considerably in 1932. Nevertheless, apart from the London painting, which is still directly dependent on fifteenth-century motifs, these works mark an adaptation to the new taste which made its appearance at the beginning of the sixteenth century, and exemplify a different style from the one studied here.
In 1932, Friedländer proposed to attribute to this artist the illustrations of the Gouda edition of *Le Chevalier Délibéré*, but this theory does not seem acceptable.

Literature: Friedländer, 1913; Schretlen, 1925B; Friedländer, X, 1932, p. 45–52; Hoogewerff, I, 1936, p. 575–81 and II, 1937, p. 388–96.

143 Triptych of the Crucifixion (Pl. 132)
Left wing: Ecce Homo
Reverse: Virgin and Child with St. Augustine
Right wing: The Deposition from the Cross
Reverse: St. Peter, St. Mary Magdalene
London, National Gallery

234

This picture is still difficult to date. By reason of its meticulous execution and fondness for anecdote, it may yet be datable to the closing years of the fifteenth century. However, we cannot exclude the possibility that it may have been influenced by certain works painted in Haarlem at the beginning of the sixteenth

century, like those of Joest van Kalkar. One may also notice the curious similarity between the group of Pilate and Caiaphas in the central panel and the riders from the *Martyrdom of the Ten Thousand* in Warsaw, which recent criticism has ascribed to a Bruges painter but which I prefer to see as north Netherlandish work. Martin Davies has also rightly pointed out how similar this composition is to the *Oultremont Triptych* by Jan Mostaert (Brussels, Musées Royaux des Beaux-Arts). The landscape adopts the principle of dividing and isolating the scenes by using the lie of the land. But it also reveals new preoccupations in its search for more natural lighting, which represents the illumination of a real landscape rather than that of an idealised sky.
If we must accept the attribution to the Master of Delft of the illustrations of the *Life of St. Lydwine* (155), the London painting must be considered earlier than this publication of 1498.

Dimensions: Wood (oak). Centre, 98 × 105.5; Wings, 102.5 × 49.5 each
Provenance: coll. of Lord Northwick, Thirlestaine House (cat. 1858, no. 474); sold London, 26 July 1859 (lot 83); acquired by Lord Brownlow c.1860; presented by Earl Brownlow in 1913.
Catalogue: London, National Gallery, 1955 (Davies) p. 80–2.
Literature: Friedländer, 1913, p. 107; Friedländer, X, 1932, no. 60; Hoogewerff, II, 1937, p. 395.

Master of the Altarpiece of St. John the Baptist (Hugo Jacobsz ?)

(Known to have been active at Leiden, Ghent and Gouda between 1480 and 1534)

The first attempt at isolating the work of the Master of the *Altarpiece of St. John the Baptist* was made by D. Hannema in 1936 after the Rotterdam exhibition. In 1955 J.Q. van Regteren Altena, after suggesting in 1939 that the panels of the Life of St. John should be seen as fragments of the Gouda altarpiece, proposed the hypothetical identification of the artist with Hugo Jacobsz.
The references to Hugo Jacobsz were published by Elsevier 1858 and 1869, Dülberg 1899 and Koning 1950. An unpublished text in the Archives of the convents of Leiden (no. 1460) informs us that in 1480 the artist lived in the Neerstraat near the Rijnburgerpoort.

Literature: Hannema, 1937; Hoogewerff, II, 1937, p. 285–6, and V, 1947, p. 57; Regteren Altena, 1939 and 1955; Wescher, 1959; Boon, 1968.

144 The Nativity
Brussels, Musées Royaux des Beaux-Arts

Regteren Altena's attribution of this panel to Hugo Jacobsz has been disputed by Karel Boon, who associated it with a *Crucifixion* in the collection of the Baronne de Descamps, with which it seems to have little connection, however. The comparison with the *Spes Nostra* of Amsterdam suggested earlier by Hoogewerff, is even less convincing.

235

Since the discovery of a second version of the same composition in the museum at Esztergom (*145*), the attribution to Hugo Jacobsz seems to have acquired more substance. This other picture is, in fact, closer to the artist's known style. What may seem surprising is the fact that the artist is following, probably very closely, a south Netherlandish original which was also copied by the Master of Schöpfingen between 1450 and 1460 (Münster, 1952, no. 28, fig. pl. 8).

Dimensions: Wood. 93 × 74.
Provenance: collection of Ch. Léon Cardon: acquired from this in 1921.
Exhibitions: 's Hertogenbosch, 1913, no. 44; Utrecht, 1913, no. 83 (attr. to Ouwater); Amsterdam, 1958, no. 65.
Literature: Cohen, 1914, p. 21; Winkler, 1924, p. 155; Kessler, 1930, p. 60; Hoogewerff, II, 1937, p. 280; Regteren Altena, 1955, p. 111; Boon, 1968, p. 12, note 5.

145 The Nativity
Esztergom, Christian Museum.

Attention was drawn to this picture by K.G. Boon (1968), who considered, however, that it should not be included in the oeuvre of the Master of the *Altarpiece of St. John the Baptist*. And yet the modelling in large areas, the jerky movements of the hands and the simple shapes of the faces are very much in that painter's style.

236

The relationship of this painting to the Brussels *Nativity* may give rise to difficulties. The composition of the former is more restrained than that of the latter. The Flemish sources, which are visible in the Brussels version, are barely noticeable in the Esztergom work, which exemplifies the handling of the artist's mature works. Hence, it is more logical to see this as a variant of the previous painting, handled with more freedom and spontaneity.

Dimensions: Wood. 40 × 30.3.
Literature: Boon, 1968, p. 12, note 5.

146 The Carrying of the Cross
The Hague, collection of Mr. J.W. Frederiks (on loan to the Boymans Museum, Rotterdam)

237

The attribution of this work to the Master of the *Altarpiece of St. John the Baptist* is due to J.Q. van Regteren Altena. It seems most convincing, by reason of the general coloration, the broad modelling of the shapes and the identity of certain figure-types. This painting, however, is more inclined towards violent and dramatic expressiveness than the panels of the *Altarpiece of St. John the Baptist*. It is close in style to the *Adoration of the Shepherds* in Vienna (*122*) attributed to the Master of the *Virgo inter Virgines*. The composition is a free and distantly-derived variant of the two Eyckian versions of the theme. The distinctive motif of the Child in the foreground may even come from the variant by Master H (*34*). Hence it is conceivable that the picture has been cut down slightly and that, in particular, it may have included a bigger procession including Pilate and Caiaphas on the right.

Dimensions: Wood. 65 × 49.5.
Provenance: collection of Lady Jekill, London; J.D. Klaassen, Rotterdam.
Exhibitions: Utrecht, 1913, no. 174; Rotterdam, 1936, no. 31; Amsterdam, 1958, no. 64.
Literature: Regteren Altena, 1955, p. 114; Wescher, 1959, p. 251 (rejecting attribution); Boon, 1968, p. 6.

147 Altarpiece of St. John the Baptist

The surviving panels indicate the existence at one time of a large ensemble consisting perhaps of several pairs of wings. But at the present time it is difficult to propose a reconstruction of this ensemble, especially as we cannot exclude the possibility of a sculpted centrepiece. The chancel of the new church at Gouda was begun in 1485 and the work of reconstruction was completed in 1493. It seems very likely that the altarpiece was painted between these two dates, and this would correspond very well both with the style of the panels and with our information on the activity of Hugo Jacobsz.

A The Birth of St. John the Baptist (Pl. 134)
Rotterdam, Boymans-van Beuningen Museum.

In this composition the artist has given an oddly prominent position to the scene of the angel's message to Zacharias. This illustration may have been dictated by the text of the *Golden Legend* devoted to the saint's Nativity (Roze, I, p. 401–10), which begins with an account of Gabriel's appearance to Zacharias in the temple (left middle ground) and of the punishment imposed on the latter for not believing the divine message: he becomes dumb and unable to explain the miracle to the people (principal scene). However, the *Golden Legend* also gives an important place to the Visitation, which is omitted. There is thus a deliberate attempt here to emphasise the rôle of Zacharias who, moreover, wears a halo. This may have been required by a special local cult.

The picture employs the device of 'mansions', probably derived from the theatre but common in painting and illumination of the second half of the fifteenth century. The figures are enveloped in robes which hang almost without folds, giving them particularly massive outlines. Prominence is given to gestures of the hands, the importance of which is also emphasised by their slight disproportion in relation to the bodies. The outline of the child in the foreground recalls the one in the left foreground of the Amsterdam *Holy Kindred* (*81*), from which it may have been borrowed.

Dimensions: Wood. 133 × 97.
Provenance: British art market; acquired in 1938 in honour of that year's jubilee exhibition.
Catalogue: Rotterdam, Boymans Museum, 1951, no. 274, p. 6.
Literature: Hannema, 1937; Regteren Altena, 1955, p. 103–4.

B The Flight of St. Elizabeth (Pl. 133)
Rotterdam, Boymans-van Beuningen Museum

This is the second panel from the *Altarpiece of St. John the Baptist* (cf. *147 A*) in the chronological order of the episodes shown; it has the same dimensions—within a few centimetres—as the first. Its subject is particularly rare and illustrates a passage from the Protoevangelium of James (*XXII-2*). Three scenes are juxtaposed here: in the foreground the flight of St. Elizabeth and St. John, on the left the murder of Zacharias by Herod's soldiers, and on the right the Massacre of the Innocents. The choice of subject still tends to emphasise the rôle of the saint's parents, who accordingly appear in the foreground. On the other hand, it also stresses the parallels between the life of the Precursor and that of Jesus by introducing an episode equivalent to the Flight into Egypt.

The infant John the Baptist is wearing a monk's habit; in this, the artist wanted to foreshadow his retreat into the wilderness, which Ludolph the Carthusian, following St. Peter Chrysologus and St. John Chrysostom, regarded as the origin of monastic life (ed. Broquin, I, p. 284–6).

In the division of his panel, the artist adopts Geertgen's principle of composition and distinguishes each group by isolating it by the lie of the land. The fragmentation of the space is perhaps stressed even more consistently here, and each area is marked out by very simple means which recall something of the methods of the Master of the *Virgo inter Virgines*.

In the background, the scene of the Massacre of the Innocents offers some dramatic faces with strained expressions verging on caricature, whose effect is heightened by the violence of the poses. In this instance the artist may be influenced by the Master of the *Virgo inter Virgines* and be thinking particularly of the illustration of the same subject in the *Epistelen en Evangelien* published at Delft in 1486 (Schretlen, pl. 57 A).

Dimensions: Wood. 132 × 95.
Provenance: Graham collection; The Hon. Mrs. Donnel Post; acquired in 1937 in commemoration of the Hieronymus Bosch Exhibition of 1936.
Exhibitions: Rotterdam, 1936, no. 25; Rotterdam, 1938, no. 15; Amsterdam, 1958, no. 62.
Catalogue: Rotterdam, Boymans Museum, 1951, no. 275, p. 6.
Literature: Baldass, 1936, p. 252; Hannema, 1937, p. 3; Friedländer, XIV, 1937, p. 98; Hoogewerff, II, 1937, p. 584; de Vries, 1938, p. 274; Regteren Altena, 1955, p. 101.

C The Meeting of St. John the Baptist and Christ (Pl. 135)
Philadelphia, Museum of Art, Johnson collection.

This panel is slightly smaller than the two preceding ones; its height has been reduced by about ten centimetres, probably by the removal of a narrow strip at the bottom and of a wider section at the top, in which the sky must originally have been extended. The paint is also much less well preserved than in the other panels from the altarpiece. A general wearing-away of the surface layers is clearly discernible and has weakened many elements of the composition.

The scene depicted is inspired by a text from the Gospel according to St. John (*1.35–7*). However, the artist has taken some liberties with the Gospel account, which runs:

'Again the next day after John stood, and two of his disciples; And looking upon Jesus as he walked, he saith, Behold the Lamb of God! And the two disciples heard him speak, and they followed Jesus.'

Although the two disciples, one of them the apostle Simon, are certainly there in the foreground and are preparing to follow Christ, they are surrounded by many other companions of the prophet. Similarly, Jesus has round him nine apostles, whose presence is in no way suggested by the Gospel. The choice of the incident is quite significant: it emphasises the Baptist's rôle as Precursor.

The composition is fairly similar to that of the panel of the Flight of St. Elizabeth. The two groups are separated by the rise and fall of the ground. Despite the rough appearance of the figures, the confrontation of the two main characters, each with his entourage of disciples, has an overall effect of great dignity.

Dimensions:	Wood. 123.5 × 94.
Exhibition:	Amsterdam, 1958, no. 63.
Literature:	Conway, 1921, p. 221; Friedländer, V, 1927, p. 137; Smits, 1933, p. 3; Hoogewerff, II, 1937, p. 285; de Vries, 1938, p. 274; Regteren Altena, 1955, p. 101; Boon, 1968, p. 5.

D St. Elizabeth and the Infant John the Baptist
Reverse: Virgin of the Annunciation?
Valencia, Museo Provincial.

238

Wolfgang Schöne made this work known in 1937 and pointed out that it might have some connection with the panels of the *Altarpiece of St. John the Baptist*. This remark seems to have gone unnoticed. And yet the very synthetic style of the forms and the very broad indication of the planes of the landscape show that this work is indeed by the same hand. Moreover, the subject and the dimensions of the panel confirm that this is a fourth fragment of the Gouda Altarpiece. The slight difference in measurements as against the Rotterdam panels raises the question of how to reconstruct the original ensemble. The reverse seems to indicate that the height of the Valencia panel has been slightly reduced, which would appear from the fact that it is eight centimetres shorter than the other wings. On the other hand, the width, which is considerably less, shows no signs of having been cut down. We must therefore imagine that some wings were narrower than others; they might have corresponded to an independent opening for the display of a sculpted effigy of the Precursor in the middle of the ensemble.

Dimensions:	Wood. 124 × 66.6.
Literature:	Schöne, 1937, p. 173–5.

148 The Entombment (Pl. 137)
Budapest, Museum of Fine Arts

This panel, compared by Horst Gerson to the work of the Master of Delft, has been justifiably attributed by Karel Boon to the Master of the *Altarpiece of St. John the Baptist*. The stylised figures and the curious attempt at foreshortening which gives the faces a squashed appea-

rance occur both in the Rotterdam panels and in the *Carrying of the Cross* in the Frederiks collection (*146*). (It can also be found in the early engravings of Lucas of Leiden). The panel is small, and is certainly a fragment of a larger composition. This is clearly confirmed by the small background figures cut off by the frame.

Dimensions:	Wood. 28.5 × 24.
Catalogue:	Budapest, 1968 (Pigler), no. 5164 (Geertgen).
Literature:	Friedländer, XIV, 1937, p. 97 (Dutch); Gerson, 1950, pl. 37 (Master of Delft); Boon, 1968, p. 5.

149 St. Anne with the Virgin and Child, and a family of donors presented by St. Francis and St. Lydwine (Pl. 136)
Amsterdam, Rijksmuseum

This panel was discovered and publicised by K. Boon. His probable identification of the female presenter with St. Lydwine (verbal comment, March 1972) would indicate that the work was probably painted for Schiedam, the home town of that saint. The composition does not have the force of that of the Rotterdam paintings and the handling also seems weaker, though this is difficult to judge because of the extreme wear suffered by the paint surface. Nevertheless, one should allow for the work's different dimensions, which do not facilitate comparison. Although the work displays obvious archaisms, especially the motif of the canopy and monumental throne which seem derived from the repertoire of the Tournai sculptors, the style appears to be later than that of the Rotterdam panels.

Dimensions:	Wood. 54.5 × 53.5.
Provenance:	British art market; acquired in 1966.
Literature:	Boon, 1968.

150 Triptych of the Adoration of the Magi
Left wing: The Flight into Egypt
Right wing: The Massacre of the Innocents
Zurich, collection of Dr. Schafrl

It is difficult to follow Karel Boon in seeing the central panel as derived from the *Monforte Altarpiece* by Hugo van der Goes. This is probably an adaptation of a more Dutch design: in fact, the arrangement of the various protagonists is closer to the *Prague Triptych* by Geertgen (*68*). The version of the Massacre of the Innocents is

239

still very similar to the one by the Master of the *Virgo inter Virgines*, and contains, like the Rotterdam *Flight of St. Elizabeth* (*147 B*), a large troop of horsemen seen from behind. The discovery of the *St. Anne* panel (*149*) serves to support the attribution of this triptych. In the former work one finds small, rather plump figures which represent a natural half-way stage between the panels of the *Altarpiece of St. John the Baptist* and the painting under discussion here. On the understanding that this needs to be seen as an effort by an aging master to adapt to the fashions of the sixteenth century, we may accept the attribution to Hugo Jacobsz.

Dimensions:	Wood. Centre: 35.5 × 26; Wings: 35.5 × 14 each.
Provenance:	acquired in Paris in 1927; Munich art market; collection of Dr. Max Emden, Hamburg; coll. of Hans Erich Emden, Porto Ronco.
Exhibition:	Amsterdam, 1958, no. 66.
Literature:	Friedländer, X, 1932, no. 127 (perhaps by the Master of Delft); Regteren Altena, 1955, p. 115–7; Boon, 1968, p. 12, note 5.

151 Abraham marrying Isaac and Rebecca
A Rotterdam, Boymans-van Beuningen Museum
B Amsterdam, Rijksmuseum

The technique of the drawing shows analogies with the methods of the painter; this is especially so in the carefully-defined shadows, handled with a network of very fine hatching but opening out on to large areas of highlight. The figures display more delicacy of detail than the paintings of the St. John series; this slight difference in handling can be accounted for either by the respective dimensions of the works, or rather by the development of the artist's style, which here is closer to the *Triptych of the Adoration of the Magi* (*150*).
The painted glass follows the drawing very closely, but makes the forms more rigid. It is very probable that it was not painted by the master himself, but by a professional glass-painter.

A Drawing
Dimensions:	Pen on paper. 22.5 × 18.3.
Provenance:	J.W. Boehler, Munich; coll. of F. Koenigs, Haarlem.
Exhibitions:	Rotterdam 1934, no. 22; Rotterdam, 1936, no. 8; Amsterdam, 1958, no. 188.
Literature:	Regteren Altena, 1955, p. 116.

B Painted glass
Dimensions:	Circular. Diameter: 22.
Provenance:	acquired with the assistance of the Rembrandt Association.
Exhibitions:	Amsterdam, 1939, no. 15 b; Amsterdam, 1958, no. 240.
Literature:	N. Beets, 1911, p. 243; Regteren Altena, 1955, p. 116.

152 Rebecca taking leave of her family
A Berlin, Kupferstichkabinett
B Amsterdam, Rijksmuseum

The Berlin drawing is no doubt the model for the painted glass in Amsterdam and displays far greater finesse, which is not due merely to the difference of medium.

240

241

The composition seems to be inspired by a lost picture by Hugo van der Goes, *David and Abigail*, the best copy of which is now in Brussels. Hence, it is interesting to recall that some painted glass by Hugo Jacobsz was produced for the Church of St. Peter in Ghent.

A   Drawing

B   Painted glass
Dimensions: Circular. Diameter: 22.
Provenance: acquired with the assistance of the Rembrandt Association.
Exhibitions: Amsterdam, 1939, no. 15 c; Amsterdam, 1958, no. 241.
Literature: Beets, 1911, p. 243; Regteren Altena, 1955, p. 116.

Workshop of the Master of the Altarpiece of St. John the Baptist

153   The Baptism of Christ
Copenhagen, Statens Museum for Kunst

The attribution to Engelbrechts, suggested by Valentiner and retained by the Copenhagen Museum, is hardly credible. The figure-types with their almost squashed faces and modelling in large areas are reminiscent of the style of the Master of the *Altarpiece of St. John the Baptist* without its force. This may be a work of his workshop or of his immediate circle.
The composition is derived from the same model as the Enschede painting (*67*). This version, however, may be closer to the lost original, which could have been by Albert van Ouwater: the landscape shows a fondness for marking out space by means of trees, and St. John's crisp drapery folds recall those in the Berlin *Raising of Lazarus* (*42*).

242

Dimensions: Wood. 42 × 26.5. A strip about 2 cm wide has been added on the left.
Literature: Copenhagen, Royal Museum of Fine Arts, 1951, no. 208.

Artist working at Gouda *c.*1486–8

154   Illustrations for Le Chevalier Délibéré by Olivier de la Marche (Pls. 138–9)

The only known copy of the Gouda edition of this book (formerly in the Alphonse de Rothschild collection; photographs in the Reserve of the Bibliothèque Nationale in Paris, M Ye 14) was identified by Holtrop as a work of the printer Gotfried van Os of Gouda. The text is dated 1483; but Holtrop thought that the printing could not be earlier than 1484, because the printer's mark is a drawing of an elephant; this was probably suggested by the exhibition of a live elephant in the towns of Holland in 1484. The years 1486–8, during which the activity of Gotfried van Os is attested, are the most likely.
The illustration follows the instructions added by the author to the manuscript now in the Bibliothèque Nationale in Paris (reproduced in an English translation in the facsimile edited by Lippmann) much more faithfully than the Paris edition of 1493.
It is tempting to compare the woodcuts to two isolated paintings, the *Carrying of the Cross* in Brussels and the *Crucifixion* in the Capilla Real, Granada (*166–7*). But alongside comparable elements (facial types, the figures' puppet-like gestures, skill in the depiction of horses), the paintings also display different characteristics: for example, greater exoticism of costume (particularly noticeable in the *Crucifixion*). Neither painting contains female faces comparable to the heads which are so characteristic of the illustrator. Even so, if the comparison did prove to be well-founded it would not tell us much about the author of the illustrations, since the paintings have not been conclusively localised.
Nor does an analysis of the illustrations provide a precise indication of where their author was trained. We can only point out that in the encounter between the Actor and Understanding, the horse (Vouloer, 'Will') is a straight copy from the panel of the *Honest Judges* in the *Mystic Lamb*.

15 illustrations of *c.*19 × *c.*13.5.

Subjects of the illustrations:
Title page   combat of the Actor with Death
p. 2   the Actor and Thought

Facsimile: Lippmann, 1898.
Literature: Holtrop, 1868, nos. 74 and 75; Campbell, 1874, no. 1083; Conway, 1884, p. 144–8; Lippmann, 1898; Schretlen, 1925, p. 51; Schretlen, 1925B; Friedländer, V, 1927, p. 62; Friedländer, X, 1932, p. 51–2; Hind, 1935, II, p. 586–90; Steinbart, 1937, p. 12–15; Hollstein, XII, n.d., p. 131–4; Boon, 1968, p. 3–5.

Artist working at Schiedam in 1498

155   The Life of St. Lydwine
(*Vita alme Virginis Lydwine de Schiedam*)
Printed at Schiedam by Otgier Pietersz Nachttegael in 1498

The 26 illustrations of this book constitute the most remarkable collection of late fifteenth-century woodcuts in Holland after the blocks for *Le Chevalier Délibéré*. The suggestion that both collections should be attributed to the same master, however, is not acceptable.

243

Still, the second artist draws his inspiration from the first in the simplicity of his means, his economical use of hatching and the clarity of his images.

Moreover, this book is less isolated than *Le Chevalier Délibéré* amongst Netherlandish woodcut work. The same master should probably be credited with the title page for a *Life of St. Lydwine* printed at Gouda in 1496 (Campbell, 1874, no. 1125), as well as the *Historie van Joseph* also printed at Gouda, but in 1500.

The illustrations display both archaisms and, to a considerable degree, a new spirit. It is noteworthy that they are very frequently set behind an architectural frame, a fifteenth-century device. On the other hand, like *Le Chevalier Délibéré* but with very different methods, they put the accent on the figures, cutting down the space in which they are set. The poses and groupings of the characters are marked by a calm and simplicity, due principally to an increased horizontal emphasis, which has nothing in common with the Gouda woodcuts. The connection between these compositions and the works of the Master of Delft is fairly evident, but one hesitates to attribute both paintings and woodcuts to the same artist.

244

245

Subjects of the illustrations:

1 the saint appearing to Jan Brugman
2 the saint receiving a branch of a rose-tree from an angel
3 initial D with St. Veronica
4 the saint prays to the Virgin to spare her from marriage
5 the saint falls on the ice
6 a doctor visits the sick saint
7 visit of Werboldus, who leaves her some money
8 the saint ill in bed
9 appearance of an angel to the sick saint
10 the saint makes clothes for the poor and has food distributed
11 the saint has a vision of despair
12 the saint asks for the sacraments
13 she receives the stigmata and is crowned by the Virgin
14 priests enquire about her
15 an angel shows her the souls in Purgatory
16 an angel shows her Paradise
17 appearance of the Virgin of the Nativity and Lactation
18 the saint has a vision of her martyrdom
19 appearance of an angel who shows her her crown
20 she receives extreme unction from the hand of Christ
21 death of the saint
22 the saint laid out in her coffin
23 burial
24 escutcheon bearing a heart pierced by two arrows
25 escutcheon bearing a lion rampant
26 the saint presents Jan Brugman to St. Anne with the Virgin and Child

Literature: Campbell, 1874, no. 383; Conway, 1884, p. 306–7; Schretlen, 1925 (Jacob Cornelisz); Schretlen, 1925 B, p. 143; Gesamtkatalog, no. 5579; Henkell, 1926, p. 8; Friedländer, X, 1932, p. 51–2; Steinbart, 1937, p. 12–15 (rejecting attribution to Jacob Cornelisz); Hollstein, XII (n.d.) p. 185–8; Sheppard, 1950.

The Master of Evert van Soudenbalch

The first attempt at isolating the work of this illuminator was made by Byvanck, and his designation was suggested by the name of the man for whom the Vienna *Bible* was intended, a canon of Utrecht Cathedral.

It was only with the discovery of the *Book of Hours of Jan van Amerongen* (the only one of his works examined here) that this master's style showed itself capable of escaping from the confines of illustration to which his other works, despite their fine quality, were restricted: the two-volume Dutch Bible of Evert van Soudenbalch (Vienna, National Library, cod. 2771 and 2772, cf. Vermeeren, 1955–7), a *Last Judgment* in a Bible in the Library at Liège (MS 13, Byvanck, 1937, fig. 206), a pen and ink illustration in a Bible in the Royal Library at The Hague (MS 78 D 39), and lastly the illustration of a Book of Hours (H.P. Krauss, cat. 108, Delaissé, 1968, p. 45 and fig. 99). The *Book of Hours of Jan van Amerongen* is dated 1460 and the colophon of the Vienna *Bible* certifies the completion of its transcription in 1468; the artist must therefore have been active between 1455 and 1475 approximately.

Several attempts have been made to link paintings with these illuminations. The most notable have been by Hoogewerff (I, 1936, p. 544–60) and by K.G. Boon (1961). The former dubs the painter 'Zeno' and wants to identify him with the artist since christened the Master of the *Manna*. The latter sees these productions as the early work of Erhard van Reuwich. Neither of these hypotheses seems to bear examination.

Literature: Hoogewerff, I, 1936, p. 544–60; Byvanck, 1937, p. 85–8; Delaissé, 1949 (Brussels Book of Hours); Vermeeren, 1955–7 (Vienna Bible); Boon, 1961; Delaissé, 1968, p. 42–8.

156 Book of Hours of Jan van Amerongen
Brussels, Bibliothèque Royale, MS II 7619

Published in 1949 by Delaissé as the *Book of Hours* of Mary van Vronensteyn, this book was actually commissioned by Jan van Amerongen (Boon, 1961, p. 51, note 2). The latter is known as having been bailiff of Utrecht in 1468–70. He was married to Mechtelt Hendricksd van Gent, by whom he had no children. The book was inherited by his niece, Maria van Raephorst, married in 1520 to Lubbaert de Wael van Vronensteyn. It is dated on folio 2, which contains a table of dominical letters beginning in 1400, amongst which the letter for 1460 is marked by a finger.

The book is very richly decorated, and contains numerous illuminated initials, in which Delaissé has discerned the work of three separate artists. The larger part of the decoration consists of twelve full-page illuminations, all executed on inserted sheets. They are the work of the Master of Evert van Soudenbalch. Delaissé has shown that the workshop which produced the secondary initials was probably that of the artist of the full-page illuminations. Only the latter will concern us here, as they are the only ones conceived in imitation of panel paintings.

The Taking of Christ (folio 17 *v.*) (Pl. 140)
The composition is based essentially on the Eyckian illumination in the *Turin Hours* (*15*). The artist has altered the pose of the servant Malchus, whose rôle in the Turin composition was very minor but who becomes here one of the most picturesque elements. The nocturne effect has almost completely disappeared. The picture has been complemented by delightful little scenes in the borders. They may also be inspired by lost Eyckian models, as they display a delicacy and elegance which could have been derived from such an example.

Christ before Pilate (folio 38 *v.*)
The composition of this illumination is very close to a page in the *Hours of Catherine of Cleves* (*37*, P. 20). Both scenes are set behind an architectural frame. With the Master of Catherine of Cleves it is conceived in the manner of fourteenth-century illuminators as a small edifice floating on the page. With the Master of Evert van Soudenbalch it is treated with much greater restraint, and resembles the device used at the same period by the Master of the *Manna*.

The Crowning with Thorns (folio 44 *v.*)
The scene has probably been devised from a combination of elements borrowed from the *Mocking of Christ* in the *Hours of Catherine of Cleves* (*37*, P. 19) and from the *Crowning with Thorns* (P. 23). From the first, the Master of Evert van Soudenbalch has notably retained the idea of a symmetrical and centred composition, as well as the figures of two Jews kneeling in the foreground.

The Nailing to the Cross (folio 49 *v.*)
The subject is handled according to a convention which seems to have been very popular in the northern Netherlands. It is the one adopted by Gerard David in a triptych whose central panel is now in the National Gallery, London (Pl. 147). The ground of Golgotha is revealed in a steeply-angled view; the Cross lies obliquely across the picture and the executioners bustle around it. Although the subject is a little different, the illumination in the *Hours of Catherine of Cleves* of *Christ awaiting His execution* contains a similar picturesque detail: an executioner drilling a hole in the base of the Cross with an enormous gimlet.

241

The Crucifixion (folio 54 v.)

The composition of this scene owes a great deal to the panel of the New York *Diptych* by Jan van Eyck (*20*). There is no direct copying, but a systematic borrowing of motifs, especially amongst the horsemen, who are often reproduced by reversal. The group of the Virgin and the holy women is set in the same place, but is arranged differently. This composition has been directly copied by a Utrecht (?) artist (*158*), either from the illumination or from a variant now lost.

The Deposition from the Cross (folio 59 v.)

This scene does not seem to have been composed with any particular model in mind. The persistence of the Eyckian motif of the horsemen in a hollow lane should be noted.

246

The Entombment (folio 67 v.)

It is unlikely that the illuminator is following a model here. For the setting he adopts the design used in the *Crucifixion* and the *Carrying of the Cross*. Rather than an *Entombment* strictly speaking, the artist here depicts another scene: the carrying to the tomb. The same theme was treated on two separate occasions by the Master of the *Virgo inter Virgines* (*129–33*).

Pentecost (folio 73 v.)

Here again, the illuminator does not seem to have taken advantage of a model. He departs from the interpretation of the subject by the Master of Catherine of Cleves (*37*, P. 51), and yet remains very close to its spirit with the spontaneity of the apostles' attitudes and the popular appeal of their faces.

Christ blessing in a church (folio 97 v.)

For Christ's pose here, the illuminator has drawn his inspiration from a page in the *Turin Hours* by hand K (folio 44 v., Durrieu, 1902, Pl. XXV). The church interior is very similar to the one in the preceding

247

illumination in the same manuscript (folio 43 r., Durrieu, 1902, pl. XXIV). However, the delicacy of the handling is greater than in the model. The artist has a particularly good command of colour, and draws from it effects of light which must be inspired by Eyckian examples.

Christ on the Cross with the Virgin and St. John the Evangelist (folio 123 v.)

This is an interpretation of an Eyckian model, the *Crucifixion* in the *Milan-Turin Hours* (*28*) painted by Master H, probably over a drawing by Jan van Eyck. One should note the curious addition behind the Virgin of a peasant with a donkey, an idea borrowed from the *Carrying of the Cross* by Jan van Eyck (*22*). This illumination was copied by a Utrecht artist between 1460 and 1467 for a Triptych now in the Centraal Museum, Utrecht (*157*).

The Last Judgment (folio 138 v.) (Pl. 141)

Despite the limited space available for the illuminator, the scene is very full. It includes the resurrection of the dead, Hell represented by the jaws of a monster, Heaven by an ornamental entrance and, in the sky, Christ the Judge flanked by the Virgin and St. John the Baptist.

Requiem Mass (folio 161 v.)

The illuminator draws his inspiration here from certain scenes by the Master of Catherine of Cleves, like that of the *Funeral Vigil* (*37*, P. 44), the *Requiem* (P. 46) or the *Communion* (P. 72).

Dimensions:	Volume of 251 folios of 18.5 × 14.
Provenance:	Mary van Vronensteyn; Cornelis van Aerssen and Anna Albertine van Beijeren; A. van Aerssen Beijeren.
Exhibitions:	The Hague, 1950, no. 27; Brussels, 1958, no. 37; Cologne, 1961, no. 3.
Literature:	Delaissé, 1949; Byvanck, 1953, p. 40–3; Pieper, 1959, p. 144–6; Boon, 1961, p. 51; Carter, 1962.

Utrecht artist working between 1460 and 1467

157 Triptych of the Crucifixion

Left wing: The Mass of St. Gregory
Right wing: St. Christopher
Reverse of the wings: The Annunciation (in grisaille)
Utrecht, Centraal Museum (on loan from the Rijksmuseum, Amsterdam)

248

The harshness of the features belongs very much to the 'rustic' tendency, and so does the somewhat loud colour harmony, with its aggressive opposition of a very strong green in the background to the bright reds of the costumes. By comparison with the inner faces, the reverse of the wings seems almost relaxed. The drapery folds are less busy, and the forms are fuller. Perhaps this part of the work is by another hand; the face of the Virgin of the *Annunciation* is very different in character from that of the Virgin in the *Crucifixion*; its form is more rounded, almost without internal modelling, and is reminiscent of those in the *Crucifixion* in Providence (*158*).

249

Dimensions:	Wood. Centre: 73 × 48; wings: 73 × 20 each.
Provenance:	purchased in 1887 by the Rijksmuseum of Amsterdam from J. H. Cremen.
Exhibitions:	The Hague, 1950, no. 27; Amsterdam, 1958, no. 7.
Literature:	Winkler, 1923, p. 139; Winkler, 1924, p. 154; Friedländer, III, 1925, p. 112; Byvanck, 1930, p. 127; Hoogewerff, IX, 1936, p. 564; Panofsky, 1953, p. 323; Boon, 1961, p. 51.

Master of the Buukerk (Hillebrant van Rewijck?)

This artist's oeuvre was isolated by Karel Boon in an article published in 1961. The key work is the large fresco of the *Tree of Jesse* in the Buukerk, Utrecht. Boon has linked this fresco with three paintings: the *Crucifixion* in Providence, Rhode Island, the *Nailing to the Cross* in the Walker Art Gallery and the *Triptych of the Crucifixion* in Utrecht. The attribution of this last picture to the Master seems difficult to accept. Only the external grisaille could perhaps be by him. The proposal to identify this Master with Hillebrant van Rewijck is based solely on the fact that this artist performed various tasks for the Buukerk between 1456 and 1469.

Literature:	Boon, 1961.

158 The Crucifixion

Providence, Museum of the Rhode Island School of Design

250

This curious painting is notable for its almost exact correspondence with the miniature on folio 55 *v.* of the *Book of Hours of Jan van Amerongen (156)*; the few discernible differences nevertheless indicate that the earlier work is not the painting — as supposed by Boon and Carter — but the illumination.

Dimensions: Wood. 69.5 × 48.
Provenance: acquired from Pieter de Boer of Amsterdam.
Literature: Boon, 1961; Carter, 1962; Delaissé, 1968, p. 88.

159   The Nailing to the Cross
Liverpool, Walker Art Gallery

This odd work, which unfortunately is in a poor state of preservation, has been associated by Karel Boon with the fresco of the *Tree of Jesse* in the Buukerk in Utrecht. The suggestion is a very attractive one, despite the difficulty of comparing two works so different in both subject and handling. But we do notice that rather awkward stiffness of the figures, the heads slightly too heavy for the bodies and the faces rendered so strangely distinctive by their large noses — all of which are characteristic of the fresco. The Providence painting, however, seems to show greater skill in execution and rather different figure-types; this gives rise to some reservations about its attribution to the same artist. This depiction of the *Nailing to the Cross* corresponds to a design which must have been known in the northern Netherlands. (Cf. *37*, P. 25; *156* folio 49 *v.*; and Gerard David).

Dimensions: Wood. 67.5 × 59.7.
Provenance: William Roscoe collection; Liverpool Royal Institution.
Literature: Fastnedge, 1954, p. 32; Boon, 1961, p. 52–3.

160   The Tree of Jesse
Utrecht, Buukerk

This fresco was discovered in 1840 in the Buukerk in Utrecht. A lithograph reproduction of it was published in 1849 by D. van Lokhorst (Carter, 1962, fig. 8). An inscription in the bottom right-hand corner beneath the portraits of the donors, now difficult to make out, should be read:

'Int iaer ons heren mcccc xlviii op sinte matheus dach sterf ghertrut flores otten wijf, bit voir de siel.'

However, the work must have been painted later than 1448, the date of the donor's death, since the chapel on whose wall it hangs does not seem to have been completed before 1453.

It is rather difficult to gauge the effect of this fresco from photographs. The extremely 'rustic' appearance of the figures, whose faces verge on caricature, still allows considerable monumentality. The illusion of space is created very simply by a device dear to illuminators — a flagstone floor whose perspective helps to locate the planes.

On a nave pier of the same church there is another fresco, of *St. Christopher*, which could well be by the same hand. A thorough-going restoration of the building might hold further surprises in store, since in many other places whitewash has flaked away to reveal the presence of hitherto hidden frescoes.

Fresco.
Literature: Faussen, 1846; Kalcken, II, 1909; Winkler, 1923, p. 135; Hoogewerff, I, 1936, p. 360–4; Boon, 1961; Carter, 1962, p. 8–9.

Utrecht artist, last quarter of the fifteenth century

161   The Mystic Marriage of St. Agnes
Utrecht, Archiepiscopal Museum

St. Agnes was held in particular veneration at Utrecht, where important relics of her were preserved in the Church of St. Martin. The saint, who is clearly pointing to the lamb on a cushion in front of her, receives the ring from the Child Jesus. The source of this transposition of the subject of the Mystic Marriage of St. Catherine is presumably the *Golden Legend*, which has the saint say to the prefect's son who wants to marry her:

'I love one who is much nobler and of better lineage than you ... He who has plighted his troth to me with the ring that he has placed on my right hand, who has put precious stones around my neck and clothed me with a mantle of cloth of gold...' (Roze transl. I. p. 140–1).

The chancel of the church visible in the background may be taken as a rough evocation of the choir of Utrecht Cathedral. The elevation is identical, the only difference being the design of the triforium arcade, which still appears as Romanesque in the painting, whereas in fact it consists of trefoiled arches. The artist's clear suggestion of the soaring vaults of the ambulatory well conveys the effect aimed at in this large building.

The device of tapestries held up by angels seems to have been very popular in the last quarter of the fifteenth century in Utrecht. It occurs both in illuminations and in the few known paintings. It may have led the Master of the *St. Bartholomew Altarpiece* to adopt it systematically in his own works.

Dimensions: Wood (oak). 31.5 × 44.
Provenance: Hellmich coll., Baak.
Exhibitions: Amsterdam, 1958, no. 42; Cologne, 1961, no. 7.

Literature: Dülberg, 1903, p. 7; Friedländer, 1926–7, p. 177; Grete Ring, 1939, p. 29–44; Busch, 1939, p. 35–6; Rath, 1941, p. 109, note 54.
Catalogue: Centraalmuseum, 1933, no. 544; Aartsbisschoppelijkmuseum, 1948 (Bouvy), no. 47 (Master of the *St. Bartholomew Altarpiece*).

162   St. Anne with the Virgin and Child
Utrecht, Archiepiscopal Museum

This painting is directly linked in both composition and style to the *Mystic Marriage of St. Agnes*. It adopts the same arrangement of the figures in a church chancel behind a stone parapet on which sits the Child. The figure-types are also very similar to those in the *St. Agnes* painting. The execution is much less fine, however, and is further weakened by the wearing away of the surface paint layers. The work thus very probably originated in the same circle as the foregoing one, perhaps even in the same workshop, but is not by the same hand. It is difficult to be precise about its date for lack of comparisons. The period *c.*1470, suggested by recent criticism in terms of the work of the Master of the *St. Bartholomew Altarpiece*, seems rather too early, however. The style of St. Anne's head-dress and the simplicity of the draperies suggest a slightly later date, *c.*1480–90.

Dimensions: Wood (oak). 42 × 31.
The frame, perhaps original, bears an inscription which is certainly a later overpainting, perhaps even modern: 'Bene vivere et laetari'
Provenance: Canon W. M. de Jongh, Utrecht.
Exhibitions: Utrecht, 1913, no. 48; Cologne, 1961, no. 6.
Catalogue: Aartsbisschoppelijkmuseum, 1948 (Bouvy), no. 106.
Literature: Dülberg, 1903, p. 8–9; Friedländer, V, 1927, p. 63 and 138, no. 39; Hoogewerff, II, 1937, p. 238; Grete Ring, 1939, p. 40–1; Rath, 1941, p. 14.

163   The Mystic Marriage of St. Agnes
(Pl. 142)
Esztergom, Christian Museum

The window opening on to a landscape is an Italianate feature similar to that used by the Master of Moulins in his *Beaujeu Triptych* of 1488 (Louvre). On the other hand, the three figures betray their origins in models by the circle of Bouts. The curious female faces with broad foreheads, small mouths and narrow chins even seem to be a clumsy transposition of Bouts's. Finally, the angel musicians are apparently peculiar to the repertoire of the Utrecht workshops of the very end of the fifteenth century. The localisation of the painting at Utrecht has been rightly suggested by Grete Ring, arguing principally from the iconography of the Mystic Marriage of St. Agnes, a tradition peculiar to the cathedral city.

Dimensions: Wood. 68 × 51.5.
Provenance: unknown.
Literature: Ring, 1939, p. 28–9; Végh, 1967, no. 24.

164 Virgin and Child with Angel Musicians
Berlin, Staatliche Museen

251

It is to Karel Boon that we owe the attribution to the Utrecht school of this painting and also the other version of the same subject (cf. following entry); he argues from the connections that it displays with clearly localised sculpture and illumination. He has also pointed out that the figure-types of the Virgin and the Child are derived from Schongauer's engraving, the *Virgin with a Parrot* (Lehrs 37), and that the angels playing the viol and the organ are also borrowed from an engraving by the same artist, that of the bishop's crozier (Lehrs 105). It is therefore difficult to date the painting earlier than the 1480s, bearing in mind these borrowings from engravings which are generally dated between 1470 and 1480.

Dimensions: Wood (pine), transferred to oak (in 1930). 80.3 × 66.
Provenance: L. Somzée coll. (sold Brussels, 24 May 1904, lot 622, as Schongauer); Hohenzollern coll., Sigmaringen; acquired in 1928.
Exhibitions: Amsterdam, 1958, no. 43; Cologne, 1961, no. 8.
Literature: Rieffel, 1924, p. 58; Mayer, 1928, p. 65; Kunze, 1939, p. 10; Boon, 1940, p. 99–103.

165 Virgin and Child with Angel Musicians
United States, private collection.

This is a variant of the preceding work, but whereas the latter was inspired by the engravings of Schongauer, this one adopts the same layout without actually using the figures from the engravings as models. Here, the Virgin holds the Child in her arms; the angels are free interpretations of those in the Berlin painting. The artist has also retained the motif of the gold filigree spandrels. It is quite possible that both works are by the same artist; the photographs seem to indicate a similarity of handling, especially in the depiction of hair.

Dimensions: Wood. 47 × 33.5.
Provenance: acquired from Pieter de Boer, Amsterdam.
Exhibition: Rotterdam, 1936, no. 76a.
Literature: Boon, 1940, p. 99–103.

Master IAM van Zwolle

It has not seemed necessary to give here a complete description of the work of this engraver, which has been examined successively by Lehrs (VII) and Hollstein (XII). It has not been possible to consult a recent American work by Elisabeth Finkenstaedt (unpublished), presented as a thesis at Havard University in 1963.

The old identification of this Master with Johann von Cöln, for which Nagler was responsible, has been conclusively refuted. It is agreed that the last word of the signature should be read as 'Zwoll' rather than 'Zwott', and that the artist should thus be presumed to have been active in the town of Zwolle. This basic assumption has allowed Th. de Vries (1954 and 1958) to identify him with Johann van den Mijnnesten.

The latter, who may have been born c.1425, died in 1504. He was granted the burghership of Zwolle in 1462, and his activities as a painter there are mentioned subsequently. The known payments are mostly for the painting of statues. His son, Johann, who was granted the burghership in 1516, signed a deed in 1531 with a monogram in the form of a house, close to the A of IAM. Johann van den Mijnnesten seems to have had another son by a first marriage, named Roger, who is mentioned as a goldsmith.

It may seem surprising to find a painter working as an engraver, but we cannot exclude the possibility of a collaboration between the father and the goldsmith son; the presence of a burnisher in the signature may signify the latter's participation.

Literature: Lehrs, VII; Hollstein, XII, p. 252–79; Th. de Vries, 1954 and 1958; Dubbe, 1970.

North Netherlandish Artist, last quarter of the fifteenth century

166 The Carrying of the Cross (Pl. 146)
Brussels, Musées Royaux des Beaux-Arts

This curious and charming painting was made known in 1923 by Winkler, who ascribed it to the circle of the Master of the *Virgo inter Virgines*. However, no specific element betrays the origin of this work or the *Crucifixion* in the Capilla Real in Granada, which is indisputably by the same hand. The attribution to Allaert van Hameel, proposed by Tolnay, is still highly problematical; there is nothing to prove that this architect from 's Hertogenbosch was a painter or even that he was the designer of the compositions of which he signed the engravings.

Dimensions: Wood. 49 × 42.
Provenance: Ch. Cardon coll., Brussels.
Exhibition: Rotterdam, 1936, no. 32.
Literature: Winkler, 1923, p. 144; Winkler, 1924, p. 156; Tolnay, 1965, p. 349 (Allaert van Hameel).

167 The Crucifixion
Granada, Capilla Real

In 1923, while drawing attention to the *Carrying of the Cross* in Brussels (cf. preceding entry), Winkler mentioned this *Crucifixion*, which he justifiably attributed to the same hand. It is quite possible that the artist knew the *Crucifixion* by Master H in the Ca' d'Oro (*32*).

252

Although he does not draw his inspiration from it in a very literal way, one notes at least that his Christ is of a similar type to that in the Venice painting and that one of the buildings of Jerusalem is crowned by an odd-looking ball similar to the one visible in the same work.

Dimensions: Wood. 53 × 36.
Provenance: collection of Isabella the Catholic (?).
Literature: Winkler, 1923, p. 144; p. 144; Angulo Iniguez, 1925, p. 111, no. 1; Friedländer, V, 1927, p. 154, no. 112, (follower of Bosch); Gallegoy Burin, 1952, p. 79–90, no. 9.

168 St. Martin
Philadelphia, Museum of Art, Johnson collection

253

Valentiner attributed this work to the Haarlem school, but its links with Haarlem painting are rather superficial. The theory is possible, but by no means established; it may be worth remembering that Utrecht had a very important church dedicated to St. Martin.

Dimensions: Wood. 45 × 31.
Exhibition: Amsterdam, 1958, no. 34.
Literature: Valentiner, 1913, no. 346; Valentiner, 1914, p. 64; Friedländer, V, 1927, p. 138, no. 43; Kessler, 1930, p. 58; Hoogewerff, I, 1936, p. 558; Boon, 1947, p. 35.

169 Portrait of Petrus Veenlant

Philadelphia, Museum of Art, Johnson collection

254

It is tempting to compare this likeness to that of the fourth figure from the right in the group of Hospitallers in the panel of the *Burning of the bones of St. John the Baptist* by Geertgen (*71*): in both cases there is the same pointing gesture, the same unfocussed gaze and a reasonable similarity in features. Valentiner has pointed out this connection and has used it to attribute to Geertgen's circle both this portrait and the *St. Martin* (cf. preceding entry), which in his view is by the same hand. There can indeed be no doubt that the artist who produced this little panel has imitated the Haarlem Master; but one only needs to compare the technique of the two hands to gauge the weakness of the imitation. Hence, there is no compelling reason for this to be considered the work of a Haarlem artist. It was not necessary to have been trained in Haarlem or to be working there to imitate a detail of one of Geertgen's paintings.

Dimensions: Wood. 42.5 × 23.5.
Literature: Valentiner, 1913, no. 354; Valentiner, 1914, p. 14; Hoogewerff, II, 1937, p. 404–6.

170 Two altarpiece wings

A   Fragment of an Adoration of the Magi
B   Ecce Homo
The Hague, J. W. Frederiks collection (on loan to the Boymans Museum, Rotterdam)

255

The altarpiece to which these two panels belonged must have been fairly large, since the artist deemed it necessary to divide the scene of the *Adoration of the Magi*

between two panels: in the surviving one, one of the Kings (Melchior?) is kneeling on the left while the Child holds out His arms towards the right, presumably in the direction of the other two Magi, who must have been shown on the adjoining panel.

In both instances the paint surface is somewhat worn, and the modelling that can be seen is, in many places (particularly the face of the Virgin in the *Adoration of the Magi*) a restoration. The work nevertheless has a very distinctive character, for which it is hard to find equivalents. The handling of drapery folds in large areas is slightly reminiscent of Hugo Jacobsz. The rather garish palette puts one in mind of the Master of the *Manna*. The heads, which are round, very large in proportion to the bodies and markedly vulgar, are expressed in volumes. Through the thin paint layers, a rather sketchy preparatory drawing can be made out in many places.

Only the figure-type of the Virgin and, to a lesser degree, that of the Child, may suggest a possible localisation: they display some affinity with the figures of Utrecht paintings. The Virgin is not dissimilar from the one in the *Mystic Marriage of St. Agnes* from Utrecht (*161*), but the two paintings correspond most closely to the version of the same subject now at Esztergom (*163*).

It is also difficult to be precise about the date of these works. In spirit they are fairly similar to the works of the Master of Aix-la-Chapelle, who seems to have been active at the beginning of the sixteenth century. In my view, these two panels could belong either to the very end of the fifteenth century or to the beginning of the sixteenth.

Dimensions: Wood. 82.5 × 70 each.
Exhibitions: Rotterdam, 1936–7, no. 41; Amsterdam, 1939, no. 75a and 110a; Laren, 1961, nos. 96 and 97.
Literature: Friedländer, XIV, p. 98.

171 The Crucifixion

Budapest, National Museum of Fine Arts

256

This very curious painting has recently been attributed to Dirck Baegert, the Westphalian master (Musper, 1965). Here, however, one does not find the delicacy and calm which mark the work of that artist. Pigler saw it as the work of a fifteenth-century north Netherlandish artist. The suggestion is easy to accept when one takes into account the nervous contortion of the poses, the 'rustic' figure-types and the jerky rhythms of the

composition. The problem here is very similar to that posed by the *Carrying of the Cross* in Brussels (*166*) and the *Crucifixion* in Granada (*167*). Like those two works, this painting combines a handling which is southern in spirit —which could mean similar to that of the Haarlem workshops— with a fondness for 'rustic' figures and violent gestures. If there were not such profound differences between the figure-types, one might have been inclined to attribute the three paintings to the same master. It is quite possible that they at least originated in the same workshop, as may be indicated by motifs as identical as the pose of the Brussels Christ and that of one the holy women in the Budapest painting. But as to whether the workshop was in Haarlem, Delft, Utrecht or Zwolle, there is no significant clue.

Dimensions: Wood (walnut). 146 × 109.
Provenance: Esterhazy collection (Inv. of 1820, no. 26, as Lucas van Leyden).
Exhibition: Düsseldorf, 1904, no. 191.
Catalogue: Budapest, Museum of Fine Arts, Pigler, 1968, no. 125.
Literature: Dülberg, 1899, p. 33–4; Scheibler, 1903, p. 562; Balet, 1910, p. 160; Hoogewerff, I, 1936, p. 560–1; Musper, 1965.

THE NORTHERN NETHERLANDS
IN THE 15TH CENTURY

(After the maps in *Geschiedkundige Atlas van Neederland*)

Ecclesiastical Principality of Utrecht

County of Holland and Zeeland

Duchy of Guelders

✕✕✕✕ Limits of the diocese of Utrecht

╌╌╌╌ Actual frontiers of the Netherlands

FRIESLAND

Groningen

Northern province of the
ecclesiastical Principality

Zwolle

Deventer

Haarlem Amsterdam

HOLLAND

GUELDERS

Leiden

The Hague

Oudewater   Utrecht

Delft   Gouda

Arnhem

Rotterdam

Gorinchem

Nijmegen

Dordrecht

ZEELAND

's Hertogenbosch

BRABANT

Antwerp

Bibliography

This study was first published as Gérard de Saint Jean et la peinture dans les Pays-Bas du Nord au XVe siècle *(3 vols.) by the* Service de réproduction des thèses *of the University of Lille III in 1979, as a private edition of 200 copies. The present book is an up-dated version of the original thesis, which was written in 1973, and it therefore does not seem necessary to quote it otherwise as a source. Only a single element that could aid researchers is missing from this version of the book —the corpus (vol. 2, pp. 1056–1152) of the documents known to date on the artists in the northern Netherlands. It was marred by a few minimal errors of transcription in the original version, which could not be corrected for photocomposition for technical reasons.*

This bibliography contains complete references to the works quoted in abbreviated form in the main text. They are given in alphabetical order according to the name of the author and thereafter chronologically for the works of the same author. Exhibition catalogues are listed under the name of the city where the exhibition took place and followed by the date of the exhibition; museum catalogues are listed by the name of the city where the museum is located and followed by the name of the museum.

ADHEMAR Hélène, 1961, 'La date du portrait de Jean sans Peur, duc de Bourgogne—Etude d'après un exemplaire conservé au musée du Louvre', in *La revue du Louvre et des musées de France*, II, p. 265–268.

ALBERDINGK THIJM J.A., 1881, 'Het Zoen-Offer des Nieuwen Verbonds schilderstuk van een onbekenden XV eeuwschen Meester', in C.E. Taurel, *De christelijke Kunst in Holland en Vlaanderen*, Amsterdam, p. 21.

ALGEMEINE GESCHIEDENIS DER NEDERLANDEN, III, 1951 and IV, 1952, under the direction of J.A. van Houtte, J.F. Niermeyer, J. Presser, J. Romein and H. van Werveke, Utrecht.

ALLAN F., 1870–1883, *Geschiedenis en Beschrijving van Haarlem*, 4 vol. Haarlem.

AMPZING Samuel, 1628, *Beschryvinge ende Lof der stad Haerlem in Holland*, Haarlem.

AMSTERDAM 1663, Dr. O. O. D., *Historische Beschryving der Stadt Amsterdam*, Amsterdam (Jacob van Meurs).

AMSTERDAM 1898, *Rembrandt: Collection des œuvres du maître réunies à l'occasion de l'inauguration de S.M. La Reine Wilhelmina, Stedelijk Museum.*

AMSTERDAM 1939, *Bijbelse Kunst*, Rijksmuseum.

AMSTERDAM 1950, *120 beroemde schilderijen uit het Kaiser-Friedrich-museum te Berlin*, Rijksmuseum.

AMSTERDAM 1951, *Bourgondische Pracht van Philips de Stoute tot Philips de Schone*, Rijksmuseum, 28 July–1 October.

AMSTERDAM 1958, *Middeleeuwse Kunst der Noordelijke Nederlanden*, Rijksmuseum, 28 June–28 September, catalogue written under the direction of R. van Luttervelt.

AMSTERDAM RIJKSMUSEUM 1973, *Beeldhouwkunst in het Rijksmuseum* (Jaap Leeuwenberg), Amsterdam.

ANGULO INIGUEZ Diego, 1925, 'La Crucifixion. Tabla holandesa del siglo XV en la Capilla Real de Granada', in *Archivo español de Arte y Arqueologia*, I, p. III.

ANGULO INIGUEZ Diego, 1925 B, 'El "Maestro de la Virgo inter Virgines", la tabla del prime Conde de Alba', in *Archivo español de Arte y Arqueologia*, I, p. 193–196.

ANTWERP 1930, *Exposition internationale, coloniale, maritime et d'Art flamand — Section d'Art flamand ancien*, June–September.

ANTWERP 1954, *De Madona in de kunst*, Koninklijk Museum voor Schoone Kunsten.

ANTWERP MUSÉE ROYAL DES BEAUX-ARTS, 1948, *Catalogue descriptif. Maîtres anciens*, by A.J.J. Delen.

ANTWERP MUSÉE MAYER VAN DEN BERGH, 1966, *Catalogue I*, (Schilderijen – Verluchte Handschriften – Tekeningen), Antwerp, 2nd ed., by Jozef de Coo.

ANZELEWSKY Fedja, 1971, *Albrecht Dürer. Das malerische Werk*, Berlin.

ARU C. and GERARDON Et. de, 1950, 'La galerie Sabauda de Turin', (*Les Primitifs Flamands – I – Corpus de la Peinture des Anciens Pays-Bas méridionaux au quinzième siècle*, 5), Antwerp.

AUBENAS Roger and RICARD Robert, 1951, *L'Eglise et la Renaissance (1449–1517)*, (*Histoire de l'Eglise*, directed by Augustin Fliche and Victor Martin, 15), Paris.

AVRIL François, 1974, 'La peinture française au temps de Jean de Berry', in *Revue de l'Art*, n° 28, p. 40–52.

AXTERS Stephanus, 1956, *Geschiedenis van de vroomheid in de Nederlanden, III, De Moderne Devotie, 1380–1550*, Antwerp.

BALDASS Ludwig, 1919, 'Ein frühwerk des Geertgen tot Sint Jans und die holländische Malerei des XV. Jahrhunderts' in *Jahrbuch der Kunsthistorischen Sammlungen in Wien*, XXXV, p. 1–33.

— 1919 B, 'Mabuses "Heilige Nacht" eine freie Kopie nach Hugo van der Goes' in *Jahrbuch der Kunsthistorischen Sammlungen in Wien*, XXXV, p. 34–48.

— 1922, 'Geertgen van Haarlem', (*Kunst in Holland*, V–VI), Vienna.

— 1926 'Betrachtungen zum Werke des Hieronimus Bosch', in *Jahrbuch der Kunsthistorischen Sammlungen in Wien*, N. F., I, p. 103–118.

— 1927 'Die Niederländer des 15. und 16. Jahrhunderts auf der Ausstellung flämischer Kunst in London', in *Belvedere*, XI, p. 80–85.

— 1928, 'Niederländische Bildegedanken in Werken des älteren Hans Holbein', in *Beiträge zur Geschichte der deutschen Kunst*, II, Augsburg.

— 1932, 'Die Entwicklung des Dirk Bouts: Eine stilgeschichtliche Versuchung', in *Jahrbuch der Kunsthistorischen Sammlungen in Wien*, N. F., VI, p. 77–114.

— 1934, 'Das Ende des Weichens Stiles in der österreichischen Tafelmalerei', in *Pantheon*, XIV, p. 373–381.

— 1936, 'Die früholländische Ausstellung in Rotterdam' in *Pantheon* XVIII p. 232–237.

— 1937, 'Die niederländischen Maler der spätgotisches Stiles', in *Jahrbuch der Kunsthistorischen Sammlungen in Wien*, N.F., XI, p. 117–138.

— 1950, 'The Ghent altarpiece of Hubert and Jan van Eyck', in *The Art Quarterly*, XIII, p. 140–150 and 182–190.

— 1952, *Jan van Eyck*, London.

BALET Leo, 1909, *Der Früholländer Geertgen tot Sint Jans*, The Hague.

BALTIMORE 1962; *The International Style*, Walters Art Gallery.

BALTRUSAITIS Jurgis, 1960, *Réveils et prodiges — Le gothique fantastique*, Paris.

BARCIA A.M., 1911, *Catalogo de las coleccion de pinturas del excmo sr duque de Berwick v de Alva*, Madrid.

BAUCH Kurt, 1962, 'Bildnisse des Jan van Eyck', in *Jahresheft 1961–62 der Heidelberg Akademie der Wissenschaft* (reprinted in K.B., *Studien zur Kunstgeschichte*, Berlin 1967, p. 79–122).

BAUDOUIN Frans, 1958, 'Kanttekeningen bij de catalogus van de Dieric Bouts-Tentoonstelling', in *Bulletin des Musées Royaux des Beaux-Arts*, Brussels, VII, p. 119–140.

BAZIN Germain, 1952, 'Petrus Christus et les rapports entre l'Italie et la Flandre au milieu du XVe siècle', in *Revue des Arts*, II, p. 194–208.

BEENKEN Hermann, 1934, 'Zur Enstehungsgeschichte des Genter Altars Hubert und Jan van Eyck', in *Wallraf Richartz Jahrbuch*, III, p. 176–232.

— 1941, *Hubert und Jan van Eyck*, Munich.

BEETS N., 1911, 'Aawinste Nederlandse Museum', in *Bulletin uitgeg. door den Nederlandse Oudheidkundigen Bond*, p. 243–247.

BEISSEL S., 1904, 'Un livre d'Heures appartenant à S. A. le duc d'Arenberg à Bruxelles; étude iconographique', in *Revue de l'Art chrétien*, 4th series, XV, p. 437–447.

BENESCH Otto, 1925, 'Über einige Handzeichnungen des 15. Jahrhunderts', in *Jahresbuch der Preussischen Kunstsammlungen*, 46, p. 181–190.

— 1928, *Beschreibender Katalog der Handzeichnungen in der graphischen Sammlung Albertina. Die Zeichnungen des niederländischen Schulen des XV. und XVI. Jahrhunderts*, Vienna.

BERESTEYN E. A. van, 1934, *Geschiedenis der Johanniter-Orde in Nederland tot 1792*, (Gorcum's historische Bibliotheek), The Hague.

BERGSTROM I., 1957, 'Medicina, fons et scrinium. A study in van Eyckian symbolism and its influence in italian art', in *Konsthistorisk Tidskrift*, XXVI, p. 1–20.

BERJEAU J., 1860, *Canticum Canticorum, reproduced from the Scriverius copy in the British museum*, London.

BERLIN 1975, *Pieter Bruegel d. A. als Zeichner*, Staatliche Museen.

BERLIN GEMÄLDEGALERIE 1975, *Staatliche Museen Preussischer Kulturbesitz – Berlin – Katalog der ausgestellten Gemälde des 13–18 Jahrhunderts*, Berlin.

BERLIN, KUPFERSTICHKABINETT, 1918, F. LIPPMANN, *Zeichnungen alter Meister im Kupferstichkabinett zu Berlin*, Berlin.

— 1930, E. BOCK, *Die Zeichnungen alter Meister im Kupferstichkabinett zu Berlin*, Berlin.

BERMEJO Elisa, 1955, 'El Cristo muerto' del Maestro de la 'Virgo inter Virgines', in *Archivo español de Arte y Arqueologia*, p. 261–263.

BESANÇON J. (Bouchot-Saupique Jacqueline), 1951, *Les dessins flamands*, Paris.

BIALOSTOCKI Jan, 1968, 'Le gothique tardif: désaccords sur le concept', in *L'Information d'Histoire de l'Art*, 13, p. 106–128.

BLOK P.J., 1884, *Eene hollandsche Stad onder de bourgondisch-oostenrijksche Heerschappij*, The Hague.

— 1892 and 1893, *Geschiedenis van het nederlandsche Volk*, 2 vol., Groningen.

— 1905, *Geschichte des Niederlande*, German translation of the previous work, 2 vol., Gotha.

BODE Wilhelm von, 1880, 'Die Aufweckung des Lazarus von Albert van Ouwater in der königlichen Gemälde Galerie zu Berlin', in *Jahrbuch der Preussischen Kunstsammlungen*, 11, p. 35–41.

BODENHAUSEN E. von, 1905, 'Aus des Werkstatts des Hubert van Eycks', in *Jahrbuch der Preussischen Kunstsammlungen*, XXVI, p. 111–115.

BOIS-LE-DUC, 1913, *National Tentoonstelling van oude kerkelijke Kunst te s'Hertogenbosch*, June–September.

— 1967, *Jheronimus Bosch*, Noordbrabants Museum, 17 September–15 November, catalogue in 2 vol., the 2nd of *Bijdragen* (Steppe, Pirenne, Gerlach, Bax and Schoute).

BONIFACIO Giovanni, 1616, *L'Arte de' Cenni*, Vicentia.

BOON K.G., 1939, 'Geertgen tot Sint Jans. Stimmung und Inhalt seiner Kunst', in *Pantheon*, XXIV, p. 334–340.

— 1940, 'Eenige opmerkingen naar aanleiding van vroege nederlandsche Schilders', in *Oud Holland*, LVII, p. 96–108.

— 1947, *De Erfenis van Aelbert van Ouwater*, in *Nederlandsche Kunsthistorisch Jaarboek*, I, The Hague, p. 33–45.

— 1950, 'Een hollands Altaar van omstreeks 1470', in *Oud Holland*, LXV, p. 207–215.

— 1950–51, 'Naar aanleiding van tekeningen van Hugo van der Goes en zijn school', in *Nederlandsche Kunsthistorisch Jaarboek*, III, The Hague, p. 82–101.

— 1958, 'De eerste bloei van de Noord-Nederlands Kunst', in catalogue *Amsterdam 1958*, p. 16–17 (English translation of prefaces published as off-prints).

— 1961, 'Een Utrechtse Schilder uit de 15 de eeuw, de Meester van de Boom van Jesse in de Buukerk', in *Oud Holland*, LXXVI, p. 51–60.

— 1963, 'De Meester van de Virgo inter Virgines', in *Oud-Delft*, 2, Rotterdam–The Hague, p. 5–35.

— 1964, 'Nieuwe gegevens over de Meester van Katharina van Kleef en zijn atelier', in *Bulletin van de koninklijke Nederlandse oudheidkundige Bond*, 6th series, 17, p. 241–254.

— 1966, 'Geertgen tot Sint Jans of Mostaert', in *Oud Holland*, LXXXI, p. 61–72.

— 1967, 'Geertgen tot Sint Jans', (*Art and Architecture in the Netherlands*), English and Dutch eds., Amsterdam.

— 1968, 'Werk van een vroege Goudse of Leidse schilder in het Rijksmuseum', in *Bulletin van het Rijksmuseum*, 16, p. 3–12.

— 1968 B, 'De Schilder van de triptiek in de Disputacion Provincial te Avila', in *Miscellanea Josef Duverger*, Ghent, p. 110–124.

BORENIUS T., 1929, 'Die holländische Ausstellung in London', in *Pantheon*, III, p. 134–137.

BOUCHOT Henri, 1904, *Les Primitifs français, 1292–1500*, (Suppl. documentation for official exhibition catalogue), Paris.

— 1905, *L'exposition des Primitifs français: La peinture en France sous les Valois*, Paris (n.d.).

BOUVY D.P.R.A., 1947, *Middeleeuwsche Beeldhouwkunst in de Noordelijke Nederlanden*, Amsterdam.

BRIÈRE Gaston, 1919, 'Un nouveau primitif français au musée du Louvre', in *Gazette des Beaux-Arts*, 4th period, XV, p. 232–244.

BRUCK Robert, 1903, 'Friedrich der Weise als Forderer der Kunst', in *Studien zur Deutschen Kunstgeschichte*, 45, Strasbourg.

BRUGES 1867, *Gilde de St-Thomas et St. Luc. Tableaux de l'ancienne école néerlandaise exposés à Bruges dans la grande salle des Halles*, (cat. de Weale).

— 1902, *Exposition des Primitifs flamands et d'art ancien*, 15 June–15 September, catalogue prefaced by W. H. J. Weale.

— 1956, *L'Art flamand dans les collections britanniques*, Museum of Groningen, August–September.

— 1958, *L'Art flamand dans les collections espagnoles*, Museum of Groningen, July–August.

— 1960, *Le siècle des Primitifs flamands*, Museum of Groningen, 26 June–11 September.

BRUSSELS 1935, *Exposition universelle et industrielle – Cinq siècles d'art*.

— 1937–38, *Dessins hollandais de Jérôme Bosch à Rembrandt*.

— 1946, *La peinture hollandaise de Jérôme Bosch à Rembrandt*, Palais des Beaux-Arts.

— 1950, *Chefs-d'œuvre des musées de Berlin*, Palais des Beaux-Arts, 27 September–27 December.

— 1951, *Le siècle de Bourgogne*, Palais des Beaux-Arts, 13 October–16 December.

— 1958, *Rijkdom van de Koninklijke Bibliotheek van Belgie*.

— 1959, *La miniature flamande — Le mécénat de Philippe le Bon*, Palais des Beaux-Arts, April-June, catalogue by L. M. J. Delaissé.

— 1977, *Mémoriaux d'Antoine Succa* (cat. de Micheline Comblen-Sonkes et Christiane van den Bergen-Pantens), Bibliothèque royale Albert Ier.

BRUSSELS and DELFT 1957–58, *Dieric Bouts*, catalogue by Frans Baudouin (paintings), K. G. Boon (drawings).

BRUYN Josua, 1963, 'Vrederick Hoon anno 1465 – Een Haarlemse primitief in effigie in het Rijksmuseum', in *Bulletin van het Rijksmuseum*, XI, p. 31–38.

— 1966, 'De Abdij van Egmond als opdrachtgeefster van kunstwerken in het begin van de zestiende eeuw', in *Oud Holland*. LXXXI, p. 145–172 and 197–227.

BRUYN Josua and MILLAR Oliver, 1962, 'Notes on the Royal Collection, III: the "Dutch Gift" to Charles I' in *The Burlington Magazine*, CIV, p. 291–294.

BUDAPEST MUSEUM DER BILDENDEN KUNSTE, 1968, *Katalog der Galerie, Alter Meister*, by A. Pigler, Tübingen.

BÜRGER Willy, 1869, 'Nouvelles études sur la galerie Suermondt à Aix-la-Chapelle', in *Gazette des Beaux-Arts*, 2nd per., XI, p. 5–37.

— 1925, *Die Malerei in den Niederlanden, 1400–1500*, Munich.

BURCKARDT Jacob, 1898, *Der Cicerone*, 7th rev. ed. by Wilhelm Bode, Leipzig, 3 vol.

BURROUGHS Alan, 1938, *Art Criticism from a Laboratory*, Boston.

BUSCH Harold, 1939, 'Das Triptychon in Djursdala; Probleme zwischen Lübeck und Köln; Neues, über dem Meister des Bartholomäus-Altars', in *Konsthistorisk Tidskrift*, 8, p. 33–47.

— 1943, *Meister des Nordens. Die altniederdeutsche Malerei 1450 bis 1520*, Hamburg.

BYVANCK A. W., 1923, 'Utrechtse miniaturen', in *Het Gildeboek*, VI, p. 106–117.

— 1930, 'Aanteekeningen over handschriften met miniaturen', in *Oudheidkundig Jaarboek*, X, p. 93–139.

— 1931, 'La miniature dans les anciens Pays-Bas pendant la première moitié du XVe siècle, in *Mélanges Hulin de Loo*, Brussels, p. 74–80.

— 1937, *La miniature dans les Pays-Bas septentrionaux*, Paris (Dutch ed., *De middeleeuwsche Boekillustratie in de Noordelijke Nederlanden*, Antwerp, 1943).

— 1953, 'Noord-nederlandse Miniaturen', in *Bulletin van de Koninklijke Nederlandse oudheidkundige Bond*, 6, p. 40–43.

BYVANCK A. W. and HOOGEWERFF G. J., 1926, *La miniature hollandaise dans les manuscrits des 14e, 15e et 16e siècles*, The Hague. 1 vol. (text) et 2 vols. (plates).

CAESARIUS ed. STANGE Joseph, 1851, *Dialogus miraculorum*, Cologne.

CALKINS Robert G., 1978, 'Parallels between Incunabula and manuscripts from the circle of the Master of Cleves', in *Oud Holland*, 92, p. 137–160.

— 1979, 'Distribution of Labor: the Illuminators of the Hours of Catherine of Cleves and their Workshop', in *Transactions of the American Philosophical Society*, vol. 69, part. 5.

CANTICUM CANTICORUM, 1921–1922, Facsimile by Marées-Gesellschaft, Berlin.

CAOURSIN, 1496, *Guillelmi Caoursin Rhodiorum Vice cancellariis obsidionis Rhodie Urbis descriptio,* Ulm (Joanne Reger).

CARDERA Y SOLANO D. Valentin, 1877, *Catalogo y descripcion sumaria de retratos antiguos,* Madrid.

CARTER D.G., 1962, 'The Providence Crucifixion: its place and meaning for Dutch fifteenth century Painting', in *Bulletin of Rhode Island School of Design, Museum notes,* May, p. 1–40.

CASTELFRANCHI VEGAS Liana, 1975, 'Il libro d'Ore Bodmer di Michelino da Besozzo e i rapporti tra miniatura francese e miniatura lombarda agli inizi del Quattrocento', in *Etudes d'art français offertes à Charles Sterling,* p. 91–103.

CHAMPEAUX A. de, 1898, 'L'ancienne école de Bourgogne', in *Gazette des Beaux-Arts,* 3rd per., XIX, p. 36–44 and 129–142.

CHASTEL André, 1969, *Le Mythe de la Renaissance, 1420–1520,* (Arts, Idées, Histoire), Geneva.

CHASTELLAIN ed. de KERVYN DE LETTENHOVE, 1863–1866, *Œuvres de Georges Chastellain,* Académie royale de Belgique, Brussels, 8 vol.

CHATELET Albert, 1951, 'A propos des Johannites de Haarlem et du retable peint par Geertgen tot sint Jans', in *L'Architecture monastique,* special edition of *Bulletin des relations artistiques France-Allemagne,* Mayence, May (n.p.).

— 1956, 'Les étapes de l'enluminure des manuscrits dits de Turin et de Milan-Turin', in *La revue des Arts,* 6, p. 199–206.

— 1957, 'Les enluminures eyckiennes des manuscrits de Turin et de Milan-Turin', in *La revue des Arts,* 7, p. 155–164.

— 1960, 'Albert van Ouwater', in *Gazette des Beaux-Arts,* 6th period, LV, p. 65–78.

— 1962, 'A plea for the Master of Moulins', in *The Burlington Magazine,* CIV, p. 517–524.

— 1963, 'Le retable du Parlement de Paris', in *Art de France,* IV, p. 60–69.

— 1965, 'Sur un Jugement dernier de Dieric Bouts', in *Nederlandsch Kunsthistorisch Jaarboek,* 16, p. 17–42.

— 1966, 'Rogier van der Weyden et Jean van Eyck', in *Koninklijk Museum voor Schone Kunsten,* Jaarboek 1966, p. 7–37.

— 1967, 'En guise de postface en 1967', in re-ed. by Comte Paul Durrieu, *Heures de Turin,* Turin.

— 1970, Review by Millard Meiss, 'French Painting in the Time of Jean de Berry' I, 'The late Fourteenth- century and the Patronage of the Duke'; II, 'The Boucicaut Master' in *Revue de l'Art,* 8, p. 81–83.

— 1970 B, 'XVᵉ et XVIIᵉ siècles' in *Chantilly – Musée Condé – Peintures de l'école française* (Inventaire des collections publiques françaises, 16, Institut de France), Paris.

— 1973, 'Geertgen tot sint Jans dessinateur: une proposition', in *Album Amicorum J. B. van Gelder,* The Hague.

— 1974, 'Deux points controversés de la vie de Rogier', in *Rogier van der Weyden en zijn Tijd,* (Koninklijke Academie voor Wetenschappen, Letteren en Schone Kunsten van Belgie, Klasse der Schone Kunsten), p. 37–41.

— 1975, 'Dürer und die Nördlichen Niederlande', in *Anzeiger des Germanischen Nationalmuseum,* p. 52–64.

— 1979, *Les Primitifs septentrionaux – La peinture dans l'Europe septentrionale et la péninsule ibérique au XVᵉ siècle* (Histoire universelle de la peinture), Geneva.

— 1979 B, *Van Eyck* (Collana d'Arte Paola Malipiero 4), Bologna (in Italian).

— 1980, 'Un collaborateur de Jean van Eyck en Italie', in *Mélanges en l'honneur de Mademoiselle S. Sulzberger* (Etudes d'histoire de l'art publiées par l'Institut historique belge de Rome IV), p. 43–60.

CHATELET Albert and THUILLIER Jacques, 1963, *La peinture française – De Fouquet à Poussin,* Geneva.

CHATELET Albert and FAGGIN Giorgio T., 1969, *Tout l'œuvre peint des frères van Eyck,* Paris.

CHICAGO 1933, *A century of Progress Exhibition of Paintings and Sculpture lent from American Collections,* The Art Institute of Chicago.

CLEMEN Otto, 1910, *Canticum Canticorum – Holztafeldruck von c. 1465,* (Zwickauer Facsimiledrucke no. 4), Zwickau.

CLEMEN Paul, 1892, *Die Kunstdenkmäler des Kreises Kleve,* (Die Kunstdenkmäler der Rheinprovinz,* I, 4), Düsseldorf.

CLEVELAND 1936, *Twentieth Anniversary Exhibition of the Cleveland Museum of Art.*

COHEN W., 1914, 'Die Ausstellung frühholländischer Malerei und Plastik in Utrecht', in *Zeitschrift für Bildenden Kunst,* N.F. XXV, p. 25–35.

COLOGNE 1961, *Der Meister des Bartholomäus altares – Der Meister des Aacheneraltares,* Wallraf Richartz Museum, 25 March–28 May, Catalogue with introductions by K.G. Boon, Paul Pieper and Hans Kinsky.

CONWAY William Martin, 1884, *The Woodcutters of the Netherlands in the Fifteenth Century,* Cambridge.

— 1887, *Early Flemish Artists and their Predecessors on the Lower Rhine,* London.

— 1921, *The van Eycks and their Followers,* London.

— 1922, 'Albert van Ouwater', in *The Burlington Magazine,* XL, p. 120.

COO Josef de, 1958, 'De unieke voorstelling van de "Josefhousen" in het weelluik Antwerpen-Baltimore', in *Oud Holland,* LXXIII, p. 186–198.

— 1960, 'De vorstelling met de "Josefhousen" in het weelluik Antwerpen-Baltimore toch niet uniek', in *Oud Holland,* LXXV, p. 222–228.

— 1965, '"In Josephs Hosen Jhesus ghewonden wert", ein Weihnachtsmotiv in Literatur und Kunst', in *Aachener Kunstblätter,* 30, p. 144–184.

— 1965 B, 'L'ancienne collection Micheli au musée Mayer van den Bergh', in *Gazette des Beaux-Arts,* 7th period, II, p. 345–370.

COPENHAGEN ROYAL MUSEUM OF FINE ARTS, 1951, *Catalogue of Old Foreign Paintings.*

CORNETTE A.H., 1947, *De Portretten van Jan van Eyck.*

COX M.L., 1911, 'Inventory of pictures in possession of Alethea countess of Arundel at the time of her death in Amsterdam in 1654', in *The Burlington Magazine,* XIX, p. 282–286 and 323–325.

CROWE J. A. and CAVALCASELLE G. B., 1899, *Storia dell'antica Pittura fiamminga,* notes by Alexandre Pinchart, Florence (Italian trans. and last ed. of *The early Flemish Painters,* London, 1872).

CUST Lionel, 1898, *The Master E. S. and the Ars Moriendi. A chapter on the history of engraving during the XVth century,* Oxford.

CUYPERS P.J.H. and GONNET C.J., 1894, *De St. Bavoverk te Haarlem,* Haarlem.

DAVIES Martin, 1937, National Gallery notes I: 'Netherlandish Primitives: Geertgen tot Sint Jans' in *The Burlington Magazine,* LXX, p. 88–92.

— 1954, *Les Primitifs Flamands, Corpus II; The National Gallery,* Brussels.

DEBONGNIE Pierre, 1954, 'Dévotion moderne', in *Dictionnaire de la Spiritualité,* III, Paris, col. 727–747.

DEHAISNES, 1886, *Documents et extraits divers concernant l'histoire de l'Art dans la Flandre, l'Artois et le Hainaut avant le XVᵉ siècle,* Lille, 2 vol.

DELAISSÉ L.M.J., 1949, 'Le livre d'heures de Mary von Vronenstevn, chef-d'œuvre inconnu d'un atelier d'Utrecht, achevé en 1460', in *Scriptorum,* III 2, p. 230–245.

— 1956, 'Le manuscrit autographe de Thomas à Kempis et "l'Imitation de Jésus-Christ"', Paris, Brussels, Antwerp, Amsterdam, 2 vol.

— 1959, *Miniatures médiévales,* Geneva.

— 1963, 'Remaniements dans quelques manuscrits de Jean de Beryy', in *Gazette des Beaux-Arts,* 6th series, LXII, p. 123–146.

— 1968, *A Century of Dutch Manuscript Illumination,* Berkeley and Los Angeles.

— 1972, 'The Miniatures added in the Low Countries to the Turin-Milan Hours and their political significances', in *Kunsthistorische Forschungen Otto Pächt zu seinem 70. Geburtstag,* Vienna.

DELEN A.J.J., 1924, *Histoire de la gravure dans les anciens Pays-Bas,* Paris.

— 'Wie was de "Meester van Francfort"?' in *Miscellanea Leo van Puyvelde,* Brussels, p. 74–85.

DELISLE Léopold, 1884, 'Les Livres d'Heures du duc de Berry', in *Gazette des Beaux-Arts,* 2nd period, XXXVI, p. 290–291.

DE MONT Pol, 1905, *De paneelschildering in de Nederlanden gedurende de 14., 15. en de eerste helft van de 16. eeuw. Naar aanleiding van de in 1902 te Brugge gehouden tentoonstelling gezeid 'Van Vlaamse Primietieven',* Haarlem.

DEMONTS Louis, 1926, 'Le Maître de la Sainte Famille avec sainte Anne du musée du Louvre', in *Gazette des Beaux-Arts,* LXXVIII, p. 13–20.

DENIS Valentin, 1957, *Thierry Bouts,* (Connaissance des Primitifs flamands, 2), Brussels.

DENUIT Désiré, (S. d.), *Jacqueline de Bavière, princesse infortunée,* Brussels.

DETROIT 1960, *Flanders in the Fifteenth Century: Art and Civilization,* The Detroit Institute of Arts, October–December.

DETROIT, INSTITUTE OF ARTS; 1954, *Catalogue of the Paintings and Sculpture given by Edgar B. Whitcomb and Anna Scripps Whitcomb to the Detroit Institute of Arts,* catalogue by E. P. Richardson, Detroit.

DICTIONNAIRE DE LA SPIRITUALITÉ, *Ascétique et mystique. Doctrine et histoire.* Published under the direction of Marcel Viller, Paris, 1937.

DIJON 1951, *Le Grand Siècle des Ducs de Bourgogne,* Musée des Beaux-Arts.

DIMIER Louis, 1938, 'Les œuvres des écoles des Pays-Bas en France, l'exposition des chefs-d'œuvre de l'art français', in *Oud Holland,* LV, p. 171–174.

DOGSON Campbell, 1899, *Grotesque Alphabet of 1464,* London.

— 1910, 'Two Woodcut Alphabets of the 15th century' in *The Burlington Magazine,* XXVII, p. 362–365.

DOLLEMAN M. Thierry de Bye, 1963, 'Jan Jansz Mostaert, schilder en beroemd Haarlemer', in *Jaarboek van het Centraal Bureau voor Genealogie,* XVII, p. 1–15.

DOLLMAYR Hermann, 1894, 'Hieronymus Bosch und die Darstellung der vier letzten Dinge in der niederländischen Malerei des XV. und XVI. Jahrhunderts', in *Jahrbuch der Kunsthistorischen Sammlungen der allerhöchsten Kaiserhauses,* 19, p. 284–343.

DOLS J. M. F., 1941, *Bibliographie van de Moderne Devotie*, Nijmegen.

DONAT DE CHAPEAUROUGE, 1977, 'Ouwaters Lazaruserweckung als politischer Dokument', in *Pantheon*, 35, p. 108–115.

DRIESSEN Robertus Keuchenius, 1882–1830, *Monumenta Groningana veteris aevi inedita*, Groningen.

DUBBE B., 1970, 'Is Johan van den Mynnesten de "Meester van Zwolle"? Nieuwe gegevens over zijn leven en werk', in *Bulletin van het Rijksmuseum*, 18, p. 55–65.

DUBY Georges, 1966, *Fondements d'un nouvel Humanisme, 1280–1440*, (Arts, Idées, Histoire), Geneva.

DÜLBERG Franz, 1899, *Leydener Malerschule, I Gerardus Leydanus, II Cornelis Engelbrechtsz*, (Inaugural dissertation in the faculty of philosophy), Berlin.

— 1899 B, 'Die Persönnlichkeit des Lucas van Leyden', in *Oud Holland*, XVII, p. 65–83.

— 1903, *Die Frühholländer, 2: Altholländische Gemälde im Erzbischöflichen Museum zu Utrecht*, Haarlem.

— 1907, *Die Frühholländer, 3: In Italien*, Haarlem.

— 1929, *Niederländische Malerei des Spätgotik und Renaissance*, (Handbuch der Kunstwissenschaft), Wildpark-Potsdam.

DÜRER Albrecht, 1956, *Schriftlicher Nachlass*, I, Hans Rupprich (ed.), Berlin.

DÜSSELDORF 1904, *Kunsthistorische Ausstellung*.

DUPONT Jacques, 1937, 'Les peintures de la Chartreuse de Champmol', in *Bulletin de la Société de l'Histoire de l'Art français*, II, p. 155–157.

DURAND GREVILLE E., 1904, 'La peinture hollandaise du XVᵉ siècle; Albert van Ouwater et Gérard de Saint Jean', in *Revue de l'Art ancien et moderne*, XVI, p. 249–267 and 373–390.

— 1906, 'Les Primitifs Flamands à l'exposition du Guildhall', in *Les Arts anciens de Flandre*, II, p. 53–72, 139–152 and 176–197.

— 1910, *Hubert et Jean van Eyck*, Paris.

DURRIEU Comte Paul, 1901, summarized in *Bulletin de la société nationale des Antiquaires de France*, pp. 208–209 and 227–228.

— 1902, *Heures de Turin, quarante-cinq feuillets à peintures provenant des Très Belles Heures de Jean de France, duc de Berry*, Paris (re-ed., Turin, 1967).

— 1903, 'Les débuts des van Eyck', in *Gazette des Beaux-Arts*, 3rd period, XXIX, p. 5–18 and 107–120.

— 1904, *La peinture à l'exposition des Primitifs français*, Paris (off-print of *Revue de l'Art ancien et moderne*, XV, p. 81–97, 161–178, 241–262 and 400–422).

— 1907, 'La peinture en France', in André Michel, *Histoire de l'Art*, I–III, Paris, p. 101–171.

— 1910, 'Les "Très Belles Heures de Notre Dame" du duc Jean de Berry', in *Revue archéologique*, 4th series, XVI, p. 30–51 and 246–279.

— 1910 B, 'Quelques portraits historiques du début du XVᵉ siècle', in *Gazette des Beaux-Arts*, 4th period, III, p. 451–469.

— 1918–1919, 'Une "pitié de nostre Seigneur", tableau français de l'époque du règne de Charles VI, donné au musée du Louvre', in *Monuments Piot*, XXIII, p. 63–111.

— 1920, 'Les van Eyck et le duc Jean de Berry', in *Gazette des Beaux-Arts*, 5th period, I, p. 77–105.

— 1922, *Les Très belles Heures de Notre Dame du duc Jean de Berry*, (Société française de reproductions de manuscrits à peintures), Paris.

DUVERGER J., 1955, 'Brugse Schilders ten tijde van Jan van Eyck', in *Musées royaux des Beaux-Arts, Bulletin*, (Miscellanea Erwin Panofsky), Brussels, p. 83–120.

DVORACK Max, 1904, 'Das Rätsel der Kunst der Brüder van Eyck', in *Jahrbuch der Kunsthistorischen Sammlungen der allerhöchsten Kaiserhauses*, XXIX, p. 161–317.

— 1918, 'Die Anfänge der holländischen Malerei', in *Jahrbuch der königlichen Preussischen Kunstsammlungen*, XXXIX, p. 51–79.

— 1925, re-ed. of 1904 work, followed by 1918 one, 1918, Munich.

DYNTER Edmond de, 1854–1860, *Chroniques des ducs de Brabant*, ed. by P.E.X. de Ram, (Académie royale de Belgique. Collection de documents inédits), Brussels, 3 vol.

EISLER Colin et MEISS Millard, 1960, 'A New French Primitive', in *The Burlington Magazine*, CII, p. 233–240.

ELSEVIER Rammelmar, 1850, article in *Kroniek van het Historisch Genootschap*, VI, Utrecht, p. 82.

— 1852, article in *De Navorscher*, II, Amsterdam, p. 251.

— 1858 'Hugo Jacobsz', in *De Navorscher*, VIII, p. 245–246.

— 1875, 'Schilderijen in olivierw door Jacob Clemensz in het Jerusalemhofje te Leiden', in *De Nederlandsche Spectator*, 22 (29 May), p. 170.

ELSLANDER A. van, 1965, *Den Spyeghel der Salicheyt van Elckerlijc*, Amsterdam.

ENGELBRACHT J. H. A. (O.F.M.), 1963, 'Het glorievolle rozenkransgeheim van Maria's kroning in de hemel door Geertgen tot Sint Jans', in *Album Discipulorum J. G. van Gelder*, Utrecht, p. 31.

EPINEY-BURGARD Georgette, 1970, *Gérard Grote (1340–1384) et les débuts de la Dévotion moderne*, (Veröffentlichungen des Instituts für europäische Geschichte Mains, 54), Wiesbaden.

EVEN Edward van, 1870, *L'ancienne école de peinture de Louvain*, Brussels and Louvain also published as articles in *Messager des Sciences Historiques de Belgique*, Ghent, 1866, p. 1–55, 241–338; 1867, p. 261–315, 439–497; 1868, p. 454–486; 1869, p. 44–86, 147–195 and 277–341.

FASTNEDGE Ralph, 1954, 'A note on the Roscoe collection' (The pictures formerly at the Liverpool Royal Institution) in *Liverpool Bulletin*, 4, p. 23–46.

FAUSSEN L. J. F., 1846, 'Utrecht voorhen en thang', in *Tijdschift voor Geschiedenis, Oudheden en Statistiek te Utrecht*, 2nd series, 3rd year, p. 141–159.

FERGUSON Georges, 1954, *Signs and symbols in Christian art*, New York and Oxford (2nd ed., 1961).

FIERENS-GEVAERT and FIERENS Paul, 1927–1929, *Histoire de la peinture flamande des origines à la fin du XVᵉ siècle*, Paris and Brussels, 3 vol.

FINKE Ulrich, 1963, 'Utrecht, Zentrum nordniederländischer Buchmalerei', in *Oud Holland*, LXXVIII, p. 27–66.

— 1965, 'Anmerkungen zu einem van Eyck-Problem', in *Berliner Museen*, 15, p. 46–49.

FISCHEL Lilli, 1952, *Die Karlsruher Passion und Ihr Meister*, Karlsruhe.

FLORENCE 1947, *Mostra d'arte fiamminga e olandese dei secoli XV e XVI*, Palazzo Strozzi, May-October; catalogue, Florence, 1948.

FOUREZ Lucien, 1949, 'Deux miniatures de Jean van Eyck à l'exposition des Arts religieux de Tournai', in *Savoir et Beauté*, p. 470–474.

FRANCIS Henry S., 1952, 'Two Dutch fifteenth-century panels gift of the Hanna Fund', in *The Bulletin of the Cleveland Museum of Art*, p. 3.

FRIEDL Antonin (n.d.), 1948, *Master Theodoricus; On his style of painting*, Prague.

FRIEDLÄNDER Max J., *Die Altniederländische Malerei*, Berlin, in Leiden, 14 vol., 1924–1937: mentioned as Friedländer followed by a volume number, the following are quoted extensively.

  1. *Die van Eyck, Petrus Christus*, 1924.
  2. *Rogier van der Weyden und der Meister van Flémalle*, 1924.
  3. *Dieric Bouts und Joos van Gent*, 1925.
  4. *Hugo van der Goes*, 1926.
  5. *Geertgen van Haarlem und Hieronymus Bosch*, 1927.
  6. *Memling and Gérard David*, 1928.
  14. *Pieter Bruegel und Nachträge*, 1937.

'FRIEDLÄNDER (a)' Max J. FRIEDLÄNDER, *Early Netherlandish Painting*, Leiden and Brussels: translation of the preceding volumes (by Heinz Norden), with, for the first 6 volumes, comments and notes by Nicole Veronese-Verhaegen. Dates of publication: 1, 1967; 2, 1967; 3, 1968; 4, 1969; 5, 1970; 6A and B, 1971.

— 1903, 'Geertgen tot Sint Jans', in *Jahrbuch der königlichen preussischen Kunstsammlungen*, XXIV, p. 62–70.

— 1903 B, 'Die Brügger Leihausstellung von 1902', in *Repertorium für Kunstwissenschaft*, 26, p. 66–91 and 147–175.

— 1906, 'Die Verzameling von Kaufmann te Berlijn', in *Onze Kunst*, X, p. 29–41.

— 1906 B, 'Die Leihausstellung in der Guildhall zu London. Sommer 1906–Hauptsächlich niederländische Bilder des 15. und 16. Jahrhunderts', in *Repertorium für Kunstwissenschaft*, XXIX, p. 573–582.

— 1906–1907, 'Compte rendu de l'ouvrage de Franz Dülberg, Frühholländer in Italien', in *Zeitschrift für Bildende Kunst*, N.F. 18, p. 79–80.

— 1910, 'Die Meister der Virgo inter Virgines', in *Jahrbuch der königlichen preussischen Kunstsammlungen*, XXI, p. 64–72.

— 1916, *Von Eyck bis Bruegel*, Berlin (2nd ed. 1921; Fr. trans., *De Van Eyck à Breughel*, Paris, 1964).

— 1923, 'A painting by Geertgen tot Sint Jans', in *The Burlington Magazine*, XLIII, p. 103.

— 1925, 'Neues über Petrus Christus', in *Kunstwanderer*, VI, p. 297–298.

— 1926, *Die Kunstsammlung von Pannwitz, I, Gemälde*, Munich.

— 1926–1927, 'Neues über den Meister des Bartholomäus-Altars', in *Wallraf Richarz Jahrbuch*, 3–4, p. 174–182.

— 1927–1928, 'Drei niederländische Maler in Genua', in *Zeitschrift für Bildende Kunst*, LXI, p. 273–279.

— 1935, 'Eine Zeichnung von Hugo van der Goes', in *Pantheon*, XV, p. 99–104.

— 1949, 'Zu Geertgen tot Sint Jans', in *Maanblad voor beeldende Kunsten*, p. 186–188.

— 1950, 'Eine bisher unbekannte Epiphanie van Geertgen', in *Maanblad voor beeldende Kunsten*, p. 10–12.

FRIES Albert, 1956, 'Anna Selbdritt samt Sippe auf einem Tafelbild des Braunschweiger Diptychons', in *Das Münster*, p. 23–28.

FRIMMEL Theodor von, 1888, *Der Anonimo Morelliano* (Marcanton Michel's Notizia d'opere del disegno), (Quellenschriften für Kunstgeschichte und Kunsttechnik des Mittelalters und der Neuzeit, N.F.I.), Leipzig (The volume of comments planned was never published.)

— 1896, 'Gemälde in der Sammlung Albert Figdor', in *Kleine Galeriestudien*, N.F.IV, p. 9–14.

GALICHON Emile, 1867, 'Exposition de tableaux primitifs à Bruges', in *Gazette des Beaux Arts*, XXIII, p. 481–488.

GALLEGO Y BURIN Antonio, 1931, *La Capilla Real de Granada* (Madrid [2nd ed.] 1952).

GAMBA Carlo, 1916, 'La Ca' d'Oro e la collezione Franchetti' in *Bolletino d'Arte*, p. 321–334.

GAND, 1913, *Wereldtentoonstelling. Oude Kunst in Vlaanderen*.

GARAS Klara, 1954, 'Some problems of early Dutch and Flemish painting', in *Acta historiae Artium*, I, p. 237–262.

GAUFFRETEAU-SEVY M., 1965, *Jérôme Bosch*, Paris.

GAVELLE Emile, 1923, 'Gérard de Saint Jean et deux miniatures flamandes', in *Revue du Nord*, IX, p. 281–286.

GEISBERG Max, 1903, *Der Meister der Berliner Passion und Israhel van Meckenem*, Strasbourg.

— 1925, *Der Meister E. S.*, (Meister der Graphik, X), Leipzig.

GELDER H.E. van, 1936, *Kunstgeschiedenis der Nederlanden* with the assistance of N. Beets, G. Brom and A.W. Bijvanck, Utrecht (2nd ed., 1946).

GELDER J.G., 1951, 'Fiamminghi e Italia' at Bruges, Venice and Rome', in *The Burlington Magazine*, XCIII, p. 324–327.

— 1951 B, 'Het zogenaamde portret van Dieric Bouts op het "Werc van den Heilichen Sacrament"', in *Oud Holland*, LXVI, p. 51–52.

— 1972, 'Der Teufel stiehlt das Tintenfass', in *Kunsthistorische Forschungen Otto Pächt zu seinem Geburtstag*, Vienna, p. 173–182.

GERLACH, O.F.M., C.A.P., 1968, 'Les sources pour l'étude de la vie de Jérôme Bosch', in *Gazette des Beaux-Arts*, 6th period, LXXI, p. 109–116.

GERSON Horst, 1936, 'Hieronymus Bosch and the North-Netherlandish Primitives', in *The Burlington Magazine*, 69, p. 136–137.

— 1950, *Van Geertgen tot Frans Hals*, (De Schoonheid van ons Land – De Nederlandse Schilderkunst, I), Amsterdam.

GERSTENBERG Kurt, 1936, 'Über ein verschollenes Gemälde von Ouwater', in *Zeitschrift für Kunstgeschichte*, V, p. 133–138.

GESAMTKATALOG DER WIEGENDRUCKE, herausgegeben von der Kommission für den Gesamtkatalog der Wiegendrucke, Leipzig 1925 (Vols I-VIII published).

GLÜCK Gustav, 1931, 'Ein Gemälde des Meisters der Tiburnischen Sibylle', in *Mélanges Hulin de Loo*, Brussels, p. 193–196.

GOFFIN Arnold, 1907, *Thierry Bouts*, Brussels.

GOLDSCHMIDT Adolph, 1902, 'Gemälde des XIV. bis XVI. Jahrhunderts aus der sammlung von Richard von Kaufmann', in *Zeitschrift für bildende Kunst*, N.F. 13, p. 239–242.

— 1915, 'Der Monforte-Altar des Hugo van der Goes', in *Zeitschrift für bildende Kunst*, N.F. XXVI, p. 221–230.

GOMEZ Moreno, 1908, 'Un trésor de peintures inédites du XVe siècle', in *Gazette des Beaux-Arts*, 3rd period, XI. p. 289–314.

GORISSEN Friedrich, 1953, *Kranenburg, ein Heiligtum des Niederrheins*. Kranenburg.

— 1954, 'Jan Maelwael und die Brüder Limbourg. Eine nimweger Künstlerfamilie um die Wende des 14. Jhs', in *Gelre*, LIV, p. 153–221.

— 1957, 'Jan Maelweal, die Brüder Limbourg und der Herold Gelre. Nachträge und Berichtungen', in *Gelre*, LVI, p. 166–178.

— 1958, 'Historisch-Heraldisch Betrachtungen über ein Studenbuch der Katharina von Kleve, Herzogin van Geldern', in *Gelre*, LVII, p. 200–218.

— 1961, 'Der Kelch der Katharina von Kleve. Eine Untersuchung über das Schicksal der Burg Lobith und ihrer Schlosskapelle', in *Gelre*, LX, p. 143.

— 1963, 'Der klevische Ritterorden vom heiligen Antonius', in *Kalender für das Klever Land*, p. 29–49.

— 1965, 'Das Stundenbuch der Katharina von Kleve. Ein Beitrag zu seiner Datierung', in *Bulletin van de koninklijke nederlandsche Oudheidkundige Bond*, 6th series 18, p. 1–7.

— 1967, *Das Stundenbuch der Katharina von Kleve*, Städtisches Museum Haus Koekkoek, Cléves.

— 1973, *Das Stundenbuch der Katharina von Kleve – Analyse und Kommentar*, Berlin.

GOTTLIEB Carla, 1977, 'Disguised symbolism in the Gulbenkian "Annunciation"', in *Coloquio Artes*, 32, p. 24–33.

GRATAMA G.D., 1915, 'Tentoonstelling van oude Kunst uit het bezit van Bewoners van Haarlem en omstreken', in *Oude Kunst*, XXVIII, p. 69–91.

— 1933, 'De "Maquette" van de S. Bavo te Haarlem', in *Oud Holland*, L, p. 218–219.

GRISEBACH A., 1912, 'Architecturen auf niederländischen und französischen

Gemälde des XV. Jahrhunderts', in *Monatshefte für Kunstwissenschaft*, V, p. 207–215 and 254–772.

GRUBE K., 1886, *Des Augustinerpropstes Johannes Busch Chronicon Windeshemse und Liber de reformatione monasteriorun* (Geschichtsquellen der Provinz Sachsen und angrenzender Gebiete, XIX), Halle.

GUICCIARDINI Lodovico, 1567, *Descrittione di tutti i paesi bassi altrimenti detti Germania inferiore*, Antwerp (G. Silvio).

— 1613, *Description de tous les Pays-Bas, autrement appelés la Germanie inférieure ou Basse Allemagne, par messire Loys Guicciardin, maintenant revue par le mesme autheur... derechef illustrée par plusieurs annotations remarquables par Pierre du Mont*, Arnhem (J. Jansz).

HAARLEM 1915, *Oude Kunst uit het bezit van Bewoners van Haarlem en omstreken*, Frans Hals museum.

THE HAGUE 1945, *Nederlandsche Kunst van de XVde ende XVIde eeeuw*, Mauritshuis.

— 1950, *Het nederlandse Boek, 1300–1800*, Gementemuseum.

— 1965, *Rondom de Meester van Catharina van Cleef*, Musée Meermanno-Westreenianum, 21 January–27 February, catalogue by P.J.H. Vermeeren, 1966, *In the Light of Vermeer*, Mauritshuis, 25 June–5 September.

HALL Edwin C., 1968, 'Cardinal Albergati, St. Jerome and the Detroit van Eyck', in *The Art Quarterly*, XXXI, p. 3–34.

— 1971, 'More about the Detroit van Eyck: the astrolabe, the congress of Arras and the Cardinal Albergati', in *The Art Quarterly*, XXXIV, p. 181–196.

HAMBURG 1969, *Meister Francke und die Kunst um 1400*. Kunsthalle 30 August–19 October, catalogue by Alfred Hentzen, with studies by Jürgen Bolland, Hans Werner Grohn, Otto Pächt, Peter Strieder, Paul Pieper and L.M.J. Delaissé.

HANNEMA D., 1937, 'De Meester van het Johannes Altaar, in *Bulletin Museum Boymans, Rotterdam*, I, p. 3–4.

HASELOFF Arthur, 1903, 'Die Vorläufer der van Eyck in der Buchmalerei', in *Sitzungsberichte der Kunstgeschichtliche Gesellschaft*, I, p. 1–6.

HASLINGUIS E.J. and PEETERS C.J.A., 1965, *De Dom van Utrecht*, (De Nederlandse Monumenten van Geschiedenis en Kunst; II, De Provincie Utrecht, 2), The Hague.

HAVERKAMP BEGEMANN E., 1951, 'Een noord-nederlandse Primitief', in *Bulletin Museum Boymans Rotterdam*, II, p. 51–57.

— 1953, 'Een Aanwinst bij een Aanwinst', in *Bulletin Museum Boymans Rotterdam*, IV, p. 9–11.

HEILAND Paul, 1908, *Dirk Bouts und die Hauptwerke seiner Schule. Ein stilkritischer Versuch*, Potsdam.

HEINS, 1906, 'Essai d'identifications de vues de villes dans les miniatures de Turin attribuées aux van Eyck', in *Bulletin van den geschieden oudheidkundigen Kring van Gent*, XIV, p. 246–250.

HEINZ Günther, 1960, 'Das Bild der Verkündigung vom Meister der Virgo inter Virgines im salzburger Museum Carolino Augusteum, in *Salzburger Museum Carolino Augusteum-Jahresschrift*, p. 51–62.

HELD Julius S., 1955, 'Review of Erwin Panofsky, *Early Netherlandish Painting*', Princeton, 1953, in *The Art Bulletin*, 37, p. 205–234.

HENKELL O.D., 1926, 'Review of M.J. Schretlen, *Dutch and Flemish Woodcuts of the fifteenth century*, in *Oud Holland*, XLIII, p. 80–90.

HILDESHEIM Johannes von, 1963, 'Die Legende von den Heiligen Drei Königen', trans. by Elisabeth Christern, Munich.

HIND Arthur M., 1935, *An introduction to a History of Woodcut*, New York, 2 vol. (paperback, New York, 1953).

HOFFMANN D.M., 1950, 'Our Lady of the Sanctus', in *Liturgical Arts*, 18 p. 43–45.

HOLLSTEIN F.W.H. (s.d.) *Dutch and Flemish Etchings, Engravings and Woodcuts, XII – Masters and Monogrammists of the 15th century*, Amsterdam.

HOLTROP J.W., 1868, *Monuments typographiques des Pays-Bas au XVe siècle*, The Hague.

HOOGEWERFF G.J., 1935, *Vlaamsche Kunst en Italiaansche Renaissance*, Malines-Amsterdam.

— 1936 et 1937, *De Noord-Nederlandsche Schilderkunst*, vol. I and II, The Hague.

— 1961, 'Gelderse Miniatuurschilders in de eerste helft van de XVe eeuw', in *Out Holland*, LXXVI, p. 3–49.

HOTZ Walter, 1953, 'Der "Hausbuchmeister" Nikolaus Nievergalt und sein Kreis'', in *Der Wormsgau*, III, p. 97–125.

— 1956, 'Nicolaus Nievergalt von Worms in der spätgotischen Malerei. Neue Beiträge zur Hausbuchmeisterfrage', in *Der Wormsgau*, III, p. 306–316.

HOUSTON 1952, *Masterpieces of painting through six centuries*, Allied Art Association.

HUIJBEN Jacques and DEBONGNIE Pierre, 1957, *L'auteur ou les auteurs de l'Imitation*, (Bibliothèque de la revue ecclésiastique, 30), Louvain.

HUIZINGA Johann, 1905–1906, 'De opkomst van Haarlem', dans *Bijdragen voor Vaderlansche Geschiedenis en Oudheidkunde,* 4th series, IV, p. 412–446 and V, p. 16–175.

— 1919, *Herfsttij der Middeleeuwen. Studie over levens-en gedachten-vormen der veertiende en vijftiende eeuw in Frankrijk en de Nederlanden.* Haarlem, (quoted from French ed. *Le déclin du Moyen Age,* Paris, 1948).

— 1930–1931, 'L'Etat bourguignon. Ses rapports avec la France et les origines d'une nationalité néerlandaise', in *Le Moyen Age,* XL, p. 171–194 et XLI, p. 11–35 and 83–96.

HULIN DE LOO Georges, 1902, *Bruges 1902. Exposition de tableaux flamands des XIVᵉ, XVᵉ et XVIᵉ siècles. Catalogue critique.* Ghent.

— 1902 B, 'L'atelier de Hubrecht van Eyck et les Heures de Turin', in *Annuaire de la société pour le progrès des études philologiques et historiques,* p. 69–74.

— 1911, *Les Heures de Milan,* Paris-Brussels.

— 1911 B, 'A propos de "Quelques portraits historiques du XVᵉ siècle"', in *Bulletin van geschied-en oudheidkundigen Kring van Gent,* p. 39–53.

— 1926, 'Sur la biographie de Dieric Bouts avant 1457', in *Mélanges d'Histoires offerts à Henri Pirenne,* Brussels-Paris, p. 257–262.

— 1932, 'Les voyages des frères van Eyck avant 1425', in *Bulletin de la classe des Beaux-Arts de L'Académie de Belgique,* XIV, p. 123–134.

— 1943–44, 'Traces de Hubert van Eyck. Empreintes contemporaines en Suisse et en Allemagne', in *Annuaire des Musées Royaux des Beaux-Arts de Belgique,* 14, p. 3.

HYMA Albert, 1924, *The Christian Renaissance. A history of the 'Devotio Moderna',* Grand Rapids, Mich.

HYMANS Henry, 1883, 'Un tableau retrouvé de Jean van Eyck', in *Bulletin des Commissions royales d'Art et d'Archéologie,* XXII, p. 108–116.

— 1888, 'Le St François d'Assise de Jean van Eyck', in *Gazette des Beaux-Arts,* 2nd period, XXXVII, p. 78–83.

JACOBSEN Emil, 1897, 'La Regia Pinacoteca di Torino', in *Archivio Storico dell'Arte,* 2nd series, III, p. 206–221.

JOHANNSEN, 1932, 'Un compagnon d'atelier de van Eyck', in *Revue belge d'Art et d'Archéologie,* II, p. 325–329.

JONGH Jacobus de, 1764, *Het leven der doorluchtige Nederl. en eenige Hoogd. schilders... door Karel van Mander... en vollediger gemaakt,* Amsterdam, 2 vol.

JONGH Johanna de, 1903, *Het hollandsche Landschap in ontaan en wording,* The Hague.

KAEMMERER L., 1898, *Hubert und Jan van Eyck,* Bielefeld.

KALCKEN Gustaaf van, 1914, *Peintures ecclésiastiques du Moyen Age. Troisième partie: église Ste Walburge de Zutphen,* Haarlem and The Hague.

KATZENELLENBOGEN A., 1949, 'The mission of the Apostles', in *Gazette des Beaux-Arts,* 6th series, XXXV, p. 81–98.

KELLEN van der Jr., 1861, *Muurschilderingen in de Groote- of St. Bavo's-kerk te Haarlem,* The Hague.

KELLER Karl, 1969, *Zwei Stundenbücher* (Veröffentlichung des historischen Vereins für Geldern und Umgegend, no. 68), Geldern.

KEMPIS Thomas à, 1858–1861, *Œuvres spirituelles,* trans. from Latin by P. P. M. B. Saintyves, Paris, 8 vol.

KERBER Ottmar, 1937, *Hubert van Eyck – Die Verwandlung der mittelalterlichen in die neuzeitliche Gestaltung,* Frankfurt.

— 1968, 'Hubert van Eyck "Anbetung der Könige"', in *Amici Amico – Festschrift für Werner Gross zu seinem 65. Geburtstag,* Munich, p. 138–153.

— 1972, 'Die Hubertus-Tafeln von Rogier van der Weyden', in *Pantheon,* 30, p. 292–299.

KERN G. J., 1926–1927, 'Die verschollene Kreuztragung des Hubert oder Jan van Eyck', in *Kunstwanderer,* VIII, p. 309–312, 357–362 and 415–420 (also published, Berlin, 1927).

KESSLER J. J. H., 1930, *Geertgen tot Sint Jans, zijne herkomst, en invloed in Holland,* Utrecht.

— 1933, 'De "Maquette" van de S. Bavo te Haarlem', in *Oud Holland,* L. p. 71–76.

KLAVEREN G. van Pzn., 1935, 'Utrechtse Schrijvers en Verlichters', in *Maanblad van Oud-Utrecht,* X, p.35.

KOCH Robert, 1951, 'Geertgen tot Sint Jans in Bruges' in *The Art Bulletin,* XXXIII, p. 259–260.

— 1977, 'New criteria for dating Netherlandish Biblia Pauperum Blockbook', in *Studies in late medieval and renaissance painting in honour of Millard Meiss,* Princeton, p. 283–286.

KRAMM Christiaan, 1857–1861, *De Levens en Werken der hollandsche en vlaamsche Kunstschilders, Beeldhouwers, Graveurs en Bouwmeesters van den vroegsten tot op onzen tijd,* Amsterdam, 3 vol.

KRÖNIG J.O., 1909, 'Trois primitifs néerlandais de la collection du comte de Valencia de San Juan', in *Les Arts,* 87, p. 2–6.

KRÖNIG W., 1950, 'Geertgens Bild Johannes des Täufers', in *Das Münster,* III, p. 193–206.

KUNZE Irene, 1939, 'Neuerwerbungen niederländischen Gemälde', in *Berliner Museen,* p. 8–13.

KURZ Otto, 1956, 'A Fishing Party at the Court of William VI Count of Holland, Zeeland and Hainaut', in *Oud Holland,* LXXI, p. 117–131.

LACLOTTE Michel, 1961, 'Peinture en Bourgogne au XVᵉ siècle', in *Art de France,* I, p. 287–288.

LAMPSON Dominique, 1956, *Les effigies des peintres célèbres des Pays-Bas. Edition critique de Jean Puraye,* Paris.

LAMPSONIUS Dominicus, 1572, *Pictorum aliquot celebrium Germaniae inferiorae effigies. Una cum doctiss. Dom. Lampsonii hujus artis peritissimi Elogiis,* Antwerp (H. Cock).

LANDELIN-HOFFMANS P.O.M.C., 1948, *Un Rogier van der Weyden inconnu?* Enghien.

LANE John, 1908, 'Review by W. H. J. Weale, 'Hubert and Jan van Eyck, Their Life and Work', in *The Athenaeum,* 4199, p. 484–486.

LANE Barbara G., 1973, 'The "Symbolic" Crucifixion in the Hours of Catherine de Clèves', in *Oud Holland,* p. 4–26.

— 1973 B, 'An immaculist cycle in the Hours of Catherine de Clèves', in *Oud Holland,* p. 177–204.

LAREN 1961, *Nederlandse Primitieven uit nederlands particulier Bezit,* Singer Museum, 1 July–10 September.

— 1966, *Het Kunst van het Verzamelen. Kuize uit twee nederlandse Collecties,* Singer Museum, 18 June–18 September.

LASSAIGNE Jacques, 1957, *La peinture flamande. Le siècle des van Eyck,* Geneva.

LAVALLEYE Jacques, 1936, *Juste de Gand, peintre de Frédéric de Montefeltre,* Louvain.

— 1947, 'La peinture et l'enluminure des origines à la fin du XVᵉ siècle', in *L'Art en Belgique,* under the direction of Paul Fierens, Brussels, p. 91–151.

LEEUWENBERG Jaap, 1948, 'Het werk van den Meester der Musiceerende Engelen en het vraagstuk van Jacob van der Borch opnieuw beschwoud', in *Oud Holland,* LXIII, p. 164–179.

— 1950, 'Een werk van den Virgomeister en zijn copien', in *Oud Holland,* LXV, p. 117–119.

— 1967, 'Vier onbekende norrdnerderlandse beeldhouwerken', in *Bulletin van het Rijksmuseum,* XV, p. 54–63.

LÉGENDE DORÉE, 1967, Jacques de Voragine, *La Légende dorée,* trans. by J. B. M. Roze, 2 vol., Paris.

LEHMANN-HAUPT Hellmut, 1966, *Gutenberg and the Master of the Playing Cards,* New Haven and London.

LEHRS Max, 1890, 'Der Künstler der Ars Moriendi und die wahre erste Ausgabe derselben', in *Jahrbuch der königlichen preussischen Kunstsammlungen,* XI, p. 161–168.

— 1908–1934, *Geschichte und kritisches Katalog des deutschen, niederländischen und französischen Kupferstiche im XV. Jahrhunderts,* Vienna, 9 vol., quoted as Lehrs.

LEJEUNE Jean, 1968, 'Les van Eyck et le premier paysage luxembourgeois', in *Revue belge d'archéologie et d'histoire de l'Art,* XXXVII, p. 137–191.

LEMOISNE Paul-André, 1929, 'XIVᵉ, XVᵉ, XVIᵉ siècles', in *La peinture au musée du Louvre,* I, Ecole française, Paris.

— 1931, *La peinture en France à l'époque gothique,* Paris and Florence.

LEURS S., 'Het Koor van de Sint-Donatiukerk te Brugge geschilderd door Jan van Eyck en Albert van Ouwater', in *Gentse Bijdragen tot de Kunstgeschiedenis,* XV, p. 211–221.

LIEFTINCK G. I., 1959, 'Windesheim, Agnietenberg en Marienborn en hun Aandeelin de Noordnerderlandse Boekverluchting', in *Dancwerc opstellen aangeboden aan Prof. Dr. Th. Enklaar,* Groningen, 1959, p. 188–207.

LIJTENBERG R. O. F. M., 1929, 'De genealogie van Christus', in *Oudheidkundige Jaarboek,* IX, p. 2–54.

LIPPMANN F., 1898, *Le Chevalier Déliberé by Olivier de La Marche,* (Illustrated Monographs issued by the Bibliographical Society, V), London.

LÖHER Franz von, 1869, *Jakobäa von Bayern und ihre Zeit,* Nördlingen, 2 vol.

LOENEN Jacques Cornelis van, 1950, *De Haarlemse Brouwerindustrie voor 1600,* (Thesis), Amsterdam. 'Antonio da Ancona', in *Arte veneta,* I, p. 185–186.

LONDON 1858, *Ancient Masters,* British Institution.

— 1865, Exhibition at the British Institution.

— 1886, *Old Masters,* Burlington House.

— 1906, *Netherlandish Masters,* Guildhall.

— 1927, *Exhibition of Flemish and Belgian Art, 1300–1900,* Royal Academy of Arts.

— 1929, *Exhibition of Dutch Art,* Royal Academy of Arts.

— 1932, *Exhibition of French Art 1200–1900,* Royal Academy of Arts.

— 1952, *Dutch Pictures, 1450–1750,* Royal Academy of Arts.

— 1953–1954, *Flemish Art, 1300–1700*, Royal Academy of Arts, Winter exhibition (catalogue by M. W. Brockwell).

LONDON, NATIONAL GALLERY, 1955, *Early Netherlandish School*, 2nd ed. by Martin Davies.

LONGHI Roberto, 1945, 'Calepino veneziano VI: Gli Inizi di Nicola di Maestro.

LOUVAIN, 1975; *Dirk Bouts en zijn Tijd*, Eglise Saint-Pierre.

LUDOLPH THE CARTHUSIAN, 1891, *La Grande vie de Jésus-Christ*, completely new trans. by Dom Florent Broquin, Paris, 6 vol.

LUGT Frits, 1968, *Musée du Louvre — Inventaire général des dessins des écoles du Nord — Maîtres des anciens Pays-Bas nés avant 1550*, Paris.

LUTTERVELT R. van, 1951, 'Schilderijen met Karthuizers uit de late 15de en de vroege 16de eeuw', in *Oud Holland*, LXVI, p. 75–92.

— 1952; 'De Herkomst van de Meester van de Virgo inter Virgines', in *Bulletin Museum Boymans*, III, p. 57–71.

— 1957, 'Bijdragen tot de Iconographie van de Graven van Holland naar aaleiding van de beelden uit de Amsterdamsche vierschaar, II: Een Beiers-Hollandse familiegroep', in *Oud Holland*, LXXII, p. 139–149.

LYNA Frédéric, 1933, *De Vlaamsche miniatuur van 1200 tot 1530*, Brussels and Amsterdam.

— 1946–1947, 'Les miniatures d'un mss du "Ci Nous dit" et le réalisme preeyckien', in *Scriptorium*, I, p. 106–118.

— 1955, 'Les van Eyck et les "Heures de Turin et de Milan"', in *Musées Royaux des Beaux-Arts — Bulletin*, (Miscellanea Erwin Panofsky), 1–3, p. 7–20.

— 1961, 'Elisabeth de Görlitz et les "Heures de Turin et de Milan"', in *Scriptorium*, 15, p. 121–125.

— 1962; 'L'œuvre présumé de Jean van Eyck et son influence sur la miniature flamande', in *Scriptorium*, 16, p. 93–94.

MAETERLINCK, 1913, *Une école primitive méconnue. Nabur Martins ou le Maître de Flémalle (Nouveaux documents)*, Brussels and Paris.

— 1925, *Une école préeckienne inconnue*, Brussels.

MÂLE Emile, 1905, *L'art religieux de la fin du Moyen Age en France*, Paris.

— 1958, *Les saints Compagnons du Christ*, Paris.

MANCHESTER 1857, *Art Treasures of the United Kingdom*.

MANDER van Karel, 1604, *Het Schilder-boeck*, Haarlem and Alkmaar.

— 1884, *Le Livre des peintres*, Fr, trans. by Henry Hymans, Paris, 2 vol.

MARIJNISSEN R. H., 1969, 'Note sur l'enluminure eyckienne "La Naissance de Saint Jean-Baptiste" des "Heures de Milan-Turin"', in *Scriptorium*, XXIII (Miscellanea F. Lyna), p. 225–226.

— 1979, 'On Scholarship — Some Reflections on the Study of Early Netherlandish Painting', in *Medelingen van de Koninklijke Academie voor Wetenschappen, Letteren en schone Kunsten van Belgie* (Klasse der Schone Kunsten), XL, no. 4, p. 3-14.

MARLE Raimond van, 1908, *Le comté de Hollande sous Philippe le Bon*, The Hague.

MARROW James, 1966, 'Pictorial reversals in the Turin-Milan Hours', in *Scriptorium*, XX, p. 67–69.

— 1968, 'Review of the reprinting of the "Turin Hours" by Count Paul Durrieu and the Postface by Albert Châtelet (1967)', in *The Art Bulletin*, L., p. 203–209.

MARTENS Bella, 1929, *Meister Francke*, Hamburg.

MARTIN W. et MOES E. W., 1912, *Oude Schilderkunst in Nederland*, The Hague.

MATHER F. J., 1906, 'Recent additions to the collection of Mr. John G. Johnson, Philadelphia', in *The Burlington Magazine*, 9, p. 351–363.

MAYER August L., 1926, 'A van Eyck Problem' in *The Burlington Magazine*, 49, p. 200–205.

— 1928, 'Die Fürstlich-Hohenzollernschen Sammlungen in Sigmaringen. I Die Gemälde', in *Pantheon*, I, p. 49–85.

MECHEL Christian van, 1781, *Verzeichnis der Gemälde der Kaiserlich königlichen Bilder Galerie in Wien*, Vienna.

— 1784, *Catalogue des tableaux de la galerie impériale et royale de Vienne*, Basle (French ed. of previous volume).

MEISS Millard, 1967, *French painting in the time of Jean de Berry — The late fourteenth century and the patronage of the duke*, London.

— 1968, *French painting in the time of Jean de Berry - The Boucicaut Master*, London.

— 1968 B, 'La mort et l'office des morts à l'époque du Maître de Boucicaut et des Limbourg', in *Revue de l'art*, 1–2, p. 17–25.

— 1974, *French painting in the time of Jean de Berry — The Limbourgs and their contemporaries*, New York.

MEISS Millar and EISLER Colin, 1960, cf. EISLER Colin.

MEISS Millard and OFF Sharon, 1971, 'The Bookkeeping of Robinet d'Estampes and the chronology of Jean de Berry's Manuscripts', in *The Art Bulletin*, LIII, p. 225–235.

MICHEL Edouard, 1924, 'La collection Mayer van den Bergh à Anvers', in *Gazette des Beaux-Arts*, 5th period, II, p. 41–58.

— 1944, *L'école flamande du XVe siècle au musée du Louvre*, Brussels.

MIERIS Frans van, 1756, *Groot Charterboek der Graaven van Holland van Zeeland en Heeren van Vriesland*, Leiden, IV.

— 1760, *Beschryving der stad Leyden*, Leiden, 2 vol.

MOES E. W., 1890, 'Geertgen tot Sint Jans' in *Eigen Haard*, 34, p. 532–534.

MOLANUS Joannes, 1861, *Historiae Lovaniensium, libri XIV, ex codice autographo exdidit, commentario praevio de vita et scriptis Molani, notis et apprendicibis illustravit P. F. X. de RAM*, (Collection de documents inédits relatifs à l'histoire de la Belgique, 24 and 25), Brussels, 2 vol.

MONGET Cyprien, 1896–1905, *La Chartreuse de Dijon d'après les documents des archives de Bourgogne*, Montreuil-sur-Mer, 3 vol.

MONT Pierre du, 1613, cf. GUICCIARDINI.

MORELLI Jacopo, 1800, *Notizia d'opere di disegno della prima metà del secolo XVI esistenti in Padova, Cremona, Milano, Pavia, Bergamo, Crema, Venezia, scritta da un anonimo di quel tempo*, Bassano.

MULLER S. Fzn., 1880, *Schilders-Vereenigingen te Utrecht bescheiden uit het Gemente-Archief, (De Utrechtse Archieven I)* Utrecht.

MUNICH 1930, *Sammlung Schloss Rohoncz Gemälde*, Neue Pinacothek.

MÜNSTER 1937, *Der Maler Derick Baegert und sein Kreis.* Landesmuseum, catalogue by Robert Nissen.

— 1952; *Westphalische Maler der Spätgotik, 1440–1490*, Landesmuseum, catalogue by Paul Pieper.

MURR Christophe Théophile de, 1797, *Description du cabinet de Monsieur Paul de Praun à Nuremberg*, Nuremberg.

MUSPER Theodor, 1938, 'Die Datierung und Lokalisierung der ältesten gedruckten Bücher und Laurenz Janszoon Coster', in *Die Graphischen Künste*, N.F. III, p. 41–52.

— 1938 B, 'Das Original des gothischen Figuren-Alphabets von 1464', in *Die Graphischen Künste*, N.F. III, p. 98–101.

— 1948, *Untersuchungen zu Rogier van der Weyden und Jan van Eyck*, Stuttgart.

— 1950, 'Die "Ars Moriendi" und der Meister E.S.', in *Gutenberg Jahrbuch*, p. 57–66.

— 1961, *Die Urausgabe der holländischen Apokalypse und Biblia Pauperum*, Munich 3 vol. (2 are facsimiles).

— 1965, 'Eine Kreuzigung von Dirck Baegert in Budapest', in *Bulletin du musée hongrois des Beaux-Arts*, 26, p. 35–38.

NAGTGALS F., 1878, *Zelandia illustrata*, Middelbourg, 2 vol.

NAHUYS N., 1877, 'Peinture à l'huile sur parchemin du XVe siècle représentant Elisabeth de Duvenvoorde, épouse de Simon d'Adrichem', in *Bulletin de l'Académie d'Archéologie de Belgique*, II, p. 199–206.

NEEFS E., 1875, *Histoire de la peinture et de la sculpture à Malines*, Ghent, 2 vol.

NEW YORK 1939, *Masterpieces of Art. European Paintings and Sculpture from 1300–1800*, New York World's Fair.

NEW YORK, METROPOLITAN MUSEUM OF ART, 1947, *A catalogue of early Flemish, Dutch and German paintings*, by Harry B. Wehle and Margareta Salinger, New York.

OBREEN F. D., 1877–1890, *Archief voor Nederlandsche Kunstgeschiedenis*, The Hague, 7 vol.

— 1903, *Geslacht van Wassenaar*, Leiden.

O'CONNOR Sr. Mary Catherine, 1942, *The Art of Dying Well*, New York.

OETTINGER Karl, 1938, 'Das Rätsel der Kunst des Hugo van der Goes', in *Jahrbuch der Kunsthistorischen Sammlungen in Wien*, N.F. XII, p. 43–76.

OOSTERBAAN D. P., 1956, Articles in *Delftse Courant*, 18 and 25 February.

— 1958, 'Kroniek van de Nieuwe Kerk te Delft', in *Haarlemse Bijdragen*, 65, p. 3–336.

OPMEER (OPMERUS), 1611, *Opus chronographicon*, Leiden.

ORLERS Jan Janszoon, 1641, *Beschrijvinge der stad Leyden*, Leiden.

OS H. van, 1964, 'Coronatio, Glorificatio en Maria in Sole', in *Bulletin Museum Boymans*, XV, 2–3, p. 22–38.

OUDENDIJK PIETERSE F. H. A. van, 1935, *Dürer's Rozenkranzfest*, Amsterdam-Antwerp.

OZINGA M. D., 1953, *De Gotische Kerkelijke Bouwkunst, (De Schoonheid van ons Land, XII)*, Amsterdam.

PÄCHT Otto, 1921–22, 'Ein neuer Ouwater?' in *Kunstchronik*, N.F. XXXIII, p. 820–821.

— 1927, 'Review of Max J. Friedländer, *Dierick Bouts und Joos van Gent*, Berlin 1925', in *Kritische Berichte zur kunstgeschichtlichen Literatur*, I, p. 37–54.

— 1956, 'Panofsky's "Early Netherlandish Painting"', in *The Burlington Magazine*, XCVIII, p. 110–116 et 267–279.

PÄCHT Otto and JENNI Ulrike, 1975, *Holländische Schule (Österreichische Akademie der Wissenschaften — Philosophische-historische Klasse, Denkschriften, 124 Band, Die illuminierten Handschriften und Inkunabeln der Österreichischen Nationalbibliothek, Band 3)*, Vienna.

PANOFSKY Erwin, 1927, '"Imago Pietatis", ein Beitrag zur Typengeschichte des "Schmerzenmann" und der "Maria Mediatrix"', in *Festschrift für Max J. Friedländer zum 60 Geburtstag*, Leipzig, p. 261–308.

— 1927–1928, 'Review of G. J. Kern, *Die verschollene Kreutztragung des Hubert oder Jan van Eyck*, Berlin, 1927, in *Kritische Berichte zur kunstgeschichtlichen Literatur*, p. 74–83.

— 1943, *The Life and Art of Albrecht Dürer*, Princeton (2nd ed. 1945, 3rd ed. 1948, 4th ed. 1955).

— 1953, *Early Netherlandish Painting*, Cambridge.

— 1953 B, 'Guelders and Holland: a footnote on a recent acquisition of the Nationalmuseum at Stockholm', in *Kunsthistorisk Tidskrift*, XXII, p. 90.

— 1954, 'A letter to St. Jerome. A note on the relationship between Petrus Christus and Jan van Eyck', in *Studies in Art and Literature for Bella da Costa Greene*, Princeton, p. 102–108.

— 1956, 'Jean Hey's "Ecce homo" – Speculation about its author, its donor and its iconography', in *Bulletin des Musées Royaux des Beaux-Arts*, Brussels, p. 94–138.

PARDIAC Abbé Jean-Baptiste, 1886, *Histoire de saint Jean-Baptiste et de son culte*, Paris.

PARIS 1904, *Exposition des Primitifs français*, catalogue by Henri Bouchot, Léopold Delisle, J.-J. Guiffrey, Frantz-Marcou, Henri Martin and Paul Vitry.

— 1935, *De van Eyck à Bruegel*, musée de l'Orangerie, catalogue by Jacques Dupont and Jacqueline Bouchot-Saupique, préface by Paul Jamot.

— 1937, *Chefs-d'œuvre de l'art français*, Palais national des Arts.

— 1950, *La Vierge dans l'Art français*, Petit Palais.

— 1951, *Chefs-d'œuvre des musées de Berlin*, Petit Palais.

— 1952, *Chefs-d'œuvre de la collection D. G. van Beuningen*, Petit Palais, catalogue by D. Hannema.

— 1956, *Chefs-d'œuvre du musée de Douai*, Galerie Heim.

— 1966, *Dans la lumière de Vermeer*, musée de l'Orangerie, 25 September–28 November.

— 1972, *Cent dessins du musée Teyler de Haarlem* (cat. by J.Q. van Regteren Altena).

PASSAVANT J. David, 1841, 'Beiträge zur Kentniss der alt Nederländischen Malerschulen', in *Kunstblatt*, XXII, p. 9, 10, 14 and 15 (also in French in *Messager des Sciences*, Ghent, 1842, p. 20–211).

— 1853, *Die christliche Kunst in Spanien*, Leipzig.

PELINCK E., 1949, 'Het gebortejaar van het "wonderkind Lucas van Leyden"', in *Oud Holland*, LXIV, p. 193–196.

PETERS Heinz, 1968, 'Zum New Yorker "Diptychon" der Hand G', in *Munuscula discipulorum* (*Kunsthistorische Studien Hans Kaufmann zum 70. Geburtstag*, 1966), Berlin, p. 235–246.

PHILIPPOT Albert and Paul, 1958, 'Examen stylistique et technique' (La Justice d'Othon de Thierry Bouts), in *Bulletin de l'Institut Royal du Patrimoine Artistique*, I, p. 31–48.

PHILLIPS Claude, 1886, 'Expositions d'hiver de la Royal Academy et de la Grosvenor Gallery à Londres', in *Chronique des Arts et de la Curiosité*, p. 14–15.

PIEPER Paul, 1953, 'Miniaturen des Bartholomäus-Meisters', in *Wallraf Richartz Jahrbuch*, XV, p. 135–156.

— 1959, 'Das Studenbuch des Bartholomäus-Meisters' in *Wallraf Richartz Jahrbuch*, XXI, p. 97–158.

— 1964, *Das Westfälische in Malerei und Plastik*, (*Der Raum Westphalen*, V, 3), Münster.

— 1965, 'Der Meister der Katharina von Kleve. Zu den Austellungen in New York und den Haag', in *Kunstchronik*, 18, p. 57–62.

— 1966, 'Das Stundenbuch der Katharina van Lochorst und der Meister der Katharina von Kleve', in *Zeitschrift Westfalen. Hefte für Geschichte Kunst und Volkskunde*, 44, 3 p. 97–163.

PIGLER Anton, 1950–1951, 'Das Problem der Budapester Kreuztragung', in *Phoebus*, III, p. 12–24.

— 1954, 'Some comments on Klara Gara's article' in *Acta Historiae Artium*, I, p. 265–267.

— 1968, cf. BUDAPEST, MUSEUM DER BILDENDEN KÜNSTE.

PIRENNE Henri, 1903 and 1908, *Histoire de Belgique, II Du commencement du XIVᵉ siècle à la mort de Charles le Téméraire* (2nd ed. 1908) III *De la mort de Charles le Téméraire à l'arrivée du duc d'Albe dans les Pays-Bas* (2nd ed. 1912) Brussels.

PIT A., 1891–1892, 'La gravure dans les Pays-Bas au XVᵉ siècle et ses influences sur la gravure en Allemagne, en Italie et en France', in *Revue de l'art chrétien*, 34, p. 486–497 and 35, p. 29–36 and 126–132.

— 1894, *Les origines de l'art hollandais (essai de critique)*, Paris.

PLUMMER John, 1964, *The Book of Hours of Catherine of Clèves* (catalogue of an exhibition at the Pierpont Morgan Library with introductions by Harry Bober, L. M. J. Delaissé, Millard Meiss, Erwin Panofsky and Frederick B. Adams, Jr.), New York.

— 1966, *The Hours of Catherine de Clèves*, New York (French and German ed., Paris and Berlin).

POORTER A. de, 1931, 'Testament van Anselmus Adornos, 10 Febr. 1470', in *Biekorf*, XXXVII, p. 225–239.

POORTENAAR Jan, 1947, *Coster niet Gutenberg*, Naarden.

POPHAM A. E., 1926, *Drawings of the early Flemish school*, London.

— 1932, *Catalogue of drawings by Dutch and Flemish artists preserved in the department of prints and drawings in the British Museum*, London and Oxford.

POR Jacob, 1929, 'Een olieverf schildering van omstreeks 1420,' in *Oudheidkundig Jaarboek*, IX, p. 150–153.

PORCHER Jean, 1961, 'Le portrait de Louis II d'Anjou', in *Art de France*, I, p. 290–292.

POST Chandler R., 1942, 'A second retable by Jan Joest in Spain', in *Gazette des Beaux-Arts*, 6th series, 22, p. 127–134.

POST M., 1919, 'Das zeitliche und künstlerische Verhältnis der Turin- Mailänder Gebetbuches zum Genter Altar', in *Jahrbuch der preussischen Kunstsammlungen*, XL, p. 175–205.

POST R. R., 1957, *Kerkgeschiedenis van Nederland in de Middeleeuwen*. Utrecht and Amsterdam, 2 vol.

— 1967, *Geert Grootes tractaat Contra turrim traiectensem teruggevonden*, The Hague.

— 1968, *The Modern Devotion – Confrontation with Reformation and Humanism, (Studies in Medieval in Reformation Thought*, III), Leiden.

PROST Bernard, 1891, *Artistes dijonnais*, Paris.

— 1902 et 1913, *Inventaires, mobiliers et extraits des comptes des ducs de Bourgogne de la maison de Valois (1363–1477)*, Paris, 2 vol. published.

RADINGER K. von, 1910–1911, 'Gemälde im städtischen museum in Salzburg', in *Blätter für Gemäldekunde*, VI, p. 131–132.

RATH Karl vom, 1941, *Der Meister der Bartholomäus-altars, (Kunstgeschichtliche Forschungen des Rheinischen Heimatbundes*, 8), Bonn.

REAU Louis, 1939, *La peinture française du XIVᵉ au XVIᵉ siècle*, Paris.

REGTEREN ALTENA J. Q. van, 1939, 'Review of G.J. Hoogewerff, De Noordnederlandsche Schilderkunst', vol. I and II, The Hague, 1936 and 1937, in *Tijdschrift voor Geschiedenis*, 54, p. 61–63.

— 1955, Hugo Jacobsz, in *Nederlands Kunsthistorisch Jaarboek*, VI, p. 101–117.

— 1959, 'The Glorification of the Virgin by Geertgen tot Sint Jans – Postscriptum', in *Oud Holland*, LXXIV, p. 169–173.

— 1966, 'Wanneer verbleef Geertgen tot Sint Jans in Vlaanderen?' in *Oud Holland*, LXXXI, p. 76–83.

— 1974, 'The high altar of the Church of St. Bavo in Haarlem', in *Liber amicorum Karel G. Boon*, Amsterdam, p. 122–135.

REINACH Salomon, 1905–1923, *Répertoire des peintures datées du Moyen Age et de la Renaissance*, Paris, 6 vol.

REINCKE Heinriche, 1958, 'Genealogische Fragen um den Meister Francke', in *Zeitschrift für Niedersächsische Familienkunde*, 33, p. 49.

— 1959, 'Probleme um den "Meister Francke"', in *Jahrbuch der Hamburger Kunstsammlungen*, 4, p. 9–26.

REISET Frédéric, 1878, *Musée du Louvre – Notice des Dessins. Cartons... Première partie: écoles d'Italie, écoles allemande, flamande et hollandaise*, Paris.

REIS SANTOS Luis, 1953, *Obras Primas da Pintura Flamenga do Seculos XV et XVI em Portugal*, Lisbon.

RENDERS Emile, 1931, *La solution du problème van der Weyden-Flémalle-Campin*, Bruges, 2 vol.

— 1933, *Hubert van Eyck, personnage de légende*, Brussels and Paris.

RENOUVIER Jules, 1857, *Les peintres de l'ancienne école hollandaise*, Paris (also published in *Revue universelle des Arts*, 1858, p. 113–121).

RENSING Theodor, 1967, 'Über die Herkunft des Meisters Francke', in *Wallraf Richartz Jahrbuch*, XXIX, p. 31–60.

REUTERSWÄRD Patrik, 1971, 'Den unge Johannes Dopären i öken Kring en teckning av Filippino Lippi', in *Konsthistoriska Studier tillägnade Sten Karling*, Stockholm.

REYNAUD Nicole, 1961, 'A propos du Martyre de saint Denis' in *Revue du Louvre et des musées de France*, II, p. 175–176.

— 1970, 'Maître Francke et l'art autour de 1400', review of the exhibition at Hamburg, 1969, in *Revue de l'art*, 9, p. 89–91.

RICHARDSON E.P. 1936, *The Detroit Institute of Arts – Flemish Painting of the Fifteenth and Sixteenth Centuries*, Detroit.

— 1956, 'The Detroit "St. Jerome" by Jan van Eyck', in *The Art Quarterly*, XIX, p. 226–235.

RICKERT Margaret, 1949, 'The Illuminated Manuscripts of Meester Dirc van Delft's Tafel van den Kersten Ghelove', in *The Journal of the Walters Art Gallery*, p. 78–108.

RIEFFEL Franz, 1924, 'Das fürstliche hohenzollernsche Museum zu Sigmaringen, Gemälde und Bildwerke', in *Staedel-Jahrbuch*, 3–4, p. 55–74.

RIEGL Alois, 1902, 'Das holländische Gruppenporträt' in *Jahrbuch der Kunsthistorischen Sammlungen des Allerhöchsten Kaiserhauses*, XXIII, p. 71–278 (2nd ed., Vienna, 1931).

RIEMER J. de, 1730, *Beschrijving van 's Gravenhage*, The Hague.

RING Grete, 1939, 'Die Gruppe der heiligen Agnes', in *Oud Holland*, LVI, p. 26–47.

— 1949, *A Century of French Painting, 1400–1500*, London (French ed., *La peinture française du XVᵉ siècle*, London).

— 1952, 'Attempt to Reconstruct a Lost Geertgen Composition', in *The Burlington Magazine*, XCIV, p. 147.

ROGERS Meyric (M. R. R.), 'The Entombment by "The Master of the Virgo inter Virgines", Netherlandish, late 15th century', in *Bulletin of the City Art Museum of Saint Louis*, XX, p. 46–48.

ROLLAND Paul, 1932, *Les Primitifs tournaisiens*, Brussels.

— 1949, 'Review of P. Landelin-Hoffmans O.M.C., *Un Rogier van der Weyden inconnu*, Enghien, 1948', in *Revue belge d'Archéologie et d'Histoire de l'Art*, 18, p. 90–92.

ROMBOUTS P. and LERIUS T. van, 1872, *De Liggeren en andere historische archieven der Antwerpsche Sint Lucasgilde*, Antwerp, 2 vol.

ROTTERDAM 1930, *Kersttentoonstelling*, Museum Boymans.

— 1934, *Nederlandse teekeningen 15ᵉ tot 17ᵉ eeuw uit de verzameling F. Koenigs*, Museum Boymans.

— 1936, *Jeroem Bosch – Noord-Nederlandsche Primitieven*, Museum Boymans, catalogue by D. Hannema and J.G. van Gelder.

— 1936–37, *Rotterdamse Kunstring*.

— 1938, *Kersttentoonstelling. Schilderijen, tekeningen en beeldhouwerken uit particuliere Nederlandse verzamelingen*, Museum Boymans.

— 1949, *Mesterwerken uit de Verzameling van Beuningen*, Museum Boymans.

— 1955, *Kunstschatten uit Nederlandse Verzamelingen*, Museum Boymans, 19 June-25 September, catalogue by E. Haverkamp-Begemann and B. R. M. de Neeve.

ROTTERDAM, MUSEUM BOYMANS, 1951, *Gilds Schilderkunst en Beeldhouwkunst*, Rotterdam.

RYLANDS W. Harry, 1881, *Ars Moriendi; A reproduction of the copy in the British Museum with an introduction by George Muller*, London.

SANTOS Reynaldo, 1957, *Os Primitivos Portugeses*, Lisbon.

SAXL Fritz, 1926, 'Studien über Hans Holbein d. J. I: Die Karlsruher Kreuztragung', in *Belvedere*, 10, p. 139–154.

— 1942, 'A spiritual Encyclopedia of the later Middle Ages', in *Journal of the Warburg and Courtauld Institutes*, V, p. 82–134.

SCHABACKER Peter H., 1975, 'The Holy Kindred in a Church: Geertgen and the Westphalian Master of 1473', in *Oud Holland*, LXXXIX, p. 225–242.

SCHÄFER Joseph, 1949, *Les primitifs français du XIVᵉ et du XVᵉ siècles*, Paris.

SCHAPIRO Meyer, 1945, 'Muscipula Diaboli', the Symbolism of the Merode Altarpiece', in *The Art Bulletin*, XXVII, p. 182–187.

SCHEIBLER, 1903, 'Zu altdeutsche und altniederländischen Gemälden des Museum', in *Denkschrift aus Anlass des 25 jähr Bestandes des Suermondt Museums*, Aachen, p. 28–33.

SCHENDEL A. van, 1957, 'De boom van Jesse en het problem van Geertgen tot Sint Jans', in *Bulletin van het Rijksmuseum*, 5–3, p. 75–83.

SCHILLING Rosy, 1961, 'Das Llangattock-Stundenbuch, sein Verhältnis zu van Eyck und dem Vollmar des Turin Mailander Studenbuches', in *Wallraf Richartz Jahrbuch*, XXIII, p. 211–236.

SCHMARZOW August, 1899, 'Der Meister E. S. und das Blockbuch Ars Moriendi' in *Berichte über die Verhandlungen der königlich sächsischen Gesellschaft der Wissenschaft zu Leipzig*, I, p. 1–29.

— 1900, 'Ist der Bildercyclus "Ars Moriendi" deutschen oder niederländischen Ursprungs?', in *Repertorium für Kunstwissenschaft*, XXIII, p. 123–142.

SCHMIDT-DEGENER F., 1911, 'Notes on some fifteenth century silver-points', in *The Burlington Magazine*, XIX, p. 255–261.

SCHNEIDER Friedrich, 1913, 'Herzog Johann von Baiern, erwählter Bischof von Lüttich und Graf von Holland, 1373–1452', (*Historische Studien*, published by E. Ebering, 104) Berlin.

SCHÖNBRUNNER Joseph and MEDER Joseph, 1896–1908, *Handzeichnungen alter Meister aus der Albertina und anderen Sammlungen*, Vienna.

SCHÖNE Wolfgang, 1937, 'Über einige altniederländische Bilde vor allem in Spain', in *Jahrbuch der Preussischen Kunstsammlungen*, 58, p. 153–181.

— 1938, *Dieric Bouts und seine Schule*, Berlin and Leipzig.

— 1942, 'Albert van Ouwater', in *Jahrbuch der Preussischen Kunstsammlungen*, 63, p. 1–42.

SCHOLDERER Victor, 1940, 'The invention of printing', in *The Library*, 4th series, XXI, p. 1–25.

SCHOUTE Roger van, 1963, *La Chapelle royale de Grenade*, (Les Primitifs flamands. I: Corpus de la peinture des anciens Pays-Bas méridionaux du quinzième siècle, 6).

— 1970, 'Le dessin de peintre chez Thierry Bouts', in *Mélanges d'archéologie et d'histoire de l'art offerts au professeur Jacques Lavalleye*, Louvain, p. 327–333.

SCHRADE H., 1932, *Ikonographie der christlichen Kunst. I: Die Auferstehung Christi*, Berlin and Leipzig.

SCHREIBER W. L., 1891–1911, *Manuel de l'amateur de la gravure sur bois et sur métal au XVᵉ siècle*, Berlin, 5 vol.

SCHRETLEN M. J., 1925, *Dutch and Flemish Woodcuts of the Fifteenth Century*, London (reprinted, New York, 1969).

— 1925 B, 'Het vroege werk Jacob Cornelis', in *Oudheidkundig Jaarboek*, V, p. 143–149.

— 1930, 'Een Haarlemsch stadsgezicht uit de 15 e eeuw', in *Oud Holland*, XLVII, p. 122–129.

— 1938, 'Vroeg werk van Jacob Cornelisz', in *Oud Holland*, LV, p. 145–154.

— n. d. (1946), *Dieric Bouts*, (Palet Serie), Amsterdam.

SCHRYVER Antoine de, 1969, 'Study of the illumination', in Franz Unterkircher and Antoine de Schryver, *Gebetbuch Karls des Kühnen vel potius Stundenbuch der Maria von Burgund – Kommentar*, (Codices selecti, XIV), Graz, p. 21–168.

SCHÜRER Oskar, 1937, 'Wohin ging Dürers "Ledige Wanderfahrt?", in *Zeitschrift für Kunstgeschichte*, VI, p. 171–199.

SCILLIA Diane G., 1978, 'A Late Work from the Circle of the Master of Catherine of Clèves, in *Oud Holland*, 92, p. 1–6.

— 1978 B, 'Van Mander on Ouwater and Geertgen', in *The Art Bulletin*, LX, p. 271–273.

SCRIVERIUS Petrus, 1628, 'Laurecrans voor Laurens Coster van Haarlem', in AMPZING Samuel, 1628.

SEECK Otto, 1899, 'Die charakteritischen Unterscheide der Brüder van Eyck', in *Abhandlungen der königlichen Gesellschaft zu Göttingen*, N.F. III, no. I, p. 3–77.

SHEPHARD L. A., 1950, 'The Vita Lidwinae printed at Schiedam 1498', in *Gutenberg Jahrbuch*, p. 172–176.

SHESTACK Alan, 1967, *Master E. S. (Five Hundredth Anniversary Exhibition Philadelphia Museum of Art)*, Philadelphia.

SIMON Karl, 1905, 'Albert van Ouwater?', in *Repertorium für Kunstwissenschaft*, XXVIII, p. 144–146.

SIP Jaromir, 1963, *Geertgen tot Sint Jans. Die Anbetung der Heiligen Drei Könige*, (Zauber des details), Prague.

SIX Jan, 1904, 'A propos d'un repentir d'Hubert van Eyck (problème d'identification)', in *Gazette des Beaux-Arts*, 3rd period, XXXI, p. 177–187.

— 1911, 'De platselijke gesteldheid in het getijdenboek van Willem VI van Beyeren', in *Onze Kunst*, XX, p. 105–116 (also in *Art Flamand*).

— 1922, 'La ressemblance d'Hubert van Eyck', in *La revue de l'Art*, p. 1–18.

SMITAL O., 1930, *Le livre d'heures noir du duc Galeazzo Maria Sforza*, Vienna.

SMITS Carolus Maria Joseph Hubertus Ignatius, 1933, *De Iconografie van de Nederlandse Primitieven*, Amsterdam.

SNYDER James E., 1957, 'Geertgen schildert de voorouders van Christus', in *Bulletin van het Rijksmuseum*, V, p. 85–94.

— 1960, 'The early Haarlem school of painting', in *The Art Bulletin*, XLII, p. 39-55 and 113–13.

— 1971, 'The early Haarlem school of painting; Part III; The Problem of Geertgen tot Sint Jans and Jan Mostaert', in *The Art Bulletin*, LIII, p. 445–458.

SOLMS-LAUBACH Ernstotto Graf zu, 1935–1936, 'Der Hausbuchmeister', in *Städel-Jahrbuch*, IX, p. 13–96.

SPENCER Eleanor Patterson, 1940, 'The International Style and Fifteenth Century Illumination', in *Parnassus*, XII, 3, p. 30–31.

— 1969, 'The first patron of the Très Belles Heures de Notre-Dame', in *Scriptorium*, XXIII (Mélanges Lyna), p. 145–149.

STANGE Alfred, 1934–1954, *Deutsche Malerei Gothik*, Munich and Berlin, 9 vol. (reprinted, Nendeln, Liechtenstein, 1969):
V: *Köln in der Zeit von 1450 bis 1515*, 1952.
VI: *Nordwestdeutschland in der Zeit von 1450 bis 1515*, 1954.

— 1958, *Der Hausbuchmeister*, (Studien zur deutschen Kunstgeschichte, 316) Baden-Baden and Strasbourg.

— 1967, *Kritisches Verzeichnis der deutschen Tafelbilder vor Dürer*, I, Munich.

STEINBART Kurt, 1929, 'Nachlese im Werke des Jacob Cornelisz', in *Marburger Jahrbuch für Kunstwissenschaft*, p. 213–260.

— 1937, *Das Holzschnittwerk des Jacob Cornelisz von Amsterdam*, Burg bei Magdeburg.

STENGERS Jean, 1949, *Les Juifs dans les Pays-Bas au Moyen Age*, (Académie royale de Belgique – Classe des lettres et des Sciences morales et politiques – Mémoires, 2ᵉ série, XLV 2), Brussels.

STERLING Charles, 1938, *La peinture française. Les Primitifs*, Paris.

— 1942, (JACQUES Charles) *La peinture française — Les peintres du Moyen Age*, Paris.

— 1955, 'œuvres retrouvées de Jean de Beaumetz, peintre de Philippe le Hardi', in *Bulletin des Musées Royaux des Beaux-Arts*, Brussels (*Miscellanea Erwin Panofsky*), 1–3, p. 57–82.

— 1959, 'Portrait painting at the court of Burgundy in the early 15th century', in *Critica d'Arte*, VI, p. 289–312, also published, with sight changes, as 'Un tableau inédit et la peinture de portrait à la cour de Bourgogne au début du XVe siècle', in *Archives de l'Art français*, XXII, 1959.

— 1966, 'La Pietà de Tarascon et les peintres Dombet', in *La revue du Louvre et des Musées de France*, 16, p. 13–26.

— 1971, 'Observations on Petrus Christus', in *The Art Bulletin*, LIII, p. 1–26.

— 1978, 'Jan van Eyck avant 1432', in *Revue de l'Art*, no. 33, p. 7–82.

STERLING Charles and ADHEMAR Hélène, 1965, *La peinture au musée du Louvre – Ecole française XIVe, XVe, XVIe siècles*, Paris.

STEVENSON Allan, 1966, 'The *Quincentennial of Netherlandish Blockbooks*', in *The British Museum Quarterly*, XXXI, p. 83–87.

— 1966 B, 'Netherlandish Blockbooks', in *Times Literary Supplement*, 1 December.

STORCK Willy F., 1910, 'Zu den Stichen des Meisters des Amsterdam Kabinetts', and 'Über das mittelalterliche Hausbuch', in *Monatshefte für Kunstwissenschaft*, III, p. 243–244 and 185–187.

STROCKA Volker Michael, 1970, 'Albrecht Dürer und Volfgang Peurer', in *Argo, Festschrift für Kurt Badt*, Cologne, p. 249–260.

STRÜMPELL Anna, 1925–1926, 'Hieronymus im Gehäuse', in *Marburger Jahrbuch für Kunstwissenschaft*, 2, p. 173–252.

STUFFERS J.W., 1915, *De Groote of Sinte Bavokerk te Haarlem na de restauratie*, Haarlem.

SULZBERGER Suzanne, 1951, 'An aspect of Eyckian landscape', in *Scriptorium*, V, p. 40–45.

— 1952, 'Michelino da Besozzo and the relations between Italian illumination and the art of van Eyck', in *Scriptorium*, VI, p. 276–278.

— 1952B, 'Pinturicchio et les van Eyck', in *Gazette des Beaux-Arts*, 6th period, XL, p. 261–268.

— 1958, 'Geertgen tot Sint Jans and the art of the miniature. The Glorification of the Virgin by Geertgen tot Sint Jans', in *Oud Holland*, LXXIV, p. 167–169.

— 1960, 'Juste de Gand et l'école de Haerlem', in *Revue belge d'Archéologie et d'Histoire de l'Art*, 29, p. 49–62.

SWILLENS P., 1925, 'Schilders en Beeldhouwers in Oud-Utrecht', in *Jaarboekje van 'Oud-Utrecht'*, II, p. 50–71.

SWILLENS P.T.A., 1948, 'De Utrechtsche beeldhouwer Adriaen van Wesel, ± 1420 – na 1489', in *Oud Holland*, LXIII, p. 149–165.

TENENTI Alberto, 1952, '*La vie et la mort à travers l'art du XVe siècle*', Cahiers des Annales, 8), Paris.

TEREY Gabriel de, 1927, 'An unknown picture by the Master of the Virgo inter Virgines', in *The Burlington Magazine*, 50, p. 297–298.

TER KUILE E.H., 1933, 'Nog eens: de Maquette van de St. Bavo te Haarlem', in *Oud Holland*, L, p. 132.

TIETZE Hans, 1919, *Die Kunstsammlungen der Stadt Salzburg*, (Oesterreichische Kunsttopographie, 16), Vienna.

TIETZE-CONRAT Erica, 1931, 'Flemish school 15th century (perhaps Gerard David)', in *Old Masters Drawings*, VI, p. 50–51, pl. 44.

TIMMERS J.J.M., 1949, *Houten Beelden (De Houtsculptuur in de Noordelijke Nederlanden tijdens de late Middeleeuwen)* (De Schoonheid van ons Land, 5), Amsterdam and Antwerp.

TOLEDO 1935, *French and Flemish Primitive Exhibition*, The Toledo Museum of Art.

TOLNAY Charles de, 1932, 'Zur Herkunft des Stiles des van Eyck', in *Münchner Jahrbuch der bildenden Kunst*, IX, p. 320–338.

— 1939, *Le Maitre de Flémalle et les frères van Eyck*, Brussels.

— 1965, *Hieronymus Bosch*, Baden-Baden.

TOTH-UBBENS Magdi, 1963, 'Van Goude, Zelver, Juellen ende Andere Zaken', Twintig jaren haagse tresorie-rekeningen betreffende beeldende Kunst en Kunstnijverheid ten tijde van Albrecht van Beyeren, 1358–78', in *Oud Holland*, LXXVIII, p. 87–134.

TROESCHER Georg, 1966, *Burgundische Malerei*, Berlin, 2 vol.

TSCHUDI Hugo von, 1898, 'Jan van Eycks Christus am Kreuz zwischen Maria und Johannes', in *Jahrbuch der königlich Preussischen Kunstsammlungen*, 19, p. 202–205.

UTRECHT 1913; *Tentoonstelling van Noord-Nederlandsche Schilder- en Beeldhouwkunst voor 1575*, Gebouw voor Kunsten en Wetenschappen.

UTRECHT AARTSBISSCHOPPELIJK MUSEUM, 1948, *Catalogus Schilderijen*, by D.P.R.A. Bouvy, Utrecht.

UTRECHT CENTRAAL MUSEUM, 1952, *Catalogus der Schilderijen* by C.H. de Jonge, Utrecht.

VAERNEWIJCK Marcus van, 1568, *Den Spieghel der nederlandscher Audtheijt*, Ghent (2nd ed., 1574, entitled, *De historie van Belgis*).

VALENCIENNES, 1918, *Geborgene Kunstwerke aus dem besetzten Nordfrankreich*, catalogue by Theodor Demmler.

VALENTINER W.R., 1913, *Catalogue of a collection of paintings and some art objects. II: Flemish and Dutch Painting*, John G. Johnson, Philadelphia.

— 1914, *Aus der niederländischen Kunst*, Berlin (English ed., *The Art of the Low Countries*, New York, 1914 and London, 1920).

— 1925, 'Saint Jerome by Petrus Christus', in *Bulletin of the Dtroit Institute of Arts*, VI, p. 58–59.

— 1943, 'Albert van Ouwater', in *The Art Quarterly*, 6, p. 79–91.

— 1955, 'Simon van Herlam', in *Gazette des Beaux-Arts*, 6th period, XLV, p. 5–10.

VANAISE P., 1966, 'De Meester van Vatervliet en zijn Nood Gods', in *Institut royal du Patrimoine artistique, Bulletin*, IX, p. 9–39.

VANSTEENBERGHE E., 1921, *Le cardinal Nicolas de Cues (1401–1464) – L'action et la pensée*, (Bibliothèque du XVe siècle, XXIV), Paris.

VEGH Janos, 1967, *German and Bohemian paintings of the 15th century*. (Museum of Fine Art, Budapest, and Christian Museum, Esztergom), Budapest.

VENISE, CA'D'ORO, 1946, *La galleria Giorgio Franchetti alla Ca' d'Oro*, catalogue by G. Fogolari, U. Nebbia and V. Moschini, Venice.

— 1950, *La galleria Giorgio Franchetti alla Ca' d'Oro di Venezia*, catalogue by G. Fogolari, Rome.

VENTE M.A., 1961, 'Bijdragen tot de Geschiedenis van het vroegers Grote Orgel in de St. Bavo en zijn Bespelers tot 1560', in *Nederlandse Orgelpracht*, Haarlem, p. 1–34.

VERMEEREN P.J.H., 1955, 'De Nederlandse Historienbijbel der Oostenrijkse Nationale Bibliotheek Codex 2771 en 2772', in *Het Boek*, XXXII, 2, p. 101–139.

VIENNE 1962, *Europäische Kunst um 1400*, Kunsthistorisches Museum, Vienna, 7 May–31 July.

VISSER G., 1899, *Hendrik Mande. Bijdrage tot de kennis der Noordnederlandsche mystiek*, The Hague.

VOGELSANG W., 1942, *Geertgen tot Sint Jans*, (Palet Serie), Amsterdam.

VOLL Karl, 1900, *Die Werke des Ian van Eycks, eine kritische Studie*, Strasbourg.

— 1906, *Die altniederländische Malerei von Jan van Eyck bis Memling – Ein entwicklungsgeschichtlicher Versuch*, Leipzig (2nd ed. 1923).

VOLSKAJA V.N., 1960, 'Kartina Niderlandskogo Khudoznika XV v.v. Gosudarstvennom Muzee Isobrazitelnvkh Iskusstv im A.S. Puskina', in *Ist. Russ. Zapadnoevrop Iskuss*, p. 232–242 (conclusions mentioned in Jan Bialostocki, 'The Literature of Art. Recent Research: Russia Early Periods', in *The Burlington Magazine*, CVII, 1965, p. 432).

VOS Dirk de, 1976, 'Nieuwe toeschrijvinge aan de Meester van de Lucialegends, alias de Meester van de Rotterdamse Johannes op Patmos', in *Oud Holland*, 90, p. 137–161.

VOSS Hermann, 1909, 'Het Maria-altaar van den Meester der Virgo inter Virgines in het museum te Salzburg', in *Onze Kunst*, XX, p. 101–104.

VRIES A.B., de, 1938, 'Vier Jahrhunderte Malerei 1400–1800 aus holländischem Privatbesitz. Ausstellung im Museum Boymans, Rotterdam', in *Pantheon*, XXII, p. 270–278.

VRIES T. de, 1954, 'Meester van Zwolle, Johan van den Mynnesten 450 jaar geleden te Zwolle overleden', in *De Mars, Maanblad voor Overijssel*, II, 12 p. 280.

— 1958, 'Meester van Zwolle, Johann van den Mynnesten's levensgeschiedenis', in *Overijssele Portretten*, Zwolle, p. 7–12.

WAAGEN G.F., 1837 and 1838, *Kuunstwerke und Künstler in England*, Berlin, 2 vol.

— 1839, *Kunstwerke und Künstler in England und Paris*, III, Berlin.

— 1863, *Treasures of Art in Great Britain*, VI, London.

1864, *Die Gemäldesammlung in der kaiserlichen Eremitage zu St. Petersburg*, Saint Petersburg.

WALVIS J., 1714, *Beschryving der stad Gouda, door J.W. (alvis)*, Leiden.

WATERHOUSE E.K., 1953, 'Some Old Masters other than Spanish at the Bowes Museum', in *The Burlington Magazine*, 45, p. 120–123.

WEALE W.H.J., 1872–1873, 'Documents inédits sur les enlumineurs de Bruges', in *Le beffroi*, IV, p. 238–337.

— 1903, 'The early painters of the Netherlands as illustrated by the Bruges exhibition of 1902', in *The Burlington Magazine*, I, p. 41–52, 202–217, 329–336 and II, p. 35–40 and 326–332.

— 1904, 'Paintings by John van Eyck and Albert Dürer formerly in the Arundel collection', in *The Burlington Magazine*, VI, p. 244–249.

— 1908, *Hubert and John van Eyck*, London and New York.

— 1910, 'Notes on some portraits of the early Netherland school', in *The Burlington Magazine*, XVII, p. 174–177.

WEALE W. H. J. and BROCKWELL M., 1912, *The van Eycks and their art*, London, New York and Toronto.

WEHLE Harry B. and SALINGER Margareta, cf. NEW YORK METROPOLITAN MUSEUM, 1948.

WEIGEL T.O., 1869, *Ars Moriendi, Editio princeps. Facsimile des Unicum im Besitze von T. O. Weigel in Leipzig*, Leipzig.

WESCHER Paul, 1930, 'Nachrichte-Berlin', in *Pantheon*, 6, p. 574–580.

— 1936, 'Zur "Madona mit dem Karthäuser" von Jean van Eyck in der Sammlung Robert de Rothschild', in *Pantheon*, XVII, p. 34.

— 1942, 'Der Meister der Heiligentafeln', in *Oud Holland*, LIX, p. 65–71.

— 1959, 'Drawing by the Gouda Master of the St. John Altar', in *The Art Quarterly*, XXII, p. 249–254.

WESE Arthur, 1927, *Skulptur und Malerei in Frankreich im XV. und XVI. Jahrhundert*, (Handbuch der Kunstwissenschaft), Wildpark-Potsdam.

WIERSUM E. and LE COSQUINO DE BUSSY A., 1927, 'Visitatie-Verslagen van de Johanniter-Kloosters in Nederland (1945, 1540, 1594)', in *Bijdragen en Mededeelingen van het historisch Genootschap*, 48, p. 146–339.

WILLIGEN A. van der, 1866, *Geschiedkundige aanteekeningen over Haarlemsche Schilders*, Haarlem (French ed., Haarlem, 1870).

WINKLER Friedrich, 1915, 'Zwei Utrechter Miniaturisten aus der Frühzeit der Holländischen Malerei und die Heures de Turin', in *Jahrbuch der Kunstsammlungen der allerhöchsten Kaiserhauses*, XXXII, p. 324–333.

— 1916, 'Über verschollene Bilder der Brüder van Eyck', in *Jahrbuch der preussischen Kunstsammlungen*, 37, p. 287–301.

— 1922, 'Der Meister der Anna Selbdritt im Louvre', in *Kunstchronik und Kunstmarkt*, N.S. XXXIII, p. 611–617.

— 1923, 'Unbeachtete holländische Maler des XV. Jahrhunderts', in *Jahrbuch der preussischen Kunstsammlungen*, 44, p. 136–146.

— 1924, *Die Altniederländische Malerei*, Berlin.

— 1925, *Die Flämische Buchmalerei*, Leipzig.

— 1926, 'Der Meister der Habsburger. Ein unbeachteter alpenländischen Maler um 1500', in *Belvedere*, IX, p. 47–50.

— 1927, 'Neues von Hubert und Jan van Eyck', in *Festschrift für Max J. Friedländer zum 60. Geburtstag*, Leipzig, p. 91–102.

— 1930, 'Paul de Limbourg in Florence', in *The Burlington Magazine*, LVI, p. 95.

— 1958, 'Die Wiener Kreuztragung', in *Nederlands Kunsthistorisch Jaarboek*, 9, p. 83–108.

— 1959, 'Ein frühfranzösisches Marienbild', in *Jahrbuch der Berliner Museen*, I, p. 179–189.

— 1959 B, 'Zur Kenntnis und Würdigung des Jan Mostaert', in *Zeitschrift für Kunstwissenschaft*, XIII, p. 177–214.

— 1960, 'Die Anbetung der könige mit dem Baldachin von Robert Campin', in *Mouseion (Studien aus Kunst und Geschichte für Otto H. Förster)*, Cologne, p. 138–140.

— 1964, *Das Werk des Hugo van der Goes*, Berlin.

WIT Kees de, 1937, 'Das Horarium des Katharina von Kleve als Quelle für die Geschichte der südniederländischen Tafelmalerei und der nordniederländischen Miniaturen', in *Jahrbuch der preussischen Kunstsammlungen*, LVIII, p. 114–123.

WOERMANN Karl, 1896, *Handzeichnungen Alter Meister im königlichen Kupferstichkabinett zu Dresden*, 1, Munich.

WOESTIJNE Karel van de, 1904, 'Het verloren Getijdenboek van Turijn', in *Tijdschrift voor Boek- en Bibliotheekwezen*, 2, p. 123–135.

WOLTMANN Alfred, 1886, *Holbein und seine Zeit*, Leipzig.

ZEDLER Godfried, 1923, *Die neuere Gutenberg-Forschung und die Lösung der Coster-Frage*, Frankfort.

ZERNER Henri, 1971, 'L'Art au Morier', in *Revue de l'Art*, II, p. 7–30.

ZIMMERMANN Heinrich, 1917, 'Über eine frühholländische Kreuztragung', in *Amtliche Berichte aus den königlichen Kunstsammlungen*, XXXIX, col. 15–29.

WORCESTER, PENNSYLVANIA 1939, *Exhibition of Flemish Painting*, The Worcester Art Museum and The Philadelphia Museum of Art.

ZURICH 1958, *Sammlung Emil G. Bührle*, Kunsthaus.

257

Photo credits

The author assembled all the illustrative material for this book. The publishers would like to thank the museums and libraries for their help and for exempting this book, in the majority of cases, from reproduction fees.

In addition to the material provided by the photographic services of public and private institutions, photographs have been made available by the following:

Brunswick (West Germany), B. P. Keiser: Pl. 104
Budapest, Josef Horvai: Pl. 142, Alfred Schiller: Pl. 137
Ganting, Blauel: Pl. 66
Madrid, Oronoz: Pls. 59, 60
Milan, Ing. G. Molfese: Pls. 14, 16, 20, 22, 28, 29, 30, 31
Turin, Giustino Rampazzi: Pls. 15, 17, 21, 32
Vienna, Meyer: Pls. 85, 86, 87, 88, 124 and the jacket illustration
West Berlin, Jörg P. Anders: Pls. 6, 54, 57, 65, 91

INDEX

This entries in this index refer to the page numbers in the text. Entries in capital letters are for people and places; entries in italics are for major works treated (paintings and books). Catalogue pages are entered separately under the names of the artists.